KOHLER'S DICTIONARY FOR ACCOUNTANTS

PRENTICE-HALL SERIES IN ACCOUNTING
CHARLES T. HORNGREN, EDITOR

6th Edition

KOHLER'S DICTIONARY FOR ACCOUNTANTS

Edited by

W. W. Cooper

The Foster Parker Professor of Management, Finance, and Accounting
Graduate School of Business
The University of Texas at Austin

Yuji Ijiri

The Robert M. Trueblood Professor of Accounting and Economics
Graduate School of Industrial Administration
Carnegie-Mellon University

Prentice-Hall, Inc., Englewood Cliffs, N.J. 07632

Library of Congress Cataloging in Publication Data

Kohler, Eric Louis, (date)
  Kohler's Dictionary for accountants.

  Rev. ed. of: A dictionary for accountants.   5th ed.
1975.
  Includes index.
  1. Accounting—Dictionaries.   I. Cooper,
William W. (William Wager), (date).   II. Ijiri,
Yuji.   III. Title.   IV. Title: Dictionary for
accountants.
HF5621.K6   1983   657'.03'21   82-13354
ISBN 0-13-516658-6

Editorial/production supervision and interior design by *Barbara Grasso*
Chapter opening design by *Maureen Olsen*
Cover design by *Diane Saxe*
Manufacturing buyer: *Ray Keating*

Printed in the United States of America

10 9 8 7 6 5 4 3 2 1

ISBN 0-13-516658-6

PRENTICE-HALL INTERNATIONAL, INC., *London*
PRENTICE-HALL OF AUSTRALIA PTY. LIMITED, *Sydney*
EDITORA PRENTICE-HALL DO BRASIL, LTDA., *Rio de Janeiro*
PRENTICE-HALL CANADA INC., *Toronto*
PRENTICE-HALL OF INDIA PRIVATE LIMITED, *New Delhi*
PRENTICE-HALL OF JAPAN, INC., *Tokyo*
PRENTICE-HALL OF SOUTHEAST ASIA PTE. LTD., *Singapore*
WHITEHALL BOOKS LIMITED, *Wellington, New Zealand*

CONTRIBUTORS TO THE SIXTH EDITION

Earl F. Davis, The University of Georgia (Business Law)

James W. Deitrick, The University of Texas at Austin
  (Financial Accounting Theory and Practice)

William D. Haseman, University of Wisconsin at Milwaukee
  (Accounting and Management Information Systems)

Leon E. Hay, University of Arkansas
  (Nonprofit, International, and Social Accounting)

Harvey S. Hendrickson, Florida International University
  (Systems of Accounts and Bookkeeping)

Sandra A. Hibberd, AMAX Inc. (Financial Accounting Pronouncements)

James O. Horrigan, University of New Hampshire (Financial Statement Analysis)

William R. Kinney, Jr., University of Iowa (Statistics and Quantitative Methods)

John C. Lere, University of Minnesota (Cost Accounting)

Ferdinand K. Levy, Georgia Institute of Technology (Business and Economics)

James K. Loebbecke, University of Utah (Auditing)

Charles R. Purdy, University of Minnesota (Cost Accounting)

Donald H. Skadden, University of Michigan (Tax Accounting)

Robert T. Sprouse, Financial Accounting Standards Board
  (Financial Accounting Pronouncements)

Shyam Sunder, University of Chicago (Financial Management)

Mikel G. Tiller, University of Tennessee
  (Nonprofit, International, and Social Accounting)

Lawrence A. Tomassini, The University of Texas at Austin
  (Managerial Planning and Control)

Glenn A. Welsch, The University of Texas at Austin
  (Managerial Planning and Control)

Stephen A. Zeff, Rice University (Accounting History, Institutions and Persons)

Charles T. Zlatkovich, The University of Texas at Austin
  (Financial Accounting Theory and Practice)

PREFACE

There you have it: a quick summary within this allotted space of one individual's observations, participations and survival in the midst of dynamic undercurrents...[and] into the hectic preoccupations of today, some of which have already led to decisions and pronunciamentos growing out of involved concepts that will have to be retraced [and possibly reformed and simplified] if the output of accountants is to continue as assimilable reading material for the laity: a laity that may in the end include the bulk of the profession. [From *Eric Louis Kohler: A Collection of His Writings (1919-1975)*, The Academy of Accounting Historians, 1980]

This is the first edition of *Kohler's Dictionary for Accountants*. It is also the sixth edition of E. L. Kohler's *A Dictionary for Accountants*. This is more than a play on words. The first edition of the latter work appeared in October of 1952 and went through a series of revisions with the final, fifth edition, completed in April of 1975 with publication only shortly before Kohler's death on February 20, 1976.

The first edition of Kohler's original work constituted a landmark in accounting— a plateau, one might say—which brought together and succinctly summarized much of what had gone before. It was "plateaulike" in that it also provided a very broad base for further development not only by its clear and cogent summaries but also by bringing into focus the developments and concepts from a great many other fields for their possible bearing on future developments for accounting.

Kohler's interest in the possibility of contributing a systematized body of terminology and definitions to the profession and practice of accounting goes back at least as far as his experiences when serving as Chairman of the American Institute of Accountants' Committee on Terminology (1936). He had a good deal more in mind than any possible charge to that committee, however, when he finally began putting *A Dictionary for Accountants* together. For one thing he saw this work as part of a continuing effort for developing a general set of accounting principles and for improving (in every sense of the word) accounting practice. For another thing, he saw it as an opportunity to reach beyond accounting to bring in terms and concepts from related disciplines and to adjust or adapt them for use in accounting. The result was much more than a dictionary, or at least it was much more than a dictionary of accounting. At numerous points—and especially with words that he regarded as basic to accounting—Kohler filled out the definitions with brief essays and elaborations that are really gems of synoptic insight into accounting issues, problems, and practices at very basic levels. This much is pure Eric Kohler. To reach beyond accounting into other disciplines, however, he had to have help from a variety of individuals, many of whom are acknowledged in the first edition. Two who continue to deserve mention for these types of contributions to the original edition are Samuel Nakasian and David Rosenblatt, the former for his contributions from economics, especially international trade and commerical practices, and the latter for his contributions from formal logic, statistics, mathematics, and science generally.

One of the editors of this edition (Cooper) also assisted in a good deal of the work on the first edition and was thus in a position to observe Kohler's style and method of work. In such situations, Kohler quickly threw himself into each idea and, not being easily satisfied with modes of expression by others, he would re-write and rewrite each such contribution until it fitted into the grander scheme of things that he was visualizing for his dictionary. A good example is the definition (and discussion) of the term *axiom*, which has been carried forward pretty much intact from the first edition into this one. A product of collaboration between Rosenblatt and Kohler in this kind of process, it represents a marvelously succinct discussion which, characteristically, winds up with an attempt—the first we know of—to axiomatize accounting at very basic levels. In addition, in the discussion accompanying this definition, Kohler also summarizes and rationalizes (again succinctly) one whole prong of the dictionary and relates it to the rest of accounting (and science) by observing that "in an applied field, such as accounting, the axioms are identical with propositions which belong equally to other disciplines."

All parts of editions one through five of *A Dictionary for Accountants* were either contributed originally by Kohler or else filtered by him through a process such as we have just described. This continued through the fifth (and last) edition, which he conducted on his own even while the accelerating pace of change in accounting, in other disciplines, in technology, in business, in law (including tax law), and in the world in general made this increasingly difficult to do. In our case, however, and for this edition, we proceeded in a different manner and called for help from others whose names, along with the fields in which their help was solicited, appear in *Contributors to the Sixth Edition*. The additions, deletions, alterations, and expansions that are contained in this dictionary relative to the fifth edition of *A Dictionary for Accountants* could not have been accomplished—indeed, we would not even have attempted it—without the contributions from these individuals, and, in addition, the revisions to the infra structure undoubtedly reflect the influences of our long-time friends and collaborators, A. Charnes and H. A. Simon, as well as R. M. Cyert and George Kozmetsky.

Having made this acknowledgment, we also need to absolve all of the above individuals from blame for any shortcomings. Knowing that we would be preserving much of the previous edition, we secured the consent of each of these persons to edit their contributions as our own judgment might dictate in order to obtain a (more or less) uniform style and degree of coordination. Although many of the contributions from each of these individuals found their way into other parts of the dicitonary—at least by cross reference—it would really be quite impossible to track and credit them individually. With their permission, we therefore stopped at identifying each of these persons with the major fields in which their contributions were solicited. We did not check the results of our editings with any of these individuals and so we can only express our gratitude to them and hope that what they find in this dictionary meets with their approval.

We also wish to make the following copyright acknowledgments. Various terms and phrases taken from the pronouncement of the Financial Accounting Standards Board are used throughout this dictionary. They are used with the permission of the Financial Accounting Standards Board, which is hereby gratefully acknowledged. Most of the terms contributed by Leon E. Hay in the areas of nonprofit accounting came from his book, *Accounting for Governmental and Nonprofit Entities*, and permission by Richard D. Irwin, Inc., the publisher of the book, is hereby gratefully acknowledged. In both cases, they extended their kindness even further and allowed us to indulge in only blanket acknowledgments in order to accommodate the needs of a dictionary in which specific acknowledgments at various points would have been extremely difficulty to make.

Although we made a determined effort to preserve as much as possible from the fifth edition, the pace of progress noted above did force extensive changes and alterations. Some occurred in the form of new terms and the revision or elimination of older ones to reflect the many changes in accounting, auditing, tax law, etc., which have occurred since the fifth edition. Similar changes also occurred in terms from related fields, where to make room for newer developments (e.g., in statistics and computers), we found it necessary to delete or condense some of the other materials in rather drastic fashion. Some of the reasons for the latter deletions may be of interest. For instance, as a case in point, we eliminated a good deal of the material on statistical quality control that appeared in editions one through five because, in our judgment, the intentions of the original inclusion had been accomplished—as witness the widespread use of these ideas in many parts of contemporary practice. We did not omit the basic ideas of statistical quality control, however, but only some of the copious buttressing details that appeared in earlier editions, as possible aids to applications in accounting, because we believed it more important to draw in many other new and important ideas from statistics and related areas such as operations research and management science.

The impact of computers and related developments on accounting practice and research also made it imperative to find a way to bring in material pertinent to these developments without unduly expanding the resulting book. Much of this was accomplished by omitting tables—such as the logarithm, compound interest tables, and related nomographs—which appeared in previous editions. It is perhaps of some interest therefore to observe that, in our minds, the availability of such tables in a book like this one appeared much less necessary in this edition, e.g., as devices of convenience, because such information as may be required is now easily obtained not only from computers but also from the small calculators that almost all accountants now carry in their pockets or briefcases.

The fifth edition contained slightly more than 3,000 terms. This sixth edition contains 4,538 terms, of which 2,660 were carried over from the fifth edition, many being drastically revised, and 1,878 are newly defined terms, a ratio of roughly 60% old terms versus 40% new terms. While this itself indicates the considerable degree of revision that has been made, the real extent of revision might be such that more than half of the materials are new, since a significant portion of the old terms have undergone extensive changes and updating.

We have continued the tradition of the previous editions by alphabetizing compound words as though they formed a single word. All numbers are spelled out and all nonalphabet characters such as a hyphen or an apostrophe are omitted before forming the single word for the purpose of alphabetizing. Thus, for example, ''directors' report'' is alphabetized as if it were spelled directorsreport,'' hence it is placed between ''direct material'' (spelled ''directmaterial'' and ''direct overhead'' (spelled ''directoverhead''). This method of alphabetizing, which is called the letter-by-letter principle of alphabetizing (as against the word-by-word principle), has been widely used in dictionaries.

We have also continued the tradition of italicizing terms defined elsewhere in the dictionary, or else we indicate such an appearance in other ways such as ''See...'' or ''*q.v.*,'' for *quod vide* (or ''which see''). There may, however, be a variation in the word ending between the italicized word and the term defined in the dictionary (e.g., adjective versus verb, past versus present tense, singular versus plural, etc.). Also italicized are names of journals and books, foreign words, section headings, mathematical symbols, and words with emphasis, but these should be clear from the context.

As a new attempt to facilitate referencing terms in the dictionary, we have supplied an index at the end. The index is an alphabetical listing of all terms defined in the dictionary together with the page number where the term is defined and zero, one, two, or three dots to indicate the size of the definition (more dots, more detailed) as described at the beginning of the index. The idea is to allow a reader to scan the index in a fashion that should often be easier and more rapid than paging through the dictionary itself in search of a term that may perhaps appear in another form.

Finally, we would like to express our appreciation to our assistants who played an indispensable role during the entire duration of the project.

The first of our acknowledgments goes to the DEC-20 Computer System at Carnegie-Mellon University (in the spirit of our mutual friend and colleague, Herbert A. Simon, who believes that the computer is capable of acquiring a personal identity). The most typical characteristic of a dictionary project is the enormous frequency with which a need arises for classifying, sorting, searching, and referencing words or sentences. Without the aid of an efficient computer system, the amount of clerical work would have been overwhelming. Fortunately, Prentice-Hall supplied us at the beginning of the project with a magnetic tape of the fifth edition used in its composition. After a suitable character conversion and an elimination of composition marks, the tape provided a basis for the sixth edition. At the end, after entering all the changes, additions, and deletions, followed by a conversion back to the compositor's characters, we were able to supply to Prentice-Hall a magnetic tape of the manuscript in a form acceptable to the compositor that can speed up the production process considerably. This and other parts of the work were made possible by help from Ron Ledwith of Prentice-Hall, supplied in a ready and easy manner that probably belies the effort and thought he expended. To the list of such assistance from Prentice-Hall should be added the high-quality results of the efforts of Barbara Grasso and Sally Ann Clauss, who served as production and copy editors, respectively.

The excellent computer system at Carnegie (one of the best in the country) offered efficient operation for editing, sorting, checking of spelling, printing, tape processing, and tape conversion. We wrote numerous computer programs as needs arose at various phases of the project, all in APL (which stands for *A Programming Language*). This is a high-level general-purpose language particularly suitable for this type of work because it processes arrays of characters all at once, thus eliminating tedious looping and indexing in programs, while most other computer languages process one character at a time. Needless to say, our acknowledgment extends to the persons at the C-MU Computation Center who have made the system function in such an exceptionally efficient manner.

Tomo Ijiri spent laborious hours at a computer terminal, typing in all of the new and re-vised (and re-revised) materials—often helping to correct errors she detected in the proc-ess. During the more than four years that this project lasted, she continued at this effort even when the editors found it necessary to attend to other matters. Similarly, Ruth Coop-er helped with much of the cross referencing, and her experience as a practicing lawyer was drawn upon many times. This, in addition to the patience and encouragement provid-ed by Ruth and Tomo, made the continuation of this endeavor possible and often made it even pleasant or at least bearable during its long duration.

While intensive care has been exercised to minimize errors of various kinds, we are sure that some must have occurred, not only errors of a clerical variety but also more seri-ous errors of commission and omission. However, the task goes on. This is surely not the last edition of this dictionary. In the interest of perfecting future editions, we solicit the help of readers in calling such matters to our attention. Comments, suggestions, and criti-cisms will also be appreciated and may be directed to either of the editors. In this way, we may perhaps continue to progress on issues such as those mentioned in the headnote to this Preface.

W. W. Cooper

Graduate School of Business
The University of Texas
Austin, Texas 78712

Yuji Ijiri

Graduate School of Industrial Administration
Carnegie-Mellon University
Pittsburgh, Pa. 15213

KOHLER'S DICTIONARY FOR ACCOUNTANTS

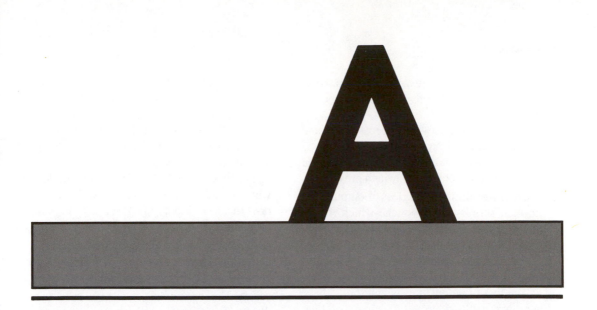

AAA = *American Accounting Association*.

Abacus See *accounting journals*.

abandonment The complete retirement of a fixed asset from service, following salvage or other reclaiming of removable parts; as, the abandonment of an exhausted coal mine or oil well, or street-railway tracks upon the institution of bus service; see *retirement*. Under the income-tax regulations, an abandonment loss deduction is allowed only on property of a capital nature (generally excluding depreciable assets employed in a business), the intention to abandon must be evident, the usefulness of the property must have been completely terminated, and there must be no possibility of any future use of the asset. Under special rules, a retirement loss may be allowed on the abandonment of depreciable business property.

A provision in contemplation of future abandonment is a provision for *obsolescence*; such a provision or the loss recognized when the abandonment occurs is not a capital loss for income-tax purposes but may be deducted in full. See *fixed asset; depreciation*.

abatement 1. The cancellation of a part or all of a past or prospective expenditure.

2. A reduction or cancellation of an assessed tax. Under the *Internal Revenue Code*, a claim in abatement is not permitted as to income, estate, and gift taxes.

3. Any item of incidental income accounted for as a reduction of a general cost; as, the income from minor sales to outsiders of electric power produced by a generating plant owned by a manufacturing enterprise.

ability to pay Having sufficient resources to liquidate or otherwise discharge obligations when due. It may be measured in terms of "wealth" or total assets; or it may also be restricted to liquid assets or even cash. "Income" is also a pertinent measure, especially in taxation, where it often assumes the form of "relative" ability to pay—a guiding principle, or justification, for graduated tax rates as in the federal income tax. It is also reflected in the timing of tax collections. In some circumstances, taxes are collected when cash is received rather than when income or sales are accrued. Thus, recognition of taxable income is postponed on installment sales, but rents received in advance are taxable when received.

abnormal costs 1. Unusual or atypical costs which are usually irregular and unexpected in their occurrence.

2. The difference between expected costs under normal conditions and the actual costs incurred.

3. The difference between expected costs and the actual costs incurred.

4. Costs which should have been avoidable under the actual conditions which prevailed.

abnormal lost units 1. The loss of output units through shrinkage or spoilage which should not have occurred under cost-efficient operating conditions. The cost of such losses is, therefore, not a necessary part of the cost of producing units of good product.

2. The loss of output units which should have been avoidable given the existing specification of raw material inputs, product outputs, and production method. See *shrinkage* and *spoilage*.

abnormal performance index (API) An index of nonsystematic changes in security prices used to study the effects on security prices of unexpected changes in accounting earnings. The index is a cumulative average of the *unsystematic risk* or unexplained *variance* of the returns on securities relative to the return on a market *portfolio*. See *capital asset pricing model*. It is usually formulated as follows:

$$ API = \frac{1}{N} \sum_{i=1}^{N} \prod_{t=1}^{T} (1 + \mu_{it}), $$

where N = number of securities; T = number of time periods; μ_{it} = the part of the return on security i in period t explained by the return on a market portfolio, or the forecast error; and

$$ \prod_{t=1}^{T} (1 + \mu_{it}) = (1 + \mu_{i1})(1 + \mu_{i2}) \dots (1 + \mu_{iT}), $$

the T-fold product of the $(1 + \mu_{it})$.

abnormal shrinkage 1. Shrinkage which should not have occurred under cost-efficient operating conditions.

2. Shrinkage which should have been avoidable in the circumstances. See *shrinkage*.

abnormal spoilage 1. The loss of usable parts or salable products which could have been avoided under cost-efficient operating conditions. The cost of such losses is not, therefore, a necessary part of the cost of producing units of good product.

2. The loss of usable parts or salable products which could have been avoided with existing raw material inputs, product outputs, and production method.

above par At a premium: applied to the market quotation or price of a security or other item of value, higher than its face amount.

abscissa The horizontal or x axis in a two-dimensional *coordinate system* or chart.

absorb 1. To merge by transfer all or part of the amounts in an account or group of accounts with another account in such a manner as to cause the identity of the first to be lost, as by the transfer of operating expense from *basic-expenditure* accounts to work in process, or from work in process to finished goods, or from finished goods to cost of sales; or by the writeoff of a bad debt against an allowance (reserve) for bad debt.

2. To include related actual costs in establishing a price or a standard cost.

3. To spread costs through *allocation* or proration (*prorate*).

absorbed costs Factory overhead and other indirect costs which are allocated to products or services. See *overhead; cost absorption*.

absorbing state A state which has a zero probability of leaving it so that, as in a *Markov process*, the probability of transiting to some other state is zero once an absorbing state is reached.

absorption account An account offsetting, in whole or in part, one or more related accounts, its purpose being to preserve the identity of such accounts, as well as accumulate periodic transfers to other accounts; thus, an account for *accumulated depreciation*; an *allowance* for doubtful accounts. See *split-account system; contra account; cost absorption; valuation account.*

absorption costing The process of allocating all (*full absorption costing*) or a portion (*direct costing* and *standard costing*) of fixed and variable production costs to *work in process, cost of sales,* and *inventory.*

abstract *adj.* Characterizing a property or relation considered apart from local or temporary contexts, or a quality considered independently of the object or event that possesses it; pertaining to (a) that which is common to a class; (b) a meaning that can be expressed by a symbol that does not refer to anything unique; (c) features not limited to a perceived object; or (d) an expression calling attention to such features. *n.* = *trial balance.*

Academy of Accounting Historians Founded in 1973, the Academy of Accounting Historians is a voluntary organization of persons interested in the study of accounting history. It publishes a newsletter, working papers, monographs, and *The Accounting Historians Journal.*

accelerated cost recovery system (ACRS) In order to stimulate investment, a new method of depreciation was prescribed in the Economic Recovery Tax Act of 1981, allowing taxpayers fast cost recovery for tax purposes. All tangible properties, new and used, that are placed in service by the taxpayer after December 31, 1980, are eligible with some exceptions. (A major item in the exceptions is property which the taxpayer elects to depreciate under a depreciation method not expressed in terms of years, such as the unit-of-production method.) Cost of eligible property is "recovered" (depreciated) over a predetermined period (one of 3, 5, 10, or 15 years based on the types of property) and at predetermined rates. The rates generally reflect the results of using the double-declining

balance method (1) with a switch to the sum-of-the-years-digits method at an optimum point, (2) with a half-year convention in the year the property is placed in service, and (3) with salvage value being disregarded. The same rate schedule is applied to both new and used property.

Thus, for 3-year property, the recovery percentage is 33% in the first year, 45% in the second year, and 22% in the third year. For 5-year property, the percentages are 20, 32, 24, 16, and 8. For 10-year property, they are 10, 18, 16, 14, 12, 10, 8, 6, 4, and 2. For 15-year public utility property, they are 7, 12, 12, 11, 10, 9, 8, 7, 6, 5, 4, 3, 3, 2, and 1. For 15-year real property, detailed percentages are specified based on the month in which the property is placed in service since the half-year convention is not used in this case. These percentages are applicable to properties placed in service after 1985 when the law is fully phased in. For those placed in service in 1981 through 1984, less accelerated percentages are specified.

Three-year property consists of autos, light-duty trucks, equipment used in connection with research and experimentation (R&D equipment), horses older than certain ages when placed in service, and personal property with an asset depreciation range (ADR) midpoint life of 4 years or less. (ADR is the depreciable life specified by the Treasury Department for classes of assets based on industry experience and had been in use before this 1981 Act.) Five-year property includes most machinery, equipment, furniture and fixtures, horses not in the 3-year class, and some short-lived public utility and real property. Ten-year property consists of public utility property with an ADR midpoint life greater than 18 but not greater than 25 years, railroad tank cars, some coal utilization property, manufactured residential homes and mobile homes, and real property with an ADR midpoint life of 12.5 years or less. Fifteen-year property is public utility property with an ADR midpoint life exceeding 25 years and real property with an ADR midpoint life of more than 12.5 years or with no ADR life.

In lieu of using the ACRS, a taxpayer may elect to use the straight-line method over the optional recovery periods of 3, 5, or 12 years for 3-year property under the ACRS; over 5, 12, or 25 years for 5-year property; over 10, 25, or 35 years for 10-year property; and over 15, 35, or 45 years for 15-year property. Such an election may help a taxpayer with expiring net operating loss carryovers or credit carryovers. A single recovery period should be used for all property in the same class and placed in service in the same year, except for 15-year real property, for which the election may be made on the property-by-property basis.

accelerated depreciation Depreciation at a larger than usual rate because of (a) plant operations at more than normal speed, use, or capacity; (b) a useful or economic life materially less than physical life, as (i) mine equipment, the physical life of which is in excess of the estimated operating period of the mine, its cost therefore being absorbed in operating expenses over the shorter period, or (ii) assets purchased for use in connection with a contract, order, or job at the completion of which the assets will have a diminished or no foreseeable remaining utility; (c) an excessive cost of construction occasioned during a period in which materials and skilled labor are at a premium, such excessive cost being written off during what is estimated to be the high-price period; (d) the decision of the Congress to stimulate investments of certain types by allowing rapid cost recovery for tax purposes, as in *accelerated cost recovery system*; (e) tax advantages arising from the use of declining-balance method

and sum-of-the-years-digits method (see *depreciation methods*); (f) other conditions giving rise to limited or lessened economic use. The federal income-tax regulations give little or no recognition to items (a) and (c), except through optional methods of *depreciation*. See *accelerated cost recovery system; depreciation; depreciation methods; obsolescence*.

acceptable quality level (statistical quality control) A predetermined degree of quality, generally in terms of number or percent of defective items in a lot or batch of goods, which is regarded as satisfactory in the sense that such quality will be accepted by the inspection procedure a high proportion (generally 95% or more) of the time; often referred to as AQL.

acceptance 1. A promise to pay, by the drawee of a bill of exchange, usually evidenced by inscribing across the face of the bill "accepted," followed by the date, the place payable, and the acceptor's signature. Any words showing the intention of the drawee to accept or honor the bill are sufficient, however. The effect of the acceptance is to make the bill equivalent to a promissory note, with the acceptor as maker and the drawer as endorser. See *bank(er's) acceptance; promissory note*.
2. A *bill of exchange* accepted by the drawee.
3. A *trade acceptance*.
4. The action of one of the parties to a contract to make it valid, following the offer of the other party. The acceptance may be made orally or in writing, depending on the nature of the contract.

acceptance sampling (statistical quality control) Use of samples to determine the acceptability of submitted lots of goods. Acceptance sampling by *attributes* is probably the predominant practice, the inspection test involving either a classification of the sample items as good or defective or a count of the number of defects per 100 units. Acceptance sampling by *variables* is also possible; where feasible it possesses greater efficiency per unit inspected than does sampling by attributes. However, both methods involve assumptions concerning the distribution of quality within the lot, and these assumptions place a real restriction on the general applicability of acceptance sampling by variables. The inspection test consists of measuring some quality characteristic of each item in the sample. Judgment on the lot is then based on the data resulting from this measurement.

Acceptance sampling by *attributes* is divided into four types, according to whether single, double, multiple, or sequential (item-by-item) samples are used. Under single sampling, a *sample* consisting of a predetermined number of items is taken at *random* from a lot. On the basis of this sample evidence of production quality, the entire lot is accepted or rejected. This scheme in many cases requires a relatively large sample. Although inspection of the sample may be curtailed in various ways, this is seldom desirable. A better alternative is to seek other sampling schemes that yield corresponding (matched) protection with lower inspection costs.

Double sampling may, in many cases, and with less expense, give the same degree of quality protection as single sampling. Double sampling proceeds in two steps. A relatively small random sample of items is taken from the lot and inspected on the basis of predetermined standards. From the evidence obtained through this first sample, it may be decided to accept or reject the lot. Since the sample is relatively small, the evidence yielded by it may prove inconclusive. When such is the case, a second sample (usually larger than the first sample) is taken at random from the remainder of the lot and the results of the two samples are combined to determine whether to accept or reject the lot.

Multiple sampling constitutes a logical extension of double sampling, except that successive samples, where needed, are the same size as the first sample. For each sample, three decisions are possible: (a) accept the lot, (b) reject the lot, or (c) take another sample because the accumulated evidence through that stage is inconclusive. In multiple sampling, the "group" or "block" samples are always small relative to the single or double plans being matched and are accompanied by acceptance and rejection numbers that maintain the specified degree of quality protection and arranged to force a decision by at most nine (and frequently fewer) blocks.

Sequential (item-by-item) sampling resembles multiple sampling in principle, the block size being simply one item, so that the three possible decisions are available after inspection of each unit rather than at the end of the inspection of a group of units. Also, in sequential sampling, inspection could continue all the way through to complete 100% sorting of the entire lot, although in practice this is never done, decisions under this scheme being consistently reached after the inspection of fewer pieces on the average than under any of the other three types. Because sequential plans are easy to design, they are extremely flexible and can therefore be "custom-built" to fit special protection requirements with greater precision than is possible under any of the other three types of sampling. The major obstacles to the practicability of sequential sampling are the highly variable inspection load it imposes, with its attendant handling costs, and the necessity for careful training and supervision of the inspection personnel to be entrusted with using it.

All four types of sampling plans are based on definite protection features in terms of calculable risks; standard tables are available covering a wide range of quality protection and providing appropriate sample sizes and acceptance and rejection criteria.

Developing experience with sampling from successive lots of goods and the maintenance of a *p* chart (see *control chart*) in conjunction with sampling may be used as a guide for sample redesign which will result in reduced or tightened inspection.

For plans with matched protection features, techniques are available for determining how the four types of plans compare as to the average amount of inspection required to reach a decision on the lot. Multiple sampling plans will generally have a decided advantage in this respect over the corresponding single or double plans at all levels of incoming lot quality, and sequential plans will be even more frugal in this respect than multiple plans.

accessions tax A proposed alternative to the present taxation of gift and estate transfers, which would levy taxes on the recipients of gifts and inheritances rather than on the transferors, with progressive rates applied to the cumulative amount of all wealth received. See *inheritance tax; death taxes; unified transfer tax*.

access time (computers) The time between which data are requested and delivered from a storage device. This includes *latency time* and *seek time* as well as time to transfer data.

accommodation endorsement An endorsement by one person, without consideration, on a note or other credit instrument to which another person is a party, for the purpose of establishing or strengthening the other's credit; as, a corporation's endorsement on the bank loan of a subsidiary. See *commitment; contingent liability*.

accommodation note (or paper) A note signed by one person as maker, endorser, or acceptor, on behalf of another whose credit standing is weak or nonexistent. As a rule, no consideration is involved, the intent of the signer being to act as a surety or guarantor. The power of a corporation to act as such a signer is often questioned. See *contingent liability*.

accommodation purchase A good or service acquired by an organization for another, or for a customer or employee, usually because of superior purchasing facilities, larger discounts, or other advantage.

account *n.* 1. A formal record of a particular type of transaction expressed in money or other unit of measurement and kept in a *ledger*.

2. = *account current*.

3. The amount owed by one person to another, often evidenced by a statement showing details. See *account stated*.

4. (governmental accounting) An *appropriation request* appearing in the annual budget of the United States.

5. Chargeable or creditable, as in the expression, "for the account of, on behalf of."

6. *pl.* = *financial statements;* as, the annual accounts of a business enterprise. In British practice, both *books of account* and year-end financial statements may be implied.

7. *pl.* The bookkeeping records (*books of account*) of any organization, including journals, ledgers, vouchers, and other supporting papers.

v., with "for": (a) To place in the books of account; (b) to furnish facts supported by explanations; (c) to return (tickets, coupons) as unsold or unclaimed; (d) (auditing) to obtain explanations that constitute *accounting evidence* concerning an expenditure; with "to": to render an *accounting* (*2*).

In practice, there are no mechanical standards, minimum or otherwise, for the account form. Required only are (a) the date, to identify the day or accounting period of the transaction or transaction group, (b) the source of the item, so that when an error is discovered or an internal or external audit is being made, original supporting data may be readily referred to, and (c) the money amount. Bookkeeping machines and the use of punched cards and data-processing equipment often make possible the replacement of formal journals and ledgers by a file of cards or a tape or by summaries of such original data as sales invoices. Making only total entries for each month in the general ledger is a frequent practice, and occasionally it will be found that the general ledger itself has been discarded in favor of "worksheet accounts," the latter being totals of classified transactions. In most instances a formal general ledger, often hand-posted, must be maintained, if for no other purpose, as an overall index of the transactions of a period (see illustration under *trial balance*). In all cases, however, whether the account forms be formal or of the less formal variety, a strict procedure must be followed to minimize error and maximize referability to source documentation. See *ledger; double-entry bookkeeping*.

accountability 1. The obligation of an employee, agent, or other person to supply a satisfactory report, often periodic, of action or of failure to act following delegated authority. See *responsibility; authority; accounting (2); feedback; property accountability*.
2. Hence (governmental accounting) the designation of the account or amount of a *disbursing officer's* liability.
3. The measure of responsibility or liability to another, expressed in terms of money, units of property, or other predetermined basis.
4. The obligation of evidencing good management, control, or other performance imposed by law, regulation, agreement, or custom. See *audit* (comprehensive audit).

accountability unit The unit selected as the basis of accountability determination. See *zero-base budgeting; property account*.

accountable 1. Having responsibility or liability for property held in trust or under some other relationship with another. See *accountability*.
2. (government accounting) Personally liable for improper payments; said of a *certifying officer* or *disbursing officer*.
3. Requiring entry on the books of account: said of a transaction not yet recorded, often with reference to its timing. See *incur; recognize*.
4. = responsible. See *responsibility*.

accountable officer (government accounting) An authorized officer, *certifying officer, disbursing officer,* or *collecting officer*.

accountable person One charged with *accountability*.

accountable warrant See *warrant (5)*.

Accountancy See *accounting journals*.

accountancy The theory and practice of *accounting*: its responsibilities, standards, conventions, and activities.

accountant One skilled in *accounting*. See *public accountant; certified public accountant; private accountant*.

Accountant, The See *accounting journals*.

accountant in charge An auditor who supervises the field work of an audit engagement, allots duties to assistants, reviews their findings, and drafts reports.

Accountants for the Public Interest An organization of volunteer professional accountants devoted to serving the public good by offering to analyze, in an objective manner, the accounting, financial, and fiscal dimensions of public policy questions. It also serves local communities by providing technical accounting assistance to small nonprofit organizations which cannot afford to pay professional fees. The first local body of Accountants for the Public Interest was founded in 1972 in San Francisco, and by 1977 a total of 15 such organizations existed in the United

States. In 1975, a national coordinating organization was incorporated, with headquarters in San Francisco. See *public interest accounting*.

Accountants International Study Group A group of representatives from the Institute of Chartered Accountants in England and Wales, the Canadian Institute of Chartered Accountants, and the American Institute of Certified Public Accountants whose purpose is to study and report on areas of accounting practice common to the three constituent groups.

Accountant's Magazine, The See *accounting journals*.

accountants' report = *auditors' report*.

accountant's responsibility The moral obligation assumed by an accountant, as a member of a *profession*, as in, for instance, the obligation assumed by a public accountant in subscribing to a financial statement from which information and guidance may be sought by management, creditors, and investors. It connotes a conduct conforming to professional, community, or individual standards of propriety as opposed to those the nonobservance of which might justify or lead to legal action.

account current Any personal account on which periodic settlements are made. Example: a consignee's periodic accounting to his consignor for sales, less agreed costs and commissions. See *account sales*.

account form The usual style followed in the presentation of a balance sheet—assets on the left and liabilities and capital, or equities, on the right, with equal totals—and less often in the case of income statements; contrasts with *report form*. See *balance sheet; income statement*.

accounting 1. The recording and reporting of *transactions*.

2. Hence, by extension, the origins, recognition, and disposition of transactions: (a) their emergence (timing, *quantification*, often in physical-unit, as well as money terms, *classification*); (b) their processing (*system design, internal check*); (c) their recording and grouping (*bookkeeping*); (d) their *feedback* (*internal reporting*); (e) the continuous critical testing of transactions (*internal auditing*); (f) the fitting of transaction groups into conventional patterns (summarization in *financial statements*); (g) professional examinations of financial statements (*audit (4)* by *public accountants*); (h) periodic reporting to investors, government agencies, and the public generally; (i) transaction *projection* (*budgeting* and other *forward-accounting* activities); (j) external reviews of and recommendations on organizational functioning (*management services*). Of these activities, (a), (b), (c), and (f) have always been traditional, though the scope of each has greatly expanded; (g) and (h) gained public recognition shortly before the turn of the century; (d) and (e) in the mid-thirties; (i) after World War II; (j) a present-day outgrowth of increasing involvement with organizational structure and management functioning.

3. A report of transactions by one responsible for acquiring, safeguarding, or administering assets or incurring expense, the disbursement of cash advanced, or the carrying out of any assigned task. Examples: an accounting of an executor to a court; an accounting between parties in the settlement of a suit; an accounting for the operation of a petty-cash fund; a report by an agent to his principal, whether or not accompanied by a cash settlement for an amount owing. See *accountability*.

4. Hence, any report embracing the transactions (including *budget* or *forecast* projections) during a designated period.

Accounting and Business Research See *accounting journals*.

accounting change A change meriting disclosure and explanation in published financial reports, seen as a change in (a) an accounting principle, (b) an accounting estimate, or (c) the reporting entity.

accounting control 1. The administrative procedures employed in maintaining the accuracy and propriety of transactions and the bookkeeping record thereof. See *internal control; internal check*.

2. An accounting procedure designed to maintain continuous internal quantitative controls over business transactions: particularly, the keeping of a duplicate account or a record of totals as a basis for proving the accuracy of the aggregate of a group of accounts; the maintenance of a property ledger. See *control account; subsidiary ledger*.

3. Any of the various accounting procedures and devices having as their purpose the supplying to management of informational records and reports essential to the administration of properties, the timing of purchases, the limitation of varied types of expenditures, and the like.

accounting convention See *convention*. Any method, procedure, or collection of methods and procedures, extensively used in accounting practice. Such conventions have the authority of custom and hence may continue to evolve and alter by adjustment to particular situations. Such conventions may also be displaced by an authoritative statement, regulation, or law as in a pronouncement by the *Financial Accounting Standards Board*, a regulation of the *SEC* in the form of an *Accounting Series Release* or a tax statute. In any case an accountant or auditor who assumes responsibility for the preparation of published financial statements and other such published reports has the duty of familiarizing himself with all such conventions as well as such formal pronouncements and principles that might be pertinent to these reports.

accounting cycle = *bookkeeping cycle*. Sequence of steps or procedures in manual accounting processes initiated by an *accounting event* (a recordable *transaction*) and completed during each accounting period: (i) record each transaction in a journal (*journalize*); (ii) *post* to a ledger; (iii) prepare a *trial balance* and possibly a worksheet (or *working trial balance*); (iv) journalize and post each *adjusting journal entry*; (v) prepare *financial statements*; (vi) journalize and post each *closing entry*; and possibly (vii) prepare a *postclosing trial balance*. See *double-entry bookkeeping*.

accounting entity = *accounting unit*.

accounting equation See *accounting identity*.

accounting event An *event* recorded in the *accounting record* of an *entity*. See *event (1); external transaction; internal transaction*.

accounting evidence See *auditing evidence*.

accounting for the public interest See *public interest accounting; Accountants for the Public Interest*.

accounting group (governmental accounting) A self-balancing set of accounts, but not a fiscal entity, therefore not a *fund (3)*. See *general fixed assets account group; general long-term debt account group*.

Accounting Hall of Fame Founded in 1950 at The Ohio State University, the Accounting Hall of Fame has the purpose of honoring individuals who have made, or are making, significant contributions to the advancement of accounting since the beginning of the twentieth century. The elections are made annually by a Board of Nominations.

Accounting Historians Journal, The See *accounting journals*.

accounting identity 1. The *identity* of the debit and credit elements of a transaction expressed in terms of double-entry bookkeeping: also known as *accounting equation*. See *double-entry bookkeeping*; see also *spread* *sheet* for illustration of two-way effect of representative transactions on bookkeeping records.

2. Hence, the *identity* of assets and equities, expressed as *assets* = *equities* (or = liabilities + capital or net worth); the consequence of the summation of a series of transactions recorded on a double-entry basis, each transaction having a total of debit and credit elements of equal amount.

Accounting Interpretations See *Accounting Principles Board*. Prepared by staff of the *American Institute of Certified Public Accountants* during the tenure of the Accounting Principles Board (APB), interpretations provided timely guidance on accounting questions having general interest to the profession; issued without the formal procedures required for an APB Opinion, they did not establish standards enforceable under the Institute's Code of Professional Ethics.

accounting journals The great number of journals published in different countries and regions which appear periodically and cover a wide range of topics in accounting and related fields. We list some of the better known (in the United States) journals as follows:

Abacus—Founded in 1965, it is a semiannual journal published in Australia by the Sydney University Press and edited by the Department of Accounting, The University of Sydney. It is devoted to accounting research.

Accountancy—Founded in 1889 under the name of *The Incorporated Accountants' Journal* as the quarterly journal of the Society of Incorporated Accountants and Auditors, it later became a monthly journal and in 1938 was renamed *Accountancy*. In 1957, when the Society was absorbed into the three chartered institutes in the British Isles, *Accountancy* became the journal of the *Institute of Chartered Accountants in England and Wales*.

Accountant, The—Founded in 1874, it is a weekly journal published by Gee & Co. (Publishers) Ltd., London.

Accountant's Magazine, The—Founded in 1897 as the monthly journal of the three chartered accountants' societies in Edinburgh, Glasgow, and Aberdeen, it became the monthly journal of the *Institute of Chartered Accountants of Scotland*, when that body came into existence in 1951. Until 1967, when the apostrophe was moved, the title of the journal was written *The Accountants' Magazine*.

Accounting and Business Research—Founded in 1970, it is a quarterly journal of the *Institute of Chartered Accountants in England and Wales* and is devoted to accounting research.

Accounting Historians Journal, The—The semiannual journal of the *Academy of Accounting Historians*, *The Accounting Historians Journal* first appeared in 1977. It was an outgrowth of the Academy's newsletter, *The Accounting Historian*, which continues to be published in reduced form.

The Accounting Review—Founded in 1926, it is the quarterly journal of the *American Accounting Association* and is devoted to publishing the results of scholarly research in accounting.

Auditing: A Journal of Practice and Theory. Founded in 1981, it is a publication of the Auditing Section of the *American Accounting Association*. Appearing semiannually (summer and winter issues), it seeks to provide a two-way flow between auditing practice and research which will also affect auditing education. An unusual feature is a book review section in which reviews are undertaken separately by an academician and a practitioner.

CA Magazine—Founded in 1921 as the *Canadian Chartered Accountant*, it is the monthly journal of the *Canadian Institute of*

Chartered Accountants (= CICA), and is devoted to the interests of accountants in public practice, industry, and government.

CPA Journal, The—Founded in 1930 as *The New York Certified Public Accountant*, it is the monthly journal of the New York State Society of Certified Public Accountants, and publishes articles of interest to practicing accountants.

Financial Analysts Journal—Founded in 1945, it is the bimonthly journal of the Financial Analysts Federation. It regularly contains articles on accounting of interest to analysts.

Financial Executive—Founded in 1934 as *The Controller*, it is the monthly journal of the *Financial Executives Institute* and is concerned primarily with articles of interest to corporate controllers and financial executives.

Government Accountants Journal—Founded in 1950 as *The Federal Accountant*, it is the quarterly journal of the *Association of Government Accountants*.

Internal Auditor, The—Founded in 1944, it is the bimonthly journal of the *Institute of Internal Auditors*.

Journal of Accountancy—Founded in 1905, it is a monthly journal of the *American Institute of Certified Public Accountants* and carries articles on accounting, auditing, and management services of interest primarily to accounting professionals.

Journal of Accounting and Economics—Launched in 1979 by the North-Holland Publishing Company, this research journal, initially to appear three times a year, is edited by the Graduate School of Management, University of Rochester.

Journal of Accounting Auditing and Finance—Founded in 1977, it is a quarterly journal published commercially by Warren, Gorham & Lamont, and is edited by the Ross Institute of New York University. It contains

articles with a research base but is oriented primarily toward professionals.

Journal of Accounting Research—Founded in 1963, it is edited and published semiannually by the Institute of Professional Accounting, the University of Chicago. Since 1966, it has included an annual supplement containing the papers presented at conferences held at the University of Chicago.

Journal UEC—Founded in 1968, the Journal UEC is the quarterly publication of the *Union Européenne des Experts Comptables, Economiques et Financiers*.

Management Accounting—1. Founded in 1919 as the *N.A.C.A. Bulletin*, it is the monthly journal of the *National Association of Accountants* and is oriented chiefly toward management accountants.
2. Founded in 1921 as the *Cost Accountant*, it is the monthly journal of the Institute of Cost and Management Accountants in the United Kingdom.

The Tax Adviser—Founded in 1970, it is a monthly journal of the *American Institute of Certified Public Accountants* and carries articles of interest chiefly to tax practitioners.

accounting manual A handbook of accounting policies, standards, and practices governing the accounts of a business enterprise or other person; it includes the *classification of accounts*.

accounting measurement *Measurements* effected for *accounting* purposes. See *measurement; measurement concept*. Such measures may be in monetary units or in other units of measurement. They are also given in a variety of different forms at the same time in order to reflect different aspects of the transactions being recorded or reported. See *management information system*.

accounting period The period of time for which an operating statement is customarily prepared. Examples: a month (the most common accounting period); 4 weeks; a quarter (of a year); 26 weeks; a year; 52 weeks; any period of time such as that covered by an *accounting (2)*. The accounting period of a year is the fiscal year ending on December 31 or the last day of any other month. An accounting period of more than one year may be required in classifications of accounts; the numbering of recurring monthly journal entries as in the case of an estate or trust. See *fiscal year*.

accounting policy 1. The general principles and procedures under which the accounts of an individual organization are maintained and reported; any one such principle or procedure. An accounting policy, as distinct from a *principle,* or professionally determined *standard,* is usually an adaptation or special application of a principle necessary to meet the peculiarities of an organization or the needs of its management. Thus, policies are required for the computation of *depreciation,* the *recognition* of capital expenditures, and the disposal of *retirements,* the general accounting principle relating to these items providing a wide latitude for individual choice. See *fixed asset; depreciation*. Occasionally an accounting policy is found to conflict with accepted principles. Any major accounting policy thus in conflict, together with an estimate of its effect on the accounts, requires disclosure in financial statements. Decisions as to the range of accounting policies and their specific formulation are often left to the controller of an organization; in large organizations, management usually participates on major policies, and the board of directors may be asked to approve them. See *principle; policy; accounting procedure*.
2. The rules or regulations such as the *S-X* Regulations of the SEC, or other regulations of this and other government agencies, as well as the statutes and court decisions bearing on their activities.

3. The opinions and pronouncements of the professional bodies such as the *Financial Accounting Standards Board* or *American Institute of Certified Public Accountants* intended to guide or control accounting practice.

accounting postulate See *postulate*. In financial accounting a postulate is generally considered to be pertinent to the development of *accounting principles*. Other parts of accounting such as managerial or cost accounting often make use of postulates from other disciplines such as economics and psychology.

accounting practice 1. The customs and predilections of accountants or auditors as expressed in their everyday activities; sometimes used in contrast with accounting theory.
2. The professional work of a public accountant; see *public accounting*. Hence, the activities of public accountants generally.

accounting principles The body of doctrine associated with accounting, serving as an explanation of current practices and as guide in the selection of conventions and procedures. The *axioms* of accounting and the *principles* deriving from them have arisen from common experiences, historical precedent, statements by individuals, pronouncements of professional bodies, and regulations of governmental agencies. The validity of accounting principles rests on their simplicity, clarity, and generality in mirroring current practices and in furnishing guidance for the conduct of practitioners and for the further development of the profession. The endorsement by a professional body of certain practices does not, however, qualify them as principles. See *accounting policy; principle; theory; convention; postulate*.

Contributions in recent years to an articulated body of accounting principles have come from three main sources. The first of these was the statement of principles underlying the preparation and presentation of financial statements, published in 1936 by the American Accounting Association (AAA). The second was a series of pronouncements of the Accounting Principles Board (APB) and its predecessor committees of the American Institute of Certified Public Accountants (AICPA) commencing in 1939 and dealing with topical problems of accounting practitioners; although not constituting a coordinated body of doctrine, they have disposed of a number of troublesome details otherwise standing as obstacles to principle formation on a broader scale. The third is the Financial Accounting Standards Board (FASB) of recent origin. The latter has expressed a need for guidance in the form of papers circulated for discussion which purport to deal with basic accounting concepts but are really only attempts at definitions of a few terms like *assets* and *liabilities*. However, as yet no full-scale summation of principles has been made, and no effort has been put forth in distinguishing fundamental *postulates*, *assumptions*, or *axioms* from principles and procedures derived from them.

The result has not been an internally consistent, reasonably comprehensive, firmly structured, interrelated body of practices, and but few of them point to principles having any conceivably universal application.

Perhaps the main difficulty in resolving principles applicable to financial statements lies in the belief that financial statements, fully footnoted and in an idealized form, will provide the information that investors and other presumed readers of such statements will find "useful." See *objectives of financial reporting*. However, the information furnished by conventional financial statements will always be limited—in some cases of minor consequence—and it has not yet been realized that current criticisms of financial statements are in a more realistic sense criticisms of the restricted information-supply system now in effect. Although the scope of disclosures in annual reports to stockholders has been steadily increasing, publication—and comparisons with operating results—the disclosure of management *forecasts* prior to the reporting period has only begun to be explored and until this route has been more fully extended, the "usefulness" of present types of financial statements will continue to be very limited.

Accounting Principles Board Founded in 1959 to replace the *Committee on Accounting Procedure*, the Accounting Principles Board was the senior technical committee of the *American Institute of Certified Public Accountants* authorized to issue pronouncements on accounting principles on behalf of the Institute. During its tenure, which ended in 1973, the Board was periodically engulfed in controversy until, in the end, its critics exceeded its supporters in influence. It was superseded by the *Financial Accounting Standards Board*.

accounting procedure One or more of the rules or practices governing day-to-day operation of a particular system of accounts.

accounting rate of return A rate of return determined by using an accrual accounting basis for determining return and the investment base. Thus, return on total assets would be derived as annual accounting net income divided by average net book value of total assets. Also see *return on investment; return on common equity*. For capital budgeting decisions, it would be computed as expected average annual accounting income from the project divided by average investment in the project.

accounting ratio See *ratio*.

accounting records The formal journals and ledgers, and the vouchers, invoices, correspondence, contracts, and other sources or support for such records; = *books of account*.

Accounting Research Bulletins A series of 59 official pronouncements issued between 1939 and 1959 by the *Committee on Accounting Procedure* of the *American Institute of Certified Public Accountants*. In 1953, the Committee issued Bulletin 43, which codified and superseded the previous 42 Bulletins on accounting procedures. The Bulletins, while not formally binding on members of the Institute, were clothed with authority by the *Securities and Exchange Commission*, which normally required that they be implemented by corporations subject to its jurisdiction.

Accounting Review, The See *accounting journals*.

Accounting Series Releases A series of official pronouncements of policy issued by the *Securities and Exchange Commission*. The Releases deal with matters of accounting and auditing policies of the Commission as well as the actions taken by the Commission regarding the rights of certain firms of certified public accountants to practice before the Commission.

accounting standard 1. A mode of conduct, imposed on accountants by custom, law, or professional body.
2. = *accounting principle*.

Accounting Standards Committee Founded in 1969-70 as the Accounting Standards Steering Committee, it is charged with drafting proposed *Statements of Standard Accounting Practice*. Its membership is composed of representatives from the six cooperating accountancy bodies in the U.K. and Ireland whose councils eventually are invited to approve the final Statements.

Accounting Standards Executive Committee Formed in 1973 as successor to the *Accounting Principles Board* as the senior technical committee on accounting principles (or standards) of the *American Institute of Certified Public Accountants*, the Accounting Standards Executive Committee began to issue *Statements of Position* on matters not occupying the attention of the *Financial Accounting Standards Board*. Since 1978, AccSEC (as it is known) has begun to integrate its pronouncement activities into those of the FASB.

accounting system 1. The *principles*, methods, and *procedures* relating to the incurrence, classification, recording, and reporting of the transactions of an organization. See *transaction*.
2. Hence, the *process* of operating, testing, and accumulating information under such a system, in accordance with controlling internal-administration policies, and with any regulatory requirements of higher authority.
3. The books, records, vouchers, files, and related supporting data resulting from the application of the accounting process; *accounting records*.

Accounting Terminology Bulletins A series of four official pronouncements issued between 1953 and 1957 by the Committee on Terminology of the *American Institute of Certified Public Accountants*. The initial Bulletin, entitled "Review and Resume," was a codification of eight of the *Accounting Research Bulletins* which dealt with terminology.

accounting transaction = *transaction*.

Accounting Trends and Techniques An annual publication of the *American Institute of Certified Public Accountants*, which first appeared in 1948 under the title "Accounting Survey of 525 Corporate Reports." It is a statistical analysis, complemented by many illustrative examples, of the financial reporting practices of a sample of 600 American public corporations.

accounting unit (or entity) 1. A business enterprise or other economic unit, or any subdivision thereof for which a system of accounts is maintained. Whether a separate accounting system for a subdivision of a business enterprise is instituted is an administrative determination dependent on such factors as distance from the general office, its degree of operating independence, reporting requirements, and the frequency, complexity, and points of origin of its transactions. Accounting records may be installed, usually without duplication or overall loss in efficiency, wherever management needs are best served. See *entity; establishment; economic unit*.

2. An individual account maintained for recording the cost or other basis of *fixed assets*, usually coinciding with a *replacement unit* or *retirement unit*; but it may also embrace the several retirement units of a single structure, and be supported by a cost report or other record from which the cost of a retirement unit may be readily obtained. See *depreciation*.

accounting valuation 1. The historical money amount attaching to any asset or expense, generally representing cost, i.e., money outlay at the time of acquisition. It is with cost and its disposition that accounting is principally concerned in both business and governmental accounting and in institutional (not-for-profit entity) accounting as well. It is sometimes said that accounting does not involve valuation; on the contrary, it may also be said that cost is itself the main, and in most instances the only, valuation employed in the day-to-day operation of business enterprise. Decisions of management are based on cost: past, present, and future. The assignment of costs to activities or products, and particularly the division of joint and common costs between the operations served by them, may be regarded as a valuation process within the larger area of *cost absorption*. The

portion of cost that is to be detached from the outlay associated with an inventory, where the rule of the lower of cost or market is being applied, likewise involves a valuation process the endproduct of which may be a partial cost which continues to attach to certain inventory items. But in all of these accounting operations, cost is the subject matter; its ultimate disposition is the central problem of cost accounting and a major problem constantly facing the general accountant. See *cost absorption*.

2. Any amount other than the historical money outlay employed as a basis of accounting, as in *current cost* accounting or *price level accounting*.

account payable 1. An amount owing to a creditor, generally on open account, as the result of delivered goods or completed services; distinguished from *accruals* and other *current liabilities* not arising out of everyday transactions. See *payable; trade account payable*.

2. Hence, a ledger account for such a liability.

3. *pl.* A general-ledger account controlling a group of such accounts. See *control account*.

account receivable 1. A claim against a debtor, generally on *open account*, its application usually limited to uncollected amounts of completed sale of goods and services; distinguished from deposits, accruals, and other items not arising out of everyday transactions. See *receivable; trade account receivable*.

2. Hence, a ledger account for such a claim.

3. *pl.* A general-ledger account controlling a group of such accounts. See *control account*.

account receivable discounted 1. An account receivable that has been assigned or sold with recourse; until paid by the debtor, the amount of the account is a contingent liability of the seller.

2. *pl.* The seller's contingent liability for customers' accounts receivable so assigned or sold: a balance-sheet term. See *balance sheet*.

account sales An interim or final statement rendered by a consignee or sales agent showing particulars of sales of goods consigned, expenses incurred, commissions, and the balance, if any, due the consignor; an *account current*.

accounts payable ratio See *days purchases in accounts payable ratio*.

accounts receivable aging schedule An analysis showing how long *accounts receivable* have been outstanding. It usually shows the percentage of receivables which are not past due and the percentages past due by various time intervals. It is used in accounting to help determine an appropriate *allowance* for uncollectibles. See *aging*.

accounts receivable collection period A measure of the average number of days it takes to collect receivables. It is compared with credit terms extended to customers to evaluate a firm's credit management. It is usually derived as receivables divided by average daily sales, i.e., annual sales divided by 365 or 360.

accounts receivable turnover A *ratio* which measures the number of times receivables are generated and collected during a time period. It is normally calculated as net credit sales divided by receivables.

account stated An *account* (3) the balance of which, as determined by the creditor, has been accepted as correct, sometimes implicitly, by the debtor. The term has significance in law, since it bars the debtor from attempting to disprove the accuracy of the computation, the bar being raised either by the debtor's explicit approval of the account and his promise to pay or by his failure within a reasonable time to indicate any exception to it.

accretion 1. An addition of principal or income to a fund as the result of a plan of accumulation; distinguished from *appreciation* and *increment*. In a pension fund, for example, an accretion may arise from payroll contributions or from revenue received on fund investments.

2. Increase in economic worth from any cause; as, the growth of timber, the aging of wines, the increase of flocks and herds.

accrual 1. The *recognition* (*1*) of *events and conditions* as they occur, rather than in the period of their incurrence, receipt, or payment.

2. The partial recognition of an item of revenue or expense and its related asset or liability: the result of the lack of coincidence of the accounting period and the contractual or benefit period.

3. An amount accrued. See *accrue*.

accrual basis (of accounting) The method of accounting whereby revenues and expenses are identified with specific periods of time, such as a month or year, and are recorded as *incurred,* along with acquired assets, without regard to the date of receipt or payment of cash; distinguished from *cash basis*. See *accrue* (*2*); *basis of accounting; accrued-expenditures basis*.

accrual costing The expensing of goods and services as they are applied or consumed. See *accrue* (*2*).

accrual date The date through which an accrual extends.

accrue *v.i.* 1. To grow; to increase; to accumulate.

2. To *recognize* in the accounts, usually at the end of a conventional period of time, as the result of the occurrence of *accountable* events or the emergence of *accountable* conditions that are in the process of continuous change. Interest on a debt, whether receivable or payable, increases day by day. The conventions of bookkeeping permit the in-

crease to be recorded daily, weekly, monthly, or yearly, in keeping with the frequency of financial statements prepared from the records or with the *closing* of the books. Other common accruing items are wages, taxes (on income or property), royalties, and depreciation of fixed assets. The term applies mostly to a continuing flow of services rather than to *physical assets*, and the process of accruing is employed by both the supplier and the recipient of the services. Upon recognizing an accruing item, a *transaction* in the form of an *adjusting journal entry* (or its equivalent) is recorded. On the books of the supplier, an asset account (e.g., interest receivable) is debited and a revenue account (e.g., interest earned) is credited,while on the books of the recipient, an expense account (e.g., interest expense) is debited and a liability account (e.g., accrued interest payable) is credited. Accruals are possible because persons who supply services have become accustomed to a period of waiting after the service has been rendered before being paid: e.g., typical bond-interest coupons become due after six months' interest has accumulated; wages are paid at the conclusion of a week's, two weeks', or month's work. *Accrue* contrasts with *prepay*. See also *accountable; recognize; transaction; double-entry bookkeeping*.

3. To come into existence; to become vested. Example: Rights to property accrue to a person's heirs upon his death; a right to a dividend accrues to a stockholder from the date of declaration.

v.t. To give effect to an accrual; to record revenue or expense in the accounting period to which it relates, notwithstanding that the required receipt or outlay may take place, in whole or in part, in a preceding or following period.

accrued asset The amount of interest, commission, services rendered to others, or other item of revenue neither received nor past due but *earned;* often a part of a larger whole. When past due, such an item, if still deemed collectible, is usually classified as an account receivable. See *accrue* (2).

accrued benefit-cost method = *unit-credit method*. An actuarial procedure for determining annual pension cost and funding requirements which credits an employee with a unit of retirement benefit, usually a fixed dollar amount or a percentage of compensation, for each period of employee service. A given year's pension cost usually is the *present value* of the increase in employees' retirement benefits resulting from that year's services. Cost is recognized as the liability for future benefits accrued through employee performance. See *aggregate level cost method*.

accrued depreciation 1. The total depreciation suffered by an asset or asset group, based on customary or fairly determined rates or estimates of useful life, now generally referred to as *accumulated depreciation*. See *depreciation; depreciation methods; fixed asset*.
2. The amount appearing in an accumulated-depreciation account.

accrued dividend The amount of unpaid and undeclared dividend on preferred stock. It differs from *dividend in arrears* by consisting of or including a provision for the period after the date on which the last dividend would ordinarily have been paid. Strictly speaking, a dividend does not accrue, since the stockholder usually has no legal claim to a dividend until it has been declared by the board of directors. See *dividend; unpaid dividend*.

accrued-expenditures basis A basis of analysis, statement preparation, or reporting characterized by the setting forth of goods received and services performed, and exemplified in a *funds-flow statement*. Such a statement contains the summary elements of an *income statement,* together with analyses of changes in assets, liabilities, and net worth, and may therefore be regarded as an *accounting* (*3*) of the differences between the items of successive balance sheets.

In federal government accounting, the term is employed in contradistinction to the *obligations* basis and the *cost basis,* the former signifying the inclusion of goods and services ordered but not received; the latter, goods and services *consumed.* The obligations basis has in the past applied primarily to *appropriations* by the Congress; at present many budgets and appropriations have been put on the accrued-expenditures basis; operating statements are said to be on a cost basis provided provisions for depreciation, if any, inventory used, and the like, replace asset acquisitions. All three bases, however, presume the *accrual* method of accounting.

accrued expense The liability covering an expense *incurred* on and before a given date, payable at some future date. Examples: accrued interest on notes payable; accrued wages; product warranties. See *expense; accrue; accrued liability.*

accrued income = *accrued revenue.*

accrued liability An amount of interest, wages, or other expense *recognized* or *incurred* but not paid; *accrued expense.*

accrued revenue Revenue earned, but neither received nor past due. See *accrued asset; accrue.*

accumulated depreciation A *contra account* or offset for a fixed asset which represents the amount of *depreciation expense* that has been charged against revenue from the date of acquisition; also known as reserve for depreciation and allowance for depreciation, it usually appears in the balance sheet, where it is subtracted from the original fixed asset cost to obtain the remaining unamortized balance. See *depreciation; depreciation methods; fixed asset.*

accumulated dividend = *dividend in arrears.*

accumulated earnings tax An additional tax assessed on accumulated taxable income of a corporation, as adjusted, which exceeds (1) $150,00 minus accumulated *earnings and profits* or (2) the amount of current year earnings and profits retained for the reasonable needs of the business, including maintenance of adequate working capital. The purpose of the tax is to discourage the corporate retention of earnings, especially liquid assets.

accumulated income (or earnings or profit) Net income retained and not paid out in dividends or dissipated by subsequent losses; *earned surplus* or *retained earnings.*

accumulation 1. The periodic addition of (a) interest or other increase to the principal of a fund, (b) annual *net income* to *retained earnings,* or (c) amortized discount to an investment or obligation in order to raise the principal sum to the amount ultimately receivable or payable. See *bond discount; deferred charge; amortization.*
2. The act of compounding. See *compound.* —accumulate, *v.t.*

accumulation factor The formula $(1 + i)^n$ applied to a principal amount bearing interest at rate *i* for the purpose of determining its total at the end of *n* periods. See *interest formulas.*

accuracy The validity of a statement, account, set of accounts, or document, such as a voucher, in portraying facts or opinions. The degree of accuracy is measured by the relative correspondence of a statement, account, or document to the *facts.* See *validation.*

The term *accuracy* has a closely related technical meaning in accounting, statistics, the natural sciences, and engineering. As contrasted with *precision,* it means the success with which the nearness to a true value is attained. Precision relates to the tendency of tests to give the same value even though the value is inaccurate. On the other hand, *relia-*

bility indicates the *probability* that a specified level of precision will be attained. Precision may be sacrificed for reliability, and vice versa, for a given sample size and method. Thus, high precision may be attained with low reliability, or low precision may be attained with high reliability for a given sample size and method.

In sampling procedures followed by an auditor, an increase in both precision and reliability requires either a larger sample or an improved sampling method, or both. For example, in certain circumstances both precision and reliability may be improved by dividing the sample into two parts, for a small part of which information is obtained with much care, time, and possibly cost per item sampled, and a larger part for which information is obtained on a more cursory, rapid, and less costly basis. The purpose of the larger part may to be secure greater *reliability* through a much larger sample size than would otherwise be used, whereas the purpose of the smaller part is to secure greater *precision* than would otherwise be obtained because of cost, time, and other considerations. The two sections of the sample may then be combined by various techniques to increase both precision and reliability. This procedure is often followed in an audit where a detailed examination is made of transactions covering a small portion of a period, while those belonging to the rest of the period are subjected only to a rapid scanning. See *verification; scan*.

achieved precision The *precision* calculated from a sample at a given reliability or confidence level.

acid-test ratio = *quick ratio*. A *ratio* which relates quick assets (current assets less inventories, mostly consisting of *cash, accounts receivable*, and *marketable securities*) to *current liabilities*. It is considered a rigorous measure of a firm's ability to pay off short-term obligations because no return is presumed from the liquidation of inventories. A minimum level of 1.0 is often prescribed for this ratio, but the ratio level of an individual firm should also be compared with the average ratio of its industry. It is typically calculated by dividing current assets less inventories by current liabilities.

acquire To come into the ownership and possession of property or services.

acquired surplus 1. The *surplus* of an enterprise existing at the date of acquisition of its control by another.
2. The excess over investment cost of dividends received by a parent or holding company from a subsidiary's earnings before consolidation; see *controlling-company accounting*.
3. The initial surplus or *retained earnings* of a successor enterprise where there has been a *pooling of interests* (i.e., no change in beneficial interests) and no full capitalization of prior retained earnings. The initial surplus may be paid-in or earned surplus (retained income) or both, depending on the nature of the surplus of the predecessor: paid-in surplus to the extent necessary to recognize the full paid-in capital of the predecessor; earned surplus in an amount not in excess of the predecessor's earned surplus, diminished by any increase in the amount attributed to paid-in capital. Example: Corporation *A*, having outstanding par-value capital stock amounting to $100,000, paid-in surplus of $50,000, and earned surplus of $25,000, is acquired by Corporation *B*, an existing company, in exchange for a block of the latter's capital stock the stated value of which is $150,000. Before the merger, *B*'s paid-in capital was $600,000 and its earned surplus $100,000. After the merger, with the capital stock at $750,000 and combined earned surplus at $125,000, the amount of each stockholder's equity in paid-in capital and

earned surplus remains unchanged. Had relative equity altered in the process, the transaction would have been a sale rather than a pooling of interests, in which case the earned surplus would be classified as capital paid in, thereafter not available for dividends. Continuing the illustration, if Corporation *B*'s original capital stock and earned surplus had been $900,000 and $100,000, respectively, *A*'s stockholders would have retained only a 150/1050 or 1/7 interest (instead of a 1/5 interest) in the combined surplus of $125,000. Under such circumstances, a purchase rather than a pooling of interests would have occurred, *A*'s earned surplus thus acquiring the status of paid-in surplus in *B*'s accounts. See *merger; consolidation; pooling of interests; earned surplus*.

acquisition The process of coming into ownership, control, or possession of something.

acquisition adjustment (public utility accounting) An account in which is recorded the difference between the cost of utility plant to the owning utility and original cost to any preceding owner who first dedicated it to public use. See *original cost* (2).

acquisition cost The *outlay* required as goods or services are purchased.

acquisition excess See *goodwill* (2); *consolidation goodwill*.

ACRS = *accelerated cost recovery system*.

activity 1. The work, or one of several lines of work, carried on within any organization or organizational subdivision.
2. Specifically, that portion of the work of an *organizational unit* relating to a specific function or class of functions: any point where organizational and functional lines intersect. See *function; activity account; program; project*.
3. The whole of the work carried on by any organization or individual.

activity account An income or expense account containing transactions over which an activity supervisor assumes responsibility and maintains control. The transactions may include both materials and services, but not overhead or other items that are the responsibilities of other persons. To insure the following of a performance design predetermined by higher authority, limitations in the form of permissible objects and ranges of expenditure, the number and qualifications of employees, and the adherence to standards of operation and output are commonly imposed on the activity and become a part of its definition. The propriety, correctness, and ''fit'' of every item of operating income or cost are then the responsibilities of the activity head. Because the person must be familiar with and approve such detail, he or she is normally supplied with a monthly or other periodic summary or copy of the activity account, and the latter must therefore contain whatever information is required by him or her for a critical review. There may thus be differences in the variety of detail furnished, depending on the nature of the activity and the needs of the activity head. See *activity; activity accounting*.

activity accounting See also *responsibility accounting*. The classification and operation of activity accounts with the object of aiding in the process of conforming organizational performance to plan; accounting by *functions*. Its principal application is to situations where forward planning, *authority, responsibility*, and *accountability* can be associated with operating units or centers each of which is identified in the organizational structure with an *organizational unit* or section of such a unit. By emphasis on transaction responsibility and accountability, activity accounting supplies substance as well as incentive to the delegation of management authority; further, it provides a series of well-defined focal points for the application and maintenance of budgetary and other operational controls. Following is a summary of definitions and principles adopted in one instance but having general application to any other operating establishment:

1. The work or tasks of a private or public enterprise, such as a corporation, consist of *projects* and *programs*, each of which is carefully defined before its commencement.

2. A *project* is a major property acquisition. Expenditures under a project are asset additions. Such an expenditure may involve the purchase of different kinds of assets, all contributing to a common function, or it may relate to "own" construction.

A project budget, the result of planning and programming, bears the approval of top management in advance of commitment; prospective unit costs are a feature. Examples of such units are material weights, labor hours, types of operation, and completed parts of structures.

As the project is being acquired or built, quantity and cost records are maintained; where construction is being carried on, frequent conferences are held between engineers and accountants on emerging unit and total costs and their relation with the project budget and, ultimately, with the completed-project cost report. Total reported cost is identical with the project cost reflected in financial statements at the end of the fiscal year during which the project is completed. The report breaks down total cost by subactivities or sections; for each section the unit costs, wherever possible, are compared with their budgeted counterparts and with costs obtaining on similar projects carried on elsewhere (variances explained in detail).

Property records for the completed project are based on and initially tie in directly with the cost report. See *plant ledger*.

Proposed minor acquisitions for a fiscal year are grouped under a single project designation. Minor replacements of equipment are given a separate project designation in order to surround them with special safeguards.

3. A *program* is a major operation. Expenditures under a program are operating costs. A program is "short-term" if it is to be completed within a fiscal year and "long-term" if it extends into a future period.

4. Subprojects and subprograms are defined (e.g., geographical) breakdowns of projects and programs, fitted to expedient delegations of management controls.

5. An activity is thus a project or program, a subproject or subprogram, or any convenient division to which authority is delegated. It is the lowest practicable coincident level of function, budgeting, and accounting.

An activity is always a unit of functional and organizational control; its orderly establishment and operation are dependent equally on specific, defined delegations of authority and on clear, nontechnical assignments of objectives.

Responsibility for the conduct of an activity, strictly within prescribed limits, must always be assumed by one person (the activity head) designed by higher authority and known to associates and outsiders to have accepted such responsibility.

The activity head often takes the initial step in the preparation of a budget; subsequently he administers the portion of the budget determined by higher authority to be applicable to his activity.

The lines of authority and the flow of information between activity head and top management are as simple and direct as possible.

6. An *organizational unit*, the smallest administrative subdivision, is designated to carry on one or more activities.

An organizational unit is one of the subgroups within an administrative (as contrasted with functional) division of the enterprise.

An organizational unit may be charged with a number of activities, but an activity may not extend beyond a single organizational unit; that is, the activity is to be generally recognizable as the exclusive task, or as one of the exclusive tasks, of such a unit.

The activity head is invariably the head of the organizational unit in which the activity is carried on.

The activity is the function, and the organizational unit the manpower, assigned to carry out an enterprise task.

7. At least one account is maintained for each activity, and no item of income or cost of an economic unit can escape assignment as the direct income or direct cost of an activity for which some one person is responsible. Once carried to an activity account, it remains there.

The one account may contain material, labor, and other *objective* items of cost, a distinctive symbol being given to each object class for overall recapitulation; but income always necessitates a separate account.

Several accounts may be required to facilitate the yield of component unit costs. No proration of the time of any individual or of the cost of any supply or service is subsequently made, excepting only prepayments, accruals, or deferrals.

A copy of each activity account, showing individual transactions, is given to the designated activity head periodically (e.g., monthly) and he or she is looked to by top management as the one responsible for the accuracy, propriety, and meaning of its content.

Explanations of transactions and other transaction data appear in such detail as may be arranged with the activity head.

8. One synthesis of activity accounts yields *financial* (functional) *statements* of projects and programs; another, capital outlay, income, and expense by organizational divisions, ordinarily required for budget comparisons.

9. The analysis of any activity account yields expenditures by *objects*; its recapitulation and comparison with quantities yield one or more unit costs.

10. Where activity accounting is carried on, a *budget* is a forward estimate of the income and cost of individual activities, with subtotals by projects and programs and by organizational divisions, or combinations of both.

11. *Accountability* may be supplied by oral or written reports to superior authority and by any of numerous other devices, such as group meetings of supervisors (e.g., factory foremen) where individual as well as interrelated problems may be discussed and solutions may be proposed and recommended.

activity base A measure of output or performance selected as a basis for planning and control of specific organizational units in a *responsibility accounting* system and used to express planned outputs and measure performance. See *activity accounting*.

activity ratios See *turnover ratios*.

activity variance = *volume variance*.

act of bankruptcy See *bankruptcy*.

act of God (insurance) An event leading to a property loss caused by forces of nature that could not have been prevented by reasonable care or foresight, e.g., flood, lightning, earthquake, hurricane.

actual cost 1. Cost, as of acquisition or production, the former net of discounts and allowances but including transportation and storage, and often averaged for internal-transfer or inventory purposes; the latter consisting of direct material, labor, and variable overhead. See *direct cost; inventory valuation*.

2. A term suggesting a degree of accuracy in a cost computation not insured by the approximations inherent in appraised, average, estimated, or standard costs; *historical cost*. When applied to product costs, it often means directly measured material and labor cost, but since these measures frequently involve prorations, averages, and varying lot quantities, the realism intended by ''actual'' may be somewhat illusory. See *joint cost; standard cost; historical cost; specific cost*.

3. Cost based on completed rather than estimated transactions.

actuarial Relating to insurance mathematics and statistics.

actuarial asset value A value assigned by an actuary to the assets of a plan, generally for use in establishing the amount and incidence of accounting charges for pension cost. See *actuarial basis; actuarial cost method*.

actuarial assumptions Conditions used to resolve uncertainties in the absence of information concerning future events affecting insurance, pension costs, etc.

actuarial basis A basis compatible with principles followed by actuaries; said of computations involving compound interest, retirement, mortality estimates, and the like.

actuarial cost method A technique used by actuaries for establishing the amount and incidence of employer contributions and/or accounting charges under a pension plan.

actuarial liability The amount by which the *present value* of prospective pension benefits and administrative expenses exceeds (1) the amount presently in a pension fund plus (2) the present value of future contributions. The latter is usually calculated on the basis of *normal cost* (or annual actuarial value) determined by any of several actuarial methods.

actuary One skilled in insurance mathematics and statistics.

addition (as relating to fixed assets) = *capital expenditure*. See *fixed asset*.

additional markon (retail accounting) An addition to a previously established *markon*.

additional paid-in capital Contributions of stockholders credited to accounts other than *capital stock*; sources: an excess over *par* or *stated value* received from the sale or exchange of capital stock, an excess of par or stated value of capital stock reacquired over the amount paid therefor, or an *excess from recapitalization*; often displayed on the balance sheet as a separate item or in combination with par or stated value and designated *paid-in capital*; on the books a separate account may be maintained for each principal source. Known also as *paid-in surplus*.

address 1. (computers) A label, name, or number that identifies the location of a register or datum in storage.

2. A label, name, or number used to identify a geographic or physical location.

adequate Fulfilling minimal requirements; satisfactory; acceptable; sufficient.

adjunct account = *absorption account*.

adjusted bank balance Corrected amount of *cash* in an entity's bank account at a given date; usually derived from a *bank reconciliation* that begins with the balance reported in the bank statement to which such items as deposits made but not recorded by the bank are added and such items as *outstanding* checks and corrections are subtracted and to which bank errors are added and subtracted; must equal *adjusted book balance*; often called *bank balance*.

adjusted basis (federal income taxes) Cost or other *basis* increased by improvements and other capitalized additions and reduced by depreciation and other recoveries. Adjusted basis is used in computing depreciation and gain or loss on sales of fixed assets.

adjusted book balance Correct amount of *cash* in an entity's account at a given date; derived in the portion of a *bank reconciliation* that begins with the balance shown in the entity's ledger account for *cash in bank* to which such items as previously unrecorded notes collected by the bank or corrections of book errors are added and such items as previously unrecorded service charges or corrections of book errors are subtracted; must equal *adjusted bank balance*; often called *bank balance*.

adjusted gross income (federal income taxes) The *gross income* of an individual reduced by those items listed in Section 62 of the *Internal Revenue Code*. Deductions to arrive at adjusted gross income include such items as trade or business expenses, expenses related to investments in rental and royalty property, certain expenses of employees, limited deductions related to capital gains and losses, moving expenses when the move is business or employment motivated and meets certain specifications, certain types of individual contributions to retirement funds, alimony, and the penalty imposed by a bank or other savings institution for early withdrawal from a time deposit. Adjusted gross income is the basis for determining the eligibility for and the amounts or limitations of various other components of the individual's tax computation, such as medical expenses and charitable contributions.

adjusted trial balance *Trial balance*, taken from the *general-ledger* accounts after *adjusting journal entries* but before *closing entries* have been *posted*.

adjusting journal entry 1. The record made of an *accounting transaction* giving effect to the correction of an error, an accrual, a writeoff, a provision for bad debts or depreciation, or the like. See *journal entry*.
2. (auditing) Any change in the accounts required by an auditor, expressed in the form of a simple or compound journal entry.

adjustment Any change in an account produced by an *adjusting journal entry*.

administered price The price per unit of commodity where the amount to be paid or received is directly established or substantially influenced by a controlling agent. Such a price, reflecting secular influences, is ordinarily the result of a planned control little influenced by short-term considerations of expanding sales and maximum profits. Administered prices may be classified by the character of the controlling agency and the nature of the control thus:

1. A government-administered price, of which there are three general classes:

(a) Ceiling price: a maximum price directly established by government decree, often used in planned economies but also used, in emergencies, in other economies. Effective ceilings limit price as an equilibrating mechanism between supply and demand and must, therefore, be accompanied by rationing or other supplementary measures.

(b) Support price: a price substantially influenced by government control of supply through production control and of trading and credit policies in an effort to maintain minimum price levels for purposes of a redistribution of income within the economy.

(c) Fixed rate: a price directly established by government decree, such as the price for the services of a public utility, usually derived by computing a fair return on the investment, the purpose being to minimize consumer costs and insure adequate service.

2. Industry-administered price: the price usually determined under oligopolistic conditions by the dominant member of an industry or group of dominant members controlling a substantial portion of the industry's production and acting as the price leader for the industry, the purpose being to stabilize the rel-

ative position of the individual concern, the group, or the industry as a whole. This price differs from a cartel price in that it is not necessarily the result of an explicit agreement but is nonetheless adopted by all the members of the industry because they recognize that it will advance their mutual interests or because each recognizes the possibility of punitive action by other dominant members who control key resources or who may resort to local price cutting. Although an industry-administered price takes any of numerous forms, it can usually be derived by formula:

(a) Base price: the price from which all other prices are computed, usually reflecting the hypothetical or actual sale of the basic grade of the commodity from a specific geographic (basing) point to customers in a specific geographic location. It may be directly established, but it is usually influenced by manipulation of the supply function of the market by the controlling agents.

(b) Computed price: the price resulting from the application of a formula usually involving an adjustment of the base price for arbitrary or hypothetical transport costs, and differentials in the grade of the commodity. This price may be on a delivered FOB or zone basis and is the price charged in transactions.

(c) Millnet or netback price: the price realized by the producer or seller resulting from the use of the computed price; it may be more or less than the base price depending on the formula used and the location of the purchaser.

Each of the foregoing is illustrated by the price system employed in the steel industry prior to 1924. Under this system all suppliers quoted a uniform delivered price at each destination, made up of the base price at Pittsburgh plus standard railroad freight from Pittsburgh to destination, regardless of the mode of shipment (truck, water, or other

means). The Pittsburgh price as established by the industry price leader was usually followed by all firms in the industry regardless of mill location. For example, a mill in Chicago would sell to Chicago customers at the computed Pittsburgh base price—including the standard freight cost to Chicago. The Chicago *millnet price* would be the price realized by the Chicago producer after deducting the actual cost of shipping from the *computed price* at which the sale took place.

3. Individual-firm price: the price established by an individual business for its own products regardless of the price charged by competitors, usually under conditions in which the firm has enough control over the market to disregard demand fluctuations and prices of competitors for appreciable periods of time. See *price*.

administration 1. That branch of management embracing the supervision and operation of any organization. One trained in the administration of business enterprise has acquired an intimate working knowledge of forms of business organization: how capital is obtained; relations with financial institutions; labor management; procurement problems; market conditions and methods of market exploitation; foreign trade; the coordination of the various parts of an enterprise so as to achieve the purposes for which the enterprise is carried on; methods of internal organization; the institution and maintenance of internal controls; methods of delegating responsibility; public and human relations; regulations of governmental bodies affecting business; how adaptations may be made to economic and social trends within the business and the industry and in the world at large; and, perhaps the most important feature of all, how any business problem may be recognized, analyzed, and solved. See *policy*.

2. The carrying on of a business, government, or other operation.

3. The collection of an intestate's assets, the payment of his debts, and the distribution of any assets remaining.

4. = *management* (2).

administrative accounting That portion of the accounting process generally associated with management; for example, the functions of the controller, internal auditing, and decisions as to prorations, valuations, reserves, charge-offs, and reporting. The term is sometimes employed in contrast with *cost accounting;* in such use, it is roughly the equivalent of *financial accounting*.

administrative action 1. Within a corporation, a decision of management (as contrasted with *corporate action*), or a decision on a matter of policy ordinarily made by the board of directors. Administrative action embraces the whole field of *administration*, or the everyday decisions that must be made promptly and as a matter of course, in order that operations may be carried on smoothly and efficiently.

2. Any act or operating policy of the executive branch of government, whether or not authorized by regulation or legislation.

administrative audit (or review) 1. = *preaudit*.

2. = *internal audit*.

administrative budget A financial plan under which an organization carries on its day-to-day affairs under the common forms of administrative *management*; a *budget*. The term is usually employed in contradistinction to *capital budget* or *fund* budget.

administrative control Those elements of internal control designed to assure adherence to management's prescribed policies and to promote operational efficiencies. (See *internal control*.)

administrative expense A classification of expense incurred in the general direction of an enterprise as a whole, as contrasted with expense of a more specific function, such as manufacturing or selling, but not including *income deductions*. Items included under this head vary with the nature of the business, but usually include salaries of top officers, rent, and other general-office expense. Typical are the following:

Salaries—officers and executives
Salaries—general-office employees
Travel expense
Legal and auditing
Office-building maintenance
Depreciation—furniture and fixtures
Stationery and office supplies
Telephone and telegraph
Postage
Light and water
Taxes other than income
Insurance on lives of officers
Subscriptions and dues
Donations
Revenue stamps

administrator 1. One skilled in *administration*.

2. One named by a court to take charge of the assets of an intestate and to dispose of them in accordance with law or ruling of the court. See *executor*.

admissible asset (insurance accounting) = *admitted asset*.

admitted asset (insurance accounting) An asset, as determined under the laws of various jurisdictions, having a value in liquidation.

ad valorem Designating a property tax, severance tax, or import or other duty computed as a percentage (rate) of the value of the property.

advance 1. A payment of cash or the transfer

of goods for which an *accounting* (*2*) must be rendered by the recipient at some later date.

2. A payment on a contract before its completion.

3. The payment of wages, salaries, or commissions before they have been earned.

advance refunding Issuance of debt instrument to refund existing debt before it matures or is callable.

advance to affiliate *Asset* account for a *loan* made by a *parent company* to its *subsidiary*.

advance to supplier An *asset* account arising from payment before a *good* or *service* is received.

adverse opinion See *opinion*.

Advisory Committee on Corporate Disclosure A special committee of experts appointed in 1975 by the *Securities and Exchange Commission* to undertake a broad and comprehensive study of the system of corporate disclosure in the securities markets being regulated by the Commission. The committee's report was issued in November 1977 and was printed by the Committee on Interstate and Foreign Commerce of the U.S. House of Representatives.

affiliate 1. A corporation or other organization related to another by owning or being owned, by common management or by a long-term lease of its properties or other control device. See *control*.

2. A close associate; said of *individuals (1)* who own property jointly or have closely related business interest. See *related party transactions*.

affiliated company = *affiliate* (*1*).

affiliation Control of, by, or under common control with another. An affiliation exists between a *holding company* or *parent company* and its *subsidiary*, or between two corporations or other organizations owned or controlled by a third. See *control* (*3*).

affirm 1. To state or assert positively; to maintain as true; to confirm or ratify; 2. (legal) to declare solemnly before a court, but without oath; 3. to ratify and accept (a voidable transaction); 4. to determine (by an appellate court) that the action of a lower court shall stand.

affreightment A contract for transporting goods by sea: a *charter party* or an ocean bill of lading.

age The number of years or other time periods an asset or asset group has remained in service at a given date. See *aging*.

aged trial balance A presentation of the details comprising an account balance where the dating (age) of the details is of significance and, therefore, set out in the presentation. The most common example is accounts receivable, where each customer balance is analyzed by aging category, e.g., current, 30, 60, 90, and 120 days and older, and totals of each category are showing for all accounts.

agency 1. The relation between principal and agent. See *agent*.

2. (governmental accounting) Any unit of government administering an appropriation, allocation, or allotment; as, a department, commission, authority, administration, or board.

agency fund A fund consisting of assets held under an agency relationship for another.

agenda 1. Work to be done; an auditor's agenda consisting of notes made in the field, inquiries, and other matters to be taken care of at a later point in the audit.

2. Any list of points for discussion or action.

agent One who represents, acts for, and accounts to another.

aggregate *n.* A collection of items supposedly related to each other or having at least some properties in common; a set. Example: An aggregate of prices. Such aggregates may be refined and submitted to processes of reduction for simplicity and processed to achieve simplicity as when, for example, each price in an aggregate of prices for consumer goods is weighted and entered into formula to obtain a single index number of consumer prices. See *consumer price index*. In general the resulting aggregation involves some loss of *information* on behavior in the underlying items. Note: This term may also be used as a verb to describe the process of forming an aggregate.

aggregate level cost method An actuarial method for projecting and allocating the cost of retirement benefits in which the pension cost is spread equally over the average service life on an employee group. This method is similar to the *individual level premium method* except that normal cost accruals are based on the covered group and not on each separate participant. See *accrued benefit-cost method; entry age normal method*.

aggregation *v*. To *aggregate*. *n*. The resulting collection or *aggregate*.

AGI (federal income taxes) = *adjusted gross income*.

aging An analysis of the elements of individual *accounts receivable* according to the time elapsed after the dates of billing or the due dates, usually the former; employed as an aid in determining an allowance or the propriety of an allowance for bad debts.—*age, v.t.* See *accounts receivable aging schedule*.

AICPA = *American Institute of Certified Public Accountants*.

AJE = *adjusting journal entry*.

algorithm 1. A set of well-defined rules or steps which lead to solution of a problem. The number of operations should be finite or a rule for stopping should be included in the operations when use on a *digital computer* is intended.

2. A systematic rule for solving arithmetic or mathematical problems in an iterative manner.

allied company = *affiliated company*.

all-inclusive income = *comprehensive income*.

all-inclusive income statement An income statement containing all items of profit and loss given recognition during a given period. It leaves little to the discretion of management and the public accountant, and is thus claimed to be more objective than a statement in which ''nonperformance'' items or prior-year adjustments are omitted. See *clean surplus rule; income statement*.

allocable Identifiable with two or more objects, activities, functions, or other *cost objectives*; said, e.g., of a *joint cost* or a *common cost* or an *overhead pool* of expense accounts.

allocate 1. To charge an item or group of items of revenue or cost to one or more objects, activities, processes, operations, or products, in accordance with cost responsibilities, benefits received, or other identifiable measure of application or consumption. Examples: to charge the amount of a voucher to an expense account; to spread fire-insurance-premium costs to departments in proportion to the insurable values of the assets located in such departments. In this sense, allocation may refer to a direct or indirect expense. See *prorate*.

2. To distribute the total cost of a *lump-sum purchase* over the items purchased or departments affected.

3. To spread a cost systematically over two or more time periods.

4. (governmental accounting) To transfer, by administrative authority, an *appropriation* or a part thereof from one agency to another.

allocation The process or result of allocating. See *allocate*.

allocation of variances 1. The assignment of differences between *standard costs* and *actual costs* to *work in process, finished goods*, and *cost of goods sold*.
2. The process of allocating *variances* to the products or activities believed to be responsible for them. See *standard cost; variance*.

allotment 1. (governmental accounting) The administrative assignment by an agency of a part of an *appropriation, allocation*, or *apportionment* to a subdivision of the agency. The authority thus conferred is to incur liabilities or obligations up to a specified amount for prescribed, often broad or discretionary, purposes.
2. An assignment of pay for the benefit of dependents.
3. The division of available or anticipated revenues among specific classes of expenditures.
4. The distribution of securities in accordance with or in proportion to applications from subscribers; the assignment of shares in a syndicate or other undertaking; the number of shares or amount so assigned.
—allot, *v.t.*

allotment ledger (governmental accounting) A subsidiary ledger containing an account for each *allotment*, showing the amount *allotted, expenditures, encumbrances*, and *unencumbered balance*.

allowance 1. Permitted tolerance in measurement, quality, or quantity of goods; also normal or permitted shrinkage, breakage, spoilage, or other loss in handling, using, or holding.
2. In the settlement of a debt, a deduction granted or accepted by the creditor for damage, delay, shortage, imperfection, or other cause, excluding discounts and returns.
3. An expenditure permitted by superior administrative authority to an organizational subdivision or to an agent. Often in the form of a round sum, it may be more or less in amount than the expense incurred, thereby obviating the need for securing proof of payment. Examples: an allowance for branch-office rent; an allowance in lieu of actual expenses, as for the maintenance and operation of an automobile owned by a salesman.
4. A *valuation account* reflecting lost usefulness, or a loss or an absorption of cost (i.e., an accumulation of expired or transferred costs). See *reserve (1); provision; depreciation; expense*.
5. A provision or an accumulation of provisions for the loss or decline in worth of an asset: a *valuation account* or an addition to a *valuation account* created by charges to expense; a *reserve (2)*. Example: an allowance for bad debts or for depreciation; on a balance sheet allowances appear as a reduction of the asset value to which they are related.

allowance for depreciation See *accumulated depreciation*.

allowance for doubtful (uncollectible) accounts A valuation account offsetting the periodic provision for estimated uncollectible accounts or bad debts; a *contra account* to *accounts* and *notes receivable* that reflects a reasonable estimate of the reported receivables that ultimately will not be collected; when specific uncollectible accounts become known, they are written off against the allowance account which has been created by charges against the revenues of previous periods. See *bad-debt* and *uncollectible accounts*.

allowance for purchase discount *Contra account* to accounts payable to show the estimated amount of *cash discount* that are expected to be taken on purchases.

allowance for sales discount *Contra account* to accounts receivable to show the estimated amount of *cash discount* on sales that are expected to be taken by customers when their receivable accounts are collected early in the next accounting period. See *cash discount*.

all-purpose financial statement A financial statement serving, as far as possible, the needs of all users. The financial statements to which professional accountants append their reports are nearly always all-purpose statements, since the accountant does not limit the use to which the statement will be put. The term is used in contrast with condensed statement (e.g., *condensed balance sheet*), which has now largely fallen into disuse, and *special-purpose financial statement*.

alpha risk The *risk* associated with a *type I error*. The risk, for example, that sample evidence will fail to support a recorded accounting balance when the same audit procedures extended to the entire population would actually support the account balance. See *beta risk*.

alteration An improvement or modification made of a fixed asset that does not represent an addition to or increase in the quantity of the services to be yielded by the asset.

alternative cost 1. Cost under conditions other than those currently obtaining, as from a change from producing to purchasing, a change in a production method, the use of a more efficient machine, the substitution of one raw material for another, a modification in a product specification, or an increase or decrease, whatever the cause, in one or more component costs. Where no plant alterations are involved, overhead remaining the same, the elements making up an alternative cost are direct and variable items. Although they may serve many purposes, alternative costs are most often estimated and compared with actual costs in testing cost-reduction proposals or in providing background for the problems of future production.
2. (economics) The usual definition of alternative cost is not in terms of any outlay but is measured in terms of the benefits that can no longer be secured; generally from the best (i.e., highest valued) of the alternatives that are foreclosed by an alternative being considered for choice. See *opportunity cost; cost*.

amalgamation A combination under a single head of all or a portion of the assets and liabilities of two or more business units by *merger* or *consolidation*.

American Accounting Association (AAA) An organization dedicated primarily to the interests of academic accountants. It was founded in 1916 under the name American Association of University Instructors in Accounting (AAUIA) and adopted its present name in 1936. Its committees issue reports on matters related to accounting education, research, and theory. Its most celebrated publication is *An Introduction to Corporate Accounting Standards*, and it publishes research studies and a journal, *The Accounting Review*. Any interested individual may become a member.

American Bar Association A professional organization of attorneys. The ABA will periodically issue policy statements which impact public accountants as to their dealings with attorneys. A primary example is their policy regarding lawyers' responses to auditors' requests for information. (See *attorney's letter*.)

American Institute of Accountants Name adopted in 1917 and retained until 1953 by the body known today as the *American Institute of Certified Public Accountants*.

American Institute of Certified Public Accountants (AICPA) A professional accounting body whose origin may be traced to the founding in 1887 of the American Association of Public Accountants, a predecessor body. The name *American Institute of Accountants* was adopted in 1917, and in 1953 its present name was taken. Through committees, the Institute provides advice to government agencies and issues technical guidance to membership once he or she becomes a certified public accountant. The Institute publishes a wide range of publications relating to the profession generally and to the practice of accounting, auditing, taxation, and management services. One of its best known publications is *Accounting Trends and Techniques*. It publishes the *Journal of Accountancy* and the *Tax Adviser*.

American Society of Certified Public Accountants (ASCPA) A professional body established by Durand Springer and other dissidents in 1921 and merged with the *American Institute of Accountants* (AIA) in 1935. It published a monthly journal, the *Certified Public Accountant*.

amortization 1. The gradual extinguishment of any amount over a period of time: as, the retirement of a debt by serial payments to a creditor or into a sinking fund; the periodic writedown of an insurance premium or a bond premium.

2. A reduction of the book value of a fixed asset: a generic term for the *depreciation, depletion, writedown,* or *writeoff* of a limited-life asset or group of such assets, an acquired intangible asset such as *goodwill*, or a prepaid expense, either by a direct credit or through the medium of a *valuation* account; hence, the amount of such a reduction. See *depreciation*.

3. = *accelerated depreciation*.

amortize 1. To write off a portion or all of the cost of an asset; to *depreciate* or deplete (*depletion*).

2. To retire (debt) over a period of years.

3. To subject any amount to a process of extinguishment.

amortized cost Cost less portions written off: the valuation basis of capital assets and of investments, inventories, and other assets where original cost has been reduced by depreciation or to an amount equal to market or other standard of valuation. See *cost absorption; depreciated cost*.

analog computer A computer which represents the value of a *variable* on a continuous basis, such as by the amplitude of a current or by voltage differences, as compared to a *digital computer*, which represents values on a discrete basis. Analog computers may be synthesized from mechanical or electrical components or by chemical, physical, or other processes.

analysis schedule A presentation of the details of an account balance showing the makeup at the beginning of the analysis period; additions, deletions, and other changes during the period; and the resultant makeup of the balance at the end of the analysis period.

analytical test A procedure which examines relationships among data as a means of obtaining substantive audit evidence (see *substantive test*) in order to point up possible areas for further audit or as a basis for determining whether special aspects of corporate (or agency) performances are adequately and fairly presented. Also termed *analytic review*. These include: (a) comparison of financial information with information for comparable prior periods; (b) comparison of financial information with anticipated results (e.g., budgets and forecasts); (c) study of relationships between elements of financial information that should conform to predictable patterns, based on the entity's experience; (d) comparison of financial information with similar information regarding the industry in which an entity operates; (e) study of the relationships of financial information with relevant nonfinancial information.

Various methods may be used to perform these procedures. They may be made using dollars, physical quantities, ratios, or percents.

Analytical tests will either support the overall reasonableness of recorded balances or they will indicate unusual fluctuations or variations which will give an auditor a basis for performing additional tests.

analytic review A use of *horizontal analysis* or *cross-section analysis* (or both) of a firm's financial statements as a guide to forming audit strategies. Such a review constitutes only one element in the formation of such strategies and, of course, these strategies are subject to change as an audit progresses and new *evidence* is uncovered. See *analytical test*.

analytic schedule (insurance) A system of evaluating the relative fire hazards involved in such matters as protection, exposure, construction, and occupancy; used as a standard in some states for determining fire-insurance rates except for dwellings, churches, and certain other structures.

analyze 1. To determine or examine the composition of an item, account, or amount, usually by reference to its historical origin; particularly (auditing) to review and set forth in a working paper the details or classified summary of items in an account, obtained or substantiated, where necessary, by reference to sources, and accompanied by explanations of major items and by cross-references to related accounts. See *scan; verify; vouch; audit*. —analysis, *n*.
2. To interpret or draw conclusions from a financial statement or statements.
3. To review a transaction or series of actual or proposed transactions to determine their effect on the accounts or on the principles to be followed in giving effect to them.

annual actuarial value = *normal cost*.

annual audit An *audit* (*4*) by a professional accountant covering a year's transactions.

annual closing The posting of *closing entries* taking place at the end of a fiscal year.

annual financial statement A balance sheet of any *accounting unit* as at the end of the last day of its fiscal year, or an income or other related statement covering the year's operations or bearing that date.

annualize (federal income taxes) To expand to an annual basis: the procedure under the *Internal Revenue Code* whereby taxable income for a fractional year is multiplied by a fraction equal to 12 divided by the number of months in the shorter period. The tax computed on the income thus expanded is then reduced by application of the same fraction reversed. This process is necessary in order to subject taxable income in the short period to the same effective tax rate as would be applicable to the proportionately larger income of a full year. This computation is required only when the fractional year is caused by a change of accounting period and is not required for a taxpayer's first or last year.

annual report 1. Any report prepared at yearly intervals.
2. A statement of the financial condition and operating results of an enterprise, prepared yearly for submission to interested parties; particularly, a report rendered each year to stockholders, and often to the employees and the public, by the board of directors or one or more of the principal officers of a corporation, summarizing its operations for the preceding year and including a balance sheet, income statement, often a funds-flow statement, and the auditor's report, together with comments by the chairman or president of the corporation on the year's business, labor relations, research program, public service, market prospects, and the like. See *reporting; auditors' report*.

annuitant The recipient of an *annuity*.

annuity 1. A series, or one of a series, of equal payments at fixed intervals and allowed to accumulate at compound interest for a specified number of periods; the right to receive such payments. An annuity may be for a specified period, as in the case of payments into a sinking fund: contingent, as in the field of life insurance, or perpetual, as in the case of an endowment fund. See *interest formulas*.

2. A periodic payment to a retired employee; a *pension benefit*.

annuity agreement (or contract) An agreement whereby money or other property is made available to another on condition that the recipient bind himself to hold and administer the property and to pay the donor or other designated person a stipulated *annuity* ceasing with a specified date or event such as the annuitant's death; also called *annuity bond*.

annuity bond A *bond* without a *maturity* date; pays interest perpetually. See *perpetual bond; perpetuity; annuity agreement*.

annuity certain An annuity payable for a stated number of periods as distinct from one dependent for its duration upon some contingency, such as marriage or death. See *annuity due; annuity*.

annuity cost A term referring to an accrual or outlay in connection with anticipatory payments under a pension plan to retired employees. In creating the fund and maintaining it, periodic contributions by the employer will ordinarily include an amount based on past as well as present services.

annuity due An annuity where payment is made at the beginning of each period, rather than at the end, as in an *ordinary annuity*.

annuity fund 1. = *Amount of an annuity*.
2. The fund created as the result of an *annuity agreement*.

annuity in advance = *annuity due*.

annuity in arrears = *ordinary annuity*. See *interest formulas*.

annuity method (of depreciation) See *depreciation methods*.

ANSI (computers) = American National Standards Institute. A national organization of computer manufacturers and users responsible for development of industry standards such as ANSI *COBOL* and ANSI *FORTRAN*.

antedate To affix a date preceding the date written or executed, as in an insurance policy, where the coverage often begins at a point of time earlier than the day the policy is officially issued.

anticipated (or anticipatory) profit A profit recorded in advance of its realization. Examples: profit on sales contracted for but not yet consummated; profit on installment sales represented by installments not currently due. See *realize; accrual basis*.

anticipatory breach An act or words, before performance of a contract is due, evincing an intent not to perform in the future, allowing the promisee to sue immediately on the breach. See *breach of contract*.

antideficiency act A federal statute directed to preventing expenditures or disbursements or incurring obligations which would create deficiencies in appropriations.

anti-dilution (dilutive) Term from APB Opinion 15 to denote that the conversion or exercise of certain securities into additional shares of common stock may increase either *primary earnings per share* or *fully diluted earnings per share*; securities are excluded from the calculation of *earnings per share* in any period when their assumed exercise or conversion would have an anti-dilutive effect.

antilogarithm The number obtained when the base of a logarithm system is raised to the power indicated by the *logarithm*; symbolized by "antilog" for the common logarithm system. See *logarithm*.

antitrust laws A body of legal statutes at both state and federal levels and related court findings designed to promote competition by outlawing or regulating monopolies and combinations of firms as well as pricing or other practices that may tend to weaken competitive market forces. Principal federal antitrust laws include the Sherman and Clayton Antitrust Acts, the Federal Trade Commission Act, and the Cellar Antimerger Act.

APB = *Accounting Principles Board*.

API 1. Accounting for the Public Interest, an organization of accountants pursuing public interest projects. See *public interest accounting*.
2. Also American Petroleum Institute, an oil industry trade association.
3. *abnormal performance index*.

APL (computers) = *A Programming Language*. A computer language suitable for mathematical or statistical problems which is designed primarily to be used on a computer terminal.

a posteriori After the fact; pertaining to the process of *reasoning* (2) whereby *principles* or other *propositions* are derived from observations of *facts*.

application of funds See *statement of sources and applications of funds*.

application program (computers) A program or list of instructions which performs a task specific to a user's needs. It contrasts with a "systems program," which is more general in nature and used for many different purposes by many different users.

applied cost Cost that has been allocated to a product or activity. See *cost; overhead*.

apportionment 1. The distribution of a cost over several periods of time in proportion to anticipated benefits. See *spread; overhead*.
2. (governmental accounting) The administrative assignment, subject to the approval of the Office of Management and Budget, of all or a portion of an appropriation to a part of a fiscal year or to a specific activity or object.

appraisal The act of *appraising*; the result of appraising; an appraisal report.

appraisal method (of depreciation) See *depreciation methods*.

appraisal report A statement, in summary or detail, prepared by engineers or other qualified persons, of the cost or value of an asset, asset group, or all of the fixed assets of a business.

appraisal surplus The excess of estimated depreciated replacement cost, or other basis of measurement, of fixed or other assets over their cost or book value. It is given expression as a credit on books of account when appraisal values are recorded (a practice at present rare), and thus may find its way into financial statements. It is sometimes referred to as unrealized profit, and it was customary during the inflationary period of the 1920s periodically to reduce appraisal surplus by transfers to depreciation expense, to the allowance or reserve for depreciation, or to earned surplus. In recent years such credits have been disapproved, thus leaving the account intact; but the disposal of an appraisal-surplus account, particularly after the property to which it relates is no longer in existence, presents a problem that has not yet been satisfactorily resolved. Under the laws of most states, appraisal surplus is generally not available for cash or property dividends to stockholders; at the time of its creation it is essentially a *valuation account* rather than retained income. See *retained earnings*.

appraise 1. To examine and weigh critically: a *value judgment* following studies and tests of operating conduct. See *operating performance*.
2. To establish cost or value by systematic procedures that include physical examination, pricing, and often engineering estimates.

appraised value Cost or value established by appraisal; as, cost of reproduction less observed depreciation. See *appraise*.

appraiser One who appraises property: an owner, a prospective buyer, or, more commonly, a group of professionally skilled persons holding themselves out as experts on *valuation*.

appreciation Increase in value of property: the excess of the present value of property over *book value*. The term is applied (a) to the excess of appraisal value over book value of fixed assets (= *appraisal surplus* when given expression on books of account), and (b) to the increase in the market price of securities and commodities sold or quoted on exchanges.
—appreciate, *v.t. & i*.

appreciation surplus = *appraisal surplus*.

appropriate 1. Suitable, desirable, reasonable, or necessary in a particular context; often used by accountants as signifying conformity with the value judgments implicit in current practices. See *significant; proper*.
2. *v.* The legal process of authorizing a governmental unit to incur liabilities for specified purposes, not to exceed specified amounts, and only during a specified time period.

appropriated retained income (retained earnings or earned surplus) Retained earnings earmarked on the books of account and in financial statements for some specific or general purpose, taking the form of a separate account to which retained earnings are transferred, in corporate enterprises usually by action of the board of directors or stockholders rather than by administrative direction; it remains as a subdivision of retained earnings, and is preferably shown on the balance sheet although less frequently appearing in a separate category preceding retained earnings. Its purpose is to indicate that an equivalent unearmarked amount of assets is not to be paid out as dividends but is to be retained as a safeguard against the contingency or event indicated. It is ultimately returned to retained earnings undiminished, the related expenditure, if any, having been expensed or capitalized according to its nature. Examples: an appropriation for a plant extension or for a possible future inventory shrinkage. See *retained earnings*.

appropriation 1. An expenditure authorization with specific limitations as to amount, purpose, and time; a formal advance approval of an expenditure or class of expenditures from designated resources available or estimated to be available. An appropriation may vary in binding force from an expression of intent by the management of a business concern to a restrictive limitation by the legislature imposed on a government agency.
2. The amount of future expenditures so approved.
3. The document evidencing the act and the amount, describing the purpose, and giving essential particulars concerning the character of authorized future expenditures, as in the case of appropriations for capital assets.
4. A distribution of net income to various accounts. See *appropriation of net income*.
5. An earmarking of *retained earnings*; = *appropriated retained income*.
—*appropriate, v.t.*

appropriation account 1. (governmental accounting) The account of a government agency to which the amount of a legislative appropriation is credited; it is eventually offset by expenditure or by a cancellation, return, or lapsing of any remaining balance.
2. (British usage) The account to which the profit-and-loss balance for the year is carried and taxes and dividends are charged, the balance being transferred to *revenue reserves*.

appropriation act (bill, ordinance, resolution, or order) A legal action authorizing the administration of a governmental unit to incur liabilities for the acquisition of goods, services, or facilities to be used for purposes specified in the act or ordinance, and in amounts not to exceed those specified for each purpose. The authorization usually expires at the end of a specified term, most often one year.

appropriation budget A document fixing specific allowances for the budget period.

appropriation ledger (governmental accounting) A subsidiary ledger containing an account with each *appropriation*, showing the amount appropriated, the *expenditures*, and often the *encumbrances* and the unencumbered balance of each appropriation; or, if allotments are made and a separate ledger maintained therefor, the appropriations, the allotments, and the unallotted balance of each appropriation. Appropriation ledgers have recently been replaced by records maintained on an ordinary accrual-accounting basis.

appropriation of net income The disposition of noncorporate net income by the owner or partners, or of corporate net income by resolution of the directors (or, in Britain, by stockholders), sometimes summarized at the foot of an income statement; as, the setting aside or commitment of net income for dividends, the allocation of net income to a sinking fund or other *appropriated retained income*, or the transfer of net income or the balance of net income to earned surplus (retained earnings). Among corporate enterprises there is some difference of opinion as to what items are income deductions (i.e., deductions from operating revenue before the determination of net income) and what items should be regarded as net-income appropriations; as a rule, the former are unusual expenses including losses; the latter, transactions with stockholders or an earmarking of *retained earnings*. In British practice, appropriations also include "direct" (i.e., income) taxes. See *income deduction; net income*.

appropriation period (governmental accounting) The year or other period of time during which an *appropriation* may be obligated or expended.

appropriation receipt (governmental accounting) A receipt of a special fund or trust fund, available for expenditure only for specified purposes.

appropriation refund (governmental accounting) The return of an advance or the recovery of an improper disbursement, regarded as a full or partial cancellation of the original expenditure and hence available for reobligation or reexpenditure.

appropriation reimbursement (governmental accounting) An addition to an appropriation arising from the sale of goods or services to another branch of the government or to an outsider.

appropriation request (governmental accounting) A petition for funds by an administrative or other agency of government to the legislature. Under current practices, the request, known as an *account* (5), consists of suggested appropriation language, brief schedules of anticipated costs of *programs* with a narrative *justification* for each, particulars of any financing available from other sources, and an *objective statement*.

appropriation section A final division sometimes attached to an income statement showing the disposition of net income as between dividends, surplus reserves, and earned surplus (retained earnings). See *appropriation of net income*.

appropriation (transfer) warrant See *warrant* (5).

approval of transaction An indication that the conditions required by authorization have apparently been met.

approximate Containing *error* usually small or limited in magnitude; thus a quantity, or verbal characterization, which cannot validly be claimed to coincide in all respects with results which could be secured by more precise consideration or treatment.

v.t. To attempt or effect an *approximation*.

approximation 1. A procedure designed to elicit results which are less than exact.

2. The result of such a procedure.

a priori 1. Pertaining to a line of *reasoning (2)* based on specific assumptions rather than experience; deductive.

2. Pertaining to assumptions or knowledge obtained before formulating or characterizing hypotheses, plans of actions, etc.

3. Characterizing the formulation of explicit hypotheses, definitions, axioms, and rules of inference prior to undertaking an investigation or embarking on a course of action.

arbitrage Buying and selling simultaneously the same commodity in two or more markets with the expectation of profiting from temporary differences in prices.

arbitrary Determined by individual judgment for which no better explanation can be given in terms of accepted rules or standards than for an alternative judgment.

arbitration A procedure in which contending parties submit some or all parts of the dispute to an outside impartial referee whose decision is binding on all disputants, often with a status equivalent to a legal judgment. Arbitration clauses are often found in labor contracts and contracts between buyers and sellers for pricing at the time of future delivery of a product or service.

ARIMA An acronym for "autoregressive integrated moving average" time series process. In *univariate analyses*, observations in a time series are expressed as a function of past levels of the series (autoregressive process) or as a function of past disturbances to the series (moving average process). These functions are identified with the use of *autocorrelations* and related measures of time-dependent behavior. The term integrated applies if the data need to be differenced in order to produce a stationary series by the removal of trends. Time series models are often used in accounting research to provide a benchmark forecast for comparison with more sophisticated models which use other information in addition to past observations of the series being studied.

arithmetic mean The result obtained by dividing the sum of two or more quantities by the number of items; usually denoted by a symbol such as $\overline{Y}$. It is often intended as a representative quantity or as a measure of the central tendency of a group of items. See *average; mean; geometric mean*.

Arithmetic means are of two kinds: simple and weighted. The simple arithmetic mean, or simple average, sometimes called unweighted, is the sum of a set of values divided by the number of such values. To obtain a weighted arithmetic mean, each value is multiplied by some index of importance or weight before the summation is made. The divisor is then the sum of the weights. The most widely used weights are the frequencies (such as inventory quantities) with which the values (such as inventory prices) occur. Thus, the numbers 4, 7, and 10 may occur with frequencies of 5, 3, and 2, respectively. The simple mean would be

$$\frac{4 + 7 + 10}{3} = 7,$$

while the weighted mean, using the frequencies as weights, would be

$$\frac{(5 \times 4) + (3 \times 7) + (2 \times 10)}{5 + 3 + 2} = 6.1,$$

the smaller result being attributable to the greater frequency of the smaller numbers.

arithmetic progression A numerical series the value of which increases or decreases from one term to the next by the same amount, as, $1, 3, 5, 7, 9, \ldots$; $.25, .5, .75, 1, 1.25, \ldots$ The total of such a series, where S is the total, a the first and l the last of the series, d the constant difference, and n the number of terms, is expressed as follows:

$$S = a + (a + d) + (a + 2d) + \ldots$$
$$+ (a + [n - 1]d);$$

and

$$S = l + (l - d) + (l - 2d) + \ldots$$
$$+ (l - [n - 1]d).$$

Hence,

$$2S = a + l + a + l + a + l$$
$$+ \ldots + a + l = n(a + l);$$

and

$$S = \frac{n}{2}(a + l).$$

If a, d, and n are known and l is unknown, then

$$S = \frac{n}{2}(2a + [n - l]d);$$

if both a and d are 1, then

$$S = \frac{n}{2}(n + 1),$$

in which S is the sum of the first n numbers. See *geometric progression*.

arithmetic unit (computers) The portion of the central processor of a *digital computer* in which the basic arithmetic operations are performed.

arm's-length *adj*. On a commercial basis, dealing with or as though dealing with independent, unrelated persons; competitive; straightforward; involving no favoritism or irregularity; as, an arm's-length purchase. A buyer and a seller both free to act, each seeking his or her own best economic interest and agreeing on a price, are said to have an arm's-length relationship. Transactions between affiliated companies are not ordinarily regarded as being at arm's length even though expressed in terms of market values. —*arm's length, n.*

array An ordered arrangement of data or symbols. See *vector; matrix.*

arrears Money remaining unpaid at the regular due date or a liability not discharged when due; also applies to dividends when a corporation passes or fails to declare a dividend sufficient to satisfy the claims to earnings of cumulative preferred stockholders. Dividends in arrears are usually disclosed in notes to the financial statements and not as corporate liabilities.

arrival draft See *draft.*

articles of incorporation The document prepared by the persons establishing a corporation in the United States and filed with state authorities; one copy, returned with a certificate of incorporation, becomes the corporate charter, enabling the corporation to function. The information filed with the state includes the corporate name and address, the names of the incorporators, the nature of the property to be acquired and the business to be carried on, proposed corporate powers, and the character and amount of capital stock to be authorized and issued. The older word, *charter*, at one time referred to an individual statute that through the first quarter of the 19th century was the only device employed by state legislatures for permitting the establishment of a private corporation. The corporation laws of the United States and foreign countries alike now provide for the creation and licensing of a business corporation by action of administrative authorities. See *corporation.*

articulated Joined together, as (1) when successive balance sheets are related to each other by accompanying *income* and *funds-flow statements* and *reconciliations of surplus* or (2) when the income statement and balance sheet are related to each other and the underlying trial balance with accompanying adjusting entries in a set of *working papers* or a *spread sheet*. See *articulation statement*.

articulated financial statements Two or more interrelated financial statements. See *articulated*; *articulation*.

articulation An interrelation which exists within a set of two or more financial statements when the elements of those financial statements have a common basis such as that derived from the *accounting identity (2)*. For example, articulation exists between a statement of earnings and a balance sheet if the elements in the statement of earnings (revenues, expenses, gains, losses, etc.) and related elements in the balance sheet (assets and liabilities) have been measured on the same basis.

articulation statement = *spread sheet*.

artificial intelligence The part of computer science concerned with developing methods for identifying or solving problems on computers which would be regarded as manifestations of the use of intelligence if performed by humans. Example: developing programs to identify patterns buried in complex arrays of data; uses of computers to state or prove theorems in mathematics or logic. Some form of *optimization* is often involved as in, for instance, the development of a shortest proof path for theorems in logic. See *complex information processing*.

artificial person An organization, such as a corporation, endowed by law and custom with functions or powers resembling those of individual beings; an unincorporated association may have similar characteristics, as where it can sue and be sued in its own name. The term originated with Chief Justice Marshall in the Dartmouth College Case (4 Wheat. 626 U1819e): "A corporation is an artificial being, invisible, intangible, and existing only in contemplation of law." A more modern concept is to regard a corporation as a group of natural persons authorized to act as though they were but one person.

as at = At. A phrase qualifying the date of a financial statement or an action taken, often indicating that adjustments or other decisions made after that date have been incorporated.

ASCII (computers) = American Standard Code for Information Interchange. A code for mapping upper and lower case letters, numbers, and punctuation to a series of 7-bit *binary codes* (see *BCD*).

as is In its present condition; without warranty: a designation attaching to an item held for sale which forestalls any claim on the seller after a sale has been made.

ask(-ed, -ing) price The price at which the owner of property, particularly a security or commodity, formally offers to sell, as on an exchange.

aspiration level A level of performance an individual hopes or undertakes to achieve in a familiar task, given knowledge of previous performance. The term has been borrowed from psychology and applied to budgeting and standard setting processes. The implication, supported by some research, is that managers should be aware of differences in personal aspirations and adjust their budgets, standard costs, and other controls for potential differences in their impacts on different individuals.

ASR = *Accounting Series Releases*.

assembly language (computers) A computer programming language that can be translated directly into *machine language* instructions for assembling various subprograms and languages. It usually is specifically related to a given computer system.

assessable capital stock 1. Capital stock not fully paid, and subject to *calls*. See *capital stock*.
2. The capital stock of banks formerly subject to "double liability": for the par value paid in plus an equal amount subject to call in case of insolvency. See *double liability*.

assessment 1. The process of valuing property for taxation purposes.

2. Any recurrent tax (e.g., a real-estate or personal-property tax) levied by governmental authority.

3. A tax for improvements or improvement repairs relating to such items as paving, sidewalks, sewers, or drainage constructed by municipal authority; also known as a "special assessment" or "improvement" tax.

4. Entry of a tax on an official tax roll.

5. A levy on stockholders, owners of beneficial interests, members of a club, and others, for the purpose of raising additional capital or absorbing a loss.

assessment roll or ledger In the case of property subject to *ad valorem* taxes, the official list containing the legal description of each parcel of property, its assessed valuation, and name and address of owner. Additionally, in the case of property in special assessment districts, identification of the district, amount of total assessment, amount and due date of each installment, charges for interest on each installment, and record of all collections.

asset Any owned physical object (tangible) or right (intangible) having economic value to its owner; an item or source of wealth with continuing benefit for future periods, expressed, for accounting purposes, in terms of its cost, or other value, such as current or replacement cost, and reflected in a balance sheet. Supporting schedules or accompanying explanations are customarily also supplied when values other than historical cost are used.

Financial Accounting Standards Board defines assets as probable future economic benefits that can be obtained or controlled by a particular enterprise as a result of past transactions or events affecting the enterprise.

Accounting conventionally recognizes certain sources of wealth as assets but not others. Typical examples of the former are cash, investments, claims against others (receiv-

ables), materials, supplies, goods in process of manufacture or held for sale, land, buildings, machinery, tools and other plant assets, prepaid expenses, purchased goodwill, patents, and trademarks. An item of wealth may be an asset recognized in the accounts, even though not realizable in cash, as, for example, a prepaid expense relating to an expected future activity, such an expenditure being regarded as recoverable in the form of future services or benefits. The amounts at which assets are recorded do not usually indicate their current value, but rather cost or that portion of cost allocable to succeeding periods.

Assets not conventionally recognized in the accounts are generally intangibles or are derived from costs not readily assignable to them. Thus an advertising campaign, managerial foresight, standing with the trade, or competence of its technical staff may constitute or create the most valuable sources of income of a business enterprise. Although such items are sometimes designated as assets in a broad sense, their costs, even where determinable, customarily appear as expense in the books of account and on financial statements.

Perhaps the most important characteristic of an asset recognized by the accountant is its usefulness to the owner. An object or right is considered useful if it is the source of, or can be used to secure, future services economically advantageous, not to just any person, but to its present owner. A machine, for example, is an asset if the services which the machine can perform in the future are of economic importance to the owner. If these services are not of economic importance to him or her, the machine in his or her hands has no worth beyond its trade-in or salvage values.

The monetary amount attaching to an asset, determined by the application of a number of *conventions*, is often referred to as *book value*, unamortized cost, or undepreciated cost. Assets not subject to depreciation (e.g., land and long-term investments) are customarily recorded and reported at cost to the owner. Assets subject to depreciation are similarly recorded; periodically a portion of cost is transferred to expense as the estimated economic usefulness of the asset to the owner becomes exhausted. See *fixed asset; depreciation*.

Inventories of raw materials, goods in process, finished goods, and merchandise are customarily reported at cost or, where replacement cost is lower, at something less than cost. See *inventory valuation*. Marketable securities and other assets are subject to the same general treatment; some assets are valued at what their salvage will bring. See *cost basis*.

It is customary to reflect in the balance sheet under "deferred charges" or "prepaid expenses" costs pertaining to services or benefits to be enjoyed in future periods. See *deferred charge*.

For balance-sheet purposes, assets are broadly grouped as current, fixed, or intangible, and, within such groupings, by more descriptive titles, such as receivables, inventories, investments, plant and equipment, goodwill, and patents. See *balance sheet*.

asset-accountability unit Any item of plant or equipment, separately accounted for upon acquisition, removal, transfer, sale, demolition, or abandonment.

asset depreciation range (ADR) See *class-life depreciation system; accelerated cost recovery system*.

assets cover Underlying security; British usage.

asset turnover See *turnover ratios*.

asset utilization ratios See *turnover ratios*.

assignment The transfer to another of any right or interest in real property, or of the title to and interest in an item of personal property, as a patent or a receivable.
—assign, *v.t.*

assignment for the benefit of creditors Assignment of property by an insolvent debtor to a third party (in trust) instructing payment of creditors, pro rata, with a return of any surplus to the debtor.

associated company 1. = *affiliated company*.
2. A corporation exactly 50 percent of whose voting capital stock is owned by another. See *subsidiary*.
3. A corporation in which another company holds a *trade investment*; British usage.

associated with Relates to an external auditor's responsibility for unaudited information contained in the footnotes to audited financial statements. These footnotes arise from specific requirements of the *Securities and Exchange Commission* for disclosures of such information by registrants, but which waive the requirement that they be audited. The auditor is thus "associated with" the data. Although he or she need not audit it, he or she must review it and make appropriate inquiries to consider its overall reasonableness.

association 1. An economic unit, not incorporated, owned by or existing for the benefit of a group of persons or other economic units, and carrying on transactions with or without a profit objective. See *corporation*.
2. (federal income taxes) An unincorporated business may be an "association taxable as a corporation." The regulations list six corporate characteristics or traits which may identify an unincorporated organization as an association: (a) the existence of associates, (b) an objective to carry on business and divide the profits, (c) continuity of life, (d) centralized management, (e) limited liability, and (f) free transferability of ownership interests. An organization lacking either of the first two traits will never be classified as an association. As to the remaining four traits

an organization may, generally speaking, be an association though lacking one of them. In 1964 the *IRS* issued the so-called Kintner regulations, which restricted requests for corporate classification by associations. Recently many states have enacted laws permitting professional people to set up their practice in association or corporation form, in order to qualify for tax benefits as employees of their association or corporation.

3. (statistics) The tendency for two or more sets of characteristics or classifications to display interconnections or interrelations. The term may refer to either quantitative characteristics (*variables*) or qualitative ones (*attributes*), but there is a tendency to restrict its usage to qualitative relations, reserving the term *correlation* for the study of quantitative characteristics. The term includes both the tendency toward interconnection and the deviations from that tendency. Association becomes stronger as the tendency toward interconnection becomes more pronounced and the deviations from interconnection become less pronounced. Kendall, in *The Advanced Theory of Statistics*, notes: ''It is necessary to point out...that statistical association is different from association in the colloquial sense. In current speech we say that *A* and *B* are associated if they occur together fairly often; but in statistics they are associated only if *A* occurs relatively more or less frequently among the *B*'s than among the not-*B*'s. If 90% of smokers have poor digestion, we cannot say that smoking and poor digestion are associated until it is shown that less than 90% of nonsmokers have poor digestion.'' See *coefficient (2b); contingency table*.

Association of Government Accountants Founded in 1950 as the Federal Government Accountants Association, it is dedicated to the interests of accountants employed in government. Among its publications is *The Government Accountants Journal*.

assumed liability 1. An obligation for which responsibility for payment is taken, as in the acquisition of a going concern.
2. An *absorbed cost* (*1*).

assumption A premise; a statement, accepted without proof, sometimes unconsciously, as a basis for a line of reasoning or course of action, either because its applicability is deemed to be self-evident, or because its implications appear to justify exploration. One method of judging an argument, exposition, or what appears to be an arbitrary procedure, is to identify the possible assumptions, including biases, on which they are based, and determine their acceptability by weighing the tenability of possible inferences that follow modifications or deletions. See *rule; standard; axiom; reasoning*.

assurance A positive declaration intended to give confidence.

assured A person to be indemnified by another against a risk or eventuality; any beneficiary of an insurance policy.

asymptote The line or the curve toward which a curve approaches ever more closely as the latter is extended to infinity but never exactly meets except at infinity.

at par A quotation or price identical with the face or nominal amount of a security, or of a fixed transfer rate of foreign exchange. See *par; face amount; value*.

attainable cost Any considered, realistic estimate of a future cost: for example, serving as a basis for a budgetary allowance, limitation or control, or a contract proposal; or as a *standard cost* or *standard of comparison*. See *standard*.

attained age normal method A projected benefit-cost method developed by actuaries for allocating the cost of retirement benefits to particular years for accounting and funding purposes. It is a modification of either the individual level premium method or the aggregate level cost method in that past or prior service cost is recognized as a separate component of annual pension cost. Past or prior service cost is measured individually for each employee. Normal cost for each employee or employee group is allocated to periods after inception of the plan in level amounts or as a level percentage of compensation over the employee's estimated future service life or the average service life of the employee group. Annual pension cost equals normal cost plus either an amount for amortization of past service cost or interest on the unfunded past service cost balance.

attention directing (reports) See *exceptions report*.

attest To authenticate formally, as in a report; to express, after careful investigation, an opinion of correctness or *fairness* as in the auditor's *short-form report*. (See *auditors' report*.) "Attest function" refers to extension of the public accountant's role to any situation where he or she may be called upon for an objective statement of fact or opinion that may assist in the making of judgments by others.

attorney's letter (auditing) A letter sent by an auditor to a client's attorney(s) as the primary means of obtaining corroboration of the information furnished by client management concerning litigation claims and assessments. Considered to be an essential procedure in all audits. Also referred to as "lawyer's letter" or "legal letter."

attribute 1. A quality or group of qualities reduced to quantitative form for purposes of accounting, mathematical, or statistical analysis. Quantitative data can always be reduced to attributes by a coding or classification scheme, but the reverse is not necessarily true. Thus, the attributes of a business may be determined by the results of financial and cost analysis which are combined as a basis for judging the worthwhileness or success of a venture. Also, *historical cost, current cost,* *current exit value, expected exit value,* and *present value* which result from past or anticipated transactions may be assigned to an asset as one of its attributes.

2. In *statistical quality control*, the fraction or percent defective out of the total amount of a given type of goods produced or received, constituting a measure of the quality of the production process used to manufacture the goods, or the quality of the supplier who has furnished the goods. More generally, a classificatory variable assigned a value of 1 or 0 according to whether an item possesses or does not possess a particular quality. Such sampling also extends to audit situations when the portion of the population containing the attribute is inferred from a sample.

attribute sampling See *attribute* (2).

audit 1. The examination of contracts, orders, and other original documents for the purpose of substantiating individual transactions before their settlement; = *preaudit*; *voucher audit*; *administrative audit*.

2. Any systematic investigation or appraisal of procedures or operations for the purpose of determining conformity with prescribed criteria; the work performed by an internal auditor; see *internal audit*.

3. Any inspection of accounting or other records of past or projected management activities in order to provide a basis for third-party evaluation or appraisal. This may involve analysis or tests of records and supporting documents. It may also involve interrogation of management and others for the purpose of securing confirmations or proofs of evidence that can be documented for third-party evaluation—such evaluation extending to inspection and possible alternate evaluations by other auditors.

4. Different kinds of audits are now emerging and continue to evolve in both private enterprise and governmental practice, and these may be identified as follows:

(A) *Financial audit*. Also called "attest audit," it involves reviews of statements prepared by management or others as a prelude to expressing opinions attesting to the fairness and adequacy of the representations these statements contain or imply. This involves an exploratory, critical review by a professional accountant of the underlying internal controls and accounting records of a business enterprise or other economic unit, precedent to the expression by the auditor of an opinion of the propriety ("fairness") of its financial statements; often accompanied by a descriptive adjective or phrase indicating scope or purpose, e.g., annual audit, balance-sheet audit, audit for credit purposes, cash audit.

In general, the term does not refer to specific procedures but connotes only whatever work an accountant undertakes in the way of substantiating or examining a transaction, the records of a series of transactions, a financial statement, or a schedule reflecting one or more transactions or accounts. In a narrower sense, the term refers to the particular procedures generally recognized by accountants as essential in acquiring sufficient information to permit the expression of an informed opinion as to a financial statement or statements. See *auditors' report (1)*.

Somewhat more specific objectives of an auditor, particularly in making an annual examination of a business concern, are to satisfy oneself that with respect to the financial statements and the notes or explanations accompanying them: (a) no material asset, liability, or item of net worth has been omitted; (b) no untrue item or statement appears; (c) no *material fact* is included or omitted that would cause the statements to be misleading; (d) the assets shown at the date of the balance sheet were owned and the liabilities were amounts actually owing (or contingently owing, in the case of contingent liabilities); (e)

the nature and classification of capital stock have been set forth, and the amounts shown therefore are not in excess of the amounts of capital stock issued; (f) surplus (paid in and earned) is broken down into its principal classes, with a showing of the amount applicable to each class; and (g) the income statement reflects fairly the operating results for the period indicated in the statement heading. (B) *Comprehensive audit*. Also called "extended scope audit." An extension of the audit process for the purpose of reviewing and appraising any or all parts of management activity. Unlike "attest audit," the auditor does not restrict the review to financial statements and related transactions. In comprehensive audit, the auditor also assumes responsibility for preparation and release of the resulting reports with, oftentimes, an accompanying management response in that same report. Potential third-party effects that can be identified with areas audited that may need to be considered are also an auditor responsibility in both the rendering and distribution of the audit reports resulting from such comprehensive (extended scope) audits. Aspects of management activities that might be covered may be listed as follows:

1. *Propriety* of (a) Objectives pursued and (b) Methods used.

2. *Effectiveness* in (a) Stating objectives and (b) Attaining objectives.

3. *Efficiency* of performance as measured by (a) Benefits received and (b) Resources utilized.

Sometimes the efficiency category may be decomposed further into "price efficiency" and "technical efficiency," or terms such as "economy" and "efficiency" may be used to distinguish between prices paid or received in order to identify separately outside (market-oriented) aspects of a transaction from subsequent uses made of the resulting resources. In any case efficiency is always to be accorded quantitative significance. Quantitative expression is also a "desideratum" for effectiveness, although it must be recognized that this will not always be possible as when, for instance, an objective may involve intangibles such as improvement in the moral climate of a social or corporate sector. Propriety dimensions (which may involve public attitudes and issues of morality as well as law) are even more resistant to quantitative expression. Expressions of desired directions of improvement and accomplishment may, however, be formulated in ways that are susceptible to audit.

Different aspects of such comprehensive audits may be found in activities like the following:

(a.i) Compliance audit: An audit of transactions as well as procedures and policies being followed to ascertain whether they conform to policies prescribed by other parts of management and/or applicable laws and regulations prescribed by public authorities.

(a.ii) Management audit: An audit to evaluate efficiency aspects of management activities.

(a.iii) Program audit: An audit to evaluate effectiveness as well as efficiency of management activities.

The three just listed categories may be combined in various ways, of course, and extended to issues of propriety as well. The latter, i.e., propriety, may also provide the focus of an audit, as when fraud is suspected or when a possibility of legal violations such as breach of antitrust laws is to be investigated. It is important to bear in mind, however, that there must be a need by the auditor for objective and competent professional appraisal (with its accompanying third-party orientation) in order to distinguish these audits from other investigations, e.g., of political or legal variety, that might also be conducted.

A leader in the development of comprehensive audits is the U.S. General Accounting Office—See *Comptroller General*—although such audits also occur in the internal auditing practices of many of the large multinational corporations. In the conduct of such audits, extensive use is nearly always made of interdisciplinary teams. Systems analysts, engineers, operations researchers, management scientists, and other professionals (such as may be found in the Management Advisory Services units of public accounting firms) may often become members of such audit teams. The accountant's *third-party* orientation and auditing expertise, however, is often needed in the interdisciplinary teams that are used in one or more parts for the formulation and conduct of strategy in comprehensive audits. Various parts of an accounting background are also likely to be needed in other extensions of auditing for presently developing *peer reviews* in which public accounting firms are retained to review the practices of other CPA firms. They are also often needed, although not always present, in the efficiency audits of public utilities that are being increasingly used by the regulatory commissions in various states. On the other hand, the accounting viewpoint is nearly always present in the comprehensive audits that are occurring in corporations and other private enterprise activities.

auditability The condition of the records and circumstances of an auditee which allows an auditor to conduct an effective audit examination. There are two general conditions which must exist for an economic entity to be auditable: The entity must have a system of record keeping such that adequate evidence is available for the auditor's examination (see, e.g., system of *internal accounting control*). The principals of the auditee entity must have a degree of personal integrity such that they will not knowingly and intentionally deceive the auditor. Although special types of audits can uncover *management fraud*—see, however, *audit (4B)*—it is much more difficult to accomplish audit objectives when management intends to deceive the auditor than when management is honest and cooperative.

audit adjustment An *adjusting journal entry (2)* following an examination by public accountants.

audit certificate = *auditors' report (1)*.

audit committee A subcommittee of a corporation's board of directors which serves as the focus of its *audit* activities. Under New York Stock Exchange and *SEC* rules such committees must consist of outside directors who are responsible for the selection and evaluation of the external auditors. There is a growing tendency for such committees to be recipients of internal as well as external *audit* reports and to be responsible for determining what aspects of corporate activities should be publicly disclosed. Another function of these committees is to review management representations under the *Foreign Corrupt Practices Act*.

audit cycle The pattern established for the performance of auditing procedures over time. The audit cycle may relate to (1) when various phases of an audit are performed within the audit period (e.g., inventory observation in October, confirmation in November), or (2) the frequency with which a specific audit procedure or phase is repeated (e.g., Plant A is audited every year, Plant B is audited every other year).

audited voucher A voucher that has been administratively examined and approved for payment.

audit guide A series of topical booklets published by the American Institute of Certified Public Accountants (AICPA) to supplement the Statements on Auditing Standards and statements of position on accounting principles. Similar objectives for governmental audits may be found in the U.S. General Accounting Office's (USGAO) publication, "Standards for Audit of Governmental Organizations, Activities and Functions" and by the report "Governmental Accounting, Auditing, and Financial Reporting," issued by the National Council on Governmental Accounting (NCGA).

Many of the AICPA guides relate to a specific industry, i.e., banks, brokers and dealers in securities, colleges and universities, construction contractors, employee health and welfare benefit funds, finance companies, fire and casualty insurance companies, government contractors, investment companies, savings and loan associations, state and local governmental units, stock life insurance companies, voluntary health and welfare organizations, and hospitals. Others relate to technical areas such as EDP, personal financial statements, and unaudited financial statements. The contents of these guides are generally considered authoritative, although not of the same stature as SAS and FASB pronouncements. The U.S. GAO report describes the different kinds of audits that may be performed as part of a comprehensive audit (*audit*).

auditing Act or process of making an audit. See *audit*.

auditing around the computer Refers to an approach to the audit of records which are maintained (at least partially) with the use of electronic data processing, whereby source documents and details on computer produced reports are traced back and forth as a means of verification. This is in contrast to "auditing through the computer," where data are processed, or program codes examined, as a means of verifying actual processing steps.

auditing evidence Proof obtained by any of the various devices employed by the public accountant in the course of an audit. The process of auditing may be regarded as the collection of such accounting evidence as in the opinion of the auditor is required by standard or minimum procedures and by the peculiarities of the case in hand before issuing a report. The evidence is derived from such varied activities of the auditor as a determination of the character and extent of the system of *internal control*; comparisons of current costs and cost trends with those of past periods and other organizations (see *analytic review*); detailed examinations, test checks, or scannings of certain individual accounts or groups of accounts, securing representations from management or certifications or opinions of third persons; and personal observation or inspection. Auditing evidence is measured by commonly accepted auditing standards based in part on rules of law, statistics, and other disciplines. See *audit; audit standards; evidence*.

auditing procedure An action taken by an auditor to obtain audit *evidence*. Auditing procedures include physical examination of assets, confirmation with third parties, inspection of documents, observation of company activities, obtaining representations from client management and personnel and others determining mechanical accuracy by recomputation and training, and analysis of information for reasonableness.

The performance of auditing procedures is an outgrowth of the *auditing process*. Procedures are planned and documented in the *audit program* and working papers.

auditing process The sequences of steps which constitute the approach to and accomplishment of an audit. Although the steps will differ among types of audits, all will require certain broad common activities: agreeing on the purpose of the audit with the parties involved, when pertinent, establishing specific objectives, gaining an understanding of the auditee's activities and circumstances, planning the audit procedures to be performed, conducting the procedures, evaluating the results, and reporting the results. Since audits consume economic resources and provide economic benefit, it is important to consider the cost-benefit relationships as a part of good management in the conduct of an audit. The audit process provides a framework for management and control.

Auditing Standards Board The official board established by the American Institute of Certified Public Accountants charged with the responsibility of establishing, modifying, and interpreting *generally accepted auditing standards*. See *Statements of Auditing Procedure*.

Auditing Standards Executive Committee Predecessor to the *Auditing Standards Board* prior to 1978.

audit notebook A record, used chiefly in recurring audits, containing data on work done and comments outside of the regular subject matter of working papers. It generally contains such items as the audit program, notations showing how sections of the audit are carried out during successive examinations, information needed for the auditor's office and for staff administration, personnel assignments, time requirements, and notations for use in succeeding examinations. It may be a part of the *permanent file*.

auditor 1. One who, either as a regular employee or in an outside and professional capacity, *audits* books of account and records kept by others. There is a growing tendency to extend the scope of auditing functions as in comprehensive audits and to include review and appraisal of budgetary and other predictions or *forecasts* as well as completed transactions. See *public accountant; certified public accountant; internal auditor; audit*.

2. *sing.* or *pl.* A firm of professional accountants.

3. Any person appointed by higher authority to examine and report on accounts and records.

auditors' report 1. (short form) The formal means for conveying the external auditors' opinion on the results of their examination of financial statements (see *generally accepted auditing standards*). Where the auditors' opinion is "unqualified," a standard two-paragraph report is issued:

> Board of Directors and Stockholders
> XYZ Company, Inc.
> We have examined the balance sheet of XYZ Company, Inc. as of December 31, 19—, and the related statements of earnings, stockholders' equity, and changes in financial position for the year then ended. Our examination was made in accordance with generally accepted auditing standards, and accordingly included such tests of the accounting records and such other auditing procedures as we considered necessary in the circumstances.
> In our opinion, the aforementioned financial statements present fairly the financial position of XYZ Company, Inc. at December 31, 19—, and the results of its operations and the changes in its financial position for the year then ended, in conformity with generally accepted accounting principles applied on a basis consistent with that of the preceding years.
> (signed) ABC, Certified Public Accountants

Modifications to this standard format occur in any one or combinations of the following specific situations: (1) when the *scope* of the auditors' examination is affected by conditions that preclude the application of one or more auditing procedures the auditors consider necessary in the circumstances; (2) the auditors' opinion is based in part on the report of other auditors; (3) the financial statements are affected by a departure from a generally accepted accounting principle; (4) accounting principles have not been applied consistently; (5) the financial statements are affected by uncertainties concerning future events, the outcome of which is not susceptible of reasonable estimation at the date of the auditors' report; (6) the auditors wish to emphasize a matter regarding the financial statements.

Modifications will affect the first (scope) paragraph and/or the second (opinion) paragraph as appropriate. In the above situations except (2) (reliance on other auditors), explanatory information will be presented in a separate middle paragraph added to the report.

Where situation (1), (3), (4) or (5) occurs, the auditors are said to have issued a *qualified report*, which will include their *qualified opinion*. These may be: a *disclaimer*, where the auditors state that they cannot give an opinion because of severe limitations on the scope of their examination; an *except for report*, where the auditors comment on the fairness of the financial statements other than as to the impact of one or more particular deviations; an *adverse opinion*, where the deviations are so severe as to affect the fairness of the financial statements as a whole; and a *subject to* opinion, where the auditors opine on the fairness of the financial statements subject to the outcome of a material uncertainty.

Acting on a recommendation of the Cohen Commission, the *Auditing Standards Board* in 1980 proposed the following major revision:

> The accompanying balance sheet of X Company as of December 31, 19—, and the related statements of income, retained earnings and changes in financial position for the year then ended are management's representations. An audit is intended to provide reasonable, but not absolute, assurance as to whether financial statements taken as a whole are free of material misstatements. We have audited the financial statements referred to above in accordance with generally accepted auditing standards. Application of those standards requires judgment in determining the nature, timing and extent of testing and other

procedures, and in evaluating the results of those procedures. In our opinion, the financial statements referred to above present the financial position of X Company at December 31, 19— and the results of its operations and the changes in its financial position for the year then ended in conformity with generally accepted accounting principles.

A large number of negative comments were received that centered around reactions to the omission of terms like "present fairly" and "consistency." It was believed that the proposed "scope paragraph" would be interpreted as only an attempt to protect auditors against possible legal action. The proposed revision was abandoned in 1981 in favor of the existing one.

2. (long form) A detailed report or letter prepared by an auditor following an audit. Addressed to the management or directors, it may supplement, contain, or replace the short-form report. There is no established pattern for a long-form report, but it often contains details of the audit scope, comments on operating results and financial condition, a funds-flow statement, causes of changes as compared with preceding years, and procedural suggestions.

audit period The period covered by an *audit*, e.g., a year. The audit is often performed partly within the audit period and partly in the period following.

audit program 1. The procedures undertaken or particular work done in conducting an *audit*.
2. A description, memorandum, or outline of the work to be done in an audit, and often of the time allotted and personnel assignments, prepared by a principal as a definition of audit scope, or by an auditor for the guidance and control of assistants. This serves both as a planning document and a *control* on the work to be done. It also serves to document the work performed and provides information on dates and the persons performing the work.

audit standards Standards applying to the conduct of audit work done by auditors, usually as adopted by the professional associations to which the auditors belong or as published by regulatory agencies authorizing the audit work to be done. For example, external audits by public accountants are governed by standards published by the American Institute of Certified Public Accountants (see *generally accepted auditing standards*); the Institute of Internal Auditors has published standards as guidance for internal auditors; the General Accounting Office has published standards governing federal government audits and audits of federal grants to local governments.

audit test 1. The application of an *auditing procedure* to less than all available data —for example, applying confirmation procedures to 50% of customer balances or examining 5% of all cash disbursements.
2. = *auditing procedures*.
3. Application of an auditing procedure where the objective is to determine the validity of an assertion rather than to estimate an amount. See also *hypothesis* (*3*); *test*.

audit trail The reference, accompanying a transaction *entry* or *posting*, to source records or documents. A "good" audit trail is one where the labor of tracing transactions to original documents has been reduced to a minimum; such trails are essential, built-in features of *systems of accounts*.

audit year The year covered in an annual or balance-sheet audit: usually the *fiscal year*.

authority 1. The right to perform certain acts or prescribe *rules* governing the conduct of others. Although often regarded as absolute in the sense of not requiring prior approval or consideration of the desires of those immediately affected, the *arbitrary* exercise of such rights often proves to be (a) impracticable or inefficient because of possible consequent resistance or misunderstandings, and (b) unnecessary because such alternatives as exemplary conduct, persuasion, education, and better means of communication between individuals can be employed. Successful *delegations of authority* require (a) a definition of scope capable of being understood by other persons as well as by those immediately affected, and (b) the institution of an environment that obviates the need for the arbitrary exercise of power. Under balanced schemes of corporate management, administrative authority represents the activation of corporate policy and is coupled with *responsibility* and *accountability*.

2. Hence, a person regarded as being in a position to exercise such a right. See also *incidental authority*.

3. A person commonly regarded as possessing an extensive knowledge in any given field.

4. A governmental unit or public agency created to perform a single function or a restricted group of related activities. Usually such units are financed from service charges, fees, and tolls, or they may also have taxing powers. An authority may be independent of any other government or may be dependent upon another governmental unit for its creation, existence, or the exercise of its powers.

authority bonds Bonds payable from the revenues of a specific authority. Since such authorities usually have no revenue other than charges for services, these are ordinarily revenue bonds.

authorization 1. The act of authorizing, i.e., to grant the power or right to perform the authorized act. Having the sanction or support of an *authority*. In accounting systems, authorization is either general, i.e., in the form of broad policies set by management, or specific, i.e., relative to individual transactions.

2. (governmental accounting) A program sanction created by a legislative body under which an *agency* (2) is created and permitted to operate, general policies established, and limitations, as of time, areas of authority, and relationships, specified. Funds for its operation are subsequently provided by an *appropriation*.

authorized capital stock The number of shares and usually the par or stated value of the capital stock that may be issued by a corporation under its *articles of incorporation*. In some instances the stockholders or directors may determine the stated value per share. See *capital stock*.

autocorrelation The lagged correlation of a given series with itself. See *serial correlation*. An autocorrelation coefficient thus provides a measure of the *correlation* between different observations of the same item, as in a *time series*. For example, if high sales in one month are generally followed by high sales in the next month, then the month-to-month time series for sales would be positively autocorrelated. If high sales were generally followed by low sales the series would be negatively autocorrelated, while if no relation existed between high and low sales the autocorrelation coefficient would not differ significantly from zero. Autocorrelation is also relevant for other applications such as *systematic sampling* from documents in a file or entries in a set of accounts, in which cases the term ''time'' is accorded only generic significance. A typical application is to the analysis of *residuals* in a regression equation to ascertain whether assumptions of statistical independence are violated. See *residual* (4).

automatic machine A machine which after commencing its *cycle* of operations requires no attention from the operator; sometimes called ''fully automatic'' to distinguish it from a semiautomatic machine which may require intermittent attention during its cycle of operations.

automatic reinstatement The continuance of an insurance contract, after a loss has occurred, in an amount equal to the face value of the contract.

automation 1. Technological progress that results in the substitution of machinery controlled by information-processing equipment for human labor in the manufacture of products or the performance of tasks.
2. The results of such progress.

autoregressive process A time series process for which each observation in the series is represented as a weighted additive function of prior observations. The weights can be estimated by regressing against prior observations of the series. See *regression equation*.

auxiliary activities (institutional accounting) Operations of a business character carried on by an institution for the service of its employees and patrons, but often not directly related to the primary functions of the institution. Examples: university dormitories, dining halls, infirmaries; a student union; a bookstore.

auxiliary enterprise Activities of a college or university which furnish a service to students, faculty, or staff on a user-charge basis. The charge is directly related to (but not necessarily equal to) the cost of the service. Examples include residence halls, stores and restaurants, faculty clubs, and intercollegiate athletics.

auxiliary equipment An accessory, improvement, or separately acquired addition to a major item of equipment; as, a motor or a safety device.

available assets Assets, including *available cash*, free for any general use, unencumbered, and not serving as collateral.

available balance 1. (governmental accounting) An *appropriation, apportionment*, or *allotment*, less expenditures and outstanding commitments.

2. Actual receipts, plus amounts on order, less reservations: said of an inventory item.

available cash 1. Cash in bank, excluding outstanding checks, and on hand; cash that may be used for general purposes.
2. (governmental accounting) Cash in bank and on hand in a given *fund* that can be utilized in meeting current *obligations* (2).

available earned surplus = *unappropriated retained earnings*.

average 1. = *arithmetic mean*.
2. Any central tendency of a series of quantities. See *arithmetic mean; harmonic mean; median; geometric mean; mode; moving average; progressive average; weighted average*.
3. (marine insurance) Any of certain losses or expenses arising from perils at sea, and the distribution of the loss among the several persons at interest. See *general average; particular average*.
4. (accounts) *v.* To ascertain the date upon which the settlement of an account consisting of several items due at different dates may be made without loss of interest to either party to the transactions.

averageable income (federal income taxes) The amount by which current taxable income exceeds 120% of the average of the taxable incomes of the immediately preceding four years (the base period years). See *income averaging*.

average base period income (federal income taxes) The average of the taxable incomes of the four base years, immediately preceding the current computation year. Multiplied by 120% to obtain nonaverageable income. The excess of taxable income for the computation year over nonaverageable income is termed averageable income and, if over $3,000, may be taxed as computed under the *income averaging* provisions. If the *filing status* of the taxpayer has changed between any of the four base years and the computation year, taxable income for the differing base years must be recomputed.

average collection period See *accounts receivable collection period*.

average cost 1. Total cost divided by total quantity, the latter representing usable or salable items: a generally accepted basis for *inventory valuation*.

2. = average unit cost.

3. The average of the costs incurred in each of a sequence (or collection) of periods; = average total cost.

average deviation A measure of the variation of a group of numerical data from a designated point; the arithmetic mean of the differences between each item and the arithmetic mean of the data or other selected point, where the differences are added without regard to sign. Thus the arithmetic mean of 5, 6, and 7 is $(5 + 6 + 7)/3 = 6$, and the average deviation, taken without regard to sign, is $(1 + 0 + 1)/3 = 2/3$. The smaller the result, the more representative is the average. See *standard deviation; dispersion*.

average life The estimated useful-life expectancy of a group of assets subject to *depreciation*. See *composite depreciation* and *depreciation methods* (*composite-life method*).

average outgoing quality (statistical quality control) A term applicable only to an inspection procedure that enforces good 100% inspection of each rejected lot to remove therefrom all defective items, which (in theory at least) are then replaced by good items. The term applies to the quality of material ultimately passed into stock by these procedures. Accepted lots leave an inspection station at virtually the same quality they had when submitted for inspection. Rejected lots, however, always have their quality improved by enforcement of the screening operation. The result of mixing improved lots with those already accepted is to dilute the overall fraction defective ultimately passed into stock and thus to establish an "average outgoing quality" (AOQ) for product inspected. For every sampling plan and for each level of incoming product there is a calculated AOQ value easily obtainable from the OC curve (see *operating-characteristic curve*) for the plan. Plotting these AOQ values over a scale of lot quality p gives an AOQ curve showing how this feature varies with lot quality.

average outgoing quality limit (statistical quality control) The maximum AOQ value associated with a given sampling plan when screening of each rejected lot is enforced; the maximum point on the AOQ curve for a plan. It represents the poorest quality level on the average that will exist in product ultimately passed into stock under AOQ inspection procedures.

axiom A general statement the truth of which is not questioned; a *postulate;* a principle which is itself incapable of proof but is assumed to be true in order to proceed with or test the consistency of a line of reasoning; a statement concerning relations between *primitives* in a symbolic system, such as a branch of mathematics or logic, or an exact science. Axioms may be identified in every branch of reasoned discourse, although there may be reasoned discourse without awareness of axioms; thus, the axioms of arithmetic were not completely identified until the last century. An axiom cannot be proved true or false in terms of the discipline which uses or depends upon the axiom; thus, the axiom of contradiction of classical logic cannot be proved by means of that logic. The Euclidean axiom, "between two points there passes at most one straight line," can be proved, but not by the techniques of Euclidean geometry. Prior to the 19th century, axioms were often defined as "self-evident truths." This usage has not entirely disappeared, although it is now regarded as confusing (a) the problem of achieving consistency in formal operations with a given set of symbols and (b) the empirical problem of determining which symbols accurately represent facts.

Since by definition axioms are not directly examined or criticized for their truth value, the critical study of axioms is directed at their (a) consistency, (b) independence, (c) completeness, and (d) fecundity. Statements accepted as axioms may prove to be inconsistent with one another, although the demonstration of such inconsistency may be difficult. A set of axioms is said to be independent if no one of them can be deduced from the others; complete, if any propositions which may be expressed in terms of the *primitives* of the system can be shown to follow from the axioms (i.e., if any proposition can be demonstrated to be true or false and no relevant proposition will merely be undecidable by reasoning from the axioms); and fecund, if many useful and important propositions can be deduced from them. There are, of course, many systems of logic and mathematics which are not known to be useful, although some of them have more important consequences than might be supposed. For example, the Boole-Schröoder algebra, which has only the numbers 1 and 0 in addition to algebraic numbers, and no coefficients or exponents, has done much to systematize the testing of the reasoning present in the employment of ordinary language.

In an applied field, such as accounting, the axioms are identical with propositions which belong equally to other disciplines. Some of the axioms often employed in accounting are: (a) an economic unit has an identity apart from other economic units; (b) the life of a typical economic unit extends indefinitely into the future; (c) relations between economic units are carried on by means of identifiable, separable, and measurable transactions; (d) the transactions of an economic unit are expressed in terms of a common medium of exchange; (e) transactions, collectively, measure both economic wealth and economic activity. See *principle; assumption; rule; proposition; postulate; primitive*.

backdoor financing (federal accounting) A congressional sanction giving rise to spending *authority* without formal *appropriation*, as from legislation permitting the issuance of bonds to the public or borrowing from the Treasury when need may arise.

backlog reporting The disclosure usually through footnotes (e.g., in reports to stockholders) of unfilled orders from customers. Information on backlogs is periodically supplied by some trades, and regarded as confidential in others. The present trend in improved corporate reporting to stockholders calls for comparative data on backlogs, on projections of future volumes of production, and even on operating costs: in essence, the corporate budget for future months or years, based on prospective deliveries of goods and services to customers.

back order The portion of a customer's order undelivered for any reason, but usually because the product or merchandise will be available only at a later date.

backwardation (London Stock Exchange) The fee, including interest, paid by a speculator for the delayed delivery of stock sold, pending what is hoped will be a decline in its price. See *contango; short sale*.

bad debt 1. An uncollectible receivable.
2. *pl*. Specific receivables determined to be uncollectible in whole or in part, either because the debtors cannot pay or because the creditor finds it impracticable to enforce payment, the amount being charged to profit and loss or a *reserve* or *allowance* for bad debts, where such a reserve is maintained.
3. *pl*. The account to which is charged periodically, usually with an offsetting credit to a reserve or *allowance* for bad debts, the estimated loss from uncollectible accounts based, for example, on a percentage of (credit) sales for the period, a percentage of outstanding accounts at the end of the period, or a review of the individual accounts: in each case, any balance remaining in the reserve from past periods being taken into consideration; a *provision* for bad debts.

bad-debt expense See *bad debt (3)*; *uncollectible accounts*.

bailment A delivery or transfer of possession of money or personal property for a particular purpose, as on consignment or for safekeeping or repairs. A bailment constitutes a *contract*, express or implied, that the purpose of the delivery or transfer will be carried out. The person making the delivery is the bailor, the recipient the bailee; thus, a railroad in accepting goods for transportation becomes a bailee.

balance *n*. 1. The difference between the total debits and the total credits of an *account* or the total of an account containing only debits or credits.
2. The equality of the total debit balances and the total credit balances of the accounts in a ledger, as in the expression: ''The accounts are in (or out of) balance.'' See *trial balance*.
3. Agreement of the total of the account balances in a subsidiary ledger with its general-ledger control.
v.t. 1. To determine and enter the *balance* (*1*) of an account or group of accounts so that the sum of the debit postings will equal the sum of the credit postings.
2. To prove the equality of debits and credits in a ledger or of the total of the accounts in a subsidiary ledger with the controlling account; to prepare a trial balance for which the total debits equal the total credits.

balanced budget A *budget* in which forward *expenditures* for a given period are matched by expected *revenues* for the same period. See *accrued-expenditures basis*.

balance of payments 1. The difference in a given time period between a country's payments for goods, services, and capital investment to abroad and its receipts from abroad denominated in current monetary units. This includes *balance of trade*.
2. The cumulative balance of such differences at any moment of time.
3. The portion of this amount owing to or from another country or group of countries.

balance of trade 1. The difference in a given time period between a country's imports and exports of goods and services valued in current monetary units.
2. The cumulative balance of such differences at any moment of time.

3. The portion of this amount owing to or from another country or group of countries.

balance sheet A statement of financial position of any economic unit disclosing as at a given moment of time its *assets*, at cost, depreciated cost, or other indicated value; its *liabilities*; and its ownership equities. The traditional, most followed form of the balance sheet is the *account form*, with assets on the left and liabilities and owners' equities on the right; in British and continental practice, the order of assets and liabilities is usually reversed. In recent years, experimental attempts have been made to simplify the presentation of balance-sheet information, with the result that the *report form*, with numerous variations, has been employed by some accountants for external reporting.

Standards generally observed in the structure and content of the balance sheet, aside from its form, are:
1. Current assets and liabilities are the first items shown. In the account form, they head the asset and liability sides, respectively; in the report form, current liabilities follow current assets and are subtracted in total from the current-asset total, yielding the amount of *working capital*. At one time it was common practice for fixed assets to precede current assets, as the consequence of emphasis on the ownership of property to which the investment of stockholders had been primarily devoted. Because of the growing importance of operational problems and the need for reporting first on the operating environment, the practice survives only in the utility field.
2. Items other than cash making up current assets and items of current liabilities are generally limited to those convertible into cash or payable out of cash, respectively, within the year following the balance-sheet date; where, nevertheless, long-term installment accounts, work in process, or other items are included as current assets, they are identified

and some indication of the time of their liquidation accompanies them. See *operating cycle*.

3. Current assets are listed in the order of their likely *liquidity*, commencing with cash; current liabilities, in their conventional groupings, have no such order but often appear in the following sequence: bank loans, other loans (including maturing portions of long-term obligations), accounts payable, deferred income, accruals.

4. The five major divisions of current assets are cash, temporary investments, receivables, inventories, and prepaid expenses. As a rule, no detail supplements their bare titles unless an exception to their customary definitions appears.

5. Current assets are regarded as cash (or as costs or other recognized amounts in the process of conversion into cash) available for general use. Where its withdrawal or uses are limited, cash is separately shown and qualified. If restricted to purchases of fixed assets, it is normally excluded from current assets altogether. Reductions, in the form of write-downs or the creation of or addition to reserves, are necessary for those current-asset items whose convertibility is doubtful. Thus, the amount of cash in a closed bank is reduced to the sum estimated to be recoverable; temporary investments having a market value substantially less than cost are reduced to that value; receivables are decreased by the estimated unrecoverable amounts they include; the portion of inventories replaceable or salable at less than cost are reduced to "market"; and prepaid expenses are marked down pro rata to that portion of their costs that pertains to the future services expected from them. The basis of valuing investments and inventories is disclosed. In periods of rising prices, where the *LIFO* method of valuing inventories has been followed, the outlay for inventories carried into the next period is reduced to levels sometimes materially below the more common valuation basis of "cost or market, whichever is lower," making necessary the disclosure of the amount of the understatement. See *cash; temporary investment (2); receivable (2); inventory (3); prepaid expense (2)*.

6. Investments in and advances to affiliated companies may appear on unconsolidated balance sheets, and on consolidated balance sheets where the *consolidation policy* excludes certain *affiliates*, such as one in which less than a majority of the voted stock is owned. The usual valuation basis is cost, adjusted to underlying book values if less than such cost. In some instances, the interest in the net income of a subsidiary is taken up on the books of the controlling company, but this practice is not generally favored. See *controlling-company accounting*.

7. Fixed assets are most often valued at depreciated cost. The principal breakdowns disclosed are buildings, machinery and equipment, and land. See *fixed asset; depreciation*.

8. Intangibles are no longer common items on balance sheets. They may arise at the outset of an enterprise or at a later date when a *going concern* is purchased. See *lump-sum purchase; goodwill; intangible value*. Their basis of valuation is indicated. In recent years it has been customary to write off *goodwill* by a gradual process of *amortization* or by a direct charge to *retained earnings*.

9. Other types of assets are infrequently encountered. *Deferred charges* are now limited largely to *prepaid expenses*, which in recent years have been restored to current assets; factory and office supplies are generally classified as inventory or as prepaid expense. A long-term receivable is given a classification following current assets, unless it is of the installment variety, which under customary trade practices is accorded a current-

asset classification; but, whether or not so classified, some indication of the time of collection is generally inscribed in its title. A claim for a tax refund is given a noncurrent classification if the immediacy of its collection is not known, but is omitted from the balance sheet if a basis for settlement has not yet been agreed to by the taxing authority. A *sinking fund* in which cash and investments are being accumulated to cover a future retirement of securities is occasionally met with; where the assets it contains are no longer under the control of the debtor or cannot be used for any other purpose, the amount of the sinking fund may be deducted on the face of the balance sheet from the liability to which it relates. Funds created to meet future pension obligations (see *pension fund*) have appeared in a few balance sheets during recent years. Such funds are shown as separate asset items, and the securities included therein are usually valued at cost or at less than cost if the market value is less; with a pension fund as with a sinking fund, if the control of its assets is shared with or is in the hands of others, the amount of the fund may be deducted on the balance sheet from its related liability.

10. *Current liabilities* are generally confined to amounts shortly to be paid for goods and services already received or in settlement of recognized losses. Their leading features have already been mentioned. If any current liability is secured, the nature and amount of the security is indicated, usually parenthetically or in the form of a footnote.

11. Long-term liabilities are accompanied on the balance sheet by a description that discloses their nature, security, maturity date or dates, the rate of interest they bear, and any special features, such as convertibility. Reacquired bonds or bonds held in a sinking fund for redemption are a reduction of the bond amount, as may be the remaining items in a sinking fund that can be legally employed only in the redemption of the issue.

12. Owners' equity (= *stockholders' equity* or *net worth*) is divided between capital paid in (contributions of stockholders) subdivided by classes of stock between *par value* or *stated value*, *additional paid-in capital* (capital surplus), and *retained earnings* (earned surplus). Details of changes in capital stock since the last reporting date may be covered in footnotes, and changes in *retained earnings* are reported in a separate exhibit.

balance-sheet account An account the amount of which alone or in combination with others appears in a *balance sheet*. Balance-sheet accounts remaining on a general ledger after revenue and expense accounts have been closed for a fiscal period constitute the items of a *postclosing trial balance*.

balance-sheet audit = *audit* (*1*). This term, along with *examination*, special examination, *annual audit*, and other terms designed to indicate varying responsibilities of the auditor, has now largely given way to the simpler term, *audit*.

balance-sheet equation = *accounting identity* (*2*).

bank(er's) acceptance 1. An instrument utilized in the financing of foreign trade, making possible the payment of cash to an exporter covering all or a part of the amount of a shipment made by him or her. Such an arrangement originates with the foreign importer, who instructs a local bank to provide for a "commercial acceptance credit" with, for example, a New York bank in favor of a named American exporter; the New York bank then issues an acceptance credit, in effect guaranteed by the foreign bank, to the exporter, under the terms of which he or she may draw a time bill of exchange maturing in 60 or 90 days. Supported by the required evidence of shipment, the bill of exchange is accepted by the bank, by endorsement on the face of the bill, thus signifying that it will pay the bill at maturity. The exporter may retain the bill until maturity or sell it on the so-called "discount market." See *foreign-trade financing*.

2. A similar instrument employed in domestic trade, particularly in the financing of sales of staples. The direct liability of the bank, effective upon endorsement of the bill of exchange, gives added marketability to the paper and makes available to dealers or other investors in such paper a security having a firm, short-term due date and carrying with it virtually no *risk*.

bank balance The amount remaining at a given date in a checking or deposit account, differing from the amount reported in a bank statement of the same date because of outstanding checks, deposits in transit, and sometimes other, usually minor, items. See *adjusted bank balance; adjusted book balance*.

bank charge An amount charged to a customer by a bank for collection, protest fees, exchange, checks drawn, or other services, exclusive of interest and discount. An imputed bank charge, offset by a credit of equal amount for imputed interest on demand deposits, appears in the computation of *national income*.

bank confirmation Statement obtained by an *auditor* from a client's bank reporting at a stated date on the client's bank accounts, *loans*, and other *liabilities (1)*, *collateral* pledged, and other matters. See *auditing evidence; confirmation (2)*.

bank credit The amount of borrowing at interest from commercial banks by businesses and individuals. The loans, which are represented as bank assets, also appear as *demand deposits* on the *liability* side of the banking system's *balance sheets* and are thus

included in the measurement of the economy's *money supply*.

bank discount Interest on a bank loan collected at the time the loan is negotiated.

bank loan An amount borrowed by a depositor from a bank under a *credit line* or other agreement, evidenced by a promissory note bearing interest payable at intervals or at maturity, or a promissory note (a *discount*) from which interest until maturity has been deducted. Most bank loans classify as current liabilities, notwithstanding the possibility of *rollover*.

bank note A promise to bearer made by a bank, issued under banking laws and intended to serve as money. Before 1935, national banks in the United States could issue bank notes; since then the issuance of bank notes has been confined to the *Federal Reserve Bank*.

bank overdraft The amount owing to a bank by a depositor as the consequence of checks drawn in an amount exceeding his or her deposits in a commercial account.

bank reconciliation A statement displaying the items of difference between the balance of an account reported by a bank and the account appearing on the books of the bank's customer. Among such items are outstanding checks and deposits in transit.

bankruptcy 1. The condition of *insolvency*, in which the assets of a debtor have been turned over to a receiver or trustee for administration.

2. The process of administering a debtor's assets and liabilities by a federal court, following the granting by the court of a petition on the part of the person or creditors, the purpose being to insure the full or pro rata settlement of the debtor's obligations in an orderly manner or, where possible, to reorganize the debtor's affairs so that he or she may contin-

ue or reenter business, and in some instances to relieve him or her from further liability on the unsatisfied portion of his or her obligations. See *statement of realization and liquidation*.

bank statement 1. The formal periodic statement of the assets, liabilities, and net worth of a bank.

2. The statement (usually monthly) rendered by a bank to a depositor.

barbell portfolios Bond *portfolios*, or portfolios with term investments, i.e., investments such as bonds with explicit maturity dates, which are concentrated in short-term and long-term maturities. See *laddered portfolios*. See also *risk*, especially the discussion of ways of measuring risk.

bar chart A statistical series, such as a *frequency distribution*, represented by means of relative or absolute heights of a group of rectangles.

bareboat charter A *charter* giving to the charterer the same rights and privileges to the use of a ship as would be possessed under conditions of full ownership.

bargain purchase *Transaction* in which goods are acquired at less (usually much less) than *fair market value*. See *buyers' market; forced-sale value; distress merchandise*.

bargain purchase option A provision giving a lessee the right to purchase leased property for an amount that is significantly less than the expected fair value of the property at the date of exercise.

bargain renewal option A provision giving a lessee the right to renew a lease at a rental that is significantly less than the expected fair rental at the exercise date.

barter The delivery or exchange of goods and services directly for other goods and services without the use of a medium of exchange such as money. The basis of valuation to ei-

ther seller is the market or cash-equivalent value of whatever he or she receives—its price had it been paid for in cash, or, lacking a price, the price of a competitive product performing an identical function, or the average price, suitably weighted, of products performing higher and lower functions; if no comparables are present, then the cash price of the product given in exchange; if no such cash price is ascertainable, the *book value* of the product given in exchange may be assigned to the product received without recognition of gain or loss. Some accountants advocate the last-described procedure for all barter transactions, contending that "realization" cannot be effected unless cash is to mark the termination of the deal. See *sale; exchange*.

base period 1. The period of time chosen for a *standard of comparison*.

2. (federal income tax) Under the *income-averaging* concept, the four taxable years immediately preceding the year that averaging is elected.

base-stock method (of valuing inventory) See *inventory valuation*.

BASIC (computers) = *B*eginners *A*ll-purpose *S*ymbolic *I*nstruction *C*ode. An especially simple computer programming language designed for *time-sharing* systems and used for both mathematical computing and manipulation of strings of characters.

basic dimension A theoretically exact size, such as the dimension of a shaft or hole for a machine part, to which a tolerance is applied for practical production and operation. Thus, a basic diameter for an axle might be 1 1/2″, to which a tolerance of 1/16″ may be added for practical manufacture. Axles less than 1 7/16″ or greater than 1 9/16″ would then fall outside maximum and minimum tolerance limits. Usually basic sizes or dimensions lie midway between a maximum and minimum.

In certain cases a basic size may be at a minimum limit with a plus tolerance, or at a maximum limit with a minus tolerance; in other cases, a basic size may be closer to one limit than another. Much effort has been expended in simplifying and standardizing parts dimensions, one of the most important results of this effort being the development of the American Standard for Limits and Fits for Engineering and Manufacturing. Tables of preferred tolerances and allowances and other important items, such as screw threads, have also been prepared. These tables are extensively used to reduce the total number of sizes manufactured and to standardize parts and machine manufacture. In engineering design, standard or preferred values taken from these tables are generally used, unless a good reason exists for departing from the standard.

basic expenditure A term often used to identify a cost as it is first classified in the accounting records; thus, a raw-material cost which may ultimately be reclassified as a part of the cost of work in progress. See *absorb; primary account; terminal account.*

Basic Postulates of Accounting, The Published in 1961, this was the first in a series of Accounting Research Studies published under the authority of the Director of Accounting Research of the *American Institute of Certified Public Accountants*. Its author, Maurice Moonitz, was also the Institute's Director of Accounting Research at the time. It was envisaged that this first Study would constitute the core of a theory which could be used to support future *Opinions* of the *Accounting Principles Board* coupled with *A Tentative Set of Broad Accounting Principles for Business Enterprises.*

basic standard cost 1. A *standard cost* that serves as a point of reference from which to measure changes in current standard cost as well as in actual cost. It is customarily modi-

fied only when the character of the activities carried on changes.

2. A standard cost developed from engineering studies in the light of assumed objectives; it may or may not be currently attainable.

basing point A geographical location at which the quoted price of a commodity serves as the foundation for the price of the same product in another location, the difference being the transportation cost between the two locations. See *administered price.*

basis Cost, or a value employed as a prescribed substitute for cost when an asset is acquired other than through normal purchase. Basis is the amount which must be restored to taxpayer before gain is realized. See *adjusted basis; basis point.*

basis of accounting The method employed in the recording and reporting of transactions. Two commonly recognized bases are: the *accrual* method and the *cash basis*, the latter, especially in small organizations, personal records, and the like, serving as a substitute for the former. A third is the *commitment* basis, extensively employed in governmental accounting. It may be regarded as the point at which a transaction is to be started; the cash basis recognizes when it is terminated; the accrual basis is identified with the occurrence of a transaction. See *accrual basis.*

basis point One one-hundredth of a percent; used to express differences in *yields* on *bonds.*

basket purchase The purchase, as a unit, of a group of assets, particularly capital assets, at a single negotiated price, often a round figure, that must subsequently be divided as between the various assets or asset groups usually on some arbitrary basis; = *lump-sum purchase.*

batch A specific quantity of materials or parts composing a purchase of goods; a withdrawal from stock for processing; a selection for testing, a production run, and so on. The quantity may be planned as a standard or may be the actual quantity called for or furnished in a requisition or production order.

batch costing A method of cost accounting whereby costs are accumulated by batches or runs, as in the petroleum, chemical, and rubber industries. The costs attach to a particular quantity of raw material as it is charged into a refining or other process and often, in addition to the cost of the material itself, they include the whole of the operating expenses of the plant or process during the treatment period. The resultant total, less the market value of byproducts, is sometimes spread over the major endproducts in proportion to their weight volume, or market value.

batch process 1. A method of *production* (2) in which a limited quantity of material or parts is processed during a given time interval and is identifiable with a particular output; contrasts with *continuous process*.
2. (computers) An approach to processing data whereby a number of programs or problems are collected and returned to the user after each submission.

Bayes' rule A formula, attributed to the Reverend T. R. Bayes, by which one can determine the *(posterior)* probability of various states given prior-to-experimentation probabilities about states and the results of an experiment. The formula for Bayes' rule is:

$$P(S_i \mid x) = \frac{P(x \mid S_i)P(S_i)}{\sum\limits_{j=1}^{n} P(x \mid S_j)P(S_j)} =$$

$$\frac{P(x \mid S_i)P(S_i)}{P(x \mid S_1)P(S_1) + \ldots + P(x \mid S_n)P(S_n)},$$

where S_j represents state $j = 1, 2, \ldots, n$ and x represents the experimental results. S_i represents a specifically hypothesized state from among this set, $P(S_i)$ represents its probability of occurrence, and $P(x \mid S_i)$

represents the probability of the occurrence of x on this hypothesis. (See the formulas under *probability*.) The ratio on the right gives the posterior probability of the hypothesis; i.e., the revised probability after x is observed, which is symbolized as $P(S_i \mid x)$ on the left.

Example: S_1 and S_2 represent 2 urns which are drawn with $P(S_1) = P(S_2) = 1/2$. S_1 contains black and nonblack balls in the ratio 2/5 and S_2 contains black in the proportion 1/4. A random drawing produces one black ball from the previously selected urn. In this example x represents the random drawing of one black ball and Bayes' rule gives

$$P(S_1 \mid x) = \frac{P(x \mid S_1)P(S_1)}{P(x \mid S_1)P(S_1) + P(x \mid S_2)P(S_2)}$$

$$= \frac{2/5}{2/5 + 1/4} = 8/13$$

as the probability that S_1 was drawn while the probability that state S_2 prevails is

$$P(S_2 \mid x) = \frac{P(x \mid S_2)P(S_2)}{P(x \mid S_1)P(S_1) + P(x \mid S_2)P(S_2)}$$

$$= \frac{1/4}{2/5 + 1/4} = 5/13$$

and the weight of evidence favors the hypothesis S_1. The evidence favors S_1, although S_2 may be selected if the penalties for erring in this direction outweigh the weight of the evidence. This and other aspects of choice, including rules for deciding when to acquire more evidence before making a choice, are dealt with in *decision theory*, where Bayes' rule plays a prominent role. Evidently

$$0 \leqslant P(S_i \mid x) \leqslant 1$$

and

$$\sum_{i=1}^{n} P(S_i \mid x) = 1$$

define a new probability distribution which incorporates knowledge of the evidence gained from the experiment that yielded x. These values are referred to as *posterior probabilities*, which are elements in this new posterior distribution. Alternatively these values can be interpreted as new prior probabilities in preparation for yet another experiment to obtain further improvements in the state probability estimates, the process continuing until satisfaction is achieved as in, for instance, the optimizing *strategies* obtained from a *decision* theory analysis.

BCD (computers) = binary coded decimal. A code for mapping upper case letters, numbers, and punctuation to a series of 6-bit binary codes (see also *ASCII*).

bear (security and commodity markets) One who believes that prices will fall, and sells in anticipation of that event. He or she may also speculate on *short account* through a broker, with a promise to deliver a stock or commodity at a certain date and price, hoping in the meantime to buy the item in the market at a lower price. A ''bearish'' market is one in which the prevailing trend in prices is downward; a ''bearish'' attitude is one that reflects the belief that prices are about to decline. See *bull*.

bearer bond An unregistered bond on which interest and principal are payable to the holder; on transfers, endorsement is not required.

bearer stock Corporate capital stock evidenced by certificates not registered in any name. They are negotiable without endorsement and transferable by delivery, as are coupon bonds, and carry numbered or dated dividend coupons. In European countries, capital stock is commonly issued in the form of bearer certificates. The practice is unknown in the United States. See *warrant; right*.

behavioral accounting The attempt to identify psychological or sociological effects with reporting or accounting for enterprise activities. See *inductance hypothesis*.

below par At a discount; less than face amount.

benchmark A standard of calibration or correction. Example: Use of the U.S. Census of Population for correcting or updating many other statistical compilations and estimating procedures. The National Bureau of Standards provides a series of benchmarks for units of weight and measure.

benchmark program (computers) An existing computer program or group of programs for execution on different machines in order to comparatively evaluate each machine's performance.

beneficial interest 1. An interest in property held in trust, as distinguished from legal ownership, or in the benefit arising from an insurance policy or other contract; a certificate of such interest.
2. *pl*. The proprietorship represented by the outstanding shares of stock of a corporation; the collective rights of persons having any common proprietorship interest.

benefit The service or satisfaction yielded by an expenditure. See *service, n*.

benefit-cost analysis A comparison of benefits with costs, usually in the form of a ratio (called the benefit-cost ratio) after both benefits and costs have been stated in comparable units. Examples: (1) Sales to cost of sales, in which case the dollar value of sales represents the output benefits and cost of sales measures the value of the inputs utilized. (2) Years of additional income from lives saved in an accident prevention program compared with the cost of the program. See *cost-effectiveness analysis; efficiency*.

Beta Alpha Psi Founded in 1919, Beta Alpha Psi is the national accounting fraternity in the United States. It maintains student chapters on more than 125 university campuses, and holds a national meeting each year in August. Its primary functions are to extend membership to students on the basis of their academic records and to provide a continuing forum for the discussion of subjects of current interest in the accounting profession.

beta coefficient A measure of the *systematic risk* of a security which shows the tendency of that security to move up and down with the market in general. A beta coefficient of 1.0 indicates a security with average risk because it rises and falls by the same percentages as the market on the average. A high-beta security is more volatile than the market average, while a low-beta security is less volatile than the average. See *capital asset pricing model*.

beta risk The risk associated with a *type II error*. The risk, for example, that sample evidence will support the correctness of a recorded account balance when the same audit procedures applied to the entire population would reveal an error of a material amount. See *alpha risk*.

betterment An expenditure having the effect of extending the useful life of an existing fixed asset, increasing its normal rate of output, lowering its operating cost, increasing rather than merely maintaining efficiency or otherwise adding to the worth of benefits it can yield. The cost of adapting a fixed asset to a new use is not ordinarily capitalized unless at least one of the foregoing tests is met. A betterment is distinguished from an item of *repair* or *maintenance* in that the latter have the effect merely of keeping the asset in its customary state of operating efficiency without the expectation of added future benefits. See *fixed asset; capital expenditure; repair; maintenance*.

bias 1. The propensity, often unconscious, to search for, assemble, present, or use *evidence* in such a manner as to point to a preselected endproduct or conclusion. Bias does not of necessity lead to error, since it may be anticipated and allowed for by employing adjusting or weighting devices, or

ostensibly inaccurate results may be interpreted or cross-checked in a variety of ways. It is possible to extract evidence and synthesize an objective and *valid* picture even when employing biased or potentially biased sources of information. A principal objective in the process of auditing is the search for and correction of biases. An auditor determines the presence or lack of bias in a group of accounts receivable by circularizing persons against whom claims are held. Offsetting biases are regularly taken advantage of in the construction of *internal controls*. By the operation of a normally patterned system of *internal check*, valid results are deemed to follow by placing individuals with independent, opposing interests in opposition to each other and making them participants in the recording of the same transaction. The assumption underlying any such device is that the offsetting biases are of the same relative order of magnitude.

2. (statistics) Systematic, as distinct from random, error. It may be present in the method of collecting or processing data, as when nonrandom elements are introduced into a sample, or it may be present in the method of estimation. The amount of bias in an estimating method is determined by the magnitude with which the expected value departs from its universe value. See *expected value; random*.

bicolumnar = *double-entry bookkeeping*: a term sometimes used to characterize a *balance sheet* or *income statement*.

bid An offer to buy.

bid price The price at which a prospective owner of a security, commodity, or other property formally offers to buy.

big bath A very large writeoff of assets.

Big Eight A term applied to the eight largest partnerships of independent certified public accountants in the United States: Arthur Andersen & Co.; Coopers & Lybrand; Deloitte

Haskins & Sells; Ernst & Whinney; Peat, Marwick, Mitchell & Co.; Price Waterhouse & Co.; Touche Ross & Co.; and Arthur Young & Company.

bilateral contract A contract where the promise of one party is consideration for the promise of the other; a promise for a promise. See *unilateral contract*.

bill *n.* 1. An *invoice* of charges for goods or services.
2. = *bill of exchange*.
v.t. To prepare and dispatch an invoice covering charges for goods sold or services rendered to another.

bill of exchange 1. An unconditional order in writing addressed by one person to another, signed by the person giving it, requiring the person to whom it is addressed to pay on demand or at a fixed or determinable future time a sum certain in money to order or to bearer (Uniform Negotiable Instruments Law); synonymous with *draft acceptance* when referring to a domestic transaction.
2. Any order to pay money arising out of a foreign transaction.

bill of lading A written acknowledgment issued by a carrier as bailee constituting both a receipt of goods and a contract undertaking to deliver the goods at a specified place to a named person or to his order. Title to the goods may be passed by transfer of the bill of lading.

bill of materials A specification of the character and quantity of the materials and parts entering into a particular product. Considered along with quantities to be produced and the rate of production, it forms the basis of and justification for raw-material and parts orders, minimum and maximum on-hand quantities of raw materials and parts, cost estimates, work-in-process valuations, and production planning generally.

bill of sale A written agreement by terms of which the title or other interest of one person in goods is transferred or assigned to another. See *sale*.

bill payable 1. A bill of exchange owing.
2. = *note payable*.

bill receivable 1. A bill of exchange receivable.
2. = *note receivable*.

binary code (computers) A code that uses two distinct characters, usually 0 and 1.

binary search See *search*.

binomial distribution A *statistical distribution* specifying the probabilities of different combinations of independently drawn observations for a fixed sample size from a population in which one of two mutually exclusive outcomes must occur for each item that is drawn. An urn with an infinite number of black and white balls represents one such population and an urn with a finite number of black and white balls represents another if drawing is with replacement—i.e., if each item is replaced prior to the next draw. If p, $0 \leq p \leq 1$, is the probability of drawing a black ball and $q = 1 - p$ is the probability of drawing a white ball, then the binomial distribution becomes

$$(q + p)^n = C_0^n q^n p^0 + C_1^n q^{n-1} p^1 + \ldots$$
$$+ C_{n-1}^n q^1 p^{n-1} + C_n^n q^0 p^n$$
$$= \sum_{r=0}^{n} C_r^n q^{n-r} p^r = 1$$

with *expected value np* and *variance npq* for the number of occurrences of black in a sample of size n. The characteristic term

$$C_r^n q^{n-r} p^r = \frac{n!}{r!(n-r)!} q^{n-r} p^r$$

is the probability of observing r black and hence $(n - r)$ white balls in a sample of size n. See *permutation (4)*. See also *hyper-*

geometric distribution and *multinomial distribution*.

bit (computers) An abbreviation of *Bi*nary dig*it* or *Bi*nary uni*t*. The smallest unit of information stored on a digital computer; usually represented as a 0 or a 1. See *byte*.

bivariate analysis See *multivariate analysis*.

B/L = *bill of lading*.

black market The buying and selling of commodities or foreign exchange (including local currency) in violation of governmental restrictions; also, the location of such an activity. Compare with *gray market*.

blanket appropriation An aggregate budgetary allocation made without specific details of project elements. Such appropriations are used, for example, in capital expenditure budgets for minor additions and ordinary repairs.

blanket insurance An insurance contract relating to a variegated class of property; the number of items covered may fluctuate from time to time.

blanket mortgage A *mortgage* that covers all fixed assets of a borrower instead of covering specifically named assets.

blind entry 1. An entry stating only the accounts and the amounts debited and credited, but not giving other information or explanation essential to an adequate record. See *journal entry*.
2. A posting in a ledger not supported by a journal voucher or other record.

block 1. To forestall, hinder, or prevent.
2. A related set of accounts, entries, or transactions.
3. (computers) Block (records). One or more of a set of logically related records which are to be transferred to and from auxiliary storage in one operation. Blocking records decreases auxiliary storage requirements and increases access efficiency. An *interrecord gap* occurs between blocks on magnetic tape. See *physical records (2)*.

blocked currency Money the exchange of which for the money of another country is forbidden by law.

block method (for controlling accounts) A system of subcontrol accounts maintained for ease in keeping subsidiary accounts, as with customers, where their number makes necessary a division of labor and responsibility for their accurate maintenance.

block records See *block (3)*.

block sampling 1. A method of judgment sampling where items are selected in sequence. Once the first item in the block is selected, the remainder of the block is chosen automatically.
2. See also *cluster sampling* and *systematic sampling*.

block search See *search*.

blotter 1. A memorandum record in which notations are made of business transactions as they take place, often without regard to orderly classification or form, and from which entries or entry summaries are subsequently made in formal books of original entry; a *daybook*.
2. In stock-brokerage accounting, a formal book of original entry in the nature of a cash-receipts or cash-disbursements journal, with elaborations peculiar to the business.

Blough, Carman G. (1895-1981) The first Chief Accountant of the *Securities and Exchange Commission*, Carman G. Blough became one of the most respected American authorities on the content and application of "generally accepted accounting principles." He served as President of the American Accounting Association in 1944 and as the first full-time Director of Research of the American Institute of Certified Public Accountants from 1944 to 1961. Many of his columns in the *Journal of Accountancy* on accepted accounting practice were gathered in a volume, *Practical Applications of Accounting Standards*, which was published by the Institute in 1957. Blough was a charter member of the *Accounting Principles Board* from 1959 to 1964.

blue-sky law The popular term for a state law regulating issues of securities. Kansas was the first (1911) to adopt an act of this kind. In general, these laws are coordinated, often informally, with federal acts; many of them provide for the licensing of dealers, brokers, and others offering securities for sale, and of each salesman or agent; most of them require registration of new issues, the registration varying between the filing of specified information and action leading to formal approval of the issue by the state regulatory body. Prevention of the grosser forms of fraud has often been the predominant aim of these laws.

board-designated funds *Funds* (usually of a hospital) created to account for assets set aside by action of the governing board for specified purposes. Board-designated funds are *unrestricted funds*, not *restricted funds*.

board of directors The persons elected by stockholders and charged under corporation laws with the responsibility of supervising the affairs of a corporation. Their number is dependent on the provisions of the articles of incorporation and bylaws; a minimum of three is often required, and they may or may not be stockholders. A chief function of a board of directors is generally held to be policy making, as distinct from *administration*, although many policies, initiated by management, are now subject only to the sufferance of or a nominal review by the board.

BOM = beginning of month.

bond 1. A certificate of indebtedness, in writing and often under seal. Bonds are issued in the form of coupon or bearer instruments, or are registered in the name of the owner as to principal only (registered coupon bonds) or as to both principal and interest (registered bonds). Their title usually indicates broadly the purpose for and the security upon which they are issued, also the method of payment or redemption; e.g., consolidated-mortgage bonds, equipment bonds, and first-mortgage bonds. Bonds may be classified by (a) the type of issuing body, e.g., government, state, municipal, railroad, or other utilities; (b) the nature of the project financed, e.g., farm-loan, irrigation, reclamation, or development bonds; (c) the type of currency in which they will be paid, e.g., dollar, sterling, gold, legal-tender bonds; (d) special privileges, e.g., participating or convertible bonds; (e) the type of lien, e.g., underlying, junior lien, first- or second-mortgage bonds; (f) fitness for investments, e.g., savings-bank or trustee bonds; (g) maturity, e.g., short-term or long-term bonds.

2. An obligation in writing, binding one or more parties as surety for another; a surety bond. Such a bond is often required of litigants by the courts to secure costs, damages, and debts; of receivers, administrators, executors, guardians, trustees, and others to protect the interests they represent; and by the government and other authorities and employers, of persons holding positions of public or private trust. Surety bonds may be issued by a guaranty company or by one or more individuals.

3. As used in the expression "in bond": pertaining to goods in a bonded warehouse that cannot be released except by payment of certain duties or taxes.

bond anticipation notes Short-term interest-bearing notes issued by a governmental unit in anticipation of bonds to be issued at a later date, the notes to be retired from proceeds of the bond issue. See also *tax anticipation note; revenue anticipation note*.

bond conversion The exchange of *convertible bonds* for *preferred stock* or *common stock*. See *conversion (1)*.

bond discount (and expense) The excess of the face amount of a bond or class of bonds over the net amount received when it was issued.

The cost of a bond issue, made up of identifiable costs, such as legal, accounting, appraisal, and engineering fees, costs of registration and printing, and the excess of face value over disposal price (discount) are often absorbed as an expense at the time they are incurred; or they may be combined in a single account and regarded as a *deferred charge*, allocable to the years during which the bonds are outstanding. The commission paid to a dealer for selling the security is usually regarded as a deduction in determining *net proceeds* and therefore does not find its way into the accounts as a cost and in a strict sense should not be regarded as an addition to the deferred-charge account: a situation arising where the dealer contracts to purchase the bonds at a fixed price (more or less than face value), his commission or profit arising from the addition made to this fixed price when the bonds are sold to the public.

Bond discount is a species of premium, since it is the extra payment, in addition to regular interest, that must be paid to induce the investor to loan his or her money, and it is payable at the same time that a formal premium is payable. Thus, if a corporation receives net proceeds of $99,000 from the sale of a bond issue that has a face value of $100,000 and is repayable at 102 ten years hence, the discount of $1,000, along with the redemption premium of $2,000, is to be paid out at maturity. What was borrowed was $99,000; what is to be repaid is $102,000;

and in conformity with the principles of accrual accounting, the difference of $3,000 calls for recognition in the accounts as an expense during the loan period of ten years. Following are several methods that have been advocated by various authorities for disposing of this amount:

1. Record the loan in the amount of the net proceeds received ($99,000); on a balance sheet at the time the loan is made, report as the obligation the amount received, and parenthetically state both the face value and the redemption amount; each year increase the liability by $300, at the same time charging financial expense. Thus, by a process of *accumulation*, the liability is raised to its full amount in the year of retirement. This is a preferred but seldom-followed procedure.

2. Record the loan at its face amount ($100,000). *Debit* cash $99,000 and unamortized bond discount $1,000; each year *charge* $100 to financial expense or bond discount amortized and credit unamortized bond discount; each year charge the same expense account with $200 and credit accrued bond-retirement premium. On a balance sheet include the amortized bond discount under deferred charges, show the liability for the bond issue as $100,000 and, as a separately stated addition thereto, the accumulated amount of the retirement premium. This is the procedure generally found in practice.

3. A variation of the latter procedure is occasionally found. An unamortized-bond-discount account is maintained, with periodic writedowns as described, but no provision for the accumulation of the retirement premium is made, the premium paid during the year of retirement being treated as an expense of that year.

Discount and premium on serial-bond issues may be segregated by classes or dates of maturity and the amortization or accumulation pertaining to each class may be computed separately; or the discount and expense (and premium) for all classes may be lumped together. Either method, supplying a basis for substantially similar results, is acceptable.

The usual method for spreading bond discount (and premium) over the years in which a serial obligation is in force is known as the *bonds-outstanding method*.

Considerable controversy has arisen in past years as to the disposition of unamortized discount and expense in connection with a bond issue that has been refunded. Three methods of disposition, in the order of their general preference, have been employed:

1. Charge it to expense (or retained earnings) in the year of retirement.

2. Continue to amortize it on the old basis, as though the retired issue were still outstanding.

3. Add it to any discount and expense on the new issue and thus amortize it over the life of the new issue.

Of the three methods, the first and second have often been employed; the third, but rarely, although permitted under SEC-approved practices. In support of the first it may be said that the unamortized discount and expense are deductible for income-tax purposes in the year of refunding; moreover, it is argued, when the old issue disappears, all the accounts maintained for it should be eliminated at the same time, the unamortized sum becoming a current expense (if *significant*, possibly treated as an extraordinary one) of the year of the refund. A basic objection to the second and third methods is that they result in an overstatement of subsequent interest costs, since the debt-service cost of the new issue, which is usually independent of the old, is increased by a part of the debt-service cost of an issue no longer in existence. Support is sometimes given to the second method provided the total of the periodic charge for interest and debt-discount amortization does not exceed that which would have resulted if the refunding operation had not taken place. See *deferred charge*.

bond dividend A *dividend* paid in the issuing company's own bonds.

bonded debt Debt evidenced by bonds outstanding. See *funded debt*.

bond fund (municipal accounting) A fund established by a municipality or other government agency for the receipt and disbursement of the proceeds of a bond issue. See *fund*.

bond indenture See *indenture*.

bond ordinance or resolution An ordinance, or resolution, of a governmental unit authorizing a bond issue, usually for specified purposes. The amount, date of issue, maturity date, and provisions ordinarily found in *bond indentures* are generally incorporated in the ordinance or resolution.

bond premium The net amount yielded by the sale of a bond or class of bonds in excess of its face value. On the books and balance sheet of the issuer it appears as a deferred credit and is commonly amortized over the life of the bonds by the *bonds-outstanding method*, the periodic transfer to income being subtracted from or appearing with interest expense—such treatment being justified from the supposition that, if the interest rate had been smaller, a premium would not have been realized from the sale. Upon premature retirement of the bonds and in various other situations, the unamortized premium is disposed of in a manner resembling the disposition of *bond discount*.

bond rating Quality ratings of corporate and municipal bond issues which reflect the probability of default on each issue. The two major rating agencies are Moody's Investors Service and Standard & Poor's Corporation.

Twelve alphabetic ratings ranging from AAA to AA ("high quality"), A to BBB ("investment grade"), BB to B ("substandard"), and CCC to D ("speculative") are assigned. The fourth highest rating, BBB, is particularly important because institutional investors are restricted from buying bonds below that rating. Accounting data have been found to be good predictors of new bond ratings and ratings changes.

bond redemption A transaction in which *bonds (1)* are repurchased or retired by the issuer. See *redemption*.

bond register 1. A record in which each outstanding bond and often the payment of each successive coupon are registered. Two types of bond registers are in common use. In one, separate sections are provided for the various series, each section being subdivided by the denominations of the bonds. Columns are provided for the consecutive symbols and numbers of the bonds and for coupon dates. Notations in these columns are made as coupons are paid. In the second type, a separate page appears for each outstanding bond; in addition to provision for the bond symbol and number, each page is divided into rectangles of the size of the coupons and bearing their consecutive numbers. Each coupon paid is pasted into its rectangle; the open spaces represent outstanding coupons.
2. A record kept by a bond registrar wherein outstanding bonds of a specified issue are registered in the name of the holder.

bond risk premium The difference between the yield to maturity on a corporate or municipal bond and the risk-free rate on a U.S. government bond with the same maturity date. It measures that portion of the bond's yield which compensates the investor for risk taking. The variability of long-run accounting earnings has been found to be an important determinant of bond risk premiums.

bond sinking fund See *sinking fund*.

bonds-outstanding method (of amortizing bond discount) A term referring to the spread of *bond discount* over the life of a bond issue by periodic charges to expense, determined by a ratio equal to the fraction having as its numerator the face value of bonds outstanding during the period and as its denominator the total of such face values for all the periods during which the bonds are outstanding. The same fraction may be derived from dividing interest expense for the period by all the interest to be paid on the bonds during the life of the issue, assuming no prepayments.

bonds payable = *bonds*.

bond table A book in which is tabulated, on the basis of the yield at each of an extensive series of interest rates, the *present value* of a bond of a specified maturity bearing interest at any customary rate.

bond valuation 1. The process followed by an investor in determining what to pay for a bond or, in the case of an issuer, the price that should be received; involved is the determination of a value based upon the redemption price of the bond when held to maturity or earlier fixed date, the nominal or coupon rate of interest, and the effective rate or desired yield.
2. The value resulting from the application of the process.

bonus 1. Premium or extra allowance paid to an employee or corporate officer.
2. Securities issued as a premium with a purchase of bonds or stocks.
3. A lump-sum payment for a lease, particularly in extractive industries, in addition to royalties.

bonus method See *goodwill method*.

bonus pool An amount, determined by administrative or board action, to be shared by management, or employees generally, under an incentive plan or other agreement or policy whereby additional compensation may be awarded.

book *n.* = *book of account*.

v. To record a *transaction*; to make an *entry*.

book inventory 1. An inventory which is not the result of actual stocktaking but of adding the units and the cost of incoming goods to previous inventory figures and deducting the units and cost of outgoing goods. Without units of quantity of input and output the term is usually qualified to denote its tentative character.

2. The balances of materials or products on hand in quantities, dollars, or both, appearing in perpetual-inventory accounts. See *perpetual inventory*.

bookkeeper One engaged in *bookkeeping*. The term is applied to a person who does all the bookkeeping of an enterprise, or whose work is specialized, such as one who maintains the general ledger or who works on accounts receivable. A bookkeeper may also be an accountant if, in addition, he or she prepares or supervises the preparation of financial statements from the accounts, designs and modifies the methods employed, or supervises transaction recording.

bookkeeping The process of analyzing, classifying, and recording transactions in accordance with a preconceived plan, for the purpose of (a) providing a means by which an enterprise may be conducted in an orderly fashion, and (b) establishing a basis for recording and reporting the financial affairs of the enterprise and the results of its operation. See *double-entry bookkeeping*.

bookkeeping cycle = *accounting cycle*.

book of account 1. Any *journal, register*, or *ledger* which forms a part of a *system of accounts*.

2. *pl.* All the *books of original entry* and *books of final entry*, and the invoices, vouchers, contracts, correspondence, and the like

that result from the occurrence of transactions and the operation of a *system of accounts*; often shortened to *books*.

book of final entry A record book in which the money amounts of transactions, accumulated according to a previously established classification of accounts, are transferred or *posted*; a *ledger*.

book of original entry A record book, recognized by law or custom, in which transactions are successively recorded, and which is the source of postings to ledgers; a *journal*. Books of original entry include general and special journals, such as cashbooks and registers of sales and purchases. Memorandum books, check stubs, files of duplicate sales invoices, and the like, wherein first or prior notations may already have been made, although commonly regarded as a part of the *books of account*, are also referred to as "business papers or supporting records" and are not referred to as books of original entry unless they are used as posting sources.

book of secondary entry = *book of final entry*.

book profit 1. Profit as shown by the books of account before verification or audit or as contrasted with "economic" profit or profit determined on some other basis.

2. *pl.* Profits based on book figures, especially in cases where book figures differ from actual cost.

book surplus 1. *Surplus* (retained income) before giving expression to audit corrections.

2. *Surplus* as shown by the books, on a *going-concern* basis, as distinct from a figure that would result from putting the accounts on a liquidating or some noncost basis.

book value (or cost) 1. The net amount at which an asset or asset group appears on the books of account, as distinguished from its market value or some intrinsic value. *Gross book value* is the amount appearing in an asset account; while *book value* (or *net book* *value*) is the gross book value less any applicable portion of accumulated depreciation or other *valuation account*.

2. The face amount of a liability less any *unamortized bond discount* and expense.

3. As applied to capital stock: (a) the book value of the *net assets*; (b) in a corporation, the book value of the net assets, divided by the number of outstanding shares of capital stock; it is based on the *going-concern values* customarily reflected in balance sheets. It may also mean the portion of the proceeds applicable to each share of stock following a no-gain, no-loss liquidation at a given balance-sheet date. Without specific provisions to the contrary in the articles of incorporation or the governing state law, the book value of a share of *preferred stock* would be its agreed value in involuntary liquidation plus cumulative dividends in arrears, if any, provided that the total is not in excess of the corporate net worth; to common stock would be assigned the balance, if any, of net assets. Book value attaches only to outstanding shares of capital stock, and not to unissued or reacquired shares.

book value per share A measure of the average amount of *stockholders' equity* per share of stock computed by dividing total assets minus total liabilities by the number of outstanding shares of capital stock. See *book value* (3).

boot Something in addition; specifically (federal income taxes) in a property exchange that would otherwise be tax-free (e.g., certain like-kind or reorganization exchanges), money or other property passing in the exchange; in general, if the recipient of the boot realizes gain in the exchange, the gain is taxable to the extent of the money or fair market value of the boot received.

bordereau (insurance accounting) A docket now restricted to a tabular register or report containing abstracts of insurance written.

Boston ledger A type of ledger in which the record on each account progresses horizontally in columnar sections assigned to successive accounting periods. Several accounts may be kept on a single page. This form of ledger eliminates the necessity of preparing a separate trial balance, the aggregate of balances in each section taking its place.

bottom-up approach An approach to management which is intended to emphasize the importance of lower echelons or subsidiary company (or agency) management levels. In computers it is an approach to system design which begins by building the detail foundation routines first, then working up to the top level integrating routines. It contrasts with *top-down approach*.

Box-Jenkins method A way of estimating the process which governs a *time series* by reference to the class of *ARIMA* models.

BOY = beginning of year.

boycott A refusal to perform a customary act: usually an action participated in by more than one person for a common purpose; a refusal to buy or handle goods of an organization whose employees are on strike; hence, any such refusal to buy or sell.

branch accounting An accounting which maintains a complete self-balancing set of accounting records for each branch office. The type of accounting used, however, depends on company policy about the degree of autonomy given each branch and the control retained by the home office. Accounting integration between home office and branch records is usually achieved with control or reciprocal accounts.

Bray, F. Sewell (1906-1979) An English chartered accountant who was one of the leaders of the research program of the Society of Incorporated Accountants and Auditors during the 1940s and 1950s. From 1948 to 1957, he was joint editor of the Society's journal, *Accounting Research*, and from 1952 to 1957 he held the Stamp-Martin Professorship at Incorporated Accountants' Hall, a title bestowed by the Society. He wrote several books and numerous articles, most of which reflect a keen interest in linking economic and accounting theory.

breach of contract Failure of one or both parties to perform a contract as agreed. See also *anticipatory breach.*

breakdown An analysis, usually summarized in terms of transaction classes, of an account balance or other figure; e.g., the process followed in the preparation of a *spread sheet.*

breakeven capacity See formula (1) under *breakeven point.* The breakeven point stated in terms of a capacity utilization percentage.

breakeven chart Any of several types of charts on which the *breakeven point* is shown. As employed in accounting, it is typically an important tool of *forward accounting:* a projection of a year's operations in which costs and profits are shown under varying sales volumes. The projection may involve the business as a whole, a department, an operation, or a product.

Example: the Simplex Manufacturing Company is the manufacturer of several lines of finished parts that become the raw material of other producers. During emergency periods, its volume of business has been dependent to a great extent on the availability of raw materials. The business is competitive, and the margin of net profit is, as a rule, narrow.

In November, 19-0, the company's budget committee, consisting of the chairman of the Finance Committee of the Board of Directors, the president, the controller, the sales manager, and the production vice-president, approved the figures appearing in the first six columns of the *projections schedule* shown. These were derived in part from past experience plus the expectation of increases in the prices of raw materials. The prospect of increasing selling prices was considered dim. It

PROJECTIONS SCHEDULE (*in thousands*)

Item	Fixed Costs	Original Projection Made on Dec. 12, 19-0 for the Year 19-1 — Varying Sales Volume					Reprojections Full Year after Close of Quarter Q1	Q2	Q3	Actual for Full Year*
Sales	650	1,000	2,000	3,000	4,000	5,000	4,200	4,600	4,400	4,300
Material	0	250	500	750	1,000	1,250	1,200	1,300	1,200	1,200
Labor	0	400	600	750	800	1,000	800	850	850	850
Overhead	250	250	400	500	600	650	250	300	300	300
							450	400	300	300
Selling	50	150	300	400	450	500	100	100	100	100
							350	400	350	300
Administration	150	200	300	300	350	400	150	150	150	100
							300	200	250	250
Depreciation	100	100	100	100	100	100	100	100	100	100
Interest	100	100	100	100	100	100	100	100	100	100
Income tax	0	0	0	50	300	450	300	350	300	300
Dividend	0	0	0	0	200	250	50	250	250	250
Retained income	0	−450	−300	50	100	300	50	100	150	150

*Not yet filled in on chart.

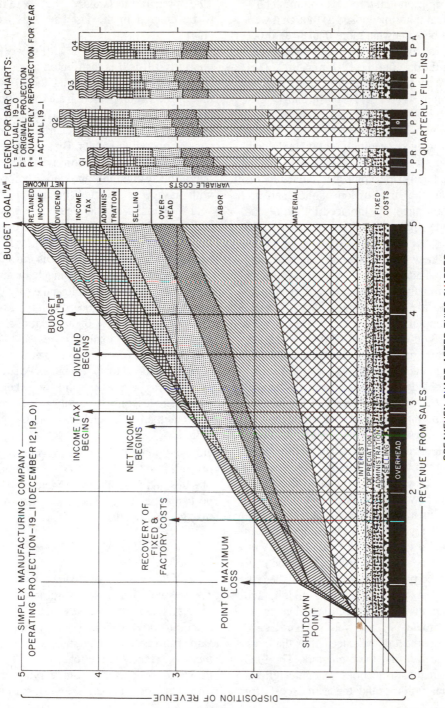

SIMPLEX MANUFACTURING COMPANY
OPERATING PROJECTION—19_I (DECEMBER 12, 19_O)

LEGEND FOR BAR CHARTS:
L = ACTUAL, 19_O
P = ORIGINAL PROJECTION
R = QUARTERLY REPROJECTION FOR YEAR
A = ACTUAL, 19_I

BUDGET GOAL "A"
BUDGET GOAL "B"
DIVIDEND BEGINS
INCOME TAX BEGINS
NET INCOME BEGINS
RECOVERY OF FIXED & FACTORY COSTS
POINT OF MAXIMUM LOSS
SHUTDOWN POINT

DISPOSITION OF REVENUE

REVENUE FROM SALES

BREAKEVEN CHART, AFTER THIRD QUARTER.

NET INCOME
RETAINED INCOME
DIVIDEND
INCOME TAX
ADMINIS-TRATION
SELLING
OVER-HEAD
LABOR
MATERIAL
VARIABLE COSTS
FIXED COSTS

INTEREST
DEPRECIATION
ADMINISTRATION
SELLING
OVERHEAD

Q1 Q2 Q3 Q4
L P R   L P R   L P R   L P A
QUARTERLY FILL-INS

73

was the opinion that the sales volume for 19-0, which at that time looked as though it were going to be somewhat more than $4,000,000 for the year, might be expanded under favorable conditions during 19-1 to $5,000,000. The primary budget goal, therefore, was set at the latter figure, *"A,"* but a budget goal *"B"* of $4,000,000 was also established as a floor below which business was not likely to drop, short of exceedingly unfavorable conditions.

Immediately the controller tabulated the figures in the first section of the chart appearing on page 73 embraced by the legend "Revenue from Sales" on the horizontal axis.

As the new year approached, an *operating budget* was adopted by the Finance Committee as summarized in column 6 of the projections schedule shown on page 72.

The supplemental bar charts Q1-Q4 were prepared within a period of two weeks following the end of each quarter of 19-1, the first bar in each case representing last year's sales (labeled *"L"*) broken down by actual costs of the principal factors of production. Both the second and third bars reflect the sum of actual sales for the first three months plus reestimated sales for the balance of the year, broken down by the originally projected factor costs extended over from the main section (*"P"*) and by factor costs for the first three months plus a reestimate of costs for the balance of the year (*"R"*), it being borne in mind that, as each quarter ends, a better vantage point is available from which the estimates of the previous November may be critically recast. In the seventh, eighth, and ninth columns of the projections schedule are the reestimates of the year's volume and costs, prepared, as indicated, after the close of each of the first three quarters. The final column in the projections schedule reflects the actual volume and the actual costs for

19-1, prepared in January 19-2; these remain to be entered in the last bar (*"A"*) of the chart.

Each quarter the chart, with newly added quarterly fill-ins, is distributed to top executives and board members at their quarterly meetings, accompanied by explanations of principal variations and by financial statements showing detailed quarterly comparisons of operating results. By supplying these persons with the latest reestimate of probable operating results and an overall comparison with last year's actual business and last year's estimate of this year's business, the chart serves to transmit one type of operating information in capsule form and at the same time provides a check on forecasting skills.

Primarily informational in character, the breakeven chart is a simple and easily understood device which proceeds on the assumptions of (1) linearity of all relations, when stated in terms of total revenues, and (2) unvarying mixes of the revenue items comprehended in these total revenues. When these assumptions are not valid or when mix changes in response to varying prices are to be studied, then more elaborate *models* are required.

breakeven point 1. The volume point at which revenues and costs are equal: a combination of sales and costs that will yield a no-profit, no-loss operation. The following formula may be employed:

$$s_0 = \frac{f}{1 - v/s}.$$

$s_0 = f/(1 - v/s)$ is obtained from $s_0/s = f/(s - v)$. Thus, the assumption of the *model* is that the breakeven level of sales stands to present dollar sales volume in the same ratio as fixed costs stand to *contribution margin*, where f is the total of fixed costs, v the total of present costs varying directly with sales, s the present sales volume, and s_0

the sales volume required to cover costs. Thus, if $f = \$90,000$, $v = \$50,000$, and $s = \$125,000$,

$$s_0 = \frac{90,000}{1 - 50,000/125,000}$$

$$= \$150,000 .$$

This means that, to cover expenses, total sales must be not less than $150,000.

The breakeven point may also be expressed in terms of a percentage of total plant capacity. This may be obtained in the above example by altering the formula to

$$r = \frac{f}{(1 - v/s)c}, \qquad (1)$$

where c is the plant capacity in terms of maximum sales volume and r is the ratio sought; if c is $200,000, the breakeven point is 150,000/200,000, or 75%. Or, if plant capacity is stated in terms of present operations, the formula becomes

$$r = \frac{fc_1}{s - v},$$

where c_1 is the ratio of present plant utilization to total plant capacity; if c_1 is 62 1/2%, then

$$r = \frac{90,000 \times .625}{125,000 - 50,000} = .75, \text{ or } 75\%.$$

2. That point in the cost of a variable factor of production at which one or more alternatives are equally economical.

3. Multiple breakeven points (or ranges). In a multiproduct firm where the production of each good is independent of that of another good and $s_1, s_2, \ldots, s_n$ are the sales volume of each good in physical units required for the firm to break even if only one good is produced, then $\alpha_1 s_1 + \alpha_2 s_2 + \ldots + \alpha_n s_n$, for all $\alpha_1 + \alpha_2 + \ldots + \alpha_n = 1$ and $0 \leqslant \alpha_j \leqslant 1$ for $j = 1, 2, \ldots n$, describes the range of all possible breakeven points when one or more products are produced.

break-up value The amount which can be obtained for assets at forced sales, upon discontinuance of their normal use; salvage value.

bribes Payments, offers, promises, or gifts given for the purpose of improperly or in an *ultra vires* manner influencing some act or a decision of another.

bring forward To inscribe the balance or the total debits and credits of an account, worksheet, or any tabular statement upon a new page or sheet or upon a cleared section of an old sheet.

broker Any agent acting as intermediary between buyer and seller of real or personal property or service; he or she does not take title to property in the typical transaction but receives a fee from either or both parties, thereby identifying himself or herself as an agent of one or both. The term is often loosely applied to *dealers*, especially in securities.

brokerage A commission, paid or accruing to a broker, arising from effecting a *deal* between seller and buyer, and borne by either party in accordance with custom, regulation, or special agreement. It may be fixed, as in stock market transactions, by trade or government bodies, and may take any of various forms, such as a percentage or modification of selling price; a (finder's) fee; an underwriting or other *discount* (4); a concession or other advantage (whether or not transaction-related).

broker's loan A borrowing from a bank by a broker or investment dealer for the purpose of purchasing or carrying securities or for carrying customers' margin accounts.

bucket shop An operation by a broker whereby customers' orders to buy and sell are not immediately executed but are held for a possible price change that will yield the broker a personal gain.

budget 1. Any financial plan serving as an estimate of and a control over future operations.

2. Hence, any estimate of future costs or revenues.

3. Any systematic plan for the utilization of manpower, material, or other resources.

Budgets assume varying forms, depending on the operating methods, scope, and complexity of an enterprise. They may, however, be divided into two main classes: capital budgets, directed toward proposed expenditures for *project* activities and often requiring special financing; and operating budgets, directed toward planning and controlling *program* activities. Operating budgets may be subdivided further into sales, advertising and marketing, production and labor, inventory and purchases, maintenance, and overhead budgets, as well as special-purpose short-term budgets, such as those constructed for job-order or batch production.

Financial budgets such as the cash budget, for planning and controlling cash receipts and disbursements, and budgets constructed for longer-range financing can be keyed directly into *pro forma balance sheets* at the end of the budget period, and into projected statements of income and expense.

Operating and capital budgets may also be classified by type into appropriation, forecast, and flexible budgets. Appropriation-type budgets, involving usually a lump-sum-expenditure ceiling with such supporting detail as may be necessary or possible, are used in governmental bodies, or for controlling capital expenditures or programs, such as advertising, where it may be difficult, because of the absence of past experience or developed standards, to relate performance to expenditure in detail. Forecast-type budgets may be used for either projects or programs. They are distinguished from flexible budgets in that budgetary estimates and controls are designed for only one level of activi-

ty. Should any wide deviation from that level of activity occur, the forecast budget loses much of its relevance. Flexible budgets, on the other hand, provide estimates as a basis for control at varying rates of activity. A flexible budget requires careful segregation of costs into fixed, semifixed, and variable; it also requires well-developed standards for relating costs to production or other enterprise activities. See *breakeven chart*.

Many business concerns employ a combination of appropriation, forecast, and flexible budgets for purposes varying from mere forecasting to the establishment of current operating controls and standards of performance. Moreover, complete budgets covering all phases of an enterprise, as well as incomplete budgets covering only certain phases, are also met with in practice.

In the federal government, extensive use has been made of the principle of the operating budget, which is called a *program* or performance budget. The aim has been to establish a form of budget which serves not only (a) as an aid to the Congress in determining the expenditure ceiling for each governmental agency but also as the basis for (b) management controls over operations and (c) performance review by both insiders and outsiders. Because of these objectives the classification of budget detail has followed the pattern of the accounts and financial statements, and the agency's controller has played a leading role in budgetary preparation and execution—with ultimate responsibility resting on the agency's administrator.

budgetary accounts (governmental accounting) Accounts reflecting budgetary operations and conditions such as those maintained for estimated revenues and appropriations. They are distinguished from *proprietary accounts*, which show actual financial condition and operations, and are exemplified by such accounts as cash, taxes receivable, vouchers payable, and bonds payable. Examples of budgetary accounts are estimated revenues, appropriations, and encumbrances.

budgetary control The control of revenue and expense, and of changes in assets and liabilities, through the use of budgetary methods. See *budget*.

budgetary fund (governmental accounting) A *fund* in which budgetary accounts are incorporated with proprietary accounts in order to facilitate legal compliance and conformity with generally accepted accounting principles. General funds, special revenue funds, and debt service funds are referred to as budgetary funds in the AICPA audit guide, *Audits of State and Local Governmental Units*. See *fund accounting*.

budgetary slack Underestimated revenues or overestimated costs in an operating budget which make it easier to meet the specified budget.

budget document (governmental accounting) The instrument used in presenting a comrehensive financial program to the appropriating or authorizing body. The budget document ordinarily includes a balanced statement of the revenues and expenditures and other exhibits reporting the current financial condition or estimated condition of the several funds (a) at the end of the last completed year, (b) at the end of the fiscal year in progress, and (c) at the close of the ensuing fiscal period.

budgeting The process of preparing and administering *budgets*.

budget limitation Projected conditions of operation prescribed for an organization or organizational unit; these may include (a) the nature and extent of authority to carry out assigned functions; (b) employment specifications and limits of numbers and grades; (c)

coordination and avoidance of overlapping with other units and with outsiders; (d) character and limitations of particular expenditures. Frequently, however, only the last-named condition is implied by the term; the other three, being of a permanent or semipermanent nature, are left to the procedural instructions of an organization manual or of management, or, in case of governmental bodies, are found in basic or authorizing legislation.

budget period The period of time covered by a budget: a year, a quarter, sometimes a month, occasionally two or more years.

budget variance Any deviation of actual from planned (budgeted) results, such as revenues earned or costs incurred compared with the level expressed in the budgetary plan.

buffer 1. To cushion or protect.
2. (computers) A storage area used temporarily to store data which are being transferred.

bulk cargo Unpackaged cargo.

bull (security and commodity markets) One who believes that prices will rise and who invests money in securities or other property or advises others to do so, thus creating a *long* position. A "bullish" market is one in which the prevailing trend in prices is upward; a "bullish" influence is one that inflates or tends to inflate prices. See *bear*.

bullion Uncoined but refined gold or silver; generally in the form of bars or ingots.

bunched cost See *lump-sum purchase*.

burden Costs of manufacture or production not directly identifiable with specific products; *factory overhead* or service cost; *indirect costs*; apportionable costs. See *overhead*.

burden center A group of accounts in which indirect costs are accumulated and subsequently allocated to final *cost objectives*. See *cost center*.

burden rate = *overhead rate*.

bureau A major organizational and functional subdivision of a department of the federal government. Examples: the Bureau of Accounts in the Department of the Treasury; the Office of Management and Budget, before 1939 a Treasury subdivision and now a part of the Executive Office of the President, reporting directly to the President.

burning ratio (insurance) The ratio of an actual loss by fire to the total value of burnable property.

business 1. The carrying on of trade or commerce, involving the use of capital and having, as a major objective, income derived from sales of goods or services; industrial and commercial activity generally.
2. The exchange of goods or services for cash, promises to pay, or other goods or services, whether or not involving gain.
3. Any establishment for the conduct of trade or commerce; a business enterprise.

business combination The bringing together of two or more business entities, usually corporations, accomplished by transferring the net assets of one or more of the entities to another of them (a *merger*) or to a new one created for that purpose (a *consolidation*). Either action may, in effect, be a purchase, with one or more groups of stockholders retiring, or a *pooling of interests* may occur in which the stockholders of all the participants share.

business corporation A corporation engaged in ordinary business pursuits, such as manufacturing or trading, as distinguished from other types, such as financial corporations (banks and insurance companies), railroads, public-service companies, schools and other nonprofit corporations, and cooperative enterprises.

business enterprise (or entity or unit) 1. A proprietorship, partnership, joint venture, trust, or corporation; a group of persons having common interests of any kind, carrying on any economic activity, and constituting a unit commonly recognized as having a separate and distinct existence in the community. See *legal entity; entity; economic unit*.
2. Business collectively.

business game A use of competitive *simulation* to educate or acquaint students or other users with consequences of their decisions under complex conditions, which include reactions from other participants. Such games are usually computerized to deal with the desired degrees of complexity and to provide reports of results of decisions from all participants, including their interaction effects, within reasonable times. Dimensions such as sales, advertising *strategies*, production, finance, and other aspects of business, including R&D strategies, make it advisable to use team rather than only individual student approaches in many of these games. The degree of complexity and detail also makes it advisable to consider alternative organizational arrangements and assignments of responsibility explicitly. This sometimes extends to board of directors arrangements which utilize experienced businessmen in a natural experience-learning capacity that can be of considerable value for student participants in such games. The games can be very complex with computer printouts of accounting and other statements resulting from all past and present decisions of "firms" competing in the same or similar markets. The markets comprehended in the underlying simulation models are not confined to sales markets where competitive interactions are to be accommodated. They also include supply (including labor) and financial markets as well.

business income The net income of a corporation or of corporations generally. See *net income*.

business-interruption insurance Insurance against continuing expense, sometimes including payroll, and loss of business net income following the partial or full interruption of business activity caused by fire or other insured peril.

business transaction 1. Any *transaction* with a business enterprise; also, a transaction governed by well-established, generally recognized commercial standards.
2. = *external transaction*.

business trust A form of organization for carrying on a joint venture or business operation; its assets are held by a trustee, and the owners or contributors of capital (*cestuis que trustent*, or shareholders) possess evidences of ownership known as certificates of beneficial interest. Like a partnership, the owners may be personally liable to creditors unless the latter are on notice that they may look only to the trust assets for the settlement of their claims. Depending on the nature of the trust declaration and the laws of the state, a trust of this character may enjoy the status of a corporation, with limited liability to creditors. A business trust is generally subject to the federal income tax applicable to corporations. It is also known as a Massachusetts or common-law trust. If, however, the *cestuis que trustent* exercise a large degree of control over daily operations, the result may be a partnership and the partners may have an unlimited liability to creditors.

buyers' market A favorable condition for buyers within an industry usually characterized by an excess of supply over demand; contrasts with *sellers' market*. Under competitive conditions among sellers, a buyers' market results in lower market prices.

buying in The practice of bidding, particularly in connection with government contracts, whereby a price or cost estimate, known to be less than the anticipated actual price or cost, is quoted with the expectation of either increasing the contract price during the performance period through the medium of one or more change orders, or obtaining future contracts at substantially higher prices.

bylaws In a corporation, the rules adopted by the stockholders setting forth the general method by which the corporate functions are to be carried on: the time, place, and nature of meetings of the stockholders and directors; how directors are chosen; the appointment of officers and their duties; the issue and transfer of capital stock; the fiscal year; the appointment of auditors; how bylaw amendments are to be made; and so on. The bylaws must not be in conflict with the articles of incorporation or the laws of the state of incorporation or domicile.

byproduct A secondary product obtained during the course of manufacture, having a relatively small importance as compared with that of the chief product or products. The cost of a byproduct is commonly regarded as indeterminable; the revenue, if any, from its sale is typically credited to the operation concerned. See *joint product*.

byte A sequence of binary *bits* used to represent a character. On a byte-oriented machine (such as IBM System 360 and System 370), one byte constitutes the smallest addressable unit of storage. On a word-oriented machine (such as DEC PDP-11) a computer word is the smallest addressable unit of storage and it is usually made up of more than one byte.

cafeteria plans (*Internal Revenue Code*) Flexible benefit plans permitting covered employees to select the fringe benefits desired from a package provided by the employer.

CAI = *computer-assisted instruction*.

call 1. A demand on a subscriber to capital stock for all or a portion of the unpaid amount of his subscription.

2. A transferable option to buy a specified number of shares of stock at a stated price (usually somewhat above current market) at any time during a specified period. Such an option is purchased by a speculator anticipating a price rise above the delivery price. Should that event occur, he or she will order delivery of the shares and sell them on the market, thus earning a profit on an investment with a cost of only the option. If the price declines, he or she will allow the option to expire, thus sustaining a loss equal to its cost. See *put; straddle*.

callable bond A bond which accords an issuer the right to redemption (often at a call premium or call price) before it is due. Same as *redeemable bond*. See *call premium; call price*.

callable security A security permitting the issuer to redeem it before maturity, usually at specified prices and times; usually callable bonds and callable preferred stock. See *redemption*.

call loan A loan terminable at will by either party. The term is confined mostly to loans made by banks to stockbrokers.

call premium The excess above par payable by the issuer of a bond if redeemed before maturity, as provided by the bond indenture. The amount of the premium may vary, usually decreasing as maturity nears.

call price The price at which a callable bond is redeemable.

call provision A contractual condition or stipulation that enables the issuer of a security to repurchase or retire it at specified prices and times. See *call price*.

CA Magazine Journal of the Canadian Institute of Chartered Accountants. See *accounting journals*.

Canadian Institute of Chartered Accountants Founded in 1902 as the Dominion Association of Chartered Accountants, it is the principal national organization of accountants in Canada. CICA is, strictly, a federation of the ten provincial institutes (or orders) of chartered accountants, and members in good standing of any of the provincial institutes are automatically members of CICA. In Canada, the regulation of the accounting profession is a provincial matter. CICA's Accounting Research Committee (formerly part of the Accounting and Auditing Research Committee), which is broadly representative of chartered accountants from across Canada, proposes and, in the end, adopts policy statements on accepted accounting practice in Canada. These statements take the form of inserts in the *CICA Handbook*, which constitutes the most authoritative reference work on accepted accounting practice in Canada. CICA publishes a monthly journal known as *CA Magazine*.

canceled check A check paid by the drawee bank and returned to the depositor; it serves as support for the bank's charge against the depositor's account and as the depositor's receipt from the payee.

cancellable lease A *lease* which the lessee (user) may cancel at any time.

cancellation 1. (of documents generally) Voiding by defacement, perforation, or other means whereby restoration is made impossible, so that any person subsequently inspecting or coming into possession of the instrument is put on notice of the voiding.

2. (of an insurance policy) The termination of an insurance contract or bond before the end of the policy period: designated as *flat* where the termination occurs on or before the effective date of the policy; pro rata where the amount of the premium as adjusted is in the same proportion as the time the policy was in force compared with the original policy life; and short-rate where the insured cancels, the net premium cost being somewhat higher than pro rata.

C and F (C&F) = cost and freight. A term indicating that the quoted price of an object of sale includes charges for handling and freight up to delivery to a foreign port, the purchaser assuming costs of insurance and unloading, transportation, and other costs at or from the foreign port. Title passes to the buyer upon delivery to the ocean carrier. See *CIF*.

C and F (C&F) price *FAS price*, plus freight to destination but excluding marine insurance. Title and responsibility are usually regarded as transferring to the buyer upon delivery to the ocean carrier. Freight is arranged by the seller for the account of the buyer.

cap To limit. Example: A state may put a "cap" on the rate at which property may be taxed by municipalities or other units of government under its jurisdiction. The state's constitution may similarly limit (i.e., cap) the state's own borrowing power.

CAP —Committee on Accounting Procedure.

CAPA —Confederation of Asian and Pacific Accountants.

capacity 1. The ability to perform under stipulated conditions.
2. The maximum performance possible under the limiting conditions of existing physical plant, labor force, method of production, etc.

capacity cost Cost when operating at *capacity* (2): said of a plant, process, department, overhead, or unit of product. Capacity cost, although generally more than partial-capacity operating cost, is not likely to vary proportionately with the rate of production, since numerous constituent items are of a fixed or semifixed character. See *fixed cost*.

capacity ratio The ratio of actual to maximum possible output. An approximate measure of maximum potential capacity is obtained by multiplying this ratio by current output. An approximate measure of maximum practical capacity is obtained by introducing adjustments for absenteeism, labor turnover, machine downtime, and similar interruptions deemed to be unavoidable.

capacity variance = *volume variance*.

capital 1. Goods intended to further production.

2. The amount invested in an enterprise—proprietorship, partnership, or corporation—by its owners; *paid-in capital*.

3. *Legal capital:* that portion of stockholders' contributions allocated to capital-stock account by the board of directors, bylaws, articles of incorporation, or agreement with stockholders; *stated capital*.

4. The amount so invested plus retained income (or earned surplus); *net worth; net assets; stockholders' equity*.

5. Net worth plus long-term liabilities; also, the equity of security holders.

6. (economics) (a) One of the factors of production: goods produced by man to further production of other goods; wealth (of an individual) devoted to obtaining money income; any wealth employed with productive intent, e.g., consumers' capital, *producers' capital*. See *capital asset*. (b) Hence, net worth plus all liabilities; total *assets*. See *asset*.

capital account 1. Fixed assets as a class. In this sense, the term is used in such expressions as "additions during the year to capital account."

2. Any permanent proprietorship account.

capital asset 1. An asset intended for continued use or possession, common subclassifications being (a) land, buildings and equipment, leaseholds, mineral deposits, timber preserves (fixed assets); (b) goodwill, patents, trademarks, franchises (intangibles); (c) investments in affiliated companies.

In economics, the term is synonymous with any *asset* capable of generating income but is sometimes restricted to *fixed capital,* with essentially the same meaning as in the preceding paragraph: assets used in production that are exhausted gradually, in contrast with *circulating capital*.

In accounting terminology, the term may be synonymous with *fixed asset,* usually indicating any tangible asset, such as plant and equipment, and sometimes an intangible, such as a patent. Capital assets are ordinarily those purchased for use in production over relatively long periods of time rather than for resale or for conversion in a single operation or within a short time period. See *fixed asset*.

2. (federal income taxes) Capital asset has a different meaning for income tax purposes than for accounting or economics. Section 1221 of the *Internal Revenue Code* defines "capital asset" as all property owned by a taxpayer except inventory-type assets, accounts and notes receivable, real and depreciable property used in a trade or business (fixed assets), and copyrights, compositions, letters, and memoranda unless such intangibles were purchased at a fair market value.

capital-asset pricing model A general framework for analyzing the relationship between risks and rates of return on securities, especially common stocks. Risk is assumed to consist of two parts, *unsystematic risk*, which is caused by events unique to a firm, and *systematic risk*, which is the relative volatility of a stock as it moves up and down with the general market. Unsystematic risk can be eliminated by diversification, that is, by adding different stocks to an investment *portfolio*, but systematic risk cannot be eliminated. Thus, only systematic risk is relevant in determining the required rate of return on a stock as in

$$k_i = R_f + \beta(k_M - R_f),$$

where k_i = the required rate of return on security i; R_f = the risk-free rate of return on U.S. government securities (usually approximated by the *Treasury bill* rate); β = beta coefficient of the stock; and k_M = the average rate of return on an investment portfolio consisting of all stocks in the market.

The slope coefficient β may be estimated in a variety of ways. Formally it is expressed as the *covariance* of the returns on security *i* and the returns in the market divided by the *variance* of returns in the market—*viz.*,

$$\beta = \frac{\text{cov}(k_i, k_M)}{\text{var}(k_M)}.$$

In this form, the beta coefficient is also referred to as *market risk*. This formulation for estimating k_i represents the capital asset pricing model. It is widely used in analytical approaches to required rates of return. For example, if a stock's beta coefficient were 1.5, the return on risk-free U.S. government securities were 8% and on a market portfolio of stocks 12%, then the required rate of return on the stock would be 14%, *viz.*, $k_i = 8\% + 1.5(12\% - 8\%) = 14\%$. The capital asset pricing model has contributed importantly to modern finance and economics and it has been a rich source of ideas in *financial accounting* research.

capital bonus = *stock dividend*; a British term.

capital budget(-ing) 1. The portion of a budget, or a separate budget, devoted to proposed additions to *capital assets* and their financing.

Techniques in capital budgeting include the *net present value, internal rate of return*, and *payback period* approaches. See *interest formulas; complete cycle costs*. The advent of electronic computer codes and models have made possible a variety of sophisticated approaches which allow the study and consideration of different investment *portfolios* as aspects of "what if" and "should cost" planning.

2. (municipal accounting) A plan of municipal improvements instituted usually for a period of 5 years or more, including the method of financing.

capital coefficient (national-income accounting) Average cost of acquiring an additional unit of annual productive capacity. Capital coefficients are usually obtained by the *least-squares method*, using a straight-line *regression equation*, $Y = a + bX$, where X and Y are *time series* of expenditures and *capacity* increases, respectively. The value obtained for b provides an estimate of the capital coefficient. Further refinements, such as *trend analysis* and adjustments for variation in dollar cost, are sometimes introduced to obtain "real" (or "physical") capital coefficients.

capital consumption allowance See *depreciation*.

capital dividend A dividend charged to and hence deemed to be paid from paid-in capital.

capital expenditure 1. An expenditure intended to benefit future periods, in contrast to a *revenue expenditure*, which benefits a current period; an addition to a capital asset. The term is generally restricted to expenditures that add fixed-asset units or that have the effect of increasing the capacity, efficiency, life span, or economy of operation of an existing *fixed asset*.
2. Hence, any expenditure benefiting a future period.

capital gain 1. The excess of proceeds realized from the sale or exchange of a noninventory asset over its book value. It is accounted for as is any other gain or profit: carried into the income statement (separately shown if material in amount) and then to retained earnings or other proprietorship account. Some economists have urged that capital gains should not be combined with gains from other sources, the supposition being that capital gains are immediately reinvested. For many years this point of view has prevailed, in varying degrees. In the computation of national income, both in the United States and abroad, capital gains of individuals are excluded. The general attitude of accountants is that this omission seriously distorts portrayals of national income behavior, since securities and other sources of capital gains are commodities differing in no essential way from other commodities, and that in times of inflation as well as depression, many capital gains find their way into the consumption stream.

2. (federal income taxes) The excess of proceeds realized from the sale or exchange of a *capital asset* over its *adjusted basis*; capital gains and losses are classified into long-term and short-term depending upon the period the asset was held by the taxpayer. From 1944 to 1977 the short-term holding period was 6 months or less and since 1977 it has been 12 months or less.

Generally speaking, long-term capital gains of individuals and corporations are taxed less severely than other types of income. Although real and depreciable assets used in a trade or business are excluded from the tax definition of capital assets, long-term losses and certain, very limited, long-term gains on such assets may be treated as long-term capital gains and losses under Section 1231 of the Code. See *capital loss, capital gain net income,* and *net capital gain.*

capital gain net income (federal income taxes) The net positive sum resulting from the combining of separate *capital gains* and losses. Given preferential tax treatment, ''capital gain net income'' is the end result of offsetting capital gains and losses, first with gains and losses of a like holding period to get a net long or short-term gain or loss with the net long-term gain or loss. See *net capital gain.*

capital goods 1. See *capital (5)*.
2. = *fixed assets*.

capital improvement fund A fund to accumulate revenues from current taxes levied for major repairs and maintenance to fixed assets of a nature not specified at the time the revenues are levied. Expenditures are made at the time specific *projects* become necessary.

capitalization of earnings 1. Process of determining the economic value of a firm by calculating the *net present value* of the firm's predicted future *net income*; used as an approximation to the *average* predicted future net *cash flow* of the firm.
2. To transfer from retained earnings to a *capital stock* or *capital surplus* account as a result of a stock dividend, or by resolution of the board of directors, with stockholder approval when required.

capitalization of interest Interest costs incurred during the time necessary to bring an asset to the condition and location for its intended use and included as part of the historical cost of acquiring the asset. See *interest on investment.*

capitalization ratio *Fixed assets* (as depreciated) divided by *net worth*. See *ratio; fixed assets-to-equity capital ratio.*

capitalization unit An expenditure for a *fixed asset* or addition thereto that has the effect of enlarging physical dimensions, increasing productivity, lengthening future life, or lowering future costs. In borderline cases, the cost, if it is to be capitalized, is often required to be well under the capitalized value of either (a) the resultant added service to be yielded, or (b) future costs saved. See *retirement unit; fixed asset; depreciation.*

capitalize 1. To record and carry forward into one or more future periods any expenditure the benefits or proceeds from which will then be *realized*. See *capital expenditure.*
2. To add to a fixed-asset account the cost of plant additions, improvements, and expenditures having the effect of increasing the efficiency or yield of a capital asset or making possible future savings in cost from its use.
3. To transfer *retained earnings* to a capital-stock account, as the result of the issue of a

stock dividend, a recapitalization, or, under the laws of some states, resolution of the board of directors. See *stock dividend; capitalized surplus; splitup*.

4. To *discount* or calculate the *present value* of the projected future earnings of an asset or business. See *capital value; capitalized value*.

capitalized expense An item of cost usually charged to profit and loss but, because related to a period of construction, added to a capital-asset account.

capitalized surplus Surplus (paid in or earned) of a corporation that has been transferred to capital stock, through the issue of a stock dividend, by increasing the par or stated value of capital stock without an issue of additional shares, or by a simple resolution of the board of directors. These actions, when authorized under articles of incorporation or amendments thereof, usually require *ratification* by stockholders. See *capitalize (3)*.

capitalized value 1. The present worth of a future service, often determined on the basis of an assumed periodic yield and unit cost.
2. = *present value*.

capital lease Also called a *financing lease*. A lease recorded as an asset acquisition accompanied by a corresponding borrowing of funds by the lessee. Both are shown on the balance sheet and expenses consist of interest on the debt and amortization of the asset in a manner similar to depreciation plus financing charges on owned assets. The lessor treats the lease as a sale of the asset in return for a series of future revenue payments.

capital leverage See *financial leverage; leverage*.

capital liability 1. = *long-term liability*.
2. = *net worth*.

capital loss (federal income taxes) The excess of *adjusted basis* over proceeds in a sale or exchange of a *capital asset*, or an asset treated as a capital asset ("Section 1231 transactions"). Capital gains and losses are separated into long-term and short-term depending on whether or not the asset has been held more than 1 year. See *capital gain net income*. A corporation may not deduct a net capital loss but may carry it back 3 years and forward 5 years and offset it against net capital gains of those years. An individual may deduct up to $3,000 of a net capital loss and carry any excess forward indefinitely. Losses which originated as short-term may be deducted in full in the current $3,000 deduction, while only 50% of losses which originated as long-term may be deducted.

capital maintenance concept A *concept* in which earnings result only after capital has been maintained or recovered. The concept of capital is therefore critical in distinguishing a return *of* capital (capital maintenance) from a return *on* capital (earnings). The two most common capital maintenance concepts are the *financial concept of capital* and the *physical concept of capital*.

capital market 1. The market for long-term financial instruments such as stocks, corporate and government bonds and mortgages.
2. A broader definition also includes the market for shorter-term loans and securities as in the *money market*.

capital outlay = *capital expenditure*.

capital-output ratio The ratio of the value of the capital stock of an economy to the value of its output of goods and services, each measured in current dollars, at a given point in time.

capital paid in = *paid-in capital*.

capital projects fund A fund created to account for all resources used for the construction or acquisition of designated fixed assets by a governmental unit except those financed by *special assessment funds*, *proprietary funds*, or *fiduciary funds*.

capital rationing The existence of a constraint or limitation on the total amount of borrowing or capital expenditures that can be undertaken by management in any period.

capital-reconciliation statement = *statement of sources and applications of funds*: a British term.

capital recovery allowance (federal income taxes) Deduction for capital used in the production of income. In tax law the allowed deduction has assumed a variety of focuses. At first it was almost exclusively restricted to the form of straight-line *depreciation* over the useful life of the asset. In more recent years, Congress has allowed more rapid recovery of cost as an incentive for investment. *Accelerated depreciation* and the use of shorter lives have been used. An example of a more rapid, and more arbitrary capital recovery allowance is the *rapid amortization* over 60 months. Immediate deduction has been used in some countries, and has been used in the United States for a few items, e.g., research and development expenditures. See also *accelerated cost recovery system*.

capital reserves (British usage) That portion, or any detail thereof, of the *total equity* or *net worth* of an enterprise consisting of such items as premium on capital stock, revaluation surplus, reserve for the retirement of capital stock, and sometimes capital gains and other items, all of which is regarded as unavailable for withdrawal by proprietors; contrasts with *revenue reserves*.

capital savings Any reduction in capital requirements such as from an invention or innovation which results in a given rate of output with a lesser amount of capital.

capital stock 1. The ownership shares of a corporation authorized by its articles of incorporation.
2. The money value assigned to a corporation's issued shares, constituting generally the legal capital of the corporation. The capital stock of a corporation may be divided into several classes of shares having various rights, preferences, and priorities. It may have a par value within limits set by law, or it may have no par value. The latter is given a declared or stated value. See *stated value; legal capital*.
3. The account maintained for such par or stated value. See *authorized capital stock; issued capital*.

capital-stock discount See *stock discount*.

capital-stock premium See *additional paid-in capital*; *premium on capital stock*.

capital structure ratio A type of *ratio* that relates long-term senior securities to total capitalization. The ratio denominator is usually defined as long-term debt plus preferred stock plus common stockholders' equity. This type of ratio purports to measure the underlying protection for senior securities and the riskiness of common stock.

capital sum The original amount or principal of an estate, fund, mortgage, bond, note, or other form of financial investment, together with accretions not yet recognized as income.

capital surplus That part of the paid-in capital of a business not assigned to capital stock; i.e., contributions by stockholders in excess of par or stated value of shares; = *paid-in surplus*. This term is falling into disuse. It is being replaced by "capital paid in in excess of par or stated value," or some variation thereof.

capital turnover The ratio of yearly sales to *invested capital*. In calculating this ratio, invested capital is usually measured as the sum of *net worth* and *long-term liabilities*. Same as *investment turnover*.

capital value The total, on a *discounted* basis, of the estimated net income stream from capital goods.

CAPM = *capital asset pricing model*.

cardinal number A symbol expressing a quantity of units: 1, 2, 3, etc.; any *digit* or combination of digits; an *integer*. See *ordinal number*.

card reader (computers) An input device which senses the holes on a punched card and translates them into binary data for a computer. See *binary code*.

carried interest (petroleum industry) The fraction of a *working interest* that advances no portion of the outlay necessary to pay for current costs, as of drilling, such costs being borne by the "carrying interest" making up the balance of the working interest. The agreement between the parties commonly provides for the recoupment of these costs out of the first proceeds from production.

carry (to) To *enter* or *post*.

carryback (federal income taxes) 1. The amount of the net (operating) loss for a given year of an individual, corporation, or other taxpayer carrying on a business, subject to certain adjustments, that may be deducted from the net income of three preceding years; if not thus fully absorbed, the balance may be treated as a *carryover*. With certain exceptions, a corporation may also treat a *capital loss* as a carryback.
2. The unused portion, if any, of the excess-profits credit that was added to the excess-profits credit of the preceding year under one-time tax laws; any amount not thus absorbed was treated as a *carryover*.

carry forward *v.* 1. To defer the classification of an item of revenue or expense as nominal until such time as the revenue is earned, or the benefit is received from the expenditure; during the interval, it appears on a balance sheet as deferred revenue or prepaid expense. A loss, i.e., an expenditure from which no commensurate benefit is being or will be received, is occasionally carried forward for absorption in some later period, although the accepted standard is to recognize its nominal character at the time the flow of benefits ceases.
2. To transfer the balance of an account from one ledger to another, from a temporary account to a permanent account, or from one period to the period immediately succeeding.
3. To transfer the total of a column of figures to another column or to another page, especially where a column or a page has been filled with entries or postings.
n. 1. The amount so deferred or transferred.
2. = *carryover*.

carry-forward working papers *Working papers,* often a part of a *permanent file*, containing running analyses or summaries of fixed assets, reserves, net worth, and other accounts the future understanding and interpretation of which are at least in part dependent on the auditor's accumulation of information concerning them.

carrying charge 1. A recurring cost incident to the possession or ownership of property, usually regarded as a current expense but occasionally added to the cost of an asset held for ultimate disposition where the market or likely disposal proceeds are judged to be sufficient to absorb the cost thus enhanced. Examples: taxes and mortgage interest on real estate; storage and insurance on merchandise; interest charged by brokers on margin accounts.
2. The addition to or *loading* of the price of merchandise sold on an installment plan.

carrying cost The cost of holding and storing a unit of inventory for a period of time. See *economic order quantity*.

carrying value 1. The amount at which a property is recorded on the books, net of depreciation, if any; *book value*.
2. A value of market or less fixed by a lending bank on a security pledged as collateral.

carryover (federal income taxes) The amount of the net (operating) loss for a given year, of an individual, corporation, or other taxpayer carrying on a business, subject to certain adjustments, that to the extent not absorbed as a *carryback* may be deducted from the taxable income of succeeding years. See *carryback*.

carryover basis (federal income taxes) The basis of valuation for tax purposes on property acquired from a decedent. Previously this was generally fair market value of inherited property at date of death. The *unified transfer tax* adopted in 1976, however, now provides that it shall be the *adjusted basis* of the property immediately before the death of the decedent (Section 1023) further adjusted as follows: (a) in the case of appreciated property, federal and state *death taxes* applicable to the appreciation may be added to the carryover basis, provided the adjustment does not increase the basis above fair market value; (b) the executor may elect fair market value as the basis for personal or household effects up to a total of $10,000 fair market value per decedent; (c) there is an exception for small estates where the aggregate carryover basis is less than $60,000; the basis in such estates will be adjusted up to an aggregate fair market value of $60,000; (d) as a transitional rule, a "fresh start" is allowed for property acquired by the decedent prior to 1977 and transferred at death occurring after 1979; Section 1023(h) provides that some or all of the appreciation in such property prior to 1977 may be added to the carryover basis.

carryover file (auditing) = *permanent file*.

cartel A group of separate business or government organizations that has agreed to institute measures to control competition.

Cartels have many forms. As common control increases in degree and duration, the cartel may pass into *monopoly*. Monopoly consists of a single legal entity exercising control of the entire production and sale of a commodity or service; *monopsony* takes the form of a single firm purchasing the entire supply.

Cartels, generally not as effective as monopolies, have difficulty in maintaining themselves. Through political or other maneuverings, they often attempt to move toward monopolistic devices. Lack of success may, on the other hand, drive cartels toward *oligopoly*, which differs from a cartel in that each of the individual firms is left to its own devices. No explicit agreement or form of control exists. Oligopoly (or oligopsony, the purchasing side counterpart) often proves less effective than the cartel.

Oligopoly, oligopsony, and like conditions are classed as phenomena of imperfect competition. Firms operating under imperfectly competitive conditions share with monopoly the characteristic that each firm is so large and furnishes so significant a proportion of the product that changes in the firm's policies will affect market prices. But such firms share with pure competition the characteristic that firms may leave or enter the industry freely, as prospects of profit seem to dictate. Only when (a) each firm is so small that it has no significant influence on market prices, and (b) free access is available to all firms that seek to leave or enter the industry, can pure competition prevail.

Cartesian coordinate system A *coordinate system*, with uniformly scaled axes at right angles to each other, devised by René Descartes, French philosopher of the 17th century, as a means of solving algebraic problems by geometry and vice versa. See *coordinate system*.

cash n. *Money*, negotiable money orders and checks, and balances on deposit with banks after deducting outstanding checks. As an unqualified balance-sheet caption under *current assets*, cash may be assumed to include time and savings deposits and cash on hand undeposited or in change funds and to be available for any ordinary use within the enterprise; hence it does not include the proceeds of security issues or other amounts that may be applied only to the acquisition of fixed or other noncurrent assets, or to the liquidation of funded debt or other non-current liabilities. Cash having such limited uses, bearing a descriptive title, is given a separate balance-sheet position. See *balance sheet; current asset.*

v. To exchange a check or other demand document for money.

cash asset Cash and any asset which may be converted immediately into cash without upsetting day-to-day operations; *marketable securities* are excluded. Examples: cash on hand; cash deposited in banks; cash in transit; demand certificates of deposit; trade acceptances. Cash in the hands of a trustee for the liquidation of debt is not regarded as a cash asset. The term should not be confused with *liquid assets* or *quick assets.* See *balance sheet.*

cash audit An audit limited to the examination of cash transactions for a stated period, its purpose being to determine whether or not all cash received and receivable has been recorded, disbursements are supported by authorized vouchers, the cash balance is represented by cash actually on hand or in bank, and the cash records and internal controls surrounding cash are in good order.

cash basis A basis of keeping accounts, in contrast to the *accrual basis,* whereby revenue and expense are recorded on the books of account when received and paid, respectively, without regard to the period to which they apply. The cash basis is a frequently unsatisfactory variation of the accrual basis, but in instances where transactions are limited to cash revenue and outgo, the two methods may virtually coincide.

cashbook A book of original entry for cash receipts, disbursements, or both.

cash budget An estimate of cash receipts and disbursements for a future period, cash requirements at various points within the period, and cash on hand at the end of the period.

cash cycle = *earnings cycle.*

cash-disbursements journal A *journal* in which are entered individual disbursements or blocks of disbursements as they occur. There are many varieties: some with a single money column, with entries made by hand; others with distribution columns that are machine-entered. See *check register.*

In a single business enterprise there may be several cash journals, e.g., a cash-receipts journal at each location receiving cash, one for each cashier or each depository. Convenience, speed in recording, the competence and bonding of receiving and disbursing clerks, the nature of protective crosschecks, recording machinery available, and methods of internal control, including the depth and frequency of internal audits, are among the factors determining the size, rulings if any, details preceding and accompanying entry, and disposition of cash records. Basic requirements call for accuracy, adequate supervision, and "built-in" good (internal and external) *audit trails.*

cash discount An amount allowed for the prompt settlement of a debt arising out of a sale. Cash discounts taken or allowed are usually shown in an income statement as reductions of sales or purchases; or, now less frequently, as financial expense or income on the theory that the prompt settlement of a receivable or payable is a prepayment, the "normal" payment being at the end of a credit period. In either case, the receivables and payables are first stated in the accounts at their gross amounts and the discounts are recorded in separate accounts as they are taken. A third method is to record in the first instance payables (or less commonly, receivables) at their net amounts and to record the *missed discounts*, those arising from customers' accounts being an item of income and those from creditors' accounts an item of expense. The last-named method presumes the "normal" payment date to be the invoice date. In recent years there has been a slight trend toward the adoption of the third method for payables, although the first method has gained considerable popularity. A discount of more than 2%, even though allowed for prompt payment, has long been conventionally classified as a *trade discount*. See *discount; allowance for sales discount*.

cash dividend A dividend paid in cash, as distinguished from one paid in corporate stock, bonds, or other obligations or in property other than cash. See *dividend*.

cash equivalent Money's worth; the immediately *realizable value* of a good or service received in an *exchange*.

cash equivalent value Amount for which an asset could be sold; the immediately *realizable value* for a good or service received in an exchange. See *fair market value; fair value*.

cash flow 1. The net cash generated by a firm's operations for a given time period, that is, cash inflows from collections of revenue minus cash outflows for payments of expenses. In security analysis, a popular, but somewhat cruder, concept of "cash flow" is net income with nonfund charges, such as depreciation, added back.

2. The tracing, in successive steps, of individual items, or of aggregates, of income or expenditure from their first recognition in the accounts to their final disposition or loss of identity. See *cash-flow statement*.

cash-flow statement A statement of cash income and outgo between two given dates, its components often identified with items appearing in *balance sheets* and intervening *income statements*. Accountants have followed a variety of ways in determining, classifying, and tabulating source-and-application amounts of sales, receivables, inventories, and payables, and occasionally other items; by means of a continuous segmentation in terms of original or primary *transactions* through split balance-sheet and operating accounts these variant practices can be noted.

Split accounts, which provide running analyses of the current period's cash receipts and disbursements, simplify the selection and determination of the particular variety of cash-flow statement desired. The practical justification for the simplest procedures (some procedures may involve a number of anticipated rather than past cash transactions) is found in the usual absence of significant differences between the possible alternatives appearing above, differences diminishing in significance still further in comparative presentations consistently derived.

Cash-flow statements are often regarded by security and credit analysts as providing a better basis for judgments concerning profits, financial condition, and financial management than the basis supplied by traditional but now often compromised income statements. One common derivative from cash-flow statements often cited by analysts has been growth trends.

A projected cash-flow statement, based on past actual experience as modified by expected price changes and other factors, provides a useful basis for both planning and budgeting, and information for stockholders and others. See *flow statement; funds-flow statement; cash basis; budget; split-account system*.

cash-flow-to-capital-expenditures ratio A *ratio* computed from the *Statement of Changes in Financial Position*, by dividing funds from operations less dividends by plant and equipment expenditures. It is intended to provide a measure of a firm's ability to continue its operations in the long run.

cash-flow-to-total-debt ratio A *ratio* which measures a firm's ability to meet its financial obligations, derived by dividing funds from operations by total debt. It has been found to be an efficient predictor of bankruptcy. Its numerator is usually taken from the *Statement of Changes in Financial Position*, and some analysts prefer to use long-term debt in the denominator.

cash fund 1. A deposit or investment of cash for any purpose, readily reconvertible into cash: a *cash asset*.
2. *pl.* = temporary investments, as in the phrase "cash and cash funds."

cashier One responsible for the handling and initial recording of cash receipts and disbursements, and of cash on hand, or of a limited class of cash transactions.

cash in bank The balance of money on deposit with a bank, subject to withdrawal, after deducting outstanding checks and adjusting for bank charges and credits; often included is a minimum amount on deposit required under a service or short-term loan agreement.

cash in transit Cash (currency and checks) in movement to or from an organization at a specific moment of time and thus not appearing on an organization's books. If the sender or receiver of the cash is a subsidiary, home office, or branch, the in-transit item, not appearing as such on the books of either, is the subject of a reclassification entry whenever *combined* or *consolidated financial statements* are prepared.

cash items Receipted bills, checks, and other vouchers for disbursements from *imprest* or other *cash funds*, held for collection or for reimbursement from general cash; checks, drafts, and other paper credited to a depositor's account, to be collected by the bank.

cash journal A cashbook; a columnar journal or equivalent in which all transactions are entered, whether or not cash is involved. See *cashbook; ledger journal; cash-disbursements journal*.

cash on delivery See *COD*.

cash on hand Cash in immediate possession, represented by coin, paper money, and negotiable checks and other paper commonly accepted for immediate credit by a bank in a deposit of cash.

cash price The price charged when payment is effected within a specified interval of time, either immediately or within a limited credit period such as 30 days. It is usually the same as *COD* price. See *price*.

cash-receipts journal A journal in which cash receipts are entered chronologically. Some forms provide for a single entry per day for cash sales and other types of receipts over which separate controls are maintained. See comments under *cash-disbursements journal*.

cash records The records and evidences of the receipt, disbursement, deposit, and withdrawal of cash. Cash records include cash-receipt, cash-disbursement, and petty-cash books; registers of receipts and disbursements; checkbooks, stubs, or registers; canceled checks; copies of deposit slips; and receipt and disbursement vouchers and subvouchers and their attachments. See *book of account; system of accounts*.

cash requirements See *estimate of cash requirements*.

cash resource = *cash asset*.

cash sale 1. The delivery of goods or the performance of service accompanied by a concurrent receipt of *cash*.
2. *pl.* A classification of sales made up of such transactions. See *sale*.

cash statement A statement rendered periodically, often daily, to management, usually showing the opening and closing balances of cash on hand and in each bank, a summary of the receipts and disbursements of the period or day, and particulars of deposits and withdrawals. The statement may be cumulative and may also contain an estimate of the resources and requirements of the immediate future. See *cash-flow statement*.

cash surrender value See *surrender value*.

cash to current liabilities ratio A *ratio* which measures a firm's immediate ability to meet its short-run financial obligations: derived by dividing the sum of cash and marketable securities by current liabilities. It is considered an extremely rigorous measure because it implicitly assumes that cash inflows from collections of receivables will be zero.

casting out nines See *check figure (1)*.

cathode-ray tube (CRT) terminal (computers) A computer terminal which contains a keyboard for input and which outputs its information on a television-like screen. It is faster than a typewriter console but usually does not make provision for hard copy without further auxiliary equipment. Most CRT terminals display printing characters and numerical data, but some also provide for plotting of lines for use in graphic displays.

caveat emptor "Let the buyer beware." Common-law maxim that buyer purchases at his or her peril; that is, that the seller makes no warranties concerning the property transferred. See *caveat venditor*.

caveat venditor "Let the seller beware." A maxim placing responsibility for defects on the seller. As existing in American law today, it is the seller's duty to do what the reasonable person would do in a similar situation.

CD See *certificate of deposit*.

ceiling Any limit in physical amounts or dollars, imposed by legal or administrative authority. Examples: a ceiling price; a personnel ceiling limiting the number of employees or their compensation. See *price*.

ceiling price See *price; administered price*.

central bank Banks in certain countries, often set up by statute, which regulate the total amount of money and credit in an economy as well as aspects of banking practice. Central banks are generally charged with promoting economic, monetary, and credit conditions favorable to commercial and industrial activity. Example: the Federal Reserve System in the United States.

central limit theorem A fundamental theorem of statistics from which the *normal distribution* derives its importance. According to the theorem, as the sample size becomes large, the distribution of the means for randomly drawn samples approaches a normal distribution with mean equal to that of the population and variance equal to the population variance divided by the sample size. This result holds irrespective of the underlying distribution of the population provided the assumptions of finite variance and independently drawn observations holds and the samples are not drawn from different parent *populations*.

central processing unit (CPU) (computers) The portion of the computer which contains the arithmetic units, logical units, instruction control units, registers, and input/output interfaces.

central tendency See *arithmetic mean*.

cents percent See *insurance premium*.

certainty equivalent The amount of benefit obtainable with certainty which one is willing to exchange for a usually larger but uncertain amount. The former is said to be the certainty equivalent of the latter.

certificate See *auditors' report*.

Certificate in Management Accounting Certificate awarded by the Institute of Management Accounting of the National Association of Accountants after passing a four-part examination and meeting education and experience requirements.

certificate of deposit 1. A formal instrument, frequently negotiable or transferable, issued by a bank as evidence of indebtedness and arising from a deposit of cash subject to withdrawal under the specific terms of the instrument.
2. A formal certificate, usually printed or engraved, ordinarily negotiable or transferable, and issued by a depository or agent against the deposit of bonds or stock of a corporation under the terms of a reorganization plan or other agreement.

certificate of incorporation A document issued by the secretary of state or other state official, establishing a corporation. See *articles of incorporation*.

certificate of indebtedness 1. One of a series of bearer obligations, usually of comparatively short term, interest-bearing, unsecured, issued by a corporation in conjunction with temporary financing, or by the Treasury of the United States, for current requirements of the government, in anticipation of taxes or the sale of long-term bonds.
2. A general term applied to a bond or other security evidencing debts owed, as distinct from a certificate of stock, which represents a share in the equity.

certified accountant (FCCA, ACCA) A title conferred by the Association of Certified Accountants (in the United Kingdom) and by similar bodies in certain other countries (as, e.g., Malaysia) which authorizes the holder to practice as an independent public accountant and thus to render an opinion on the propriety of financial statements. On having satisfied the prescribed experience and examination requirements, the candidate is entitled to use the designatory initials ACCA (for members of the Association of Certified Accountants). On meeting further requirements, the title of Fellow (FCCA) is conferred.

certified check A depositor's check on which a bank guarantees payment by endorsement, usually across the face of the check; an action accompanied by a debit against the customer's account and a credit to certified checks payable. Verbal guarantees, sometimes given by banks, may have the same effect.

certified financial statement A balance sheet or other financial statement accompanied by and related to a report of a public accountant. See *auditors' report*.

certified internal auditor (CIA) A title conferred by the Institute of Internal Auditors following the submission of an approved application and the successful completion of a four-part examination. The CIA title was awarded in 1973 on the basis of experience alone (under a "grandfather" provision) and by examination beginning in 1974.

certified management accountant (CMA) See *Certificate in Management Accounting*.

certified public accountant (CPA) A title conferred by a government agency or by a professional accounting body which, in most instances, authorizes the holder to practice as an independent public accountant and thus to render an opinion on the propriety of financial statements. In the United States, the title is given by an agency of a state or other political subdivision once the candidate has met the statutory requirements as to age, education, residence, moral character, and experience, and has passed the Uniform CPA Examination, which is administered by the *American Institute of Certified Public Accountants*. A CPA of one jurisdiction ordinarily may obtain a certificate to practice in other jurisdictions by endorsement. In other countries (including the Philippines, Malaysia, and Japan), the title is conferred either by a professional accounting body or by a government department.

certifying officer (governmental accounting) A bonded employee authorized to approve vouchers for payment.

cestui que trust (cestuis que trustent, *pl.*) "He who trusts"; a person entitled to the beneficial or equitable interest in property held in trust, the legal title being held by a trustee; the beneficiary of a *trust*.

chain 1. A *connected graph* between an initial and a terminating node without cycles (loops) and in which movement to the terminus is always effected without having to backtrack from links that lead to nodes from which access to the terminus is not possible. See *network*.
2. A group of linked symbols, records, or data items. A sequence of operations performed in a specified order as when price *index numbers* for successive years are multiplied to obtain the overall relative change between a beginning and ending year in the sequence.

chain discount A series of trade-discount percentages or their total; thus, if a list (catalog) price is subject to a 40-15-15 discount to dealers, the total chain discount is 56.65% (= .40 + .15 × .60 + .15 [.85 × .60]). See *trade discount*.

change fund Cash committed to cashiers or placed in change machines for the purpose of supplying change to customers and others, for cashing payroll checks, and sometimes for making advances to employees. It may be maintained on an *imprest-fund* basis.

changes in financial position Differences between the items of *comparative balance sheets*: a term applied to a financial statement included in the standard form of *auditors' report*. Formerly known as *source and application of funds* or *changes in working capital*, and often confused with *cash-flow* and *funds-flow statements*, it summarizes the effects of a period's transactions and resulting net gain or loss on working capital and other assets and liabilities. In comparative form, covering a series of years, historical detail is supplied that highlights modifications of financial structure and corporate growth. Because of the complexity of modern business operations, comparative statements of this sort require supplemental notes explaining trends and conditions that figures alone do not reveal.

Many variants, developed over more than a half-century of the statement's use, are found in reports to stockholders and in auditors' *short-form* and *long-form reports*.

In its present form the statement falls short of providing breakdowns of operating income and expense that lie behind the flow of funds from one balance-sheet position to another; e.g., sales increases attributable to pricing and price policies, modification of credit terms, changing demand, rising costs of labor, material, processing, and general overhead. See *flow statement; split-account system*.

changes in working capital = *source and application of funds*; now designated *changes in financial position*.

channel discount A discount comparable to a distributor's discount but differing by being applied against sales to institutional buyers, including state and federal agencies, and to purchasers who further process the product or assemble it in a larger unit. Because such purchasers distribute a different product, larger or smaller discounts than distributor discounts may be justified on the ground that a different class of customer is being served.

character A letter, numeral, or other symbol used to represent data or information.

character classification (governmental accounting) A classification used as a basis for distinguishing expenditures according to the fiscal periods they are presumed to benefit.

characteristic (of a logarithm) The integer to which the *mantissa* of a base-10 or other logarithm table must be attached in order to obtain a *logarithm*.

For the logarithm of 10 or any greater number in a base-10 system, the characteristic is equal to the total number of digits the whole number contains, less 1; for the logarithms of the numbers 1 up to 10, the characteristic is 0; for 10 it is 1 since $10 = 10^{1.0}$; for positive decimal fractions of 1, the characteristic, expressed as a minus number, is equal to the number of zeros immediately following the decimal point, plus 1, so that, e.g., for $0.1 = 1/10 = 10^{-1.0}$, which is to say that the characteristic of 0.1 is -1 and the *mantissa*, which is 0, together with the characteristic give the *logarithm* as -1.0. Thus the logarithm is the exponent to which the base 10 is raised to give 0.1 so that, conversely, the latter constitutes the *antilogarithm* of -1.0. Finally, there is no logarithm for a negative number because no exponent x will turn 10^x into a negative number. See *mantissa; logarithm; antilogarithm*.

charge *n*. A *debit*. *v.t.* To debit.

charge-and-discharge statement A tabular summary prepared for an executor, administrator, trustee, or other fiduciary, accounting for the principal and income for which he or she has been responsible and constituting a part of either an interim or final report. The statement may be in two parts: the first accounting for principal, the second for income, but only where such a division is required, as by law or court order. The ''charges'' commence with the inventory at the time the fiduciary takes over; if the fiduciary is under the jurisdiction of a court (as is generally the case), he or she seeks court approval for both the inclusiveness of the inventory items and their value. A *public accountant* may be called upon for necessary accounting records, methods of recording various types of transactions, forms of periodic reports, and, from time to time, audits of transactions and statements. Other ''charges'' appearing in the charge-and-

discharge statement will consist of assets discovered after the inventory has been taken and approved; gains (over inventory valuations) from the disposal of assets; and income from the assets or operations over which the fiduciary has jurisdiction. ''Discharges'' are composed of expenses, losses, and distributions chargeable to ''principal''; expenses and distributions applicable to income; and, if the statement is an interim one, the inventory of assets remaining at the end of the last day covered by the statement.

charge off 1. *v*. To treat as a loss; to write off; to designate as an expense or loss an amount originally recorded as an asset.
2. *n*. The elimination by a transfer to expense of a portion or all of the balance of an account in recognition of the expiration of any continuing value. Most chargeoffs are of such a nature as to require authorizations or approvals at top-management levels.

charitable contributions deduction (federal income taxes) Donations of money or property to organizations designated under Section 170 of the *Internal Revenue Code*. For individual taxpayers, the deduction is generally limited to 50% of the taxpayer's adjusted gross income. An elective 30% limitation applies to appreciated long-term capital gain property, and a mandatory 20% limitation is applied to all donations to certain private foundations listed in Section 170(1)(D). Contributions not deductible in the current year can generally be carried forward to the next five years. For corporations the amount of deduction is limited to 5% of taxable income, computed without the contribution deduction. Any excess not currently deductible can be carried forward to the next five years. The amount of potential deduction for contributions of property will differ depending upon whether the property contributed is ordinary (i.e., inventory), business (Section 1231), or capital (long-term or short-term).

charm price A price the cents portion of which is somewhat less than a dollar or terminates with a 9 or other "eye-catcher," and which is regarded as having "customer appeal"; e.g., $4.95, $ 3.98, $1.79: a term employed in retail stores and mail-order houses.

charter 1. See *articles of incorporation*. 2. See *charter party*.

chartered accountant (CA, FCA, ACA) A title conferred by the chartered institutes and certain other professional accountancy bodies in present and former member countries of the British Commonwealth (including the United Kingdom, Canada, Australia, New Zealand, India, Pakistan, Nigeria, and South Africa). Candidates must pass one or more examinations and present a prescribed kind and amount of practical experience. In some countries, they must have received a degree from a tertiary institution. Once these criteria have been met, the successful candidate is entitled to use the designatory initials CA (chartered accountant) or ACA (associate chartered accountant). In some jurisdictions, the CA or ACA may become a Fellow (thus entitled to use the designatory initials FCA) either upon the expiration of a fixed period of time (as in the case of members of the Institute of Chartered Accountants in England and Wales) or in recognition of exceptional service to the profession (as in the case of the Institute of Chartered Accountants of Ontario). A chartered accountant is entitled to practice as an independent public accountant and thus to render an opinion on the propriety of financial statements.

charter party The contract between a shipowner and the person hiring the ship. It specifies the price; the cargo to be carried; the ports of loading and destination; the period of time, including allowable *lay days*; the rate of *demurrage*, where the number of agreed lay days is exceeded; special facilities to be provided; and other conditions. The contract may be in the nature of an outright lease to the hirer or it may merely provide that transportation services be furnished by the owner.

chart for attributes (statistics) A type of statistical chart used to analyze the quality of a production or inspection process or a source of supply. The qualities are usually recorded as "percent defective" or "number of defects" of certain types. See *statistical quality control; chart for variables*.

chart for variables (statistics) A type of statistical chart used to portray the behavior of a production or inspection process in terms of one or more quantitative dimensions such as the inner or outer diameter, or the ratio of the two, for a part resulting from the process. Its focus is on continuous measures, in contrast to a *chart for attributes*, where the focus is on classification into, e.g., good or defective parts.

chart of accounts A systematically arranged list of accounts applicable to a specific concern, giving account names and numbers if any. A chart of accounts, accompanied by descriptions of their use and of the general operation of the *books of account*, becomes a *classification* or *manual of accounting*; a leading feature of a *system of accounts*.

chattel Any item of personal property or of any interest in land other than full ownership; as, a *good*, a *commodity*, a growing crop, a *lease*.

chattel mortgage A mortgage on personal property.

chattel mortgage bond *Bonds* secured by *mortgage* on movable property.

check *n*. A *bill of exchange* drawn on a bank, payable on demand.
v.t. To compare for accuracy; to test or sample; to testcheck; to verify; to gain a knowledge of. As a verb, the word lacks exact meaning and its employment without a descriptive qualification is usually avoided.

check figure A whole number, derived from and representing another, sometimes employed in verifying arithmetic operations. There are two systems, both occasionally found in bookkeeping practice and elsewhere, particularly in the absence of adding or computing machines. Both involve the determination of the check figure from the individual digits of the number represented, and its use in a "proof" operation.

1. In the 9-check-figure system, known also as "casting out the 9's," the representative (or check) figure is determined by subtracting from the sum of the individual digits of the number to be represented the highest included multiple of 9; thus, for the number 24,107, the check figure is $(2 + 4 + 1 + 0 + 7$, or 14$) - 9 = 5$; the check figure of 999 is $(9 + 9 + 9$, or 27$) - 27 = 0$; the check figure of 10 is 1. Adding these three original numbers by ordinary arithmetic gives 25,116, the check figure of which is $15 - 9$, or 6; the sum of the check figures of the three numbers is $5 + 0 + 1 = 6$; and the addition is said to be correct. Again, $348 - 95 = 253$; and the check figures for the three numbers 6 $- 5 = 10 - 9$ again indicate the correctness of the arithmetic operation. Also, $348 \times 95 = 33,060$, and $(6 \times 5) - 27 = 12 - 9$. Again, $1493 \div 124 = 12 - 5/124$, and $8/7 = (3 \times 7 + 5 - 18)/7$.

2. Under the 11-check-figure system, the check figure is obtained by subtracting the alternate digits, commencing with the second from the right, from the sum of the remaining digits, employing 11 or a multiple of 11 in such a manner as to secure a positive result of less than 11. For the three numbers illustrated above, the check figures are: $- (0 + 4) + (7 + 1 + 2) = 6$, $- (9) + (9 + 9) = 9$, and $- (1) + (0) + 11 = 10$. The total of the numbers, 25,116, has a check figure of $- (1 + 5) + (6 + 1 + 2) = 3$; the sum of the individual check figures is $(6 + 9 + 10) - 22 = 3$. The check figures of the two multiplied numbers and their product are 7, 7, and 5, respectively, and $(7 \times 7) - 44 = 5$. Finally, applying the test to the division, $8/3 = (1 \times 3 + 5)/3$.

check point (computers) A point where sufficient information about a job can be recorded so that the *program* can be restarted. This provides added flexibility which allows a program to be restarted at either the beginning of the job, or at a check point.

check register A journal in which checks issued are recorded. Where supported by a *voucher register* or its equivalent, it often takes the form of a single-column journal, containing only check numbers and amounts; see *voucher system*.

chunk (statistics) A sample selected other than on a *probability* basis. See *probability sample*.

CICA = *Canadian Institute of Chartered Accountants*.

CIF = Cost, insurance, and freight. A term indicating that the quoted price of an object of sale includes charges for handling, insurance, and freight up to delivery to a foreign port, beyond which the purchaser must assume any further handling, insurance, and transportation charges. See *C and F*. The seller may also undertake to provide insurance and transportation "for the account of" the buyer. Title passes to the buyer upon delivery to the ocean carrier unless otherwise agreed to by the parties.

CIF price Same as *C and F price*, except that the seller includes the cost of marine insurance. Title passes to the buyer upon delivery by the seller to the ocean carrier unless otherwise agreed to by the parties. Freight and insurance are arranged by the seller for the account of the buyer.

circularization = *confirmation* (2).

circulating asset = *current asset*; a British term.

circulating capital That part of a business investment that is being constantly consumed and renewed in operations, such as raw materials, labor costs, and other outlays contributing to a production process, contrasting with *fixed capital*. See *turnover; capital* (6).

circulating decimal = *repetend*.

circulation of costs 1. Allocation of costs, usually more than once into a series of accounts. Example: A portion of company overhead is allocated to subassemblies fabricated by Department A. Because the allocation is in proportion to the costs of the subassemblies, another (additional) allocation may be assigned to Department B, which carries the subassemblies to the next stage of fabrication.
2. The method employed or the amount involved in the distribution of *variances* to the products or activities believed to be responsible for them.

claim 1. A demand for payment, reimbursement, or compensation for injury or damage, under law or contract.
2. (insurance) The demand for the payment of a loss under an insurance contract or bond; the estimated amount to be paid or the amount actually paid.
3. = *equity*.

class Any group of things, characteristics of things, or events having common features, properties, or qualities.

classification The grouping of transactions, entries, or accounts under a common head or heads; a list of such groupings. See *classification of accounts; system of accounts*.

classification of accounts A list of accounts, systematically grouped (= *chart of accounts*), suitable for a particular organization, with descriptions setting forth the meaning, function, and content of each account and the relation of one to another; frequently accompanied by designs and descriptions of the records to be kept, the forms to be used in recording transactions, instructions covering their use and disposition, and the maintenance of controls. See *accounting manual; system of accounts*.

classified trial balance A *trial balance* having its component items arranged in groups, each group with its subtotal, and each subtotal constituting an item of a financial statement. The purpose of such a trial balance is to *routinize* financial-statement preparation.

class interval The number or range making up a class in a *frequency distribution*.

class-life depreciation system (federal income taxes) A tax depreciation system used before 1981. For property placed in service after 1970, taxpayers could take as a reasonable allowance for depreciation an amount based on any period of years selected by them within a 20% range above or below designated class lives (Sections 167, 263). Based on the *asset depreciation range* (ADR) system in the Treasury Regulations (Section 1.167(a)-11), the class-life system gave taxpayers assurance that their depreciation deductions would not be questioned. The system applied to all types of tangible personal property, buildings, and certain realty-like assets. The Economic Recovery Tax Act of 1981 changed the system to the *accelerated cost recovery system*, than allowed under the class-life depreciation system. See *accelerated cost recovery system*.

class rate 1. (insurance) The cost, in terms of cents per $100 of risk, of insuring against various perils, a different rate applying to different classifications of persons, properties, and hazards.
2. A rate fixed by a common carrier, usually with governmental approval, for the transportation of commodities of a given type.

Clayton Act A federal law (38 Stat. 730), passed in 1914, directed against "unfair competition'' and any act that would tend to lessen competition or create a monopoly, such as price discriminations, secret rebates, pressures on dealers not to sell competitive products, and acquisitions of competing enterprises.

clean opinion Unqualified opinion. See *opinion; auditors' report*.

clean surplus concept Idea that only two entries should be made to the *retained earnings* account in each *accounting period*. These are to record: (1) *net income* (the closing of revenue and expense accounts) and (2) *dividends* declared. Contrast this with the concept of the current *operating-performance income statement*. See *all-inclusive income statement*.

clean surplus rule (or doctrine) A rule (or doctrine) under which entries to *retained earnings* are limited to periodic income and loss and dividends, as required to be consistent with *all-inclusive income statement*.

clearing account A *primary account* containing costs that are to be transferred to other accounts; an intermediate account to which is transferred a group of costs or revenues or a group of accounts containing costs or revenues and from which a distribution of the total is made to other accounts. Examples: a construction account to which materials, payrolls, and other costs relating to the construction are carried and which is eliminated upon completion of the construction by a distribution to one or more *capital-asset* accounts; a *profit-and-loss* account set up as at the close of a fiscal period, containing income and expense account balances and closed out by a transfer to retained earnings.

clearing house A voluntary association or corporation acting as a medium for the daily settlement of transactions between its members or stockholders. It makes possible multilateral exchanges of checks, drafts, and notes as between banks of a given area, thus eliminating unilateral settlements between individual banks; and, in the case of stock and commodity brokers, it provides a means of disposing of mutual transactions promptly, safely, and uniformly, with a minimum of paper work.

clearing-house statement 1. A statement, submitted by a broker to the clearing house of a security or commodity exchange, on which are shown his or her trades on the exchange and the quantities and amounts by which purchases in each security or commodity exceed his or her sales or vice versa. On the basis of a reconciliation of the statements of the clearing-house members, the net amount due to or by each broker is paid by or to the clearing house, and the net quantity of each security or commodity deliverable or receivable by each broker is delivered to or by the clearing house, thus involving a minimum number of transfers of cash, securities, and other evidences of ownership.
2. The formal statement issued by a clearing house to show the results of its activities and its financial position.

clerical error As applied to books of account, any incorrect entry or posting, especially when involving *routine* transactions; typical causes are a mistake in coding, a faulty computation—as in an extension or footing—a failure to enter or post, a posting to a wrong account or to the wrong side of an account.

close (the books) 1. To transfer the balances of revenue and expense accounts at the end of an accounting period directly, or through a profit-and-loss or *clearing account*, to *retained earnings* or to another proprietorship account or accounts, so that only balance-sheet accounts (asset, liability, and net-worth; = *real accounts*) remain open on the general ledger. The transfer is made by means of one or more *closing entries*.

2. Hence, to give effect to adjusting entries and otherwise put the books of account in order at the end of a month, quarter, or other less-than-a-year period so that a trial balance can be extracted and financial statements prepared.

closed account An account with equal debits and credits.

closed (or close) corporation = *closely held corporation*. A corporation with a comparatively small number of stockholders, often active in the conduct of its affairs. Frequently the stockholders are also directors, a voting trust or proxies have been executed to insure continuity of management, and the articles of incorporation or bylaws restrict stock transfers. See *corporation*.

closed-end company A company maintaining an investment service for a limited group of stockholders, often specializing in a particular type of security. With no redemption privileges, for the securities in its own portfolio, investors may nevertheless sell or dispose of their interests, especially if shares are listed on a stock exchange.

closed-end mutual fund Mutual funds having a fixed number of outstanding shares that can be bought and sold through normal channels. Although shares of a closed-end mutual fund represent a proportionate interest in the fund's portfolio, their price often differs from the proportion of the market value of the fund's portfolio.

closed-loop system A system which involves one or more *feedback* loops that makes it capable of self-control, at least to some degree, by reference to its own input, output, and feedback signals.

closed mortgage (or bonds) A mortgage (or issue of bonds) against which no amount may be borrowed in addition to the total already reached.

closely held corporation See *closed corporation*.

closing The process of preparing, entering, and posting *closing entries*.

closing agreement (federal income taxes) A written agreement between the taxpayer and the Commissioner of Internal Revenue, subject to approval by higher authority, as to the settlement of a specific item or of a tax relating to a specified period of time. The agreement is regarded as final in the absence of fraud, malfeasance, or misrepresentation of a material fact.

closing date The date as of which the accounting records of an organization are made ready for a trial balance and the preparation of financial statements. In some organizations, the term is also applied to certain dates preceding the end of the period which mark cutoffs on certain classes of transactions; that is, dates after which transactions will be included in a subsequent period. Thus, the closing date for sales in a 31-day month may be established as the 28th, because the lag in recording sales for the final 3 days might delay the preparation of financial statements; with the growth of improved bookkeeping devices, this practice, at one time very common, has been largely eliminated.

closing entry 1. A periodic entry or one of a series of periodic entries by means of which the balances in revenue and expense accounts and the *nominal elements* of *mixed accounts* are adjusted for the purpose of preparing financial statements. At the end of the fiscal year, a final closing entry eliminates the year's revenue and expense (nominal) accounts, their net total being carried to *retained earnings* (earned surplus) or other proprietorship accounts.

2. An entry, usually annual, uniting separately maintained nominal elements of a split ledger account. See *split-account system*.

3. An entry having the effect of balancing an account, a set of accounts, or a ledger. See *internal transaction*.

closing trial balance = *postclosing trial balance*.

cluster sampling A form of sampling which relies on natural groupings (or clusters) of sampling units in the population. Cluster sampling involves random selection of these groups or clusters and observation of selected items in the clusters selected. The sampling is said to form a "one-stage" process if every item in each of the selected clusters is examined. If only samples of the items in the selected clusters are examined, the process is "two-stage." Further *multistage sampling* processes are also possible in which the clusters are divided into subclusters for sample selection at each stage. See *subsampling*. Suitably designed cluster sampling may yield approximately random samples with a considerable savings in "travel" cost.

CMA = *certified management accountant*. See *Certificate in Management Accounting*.

COBOL (computers) = *CO*mmon *B*usiness *O*riented *L*anguage. A programming language designed primarily for business data-processing applications. COBOL statements are English-like in nature, where a program consists of paragraphs and a paragraph consists of sentences. The language is efficient in performing record input and output, but it is cumbersome for performing mathematical calculations. See *CODASYL*.

COD 1. Cash (or collect) on delivery. An instruction attaching to a lot of goods requiring the payment of a specified amount of cash by the buyer as the goods are turned over to him or her or as services are rendered.
2. A classification of sales made up of such transactions, contrasting with *cash sale, credit sale*, and *barter*. See *sale*.

CODASYL (computers) = *CO*nference of *DA*ta *SY*stems *L*anguages. A voluntary organization of major computer users, manufacturers, and government departments. Its aim is to design and develop techniques and languages for data base analyses, design, and implementation. The specifications for COBOL were developed by CODASYL and more recently it has developed a proposed data base (CODASYL DBTG) organization and a related data description and manipulation language. Its role is to develop languages. The process of turning those languages into standards is handled by *ANSI* in America and by *ISO* on an international basis.

CODASYL DBTG (computers) = CODASYL Data Base Task Group. See *CODASYL*.

code *v*. 1. To affix a distinguishing reference number or symbol.
2. To designate on a voucher or other medium the account affected, a description of the transaction, and other data, as a condition precedent to an entry or posting.
3. The art of preparing instructions in a *computer program*.
n. The symbolization, transaction description, and other information required under a given system of accounts to be affixed to vouchers and transaction records generally for the purpose of identification and disposal; *codification*.

Code of Professional Ethics (for CPAs and CIAs) Authoritative statements establishing the guidelines of acceptable conduct for certified public accountants (CPAs) and certified internal auditors (CIAs). Codes applicable to CPAs are prepared by the American Institute of CPAs, each state society of CPAs, and each state board of accountancy and are binding on their respective members or license holders. The code for CIAs is prepared by the *Institute of Internal Auditors*.

codicil A written change in a will.

codification (or coding) A *system* of numbers or distinctive symbols attaching to accounts, entries, invoices, vouchers, or other records or documents serving as a device for distinguishing the members of a class of items from each other and as an index.

coding clerk A clerk who designates the accounts affected and the *legend*, if any, accompanying the *entry* or *posting* of completed transactions.

coefficient 1. Any one or more numbers or symbols placed before another number or symbol and serving as its multiplier; in the expressions 6*a*, 3*ab*, *abcd*, the respective coefficients of *a*, *b*, and *d* are 6, 3*a*, and *abc*.
2. (statistics) A conventional measure of the relation or lack of relation between magnitudes, of which the following are the principal types:

(a) *Coefficient of alienation*: A measure of the lack of relation between two or more variables; the value secured when the correlation coefficient is subtracted from unity. It is usually written $k = \sqrt{1 - r^2}$, where k is the coefficient of alienation and r the "coefficient of correlation" (see below).

(b) *Coefficient of association*: Any measure designed to show the degree of association between two or more sets of characteristics. Generally, the measure is chosen so that it is equal to +1 when there is complete positive association, −1 when there is complete negative association, and 0 when there is no association between the *attributes*.

(c) *Coefficient of correlation*: A measure of strength of the linear relationship between two statistical series, ranging between 0, or no relation, and +1, perfect correspondence, or −1, perfect inverse correspondence. It is the square root of the excess of 1 over a fraction, the numerator of which is the square of the standard error of estimate and denominator is the square of the standard deviation. See *least-squares method; standard deviation; correlation table.*

(d) *Coefficient of determination*: (i) The square of the coefficient of correlation; usually written r^2. It assesses the proportion of the total *variance* in the *dependent variable* that is explained or accounted for by its linear relation to the *independent variable.* (ii) Gain in efficiency as measured by least-squares regression equations relative to the *arithmetic mean.*

(e) *Coefficient of multiple correlation*: A measure of the degree of relation between several variables; usually written as R with subscripts attached to denote the variables of relation.

(f) *Coefficient of nondetermination*: A measure of the lack of relation between two or more variables; the square of the coefficient of correlation subtracted from unity; usually written $k^2 = 1 - r^2$.

(g) *Coefficient of partial correlation*: A measure of the degree of relation existing between two variables when the effect of other variables is taken into account. For example, $r_{12.34}$ is intended to show the degree of relation existing between X_1 and X_2 when the effects of X_3 and X_4 have been allowed for. The coefficient $r_{12.34}$ is sometimes referred to as the "second-order" correlation coefficient, where the order is determined by the number of subscripts to the right of the decimal point. The order thus specifies the number of other variables whose effect has been allowed for. Thus, $r_{12.3}$ would be a "first-order" coefficient, measuring the degree of relation between X_1 and X_2 when possible effects of X_3 are allowed for. The ordinary coefficient of correlation r_{12}, between X_1 and X_2, is known as a "zero-order" correlation coefficient and may be regarded as a special type of partial-correlation coefficient which does not take explicitly into account the possible effects of other variables such as X_3 and X_4 on either X_1 or X_2.

(h) *Coefficient of variation*: The *standard deviation* divided by the *arithmetic mean* of a group of figures. Combining the two in this fashion provides a relative measure of dispersion independent of units of measure and thus allows comparisons which would not be possible if either the mean or standard deviation were used alone. When the *standard error* of a statistic is expressed in this form, a measure of relative *precision* or *accuracy* is secured which is referred to as the relative standard error. If $\sigma_{\bar{x}}$ represents the standard error of the mean and σ the universe standard deviation, and N and n represent the universe and sample size, respectively, then

$$\frac{\sigma_{\bar{x}}}{\mu} = \sqrt{\frac{N-n}{N-1} \times \frac{\sigma^2}{n\mu^2}}$$

= relative standard error of the mean μ.

Such a measure also implicitly defines the degree of *reliability*; hence, the measure provides a convenient device in sample design. For a specified design, it may be used to determine the sample size necessary to obtain desired levels of *precision* and *reliability*. The equation $10\% = \sigma_{\bar{x}}/\mu$ implies that samples of size n will lie within 10% of the universe mean approximately two-thirds of the time in samples drawn from a normal universe with a *variance* σ^2. If $10\% = 1.96\sigma_{\bar{x}}/\mu$, this will be true about 95% of the time (see *normal table*). Applied in reverse, this formula may be used to determine sample size n necessary to achieve prescribed levels of precision and reliability. Suppose, for example, that this 10% precision and 2/3 probability (or reliability) is desired for samples drawn from a universe of size $N = 1,000$, $\mu = 10$, $\sigma = 10$. Using $\sigma_{\bar{x}}/\mu = 1/10$ and substituting these values gives

$$\frac{\sigma_{\bar{x}}}{\mu} = \frac{1}{10} = \sqrt{\frac{1,000-n}{1,000-1} \times \frac{100}{n \times 100}},$$

and $n = 91$ will be a sample of sufficient size to secure this precision and reliability. If it is desired to increase the reliability to .95, the above result must be multiplied by $(1.96)^2$, or approximately 4, yielding $n = 364$. The same result would be secured if the measure of reliability were left at .67, had it been desired to improve the precision from 10% to 5%.

coefficient of determination See *coefficient (2d)*.

coefficient of variation See *coefficient (2h)*.

coinsurance clause A provision in an insurance contract, such as one covering loss by fire, limiting the liability of the insurer to a proportion of loss no greater than the ratio of the amount of insurance carried to an amount equal to some stated percentage of the "cash value of the property" at the time of the loss relative to the amount of insurance carried. Example: A loss of $60,000 is incurred on property having a cash value of $150,000 on which insurance of $100,000 is carried—the policy contains an 80% coinsurance clause. 80% of $150,000 is $120,000 and $60,000 × 100/120 = $50,000; this is the amount the insurer will pay. Had the insurance been $120,000 or more, the full loss, up to the amount of the insurance, would have been covered.

collapsible corporation (federal income taxes) Under the federal income-tax law (Section 341), a corporation formed or availed of principally to manufacture, construct, or produce property, or to purchase inventory, or to hold stock in such a corporation in order that the stockholders may realize capital gain by disposing of the stock before the corporation has realized income from the property. Commencing with 1950, such gains may be taxed as ordinary income.

collateral Real or personal property pledged as part or full security on a debt. See *secured transaction*.

collateralize To secure a debt in part or in full by a *pledge*. A note is said to be collateralized if the debtor has deposited property with a creditor as part or full security for the payment of principal or interest or both.

collateral-trust bonds Bonds secured by other bonds or by stock.

collectible Capable of being converted into cash.

collecting officer (government accounting) A bonded employee authorized to receive, deposit, and report amounts owing to the government.

collection basis of revenue recognition See *installment method of accounting*.

collection float See *float*.

collection period See *accounts receivable collection period*.

collusion A secret understanding between two or more persons to take advantage of another with the object of depriving him or her of a right or property.
—collusive, *adj*. Said of bidding which occurs whenever suppliers agree among themselves (1) to submit identical or nearly identical bids to a prospective purchaser, or (2) to submit bids which will favor one or more of the colluders.

columnar system A system of bookkeeping whereby use is made of columnar records for continuous analysis and grouping of items, thus reducing the labor of posting. The use of columns is not confined to *books of original entry* but may extend to *ledgers* as well.

combination 1. An agreement between two or more business organizations, often constituting a trade group, for purposes of mutual benefit, such as a price or other trade-practice agreement; sometimes prohibited by law.
2. = *business combination*.
3. *pl*. The arrangements or *permutations* of a collection of *n* objects into two mutually exclusive classes of *r* and $n - r$ items, where *r* is the number selected for sampling or other purpose; commonly represented by the sym-

bols $C_r{}^n$ or $_nC_r$; see formula (5) under *permutation*.

combination bond A *bond* of a governmental unit payable from the revenues of a governmental enterprise which is also backed by the full faith and credit of the governmental unit.

combined attributes and variables sampling A sampling method which combines the observed error rate and monetary errors in a sample to form an upper bound on error. See *dollar unit sampling*.

combined depreciation-and-upkeep method (of depreciation) See *depreciation method*.

combined financial statement 1. A financial statement in which the assets and liabilities or revenue and expense of a group of related companies or other *entities* have been added together so as to disclose their financial position or operating results as though they were a single business unit: a *consolidated financial statement* or *group financial statement*.
2. (governmental accounting) A statement in which balance sheets, or revenues, expenditures, and changes in fund balances of all fund types and account groups are displayed without eliminating interfund transfers.

combining financial statement 1. A *group financial statement* showing constituent units, as in *segment reporting* by divisions or other organization units.
2. (governmental accounting) A statement in which all funds of a given type are combined for presentation in a *combined financial statement*.

commercial expense A general expense of operating a business, as contrasted with a cost of manufacturing or marketing. Commercial expense generally includes administrative, selling, and general expense and other general overhead, such as advertising and research. As employed in contracts, the term requires detailed specification.

commercial law That branch of law relating to business enterprise and commercial transactions generally: contracts, partnerships, negotiable instruments, estates and trusts, sales, debtor and creditor, corporations, real estate, and securities.

commercial paper 1. A type of loan taking the form of simple discount notes usually in five- and ten-thousand-dollar denominations, sold to financial houses and distributed by them to banks or investors. Issuers are mostly larger manufacturers or distributors with top credit ratings and substantial working-capital ratios.
2. Any form of *negotiable* instrument, such as a check or draft; = *bill of exchange (1)*.

commercial paper rate Annualized *yield* on *commercial paper*. Same as *open market paper rate*.

commission Remuneration of an employee, or agent, or broker relating to services performed in connection with sales, purchases, collections, or other types of business transactions, and usually based upon a percentage of the amounts involved.

commitment 1. An anticipated expenditure, evidenced by a contract or purchase order given to an outsider. Commitments are not given expression on accounting records, except sometimes on those of government agencies, since the signing of a contract or issuance of a purchase order does not give rise to a transaction. Disclosure of the amount and nature of a commitment in a balance sheet or balance-sheet footnote is, however, generally regarded as required where substantial additions to capital assets are involved or where the amount of prospective goods or services contracted for is substantially in excess of a 60- or 90-day supply or of whatever is regarded as normal to the business, or where the market price has declined or is likely to decline before delivery substantially below the contract price, thus giving rise to the likelihood of a loss. See *basis of accounting; executory contract*.
2. = *encumbrance (1)*.

Committee for Economic Development (CED) A nonprofit corporation supported by many large U.S. corporations which conducts studies and publishes timely recommendations on problems of public policy that may impact on economic activities. The CED is staffed by professional economists reporting to a board of directors consisting of prominent corporate executives and representatives from labor unions.

Committee on Accounting Procedure A senior technical committee of the *American Institute of Certified Public Accountants*, which was authorized to issue *Accounting Research Bulletins* on behalf of the Institute from 1938 to 1959. Its membership consisted primarily of partners in firms of certified public accountants, including representatives of the *Big Eight*, and also had as members several accounting professors. Its function was transferred in 1959 to the *Accounting Principles Board*.

commodity = *good*; often used as a singular for (economic) *goods*.

common average 1. = *simple average*.
2. = *particular average*.

common carrier Any *person* who undertakes and is authorized to transport persons or goods as a regular business. Under common law, such a person must provide facilities for all that apply, at fair and nondiscriminatory rates, and is held liable for any accident or damage in transit except those attributable to an act of God, a foreign enemy, or carelessness by the person transported or by the shipper of the goods. The liability of a common carrier for any loss or injury to property received by it for transportation is in effect that of an insurer. With respect to passengers, however, the common carrier is liable only for want of proper care.

common cost The cost of facilities or services employed in the output of two or more operations, commodities, or services. Thus, the premium paid for a fire-insurance contract covering unrelated lots of merchandise in a warehouse is a common cost. The resulting benefits extend to each lot. The assignment, if any, of a portion of the premium cost to any one lot is primarily an arbitrary process; insurance and other common costs applicable to a number of unrelated items are often treated as a *period cost*. Common costs of related outputs are known also as *joint costs*.

common-law corporation See *joint-stock association*.

common-law trust = *business trust*.

common logarithm See *logarithm*.

Common Market An association, usually formed by countries in a contiguous region, to promote economic activities by reducing or eliminating tariffs and trade barriers between them and, in some cases, extending to other common policies and procedures for consultation. See *EEC*.

common sense A *judgment* or set of judgments taken to be obvious or inevitable in a given social group and reflecting some definite or partially formulated general approach to problems deemed related. The *principles* of common sense are not rigorously formulated, but their applications are accepted because they have been found to work with relative success through the operation of habit or custom. From the point of view of precise logical analysis, common sense approaches to problems and their solutions often exhibit mutually contradictory elements.

common-size balance sheet See *common-size statement*.

common-size income statement See *common-size statement*.

common-size statement Also called one hundred percent statement. An accounting statement expressed in percentages of some base, rather than dollars. The base is usually net sales or total revenue in a common-size income statement and total assets in a common-size balance sheet. The percentages allow for direct comparisons between firms of different sizes, and they reveal unusual variations of individual firms from industry standards.

common stock The class of capital stock of a corporation which, after considering the rights attaching to preferred classes, if any, is neither limited nor preferred in its participation in distributions of the surplus earnings of a corporation or in the ultimate distribution of its assets; the class of stock representing the residual ownership of all the assets of a corporation after the liabilities and other proprietary claims have been satisfied.

common stock equivalent An instrument considered to be the equivalent of common stock for earnings per share computations. Common stock equivalents, such as options or warrants, often contain provisions enabling their holders to become common stockholders.

communication Any process of passing information from one person to another as by instructing or reporting; also, the initiation of a mutual interaction, human or mechanical, or both, such as that resulting from the operation of any *control (1)* or *feedback* device.

community income See *community property*.

community of interest The coordination of the policies or operations of two or more separately owned organizations by any of various devices short of actual control. Ownership of capital stock in common with others, interlocking directorates, a common source of supply, the existence of but one or a few customers, are examples; the effects are often the same as those brought about by formal controls. See *trade association*.

community property Property owned by husband and wife "in community," each sharing equally in the income derived from it.

Community-property laws are in force in states including Arizona, California, Idaho, Louisiana, Nevada, New Mexico, Texas, and Washington. Since the Federal Revenue Act of 1948, income-splitting between husband and wife has been permitted, giving a comparable income-tax benefit to married couples in all states.

company 1. A *corporation*.
2. Loosely, any organization consummating transactions in its own name.

comparability 1. The quality or qualities attributable to two or more items or groups of items whereby the presence or absence of particular conditions or tendencies may be discerned. In the preparation of comparative financial statements, the accounting objective is not only a sequential arrangement of similar elements, but also the furnishing of a basis for information that will be helpful to their joint consideration. Comparability need not connote similarity. It may often involve striking differences such as short and tall, etc.
2. Any alignment of financial or operating data against a *standard* of comparison, whereby similarities or differences may be noted, and, if significant, analyzed for causes and possible correction.

comparative advantage In economics, especially international trade economics, sometimes called the "law of comparative advantage." A doctrine under which two exchanging parties or countries will each tend to specialize in the activity wherein they are relatively most efficient. Even if one country is more efficient in all activities, it will nevertheless tend to specialize in those in which its relative efficiency is greatest. The law, or doctrine, extends to multilateral trade in which more than two countries are involved.

comparative analysis An analysis of financial statements in different (usually adjacent) time periods. Changes in each individual item in the statements are calculated either through first differences in the dollar amounts from one period to the next or the percentage changes from one period to the next. The purpose of this analysis is to isolate the causes of changes in a firm's financial patterns and to determine probable trends of a firm in the future.

comparative balance sheet Two or more balance sheets of the same organization with different dates, or of two or more organizations with the same date, customarily displayed in parallel columns to facilitate the observation of variances; supplementary columns are sometimes added to show differences. See *balance sheet*.

comparative cost A cost so computed as to be comparable with another, and obtainable by like methods of compilation, adjustment for differences in price or volume, elimination of divergent elements, and the like. See *cost*.

comparative financial statements See *comparative statements*; *comparative analysis*.

comparative statements Balance sheets, income or flow statements, or other accounting summaries juxtaposed for the purpose of contrasting the financial characteristics of an organization from one period to another. Responsibility for the adequacy of footnotes or other accompanying explanations rests with the controller, the public accountant, or other persons who expressly or impliedly subscribe to the *fairness* of the presentation.

compare (auditing) To establish the correspondences, similarities, or differences in items.

comparison schedule (auditing) A schedule or working paper which facilitates, documents, and presents the results of comparing various items of information pertinent to one or more audit objectives. For example, a schedule comparing expense items in absolute dollars and as a percent of sales between two periods.

compensation 1. Payment to an individual for services performed.

2. Reimbursement or other payment for losses or damages sustained.

compensatory balance The amount of money that a borrower must keep on deposit in a checking account or savings account or in a certificate of deposit at a lending institution as support for current borrowed funds. A compensatory balance increases the effective interest cost of borrowing. Compensatory balance arrangements ordinarily are to be disclosed in notes to the financial statements. Also called compensating balance.

compensatory time Time off allowed an employee for overtime, usually on an informal basis and at the discretion of his or her supervisor, thus obviating an overtime accrual.

competent evidential matter Audit *evidence* which is both valid and relevant for reliance thereon by an auditor in reaching his or her *opinion*. (See *generally accepted auditing standards*.) There are generally three presumptions: (1) When audit evidence can be obtained from independent sources outside an enterprise, it provides greater assurance of reliability than that secured solely within the enterprise. (2) When data are developed under satisfactory conditions of *internal control*, there is more assurance as to reliability than when they are developed under unsatisfactory conditions of internal control. (3) Direct knowledge by the independent auditor obtained through physical examination, observation, computation, and inspection is more reliable than information obtained indirectly. See *evidence*.

competitive price 1. The price established in a market by the bargaining of a considerable number of buyers and sellers, each acting independently of the other, no one of them having power enough to dominate the market. See *price*.

2. (economics) The price per unit of a commodity sold under conditions of perfect competition. Such conditions are hypothesized to be (1) a large number of buyers and sellers, as above, and (2) freedom of entry and exit into the market. A third condition in the form of an absence of *uncertainty* is also implied.

compile (computers) 1. To develop a *machine language* program from a *program* written in another, usually higher-level, language such as FORTRAN or COBOL, *q.v.* Usually one or more machine language statements are generated for each higher-level statement. The systems program which performs this task is called a compiler.

2. Assemble, group together, or arrange as in a tally of a group of vouchers.

compiler See *compile; interpreter*.

complementary products 1. Two or more types of output from the same raw material or common operation, as from the processing of crude petroleum; see *joint cost*.

2. Products possessing significantly negative *cross elasticity of demand*.

complete audit An audit of all transactions, often made for limited periods, for special transactions, or for small concerns. See *detailed audit*.

complete cycle costs See *life-cycle costs*. All costs, both fixed and variable, incurred by a project over its entire life.

completed-contract method See *revenue recognition*. A method which recognizes revenue upon completion of the project, such as a long-term construction contract. More conservative than the *percentage-of-completion method*, it is acceptable if reasonable estimates of total project cost and each period's progress cannot be developed. Although cash might be received from interim billings, revenue is still postponed to the period in which the contract is substantially completed.

completed sales basis A method of accounting under which *revenue* is recognized when a *sale* (or delivery) is made. See *revenue realization*.

complete transaction A transaction that will not normally be followed by another transaction dealing with the same subject matter; contrast with *incomplete transaction*.

complex capital structure Denotes the presence of potentially *dilutive* securities in a company's financial structure; a capital structure in the form of corporate debt and equity that includes potentially dilutive convertible securities, options, warrants, or rights that could be exercised with a resulting dilution in earnings per common share. Companies with complex capital structures must ordinarily present both *primary earnings per share* and *fully diluted earnings per share*.

complex information processing A junction between psychology and computer science in which computers are used to simulate reasoning processes of human beings, especially when complex problems are involved. The emphasis is on *heuristics* rather than optimality as in *artificial intelligence*. Example: the development of computer programs to play good and perhaps championship caliber chess against human opponents—in contrast to the *theory of games*, which provides optimal chess strategies that cannot presently be implemented, even by computer, because of the complex data processing requirements such solutions entail.

complex number A combination of two real numbers (x, y) with the *imaginary number i*, typically written $x + iy$, i being the mathematical entity whose square (i^2) is -1.

complex trust (federal income taxes) In general, a trust that may accumulate income or make a charitable contribution. See *simple trust*.

compliance audit An audit of specific activities to determine that performance has been in accordance with some specific statutory requirement, contractual agreement, or stated description. For example, audit of a hospital for compliance with Medicare reimbursement regulations; audit by an IRS auditor for compliance with tax laws; audit of a computer service center for compliance with stated systems of internal control. See *audit (4B)*.

compliance error 1. Accounting errors where a required internal accounting control procedure is omitted or deviated from in processing accounting data. Compliance errors may or may not result in a *monetary error*.
2. Departures from a procedure required to be performed by contract or statute, e.g., an improperly prepared income-tax return.

compliance test An auditing procedure or test, the purpose of which is to obtain evidence in support of the auditor's evaluation of the system of internal accounting controls of the auditee entity. Such procedures are required where the auditor intends to rely on internal controls in his or her examination; i.e., evidence supporting the controls being relied upon must be obtained (see *generally accepted auditing standards*). Compliance tests, therefore, do not relate directly to transactions or balances, but to controls (see *internal control*; contrast with *substantive test* and see also *dual-purpose test*).

Compliance tests may involve the examination of documentation or the observation of activities.

composite depreciation Method of calculating depreciation that applies a single, average rate to a number of heterogeneous assets that have dissimilar characteristics and *service lives*; e.g., where a single *depreciation rate* is used for an entire operating assembly or unit such as a refinery or a truck each consisting of separate subunits having different service lives; contrast to *group depreciation* which applies a single, average rate to a number of homogeneous assets having similar characteristics and service lives. See *composite-life method* under *depreciation methods*.

composite-life method (of depreciation) See *composite depreciation; depreciation methods*.

composition of creditors An agreement between an insolvent debtor and creditors by which the creditors agree to take less than the full amount of debts owed in exchange for an early payment of some lesser amount. Consideration is assumed to be the early collection even though a creditor is accepting less than the full amount owed.

compound 1. To add interest to principal at periodic intervals for the purpose of establishing a new basis for subsequent interest computations. Any other process of growth achieved in this manner.
2. *n*. An enclosure. Also a substance formed from other substances or elements.

compound amount of 1 The total produced by compounding the principal of 1 at a given *rate* over a given period of time. See *interest formulas*.

compound amount of 1 per period The amount, at a future date, of periodic $1 deposits drawing compound interest. See *interest formulas*.

compound discount The excess of a payment or a series of payments to be made in the future over their present value. See *present value of 1*.

compounding period Length of time between the dates that interest is paid or added *converted* to principal (compounded) for the next interest-earning period; the time period (or any portion thereof) during which *simple interest* methods and calculations are applicable. See *compound interest*.

compound interest Interest resulting from the periodic addition of simple interest to principal, the new base thus established being the principal for the computation of interest for the next following period. See *interest formulas*.

compound-interest formula See *interest formulas*.

compound-interest method (of depreciation) See *depreciation methods*.

compound journal entry A *journal entry* having three or more elements and often representing several transactions; contrasts with "simple journal entry," which contains single debit and credit elements. The compound-journal-entry form is often employed to indicate compactly the accounting effect of a series of related transactions.

comprehensive income All changes in net assets or owners' equity during a period from transactions and other events and circumstances affecting the enterprise from nonowner sources (except for capital contributions to the enterprise by owners and distributions by the enterprise to owners). Comprehensive income includes holding gains and losses as well as other asset and equity revaluations in addition to the changes reflected in the income statement accounts.

comprehensive (income) tax allocation An interperiod income-tax allocation that includes in income tax expense the tax effects of all transactions entering into the determination of pretax accounting income for the period even though some of the transactions may affect the taxes payable in a different period. Such a comprehensive allocation recognizes that the amount of income taxes payable for a given period does not appropriately measure the income tax expense related to transactions for that period. Under this view, income-tax expense encompasses any accrual, deferral, or estimation necessary to measure the tax effects of transactions included in pretax accounting income for that period.

comptroller 1. = *controller*: a misspelling of *controller*, which is derived from the French *contrôleur*, from *contre* (Latin *contra*), against; *rôle* (Latin *rotulus*, a little wheel, records at one time having been in rolled form), list, roll; and *-eur*, denoting an actor, agent; the whole originally meant a person who checks or compares one list or source of information with another. *Comptroller* has no French counterpart, but is an anglicized concoction of the French *compte* (Latin *computum*, account, *computare*, to count), account; *rôle*; and *-eur*: the combination thus arising from the confusion of *compte* with *contre*.

2. = *Comptroller General*.

Comptroller General The head of the General Accounting Office, an arm of the legislative branch of the federal government, reporting directly to the Congress on financial position, operating results, and accounting systems of government agencies. Now mainly functioning as an auditing agency and a leader in the development of comprehensive audits providing evaluations of agency and program organization and management. See *audit*.

COMPUSTAT The acronymic name of a computerized data bank which contains over 20 years of virtually complete financial accounting data for over 3,000 American and Canadian companies. Not completely free of errors, it has nevertheless become the dominant source of data for empirical research in accounting.

computed price See *administered price*.

computer 1. See *digital computer; analog computer*.

2. One who computes or calculates from numerical data.

computer-assisted audit The use of a *computer (1)* in evidence collection and testing phases of an audit process.

computer-assisted instruction (CAI) Use of a *computer (1)* to aid in teaching. The system is usually designed to deal interactively with students by asking them questions and then replying to a student's responses by asking further questions or by making corrections and asking students to repeat earlier lessons.

computer program A series of computer instructions which cause particular actions to be taken by a computer. The computer program needs to be semantically correct as well as logical in order to produce the desired results. See *semantics*.

concentration banking The practice of accelerating availability to a firm of funds collected from customers through the use of local banks in areas where receipts originate. Local banks can collect funds faster and transfer them to a designated bank account where most of the disbursements take place. See *lock box*.

concept Any abstract idea serving a systematizing function.

Conceptual Framework A major study being undertaken by the *Financial Accounting Standards Board* in order to develop the theoretical foundations of its future *Statements of Financial Accounting Standards*. One of the publications which the Board was expected to take into consideration was *Objectives of Financial Statements*, also known as the Trueblood Report. The first definitive pronouncement growing out of its Conceptual Framework study is Statement of Financial Accounting Concepts No. 1, *Objectives of Financial Reporting by Business Enterprises*, issued in November 1978.

concern Any economic unit.

conclusion The end result of a reasoning process, as distinguished from the data or the premises; in a formal system of reasoning, a theorem.

condemnation proceedings Formal legal process to determine the amount of compensation to be paid the owner of property taken by a governmental unit for public use without the owner's consent.

condemnation proceeds The amount received from a governmental unit as compensation for property taken by eminent domain. Gain from such a transaction may be postponed for federal income-tax purposes if the proceeds are reinvested in similar property. See *involuntary conversion*.

condensed balance sheet A balance sheet in which less essential detail has been combined, the purpose being to provide a quickly comprehensible picture of the main features of financial position. See *balance sheet; all-purpose financial statement*.

condition 1. A proposition that establishes or aids in establishing and delimiting the scope, applicability, or truth of another; a condition precedent, as in a contract; see *sufficient condition; necessary condition*.
2. A state of affairs at a point in time such as the liquidity or other condition of a firm as shown by its balance sheet. The state of an item of equipment, a plant, or a building. Also the physical, mental, or financial state of a person.
3. Any part or accompaniment of a *process* that is operating continuously and thus is a function of time; as, the depreciation occurring as the result of the ownership of a fixed asset. See *events and conditions*.

conditional expectation The expected value of a *variate* given other information. In regression it is common to refer to the expected value of the dependent variable Y given that a particular value of X has occurred. The conditional expectation is written $E(Y \mid X)$. See *expected value*. For a *regression* it is equal to $a + bX$, so that $E(Y \mid X) = a + bX$.

conditional probability See *probability*.

Confederation of Asian and Pacific Accountants Founded in 1957 as the Far East Conference of Accountants, the Confederation of Asian and Pacific Accountants holds international conferences every two to three years. In 1976, when the confederation supplanted the Conference of Asian and Pacific Accountants, a Secretariat was established.

Conference Board, The A nonprofit organization which undertakes analyses in economics and management with the goal of promoting business operations and the development of private enterprise.

confidence interval A range of values (i.e., an interval of values) computed from a statistical *sample* within which the *probability* achieves a specified value that the *parameter* of interest is within this range of values. The validity of the confidence interval depends upon knowledge of the underlying distribution of the *population* or assumptions about behavior of the *sampling distribution*.

confidence level The measure of probability associated with a *confidence interval*. For example, a 95% confidence level refers to the assumption that 95% of the confidence intervals computed in the same way from all possible samples of a given size will include the true value of the population *parameter*.

confirmation 1. Generally, the substantiation of a fact or condition by one having direct knowledge of it; the establishing of the truth of a statement; proof of existence, character, or amount.
2. (auditing) Substantiation of the existence and sometimes the condition and value of a claim against another or of an asset in the possession or control of another, or of the existence and amount of a liability. A confirmation usually takes the form of a written request and acknowledgment, but it may also be obtained orally, or through observation, as by the inspection of a passbook containing entries for deposits, or of records reflecting a certain transaction. See *representation*. Ei-

ther of two types of confirmation is commonly employed: a positive confirmation requesting a reply in any event, or a negative confirmation requesting a reply only in the event of a discrepancy.

conflict of interest Any relationship whereby an individual or his or her relative or trustee may benefit (by way of a present or prospective gift, gratuity, commission, discount, preference, future employment, or the like) from a transaction of that person's employer where he or she is identified with or has influenced in any way its initiation, specifications, terms, conditions, completion, or acceptance. A conflict of interest may be asserted, even where no material benefit is involved, no added cost or loss of profit is in prospect for the employer, or the relationship is known to stockholders or owners; the mere possibility of a benefit accruing to the individual at some indefinite future time is enough to justify the assertion.

conglomerate Generally, a corporation that has grown by acquiring or merging with other firms in different lines of business. The lines of business are sometimes so distinct that questions arise as to whether *consolidation* or other procedures such as *pooling of interest* or continued separate disclosure might best be employed in the preparation of financial statements.

conglomerate financial statement A *balance sheet* in which materially different financial positions of two or more business entities have been combined or consolidated; or a single *income statement* in which differing lines of products or activities, or legally separable lines of products or activities, have been merged. Current standards of disclosure in *lines of business reporting* require their separate presentation in reports to stockholders and outsiders.

connected graph See *graph*.

consent dividend (federal income taxes) A portion or all of the retained earnings of a *personal holding company*, credited to paid-in surplus rather than paid out to stockholders. The amount is reported on the stockholders' income-tax returns as an ordinary dividend, and at the same time the investment cost of the stock to which the dividend pertains is increased in like amount.

consequential loss (insurance) The indirect loss arising out of fire or other insured peril, e.g., food spoilage caused by disablement of refrigeration equipment.

conservatism A guideline which chooses between acceptable accounting alternatives for recording events or transactions so that the least favorable immediate effect on assets, income, and owners' equity is reported. Examples include the lower of cost or market method to value inventories, and the accrual of expected losses and expenses but the deferral of anticipated gains and revenues.

consideration The benefit to a contracting party that has induced a person to enter into the contract, taking the form of a promise; the performance of an act for which the performer would not otherwise be obligated; the refraining from doing something that the refrainer would otherwise be free to do; or, as is most common in commercial contracts, payment in money or transfer of property.

consignee Receiver of goods on *consignment*.

consignment Goods shipped for future sale or other purpose, title remaining with the shipper (consignor), for which the receiver (consignee), upon acceptance, is accountable. Consigned goods are a part of the consignor's inventory until sold. The consignee may be the eventual purchaser, may act as the agent through whom the sale is effected, or may otherwise dispose of the goods in accordance with an agreement with the consignor.

consignment sale See *consignment*.

consignor Owner or shipper of goods on *consignment*.

consistency 1. (auditing) Continued uniformity, during a period or from one period to another, in methods of accounting, mainly in valuation bases and methods of accrual, as reflected in the financial statements of a business enterprise or other *accounting* or *economic unit*. There are three generally recognized types: vertical consistency, within an interrelated group of financial statements bearing the same date; horizontal consistency, as between financial statements from period to period; and a kind of third-dimensional consistency, at a single date, as compared with organizations of the same type or organizations generally.

Any material change in valuation and accrual methods from one year to another demands a disclosure accompanying the financial statements of the year of change and setting forth the nature of the difference in method, the reason for the change, and the effect in dollars as compared with the result that would have been produced had the previous year's method been continued. The same sort of disclosure is required where the accounting methods of an organization are at variance with those of the industry of which it is a part, or with methods universally employed, regardless of the nature of the organization.

It has been said that the omission of inventories altogether from financial statements would have no effect on net profit, provided, and only provided, that the dollar amount thereof remained constant over the years. The same is true of accounts payable for purchases and of expense accruals. But the proviso is all-important. The quantities and valuations of successive inventories of every business enterprise do fluctuate, often substantially, and so do the dollar amounts of payables and accrued expense. Further,

without these items, the current solvency—revealed by the balance sheet—would not be disclosed. On the other hand, the failure to record small items or to allocate them between accounting periods will not affect conclusions as to operating results or financial position, and a strict application of conventional rules to such items is occasionally relaxed. The justification for relaxation, however, can rest only on the smallness of the possible fluctuation over the years and on the smallness of any one item and of the total of all other excepted items in relation to financial position at any one time.

2. The property of a set of simultaneously assumed propositions, such that no contradictions are deducible from them under prescribed rules of inference.

consolidated balance sheet A balance sheet in which the assets and liabilities of a *controlling company* are combined with the corresponding items of the organizations it owns or controls in such a manner as to disclose the financial position of the related companies as though they were a single economic unit. Minority interests in subsidiary companies customarily appear as a separate item, often expressed as a liability rather than as a part of *net worth*. *Ownership* of a subsidiary is considered to exist when a majority of the voting stock is owned by the holding company or by the same interests; *control*, a question of fact in each case, may exist with a much smaller percentage of stock ownership or even with no stock ownership, as in a situation where all or the bulk (e.g., 80%) of the fixed assets, sales, or profits of one company are under the control or direction of another.

Consolidation of financial statements of foreign corporations with those of a U.S. holding or parent company should be approached with caution because of fluctuating exchange rates, the ever-present possibility of expropriation with partial or no compensation, present and imminent restrictions on foreign-currency withdrawals, along with numerous other contingencies, new and old.

See *consolidated financial statement; consolidating financial statement; intercompany elimination; foreign currency translation.*

consolidated bond A bond issued to replace two or more outstanding issues by a single issue.

consolidated financial statement A statement showing financial condition or operating results of two or more associated enterprises as they would appear if they were one organization. The preparation of a consolidated statement involves eliminations of intercompany accounts, investments, advances, sales, and other items. See *consolidation policy; group financial statement; combined financial statement; intercompany elimination; eliminations ledger; minority interest; controlling-company accounting; subsidiary-company accounting.*

consolidated goodwill See *consolidation goodwill.*

consolidated group Affiliated corporations whose financial statements meet the tests for consolidation.

consolidated income statement A statement combining the income statements of two or more associated enterprises as a single economic unit. See *consolidating financial statement.*

consolidated mortgage A mortgage that replaces several existing mortgages of one or more creditors by a single mortgage. See *consolidated bond.*

consolidated retained earnings The combined retained earnings of all companies whose accounts are consolidated, after deducting minority stockholders' interests therein, the interest acquired by the parent company in the subsidiary companies' re-

tained earnings existing at the date of their acquisition, and intercompany eliminations.

consolidated returns (federal income taxes) The single tax return resulting from combined individual tax returns of corporations designated as "affiliated corporations" by Section 1504 of the *Internal Revenue Code.* The privilege of filing a consolidated return is elective under Section 1501, but certain intercompany adjustments and eliminations are required under Section 1502.

consolidated working fund (governmental accounting) A *fund* established by an agency for the purpose of accounting for the collective advances from two or more other agencies for particular construction services to be performed, or for goods to be delivered, usually within a single year.

consolidating financial statement A financial statement in worksheet form displaying the details that go into the making of consolidated financial statements. In its conventional form, the trial balances of controlling company and subsidiaries appear in parallel columns with one or two "eliminations" columns and "total" columns following. In lieu of the eliminations columns there may be the trial balance of an *eliminations ledger.* See *intercompany elimination.* Such a worksheet ties together book figures with published financial statements; it is occasionally furnished along with the more formal consolidated balance sheet and income statement in order to supply information as to the sources of various consolidated items, particularly where some unique financial or operating feature attaches to one of the constituent companies, the significance of which could not as readily be communicated by other means. It may be useful also where some diversity exists between individual subsidiaries but not enough to warrant independent statements, or where material intercompany eliminations are not readily determinable from other data in a report. See *grouping financial statement; conglomerate financial statement*.

consolidation 1. The combination of two or more enterprises, accomplished by the transfer of their net assets to a new corporation organized for the purpose; distinguished from *merger*.

2. The preparation of a consolidated balance sheet or other consolidated financial statement from those of related enterprises.

3. The group of enterprises (in either of the preceding senses) considered as a unit.

consolidation goodwill (or excess) That portion of the amount paid by a *parent* or *holding company* for its investment in a *subsidiary* company attributable to unusual earning power or other intangible value not recorded on the subsidiary's books; sometimes called *consolidated goodwill*. It is measured by the amount of the parent's or holding company's investment in stocks and securities less the book value reflected in the subsidiary's accounts at the time of purchase. It is common practice to reduce at once investments in subsidiaries by the amount of the consolidation excess. The writeoff becomes an *income deduction*. Equally common is the practice of amortizing the excess over a limited number of years. See *consolidation policy; goodwill (3)*.

consolidation ledger = *eliminations ledger*.

consolidation policy The policy of a *controlling company* (*parent company* or *holding company*) whereby affiliated organizations are included or excluded from consolidated financial statements. The most widely accepted policy is that consolidated statements can be justified only where the subsidiaries and the controlling company are integral parts of a single business enterprise, and where the display of the financial or operating characteristics of any one subsidiary is not material to an understanding of the group as a whole. The strongest case for consolidated statements is the situation in which a controlling company and its wholly owned subsidiaries are engaged in similar operations or together constitute an integrated line of economic endeavor under a common management.

Since the purpose of consolidated statements is primarily to give information beyond that appearing in the statements of the controlling company, their general effect is carefully weighed before publication. Included in the consolidated group are all subsidiaries regardless of the percentage of stock ownership, excepting only, where material, those that for some reason are regarded as not fitting into the integrated whole, as (a) a subsidiary whose operations are unrelated to those of its controlling company and any other subsidiary (see *conglomerate*); (b) a subsidiary about to be disposed of; (c) an uncontrolled company, even though its capital stock may be owned (see *control*); (d) a subsidiary where control is being exercised only temporarily; (e) a subsidiary the financial statements of which bear a date differing from that of the controlling company's statements; (f) a foreign subsidiary, especially where the rate of exchange has been fluctuating widely, restrictions exist on the withdrawal of funds, unfavorable legislation is in force, or the foreign government is in the process of change; (g) a subsidiary the control of which has been acquired at a figure substantially and unaccountably in excess of or less than the corresponding fraction of the recorded or appraised amount of its net assets at the date of consolidation.

Consistency in consolidation is much to be desired in order that maximum value may be obtained from comparisons of statements of successive years. New additions and omissions, if any, of consolidating units are noted on published statements, and their general effect on the total indicated. When subsidiaries are not included in the consolidated group, their separate financial statements, wherever they reflect material amounts, should accompany the consolidated statements, individually or in group form; see *combined financial statement*.

Separately published financial statements of unconsolidated subsidiaries supplementary to consolidated statements reveal in their headings the name of the controlling company and the equity owned by it.

For policies concerning items of individual statements included or omitted, see *intercompany elimination*.

consolidation surplus = *surplus from consolidation*.

constant A quantity that enters as a fixed element in the structure of an *equation* or other mathematical expression. Constants may be general and denoted symbolically by the first letters of the alphabet ($a, b, c, \ldots$), in which case they are sometimes called *parameters*, or they may by expressed as particular values, such as 1, 1/2, -10, and so on. Such "general" and "particular constants" are further distinguished from "universal constants" such as $\pi = 3.1415 \ldots$ or $e = 2.7182 \ldots$, which have the same value in every expression. See e and π; see *variable*.

constant cost = *fixed cost*.

constant dollar accounting See *general price level accounting*.

constituent company A company which is one of a group of affiliated, merged, or consolidated corporations.

constraint A limiting or boundary condition. Example: $L = 10$, the total number of labor hours available, limits production to at most $x = 5$ units when 2 labor hours per unit are required, and $2x \leq 10$ expresses the constraint on production. See *inequality*.

construction-type contracts Contracts covering construction of a specific project. Alternative accounting methods available for contractors to record costs and recognize profits or losses of construction-type contracts extending beyond one accounting period include the *completed contract method* and the *percentage-of-completion method*.

constructive dividend (federal income taxes) Payment to a stockholder construed to be a dividend because the payment is not for its stated purpose. For example, salary paid to a shareholder-employee may not be fully deductible to the corporation as compensation expense and the portion deemed excessive treated as a dividend distribution of *earnings and profits*. If a bona fide debtor-creditor relationship is not clearly established when a corporation loans money to a shareholder, it may be reclassified as a dividend distribution. Such issues usually only arise in *closely held corporations*. See *closed corporation*.

constructive receipt (of income) (federal income taxes) 1. The legal fiction whereby an item is considered to be the income of an individual on the cash basis, even though not actually received by him or her, because unconditionally available to him or her; as, matured but unclipped bond coupons; salary due a corporate official and credited to his or her account on the books of the corporation.
2. Income of one person not received by that person but paid to another; as, an exchange of items of property between persons recorded or reported at less than their fair market value; the payment of rent by a lessee to a person other than the lessor.

constructive retirement Treatment of an outstanding security as if it had been retired or repurchased at a given date and price, usually employed in the preparation of *consolidated financial statements* when one affiliate owns some or all of the outstanding debt of another affiliate. See *intercompany elimination*.

For *consolidation* purposes, the affiliates are viewed as a single *economic entity* and the debt is assumed to have been retired when it was acquired by the affiliate. This treatment is also appropriate to eliminate from consolidation a subsidiary's preferred stock that is owned by the parent firm, and any parent company stock owned by a subsidiary.

consular invoice = *customs invoice*.

consume 1. To move into production with loss of identity, as to transfer raw material to work in process; = *absorb*.
2. To destroy or diminish the utility of; said of supplies used in maintenance or of fixed assets subject to depreciation.

consumed cost 1. Any cost the benefits from which have expired or have been lost or destroyed; as the *cost of goods sold*, or of *raw materials* that make up a part of manufactured products sold, or of that portion of the cost of a *fixed asset* represented in a periodic provision for *depreciation*. Generally, a consumed cost is any cost that has been recognized as an item to be reported in an *income statement*; i.e., ''all'' costs appearing in an income statement are consumed costs and all consumed costs must be so reported.
2. Any cost transferred to a *secondary account* or a *terminal account*.

consumer demand See *demand*.

consumer(s') goods (economics) Goods satisfying human wants; contrasted with *producers' goods*, which are used to facilitate the production of other goods.

consumer sovereignty The concept under a private enterprise system by which consumers' tastes and preferences decide what goods and services will be produced.

consumer price index (CPI) A ratio of weighted prices in two periods with weights fixed in the base period. Published monthly by the U.S. Bureau of Labor Statistics and supposedly representing the change in prices over time of a typical market basket of goods and services purchased by the average consumption unit, an urban family of four with a median income. This typical market basket as determined from surveys undertaken in the base period provides the weights for all prices in the ratios until a new survey establishes a new set of weights.

consumer's risk (statistical quality control) A calculated *probability*, under a given sampling plan, that a lot of any given quality will be accepted by the plan. It is generally stated only at the *lot-tolerance-percent-defective* level or worse; hence the risk of accepting lots of unacceptable quality.

consumption The removal from the *accounts* (7) of a part or all of the cost of an *asset* (either directly or over a period of time through the medium of a *valuation account*) because of use, disposal, or loss. Examples: cleaning supplies used; a worn-out tool discarded; the portion of the total utility of a machine reflected in a provision for *depreciation* which has been added to an account for *accumulated depreciation; merchandise* or *finished goods* sold. —*consume, v.t.*

consumption function A *function* (5) relating expenditures for consumer goods and services to different levels of income. *National income* accounting sometimes uses *gross national product* in place of national income as the independent variable.

consumption taxes 1. A form of indirect taxation, this type of levy is exacted on specific commodities when purchased by a consumer, either separately or (more commonly) incorporated in the price. Examples include sales tax, *value-added tax*, and *excise tax*.
2. Viewed as an alternative to the taxation of income, taxes may be levied on the amount of wealth consumed rather than on the

amount of income received in a given period. The taxable base would be composed of all monetary receipts (including withdrawals from savings and gifts and bequests received) minus additions to investments and gifts made. Proceeds of asset sales would be includible in the tax base, and the amount of the proceeds rolled over into other investments would be deducted. The consumption base tax offers the advantages of simplicity, ease of measurement, equity based on the choice to consume resources, and encouragement of capital formation since neither income nor wealth would be taxed if they were invested and not consumed. An expenditure tax is similar in concept but measures consumption as a summation of expenditures. See *tax; regressive tax*.

Contador público A term used throughout Spanish Latin America to refer to graduates of accounting programs in universities and, in some countries, professional institutes. Holders of this title are regarded as qualified accountants in their respective countries, as there are no professional examinations given outside of the educational institutions.

contango (London Stock Exchange) The interest and other charges paid by a speculator for the delayed acquisition of and payment for stock purchased, pending what he or she hopes will be a rise in its price. See *backwardation*.

context The circumstances, environment, or disclosure out of which a statement emanates and on which a part of its meaning may depend; also, the environment or accompanying circumstances of an action.

contingency 1. A possible future event or condition arising from causes unknown or at present undeterminable. See *contingent liability; reserve for contingencies*.
2. An existing condition, situation, or set of circumstances involving uncertainty about a possible gain (gain contingency) or loss (loss contingency) to an enterprise that will ultimately be resolved when one or more future events occur or fail to occur.

contingency table (statistics) A table constructed for the purpose of analyzing or discovering associations between qualitative characteristics (*attributes*). It is distinguished from a *correlation table* by the fact that use of the latter is restricted to the study of quantitative characteristics (*variables*).

contingent annuity A periodic payment dependent on some contingency, such as the death of a person.

contingent asset An asset the existence, value, or ownership of which depends upon the occurrence or nonoccurrence of a specified event or upon the performance or nonperformance of a specified act; contrast with *contingent liability*, often growing out of such a liability.

contingent charge (or cost or expense) An outlay the incurring of which is dependent on some event or condition; as, interest on income bonds, the accrual of which is to be made only if the gross or net earnings of the business are equal to or exceed an agreed amount.

contingent fund 1. Assets set apart for use in contingencies, usually of a specified character.
2. (municipal and institutional accounting) A portion of available resources reserved for emergency expenditures or authorized transfers upon proper authority to other appropriations.

contingent issues Securities whose distribution is dependent upon future performance in the focus of specified income levels or stock market values. Example: deferred distributions to stockholders of an acquired company based on future performance of the combined company. Under specific conditions, contingent issues are included in the calculation of primary and fully diluted earnings per share. See *complex capital structure*.

contingent liability An obligation, relating to a past transaction or other event or condition, that may arise in consequence, as a future event now deemed possible but not probable. If probable, the obligation is not contingent but real (ordinarily, a current liability), and *recognition* in the accounts is required, notwithstanding that its amount must be estimated in whole or in part. The mere possibility of a future loss, as from a fire, not linked with a past event, does not give rise to a contingent liability.

contingent profit Profit the realization of which is dependent on an uncertain future event or condition.

contingent rentals Increases or decreases in rental payments (usually under a lease agreement) that result from changes occurring in the factors other than the passage of time on which rental payments are based. Examples are rental payments based on the sales of a retail outlet or automobile rental payments based on the mileage driven.

contingent reserve *Retained earnings* appropriated in anticipation of possible future losses or expenses; a *reserve for contingencies*.

contingent transaction A *contingent asset* or *liability*.

continuing account Any *asset* or *liability* (2) account carried over from one fiscal period to another.

continuing appropriation An appropriation which, once established, is automatically renewed without further legislative action until altered or revoked. These types of appropriations are distinguishable from *indeterminate appropriations*.

continuing operations Segments of a business that are expected to remain active parts of an enterprise. Operating results of continuing operations are disclosed separately from results of discontinued operations, if any.

continuity (of accounting) The assumption that in all ordinary situations an *economic unit* (*1*) persists indefinitely: an assumption basic to the preparation of *financial statements*.

continuous audit Any audit the detail work of which is performed continuously or at frequent intervals during the fiscal period, the purpose being to uncover and correct undesirable practices and errors before the end of the year as well as to relieve the auditor's workload thereafter.

continuous budget A *moving projection* of financial operations for a series of weeks, months, or quarters immediately ahead; at the end of each such period the portion of the projection then lapsed is removed and a new projection for a period of similar length is added to the series.

continuous compounding Calculation of compound interest when the *compounding period* is an instant of time so that interest is compounded an infinite number of times in one year. See *interest formulas*.

continuous inventory A process of testing inventories and of maintaining an equality between inventory-item quantities physically determined by count, weight, or measure and those appearing at the same time on perpetual-inventory records. Where the number of items is large, the full time of one or more persons (sometimes an inventory "crew") may be required to make the count, usually at times of low stocks; compare the amount with the book record maintained by the stock- or storekeeper; search for, and correct, where practicable, any observed discrepancy; suggest steps to be taken for the avoidance of future errors; and report the results. The frequency of the count will vary with the relative value per item, strictness of controls over issues, rate of turnover, possibility of alternative overall measures of consumption, as of raw materials such as steel or of purchased parts, by working back from reported factory activity or output, and other factors peculiar to individual plants. A common standard of testing frequency is once yearly. See *perpetual inventory*.

continuous process A method of *production* (2) permitting an uninterrupted flow of material and parts into a processing operation and of completed endproducts out of the operation.

continuous profit planning A planning procedure wherein a periodic profit plan (e.g., annual operating budget) is routinely revised and reprojected (e.g., on a quarterly basis). Such a procedure is typically designed for dynamic situations in which longer-range planning is unrealistic or unreliable.

contra account One of two or more accounts which partially or wholly offset another or other accounts; on financial statements, they may either be merged or appear together. Examples: an account receivable from and an account payable to a single individual; stock subscriptions, a receivable, and capital stock subscribed, a *net-worth* account; a *reserve for depreciation* and the plant and equipment to which it applies. Contra accounts include *absorption accounts*.

contra asset account See *valuation account*.

contract A legally enforceable agreement or promise. A contract normally involves an agreement between two (or more) parties created by an offer by one party and an acceptance by another, although a unilateral promise is also considered to be a contract, broadly defined. While a contract itself has not been considered a transaction and, hence, not recorded in the books of accounts under current accounting practice, it affects the financial position of the enterprise immediately upon its creation, and there seems to be a trend toward immediate recognition of contractual rights and obligations as evidenced by the accounting standards on *capital lease*.

contract authorization (governmental accounting) Permission given in an appropriation act to a governmental agency to enter into contracts or commitments involving expenditures up to a specified amount to be made in periods succeeding that covered by the current appropriation, and to be appropriated for at a subsequent date. The purpose is to avoid showing as appropriated for the current year amounts to be expended in and to benefit subsequent years. In the procurement of heavy electrical equipment, for example, delivery may follow the date of contract by two or more years, thus necessitating advance authority to purchase.

contract price The price or price formula stipulated in a contract of purchase or sale, such as:

1. Firm price: a fixed price not expected to be open to negotiation or adjustment after agreement.

2. Target price: a basis price, subject to adjustment under specified terms, generally restricted to incentive contracts under which it is adjusted by bonus and penalty provisions depending on such factors as the quality and quantity of work performed or the promptness of delivery.

3. Escalation price: the amount to which the contract price may be adjusted as specified contingencies, such as increased labor costs, occur.

4. Cost price: price based on cost, usually including a fixed fee or percentage of cost as a profit element.

5. Futures price: the price at which commodities are currently traded on an organized

commodity exchange for future delivery; the price quoted on the exchange relates to a basis grade, and the agreement to purchase or deliver follows a standard form familiar to the trade. Such prices are largely determined by the relationship between the cash price for immediate delivery (the spot price) and the purchaser's and seller's estimates of market conditions at the time of future delivery.

See *price*.

contra entry An item on one side of an account which offsets fully or in part one or more items on the opposite side of the same account.

contra liability account See *valuation account*.

contributed capital The payments in cash or property made to a corporation by its stockholders (a) in exchange for capital stock, (b) in response to an assessment on the capital stock, or (c) as a gift; *paid-in capital*; often, though not necessarily, equal to capital stock and paid-in surplus. In British usage, the term is applied to the par value of the capital stock outstanding, thus including discounts and excluding premiums; see *capital reserves*.

contributed surplus = *paid-in surplus*.

contribution 1. (federal income taxes) A gift to a charitable, religious, educational, or other institution as defined in Section 170 of the *Internal Revenue Code*. Corporations may deduct contributions up to 5% of taxable income with any excess carried forward 5 years. Individual's cash contributions to public charities are deductible up to 50% of adjusted gross income, with any excess carried forward 5 years. Individual contributions of various types of property and contributions to most private foundations are subject to more stringent limitations.

2. The payment by a person of a portion of a loss shared with others; specifically (in-

surance) an insurer's pro rata share of a loss where the insured has contracted against the same risk with two or more insurers.

3. = *stockholders' contributions*.

4. Any payment by a person to a corporation representing the purchase of capital stock, a gift, or an *assessment* (5).

5. = *benefit*.

6. See *contribution theory*.

contribution costing The application of *contribution theory* to the disposition of production costs; contrast with *full absorption costing*.

contribution margin The profit margin measured by the net difference between *sales revenue* and total *variable costs*. It provides the margin from which other costs can be recovered and profits earned. See *breakeven point* formulas. It is also an important determinant of *operating leverage*. See also *marginal income*.

contributions in aid of construction Amounts paid by customers to a regulated utility for construction undertaken at the request of the customers. Accounting treatments depend on whether the utility is regulated by the Federal Energy Regulatory Commission, or by a state commission which follows the recommendations of the National Association of Regulatory Utility Commissioners.

contribution theory The doctrine that sales of commodities or services supply a source of funds, often varying, from which production overhead and other costs are paid. Under systems of direct costing, *marginal income*—the excess of selling price over *direct costs*—is the measure of such contribution. Also involved is the notion that the determination of the amount by which the selling price is to exceed direct costs is a responsibility of top management, some products often being required to provide a greater *marginal income* in proportion to selling price than others. The practical effect of this concept is the elimination of any formal distribution of *indirect costs* and the recognition of the bulk of factory overhead as a joint cost, as is administrative overhead.

contributory pension plan A *pension plan* in which employees bear part of the cost.

control 1. Ability to influence behavior in desired amounts and directions, with the degree of conformance providing a measure of the state of control. For auditing and accounting, control may be further formalized as the process by which the *activities* of an *organization* are conformed to a desired plan of action and the plan is conformed to the organization's activities. The *concept* of control then embraces the following elements:

(a) The basic wish, need, directive, or statute, and the *authority* and capacity for its exercise;

(b) A common understanding of the purpose and consequence of the ends sought;

(c) A plan of organization and action;

(d) *Organizational units*, each with delegated, delimited authority;

(e) The assumption of *responsibility* by such units for the exercise of the authority delegated to them;

(f) Identification of the activities to be carried on within each organizational unit;

(g) *Policies* governing *operation, internal control*, including *internal audit*, and *reporting*;

(h) Operable *standards of performance* and related *standards of comparison*;

(i) Provision for continuing views by superior authority of the flow of *performance* through *internal reporting* (*feedbacks*) and direct observations, followed by *judgments* leading to action on proposed changes in purpose, scope, and procedures; and

(j) Periodic professional surveys, including *external audits* and *internal audits* and *management reviews* of the objectives of the organization, the accomplishments reflected in its activities, *appraisals* of the worth and acceptance of its *endproducts*, and the relevance of its current strategic plans and operating performance, along with suggestions for their improvement, modification, curtailment, or possible elimination.

2. Any one or more of the foregoing elements. See *control concept (of accounting)*.

3. (statistical quality control) The state of equilibrium reached when deviations from a given norm (such as the process average) are only random in character and are otherwise without assignable cause.

4. The relation whereby one or more corporations or other persons possess the power to choose at least a majority of the members of the board of directors of another corporation. The power is usually a direct one, evidenced by the ownership of a majority of the other's outstanding shares of voting capital stock, but an equally effective control may be of an indirect type: the possession of less than half of the voting stock (e.g., 20%) may be sufficient to insure the domination of meetings of stockholders, provided there exists, to the necessary degree, any one or more of the following conditions: (a) continued ability to obtain proxies from other stockholders; (b) ownership of voting stock by subsidiaries, officers, employees, nominees, or other persons having subordinated interests; (c) inactivity of passive stockholders who do not attend stockholders' meetings and do not give proxies; and (d) possession of a lease or other contract which carries with it the virtual ownership or exclusive use of assets without any formal ownership of capital stock. Occasionally instances are found where, although a majority ownership of capital stock exists, there is no domination of the other company's policies and hence no effective control, as where ownership is temporary, where a strong, self-sufficient management is in the

saddle, or where the other company is an obligor under a lease or contract of the type mentioned in the preceding sentence. Under regulations of the U.S. *Securities and Exchange Commission,* control "means the possession, direct or indirect, of the power to direct or cause the direction of the management and policies of a person whether through the ownership of voting securities, by contract, or otherwise." See *community of interest.*

5. = *internal control.*

control (or controlling) account An account containing primarily totals of one or more types of transactions the detail of which appears in a subsidiary ledger or its equivalent. Its balance equals the sum of the balances of the detail accounts.

control chart (statistical quality control) A diagram based on systematic inspection data and used to discriminate between random and nonrandom (assignable) causes of product or process variation as a means of analyzing performance and controlling quality; a *scatter diagram*, usually in the form of a *time series*, containing average and control lines for judging process performance and determining when corrective action should be taken. The importance of the methodologies followed in long-established practices of maintaining quality in production lies in the possibility of applying these practices to management controls generally.

Control charts may be constructed for data in the form of either *attributes* or *variables*. Attribute data arise from an inspection procedure that merely classifies or counts occurrences of some observable characteristic, such as the number (or percent) of defectives in a group of items or the number of defects on a unit of product; variables data arise from an inspection procedure that actually measures some characteristic of the product, such as a dimension. The most widely used control charts for variables are: (a) a chart for

averages, known as an $\overline{X}$ (*X*-bar) chart, and (b) a chart for dispersion, known as an $\overline{R}$ (*R*-bar or range) or σ (sigma) chart, depending on whether the *range* or *standard deviation* is used to measure dispersion.

As noted under *statistical quality control*, these techniques have wide areas of application, including such areas as cost, credit, and inventory control. Problems in sales and budgetary controls have also been successfully approached with these techniques and they have also been applied to standard-cost and estimated-cost control.

control concept (of accounting) The function of accounting in influencing behavior, e.g., in securing conformance between plans and actions. Example: the use of standard-to-actual cost comparisons with red and black variances calling attention to possible inadequacies in either or both. The planned (standard) and the actual cost serve as mutual *controls*. In other contexts, they may be separated as when, for instance, a standard cost is used to estimate prices for a preceding contract but actual costs are subsequently submitted to different controls such as a *budget*, which uses estimates other than the *standard costs* used for the contract.

controllability principle 1. The principle that a manager should be judged only on the performance of items subject to the manager's *control*.

2. A criterion of accounting system and report design which incorporates this principle, as in *activity accounting*.

controllable cost 1. Cost that varies with volume, efficiency, choice of alternatives, and management determinations generally; *variable cost*.

2. Any cost which may be directly regulated at a particular level of management authority.

controllable variables Elements which are subject to planning and discretionary manipulation by an organization's management. Controllability of a variable is both role-dependent and time-dependent. For example, if authority for leasing decisions is vested at the divisional level, the cost of leasing equipment is "controllable" by the division manager, but not by subordinates. Similarly, the leasing cost may be controllable prior to a contract commitment but not during the contract period.

controlled corporation (federal income taxes) The concept of control is used in the *Internal Revenue Code* to structure two types of corporate situations. The first covers "multiple corporations" which form a controlled group—deemed an "affiliated group" or "parent subsidiary group"—when one corporation controls one or more other corporations by meeting certain stock ownership tests. The second form of control in corporate situations is associated with ownership by a small number of shareholders. Two or more corporations which are owned by a common set of five or fewer persons are considered a "brother-sister group." A single corporation controlled by a small number of shareholders is also termed a "closely held" corporation. There is usually a stock ownership test with attribution of constructive ownership determined under the appropriate section of the Internal Revenue Code (e.g., Sections 318, 544, 1563).

controlled foreign corporation (CFC) A foreign corporation of which more than 50% of the total combined voting power of all classes of voting stock is owned by U.S. shareholders. The Internal Revenue Service taxes certain undistributed income of controlled foreign corporations. See Section 957(a) of the *Internal Revenue Code*.

controller An accountant in charge whose technical skills and professional interests are confined to a single organization or organizational group, and who has been given that ti-

tle by the management or directors of the organizations. The title is commonly in use in corporate enterprise, whether privately or publicly owned, and in governmental and other organizations.

Other names sometimes given to persons exercising the functions of a controller are *auditor*, chief accountant, or simply *accountant*. See *comptroller*.

Controller, The See *accounting journals* (*Financial Executive*).

Controllers Institute of America See *Financial Executives Institute*.

controlling account See *control account*.

controlling company A corporation owning or controlling one or more other corporations; it may be either a *holding company* or a *parent company*.

controlling-company accounting The method followed by a holding or parent company in recording its investment in and transactions with a subsidiary. It is usual to find an investment account in which are maintained the cost of the owned shares of the subsidiary, a current account for various types of everyday intercompany transactions, and occasionally an asset account for "profits accrued."

In general, no practical benefits are derived from accruing profit and loss from subsidiaries on the books of the controlling company; reserves for losses on investments in subsidiaries are preferably based on estimates of ultimate realization rather than on amounts of operating losses. However, accountants differ on this question. Some prefer to follow the conservative practice of adjusting for operating losses but not for profits, or for operating losses in excess of operating profits since the date of acquisition, the adjustment taking the form of a valuation reserve against the investment. This practice is unobjectionable if the addition to the reserve is a reasonable increase in the expected loss from realization. There is also support for the practice, occasionally encountered, of adjusting the investment account of the controlling company so that it will always be in agreement with its equity in the subsidiary's net worth.

A cash or stock dividend of a subsidiary effected through a credit to an account with the controlling company on the subsidiary's books and reflected as income in the amount on the books of the controlling company and as a debit to a corresponding account with the subsidiary is a financial device usually preferred over the practice of taking up the subsidiary's profit merely as an accrual. An accrual reflects only a potential right to the profit; as a dividend, the same amount becomes a creditor's equity in the subsidiary's assets.

If paid from earnings prior to the date of acquisition, dividends of subsidiaries are treated as liquidation dividends and credited to the investment account or to a valuation account applicable to the investment; should such dividends exceed the investment cost, the excess may be credited to an "acquired surplus" account in order to distinguish it from other sources of accumulated earnings.

Sales by a controlling company of subsidiary shares are best treated in the ordinary manner: their cost is average cost; the profit or loss is the difference between selling price and the average cost. On *consolidated statements* the effect is a reduction of a portion of the consolidated excess or surplus, if any, and a gain or loss differing from the controlling company's by the amount of the applicable undistributed profit or accumulated loss since the date of acquisition. See *consolidation policy*.

controlling interest (in a corporation) Any person, group of persons, or corporation(s) possessing the power to influence the actions of a *corporation*. See *controlling company*.

control model See *planning model*. A model designed to enhance *control* of activities.

control total A summation amount used to determine whether all detailed data put into a system were processed. Generally, the purpose of a control total is to make certain that no data are lost in handling or processing, but in some cases it is used to verify that the dollar amount is correct.

convention A statement or rule of practice which, by common consent, express or implied, is employed in the solution of a given class of problems or which guides behavior in a certain kind of situation. A convention, as distinct from an *axiom*, may be said to exist when it is known that an alternative, equally logical rule or procedure is available but is not used because of considerations of habit, cost, time, or convenience. Thus, the convention of omitting the characteristic in the construction of *logarithm* tables increases their convenience and saves time and cost in their compilation and publication. Placing debits on the left and credits on the right of an account supplies another example. The adoption of a particular convention may be a historical accident, but once adopted, a convention acquires value as a means of communication and cooperation. Thus, many other signs were employed for arithmetic operations when "+" and "−" were introduced by Widman in 1489; the latter were not commonly accepted until the 17th century, but they became a part of the mathematician's stock in trade because they conveyed meaning without elaborate explanations or translations.

Ultimately, the choice of axioms must be regarded as conventional. A particular set of axioms may be regarded as a set of conventions in that alternative systems can be devised in which what are now theorems are used as the starting point, and what are now axioms become theorems. Conventionality need not, however, impair the analytical usefulness of axioms; it merely implies that if an unconventional system is demonstrated to possess greater analytical power, fecundity, or simplicity, the only obstacle to its adoption is the accumulated habits of the professional community.

Convention dictates many of the activities and observances of the public accountant in such diverse matters as measures of *materiality*, the style and content of *financial statements*, the features built into *auditors, reports*, and, in general, the forms of communication an auditor follows with staff, clients, and the world at large. Modified conventions emerge in the world of accounting from time to time; they are generally ascribable to the growth of *public interest*.

conversion 1. The replacement of a holding of one class of corporate *security* with that of another class; e.g., the surrender, at the option of the owner, of one or more face-value units of long-term indebtedness or par-value units of preferred stock in exchange for a fixed number of shares of common stock; a feature often accompanying the financing of an expanding enterprise, designed to provide for an investor present security and a prospect of future gain through sharing in profits at a rate in excess of the interest return, or through an increase in the market price of the common stock beyond the agreed level of exchange. To the corporation, advantages lie in the possibility of relief from accumulating funds for repayment of the obligation and in the reduction of fixed costs; a full conversion would also lift the operating and financial restrictions that are often attached by underwriters to loan agreements; see *restricted retained earnings*.

2. The substitution of one valuation for another; as, the adjustment of *historical cost* for inflated prices or its replacement by *current costs*; e.g., in the preparation of information supplementing conventionally based financial statements in reports to stockholders.

convert 1. To substitute one form of property for another, as by sale or exchange. Examples: the sale of goods for a promise to pay; the liquidation of such a promise by the payment of cash; the exchange of a bond of an original issue for one of a related refunding issue.

2. = *compound*.

3. To misappropriate, as the funds of others for one's own use.

4. To process raw material, thereby giving it a new form or utility.

—*conversion, n.*

convertible bond A *bond* that under the terms of the bond indenture may be exchanged, at the option of the holder, and subject to specified limitations of time, rate of exchange, and other conditions, for common stock or another security of the issuer; the exchange may involve a contribution of an additional amount of cash by the investor. See *bond*.

convertible debt *Convertible bonds* or other indebtedness that may be voluntarily exchanged for the corporation's capital stock. See *convertible bond* and *convertible securities*.

convertible preferred stock Preferred stock that may be exchanged for common stock (or other security) of an issuer at the option of the holder but subject to limitations of time, rate of exchange, and other conditions stated in the contract; occasionally the exchange also may involve an additional contribution of cash by the investor-holder. See *convertible securities; preferred capital stock*.

convertible securities *Securities* which may be voluntarily exchanged for corporate capital stock during a designated conversion period at a specified exchange ratio; examples are convertible bonds and convertible preferred stock. Such securities are assumed to be converted at the start of the period or when issued, whichever is later, in computing *primary earnings per share* (if the convertible security is a common stock equivalent) and *fully diluted earnings per share* (if the convertible security is a common stock equivalent or if its assumed conversion is dilutive).

cooperative A form of organization, permitted under state laws, its purpose being to gain for producers or consumers the profits or savings which would otherwise accrue to middlemen. Its capital is contributed by its stockholders or members, who appoint a general manager; where its net income is periodically distributed to them in proportion to individual purchases or other transactions rather than in proportion to their investments, the cooperative is not subject to federal income tax. Buyers' and sellers' cooperatives, particularly in farm communities, have been in existence for many years; there are also cooperatives that distribute power; others refine and sell at retail petroleum products; still others can and market fruits and vegetables; and so on. The "Rochdale principles" under most or all of which a cooperative operates are: (a) membership open to any individual paying in a nominal amount for a single share; (b) one vote per member present at a meeting, no proxies being allowed; (c) a cash basis for sales to members and others; (d) a moderate interest return per share; (e) net income returned to members as above mentioned; (f) neutrality on religious and political issues; (g) education of members in cooperative principles and benefits.

cooperative bank See *savings-and-loan association*.

coordinate 1. *v.t.* To bring together or fashion to common purposes; to synchronize.
2. *adj.* Of equal rank, importance, or authority.

3. *n.* (mathematics) Any of two or more magnitudes that determine the location of a point. See *abscissa; variable*.

coordinate system Any method of locating or designating points in space by reference to axes. If scaled, the axes start at a common point called the "origin," and are so oriented and scaled that points can be related to them. The number of axes necessary to locate every point uniquely is called the "dimension" of the system. Two axes are required to locate each point on a plane. Three axes would be required to locate every point between the covers of this book. The axes may be at right angles, with the same scale on each, thus conforming to a *Cartesian coordinate system*. Other coordinate systems may employ obliquely tilted axes and different scales.

co-partner = *partner*. See *partnership*.

copyright The exclusive right conveyed by federal statute to reproduce and sell a book, pamphlet, drawing, design, formula, musical composition, map, photograph, or other creation, and to forbid the publication of excerpts, digests, or other imitations thereof. An account for copyrights seldom appears, since the cost of procuring a U.S. or international copyright is nominal and is usually absorbed at once as an operating expense. An exception occurs when a copyright, already established, is purchased, as by one publisher from another; here the cost is customarily spread over a relatively short period of time, such as 2 or 3 years, in accordance with estimates of revenue-producing life, or is expensed at once. A copyright extends over a 28-year period, with a renewal privilege thereafter for a similar period. See *intangible; balance sheet*.

corollary cost A cost arising from and not anticipated by the incurrence of another cost nor necessarily benefiting the purpose of the other cost.

corporate action A policy decision made by or receiving the approval of the stockholders or the board of directors of a corporation, as contrasted with *administrative action*, or decision of management; the distinction between the two fields of action is dependent on the requirements of corporate law, the provisions of bylaws of the corporation, and local or general custom. Thus, a recapitalization, including a *quasi-reorganization*, requires the approval of stockholders under the laws of most states; the appointment of a controller can be a prerogative of the board of directors imposed on it by the bylaws; a proposal to alter a product line, or to sell a major item of equipment, might be referred, by custom within the corporation, to the board of directors for decision. The term may also be applied to decisions of management, where management has assumed, or has been given by the board of directors, sometimes tacitly, broad powers of policy making. The professional accountant is frequently in the position of advising clients on matters requiring corporate action on either of these levels. See *administrative action; policy; administration*.

corporate equity Any right or claim to corporate assets subordinate to general creditors, as the equities of bondholders and stockholders. See *stockholders' equity*.

corporate joint venture A corporation created by two or more businesses which is to be terminated once the specified purposes have been served.

corporate-level controls *Internal controls* which cut across particular systems and are designed to assure that systems-wide controls are operating as intended. Corporate-level controls include such things as internal audit, budgeting and reporting systems, and standardized procedural manuals.

Corporate Report, The A discussion paper issued in 1975 by the Accounting Standards Steering Committee (today known as the *Accounting Standards Committee*) in the United Kingdom. The committee recommended an expansion of corporate disclosures, including a statement of *value added* and a statement of future prospects, as part of a comprehensive corporate report with expanded accountability to audiences other than management and investors.

corporate social report A *report* of activities by a corporation in one or more areas of *social concern*. Practice is not yet standardized as is the case for corporate financial reports for use by investors and others in the financial community. Hence, a corporate social report may be comprehensive in character or it may be directed only to selected topics where activities are reported without consideration for the information requirements of audiences with differing interests. An example of the latter is provided by the following exhibit from the report of one corporation (stated in $000):

	OSHA	Environment	Total
19-2	$ 543	$ 751	$1,294
19-3	350	525	875
19-4*	565	935	1,500
	$1,458	$2,211	$3,669

*Projected.

Even though accompanied by verbal interpretations, this summary remains inadequate not only in scope but also in its failure to go beyond the dollar expenditure in these programs. Compare it, for instance, with the integrated format for a statement like the one shown on page 130. All data are tied into the statement of revenues and expenses on the left. The dollar dimensions both public and private on the left, as represented by the statements of revenue and expenses and funds flow, followed by the *value-added*

Economic Environment		Physical Environment			Social Environment		
Private	Public	Air	Water	Other	Employment		Total
					Black	Women	
Funds flow	Value added to GNP	Particulate emissions	Acid discharge	Soil removal and restoration	(% of total)	(% of total)	Man- and woman-years
Revenues and expenses ($)	($)	(tons)	(gal)	(acre feet)	($)	($)	($)

statement, are then augmented by reports of related activities for the physical and social environments stated in units that are intended to be immediately meaningful for persons interested in these aspects of corporate activities.

Of course the articulated statement should be accompanied by more detailed exhibits and verbal interpretations along with presentations for past trends and projected future activities. One point that might be observed is that all of the above represent flow activities such as man- and woman-years employed during the period (along with percentages for blacks and women) and are directly related to the statement of revenues and expenses by reference to accounts such as cost of goods manufactured or sold. Balance-sheet categories are reported only in dollar denominations, as usual, since changes in the definitions of assets and equities are not contemplated in this form of corporate social report.

corporate strategy 1. An overall corporate plan used to guide or *control* all other plans. See *strategy* (2). Example: An R&D plan must conform to a corporation's overall strategy for moving from government military contracts which are presently predominant in its sales.

2. A corporate-wide plan for some function such as a corporate-wide sales strategy.

corporation A legal entity operating under a grant of authority from a state or other political authority in the form of articles of incorporation or a charter. In the United States, each of the states, territories, and possessions has its own general- or business-corporation act. The basic attributes of the corporation are: (a) an exclusive name, in which it can hold property, contract, and sue or be sued; (b) continued existence within the limits established by its articles of incorporation, independent of that of any of its stockholders or members; (c) paid-in capital represented by transferable shares; (d) limited liability, in that its stockholders or members, except in special cases, are not liable for its debts and obligations beyond the amount of full-paid capital stock; and (e) overall control vested in the directors, whose authority is subject to restrictions imposed by law, the articles of incorporation, the bylaws, and the stockholders or members who appoint them.

A corporation with a single shareholder is possible. Under federal revenue acts, the term includes associations, joint-stock companies, and certain types of limited partnerships.

corpus The principal or capital of an estate, fund, or trust, as distinguished from the income or proceeds. See *trust; estate accounting.*

correlation See *coefficient* (2c).

correlation table A frequency table designed to assist in determination of the relations, if any, between variables. It differs from a *contingency table* in that the latter is concerned with *attributes*, while the correlation table is concerned with *variables* or quantitative classifications. In a correlation table, the order of rows and columns is determined by the values of the variables, whereas in a contingency table, the order of the rows and columns is arbitrary.

corroborating evidence *Evidence* of secondary importance which is obtained to support other evidence upon which the auditor is placing primary reliance. See *evidence* and *generally accepted auditing standards.*

cost *n.* 1. An *expenditure* or outlay of cash, other property, capital stock, or services, or the incurring of a liability therefor, identified with goods or services acquired or with any loss incurred, and measured by the amount of cash paid or payable or the market value of other property, capital stock, or services given in exchange or, in other situations, any commonly accepted basis of valuation. Implicit in the concept of cost is the *accrual basis* of accounting. See *cost basis; accounting valuation; barter*.

2. Hence, the object of any such expenditure or outlay; e.g., direct labor in the expression "direct-labor cost."

3. = *residual cost*; thus, an inventory, or inventory item, priced at the lower of cost or market, is said to be valued at cost, the inference being that, where market price is the basis, a portion of cost equal in amount to the market price is retained in the inventory account, the balance of cost being absorbed as an expense in the year the price fell.

4. (economics) Payments or commitments for factors of production, and to suppliers of commodities or services, the conditions of which, if modified, will alter the relative quantity or rate at which the supplies of factors, products, or services are forthcoming. Costs, as distinct from *profits*, are known, with certainty, in advance; as distinct from rents, they represent payments, for a given time and place, necessary to obtain the benefit of productive services at a specified rate or volume. That is, rents are payments or commitments, the terms of which if altered will not alter the total supply of factors or products that will be forthcoming.

Expenditures are classified in accounting records and reported for management use by functions (e.g., manufacturing, selling, and financing); by organizational units or departments of a business; by product lines; or by location of operations; or in other ways suited to the operations of a particular enterprise.

Where "cost" appears in published financial statements without a qualifying adjective or phrase—as in "the lower of cost or market"—it means actual "delivered cost" or the same *standard, average*, or other commonly accepted approximation of actual cost

that has been consistently followed both in the past and in the present period. Any recent change (as within two years) in accumulations of cost or in cost reporting calls for a footnote explaining the change and, if material, its effect on current income determination.

Used in valuation and rate problems of public utilities, "cost" has a restricted meaning as the result of court decisions and rulings of regulatory commissions of the several states and the federal government. See *original cost* (2); *cost absorption* (2).

v.t. To determine the cost of something.

cost absorption 1. The expensing of an added cost, such as freight, not passed on to a customer, replacement or repair under a *guarantee* of quality or period of performance.

2. The recognition of an expenditure as an operating cost or expense, either at the time incurred and first given expression to in the accounts, or at a subsequent point of time; at the end of the period in which it is designated as an expense it is transferred with other like items to a *profit-and-loss* or other *clearing account*, and thence to *retained earnings* (= earned surplus). An income statement may be regarded as reflecting the costs absorbed during the period to which it relates. The cost-absorption process involves the recognition of expense under the following conditions:

(a) Correspondence with physical movement. The bulk of transactions in most business enterprises fall into this category, as where merchandise is bought and sold within the same year. A sale is made, and the cost of the merchandise sold is transferred from an asset status to one of expense; the whole of the expense thus recognized in an accounting period is the summation of the costs customarily associated with individual units sold. In a merchandising concern, the unit cost is invoice cost plus minor items, such as freight, sometimes added to invoice cost; in a manufacturing enterprise, material, labor, and overhead would in most instances be involved. But in both cases, the unit cost attaches equally in amount to each item sold; and on hand, out of the same lot, or produced in the same batch. See, however, (c) below.

(b) Service or benefit yielded. Fixed assets supply a stream of services the costs of which are measured by provisions for depreciation; that is, the cost of fixed assets is divided into two parts—one representing services yielded or otherwise lost to the business, the other, services expected to be yielded to the business in the future—the accounting aim in both cases being to attach an aliquot portion of cost to each unit of service yielded or lost and remaining to be yielded. Again, the annual benefit from a long-term loan is measured by a year's interest expense, the amount of which, on an accrual basis, bears a constant relationship with the principal outstanding. Operating expenses generally come under this head. Accounting seeks here to reach the same objective as in (a) above; that is, to spread costs ratably over units of acquired goods and services and to expense the unit costs thus assigned as the units are consumed.

(c) Most recent costs. *LIFO* methods of *inventory valuation* have the effect of transferring the latest costs of merchandise or raw materials to the physical units of inventory sold or put into production, regardless of when the units were acquired, or whether sales prices have increased or remain unchanged. See *inventory valuation*.

(d) Market declines. By following the basis of the lower of cost or market for inventories, investments, and sometimes other current assets, a portion of their cost may be recognized as an expense before they have been disposed of, in order that the future may bear as an expense an amount no greater than

it would have been if the inventory carried forward had been purchased or manufactured in its entirety on the final date of the accounting period. An exception is generally noted for items purchased and applied to sales contracts in which prices remain unchanged by subsequent market declines.

(e) Period charge. A property tax is a typical item here; it is usually accrued as an expense on the books of account over the year preceding the date it falls due. A "benefit-yielded" basis would be difficult—in most cases, impossible—to apply, since the services received are of an indirect character and are not measurable in their effect on operations. Depreciation and interest may also be regarded as period charges, but the primary effort in accounting for both items is to put them on a service basis. The periodic regularity of their accrual simply denotes a coincidence of the two bases. Another type of period charge is illustrated by selling expenses: in the clothing industry, for example, the selling effort for a succeeding season is usually completed before the end of the fiscal year. At one time, in an effort to follow a service-yield basis, the selling expense relating to this effort was temporarily capitalized; today the prevailing practice is to regard next season's selling expenses already incurred as a period charge, the change being attributable to the conviction that the bulk of selling cost relates as much, perhaps more, to the maintenance of continuous relations with customers and hence is logically a current expense. In recent years some attention has been given to the notion of factory overhead as a period charge, thus giving primary recognition to its components as organizational rather than product costs. Because overhead can be attached to product only by arbitrary methods of allocation, and such attachment can so often be justified only by severely straining the service-yield basis of expense recognition, the movement has gained ground, and doubtless will continue to do so.

(f) Losses. Losses are a type of expense that often stands in a class by itself. Arising in various forms in every business enterprise, losses become an expense the moment they occur, although in certain types of enterprise, such as public utilities, there was at one time a tendency to carry forward any major loss for gradual amortization over succeeding periods, thereby softening its impact against income from ratepayers. Distinction is sometimes drawn between ordinary and extraordinary losses, current expense and adjustments of past periods, and recurring and nonrecurring costs, some accountants regarding the one as expense that should appear in the current income statement, the other as a surplus charge. An alternative practice is to make such a distinction only for purposes of classification within an income statement, the more important items in any of the indicated categories appearing under *income deduction*.

(g) Minor asset purchases. New equipment or replacements, the cost of which does not exceed a stated limit, may be classified as an expense when given expression on the records. In some business concerns, the limit is $50 or $100; in larger companies, it may be $1,000 or even more. Similarly treated are various types of improvements, office supplies, and bookkeeping forms, a single purchase often yielding benefits extending beyond the current year. Nevertheless, in the interests of simplicity and savings in inventorying and recordkeeping, minor items may be expensed immediately; accountants generally approve such policies provided that the cumulative effect at any one moment of time has no important relation to total assets, and provided that the same policy is followed over the years. The quantitative effect on net income is, of course, much less than the effect on assets, since it must be measured by the difference between this year's total and last year's total of such items.

cost accountant One skilled in cost accounting.

cost accounting That branch of accounting dealing with the classification, recording, allocation, summarization, and reporting of current and prospective costs. Included in the field of cost accounting are the design and operation of cost systems and procedures; the methods of determining costs by departments, functions, responsibilities, activities, products, territories, periods, and other units, and of forecasted future costs and standard or desired costs, as well as historical costs; the comparison of costs of different periods, of actual with estimated, budgeted, or standard costs, and of alternative costs; the presentation and interpretation of cost data as an aid to management in controlling current and future operations. See *standard cost; direct costing; inventory valuation; cost absorption*.

cost-accounting standards The basic *principles* and *policies* of cost estimating, cost recognition, cost keeping, cost uses, and cost reporting. See *cost*. Standards for contracting federal agencies have been promulgated by the U.S. *Cost Accounting Standards Board*.

Cost Accounting Standards Board (CASB) An organization created by the U.S. Congress in 1970 (PL 91-379). Discontinued in 1981, its purpose was to establish uniform cost-accounting standards for application to negotiated federal government (defense as well as nondefense) contracts and subcontracts exceeding $100,000.

cost accounts A group of accounts constituting the record of *production, cost, allocation,* and, often, *distribution* activities.

cost allocation The transfer of the cost of a

good or service or the total of a group of such costs from a *primary account* to one or more *secondary accounts*, the purpose being to identify the cost with the product or other *cost objective* to which the goods or services have contributed.

cost basis (of accounting) The valuation basis followed in recording and reporting expenditures. It rests on the assumption that cost or depreciated cost is a valid and workable quantitative measure of economic activity, both for decisions of management and for the conclusions and opinions of those who rely on reports prepared from accounting records. It embraces the following conventions:

1. (a) Cost is net cash outlay; (b) where assets or services are acquired with capital stock, it is the market value of the stock; (c) if there is no such market value, it is the fair market value of the asset or service acquired; and (d) if the asset or service has no fair market value, then it is the depreciated cost of the acquired asset or the best estimate thereof in the hands of the seller. See *unit cost; stock dividend*.

2. Depreciated cost is cost less accumulated (accrued) depreciation or less any other related valuation account representing an absorption of cost: a residual amount, carried forward to the succeeding period and believed to be the source (a) of exchange value or (b) of services at least equal to such value. Besides accumulations of (reserves for) depreciation, valuation accounts may include reserves for bad debts, and reserves having the effect of marking down cost to an amount not in excess of market value, as in the case of reserves covering temporary investments and merchandise inventories. See *inventory reserve*.

3. Depreciated original cost is a standard valuation basis for assets acquired by a public utility whether from affiliated or nonaffiliated predecessor owners. See *original cost* (2).

The term is sometimes employed to indicate the *consumption* elements of the *accrual* method of accounting. See *accrued-expenditures basis*.

cost-benefit analysis The weighing of benefits against costs usually expressed as a ratio of dollar benefits to dollar costs for each of a variety of alternatives to provide a comparable basis of choice among them.

cost center An organizational division, department, or unit of machines or persons (or both) having common supervision; a single machine and its operating force; any *activity* within a manufacturing plant or other operating unit; for each such center, accounts are maintained containing direct costs for which the center's head is accountable. See *activity accounting*.

In a *cost pool*, sometimes distinguished from a cost center, the supervisory factor may not be centralized, and the items of cost are incidental in amount.

By means of an *absorption account* or other device, a center's expense totals in a manufacturing plant may be distributed, on a benefits-received, direction-of-effort, or *judgment* basis to work in process; or where, for better management control or other reason, such expenses are better classified as *terminal accounts*, they may remain undistributed as *period costs* and become an element of *cost of sales*. See *responsibility center*.

cost conscious Evidencing awareness of the need for keeping *costs* under a specified ceiling or at the lowest possible level consistent with the performance of a specified task; endeavoring to reduce cost or to incur a minimum of cost.

cost control The employment of management devices in the performance of any necessary operation so that preestablished objectives of quality, quantity, and time may be attained at the lowest possible outlay for goods and services. Such devices include carefully prepared and reviewed bills of materials; instructions; standards of performance; cost limits on items and operations; and studies, interim reports, and decisions based on these reports.

cost depletion (federal income taxes) See *depletion*. For tax purposes, cost depletion is the minimum deduction allowed for the consumption of a natural resource. For certain types of natural resources, most taxpayers may deduct *percentage depletion* if it is higher than cost depletion.

cost distribution = *cost allocation; overhead*.

cost effectiveness A policy or process is said to be cost effective when the desired results or products cannot be produced at a lower cost.

cost-effectiveness analysis A comparison of costs with measures of *effectiveness* usually in the form of a ratio. Often used in engineering designs, such ratios differ from those in benefit-cost analyses (*q.v.*) in that effectiveness need not be (and ordinarily is not) measured in the same units as cost. Examples: (1) firepower per dollar expended, as in "more bang for a buck"; (2) computation speed per dollar as a method of evaluating computers or computer codes; (3) reliability or maintainability as measured by *probability* of being ready to use as needed (reliability) or *probability* of being returned to use in a stipulated time (maintainability) relative to the cost of securing these properties.

cost finding Determination of the cost of an operation or product by allocation of *direct costs* and proration of some or all *indirect costs*; often synonymous with *absorption costing*. Cost finding often involves assumptions as to methods of parceling out *common costs* that vary materially as between the individuals who make them. The questioning of such assumptions may lead to the adoption of *direct-costing* methods.

cost flow The movement, within one or more economic units, of a *cost* or group of costs, through a series of *functions (2)* with which it has been identified. Thus, in a manufacturing unit, a particular cost and its *object* may be traced through planning, programming, requisition, purchase, receipt, stores, processing, product, inventory, sales, and collection.

cost-flow concept (of accounting) The association of costs with functions, productive processes, endproducts, and other operational objectives, by direct identification of constituent materials and services, or, in the case of *overhead*, by any of a variety of *allocation* methods based on value judgments, administrative fiat, or established convention: essentially a cycling concept beginning, for example, with planning and ending with cash; see *cost flow; cash-flow statement*.

cost fraction 1. The cost identified with a unit of operation or production, as by dividing total direct costs by the number of units of operation or production.
2. Any portion of the outlay for an asset or expense; as, the cost fraction of an asset recovered through cumulating depreciation, or of an expense that has been prorated to one of several accounts.

costing The process of ascertaining the cost of activities, processes, products, or services; *cost accounting*.

costing unit = *cost unit*.

cost ledger A subsidiary ledger containing accounts used in computing or summarizing the cost of goods manufactured or of services produced.

cost method 1. (for treasury stock) One of two generally accepted ways of accounting for shares of capital stock that have been reacquired by the issuing company. See *treasury stock method* for the other method, known as the par-value method. In the cost method, the entire amount paid to reacquire the shares is debited to the account, *treasury stock*, and shown in financial statements as a *contra account* to all other items of *stockholders' equity*; also referred to as the one-transaction concept (or method) because the reacquisition and subsequent reissue of the treasury stock is viewed as a "holding" account.

2. (for investments) An accounting for investments in equity securities that maintains the investment account at acquisition cost (or at a lower amount if the investment has been permanently impaired in value) and recognizes related dividends as income. Generally, the method is used for long-term equity investments of less than 20% of an investee's outstanding voting stock.

cost objective The *activity, organizational unit*, intermediate product or service, or ultimate endproduct with which a cost is identified.

cost of capital 1. The annual rate of return of a firm expected (or required) by investors. It is used as a cutoff rate of return in *capital budgeting*. If the *net present value* of the cash flows associated with a project or investment discounted at the cost of capital is positive, the acceptance of the project will result in an increase in the value of the firm to the investors, provided that the *risk* of the project is the same as the risk of the firm.

The returns expected (or required) by a firm's investors are usually not directly observable. Past data on the firm's securities or securities of comparable risk classes are then used to secure estimates by means of *capital asset pricing models* to obtain the *weighted average cost of capital* consisting of the average of the annual rates of return expected by holders of the firm's equity (cost of equity capital) and fixed-income securities (cost of debt capital), each weighted by their respective values.

2. For a new project; it is the rate of return required to leave the market price of the firm's stock unchanged. Deviations in project *risks* may raise the required rate, especially if the investment is substantial. See *risk; portfolio; risk analysis*.

cost of debt See *cost of capital*.

cost of equity See *cost of capital*.

cost of goods manufactured The *cost* of all goods whose production was completed during the period. This includes units started in a prior period and completed in the current period. All costs associated with these units including the work-in-process costs accumulated in prior periods are included.

cost of goods manufactured statement A statement which systematically portrays the particulars of cost of goods manufactured. These particulars usually include the cost of materials used plus the cost of labor incurred during the period as well as the overhead applied to production during the period with the resulting amounts adjusted to reflect an increase or decrease of work in process during the period.

cost of goods purchased The purchase price of goods bought, plus the cost of storage, transportation, and delivery to the point where they are to be used, and other costs pertaining to their procurement and receipt.

cost of goods sold *Cost of sales (2)*. It consists of the following elements: *cost of goods manufactured* plus finished goods inventory at beginning of the period minus finished goods inventory at the end of the period.

cost of preferred stock (1) Purchase price or price received by a corporation for its preferred stock. (2) Annual rate of return expected or required by holders of preferred stock in a firm. See *cost of capital*.

cost of production Expense incurred in and allocated to a manufacturing operation: the cost of materials, labor, and often overhead charged to work in process.

cost of reproduction The estimated present cost of replacing existing property as it was when new.

cost of sales 1. (retail) (a) The total cost of goods sold during a given accounting period, determined by ascertaining for each item of sale the invoice and such other costs pertaining to the item as may have been included in the *cost of goods purchased*. (b) The cost of goods purchased adjusted by the *inventory variation*.
2. (manufacturing) The *cost of production* of finished goods sold. In some instances overhead, especially fixed items of overhead, is excluded; rarely, certain selling and administrative expenses are included.
Cost *variances (2)* arising from *standard-cost* valuations of work in process and finished stock may also be included in toto.

cost-or-less principle A principle under which the cost of a good or service destined eventually to be expensed may under certain well-recognized conditions be written down or eliminated in part. These partly amortized costs may not be restored, notwithstanding enhancement in price or increased value in use. Writedowns of current-asset costs are customary when market or anticipated selling prices have declined; fixed assets are regularly amortized through periodic provisions for *depreciation*. See *accounting principles*.

cost or market, whichever is lower A valuation rule that recognizes impairment of asset values but avoids anticipating gains. The rule typically is applied to individual items or groups of like items such as inventory or marketable securities. In this rule, "cost" refers to historical cost and "market" refers to the current replacement cost by purchase or reproduction. See *inventory valuation; cost-or-less principle*.

cost-plus A term indicating a method of determining the selling price of goods produced or services performed under a contract whereby the cost of the goods or service is increased in the amount of a profit equal to an agreed increment to such cost. Usually the factors entering into the determination of cost (including overhead) under a cost-plus contract are strictly defined and subject to verification by the recipient of the goods or service. The method is often used when costs and other factors cannot be estimated in advance without undue risks to the contracting parties. See *cost-plus pricing*.

cost-plus pricing The practice of determining selling price by adding a profit factor to costs. When employed as an internal-control device, as in the heavy-capital-goods industries, the resulting price is in the nature of a *target price*, which is subject to reduction in the negotiation of sales. See *contract price*. Cost-plus pricing is often employed in arriving at a contract sales price where the supplier wishes to avoid the risks of cost prediction. It is likely to be used in experimental or developmental contracts for the production of new units or in purchase contracts for large machinery units requiring an extended period of production.

Cost-plus pricing may be either of the cost-plus-a-fixed-fee or cost-plus-a-percentage-of-cost-fee variety. The latter type of cost-plus pricing in contracts let by federal agencies is prohibited by law.

cost pool A group of accounts serving, as a group, to express the cost of goods and services allocable to departments, products, or other *cost objectives*. See *overhead; cost center*.

cost price 1. = *cost*.
2. See *contract price*.

cost rate = *overhead rate*: a term sometimes employed to indicate the inclusion of fixed as well as variable overhead costs.

cost records Ledgers, supporting and supported by records, schedules, reports, invoices, vouchers, and other documents evidencing the cost of a project, job, production center, process, operation, product, or service.

cost recovery 1. The recapture of cost through expense recognition; *cost absorption*.
2. See *accelerated cost recovery system*.

cost-reduction programs The employment of management devices in the performance of any necessary operation so that a decrease in cost as compared with past cost or standard cost may be attained. Such devices include the search for cheaper materials, improved methods of production and inspection, and improved standards of quality and timing.

cost saving A reduction of cost brought about by some special act, such as the taking of a cash discount on a purchase, the elimination of a specification involving an unnecessarily narrow tolerance in an article of manufacture, or the adoption of a more efficient method of production or distribution.

cost sheet A statement showing a summation of the elements entering into the cost of a product. Collectively, cost sheets may serve as a subsidiary ledger supporting a *goods-in-process* or *finished-goods* control.

cost standard A predetermined cost estimate, as of a product, with which actual cost performance may be compared. It usually represents an attainable goal and thus serves as a basis for management information and *control*, measurement of *efficiency, inventory valuation*, and reporting.

cost system A system of accounts, often subsidiary to the general ledger, by means of which the cost of products, processes, or services is determined. Cost systems are usually regarded as falling into two broad classes: *job-order* and *process-costing* systems; *estimated costs* or *standard costs* may be a feature of either. See *cost accounting*.

cost-type *adj.* (governmental accounting) Employing the accrual basis of accounting; said of a budget, an accounting system, or a financial or statistical schedule. Inherent in the concept is the recognition of *expense* as contrasted with *expenditure*, the former signifying a good or service consumed and associated with output, the latter a good or service acquired for future use or consumption. The application of the term is often limited to the affairs of noncorporate government organizations.

cost unit The quantity or amount selected as a standard for the measurement of the cost of a given product or operation. Examples: a square yard of pavement; a barrel of flour; a thousand pounds of steel; machine output per hour. The determination of cost per unit facilitates comparison with a standard cost, a past cost, or the cost of a similar unit. See *unit cost*.

cost-utility analysis A term often used interchangeably with *cost-effectiveness analysis* or *cost-benefit analysis*.

cost value *Cost*: a term used to indicate that cost is a value; contrast with *market value* or *scrap value*.

cost-volume-profit relationship The area of interest, within an organization, of management and accountants in observing and controlling the relations between prospective and actual manufacturing costs (both fixed and variable), rates of production, and gross profits. *Breakeven charts* epitomize these relationships at planning and forecasting stages, and various types of comparative cost statements provide information as the basis for action.

coupon rate of interest The annual interest payment for a coupon bond divided by its par or face value; a coupon bond's stated or fixed annual rate of interest as opposed to its *effective rate of interest*.

covariance A measure of the relation between two statistical variables. Usually symbolized σ_{xy} and defined via

$$\sigma_{xy} = E(x - \bar{x})(y - \bar{y})$$
$$= Exy - E\bar{x}E\bar{y},$$

it represents the *expected value* of the product of the deviations of the two *variates*, x and y, about their respective means. It is related to ρ_{xy}, the *correlation coefficient*, by means of the formula

$$\rho_{xy} = \frac{\sigma_{xy}}{\sigma_x \sigma_y},$$

where σ_x and σ_y are the *standard deviations* of x and y, respectively. See *coefficient (2c)*.

coverage 1. The extent or range of subject matter; scope; as, audit coverage; see *scope*.
2. (insurance) The amount of insurance carried against any risk.
3. (statistics) The portion of the universe included in a survey.

coverage ratios A *ratio* that measures a firm's ability to meet its debt charges. The numerator consists of some earnings measure, and the denominator contains the debt charges. See, for example, the *times-interest-earned ratio*.

covering entry 1. The record made in a journal or journals of all the elements of any transaction; the journalization accompanying a transaction.
2. The concealment of a transaction by giving expression to an entry for a fictitious transaction of equal amount.

covering warrant (governmental accounting) A document, issued by the Secretary of the Treasury and countersigned by the Comptroller General, accompanying a deposit of cash receipts within the federal government. A similar document is used by some state and local governmental units.

cover into (governmental accounting) To transfer to: said of receipts and appropriation and fund balances deposited in or relinquished to the U.S. Treasury.

CPA Journal, The See *accounting journals*.

cpm $=$ *critical path method*. See also *critical path accounting*.

CPU See *central processing unit*.

cr Abbreviation for *credit*.

cradle-to-grave test *Walk-through test*.

credit *n.* 1. The ability to buy or borrow in consideration of a promise to pay within a period, sometimes loosely specified, following delivery.
2. The source of a transaction.
3. A bookkeeping entry recording a reduction or elimination of an asset or an expense, or the creation of or addition to a liability or item of net worth or revenue; an entry on the right side of an account; the amount so recorded. Compare with *debit*.
4. The balance of a liability, net-worth, revenue, or valuation account. *v.t.* To record a credit by a bookkeeping entry.

credit agreement An arrangement between a bank and a potential business borrower whereby a *term loan*, often limited by specified applications and other restrictions, may be made as need arises; interest is specified at somewhat above the *prime rate* or other commercial rate; there are varying conditions of repayment or conversion into other obligations. The principal features of such an agreement are required disclosures in annual reports to stockholders.

credit analysis Evaluation of an application for loan, credit line, or credit card. Applications from business firms are usually evaluated through analysis of their financial statements, especially the cash flow and funds statements. In analysis of applications from individuals, financial data on personal assets, liabilities, and income are often combined with demographic data. When a large number of applications for relatively small loans or credit lines are involved, credit analysis is frequently carried out using *discriminant analysis* on *computers*.

credit line An agreement by a bank, usually informal and of indefinite span, to make a loan not to exceed a specified amount, when needed by a customer. Continuance of the line is usually dependent on the customer's maintaining in a commercial account at all times a *compensatory balance* equal to a substantial fraction of the prospective loan and keeping the bank informed of financial condition, operating results, and major operating developments.

credit memorandum A notice to a purchaser that the seller has decreased an amount owing to him or her; the effect is usually the reduction of an invoice previously rendered.

creditor One to whom a debt is owed.

creditors' equity The collective amount of *liabilities* (2) or amounts owing to outsiders other than stockholders.

creditors' ledger A ledger containing accounts with creditors. The total of the accounts which contain mostly credit balances is usually supported by the credit balance of a control account in the general ledger.

credit policy 1. A statement of conditions under which credit is extended by a firm to its customers. Such a policy usually classifies customers on the basis of certain criteria and specifies the amount, the term, and the conditions of credit to each class of customers. 2. In wholesale trade, the policy of allowing a customer to deduct a specified percent of invoice amount if the payment is made within a specified number of days. 3. Organization and distribution of duties in the credit department.

credit rating A measure of eligibility of a borrower to receive short-term credit. Credit reporting bureaus provide information on credit records of individuals, and mercantile

agencies distribute information on the credit-worthiness of business. Moody's, Standard & Poor's, and Fitch Investors Service provide ratings of *commercial paper* and other *money market* instruments. See *bond rating*.

credit sale 1. The delivery of goods, or the performance of a service, accompanied by the receipt of a *promise to pay*. See *sale*. 2. *pl*. A classification of sales made up of such transactions.

credit system A feature of any form of economic organization of society which permits future payments of cash by consumers and other persons in exchange for the present receipt of *goods* or *services*.

credit union A type of *cooperative* having as its purposes the promotion of thrift and the making of small loans to members. Many are federally incorporated, coming under the jurisdiction of and audit by the Federal Deposit Insurance Corporation.

cremation certificate A sworn statement by a trustee or other appointed agent that reacquired and retired securities have been destroyed.

critical path The most time consuming of any of a series of operative stages contributing to a given endproduct; or any stage in which a possible obstruction in performance would delay the programmed time or add to the cost of completing the endproduct. See *critical path method; network; graph*.

critical path accounting A procedure for collecting and dispensing information essential to the management of a project or program where the *critical path method* (cpm) has been instituted; involved are detailed projections of material, labor, and overhead costs by activities and stages, time schedules for beginning and completing each activity, prompt reporting, and close study of results, including the ascertainment of causes of variances. The objectives include the determination of the timing and amounts of financing requirements, tight controls over costs and completion dates, the timely discovery of possible bottlenecks, and the accumulation of experience in similar future operations.

critical path method An alternative name for *PERT* (= *program evaluation review technique*). A method for locating *chains* formed from all of the tasks that enter as active elements into estimates of minimum completion times for a project. See *network; graph.*

crop insurance Insurance against failure of or damage to a crop, the value of the crop being usually predetermined; a frequently insured risk is loss from hail.

cross-check 1. To add horizontally as well as vertically in order to assure the accuracy of totals.
2. To perform one operation, as in auditing, which will have the effect of aiding in determining the accuracy, propriety, or other characteristic of another operation.

cross elasticity of demand An expression showing the relationship or lack thereof between the demands for two commodities in response to a variation in the price of one of them. Letting A and B be the commodities, the cross elasticity of A with respect to B is denoted by η_{BA} and is defined by the quotient derived by dividing $\Delta q_A/q_A$ by $\Delta p_B/p_B$. Here, p_B is the price of B and q_A is the quantity of A while Δp_B and Δq_A are the magnitudes of the changes in p_B and q_A, respectively.

$$\frac{\frac{\Delta q_A}{q_A}}{\frac{\Delta p_B}{p_B}} = \frac{\Delta q_A}{\Delta p_B} \frac{p_B}{q_A} = \eta_{BA}$$

Thus, in the foregoing equation, the numerator is the relative change in the quantity of A bought as a result of the relative change in commodity B's price as portrayed in the denominator. If η_{BA} is close to zero, the prod-

ucts are unrelated; if significantly positive, the products are substitutes; and if significantly negative, the products are complements. See *elasticity.*

crossfooting test An auditing procedure where the mechanical accuracy of a total for a *matrix* is verified by reading both the row and the column totals. Usually, one or more of the columns is also read to test other column totals. See *test; cross-check (1).*

cross-section analysis A comparison effected across different firms at the same point (or period) in time. See *horizontal analysis; analytic review.*

cross-section study Study of the properties of component segments of a complex entity or of the structural relations between the segments of the entity, for some definite time period, e.g., study of the income, expenditure, and savings characteristics of two-person families in the continental United States for some designated annual period; or an analysis of a set of accounts for selected months in order to determine the probable structure of relevant transactions in other periods.

crosswalk table A two-way arrangement which shows both activity costs and the programs to which they are assigned. See Exhibit III under *program planning budgeting system.*

CRT See *cathode-ray tube terminal.*

cum dividend A term indicating that the quoted price of shares of capital stock on which a dividend has been declared includes the right to receive the dividend. The term attaches from the date of declaration to the date appearing in the resolution on which the holders are said to be of record; see *ex-dividend.*

cumulative dividend A dividend on *cumulative preferred stock* payable under the terms of the issue at stated intervals and before any distribution is made to the holders of common stock. Unpaid cumulative dividends are a part of the obligation to preferred stockholders in the event of liquidation. See *dividends in arrears*.

cumulative preferred stock Capital stock on which unpaid dividends accumulate as a claim upon past and future earnings and generally, in the event of liquidation, to the extent of available earned surplus, before any distribution can be made to the common stockholders. The right to cumulative dividends is generally expressly provided or is inferred from a guaranty of the dividends. Where there is no indication of intent, some courts have held preferred stock to be cumulative.

cumulative voting A method of voting for the election of the board of directors of a corporation whereby a minority stockholder or minority group of stockholders may, by concentrating its votes, endeavor to elect one or more members of the board. The owner of any one share is allowed as many votes for one or more candidates as there are directors to be elected.

In noncorporate bodies, or corporate bodies having no capital stock, the common-law rule of voting is that each member is entitled to one vote, regardless of the size of his or her investment; in corporate bodies, a stockholder is entitled to as many votes as he or she has shares. To permit representation from minorities, a number of state corporation laws require that, when directors of stock corporations are elected, a stockholder is permitted to distribute his or her individual votes for directors in whatever way he or she pleases. In other states, cumulative voting is permitted if provided for in the articles of incorporation. Thus, if there are two stockholders or two stockholder groups in a corporation, one owning 600 shares and the other 400 shares, and 5 directors are to be elected, the votes may be cast thus:

Voters	Shares Owned	Number of Directors Voted for				
		1	2	3	4	5
A (majority)	600	3,000	1,500	1,000	750	600
B (minority)	400	2,000	1,000	667	500	400

It will be observed that if *B* votes for candidates differing from those nominated by *A*, he or she can elect 2 directors, and even 3 (667 each), thus winning control, if *A* scatters votes equally for each of 5 candidates (600 each). *A* is more likely, however, to divide his or her votes as between 3 candidates (1,000 each) or 4 candidates (750 each), thus permitting *B* to have but 2 representatives on the board.

The number of shares necessary to elect a desired number of directors can be obtained from the following formula:

$$n = \frac{dN}{D + 1} + 1,$$

where *n* is the number of shares necessary, *d* the desired number of directors to be elected, *N* the total number of voting shares, and *D* the total number of directors to be elected. Thus, if 7 directors are to be elected, a majority group of stockholders wishes to elect not less than 5, and the total shares to be voted are 1,000, the minimum number of shares required will be

$$n = \frac{5 \times 1,000}{7 + 1} + 1 = 626.$$

Again applying the formula, if the majority group wishes to elect all 7 directors, 876 shares out of the 1,000 will be required; if a minority group wishes to elect 1 director, it will have to cast a vote of 126 shares. If the division happened to be exactly 875 and 125, and the majority casts equal votes for each of 7 candidates and the minority its entire vote for 1 candidate, a deadlock would result; but there is no record that any comparable situation has ever developed in practice. In terms of percentages of the total number of voting shares, the minimum required to elect 1 director is given in the following table:

Directors to Be Elected	One Share More Than (%)
3	25
5	16⅔
7	12½
9	10
11	8⅓
13	7⅐
15	6¼

currency Paper *money* and coin; see *cash; money*.

currency exposure See *foreign exchange exposure*.

current 1. Existing in the present but having a transitory or shifting character. Examples: current assets; current funds.

2. Relating to the present, in contrast to the past or future. Examples: the current year; the current budget.

current account 1. A running account, usually between two related companies, reflecting the movement of cash, merchandise, and other items in either or both directions; a periodic settlement is not usually required; it may differ from an *account current*.

2. An account with a partner reflecting salary withdrawals and other transactions. The balance of the account may be transferred periodically, as at the end of the fiscal year, to the partner's capital account.

current asset Unrestricted cash, or other asset held for conversion within a relatively short period into cash or other readily convertible asset, or currently useful goods or services. Usually the period is one year or less, but for some items, e.g., installment receivables, the period may be much longer. In some enterprises the period may be extended to the length of the *operating cycle*, which may be more than a year. The five customary subdivisions of current assets are cash, temporary investments, receivables, inventory, and prepaid expenses. See *balance sheet*.

current budget 1. The projection of income and expense at anticipated levels of activity rather than in terms of ideal goals.

2. An operating budget. See *budget*.

current cost The amount of cash (or its equivalent) that would have to be paid if the same asset—either an identical asset or an asset with equivalent productive capacity—were acquired currently, computed by applying to *historical cost* one or more *index numbers* (= adjusted *historical cost*) or by substituting for historical prices prevailing prices of equivalent goods and services (= *replacement cost*). See *fixed asset; inventory valuation*.

current exit value = *current market value*. The amount of cash or cash equivalent that could be currently obtained by selling an asset in orderly liquidation or by the cash outlay that would be currently required to eliminate a liability.

current expenditure An expenditure covering an operating cost or an addition to plant during a given period.

current expense 1. An expense of a given period.

2. A normal operating expense, as compared, e.g., with a *nonrecurring charge*.

current fund 1. = *general fund*.

2. *pl*. Cash and other assets convertible into cash within a short time; included are temporary investments, short-term notes, and accounts receivable—current funds thus differing from *current assets; quick assets*.

current income 1. Income of a given accounting period.

2. (institutional accounting) Receipts and accruals of the present fiscal period expendable for general operations, or for designated specific activities, exclusive of receipts for

plant additions or receipts designed to increase the principal of a fund.

current investment An expenditure for readily marketable securities having as its purpose the profitable use of cash temporarily in excess of immediate requirements; *temporary investment*.

current liability A short-term debt, regardless of its source, including any liability accrued and deferred and unearned revenue that is to be paid out of current assets or is to be transferred to income within a relatively short period, usually one year or less, or a period greater than a year but within the business cycle of an enterprise. The currently maturing portion of a bond issue is thus classified unless it is to be paid from a sinking fund or other noncurrent asset source. See *liability*.

Current liabilities, assuming a business cycle of one year, may thus consist of:

Trade accounts and notes (i.e., arising from transactions with suppliers of goods and services common to the business).

Bank loans (repayable within a year).

Current maturities (i.e., of long-term debt, payable within a year).

Loans from other financial institutions.

Deposits and advances from customers, including deposits on containers.

Dividends declared but unpaid (including unclaimed dividend checks from prior declarations).

Accruals (both due and not due) of interest, income and property taxes, payrolls, payroll and social-security taxes, commissions, royalties, vacation pay, bonuses, realized profits shared, and the like. Accruals are often *rounded off*, without affecting *significant amounts*, especially where minor portions of the accrual may be contingent on future events and conditions.

Purchased tax-anticipation notes are the only class of assets that may offset taxes payable, but even there the notes must be of the type that cannot legally be used for any other purpose.

currently attainable standards = *current standard cost*.

current market value The price that would be received or paid for the sale or liquidation of an asset (such as an item of inventory) under current conditions.

current maturity The portion of a long-term obligation to be retired during the ensuing 12 months, usually classified as a *current liability*.

current-noncurrent method A method of foreign currency translation whereby current assets and liabilities are translated into their domestic currency equivalents at the exchange rate in effect at the balance-sheet date, noncurrent assets and liabilities are translated at the exchange rate prevailing when the assets or liabilities were acquired, income statement items (except depreciation and amortization) are translated at some average of current period exchange rates, and depreciation and amortization expenses are translated at the exchange rate in effect when the related balance-sheet items were acquired. See *current rate method*.

current operating performance A term used, for instance, in *AICPA* publications to characterize *operating-performance income statements*.

current-outlay cost A cost requiring a current cash expenditure; a present out-of-pocket cost; contrast with *sunk cost*.

current price The price of record at the time of sale. See *price*.

current proceeds 1. Current *income* or receipts.

2. The amount that would be obtained if an existing obligation were incurred currently.

current rate method A method of foreign currency translation which requires that all financial statement items be translated into their domestic currency equivalents at the exchange rate in effect at the balance-sheet date. See *current-noncurrent method*.

current ratio A *ratio* which measures a firm's ability to meet its short-run obligations. It is calculated by dividing *current assets* by *current liabilities*. A minimum value of 2.0 is often prescribed for this ratio, but an individual firm's ratio level should also be compared with its industry average. This popular ratio is purported by accounting historians to be the first financial ratio developed.

current replacement cost Amount required currently to acquire (1) an asset that is identical (i.e., one of the same age, in the same condition, and with the same *service potential*) to the existing one, or (2) another asset (usually a new improved asset) that can give the same service as the existing one. Approach (2) involves estimating the buying price of the improved asset from which is deducted an allowance for the operating disadvantage of the existing asset (higher operating costs and/or lower output potential) and an allowance for depreciation calculated according to an acceptable accounting method; this yields a measurement of the current cost of the service potential of the existing asset. If (1) and (2) differ, usually the lower amount is used. See *replacement cost*; *reproduction cost*.

current resources 1. Current assets such as accounts or notes receivable which are potentially available to meet current obligations.
2. (governmental accounting) Resources to which recourse can be had to meet current obligations and expenditures. Examples are estimated revenues of a particular period not yet realized, transfers from other funds authorized but not received, and, in the case of certain funds, bonds authorized and unissued.

current return A percentage based on the ratio of annual per-share dividends paid during the 12 months immediately preceding and the market price per share at the end of the period. Employing the average price during the period, sometimes advocated, is regarded as misleading.

current standard cost A *standard cost* based on anticipated outlays for materials and services and the best performance efficiency reasonably attainable under existing conditions of production.

current taxes Taxes from the date the assessment rolls are approved by the taxing or tax-review authority to the date on which a penalty for nonpayment is attached.

current value A method of accounting under which the economic resources and obligations of an enterprise are periodically revalued. The phrase "current value accounting" is often used generically to refer to one or more of the four following measures: (a) *current cost, current proceeds*; (b) *current exit value*; (c) *expected exit value*; or (d) *present value*.

current value accounting Accounting *model* or approach in which the valuation basis for all assets is *current replacement cost (entry value)* or current *exit value* or *net realizable value (current exit value)* and for all liabilities is *present value*. General agreement is lacking on the meaning of current value accounting as to whether it means entry value or exit value. Contrast to *cost basis*.

current yield to maturity The *discount* rate that makes the current market value of a *bond* equal to the net present value of cash flows associated with the bond. See *bond valuation*.

curve The *graph* of a mathematical expression, either a function or a relation, usually drawn to scales provided by a *coordinate system*.

curve fitting The process of associating curves of mathematical functions with empirical information on the basis of a criterion or *hypothesis*. Frequently, the data are put in graphic form before fitting.

The process of fitting may be either (a) exact (as when a straight line is fitted to two points), in which case all points for which observations are obtained lie directly on the curve, or (b) statistical, in which case few, if any, points lie directly on the curve. In statistical fitting, the data are viewed as being subject to various "errors" which mask or conceal the underlying relation. In either exact or statistical fitting, the process may proceed "empirically" or by known laws or theories from which the behavior of the data is deduced. See *least-squares method*. Casual methods, such as visual inspection, freehand drawing, or use of threads may also be used in curve fitting.

customary form Said of financial statements and meaning the *account form* of balance sheet and the *report form* of income statement.

customer default *Default* by a buyer or client.

customers ledger A ledger containing accounts with customers. The total of the accounts, which mostly have *debit* balances, is usually supported by a debit balance of equal amount in a general-ledger control account.

customs duties A *tariff*.

customs invoice An invoice covering goods shipped from one country to another, made in prescribed form to give the information required by the country to which the goods are sent, sworn to before a consular officer stationed in the exporting country and bearing his or her visa. Also known as *consular invoice*.

cutoff An interruption of the continuity of recording transactions for the purpose of comparing book records with totals available from external sources. The interruption may relate to the flow of transactions in books of account or to the intermingling of physical goods. See *cutoff date*.

cutoff date 1. The date selected for stopping the flow of cash, goods, or transactions entries generally, for closing or audit purposes. Thus, when a physical inventory is taken, a cutoff date for both purchases and sales is customarily selected. This may involve a brief closing of receiving and shipping rooms, permitting a count of goods on hand, or the special labeling of items so that the transactions of one period may be kept apart from those of the succeeding period. The idea of a cutoff date carries with it the likelihood of the omission from the current year's transactions of items properly belonging there but relegated to the succeeding period—a situation tolerated even under rigorous methods of accounting—where the effect on the balance sheet is minor and the effect on the income statement is virtually nil because of the existence of a similar situation at the close of the preceding period. See *physical inventory*.

2. (auditing) The date selected by an auditor, such as one ten days after the close of a period under audit, for a supplementary verification of a cash balance. The procedure may involve obtaining from the client's bank a *cutoff statement* (with canceled checks) covering the brief period, preparing a schedule reconciling the transactions reported by the bank with those appearing on the books, tracing through deposits in transit at the end of the period, examining returned checks outstanding at the end of that period, and making other inquiries, comparisons, and reviews. The object of the supplementary examination is to strengthen the auditor's conclusions as to the propriety of the cash balance at the end of the period under audit. Comparable cutoff dates may be established for inventory additions and other transaction groupings.

cutoff errors *Errors* which result from recording transactions in a period other than when they actually occur. See *cutoff*.

cutoff statement An interim statement of transactions between two persons, prepared by one at the request of the other, usually for audit purposes. See *cutoff date* (2).

CVP = *cost-volume-profit relationship*.

cybernetics A term (from the Greek *kybernetes*, meaning "steersman" or "governor") connoting the use of *feedback* information to correct performance and direct it to predetermined goals. Initially associated with gun-control-radar aiming mechanisms in World War II, it has since spread to a variety of fields, such as automation and operations which are computer controlled with sensing devices.

cycle 1. Any of a series of operational sequences having similar endproducts of goods or services: applied to a machine, process, or plant, or to business operations generally. The elapsed time from start to finish is the cycle time.

2. Hence, the time required for such a sequence. Thus, a clock cycle is 12 hours; a lunar cycle, 28 days; a business cycle, a period beginning with an "upswing" and lasting through a depression. See *cyclical movement*.

3. (computers) A machine cycle is the time interval during which a computer can perform a specified operation (such as an addition).

4. An *accounting cycle* or *business cycle*.

cycle billing A method which divides a total billing operation into segments, each of which is billed on a different day (or unit of time) in the billing interval.

cycle count A count completed within a given period of time, such as a month or a year, the reference being to a method of more or less continuous verification of inventory quantities where each inventory subdivision or location is physically inspected at least once during the period.

cyclical movement Movement through a cycle, as in the movement from economic prosperity through inflation, recession, depression, recovery, and finally back again to prosperity. The usual movement is measured from peak to peak or trough to trough for one complete cycle.

data (*sing*. datum) 1. *Facts.* See *evidence* (*2*). 2. (computers) A collection of words or figures which can be stored and processed on a computer.

data base A collection of *data* intended to serve the needs of all of its users and organized to facilitate reporting or modeling relationships of potential interest.

data base administrator A role given to an individual or group which includes the definition, organization, and protection of a *data base*.

data base dictionary A collection of descriptions of each item stored in a *data base* including such things as data type, size, units of measure, and data relationships.

data base management system A system or collection of programs which allows a user to organize, access, and modify a data base.

data description language A computer language used to describe the data contained in a data base. This involves defining the data items and their attributes along with the data structure relating the data items.

data file See *data set*.

data independence A process by which logical and physical definitions of a *data base* are separated. With data independence an *application programmer* need only know the logical structure to develop programs while allowing the physical structure to change over time.

data integrity maintenance (DIM) The protection of a data base from accidental or intentional falsification.

data item The smallest unit of data.

data manipulation language (computers) A language used in *application programs* to access, modify, and store data in data base systems. It may be self-contained or it may serve as an extension to an existing host language such as *COBOL*.

data privacy Protection of data from being accessed or modified by an unauthorized person.

data processing 1. Any treatment of *data* such as preparation of invoices or extracting data from original documents for entry into books of account.
2. A term sometimes used to distinguish computer treatment of business type data (such as account entries) from other types of computer treatment such as statistical or algorithmic manipulations.

data record See *record* (*3*).

data security See *data integrity maintenance*.

data set A collection of similar *data records*. Sometimes referred to as a data file.

data structure A user's view of how a data base should look in terms of logical descriptions, including *data items* and their relationships. This view need not represent the way data are actually stored and treated.

dated earned surplus Earned surplus (*retained earnings*) of a corporation accumulated from the date of a *reorganization* or *quasi-reorganization*. On a balance sheet or statement of surplus, the date appear as an integral part of the title, as "Retained earnings from July 1, 19-1, $. . . ," and this title is repeated over a period of years.

date of acquisition 1. The effective purchase date of an asset. From the date of acquisition, the asset must appear in the accounts and in financial statements, and its gradual decline in usefulness (*depreciation*), if any, must be offset against it. Usually, this is the date title is acquired or the burdens of ownership are assumed and the asset is in possession.
2. The date on which the control of a subsidiary was obtained as the result of a stock purchase or otherwise by a parent or holding company. See *control*.

daybook A chronological record of business *transactions*; a *blotter*; a business diary. Transactions recorded in a daybook are subsequently translated into bookkeeping terms to show the accounts affected, and in this revised form they are entered in a *journal* and posted to a *ledger*. A daybook is now rarely used; the *journal*, in varied forms, is the *book of original entry*. Original invoices and other supporting documents have largely replaced the descriptive detail formerly inscribed in daybooks. See *journal*.

days purchases in accounts payable ratio A *ratio* which measures the extent to which ac-
counts payable represent current rather than overdue obligations. It is derived by dividing accounts payable by average daily purchases, i.e., annual purchases divided by 365 or 360.

days sales outstanding See *accounts receivable collection period*.

days to sell inventory A *ratio* which measures the average number of days it takes to sell inventory in a given year. It is derived by dividing inventory by average daily cost of sales, i.e., annual cost of sales divided by 365 or 360.

DDL data description language. See *data* (*2*).

deadlock 1. Inability to resolve two or more competing claims or arguments.
2. (computers) A situation in which two or more programs are competing for resources to which the other currently has exclusive access. For example, Program A has exclusive access to File 1 and needs access to File 2, while Program B has exclusive access to File 2.

deadweight The weight of a vessel or other means of transportation, without cargo.

deal An agreement, such as an accepted *purchase order*, between buyer and seller, which, when fulfilled, will give rise to one or more *transactions*, but which in the unfulfilled state does not give rise to an entry in the formal books of account. See *commitment; transaction*. A purchase on credit, paid for on a later date, constitutes one deal but two transactions.

dealer (in securities) A person who buys securities and holds them until sold, as distinguished from a *broker*, who characteristically buys or sells only upon a customer's order and does not take title. Over-the-counter transactions are generally handled by dealers; transactions on exchanges, by brokers. The title "dealer" is often used in referring to either type of person, since brokers, under certain conditions, may acquire and sell securities in their own name.

Dean schedule (insurance) = *analytic schedule*.

death benefits (federal income taxes) Receipts from the proceeds of life insurance, and receipts by an employee's estate or beneficiaries from or on behalf of an employer because of the employee's death; under the current *Internal Revenue Code*, the former are tax exempt and the latter exempt in an amount not exceeding $5,000.

death taxes The taxes levied by the federal government or a state government on the event of a person's death. The federal death tax is the *estate tax* portion of the *unified transfer tax*, levied against the decedent's estate. A few states also levy estate taxes, but most levy an *inheritance tax*.

debenture (bond) A security ranking ahead of preferred stock and not protected by collateral or a lien on tangible assets but only by the general credit of the issuer; the underlying indenture may require such protective measures as the maintenance of a specified working-capital ratio, the immediate maturity of the issue in case of default in the payment of interest, the placing of a prior lien on the assets of the issuer in favor of debenture holders when a subsequent issue of bonds is made, limitations on the amount of any additional funded debt, restrictions on dividends to stockholders, and protection of debenture holders (in various forms) in case corporate assets are sold or transferred. Interest on debentures is a prior lien on the net income, is payable before dividends are distributed, and may be cumulative. See *income bond*.

debenture capital Proceeds derived from the sale of debentures.

debenture stock = *debenture*; a British term.

debit *n.* 1. A bookkeeping *entry* or *posting* recording the creation of or addition to an *asset* or an *expense*, or the reduction or elimination of a liability, credit, *valuation account*, or item of *net worth* or *revenue*; an entry on the left side of an *account*; the amount so recorded. Compare *credit*.
2. The balance of an asset, expense, or debit *valuation account*.
v.t. To *enter* or *post* a debit.

debit memorandum A document, other than an invoice, showing the reason and authority for creating a *debit*; issued, e.g., by a bank, having the effect of reducing a depositor's or customer's account, or by a customer to his supplier for goods returned to the latter; contrasts with *credit memorandum*.

debt Money, goods, or services owing to another by virtue of an agreement, express or implied, giving rise to a legal duty to pay. See *incur*.

debt discount The excess of face value over the net proceeds of a loan. See *bond discount*. When the discount relates to a loan (e.g., a bank loan) standing as a current liability, it is treated as a *prepaid expense*, or, less frequently but more accurately, as a debit *valuation account*, deductible on the balance sheet from the face value of the loan. See *bond discount*.

debt-equity ratio 1. A *ratio* which measures the margin of safety that protects creditors of a firm against losses in the event of a liquidation. It is normally calculated by dividing total liabilities by total equities or total assets. However, many other versions of this ratio are used. Some analysts prefer long-term debt as the numerator, and some analysts prefer long-term equities or just stockholders' equity as the denominator. Also, many analysts prefer to use a reciprocal version of this ratio, i.e., equity to debt.
2. When used to measure a firm's capital structure, market values, rather than accounting values, are usually employed. This version has been important in the development of financial management theory.

debt limit (municipal accounting) The maximum amount of indebtedness that a governmental unit may legally incur. The difference between the maximum amount of debt which a municipality is legally permitted to incur and the amount of outstanding debt applicable to the debt limit is designated as the "legal debt margin." See *overlapping debt*.

debt margin Difference between the amount of a debt limit and the net amount of outstanding indebtedness subject to the limitation.

debtor 1. One who owes a debt and has a legal duty to pay it; contrasts with *creditor*.
2. *pl.* = *receivables*.

debt ratio See *debt-equity ratio*.

debt restructuring Restatement of debt to reflect concessions granted to a debtor by a creditor for reasons related to the debtor's financial difficulties. Such concessions may stem from an agreement between the creditor and the debtor or it may be imposed by law or a court. For example, a creditor may agree to restructure the terms of a debt to alleviate the burden of the debtor's near-term cash requirements, or a state legislature or a court may restructure the debt of a municipality to reduce or defer required cash payments.

debt service The payment of matured interest and principal; the outlay needed, supplied, or accrued for meeting such payments during any given accounting period; a budget or operating-statement heading for such items.

debt service fund (governmental and institutional accounting) A *fund* established for the payment of interest and principal on all debt, other than that payable exclusively from special assessments, revenues of proprietary funds, or revenues of fiduciary funds.

decentralization To *decentralize*.

decentralize 1. To delegate *authority* to subordinate levels within an administrative hierarchy or over different geographical regions, and to fix areas of *responsibility* for the propriety of actions taken thereunder.

2. To increase the authority and responsibility of field units geographically removed from a central office or headquarters.
3. Loosely, to establish an operating entity to which delegations are made beyond the purview of previous norms or experience.

decile Any of the values that divide a *frequency distribution* into ten parts; there are nine deciles, four preceding the *median*, the median, and four following the median. See *quantile*.

decision 1. A choice, followed by a related action, taken in preference to an alternative; the coupling of action with intent.
2. An act or preference that terminates a discussion, controversy, or period of reflection or hesitation.
3. A collection of acts, statements, and intentions, explicit or implicit, which, from the point of view of a particular *model*, and apart from the randomness defined by or implied in that model, displays a systematic pattern or sequence of patterns.

decision center An organizational unit (or subunit) which is identified with a decision-maker (manager) who has primary *responsibility* and *authority* for its activities. A *responsibility center*, a *cost center*, *revenue center*, or an *activity* (as in *activity accounting*).

decision making The process of selecting from possible (or available) alternatives a *policy* outlook or course of action under constituted authority: a principal function of *management (1)*.

decision package A document that identifies and describes a specific activity (function or operation) in such a manner that management can (1) evaluate it and rank it against other activities, also represented in decision packages, in competition for limited resources, and (2) decide whether to approve or disapprove it. This identification should include a statement of purpose (goals or objectives), estimates of the costs of performing its activity, and a list of consequences which might result from not performing the activity. Measures of performance for the activity, alternative ways of performing the activity, different levels of effort which may be required to perform the function, and the costs and benefits of carrying out the activity also form a part of the decision package. See *zero-base budgeting*.

decision table A systematic layout of possible alternative approaches to a problem, as in *decision making*, along with the action and resulting output estimated to flow from each alternative. Oftentimes used in developing or correcting logic for a computer program.

decision tree A *tree* in which the links leading from each node represent alternative choices for decision and net payoffs (benefits less costs or penalties) are assigned to the terminal nodes that may be reached by *chains* from the initial node. The nodes may be divided into two types: (1) decision nodes and (2) chance nodes where choices are made by chance in accordance with specified probabilities. The net payoffs at the terminal nodes are then represented either as *expected values* or entire *probability distributions*. See the example under *risk analysis*. Actually a *decision tree* is a special type of *game tree* involving only one player, although it may also be given an interpretation in which ''nature'' is a second player.

declaration 1. The formal action of a board of directors by which the liability for the payment of a dividend is created; see *dividend*.
2. *pl.* (insurance) That part of an insurance contract containing the insured's statement of underwriting information pertinent to the risk covered.

declared capital = *stated capital*.

declared dividend A dividend, formally authorized by a corporation's board of direc-

tors, for payment on a specified date; see *dividend*.

declared value 1. = *stated value*.
2. The value given by a corporation to its capital stock for any of various taxation purposes.

declassified cost The cost, as of a manufactured product, restated in terms of material, labor, and other basic objects of expenditure. See *disaggregated cost*.

decline in economic usefulness See *depreciation*.

decoding To reverse the process of *encoding*, that is, to transform a signal back into its original form. See *encoding*.

decommissioning cost A cost associated with retiring a commissioned plant from service. Example: Retiring a previously commissioned nuclear energy plant in a manner which will remove any threat to public safety. Dismantling fuel assemblies and entombing all radioactive waste are example of such costs, which can be considerable, and may result in a negative *salvage value* for addition to a *depreciation base*.

decomposition analysis In financial analysis, a technique for investigating the process underlying changes in the relative shares of *financial statement* items. Basically, percentage values of individual items from *common-size statements* are analyzed for two time periods to determine if the financial structure of a firm is changing significantly. The analysis is summarized as a simple number I, called the ''decomposition measure,'' defined as:

$$ I = \sum_{i=1}^{N} q_i \log \frac{q_i}{p_i}, $$

where I = decomposition measure; N = number of items in the part of the accounting statement being analyzed; i = an individual accounting statement item, $i = 1, 2, \ldots, N$; q = relative percentage share of each item in the second year; p = relative percentage share of each item in the first year; and log refers to logarithm, usually to the base 10. See *logarithm*. See also *information theory; information statistic*. Comparisons of these decomposition measures with standard values, such as industry averages, will help determine if significant changes are taking place in a firm's financial statement and where most of those changes are located. Decomposition analysis has been found useful for predicting a wide variety of financial events, such as impending bankruptcy.

decomposition measure See *decomposition analysis; information theory; information statistic*.

decrement See *increment*.

deduction 1. (logic) Reasoning for which there is a necessary conclusion, i.e., a conclusion completely implied by the premises. Strictly, necessary conclusions are possible only within sets of symbols. Whether true, and thus applicable to an existing condition, must be determined empirically.
2. Any cost or expense set off against revenue.
3. (federal income taxes) A subtraction from gross income allowed by the *Internal Revenue Code* to arrive at *taxable income*. Deductions allowed individual taxpayers are categorized as deductions to arrive at *adjusted gross income* or as itemized deductions from adjusted gross income. Deductions for arriving at adjusted gross income are listed in Section 62 of the Internal Revenue Code. Only the excess of itemized deductions over the *zero bracket amount* are deductible, and this excess is subtracted from adjusted gross income to arrive at taxable income. See *adjusted gross income; zero bracket amount*.

deductions from gross income 1. A classification prescribed by the Interstate Commerce Commission in its uniform system of accounts for carriers and other utilities, consist-

ing of deductions from gross operating and nonoperating income in the determination of net income. The classification includes such items as rents, taxes, interest, and amortization of debt.
2. In general, any item deducted before arriving at *operating income*.
3. (federal income tax) Those items identified in Section 62 of the *Internal Revenue Code* as deductible by individuals to arrive at *adjusted gross income*.

deductions from income = *income deductions*.

deductions from net income A classification prescribed by the Interstate Commerce Commission in its uniform system of accounts for carriers and other utilities, consisting of deductions from and the disposition of net income; included are such items as appropriations for reserves and dividends.

deed A written instrument under seal, conveying an interest in real property.

deed of trust A conveyance of property to a trustee, subject to release or disposal under prescribed terms; usually equivalent to a mortgage; = *trust deed*.

de facto In fact, actually; a corporation *de facto* is a group of persons or an organization that is conducting its affairs as a corporation but has no lawful authority to do so because of delay in filing incorporation papers, failure to comply with state law, lapse of charter, or other cause. See *de jure*.

defalcation See *embezzlement*.
—defalcate, *v.i.*

default Failure to pay debt interest or principal when due, or to perform any other obligation required by contract.

defensive interval A *ratio* which measures the margin of protection a firm's liquid assets would provide for reductions in its cash flows, usually calculated by dividing total defensive assets by daily operating expenditures, i.e., annual operating expenditures divided by 365 or 360. The "defensive assets" in the numerator include cash, marketable securities, and accounts receivable. The denominator includes all cash operating costs. The ratio value shows the number of days the defensive assets could service daily operating costs.

deferral (or deferment) The accounting treatment accorded the receipt or accrual of revenue before it is earned, or the incurrence of an expenditure before the benefits therefrom are received. Such items are balance-sheet liabilities or assets and are carried forward to the income account of succeeding periods as the revenue is earned or as the benefits are received from the expenditure.

defer, *v.t.*; deferrable, *adj.*

deferral method See *flow-through method*.

deferred asset = *deferred charge; prepaid expense*.

deferred charge An expenditure not recognized as a cost of operations of the period in which incurred but carried forward to be written off in one or more future periods. There are four main types: outlays the benefits from which will be enjoyed over an indefinite number of succeeding periods; outlays in the nature of long-term prepaid expenses for research and development (R&D) that are presumed to be of benefit over a fairly well defined number of future periods; *prepaid expenses* or costs—the only type of deferred charge that is classified as a current asset; and expenditures or losses that benefit no past, present, or future period.

deferred compensation (federal income taxes) Provisions for pension plans, profit-sharing plans, stock bonus plans, bond purchase plans, individual retirement plans, and Keogh (HR-10) plans as described under Subchapter D of the *Internal Revenue Code*. In all of these plans the Code contains detailed and complex rules under which compensation earned

currently can be taxed in a later year when the compensation is actually received.

deferred credit = *deferred revenue*; also a tax credit such as the treatment of depreciation under the *investment tax credit*.

deferred debit = *deferred charge; prepaid expense*.

deferred dividend A dividend declared and recorded as a liability but not payable until a specified time has elapsed beyond the usual date of payment or until a specified event has occurred.

deferred expense = *deferred charge; prepaid expense*.

deferred income tax Estimated income tax on the excess of net revenues, recognized for accounting purposes, over that reported for tax purposes. Examples: income from installment sales, undistributed earnings on foreign investments, deductions for depreciation in excess of straight-line depreciation, property taxes, product warranties, development costs.

deferred investment tax credit An accounting method which allocates the amount of *investment tax credit* to income in years subsequent to the acquisition or installation of qualified property; the allocation period usually coincides with the useful life. The argument for deferral rests on the premise that tax credit results from the use of an asset and not from its purchase. Deferred recognition of the investment tax credit is preferred under generally accepted accounting principles, but the more widely used *flow-through method* is also acceptable.

deferred liability 1. A debt the payment of which is deferred beyond a legal or customary date; e.g., a *deferred tax*.
2. Any long-term liability.
3. = *deferred revenue*.

deferred maintenance Delayed repairs, or upkeep, measured by the outlay required to restore a plant or individual asset to full operating characteristics. Through planned maintenance, depreciation, although not stopped, can usually be kept within normal limits. Deferred maintenance arises from such causes as (a) the inability to close a plant or remove a machine for repair without interfering with a production schedule; (b) the scheduling of periodic repair periods during which accumulated repairs and overhauls are made; (c) the relatively high cost of pulling out a single item for an overhaul as compared with the collective overhaul of a group of such items following an operating period; (d) the lack of need for future efficiency, as in the case of an item about to be sold; (e) the lack of funds to make needed repairs. In every operating plant and machine, there is always some element of deferred maintenance, and a combination of engineering and management skills is necessary if undue wear, plant breakdowns, or other undesirable results of less-than-maximum efficiencies are to be avoided. The decision of when to repair is usually based on whatever action (or inaction) as to maintenance will produce the minimum effect on cost, or the maximum effect on profit. See *maintenance; depreciation*.

During a fiscal year, a reserve for (deferred) maintenance is often employed to equalize as far as possible the year's maintenance cost. This is a particularly useful device where reliance is had on monthly financial statements. Under a typical procedure, total maintenance costs are first estimated for the year, and monthly accruals equal to one-twelfth of the estimate are made by debiting maintenance expense and crediting the reserve; then, as actual maintenance costs are incurred, they are charged against the reserve, and at the year end the debit or credit balance of the reserve is spread pro rata over the maintenance-expense accounts.

deferred-payment sale 1. An *installment sale*. 2. Any sale the settlement of which is extended beyond a customary credit period.

deferred repairs = *deferred maintenance*.

deferred revenue (or income) 1. Revenue or income received or recorded before it is earned, i.e., before the consideration is given, in whole or in part, for which the revenue is or is to be received; also known as *deferred credit, unearned revenue*, and *unrealized revenue*. Examples: rent received in advance, transportation sold in advance, unearned subscriptions. Like deferred charges, their classification as a current liability (and, hence, as working capital) depends upon the period of time to which they relate. Advance ticket sales are in effect temporary deposits and hence a current liability. Prepaid rent covering an immediately following period, even though not refundable except in the event of the destruction of the property, similarly constitutes a current liability in that it, too, has the characteristic of a deposit out of which maintenance and other expenses are to be paid, leaving a balance, if any, that is to be regarded as income. On the other hand, rental received for the last year of a lease running for ten more years is in the nature of a long-term debt and may be shown as a special item below current liabilities. As indicated, rent is a mixture of future income and of liability for the expenses of maintaining the property during the same period, and, if the amount involved is material, it may be divided between prospective cost, to be included as a current liability, and the remainder, constituting estimated income that may be excluded from that category. Thus, if rental of $10,000 is received for a year in advance and it is known that the only costs are insurance and taxes totaling $3,000, that amount may be shown as a current liability and the balance of $7,000 as deferred income ''below the line.''

2. Income subject to adjustment or held in suspense until offsetting charges have been determined and deducted, until a period of time has been completed, or until it has been fully identified.

deferred tax A *deferred credit* or *long-term liability* is a form of *equalization reserve (2)*: an income-leveling device having the effect of taking the "bumps" out of corporate annual earnings and per-share analyses, and thus widening the differences between net income and income derived from statements of cash (and fund) flows.

deficiency 1. The amount by which the *liabilities (1)* of an enterprise exceed its assets. See *deficit; insolvency*.
2. (federal income taxes) The excess of a tax as computed by the Commissioner over the amount shown on the taxpayer's return plus any amount previously assessed or collected.

deficiency account (or statement) A statement accounting for an estimated or actual loss to creditors and owners, usually prepared by creditors of a financially embarrassed debtor in connection with a statement of affairs in the course of bankruptcy proceedings or at the close of an investigation.

deficiency appropriation (governmental accounting) A legislative grant of spending power to meet obligations incurred in excess of a previously enacted *appropriation*. Like a *supplemental appropriation*, it is added to and identified with the original appropriation.

deficiency letter 1. An informal notice by the U.S. *Securities and Exchange Commission* questioning one or more items in a formal filing.
2. (federal income taxes) A notice from the *IRS* permitting an appeal by a taxpayer to the *Tax Court* within a 90-day period concerning a proposed additional tax (Regulations Sections 301.6212 and 301.6213).

deficit 1. Expenses and losses in excess of related income; an operating loss.
2. An accumulation of operating losses ("negative" *retained earnings*).
3. Impairment of capital; the excess of an organization's *liabilities* and *paid-in capital (proprietorship)* over the *going-concern value* of its *tangible assets*.
4. The ledger account or balance-sheet designation for such an excess.

deficit account A ledger account for a deficit; an earned-surplus account with a debit balance.

defined-benefit pension plan A *pension plan* that specifies a determinable pension benefit, usually based on factors such as age, years of service, and/or salary. A plan funded pursuant to periodic agreements that specify a fixed rate of employer contributions (e.g., a collectively bargained multiemployer plan) may still be a defined-benefit pension plan if, for example, the plan prescribes a scale of benefits and experience indicates that employer contributions will be periodically adjusted to enable such stated benefits to be maintained.

defined-contribution plan A pension plan in which an employer's contributions are determined and allocated with respect to specific individuals, usually as a percentage of compensation; the resulting benefits for each employee are the amounts that can be provided by the sums contributed for him or her.

definition A statement that sets forth and delimits the meaning of a word, phrase, or other symbolic expression, as used in a given discourse or context. Definitions serve to instruct persons who are ignorant or uncertain of a usage, to determine the consistency of usage and of reasoning in which a term or symbol is used, and to help systematize a body of knowledge. Depending upon the purpose, one or another of the following types of definition may be employed:

1. Ostensive: a mere pointing to the object or series of objects intended.

2. Synonymous: an alternative term or symbol, presumably better known by the person to whom the definition is presented.

3. Extensive or denotative: an enumeration of all of the objects covered by the defined term.

4. Operational: a specification of the procedures which lead unequivocally to the item defined, the definition of *arithmetic mean* being an example: given any set of numbers, if the operations of addition and division are performed on them in a prescribed manner, the result will be the arithmetic mean of the numbers. See *mean*.

5. Intensional or connotative: identification of the essential characteristics of the defined object or event; the traditional method of intensional definition is to treat the *definiendum* (that which is to be defined) as a class (species) included in a larger class (genus), from whose other members the species is distinguished by some characteristic attribute or quality (called the "differentia"): thus, man (species) is an animal (genus) that is rational (differentia); an insurance claim (species) is a demand for payment of a debt (genus) which is said to be incurred under a contract to protect the claimant against a loss (differentia); paid-in surplus (species) is proprietorship (genus) which represents the excess of invested funds over the investment required by law, agreement, or resolution (differentia).

6. Recursive: the application of a primitive form to synthesize a more complete, complex, or precise expression; the primitive notions of "zero" and "successor of" in Peano's *axioms* of arithmetic have been used to define the system of positive integers and the operations of addition and multiplication.

When the purpose of definition is to systematize a body of knowledge, great care is exercised in relating one definition to another. Among ancient scientists and philosophers, such systematic definitions (usually of the intensional type) were believed to identify the "essence" of the thing defined, and some infallible connection between the definition and the thing defined was supposed to constitute scientific knowledge. Such an interpretation of definition is now regarded as (a) based upon a misconception of language, (b) contributing to the delusion that knowledge of fact can be increased by the activity of defining without reference to factual evidence, and (c) conducive to the treatment of differences in word preferences as if they were disagreements regarding facts. These abuses of definition are avoided by using the form, "By *X* I mean *Y*" instead of the classical form of definition, *"X is Y."*

deflation (economics) A general decrease in the overall price level in an economy. (accounting) An application of *index numbers* or other valuation to adjust the values of various financial statement categories.

defraud To deprive of a right or property in an illegal manner. See *fraud*.

de jure By right; under authority of law: a corporation *de jure* is an organization that has complied fully with state law in establishing and maintaining itself as a corporation. Compare with *de facto*.

del credere Of or pertaining to the obligation to make good a loss arising from failure of a purchaser to pay, undertaken by (a) a sales agent with respect to his or her principal, or (b) any assignor with respect to one who buys or advances cash against the assignor's accounts receivable. Under (b), when the goods are sold or shipped, the accounts may be formally assigned and made payable to a financial institution or a commission house, which immediately advances an agreed portion of their amount, less commission and discount based on the net amount collectible from the customer; the balance of the account is paid to the assignor upon collection of the account. In some instances, the assignee may assume the credit risk and may purchase the accounts outright. Commission houses often add to their function of selling agent those of financing the sales of their principals and of guaranteeing their accounts.

del credere agent An agent who agrees to protect his or her principal against loss resulting from the extension of credit to third parties by the agent on behalf of his or her principal. In the absence of an agreement, an agent has no responsibility to a principal for default on the part of third parties.

delegation of authority An authorization by a superior to a subordinate to reach *decisions* within a defined area, subject only to *post-audit* or review.

deliberation The process of thinking preceding and leading to a *decision*. Deliberation involves the review of alternative decisions in such a way as to minimize at a later date the possibility of overlooked purposes or interests, or with other consequences; it requires an investigation of fact, and consideration of established policies, standards, and interests that serve as guides or warnings in determining the relevance of facts.

delinquent tax (real estate or personal-property) A tax remaining unpaid on or after the date on which a penalty for nonpayment attaches. Even though the penalty may be subsequently waived and a portion of the tax may be abated or canceled, the unpaid balance of the tax continues to be delinquent until abated or canceled.

delivered price A quoted or invoice *price* that includes delivery costs to the *FOB* point, the latter being a freight terminal, a warehouse, or another location commonly accepted in the particular trade or specifically agreed to between buyer and seller; to eliminate misunderstanding, a price quotation is often followed by parenthetical notation of the *FOB* point.

delivery The passage or transfer of possession of goods or services from one person to another.

delivery basis (of revenue recognition) A method of accounting in which delivery, rather than sale, becomes the critical event in determining when revenue should be recognized. It is appropriate if completion of the earnings process is better identified with delivery of goods to a location specified by the buyer.

demand 1. The desire by any person for an economic good or service.
2. The sum total of such desires by all persons, contrasting with supply: in economics, such totals are related to prices at which consumers are willing to buy—sometimes distinguished as "effective demand"—or, when precision is required, it represents a schedule of the maximum amounts that will be bought at each of a number of different prices. Each such amount is called a "quantity demanded" and distinguished from the schedule which is called a "demand curve." At an aggregate level, as in *national income accounting*, the total of all goods and services bought by consumers at current prices.
3. The action of a creditor causing the maturity of a debt, as of a note payable on demand.

demand deposit A deposit in a financial institution, such as a bank, that may be withdrawn without notice and is usually subject to check; a commercial checking account. See, however, *compensatory balance*.

demand loan *Loan* that is due whenever the lender requests payment.

demurrage A charge by a carrier for loading or unloading time in excess of agreed or customary limits. See *lay days*.

denominator variance = *volume variance*.

density 1. (computers) The number of characters or *bytes* of data stored per inch of tape. For example, a tape might have a recorded density of 1,600 bytes per inch (BPI).
2. (statistics) A mathematical *function* used to define (or generate) the *probabilities* for members of a class of *events*.

deobligation *n.* (governmental accounting) The cancellation of an encumbrance (e.g., a purchase order for supplies), thereby releasing, to an unencumbered balance, funds previously reserved.
deobligate, *v.t.* or *i.*

department A cost center, operating unit, or area; a *function*; an *activity*.

departmental burden = *departmental overhead*.

departmental charge A charge additional to the direct cost of a particular production or operation, directly or indirectly applicable to a department, such as departmental overhead or a portion of general overhead. See *overhead*.

departmentalization The subdivision of an accounting process by departments or centers of activity, for the purpose of allocating operating costs.

departmental overhead The overhead directly and indirectly charged to a department, often including a portion of the general overhead as well as direct costs. See *overhead*.

departmental profit 1. Profit on the sales or operations of a department derived from dealings with customers, after deducting direct departmental costs and expenses and sometimes a proportion of general-overhead charges.
2. The profit attributable to a sector of an integrated business enterprise when charged with operating costs and credited with the amount at which its product could immediately have been sold to outsiders. Thus, in an integrated oil enterprise, crude oil produced may be credited to the production division at the current market price and charged to the refining division at that figure, thereby making possible the obtaining of a current "profit" on the output of the production division regardless of the timing of the sale of finished product to the public. See *interdepartmental profit; profit center; transfer price*.

dependent (federal income taxes) A relative or nonrelative, as defined in Section 151 of the *Internal Revenue Code*, receiving more than half of total support from the taxpayer (either alone or with certain others under a multiple-support agreement); under current provisions a deduction of $1,000 is permitted for each dependent whose gross income is less than $1,000 or who is a child under 19 years of age or a student (regardless of how much income such a child may have) over half of whose support is furnished by the parent. For 1985 and later years, the exemption amount will be adjusted according to the rate of inflation.

dependent variable A variable the value of which is determined or delimited by other elements (*variables* or *constants*) in the structure of an equation or other mathematical expression. See *variable; function; equation*. When a *regression analysis* has been correctly identified, the dependent variable is "caused" or "explained" by the independent variable(s). They are also called "regressand" and "regressor" variables, respectively.

depletable Subject to *depletion*; wasting; said of a natural resource such as a mineral deposit or timber tract.

depleted cost *Residual cost* after deducting accrued depletion. The term is applied to mineral, coal, oil, natural-gas, and timber properties.

depletion 1. The exhaustion of a natural resource: applied to an oil or mineral deposit, standing timber, and the like.
2. The amount of prorated cost or other indicated value assigned to the extracted or otherwise removed portion of a natural resource owned or under lease.
3. The periodic assignment of cost made in the accounts for the exhaustion of a natural resource.
4. = *percentage depletion*.
5. The process of measuring and recording the exhaustion of a mineral resource.

Depletion differs from *depreciation* in that the former implies removal of a natural resource (i.e., a physical shrinkage), while the latter implies a reduction in the service capacity of an asset through use, obsolescence, or inadequacy. See *depreciation*.

deposit 1. Currency, checks, or coupons presented to a bank by or for a customer for credit to his or her account. The deposit may be credited to a "commercial" account, from which unrestricted withdrawals are made by means of checks, or it may be credited to a special account, established for some specific purpose, and subject to withdrawal in accordance with the terms of the deposit arrangement.
2. Money, securities, or other valuables temporarily lodged with others.

depositary A bank or other institution accepting cash deposits from customers; also, an individual or organization that receives and safeguards property in any form. "Depositary" and "depository" are interchangeable; originally, the former referred to a *person* and the latter to a place.

deposit warrant A financial document authorizing the treasurer of a governmental unit to accept for deposit sums of money collected by various agencies of the governmental unit.

depreciable Subject to *depreciation*; said of buildings, machinery, equipment, and other limited-life *fixed assets*.

depreciable cost That part of the cost of a *fixed asset* that is to be spread over useful life; i.e., cost less the estimated recovery from resale or salvage. See *service cost; depreciation base*.

depreciate 1. To diminish in service capacity or utility.
2. To reduce a fixed-asset cost by entering in the accounts a provision for *depreciation*.

depreciated cost 1. *Cost* less accumulated *depreciation*, if any, and less any other related valuation account having the effect of reducing original outlay to a recoverable cost; the *book value* of a fixed asset. The net amount remaining, although equal to a fraction of original cost or to market value, is *unrecovered cost*—that portion of cost judged to be fairly assignable against likely recoveries or against operations of future years. Compare with *depreciable cost*.
2. Cost that has been expensed; depreciation expense.

depreciated original cost *Original cost* less *accumulated depreciation*.

depreciated value 1. *depreciated cost*.
2. In public-utility accounting, *depreciated original cost*, unless otherwise defined by local law or regulation with reference to specific applications.

depreciation 1. Lost usefulness; expired utility; the diminution of service yield from a *fixed asset* or fixed-asset group that cannot or will not be restored by repairs or by replacement of parts; caused by numerous factors, as recounted below. See *depreciation methods; depletion; amortization*.
2. The cost of lost usefulness: (a) = *depreciation expense*; (b) = *accumulated depreciation*.
3. Loosely, any wasting away of a physical asset and hence its cost, especially where not

accompanied by a change in outward appearance, as in a slow-moving inventory of styled goods; functional loss of value. Usually, as hereinafter, the term is limited in its application to fixed assets.

4. The process of estimating and recording lost usefulness. In the paragraphs that follow, periodic *provisions* and *accumulations* have been determined on the *straight-line method*; less common methods are described under *depreciation methods* (other than straight-line).

Depreciation basically is that part of the bundle of services believed at an earlier date to have been obtainable from a limited-life asset or, more commonly, a group of limited-life assets, and now found (a) *consumed* as originally estimated; (b) consumed, at a greater or lesser rate, from anticipated causes; (c) physically dissipated by accident or other unanticipated cause; (d) uneconomical when compared with the same or similar services available from other sources; or (e) following changes in product, product demand, or operating methods, unsuited to the future needs of the owner. In these senses, the term does not involve dollar costs but simply has reference to the physical dysfunction—past, present, and future—of the limited-life asset to which it is applied. A machine in use for some time is said to be partly depreciated; a machine worn out or for any other reason incapable of profitable use by its owner is said to be fully depreciated with respect to that owner, and hence ready for resale to a new owner who has some residual use for it; or, perhaps, ready for the junk heap.

Depreciation, as of a machine, may thus be regarded as a function of

1. Use: A machine wears when operated from day to day, and it is usually expected to wear out at least twice as fast when used 16 hours a day. This loss of serviceability is commonly regarded as the primary cause of depreciation, often being referred to as "ordinary wear and tear."

2. Disuse: A machine standing continuously idle becomes potentially less and less useful as time goes on; in fact, certain machines, like farm implements standing in the open, may age even more speedily from disuse than from use.

3. Maintenance: A high standard of maintenance prolongs the life of a machine; from lack of maintenance, or for want of skilled maintenance or operation, a machine may deteriorate rapidly.

4. Change in production: If the manufacturing process in which the machine is used is altered—for example, in the interest of increased overall efficiency or because of a change in a product—a machine may not be adaptable to the change, and its future productivity to its owner may be greatly lessened.

5. Restriction of production: When the source of supply of a raw material on which a machine operates becomes less or ceases altogether (as from a natural cause or governmental order), the machine may have fewer employable service units to yield in succeeding periods.

6. Decrease in demand: The falling off in consumer use of products to which the machine contributes or the emergence of increased competition may also curtail its future employability.

7. Progress of the arts: When new devices are perfected and another machine has become available that will perform the same operation more simply, more quickly, or more cheaply, a machine's future usefulness to any owner may be seriously limited or cease altogether.

Obsolescence is loss of usefulness occasioned by improved production methods or by such other external causes as changes in demand, and in legislation or regulation leading to the reduction of future production (items 5, 6, and 7 above). *Inadequacy* is loss of usefulness brought about by business change; a building or machine may have to be replaced because it cannot be adjusted to an alteration in the character or rate of output (item 4 above). Since obsolescence and inadequacy relate to conditions common to all business, they are normally allowed for in periodic estimates of future usefulness. Where the advent of any of these factors is sudden and cannot reasonably be anticipated, the obsolescence or inadequacy is referred to as "extraordinary" and may be of such material amount as to require special treatment in the accounts and a separate disclosure in the income statement, rather than as an increase in production costs.

Because these numerous factors affect in varying degrees the carry-forward costs of machines, buildings, and other limited-life fixed assets of every enterprise, and because they are interrelated and often inseparable, the reckoning of expired services normally proceeds, as described below, on an averaging basis, as though they were a function only of time. Furthermore, depreciation factors of a related group of fixed assets may be measured compositely more accurately than individually, not only because of their interrelated character, but also because the averaged collective experience from which future estimates of usefulness necessarily derive has a more accurate application to a group than to an individual item.

In everyday business accounting usage, the term *depreciation* is applied to the estimated *cost* of expired usefulness and to making or accumulating book entries based on the application of depreciation rates in recognition of the cost of the services which a limited-life asset or asset group will no longer yield, regardless of whether such services have actually been yielded, or, if yielded, whether they have benefited production. *Rates* of depreciation are percentages the application of which to cost yields an annual amount of depreciation expense. It is always best, therefore, to couple the word with another in order to make the meaning clear—for example, "depreciation rate," "depreciation expense," "accumulated depreciation."

Depreciation-expense computations are thus based on the assumption that every fixed asset, with the exception of land, can yield a limited quantity of useful services and has a limited life. The cost of the asset, less whatever can be anticipated in the way of resale or scrap yield, is a prepaid expense that by some method must be spread over its operating life while in the hands of and in use by its present owner. If the quantity of service units is measurable, the first method that suggests itself is reflected in the following formula for periodic depreciation expense:

$$d = \frac{q}{Q}(c - s), \qquad (1)$$

where d is the periodic expense; q, the actual quantity of service units given off during the period; Q, the estimated quantity of utilizable service units that will be yielded during the whole life of the asset; c, the original cost of the asset; and s, the portion of original cost estimated to be recoverable from salvage, i.e., resale or scrap. The application of the formula is usually impracticable, however, since only in the rarest instances can the quantity of service units of ordinary fixed assets or fixed-asset groups found in a manufacturing enterprise be measured. For most fixed assets, there is no determinable unit of service.

Formula (1) is, nevertheless, basic for such wasting assets as coal, timber, and other natural products, in which d becomes *depletion* expense; q, the quantity of such units currently extracted; and Q, the estimate of tons, square feet, or barrels extractable (including q). But since Q changes as new "proven" areas are developed under or on the land or lease of which c is the cost, the rate q/Q may have to be reestablished from time to time; and the formula becomes

$$d = \frac{q}{Q_1}(c - s - y), \qquad (2)$$

Q_1 being the estimate of quantities removed and to be removed in the current year and future years, and y the balance of accumulated depletion carried over from prior years. When rates change because of reestimates of remaining available serviceability, it is customary (a) to include all of the year of the change in the new computation, and (b) not to alter accumulations of previous years, a procedure also applicable to any depreciation recomputations.

In present-day depreciation accounting, the simplest and most prevalent practice in determining annual depreciation expense is to apply a percentage rate to the cost of an asset group like "machinery," the formula being

$$d = \frac{1}{n}c, \qquad (3)$$

where n is the estimated average number of years during which the group of assets is expected to be in use. The ratio $1/n$, expressed as a percentage, is a composite rate—one that may have application to many items of the same class and even to many enterprises. Thus, a depreciation rate that may be found in all sorts of businesses is the furniture-and-fixture rate of 10%. As a composite rate, it has evolved from general experience with large groups of fixed assets; applied to a particular enterprise or to a small asset group, it may prove more conventional than accurate. It is not uncommon to find the cost of an asset group such as furniture and fixtures completely offset by accumulated provisions,

notwithstanding that the assets are still in use. Similarly, conventional rates may be applied to other classes of assets; these, too, may be found to be inaccurate when utilized in individual enterprises, even though they may represent a reasonable average for an industry.

The above three formulas are so-called "straight-line" formulas, as are the following two variants:

$$d = \frac{1}{n}(c - s) \qquad (4)$$

and

$$d = \frac{1}{n_1}(c - s - y), \qquad (5)$$

where n is the estimated number of years of useful life, n_1 the estimated number of years of remaining life including the current year, and y the depreciation accumulated in and brought forward from prior years. In most instances these variants yield substantially the same results, notwithstanding theoretical distinctions. Of the five depreciation formulas, (5) is probably the most accurate, provided that its application is accompanied by periodic remaining-life studies leading to the frequent correction of n_1.

A further variant arises from the use of a *lapsing schedule*, a practice sometimes followed by federal internal-revenue agents where no running inventory of a fixed-asset group is maintained; it is essentially the separate application of formula (3) to each year's acquisitions, a separate schedule being prepared for each principal class of fixed assets.

Where depreciation has been accumulated by the application of composite rates to asset groups, experience indicates that retirements are best charged in full against the accumulation, exceptions being made only in the case of individual major assets that have been in use substantially less than the average life of that class, as reflected in the depreciation rate. A "major" asset might be regarded for this purpose as one whose cost is greater than 20% of the accumulated depreciation applicable to that class of assets; a "substantially less" life might be one that does not exceed half of the average for that class. These are not presented as general standards but as types of tests that an auditor, for example, might employ in discussing the effects of varying procedures with clients. A more common but statistically less desirable practice is to regard as current expense or income every variation between the original cost of an asset retired, less scrap value, and the proportional depreciation accrued during the years an asset has been in use. Thus, a machine acquired at a cost of $1,000 and scrapped seven years later belongs to a group of 100 machines against which an annual composite depreciation rate of 10% has been applied. If a half-year basis is followed for additions and retirements, or if the balance at the beginning of each calendar year is the basis for applying the depreciation rate, seven years' depreciation will have been accumulated. With a scrap-value allowance in each year's computation equal to 5% of cost and with, say, a presently expected realization of $100 from the sale of the machine, the problem of classifying the "unrecovered" cost of $235 remains. Is this (a) a charge against the accumulated depreciation on machinery, (b) additional depreciation for the year, or (c) a loss on the disposal of fixed assets? Preference is given to the first alternative because a composite rate of depreciation will often result in apparent overprovisions in the case of assets in use for periods longer than the average, and the remaining cost of $235 will ordinarily be absorbed where such averages are in use.

On the whole, the preferable standard of depreciation practice is to use a composite rate for each of the main fixed-asset groups;

to charge against the accumulated provisions the full cost, less recoveries, of each asset retired, except under conditions described above; and to test the adequacy of accumulations periodically and revise the composite rate where tests reveal an accumulation of material over- or underprovisions.

To test the propriety of an annual provision for depreciation, an engineering survey may be made by examining each asset covered by the reserve and estimating its remaining years of useful life. A "book value" for each asset, consisting of original cost less accumulated depreciation at rates in force since its acquisition, is then determined and divided by a newly estimated years of remaining useful life. The sum of the quotients thus obtained, divided by the total original cost of the same asset group, indicates the theoretical percentage of accumulations that should have been recorded. The same basic data will also serve in a test for accumulation adequacy. Sampling methods applied to asset groupings containing large numbers of components of the same class yield equally satisfactory results.

Many accountants accept the practice of removing from the accounts the costs of fixed assets shown by *lapsing schedules* to be wholly depreciated. This practice may be modified in instances where larger retirements are individually recorded, but the practice is recognized as a much less desirable alternative to the full reporting and recording of each retired asset. A lapsing schedule is never a good substitute for a *plant ledger*.

Management attention to depreciation is weakened by the not uncommon assertion that the annual provision for depreciation is at best a crude and arbitrary estimate—an estimate that has wide flexibility. See *depreciation methods (appropriation method)*. This attitude leads occasionally to the manipulation of depreciation provisions in the interest of "making a showing"—decreasing provisions in years of poor profit margins and increasing them in good years. Attempts to modify the depreciation charge to correspond with units produced are not often successful, as already noted. Nevertheless, where such an attempt is made, the worth of the result produced depends on the care with which the altered rates have been arrived at after a study of relevant engineering reports and such factors as the actual use of the assets, rates for normal years, the ability of normal and abnormal rates to absorb cost during useful life, and the effect of possibly mounting obsolescence and inadequacy on such rates. The latter factors are almost invariably present and operate inexorably to shorten economic life, notwithstanding nonuse.

Management policy on depreciation is best kept on an objective level, with periodic engineering studies and internal reviews of depreciation rates and accumulations adequacy as a major feature of information and control. See *depreciation committee*.

In the income statement, the amount of depreciation expense is shown on the face of the statement or in a footnote. The amount of any amortization provided under permissive tax laws or of any other form of extraordinary depreciation or obsolescence should also appear as a separate item, with explanations.

Depreciation accumulations (often termed "reserves" or "allowances") on the balance sheet are subtracted from the assets to which they relate. The principal exception may be found in the balance sheets of certain public utilities, a few of which are still not on a full "depreciation basis"—that is, their reserves cover only fairly immediate replacements and have sometimes been classed with other "reserves" on the liability side of the statement; but the better practice, reflected in the requirements of regulatory bodies, is to subtract the accumulations (reserves) from the assets even though they may not have reached their full level, since they are still *valuation accounts*, notwithstanding their insufficiency.

depreciation accounting The *policy*-directed, periodic writedown or allocation, most frequently on a *straight-line method*, of the cost of a limited-life asset or asset group, in conformity with the best available estimates of usefulness lost to date, remaining usefulness, and recovery values; contrasts with *replacement* or *retirement* accounting, as described under *depreciation methods*.

depreciation adequacy Sufficiency of *accumulated depreciation*, with due regard for the fairness of prospective allocations of cost to future operations; see *depreciation; depreciation policy*.

depreciation base The recorded cost or other basis of a fixed asset or fixed-asset group that is to be recovered through depreciation, excluding estimated recovery from resale or salvage; *depreciable cost*.

depreciation committee A staff group of engineers and accountants or other qualified personnel whose functions are to (a) formulate, recommend, and maintain *depreciation policies*; (b) determine and redetermine, at frequent intervals, *provisions* and *accumulations* of depreciation for accounting purposes; (c) further determine similar elements for tax purposes should these differ; (d) provide information and opinions to operating personnel, management, directors, stockholders, and regulatory bodies. See *depreciation policy*.

depreciation expense 1. That portion of the cost or other basis of a fixed asset or fixed-asset group charged against the operations of an accounting period. 2. For a single year, the *depreciation base* times the *depreciation* *rate*. 3. Any provision for depreciation. See *depreciation*.

depreciation fund Money or marketable securities set aside for the purpose of replacing or providing assistance in replacing depreciating fixed assets. Modern financial practice no longer recognizes the need for such a fund; the concurrent additions to working capital that normally accompany depreciation provisions are now regarded as available for both fixed-asset additions and operating activities.

depreciation methods (other than *straight-line method*; see *depreciation*) The varied arithmetic processes of determining periodic provisions for depreciation and their accumulation over the useful life of limited-life fixed assets. Under *depreciation* the process followed throughout is the near-universal *straight-line method*. Other methods sometimes advocated or approved by accountants (often with qualifications) for income-tax and other purposes are described below. See also *accelerated cost recovery system*, a system of depreciation for tax purposes introduced in the Economic Recovery Tax Act of 1981, under which assets are depreciated over periods that are substantially shorter than their economic lives.

Age-life method: Under this method, the periodic provision for depreciation of an asset or asset group is determined by dividing its unrecovered cost at the beginning of the period (to which one-half of any additions during the period have been added) by the number, plus one, of the anticipated periods of remaining life at the end of the period. This method, essentially a variant of the *straight-line method*, is a technically correct one; the term may be applied to any situation where *depreciation rates* are periodically redetermined for future periods in the light of judgments as to remaining life expectancy. Compare with *composite-life method*, below.

Annuity method: Under this method, a constant annual amount that, when invested at a given interest rate, i, will accumulate to the original cost A of the asset (less salvage value, if any) at the end of the service life, is first computed by using a formula for sinking fund, $Ai/[(1 + i)^n - 1]$ (see *interest formulas*). This annual amount is increased by the interest at rate i on the beginning balance of accumulated depreciation. For a three-year asset costing $1,000 with no salvage value, the annual amount of sinking fund when i is 10% is $1,000 \times .1/[(1.1)^3 - 1] = \$1,000 \times .1/.331 = \$302$. Thus, the depreciation expense in the first year is $302. The depreciation expense in the second year is $302 plus interest at 10% on the beginning balance of the accumulated depreciation, which is $302, namely $302 + .1 \times \$302 = \$332$. The depreciation in the third year is likewise $302 + .1 \times (\$302 + \$332) = \$366$ (a rounding error adjusted), making the accumulated depreciation equal to the original cost of $1,000 at the end of the asset life ($302 + $332 + $366).

The same depreciation figures may be obtained by using a capital recovery factor $Ai/[1 - (1 + i)^{-n}]$ instead of the sinking-fund factor. (See *interest formulas*.) For the same asset, the capital recovery factor is $1,000 \times .1/[1 - (1.1)^{-3}] = \$1,000/2.487 = \$402$. That is, at 10% rate of return on the original investment of $1,000, annual cash recovery of $402 is expected. The return of 10% on the unrecovered investment ($1,000) is $100. Hence, $402 - $100 = $302 is the depreciation expense, leaving unrecovered investment at $1,000 - $302 = $698. Out of the cash recovery of $402 in the second year, 10% on the unrecovered investment ($698), or $70, is a return on investment, hence $402 - $70 = $332 is the depreciation expense in the second year, leaving the unrecovered investment at $698 - $332 = $366. Out of the cash recovery of $402 in the third year, 10% of $366 or $36 (a rounding error adjusted) is a return on investment, hence $402 − $36 = $366 is the depreciation expense in the third year, thus recovering the original investment fully.

The annuity method is also called the "sinking-fund method" but a distinction is sometimes made between the two, under which the above approach is designated as the sinking-fund method and an approach that adds some interest charges on top of the depreciation computed above is designated as the annuity method. In this case, the latter approach yields accumulated depreciation greater than the original cost. Neither approach, however, has been accepted in practice in any significant degree.

Appraisal method: The annual depreciation expense is the difference between the appraisal value of the fixed assets at the beginning and end of the period. This method has disappeared from practice. See *appraisal*.

Appropriation method: Depreciation expense is a fraction of sales or other income amount, or is otherwise arrived at without regard to the concept of lost usefulness: a method occasionally followed in the belief that the determination of the annual amount of depreciation is a matter of financial policy—an amount that might well depend on and vary with available profits. In some instances, amounts provided have been roughly proportional to asset use, particularly where the amount of profit has more or less reflected business activity. Although universally criticized by accountants, the method is still occasionally followed in practice.

Combined-depreciation-and-upkeep method: The usual *depreciation base* is increased by estimated total maintenance cost over the useful life of the asset, maintenance costs as incurred being charged directly to the reserve. The purpose is to equalize maintenance charges, which often occur irregularly, over the years the asset is in use, but the method is no longer in use, since in most situations maintenance costs do not vary greatly or cannot be estimated.

Composite-life method: The application of a single rate to a large group of assets, usually of the same general class, such as buildings, machinery, or trucks; details of this method appear under *depreciation*; see also *age-life method*, above. Essentially an application of straight-line depreciation, it is deemed by many accountants to yield more dependable results than other methods. Under federal income-tax regulations, the composite-life method may be applied not only to individual classes of assets but to all classes combined. Such an extension of the method would find practical application, however, only in cases where the whole asset group remained relatively stable over a long period of time and where frequent tests are made of average remaining life. The term *group depreciation* is also used, especially when a group of assets which are homogeneous in service life is depreciated under a single rate.

Declining-balance method or *diminishing-provision method*: The annual charge for depreciation is the amount obtained (a) by applying a fixed percentage to the diminishing balance of the asset account, that is, the balance after deducting preceding depreciation provisions; or (b) by applying a diminishing rate to the original cost of the asset. An illustration of (a) may be observed in the example on the next page, where a constant rate of 10% has been applied.

At the end of the tenth year, more than one-third of the cost remains; the process goes on until the balance is arbitrarily absorbed in a single year or a switch to another method, such as the straight-line method or the sum-of-the-years-digits method, is made.

Year	Annual Depreciation	Balance of Asset Cost
Cost	—	$1,000.00
1	$100.00	900.00
2	90.00	810.00
3	81.00	729.00
4	72.90	656.10
5	65.61	590.40
6	59.05	531.44
7	53.14	478.30
8	47.83	430.47
9	43.05	387.42
10	38.74	348.68

Year	Annual Depreciation at 20.5672%	Balance Remaining
Cost	—	$1,000.00
1	$205.67	794.33
2	163.58	630.75
3	129.73	501.02
4	103.04	397.98
5	81.84	316.14
6	65.02	251.12
7	51.64	199.48
8	41.02	158.46
9	32.59	125.87
10	25.87	100.00

If the constant rate (10% in the above example) is set at twice the rate under the straight-line method (5% of acquisition cost when service life is 20 years), the method is called *double-declining-balance method*.

A formula sometimes suggested for this method is

$$r = 1 - \sqrt[n]{\frac{s}{c}},$$

where r is the annual rate of depreciation, n the number of years of expected life, s the salvage value, and c the asset cost. Thus, the rate applicable to the declining value of an asset purchased for $1,000, having an expected life of 10 years and salvage of $100, would be

$$r = 1 - \sqrt[10]{\frac{100}{1,000}}$$

$$= 1 - \text{antilog}\ \frac{2-3}{10}$$

$$= 1 - \text{antilog}\ (.9 - 1)$$

$$= 1 - .794328$$

$$= .205672,$$

where *logarithms* to the base 10 were employed.

The balance at the end of each year of the ten-year period would then be:

which is exact, since $s = \$100$, the *scrap value*. In fact, the formula is exact for any $0 < s \leqslant c$.

A diminishing-rate variant known as the *sum-of-the-years-digits method* (SYD) involves the determination of an annual depreciation provision by the application to the asset cost of a fraction the numerator of which is the number of years remaining (including the current year) in the estimated life of the asset, and the denominator, the sum of all such numbers. Thus, if an asset has a life of n years, then the denominator is $n(n + 1)/2$ and the successive numerators are $n, n - 1, \ldots, 2, 1$. For instance, a life expectancy of 5 years would yield $5 \times 6/2 = 15 = 5 + 4 + 3 + 2 + 1$, with 5/15 for the initial fraction followed by 4/15 for the second fraction and finally 1/15 for the final fraction. Moreover, $(5 + 4 + 3 + 2 + 1)/15 = 1$, so that the SYD allocation also accounts for all of the amount to be depreciated.

At one time in common use in the United States and in England, particularly when depreciation provisions were being credited directly to the asset accounts on which they were based, this method had nearly disappeared from American practice. However, some years ago, interest in diminishing-provision methods has been revived. There have been several reasons: (a) buildings and equipment may have been acquired at inflationary prices, and management may desire to amortize such costs—or the inflationary portions of them—as quickly as possible in order that future periods will not be burdened with costs ascribable to the present; (b) the current revenues of the owner of the assets may be regarded as reflecting an economic condition that cannot continue—hence, cost inflations in some degree match and ought to offset revenue inflations; (c) a greater amount of depreciation, made possible by declining-balance methods, has been regarded by some business managements and their accountants as an acceptable substitute for straight-line depreciation on replacement costs—the expression of the last-named in financial statements, other than in footnotes or supplementary schedules, having met with professional opposition; (d) large amounts of depreciation should be provided in years when income-tax rates are high, thus in some measure equalizing the tax burden over the years; (e) as the depreciation base becomes exhausted, the pressure on the Congress to permit depreciation on current replacement costs in income-tax returns will become virtually irresistible; (f) the federal income-tax law and regulations now permit an even faster recovery method called the *accelerated cost recovery system.*

Policy method: A method dictated by financial or social *policy* rather than service yields. In some instances, as in public-works projects, the costs of improvements having service lives extending indefinitely into the future are *allocated* (3) against the income derived from the projects over a period known to be less than their useful lives. The policy leading to this foreshortening of the period of depreciation originates with the governing body. Thus, the cost of projects

financed with serial bonds (e.g, those of the St. Lawrence Seaway Development Corporation) may be depreciated in amounts equal to the repayment installments as they fall due, although the project may live on and yield services for many years thereafter.

Production method (Production-unit-basis method; Service-output method; Unit-of-production method): The provision for depreciation is computed as a fixed rate per unit of product, based on an estimate of the total number of units the property will produce during its service life. See *depreciation.*

Replacement method: (a) An estimate is made of the cost of replacing the limited-life assets actually in use; the amount of current depreciation expense, usually on a straight-line cost basis, is increased by a percentage derived from a comparison of the anticipated replacement cost with recorded cost. (b) Another practice given this designation is occasionally found where the cost of major replacements is disposed of in the same manner as that accorded minor replacements under approved methods of depreciation: the cost of replacements is charged to expense, the asset account remaining unchanged except for additions; no depreciation, as such, is provided. This method now stands wholly discredited.

Retirement method: Provision is made only for the value of property units shortly to be retired. This method, at one time in vogue among public utilities, has now been generally abandoned.

Service-capacity method: = *declining-balance method*, above.

Sum-of-the-years-digits method: See *declining-balance method*, above.

Unit method: Composite depreciation is calculated, as on a straight-line basis, for each item rather than the group.

Unit-summation method: Under this method, the depreciation rate is calculated anew each year for application to the book cost of the units in a property group. The rate is calculated in such a manner as to produce a total charge equal to the sum of the accruals which would be obtained if individual rates had been applied to each item in the group; a variant of the *straight-line method*.

Working-hours method: The computation is based on a fixed rate per hour of use, determined by estimating the total number of hours the property will be in use during its service life. Except in rare cases this method is inapplicable because total operating hours cannot be estimated with any degree of accuracy.

depreciation policy The determination, recordation, and reportage of fixed-asset depreciation: (a) the process of arriving at *provisions* (*1*) therefor; (b) the frequency and method of testing of current provisions and *accumulations*; (c) applications of *accumulations* to fixed-asset retirements and disposals; (d) provisions and *accumulations* (unrecorded) for tax purposes and their disclosure in periodic reports; and, (e) the display of recorded provisions, *accumulations* and explanations on income statements and balance sheets. See *depreciation; depreciation committee*.

depreciation provision The amount determined as *depreciation expense* for a specified period; a charge to *expense* and a credit to the *valuation account; accumulated depreciation*.

depreciation rate A percentage which when applied to the *depreciation base* will yield *depreciation expense* for a year.

depreciation ratio A *ratio* which measures the average rate of depreciation being charged by a firm, calculated by dividing depreciation expense by gross assets subject to depreciation. The ratio is used to evaluate the adequacy of the depreciation rate and to detect attempts at income smoothing.

depreciation recapture (federal income taxes) The portion of gain on disposal of business assets which is treated as ordinary income because it represents the recapture of prior depreciation deductions. On sale or exchange of equipment, Section 1245 provides that all depreciation deducted since 1961 is recaptured as ordinary income. On sale or exchange of buildings, the recapture applies only to depreciation in excess of straight-line and depends on the nature and holding period of the building. Section 1250 provides that varying percentages of excess depreciation will be recaptured as ordinary income.

depreciation reserve = *accumulated depreciation*: a term now increasingly avoided in published balance sheets.

depreciation unit The asset or asset group against the cost of which the depreciation rate is applied. It may be an individual asset or asset part, such as a machine or the walls of a building, in which case the depreciation method is referred to as "unit depreciation," or it may be a number of similar assets, where a single rate can be applied to their collective cost (*group depreciation*). See *depreciation; fixed asset*.

derivative suit (or action) A suit in equity by a shareholder for, or on behalf of the corporation, against directors or officers who have acted against the best interests of the shareholders.

derived demand (economics) The *demand* for a good or service which occurs because it will be employed in the production of another product. Consumer demand for one product may give rise to demands for other products used in its fabrication. The former is referred to as a final demand and the latter, derived demands. See *demand*.

descent The disposition of the real property of an intestate.

descriptive financial statement An embellished form of financial statement, now seldom employed, in which a brief explanation follows each item in the statement, the purpose being to assist the reader in grasping the meaning of the item. It was found, however, that brief explanations of certain items might, without some knowledge of accounting and business practices, lead to incorrect inferences; with such knowledge, most of the explanations were superfluous.

descriptive model See *model, n.*

descriptive statistics That branch of statistical studies devoted to the summarization of the group characteristics of particular sets of observed data. See *statistical inference.*

descriptive theory See *normative theory.*

detail account One of a group of accounts that constitute a *subsidiary ledger.*

detailed audit An examination of the books of account, or a portion thereof, whereby all or substantially all entries and transactions are reviewed and verified, as contrasted with the more usual examination by means of tests or samples. See *audit; sample; testcheck.*

determine To conclude; particularly (auditing), to reach an opinion consequent to the observation of the fit of sample data within the limit, range, or area associated with substantial conformance, accuracy, or other predetermined standard. The process of auditing may be regarded as a series of lesser determinations contributing to a major overall determination.

deterministic equivalent A *deterministic model* with solutions that satisfy optimization or other properties of a related *stochastic* model.

deterministic model A *model* which contains no *random* terms.

developing countries See *less developed country.*

development expense 1. An expenditure made in opening up and developing mineral properties, oil wells, timberlands, and the like. Development expense may be capitalized and written off at a fixed rate per unit of product or over a limited initial period of operations; or it may be written off as incurred.

2. = *promotion expense.*

development stage enterprise An enterprise devoting substantially all of its efforts to establishing a new business without generating significant revenues from the planned principal operations.

devise The disposition of real estate by will. —*devise, v.*

devolution A British term meaning to *decentralize*, with emphasis on geographical divisions.

Dicksee, Lawrence R. (1864-1932) The first occupant of an accounting chair in a U.K. university, Lawrence R. Dicksee was a prolific and influential author. His *Advanced Accounting* and books on goodwill and depreciation and reserves were widely cited in the first decades of the present century, and his classic treatise, *Auditing*, first published in 1892, is now in its eighteenth edition. Dicksee's *Auditing* served as the prototype for the series of auditing textbooks written in the United States by *Robert H. Montgomery.*

difference estimator An estimator (or sample evaluation method) in which auxiliary information in difference form is used to project sample results to the population. For example, the difference between the sample value of x and y and the population x value can be used to estimate the population value for y. In auditing, x is typically the book value of an item and y is the audited value.

differential analysis See *incremental analysis.*

differential cost 1. = *marginal cost.* See *incremental cost.*

2. The excess of estimated or alternative cost of an operation or product from which the cost of some factor or refinement has been removed or added.

3. That portion of the cost of a *function* attributable to and identifiable with an added feature: cost including the added feature less cost without the added feature. If the addition becomes permanent, the added cost tends to merge with other costs and lose its identity.

differential investment Difference between cost or carrying value of an investment in equity securities and an investor's (parent company's) proportionate share of the net book value of the affiliate; also referred to as the excess of investment cost over book value or the excess of book value over investment cost. In consolidated financial statements the difference in the first case becomes "excess from consolidation" and "consolidation surplus" in the second. See *intercompany elimination*.

digit One of the symbols used to represent a value smaller than N for a system with base N. For example, the digits 0, 1 are used for the binary (base 2) system and the characters 0, 1, 2, 3, 4, 5, 6, 7, 8, 9 form the digits for the decimal (base 10) system. All other characters in a system using this base are formed from these digits.

digital computer A computer in which data are mainly represented by discrete values usually in *binary code*. The computer is designed to perform both arithmetic and logical operations on data in this form. This is in contrast to an *analog computer* which represents data values continuously.

digraph Directed graph. See *graph*.

dilution Relative loss or weakening of *equity (3)* position.

dilutive Possessing a potential for *dilution*. See also *anti-dilution*.

diminishing-provision method (of depreciation) See *depreciation methods*.

direct access (computers) A storage organization which allows data to be located directly as opposed to going through some location relative to the previous access.

direct cost 1. The cost of any good or service that contributes to and is readily ascribable to product or service output, any other cost incurred being regarded as *indirect cost*. Commonly recognized direct costs of manufactured product are outlays for labor, material, and overhead that vary with the volume of production. Under recent trends in concepts of management controls, every cost is a direct cost, and is identifiable with or contributes to an endproduct or intermediate service.

2. = *variable cost*.

direct costing 1. The process of assigning costs as they are incurred to products and services.

2. The doctrine that *direct cost* is the basis of valuing output. Direct costing in a business enterprise requires a classification of accounts in which recognition is given (a) to the separability and assignment to output of *direct costs* or *variable costs*, the amounts of which fluctuate with output volume; and (b) to unallocated *fixed costs* or *period costs*, which reflect the maintenance of a readiness to manufacture and to sell, and which remain relatively unaffected by volume changes. Often included in the concept is the valuation of inventories. Sales less the direct cost of sales is known as contribution margin or contribution to profit and overhead. In *absorption costing*, which contrasts with direct costing, no distinction between fixed and variable costs is made in the accounts, and supplementary statistical analyses are required to bring out relationships between costs, volume, and profit. Direct costing is not a complete costing plan in itself, but it is a feature that may be introduced into either *process-costing* or *job-order-costing* systems, and *standard costs* may or may not be employed. Direct costing is sometimes re-

garded as a return to primitive cost accounting, under which only the prime cost of products was determined.

Early applications of direct costing were made independently by a number of organizations. A *National Association of Accountants* research report (*Direct Costing*, Research Series No. 23) states that the earliest published description of direct costing was contained in an article written by Jonathan N. Harris and published in an NAA Bulletin of January 15, 1936. The term "direct costing" appears to have been originated by the author of that article, and since then the concept of direct costing has expanded rapidly. In the United Kingdom, the equivalent term is *marginal costing*.

Under direct costing, separate accounts are provided for the accumulation of fixed and variable costs. Direct material and direct labor are ordinarily variable with production volume, and no change is usually made in methods of accounting for them. Manufacturing overhead, however, contains both variable and fixed components and only the former represents a direct cost.

Income statements prepared for individual product classifications commonly show separately fixed costs directly traceable to a product group and fixed costs of a general nature associated with products only by allocation.

Direct costing has four principal areas of usefulness corresponding to the following purposes for which cost data are used: (a) controlling current costs; (b) period or project profit planning; (c) determining periodic income and financial condition; and (d) estimating periodic inventories.

Where control over current costs is the objective, experience shows that control is more effective if costs associated with current volume are separated from those that are independent of current volume. Techniques of *flexible budgeting* developed for this purpose rest upon classifications of costs according to variability with volume in both budgets and departmental cost ledgers.

In predicting profit consequences of decisions to approve or reject a sales-promotion idea, an order at a special price, a proposal to make rather than to buy, or other proposals causing changes in volume, the ready availability of relevant cost data simplifies and speeds decision making. It may also improve the quality of decisions. Key figures for this purpose are rates of change in variable cost and marginal income per unit of volume and the periodic amount of fixed cost.

Under direct costing, periodic net profit varies directly with sales volume, provided that factors other than sales volume remain constant. In contrast, under absorption costing, changes in the fixed-cost component of inventories tend to obscure relationships between sales volume and profits. For any given period, the difference in profits shown by the two methods is equal to the amount of fixed cost taken out of inventory or added to inventory through inventory reduction or buildup. Profit differences tend to be greater for short periods than for long periods, because production and sales tend to be more nearly in balance over long periods. The literature on direct costing has presented considerable evidence to show that those who use income statements often fail to understand the influence exerted on profits by changes in inventory.

direct debt Debt which a governmental unit has incurred in its own name or assumed through the annexation of territory or consolidation with another governmental unit. See also *overlapping debt*.

direct expense = *direct cost*.

direct financing A financing agreement arrived at through direct negotiations between borrower and investor without intermediation by an *underwriter*.

direct financing lease A lease accounted for as a financing transaction by a lessor.

directive A call for conformity to a specified plan or procedure; a limited or general grant of *authority*; any oral or written communication requiring compliance, action, or restraint of action.

direct labor Labor as an element of *direct cost* applied directly to a product; the cost of such labor. Compare with *indirect labor*.

direct labor hour rate An overhead rate used to allocate factory overhead to the units of product produced. It is derived by dividing the budgeted overhead costs at the budgeted volume level as measured by direct labor hours by direct labor hours, where the numerator is the sum of fixed overhead and variable overhead per direct labor hour times budgeted direct labor hours. See *overhead; machine-hour rate*.

direct liability An obligation of a debtor arising from money, goods, or services received by him or her from another person; excluded would be assumed or contingent liabilities.

direct material Material as an element of *direct cost* entering into and becoming a constituent element of a product; the cost of such material.

directors' report Any financial report prepared primarily for corporate directors; specifically, quarterly and annual reports, often unaudited, addressed to directors, containing many breakdowns, analyses, and summaries not normally supplied in reports to stockholders.

direct overhead Factory, selling, or other expense attributed solely to a certain product, and thus constituting a *direct cost*.

direct shipment = *drop shipment*.

direct tax A tax which is borne entirely by the *entity* on which it is levied. A tax which is not shifted from its original point of impact. Examples: (1) a lump-sum tax per capita; (2) an individual income tax. Until passage of the 16th Amendment the use of an income tax was constitutionally forbidden to the U.S. government along with other direct taxes. An individual income tax is a direct tax only on the assumptions (1) that individuals strive to maximize their incomes and (2) that the rates are below 100%. Even a lump-sum tax per capita may lose some or all of the properties of a direct tax if political or geographical differentials provide incentives for individuals to move from the jurisdiction imposing this tax. See *indirect tax; incidence*.

direct test of financial balance A substantive auditing procedure which is applied to a recorded account balance rather than to a transaction. These may be balances recorded as of the date of the audited financial statements or as of an interim date, where additional audit work is required for the intervening period.

disaggregated cost A breakdown of cost into subcategories as when, for example, product cost is divided into material, labor, and overhead.

disaggregation A process or state that is the opposite of *aggregation, q.v.* A process or the result of decomposing an aggregate into further divisions.

disallowance (governmental accounting) See *exception* (2).

disbursement Payment in currency or by check. The term is not synonymous with *expenditure*.

disbursing officer (governmental accounting) A bonded employee authorized to pay out cash or issue checks in settlement of vouchers to the propriety of which a *certifying officer* has attested.

DISC = *Domestic International Sales Corporation*.

disclaimer A statement in an *auditors' report* indicating the inability of the auditor to express an opinion on the *fairness* of the financial statements referred to in the report. A disclaimer is appropriate when an auditor has not performed an examination sufficient in scope to enable him or her to form an opinion or, in certain cases, involving material uncertainties.

disclosure An explanation, or exhibit, attached to a financial statement, or embodied in a report (e.g., an auditor's) containing a fact, opinion, or detail required or helpful in the interpretation of the statement or report; an expanded heading or a footnote.

discontinued operations Term applied to the result of a sale, abandonment, disposal, or formally planned disposal of an important part of an entity's operations. Under *GAAP*, a section of the income statement between *income from continuing operations* and *extraordinary items* that reports both income (loss) from disposed segments and gains (losses) from *disposal of a business segment*.

discount 1. The difference between the estimated worth of a future benefit and its present value; a compensation for waiting or an allowance for returns from using the present value of these returns in other ways. See *interest formulas*.
2. An allowance given for the settlement of a debt usually as a result of payment before it is due. See *cash discount; trade discount*.
3. The excess of the par or face value of a security over the amount collected or paid for it. See *debt discount; bond discount; stock discount*.
4. Commission deducted by a banker or broker for selling an issue of securities.
5. A promissory note acquired by a bank at a discount and rediscounted with another bank or held as an asset under a title that distinguishes it from other classes of loans.

discount earned 1. A reduction in the purchase price of a good or service because of early payment. See *cash discount*. Today it

is usually deducted in arriving at invoice cost regardless of the time of payment; under such circumstances, it does not appear as a separate item in an income statement. If the deduction is taken only when payment is made, it is customary to regard it as miscellaneous income.
2. *pl.* (retail accounting) Cash discounts applicable to merchandise sold; the equivalent of cash discounts taken, adjusted for opening and closing discount allowances applicable to unsold merchandise.

discounted cash-flow method In *capital budgeting*, evaluation of projects by calculating the *present value* of cash flows associated with each project. If *cost of capital* to the firm, adjusted for the difference between risk of the project and the firm, is used as the discount rate, then the project should be added to the pool of acceptable projects when the net present value of a project is positive.

discount lost 1. A cash discount on a purchase, not taken advantage of because of failure to pay before the expiration of the discount period.
2. *pl.* Hence, an expense account maintained for the purpose of recording such discounts. Where this practice is followed, the purchase is recorded at the net amount, i.e., less the cash discount. Should it be necessary to pay the gross amount, or should the amount of the discount be paid to the creditor at a later date, the additional charge, representing the discount lost, is carried to an account bearing that name.

discovery period (insurance) The period of time allowed the insured after the termination of an insurance contract or bond in which to discover losses occurring during the time the coverage was in force and coming under the terms of the contract.

discovery sampling A procedure for determining the sample size required to achieve a given probability of observing at least one occurrence of a particular characteristic.

discovery-value accounting Accounting for reserves of gas, oil, or other natural resources that have been explored but not extracted which are *capitalized (4)* at the asset's *net realizable value*; contrast to *full-cost method* and *successful efforts method*, which capitalize *costs* incurred in the exploration. See also *reserve recognition accounting*.

discrepancy Any observed difference between opinions or facts, often with the implication of error or other impropriety.

discretionary costs A cost which may be varied at the discretion of a *responsibility center* manager; cost appropriated in relation to top management policies which has no direct relation to volume of activity. For certain expenditures (e.g., research and development, personnel administration, legal advisory services) no clear relationship exists between the amount spent and the benefits gained. Hence, management discretion typically determines the amount budgeted for such items. See *managed costs*.

discriminant analysis A statistical technique used for the prediction or qualitative classification of variables. The subjects being analyzed are first classified into *a priori* qualitative classes. Data are then collected for independent variables which seem relevant for predicting the classes to which each subject belongs. Discriminant analysis techniques are used to determine, from past data, a linear combination of the independent variables that best discriminates between the qualitative classes, in which case the discriminant function takes the form

$$Z = B_1X_1 + B_2X_2 + \ldots + B_nX_n,$$

where Z = discriminate score; B_i = discriminant coefficients; X_i = independent predictor variable, $i = 1, 2, \ldots, n$. Thus, discriminant analysis transforms the independent

variables into a single discriminate score, Z, which is used to classify the subjects into their respective qualitative classes. Discriminant analysis has been used to test the ability of accounting variables to predict the failure of firms. It has also been used to classify potential credit risks when there are large numbers of applicants for relatively small loans. See *credit analysis*.

discussion memorandum A document issued by the Financial Accounting Standards Board for public comment which is intended to provide a comprehensive discussion of issues and alternative solutions to a problem of practice along with arguments for and against each alternative solution.

dishonor To refuse *acceptance (1)* or payment: said of the drawee of *checks* and other *commercial paper (2)*.

disintermediation Withdrawal of funds from savings accounts or other types of time deposits for reinvestment, usually at higher rates of interest.

disinvestment 1. The sale or divestiture of part of a business enterprise.
2. More generally, liquidation or movement out of any investment or line of business.

dispatch earning A saving in shipping costs arising from prompt unloading at a destination.

dispersion A measure of the variation of a group of numerical data from a central tendency, such as an arithmetic mean, by determining the *range* of such data or their *average deviation* or *standard deviation*.

disposable income (national income accounting) *Personal income (2)* less income and other taxes paid by individuals, the balance being available for consumption or savings. See *national income accounting*.

disposal of a business segment Actual or formally planned elimination of a major operation of a segment of a business through sale, abandonment, discontinuance, condemnation, or expropriation. Separate disclosure on the income statement of the discontinued segment's identifiable income or loss plus gain or loss from its disposal is required under *GAAP*. Disclosure should be under the caption discontinued operations and not listed as an extraordinary item. See *discontinued operations*.

disposition of net income (or net profit or net earnings) A financial statement sometimes appearing in auditors' reports and annual reports to stockholders or owners showing dividends declared or profits withdrawn, provisions for and returns from appropriated surplus, and other items, together with the balance added to *retained earnings* or *proprietorship*. See *income statement*.

distort *v.* To create a false impression; specifically, to overstate or understate a conclusion, amount, or other representation of opinion or fact to a degree that may lead to faulty conclusions; to mislead. See *misleading*. —*n.*, distortion.

distraint (federal income taxes) The procedure under which the property of a taxpayer may be seized after he or she has neglected or refused to make payment within ten days after notice and demand.

distress merchandise Merchandise marked down in order to make possible its rapid disposal: a situation brought about by a financial stringency or other emergency demanding a quick *turnover (1)*. The term may also relate to a job lot of merchandise acquired by one dealer from another.

distributed computer systems A configuration of interconnected computers at several different locations as compared to all computers being centered at one location.

distributed system See *distributed computer systems*.

distribution 1. Any payment to stockholders or owners of cash, property, or shares, including any of the various forms of dividend; in noncorporate enterprise, a *withdrawal*.
2. A spread of revenue or expenditure or of capital additions to various accounts; an *allocation*.
3. Disposal of a product by sale.
4. The function of promoting sales and making deliveries.
5. = *statistical distribution*.
6. The apportionment and disposition, by authority of a court, of the balance of an intestate's personal property after payment of debts and costs.

distribution column A money column, often one of several, in a worksheet, journal, or ledger, providing some desired analysis or breakdown of each entry or posting.

distribution expense (or cost)—*selling expense*, including advertising and delivery costs.

distributor discount An allowance usually determined as a fixed percentage of the list of retail price; *trade discount*. By the use of discounts, sellers may limit publication to a single price—in most cases, the retail price—which the consuming public identifies with the product. Discount schedules are released only to the distributor trade and do not become general public information. The amount of discount is the gross margin to compensate distributors for selling and servicing the product. Frequently, distributors share the gross margin by rediscounting to subdistributors and retailers. The practice is generally employed in the sale of nationally advertised branded products under fair-trade laws. The manufacturer in such cases places considerable emphasis on identifying the product with a fixed or "suggested" price to consumers.

diurnal *n.* An old name for *journal* or *daybook*.

diversification 1. A process of investing in assets of different risks and maturities in order to reduce variations in the returns that might be experienced.

2. The acquisition of different lines of business for reasons such as control over supplies, smoothing earnings, etc. See *portfolio balancing*.

diversified A state in which *diversification* has been achieved.

diversified companies A *diversified* collection of companies subject to common control often involving dissimilar services or production activities and markets.

diversified enterprise (or business) Firm engaged in distinctly different lines of business (or industries) either on its own account or through subsidiaries.

diversify To introduce heterogeneity into a product line or an investment *portfolio* as a means of reducing risks. *Risk* may be further reduced if selected members of the portfolio are negatively correlated in their profit or other performance behavior. See *coefficient (2c)*.

divided account See *nominal account (2)*.

dividend 1. Cash or other assets, evidences of corporate indebtedness, or shares of the issuer's capital stock constituting a *distribution* to a class of stockholders of a corporation, the amount ordinarily being charged to *retained earnings (earned surplus)*. A liability for a dividend is expressed in corporate accounts only after formal action (*declaration*) has been taken by the board of directors. This action is authorized by a resolution by the board setting forth (a) the medium of payment, (b) the account to be charged, (c) the rate (in dollars per share or percentage), (d) the date of declaration, (e) the date the stock records are to be closed for the purpose of determining the particular stockholdings against which the dividend is applicable, and (f) the date of payment. A dividend occasionally consists of assets other than cash. A dividend of cash or property charged to an ac-

count other than *retained earnings (earned surplus)*, such as paid-in surplus, revaluation surplus, or a depletion or depreciation reserve is termed a *liquidating dividend (2)* and *(3)*.

2. A payment made to creditors during or following involuntary liquidation; see *liquidating dividend (1)*.

dividend-equalization reserve An appropriation, now obsolete, of *retained earnings* for the payment of future dividends in periods when current profits may not be adequate for the purpose.

dividend in kind = *property dividend*.

dividend payable 1. The unliquidated liability for a cash or property *dividend* created by the declaration of the dividend, ranking in case of liquidation with liabilities to general creditors. See *dividend*.

2. The balance-sheet heading for cash or property dividends declared but unliquidated either because the due date is subsequent to the balance-sheet date or because of inability to make delivery to stockholders.

dividend payout A *ratio* which measures the percentage of net income paid out in cash dividends. This ratio is considered the basic indicator of a firm's dividend policy. It is calculated by dividing dividends by net earnings available to the common stockholders.

dividends in arrears The amount of undeclared dividends accumulated on *cumulative preferred stock*, expressed as dollars per outstanding share or as a total amount.

dividend yield A market measure of the return on a stock from dividends. It is normally calculated by dividing current annual dividends by the current market price of a share of stock.

divisional reporting See *line of business reporting; segmental reporting*.

divisive reorganization Division of a business enterprise into two or more separate entities.

The more common types of divisive reorganization are *split-up, split-off, and spin-off*.

dollar accountability (not-for-profit organization accounting) In organizations having a nonprofit objective, the accounting focus is traditionally on the flow of liquid assets—dollar accountability. Thus, a statement of revenues and expenses, the sources of liquid assets and the activities for which they were used.

dollar error See *monetary errors*.

dollar unit sampling (DUS) A *probability proportionate to size sampling* of "audit units" with an upper bound estimate of potential error based on monetary errors found in the sample combined with an attribute based probability measure. The name derives from the analogy of an audit item (such as a customer account) with a book value of $10 representing 10 "dollar units" and a comparable audit item with $50 book value representing 50 "dollar units." A random sample of such "dollar units" is selected with probabilities proportionate to size and the audit units to which the sampled dollars attach are then audited. Any monetary error found in a sampled item is converted to a "per-dollar" basis and the result projected to the population. See *probability proportionate to size sampling*.

dollar-value LIFO A method of computing LIFO ending inventory by use of cost figures without the necessity of identifying, pricing, and counting units. Essentially, the inventory is divided into appropriate "pools" of similar items, and the ending inventory of each pool, priced at then current costs, is deflated to beginning-of-year costs. If the result is greater than the beginning inventory, the increase is considered to be a change in quantity. This increase in quantity ("layer") is then converted back to end-of-year prices and added to beginning inventory to get a LIFO ending inventory. The two price conversion calculations may be accomplished through the use of price indices published by the government or through internally generated price comparisons. Section 1.472-8 of the income-tax regulations contains an extensive discussion of dollar-value LIFO and authorizes use of the index method, the *double-extension method*, and the link-chain method.

domestic corporation A corporation created under the laws of a given state or country. In the federal *Internal Revenue Code* (Section 7701U4e), the term refers to a corporation established under the laws of the United States or of any of the states or territories; in a state corporation law, the term relates to a corporation created under a law of the state. See *association; corporation; foreign corporation*.

Domestic International Sales Corporation (DISC) (federal income taxes) DISCs were authorized by the 1971 Revenue Act in an effort to spur exports and improve the balance of trade. DISCs are domestic corporations that satisfy various requirements, including: (1) at least 95% of gross receipts must consist of qualified export receipts; (2) at least 95% of the adjusted basis of all assets must be qualified export assets; (3) only one class of stock may be outstanding with a par or stated value of $2,500 or more. The DISC itself is not subject to tax, but it must file an information return. The shareholders of the DISC are taxed currently on 50% of the DISC's taxable income. Two of the principal tax advantages that accrue to a DISC are: (a) Tax on 50% of the DISC profits may be deferred indefinitely until they are distributed to the shareholders, the shareholders dispose of their stock, or the DISC loses its special status. (b) The DISC can use the "untaxed" profits for investment in the United States, thereby increasing its base of operations.

donated assets *Contributions*, usually of a noncash variety such as securities, land, buildings, or equipment and materials.

donated services Services of volunteer workers who are unpaid, or paid less than market value for their services.

donated (capital) stock Issued shares of capital stock donated to the issuing corporation, usually for resale at an amount not subject to legal restriction: a practice now obsolete. Where the stock was originally issued in exchange for fixed assets or an intangible, the proceeds of its resale were credited against the recorded amount of the property so acquired; if the property originally acquired was cash or some asset subsequently sold, or if the recorded value of tangible assets acquired was independently and fairly determined, the proceeds of resale were credited to the recorded amount of any intangible assets acquired, or, in the absence of such assets, to a donated or paid-in surplus account. See *additional paid-in capital*.

donated surplus Surplus arising from contributions without consideration, by stockholders and others, of cash, property, or the company's own capital stock. Donated surplus is a form of *additional paid-in capital*.

donation 1. A return of capital stock to an issuing corporation at no cost to the corporation; see *donated stock*.
2. Any gift, particularly to an incorporated charity or other institution serving the public on a nonprofit basis.

donee beneficiary A third party to whom the promisee of a contract intends to benefit, by way of a gift, by contracting with the promisor for a performance to be rendered to the third party as though a party to the contract.

double-account-form balance sheet A balance-sheet form, based upon the double-account system sometimes used in the United Kingdom, having two sections: capital or financing, and operating or general. The capital section is on a cash basis and reflects the capital receipts and expenditures as shown by the capital-account ledger. On the one side are shown the proceeds from the shares of stock and debentures, including any premiums, and on the other side the various fixed assets on which the proceeds have been expended, including legal charges in the procurement of land and, at an earlier date, Parliamentary expenses in promoting special Acts of Parliament. The balance of the capital account is carried down to the second section or "general balance sheet." The general balance sheet consists of current assets and liabilities, reserve fund, retained "profit and loss," and all other items. The fixed assets are never depreciated in the capital account, but depreciation may be provided by charging operations and crediting a reserve account that appears in the general balance sheet, such accounts having been compulsory in some classes of companies. See *balance sheet*.

double-account system A system of accounting, prescribed in the United Kingdom for companies formed to undertake public works, such as railroads and gas companies, under sanction of special Acts of Parliament. Its distinctive feature is the separation of the fixed from the current assets and liabilities of the undertaking so as to show clearly that the capital, whether contributed by shareholders or otherwise obtained, has been provided for the special purpose of acquiring or constructing the fixed property. See *double-account-form balance sheet*.

double distribution The redistribution or proration of any expense, expense group, or other cost whereby, from an initial classification, as by *object*, the cost is transferred to another account or spread over several accounts.

double-entry bookkeeping The method usually followed for recording *transactions* under which each transaction is always entered into two or more *accounts*. Formal bookkeeping records consist of *journals, ledgers*, or their equivalent, and supporting documents and files. These records are necessary for the purpose of giving expression promptly, systematically, and conventionally to the thousands of transactions that even a relatively small organization enters into. The ultimate repository of the amounts of individual transactions or groups of similar transactions is the "account"—one of the classified pages of a ledger on which appear dates, monetary amounts, and often other essential transaction data.

Thus, in a retail establishment one would expect to find in a ledger a "sales" account in which the money amounts of daily, weekly, or monthly sales (or other income) would appear, with totals, probably, for the year to date; a "purchases" account listing the money amounts of individual merchandise purchases or groups of purchases; a series of "expense" accounts containing money amounts of individual expenses or expense totals. These three types of accounts are often called "nominal" accounts because at the end of the year or other period the account pages are removed and the total money amounts reflected on them are transferred to a single "net-result" account.

In addition to the nominal accounts, there is a group of "real" accounts, the hardy perennials among accounts that outlast the annuals or nominal accounts because they are maintained through the years, some of them changing, like cash, each day, week, or month, some decreasing, some increasing, others remaining the same; the real accounts reflect separately such items as cash balances, amounts owing from customers, the cost of merchandise left over at the end of a period, the cost of store fixtures and of other property to which the establishment lays claim, all these being "assets," or things "owned"; a second class of real accounts reflects the liabilities or the amounts "owing to" creditors for purchases or services received from them but not yet paid for, and to the owners of the business for their original investment and for the retained profits that swell their investment.

There are thus income and expense, or nominal accounts; and asset and liability, or real accounts; each account will be found occupying one or more pages in a ledger—a book containing only accounts. The accounts are arranged alphabetically according to the formal names given them, or in four main sections following the fundamental groupings just recounted.

A journal is a means of giving first expression to transactions; it exists in various forms, but is always essentially a chronological record containing lists of individual transactions added to as they occur. It keeps on growing during the day, week, month, or year of its active existence; and its details, or more often its totals, reflecting transactions of various types, are periodically transferred to whatever accounts in the ledger are affected. A journal is thus a chronological transaction-recording device and a medium for obtaining transaction details or totals that, often in classified form, go into the ledger. No amount gets into a ledger without also appearing in a journal, and every money figure appearing in a journal that represents the amount of a transaction also appears in some account in a ledger.

The recording of the amount of a transaction in a journal is called an *entry*; its transfer in detail or total to an account in a ledger, a *posting*. For every transaction or group of similar transactions, there must be an entry; for every entry or group of similar entries, there must be a posting. Traditionally the transaction is first recorded in a journal, thence posted to a ledger; under many modern bookkeeping systems, the journal entry may take place at the same time as the ledger posting. In some instances, the journal itself has virtually disappeared, its main function being to "prepare" a transaction for a ledger posting; and, since the ledger has significance only to the extent that it yields financial statements and other reports, abbreviated and time-saving forms to replace the ledger are sometimes adopted.

In double-entry bookkeeping, each transaction involves a two-way, and hence self-balancing, entry and a two-way, self-balancing posting. This identity of transaction elements arises from the nature of the transaction itself, of which there are two basic kinds: the business (or external) transaction, and the accounting (or internal) transaction. In a retail establishment owned by an individual, the following principal types of business transactions or transactions with outsiders will be found:

Cash and property coming in from owner (original and subsequent investments)

Cash going out to owner (salary; profits)

Purchases of merchandise (cash or credit)

Payments of credit purchases

Sales to customers (cash or credit)

Receipts from credit sales (cash or goods returned)

Salaries of clerks, rent, and other expenses (cash or credit)

A business transaction nearly always involves the ultimate outgo or income of cash; if not immediately, it is followed by a cash settlement at a subsequent date. Where credit is received or extended, and the eventual recording of two transactions is necessary, the two transactions together may be referred to as a "deal." Each business deal, upon analysis, is thus found, with infrequent ex-ceptions, to affect in the end the size of the cash balance in the business and at the same time to effect a corresponding but opposite change in some other account.

The two-way characteristic each transaction possesses in common with every other transaction may be expressed in the form of the simplest of identities, $a = b$. That is, in double-entry bookkeeping, two identical money elements are given expression following the *recognition* of each transaction. Since the two elements are to be recorded in the same records and the notion of equality is to be preserved throughout, the identity takes the derived form $a - b = 0$; one element is positive, the other negative. The positive element is called a *debit*; the negative element, a *credit*. Including amounts owing to owners as liabilities, a debit may be: (a) An asset increase: Cash received from a customer; merchandise received from a supplier. (b) A liability decrease: An obligation paid off. (c) An expense increase: A salary paid. (d) An income decrease: A sale, previously recorded, canceled. On the other hand, a credit may be: (e) An asset decrease: Merchandise sold; cash paid out for any purpose. (f) A liability increase: A promise to pay in exchange for merchandise purchased from a supplier. (g) An expense decrease: An expense reduced upon refund of an overpayment. (h) An income increase: A sale.

Both journals and ledgers have separate money columns for debits and credits; in a ledger, individual accounts are "balanced" periodically, an excess of debit postings over credit postings within an individual account being termed a *debit* balance, and an excess of credit postings over debit postings a *credit* balance.

Because the amount of every transaction is twice expressed in the accounts (once as a debit and again as a credit), it follows that the sum of all account balances should be zero:

that is, the total of debit balances is equal to the total of credit balances. See *dualism*.

See also *debit; credit; journal; ledger; transaction; trial balance*.

double-extension method Basic approach in federal tax regulations for implementing the *dollar-value LIFO* method of inventory valuation in which the quantity of each item in an inventory pool is extended (1) at base-year unit cost and (2) at current-year unit cost. The total of the base-year dollar cost of the ending inventory is compared to the total for beginning inventory to determine whether the total inventory quantity (= dollar-value basis) has changed. If the quantity has increased, then a current *LIFO inventory layer* will be added. The second extension must then be made to obtain the comparable current cost value of the ending inventory. This total becomes the numerator and the base-year cost total for the ending inventory becomes the denominator of an internal price index that is used to adjust the current *LIFO inventory layer* from base year to current cost. This adjusted cost then becomes the LIFO cost of the current layer, which is added to the LIFO cost of the beginning inventory to calculate the LIFO cost of the ending inventory. If the quantity as measured above has decreased, the second extension need not be made since the LIFO cost of the ending inventory will be calculated from layers accumulated in the past for which the relevant price indexes were calculated previously. See *inventory valuation*.

double liability The personal liability formerly attached to shareholders in national banks and, in some states, attaching to the stockholders of other types of corporations, for additional contributions equal to the amounts originally paid in or subscribed. It is a contingent obligation of stockholders only if the corporation is unable to pay its obligations in full.

double taxation Imposition of the same tax, or a similar tax, more than once. Usually restricted to taxes on income to the final recipient, e.g., the U.S. tax on corporate income followed by the individual income tax on dividends received. The impact is somewhat lessened by excluding the first $100 of dividends received from domestic corporations. Other countries grant a credit for the tax already paid on the distributed income by the corporation. The potential multiple tax on corporate income is substantially reduced by allowing a corporate recipient of dividends an 85% deduction. The term is also applied to a ''tax on a tax'' as occurs with *excise taxes* imposed in successive transactions. The *value-added tax* is used by many members of the European Economic Community to avoid this compounding effect.

downstream merger (federal income taxes) A merger of a parent corporation into a subsidiary.

down time The time required for setup (see *setup time*), overhaul, or maintenance; or lost time attributable to idleness.

dr Abbreviation for *debit*.

draft A written order drawn by one party (drawer) ordering a second party (drawee) to pay a specified amount of money to a third party (payee). See *bill of exchange; check; sight draft; time draft*. The draft of commercial practice is an ''arrival'' draft: a means of completing a transaction, without the necessity of handling currency, between a seller and a buyer, following an understanding between them as to the method of settlement. The initiative is taken by the seller, who prepares the instrument and deposits it at his or her bank accompanied by an invoice and a shipping receipt. These papers, forwarded by the bank to a designated bank at the destination point, are surrendered to the buyer upon acceptance or payment of the draft by him or her.

drop shipment A shipment from a manufacturer or supplier direct to the customer of a distributor or other supplier without passing through the hands of the latter.

dualism The basic twofold characteristic of various concepts, as the debit-and-credit dualism of double-entry bookkeeping.

dualism concept (of accounting) The recognition of source and disposition (or *credit* and *debit*) as the two basic elements of *transactions*, both external and internal; the unvarying equality of these elements facilitates their immediate separation and regrouping, and leads to the recording and reporting of the cost-and-yield flows dominating the operation of *economic units*.

duality Axiom or concept of *double-entry bookkeeping* that equality in debit and credit amounts must hold for every recorded transaction. See *dualism concept*.

dual presentation of earnings per share The presentation with equal prominence on the face of an *income statement* of *primary earnings per share* and *fully diluted earnings per share* of common stock. See *earnings per share*.

dual-purpose test An auditing procedure which is designed to obtain both compliance and substantive audit evidence.

due *adj.* 1. Matured and payable (owing to others) or receivable (owing by others) now or in the immediate future.
2. Maturing; in this sense, the word is accompanied by some reference to a particular date.

due from other funds (governmental and institutional accounting) A receivable for money loaned, stores issued, work performed, or services rendered to or for the benefit of another fund.

due to other funds (governmental and institutional accounting) A payable for money borrowed, stores received, work performed, or services from another *fund*.

dummy variable A classificatory variable which indicates the presence or absence of a particular qualitative characteristic. Usually the values of 0 or 1 are used for this variable to indicate the presence or absence of the characteristic.

dumping The practice by a vendor, particularly in international trade, of selling goods at or below generally recognized market prices while maintaining higher prices in areas where government protection or other preferred treatment can be secured. Such vendors often allocate their fixed and overhead expenses to goods sold in protected areas and, because of the risks involved, regard returns on dumped goods less direct costs as net profit.

duplex (computers) (1) Full: A communication loop which allows a terminal to transmit and receive simultaneously. (2) Half: A communication loop which only allows a terminal either to transmit or receive via an arrangement which allows the terminal to switch from transmit to receive.

du Pont chart system A system of *ratio* analysis which is designed to show the relationship between *return on investment*, *turnover ratios*, and *profit margin*. Its basic formulation is that return on investment equals total assets turnover times net income per dollar of sales. Total assets turnover is derived by dividing sales by total assets while net income per dollar of sales is net income divided by annual sales. The sales to total assets ratio can be broken down further into various asset categories and the net income to sales profit margin into various cost items. The system was originally designed to evaluate the operating performance of managers, but it is now widely used in general financial analyses.

DUS See *dollar unit sampling*.

duty = *tariff*. Also, a moral, legal, administrative, social, or professional obligation.

duty drawback A *tariff* concession allowing a rebate of all or part of the *duty* on goods imported for processing prior to their reexport.

e The base of natural (Napierian) logarithms: 2.718281828459+. See *logarithm*.

E and OE (E&OE) Errors & Omissions Excepted. An abbreviation sometimes placed at the foot of an invoice or statement for the purpose of reserving to the maker of the statement the right to amend the document should it subsequently prove to be incorrect in any particular.

earmark 1. To give expression to a restriction imposed by law, by contractual agreement, or by corporate or administrative action, on the use of an account or of an equivalent amount of assets represented by an account, as where, following the purchase of treasury stock, earned surplus becomes unavailable for dividends. Other illustrations are found in separate accounts maintained for the proceeds from the sale of security issues, available only for specified purposes; cash segregated for investment in some noncurrent asset; sinking-fund cash and reserves; a reserve for working capital.

2. To transfer temporarily a portion of one account to another, as in the creation of a sinking-fund reserve out of earned surplus.

earn To become entitled to income as the result of services performed for another; also often applied to revenue from the sale of goods, or to interest from investments. See *income*.

earned Realized or accrued as revenue through sales of goods, services performed, or the provision of capital in the form of an investment or a loan.

earned income 1. Income derived from personal services as distinct from other kinds of income.

2. = *realized revenue; earnings*.

earned surplus = *retained earnings*.

earning-capacity value = *earning power*.

earning power Present value equal to the assumed worth of estimated *earnings* (2). The term may be used in the valuation of a whole enterprise or a class of securities.

earning process 1. All of the steps, activities, operations, and/or transactions that are needed to acquire or produce and provide a good or service to the customer, to collect the cash, and to pay suppliers.

2. The process or activities that are completed in an *earnings cycle* or an *operating cycle*. See *earnings cycle*.

earnings 1. A general term embracing *revenue*, *profit*, or *income*.

2. *Net income*; both *earnings* and *net earnings* are used in this sense by financial writers and in the term *retained earnings*.

3. *Revenues* commonly associated with a natural person, as wages, interest, rent; = *income (3b)*.

4. = *earned income (1)*.

earnings and profits (federal income taxes) The economic income of a corporation or its current earnings which could be paid out in dividends without decreasing its net worth. For this computation taxable income is increased for various types of tax-exempt income (including interest on municipal bonds) and reduced for nondeductible expenses (including federal income taxes) in arriving at earnings and profits. Additional adjustments may also be made, such as adding back to taxable income any depreciation deducted in excess of straight-line depreciation. The computation can be extremely complex, but it is often quite significant in that dividend distributions are treated as ordinary income to the recipients only to the extent of current and accumulated earnings and profits. The computation of earnings and profits is also required under the *Internal Revenue Code* for the accumulated earnings tax, one-month liquidations, Subchapter S distributions, and controlled foreign corporations.

earnings covariability A statistical measure of the sensitivity of a firm's earnings to changes in earnings of all other firms. Analogous to the *beta coefficient* of the *capital-asset pricing model*, it is a useful accounting measure of risk. It is determined statistically by regressing a time series of a firm's earnings on a measure of average earnings in the entire economy.

earnings coverage ratios See *coverage ratios*.

earnings cycle = *cash cycle*; *operating cycle*. The series of transactions in a given entity whereby *cash* is converted into *goods* and *services*, goods and services are sold to cus-

tomers, and cash is collected from customers. See *earning process*.

earnings per share (of common stock) *Net income* of a stated period, less preferred stock requirements, divided by the average number of common shares during a period or by the number of common shares outstanding at the end of the period. This simple computation, easily understood, does not take into account outstanding stock options, convertible securities, or warrants, if any, or other possible future transactions, the assumptions being that until exercised, they have no effect on current EPS which is commonly regarded as an earnings figure measuring past performance. *Fully diluted earnings per share* adjusts the earnings per share to allow for the dilution (or diminution) of earnings per share that would have resulted from the exercise of conversion rights of convertible securities, stock options, warrants, and other such contingent claims to earnings that might be exercised. The maximum dilution possible from these sources is generally used in these calculations and issuances are generally assumed to have taken place at the beginning of the period. *Primary earnings per share* = earnings per share when (1) the denominator has been augmented by *common stock equivalents* and (2) the numerator has been augmented by the interest or other income assigned to these equivalents. On occasion both primary and fully diluted earnings per share are shown in a dual presentation of earnings per share.

earnings statement 1. = *income statement*.

2. Any analysis or presentation of earnings in statement form.

earnings variability Any measure that describes the fluctuations of a firm's earnings over time. The *standard deviation* and the *coefficient of variation* are popular measures for this purpose. See *risk index*.

easement The right to erect or make use of a road, power line, water, or other benefit on adjacent land.

economic 1. Pertaining to *economics*; contributing to production or other business activity.
2. Lowest-cost; economical.

economic activity 1. The *production* and *distribution* of *goods and services*.
2. The contribution of one or more persons to the production of useful goods or services: applied to work performed by a person or other economic unit; see *activity*.

economic cost 1. The alternatives forgone when an economic resource is used in a specific manner. See also *alternative cost*.
2. = *current cost*.

economic efficiency Also called Pareto efficiency or *Pareto optimality*. The state which obtains in an economy when resources are allocated such that one individual's lot cannot be improved either through production or exchange without causing at least one other individual to be worse off. See *efficiency (4)*; *efficiency frontier*.

economic entity = *entity (2)*; used in contradistinction to *legal entity*.

economic events Occurrences which are the occasion (perhaps anticipated) for the production, distribution, and/or sale of goods or services or for the accumulation of *wealth* and related activities such as finance and taxation. More generally, occasions which give rise to wealth flows among and within entities. The universe of economic events coincides approximately with *transactions*, of which *accounting events* are a subset. See *event*; *condition*.

economic good A commodity or service having exchange value and the capacity to satisfy or aid in satisfying human wants. See *good*.

economic interest The ownership of all or part of a business enterprise; also, the ownership of an obligation of a business enterprise.

economic life The period during which a fixed asset is capable of yielding services of value to its owner; contrast with *physical life*, a period often longer, during the whole of which it can continue to function notwithstanding obsolescence or inadequacy; a common basis for determining *depreciation expense;* see *service life; depreciation; accelerated depreciation*.

economic lot size The number of units to be ordered in a single purchase, or to be produced in a single run before machines are reset for another item, such that minimum costs are incurred or maximum benefits are secured. See *economic order quantity*.

economic order quantity The quantity of a storable good to be ordered for the purpose of minimizing the cost of the inventory which will be used to service projected demands. The costs or penalties for ordering, holding, and running out of that good are usually assumed to be known in which case the following simple formula is applicable: $q = \sqrt{2Sk/pi}$, where S = expected yearly sales, k = ordering cost per order to be placed, p = price per unit of good to be ordered, and i = interest and other costs of tying up funds in inventory.

economic resource A scarce productive factor, e.g., land, labor, knowledge, material, capital, etc., that can be used to satisfy human wants and hence has value in exchange. See *resource*.

economics The discipline whose major focus of study is the allocation of scarce resources in the satisfaction of human wants, the description of the functioning of past and present social schemes for effecting the allocation, the establishing of criteria of efficiency and stability necessary for judging such schemes, and the development of methods for their improvement.

economic unit 1. Any *person* or group of persons having a name, common purpose, and transactions with outsiders; examples: a natural person, a family, a profit or nonprofit enterprise, a governmental organization; see *business enterprise*.

2. A group of business enterprises operating under a common control, especially where there are numerous transactions between members of the group. A parent company and its subsidiaries furnish a common example; their involvement in intercompany transactions and other relationships leads to the preparation of *consolidated financial statements*. See *entity; controlling company*.

economic usefulness Amount or value of the *benefits* or *services* that are expected to be received from an *asset* or *resource*; usually measured by the *net realizable value* or *present value* of the benefits or services that are expected from an asset or resource.

economy The activities of production and distribution in a region or country.

education (for accounting) The education of an accountant may be regarded as technical, professional, and general. Some courses of study contribute to all three types. Technical education or training includes learning the vocabulary and skilled operations required in accountancy as distinguished from other occupations. Professional education is the acquisition of those attitudes and understandings which enable the accountant to work without detailed supervision, to adjust his or her performance to the needs and conditions of other occupations, and to solve intelligently novel and nonroutine problems. General education comprises all other learning from preschool conditioning to advanced studies in the liberal arts and sciences that assists the accountant in developing intellectual interests along varied lines, finding solutions for personal problems, and participating in community life.

EEC = *European Economic Community*.

effective See *effectiveness*.

effective interest method A method of accounting for bond premiums or discounts in which the interest expense for each period is determined by multiplying the carrying value at the beginning of the period (the face or maturing value minus the discount or plus the premium) of a bond or note by the *effective rate*. The following example is illustrative: a loan of $800 is received in exchange for a note to pay $100 at the end of each of two years with final payment of $1,000 at the end of the second year extinguishing the note. The nominal rate is 10% (on the $1,000 note) and the effective rate is approximately 23.7%, so the year 1 interest is 23.7% of $800 or $190, which is charged to interest expense, crediting accrued interest $100 and amortization of discount $90. The year 2 interest would be 23.7% of $890 = $210. Deducting the $100 interest due would leave $110 to be credited to the remaining unamortized discount of $110. In general the rate remains constant but the amounts of interest expense and discount amortization vary from year to year under the effective interest method. See *interest formulas* for a method of computing the effective interest rate given a series of cash flows.

effectiveness 1. Ability to (a) state and (b) achieve *objectives*. See the discussion of comprehensive audit under *audit*. In this usage an organization may be effective and inefficient. For example, a government agency may consume excessive resources while achieving all of the objectives stated in the legislation underlying its programs. In other usages, the two terms may be used interchangeably as in 2 below.

2. The quality, quantity, service yield, consumed time, or other attained performance as compared with a predetermined standard; = *efficiency*.

3. Actual *direct cost* of a product compared with its *standard cost*; actual output compared with a budgeted output; time of per-

formance compared with an anticipated time lapse. Quantitative effectiveness may be expressed as a percentage relation of the actual with the hoped for. Without reference to such means of measurement, the word means little more than "quality".

effective pay rate The rate of pay (e.g., weekly) after adding back deductions from basic pay (e.g., withholding and social-security taxes) and including insurance and other fringe benefits not deducted from basic pay.

effective rate (of interest) 1. = economic return or economic rate of interest.
2. The interest rate obtained when the *nominal rate* is divided by the actual price paid for a bond or by the actual amount of a loan. See *effective interest method*. Thus if a one-year bank loan of $1,000 is discounted at 10% by deducting the interest in advance, then the effective rate of interest is slightly in excess of 11% (= $100/$900). See *interest formulas*.

efficiency 1. A conventional measure of performance expressed in terms of a *standard of comparison*; applied to a machine, operation, individual, or organization.
2. The ratio of output to input. Called "relative efficiency" when compared to some reference standard which cannot be exceeded so that the resulting ratio is a dimensionless number which will not be greater than unity (= 100% efficiency). For instance the efficiency of a furnace may be rated relative to the number of BTUs of heat produced per ton of fuel consumed relative either (a) to some other furnace known to be efficient or (b) to the number of BTUs of heat known to be available from the fuel, as determined by chemical and/or physical consideration.
3. In its popular sense, rate of profitability.
4. (economics) (a) *Cost efficiency*: the relative ability to produce at a given rate with lower costs than other producers; or, with the same total cost, to produce at a higher rate. (b) *Technical efficiency*: the ability to obtain the greatest possible output from a given input; or to produce a given output with the lowest possible amounts of input. Note: the comparison may be with respect to a theoretically known production technology or with respect to a comparison set of other producers. In the latter case the resulting ratio is said to be a measure of relative (technical) efficiency. In any case the measure is distinguished from *price efficiency*, which is manifested not only by payment of the lowest possible prices but also by utilization of factor inputs in the optimum proportions that accord with these prices. The latter, also called allocative efficiency, is further distinguished from scale efficiency, which results from producing at the optimum scale under the given prices. In summary, technical efficiency requires obtaining the greatest possible output from the input amounts utilized; allocative efficiency requires use of the best mix proportions of inputs at prevailing market prices; scale efficiency occurs at the optimum scale under these mix and technical efficiency conditions.

efficiency-effectiveness audit See *audit* (4B).

efficiency frontier A collection of points (whose *coordinates* represent amounts of desirable and/or undesirable properties) where every point has the property that it is not possible to exchange one of these points for another without worsening some of the coordinate values. Examples: (1) The *mean-variance frontier* in *portfolio analysis*, where the investment opportunities allow portfolio selections which will improve the mean return only if accompanied by greater risks, as measured by an increased *variance* in these portfolio returns. (2) In the branch of economics known as "welfare economics" a Pareto optimum is also called a Pareto-efficient frontier because it has the property that there is no economic policy which will improve the lot of some person or group without worsening the lot of other persons or groups in a society. See *economic efficiency*.

efficiency ratios See *turnover ratios*.

efficiency variance 1. Given the actual output achieved, it is the difference between the actual input used and the input which should have been used under efficient operating conditions.

2. A *variance* resulting from causes other than a change in the price of direct costs of materials or labor. The latter are also referred to as *material usage variance* and *labor quantity variance*, respectively.

efficient capital markets See *efficient market hypothesis*.

efficient market hypothesis A general hypothesis that security prices always fully reflect all publicly available information concerning traded securities. In efficient capital markets, security prices adjust rapidly and unbiasedly to any newly released information. As a result, price changes in efficient markets behave as *random walks* over time, which is to say that there is no discernible systematic pattern which one could use to advantage as an investor. Extensive empirical research has supported the efficient market hypothesis, especially for stock markets. "Weak form" tests have established that current security prices fully reflect historical price information, and "semistrong form" tests have determined that security prices fully reflect all publicly available information, especially accounting data. However, some "strong form" tests have revealed that certain "insider information" is not always reflected in security prices. The implications of the efficient market hypothesis for accounting are far-reaching because it suggests that efforts put into financial statement analysis will not necessarily result in superior returns on investments.

efficient portfolios See *portfolio analysis*.

EFTS (banking) Electronic funds transfer system.

elasticity = *elasticity of demand* or *elasticity of supply*. Economics: The proportioned change in the quantity demanded (or supplied) in response to a proportionate change in its price. Calculated as a ratio, this becomes:

$$-\frac{\frac{\Delta q}{q}}{\frac{\Delta p}{p}} = -\frac{\Delta q}{\Delta p}\frac{p}{q} = \eta,$$

in which η, the almost universally used symbol for elasticity, is a dimensionless number. The symbols Δq and Δp refer to the change in quantity and the resulting change in price from their initial values of q and p so that $\Delta q/q$ and $\Delta p/p$ represent the proportional changes in these base quantities and prices, respectively.

Because an increase in price generally results in a fall in quantity demanded and vice versa, the negative sign in the above expression defines η as a positive number. Elasticity of supply is, however, represented by this same formula but with the negative sign omitted since it is not needed to produce a positive value for the resulting activity because an an increase in price is generally accompanied by an increase in the quantity supplied.

In any study of empirical data it is important to arrange to hold other factors constant, e.g., by *regression analysis* techniques, since otherwise incorrect values of η will generally be secured. See *cross elasticity of demand*.

With this convention, a further division is made between inelastic demands in which η is less than unity and elastic demands in which the value of η exceeds unity. In the latter case, a decrease in price will result in an increase in total revenue while in the former case it will decrease the total revenue that can be secured from the sale of the affected good or service.

elasticity of demand See *elasticity*.

elasticity of supply See *elasticity*.

electronic data processing (computers) Any of the varied methods of accumulating, assembling, and recasting transactions and other data by electronic devices, with the object of speeding the processes of recording, analyzing, and reporting.

elimination See *intercompany elimination*.

eliminations ledger A ledger maintained by a controlling company as an aid in providing an orderly, consistent record of *intercompany eliminations* when *combined financial statements* are prepared. The accounts in such a ledger increase or decrease balance-sheet and income statement items and are built up historically, following the classification appearing in the combined statements; they are modified from time to time for sales or purchases of subsidiary securities, and, on statement dates, for intercompany profits and other items.

embezzlement The fraudulent appropriation of property lawfully in one's custody, as of cash or securities by a cashier or trustee (a *defalcation*) or of stores by a stock clerk. It may be accomplished by such devices as pocketing receipts from cash sales or from customers *on account*; shipping merchandise to nonexistent customers; and preparing false disbursement vouchers. Fraudulent attempts are often made to cover up such transactions by *kiting*, *lapping*, not appropriating items in excess of some broadly established tolerance limit for breakage, spoilage, shrinkage, weighing, or counting. Although professional auditors are careful to follow many procedures designed to uncover such frauds, the detection of frauds is no longer a major or even minor objective of an audit. Guards against frauds are rather one of the principal features of modern systems of *internal control*, and therefore a prime management responsibility. See *Foreign Corrupt Practices Act*.

—embezzle, *v.t.* or *i*.

emolument Compensation and remuneration, both monetary and nonmonetary, for personal services; a salary, wage, fee, commission, award, noncontractual expense reimbursement, price concession, illegal fees, or other personal benefit received or accrued.

empirical Derived from experience; sometimes contrasted with "rational" or "deductive" (i.e., derived from some plan or principle).

employee As distinguished from an independent contractor, a person subject to the will and control of an employer with respect to what the employee does and how he or she does it. Under federal income-tax and social-security-tax procedure, if the "how" is absent, the individual is regarded as an independent contractor.

employee liabilities Bonuses, deferred compensation, pensions, retirement grants, or other amounts held for eventual payments to employees, often appearing on balance sheets between long-term obligations and stockholders' equity.

Employee Retirement Income Security Act of 1974 (ERISA) Legislation enacted to provide employees with the assurance that employer-provided retirement plans are equitable and secure. Major provisions include:

(1) Participation—An employee at least 25 years old with one year of service cannot be excluded from the plan. Exceptions are provided in the case of part-time employees and new employees within 5 years of normal retirement age.

(2) Vesting—The plan must meet one of three minimum standards on employers' contributions (employee contributions are automatically 100% vested): (a) a 5- to 15-year graduated scale with vesting of 25% at 5 years, 50% at 10 years, and 100% at 15 years; (b) 100% vesting after 10 years of service; (c) the rule-of-45 standard: 50% vesting of accrued benefits of an employee

with at least 5 years of service when age plus years of service equal 45, with 10% additional vesting for each of the following 5 years.

(3) Funding—Funding requirements have been established for defined-benefit plans which provide that the nominal cost, amortization of past service liabilities ($\leqslant 30$ years), experience loss amortization ($\leqslant 15$ years), and other items must be funded currently.

(4) Transferability—A lump-sum distribution from a qualified retirement plan will be tax free if it is reinvested within 60 days in a qualifying individual retirement account, or, in certain situations, transferred to another qualified retirement plan.

The Act also provides detailed rules for maximum contributions, maximum benefits, fiduciary responsibilities, and termination insurance.

employee stock option Right granted to an employee to acquire a corporation's capital stock under stated conditions of time, price, and number of shares. See *stock option*.

encoding The process of putting a message in code. An opposite process is called *decoding*.

encumbrance 1. (governmental accounting) An anticipated expenditure, evidenced by a contract or purchase order, or determined by administrative action.

2. = *commitment*.

3. Any lien or other liability attaching to real property.

endorsement Signature of the payee on a *draft* or *check* prior to transfer to a third party such as to the payee's bank.

endowment fund A *fund*, usually of a nonprofit institution, arising from a bequest or gift the income of which is devoted to a specified purpose.

endproduct 1. The result consequent on the application of a method of reasoning or action.

2. Any output of goods or services. See *product*.

engineered (variable) costs Those categories of variable costs that have a specified physical relationship to volume. For example, an engineering analysis should be capable of stating the quantity of raw material necessary for one unit of output.

enter 1. To record a *transaction* in a *journal*; to make an *entry*; to *journalize*.

2. = *post*.

enterprise 1. Any business undertaking; a *business enterprise*; without qualification, the term refers to an entire organization rather than a subdivision thereof; see *entity*.

2. Collectively, all business organizations.

3. The quality of management characterized by energy, initiative, resourcefulness, and adaptability.

enterprise accounting Accounting for a whole enterprise, as contrasted with accounting for the several entities, branches, or departments.

enterprise cost Cost to present owners of an asset, as distinguished from its cost to prior or subsequent owners. See *original cost*.

enterprise fund A fund established for the acquisition, operation, and maintenance of governmental facilities and services which are entirely or predominantly self-supporting by user charges; or where the governing body of a governmental unit has decided that periodic determination of revenues earned, expenses incurred, and resulting net income is appropriate. Government-owned utilities and hospitals are ordinarily accounted for by enterprise funds.

Enterprise Standard Industrial Classification (ESIC) A system with an accompanying 4-digit code for classifying enterprises (companies, firms, partnerships, etc.) by the type of economic activity in which they are engaged. The structure of ESIC follows closely the structure of the SIC codes (=

Standard Industrial Classification) which classify establishments (plants, stores, banks, etc.) rather than total enterprises for purposes of collecting and releasing statistics by the Census Bureau and other federal government agencies. The ESIC includes eight classes of enterprises at the 1-digit level, 67 at the 2-digit level, 216 at the 3-digit level, and 252 at the 4-digit level. See *Standard Industrial Classification*.

enterprise value = *going-concern value*.

entitlement 1. A payment to which a state or local government is entitled as determined by the federal government pursuant to an allocation formula contained in applicable statutes.
2. Payments to which individuals are entitled under statutes such as the social-security acts.

entity 1. A division of the activities of a natural person, partnership, corporation, or other organization, separate and complete in form, usually distinguished from a larger identity such as a head office, controlling corporation, or other more inclusive economic unit; an *establishment*. An entity is often an *accounting unit*. See *economic unit; business enterprise*.
2. Two or more corporations or other organizations operating under a common *control*, their individual financial positions and operating results often being susceptible to consolidation into *combined financial statements*. See *consolidation policy*.

entity accounting Accounting for an entity, independent of that of a predecessor or controlling organization.

entity concept The concept of a business firm or other organization having an identity separate from that of its owners or managers.

entity theory View of the relationship between the *accounting unit* (or *entity*) and its owners and other equity holders which accords it a separate identity. Although the relationship has legal and institutional support in the cor-

porate form of business enterprise, it also is found in unincorporated enterprises and nonbusiness enterprises having a continuity and existence separate from owners or organizers (e.g., governmental units, hospitals, and universities); and is said to have preceded the *corporation*. This view is based on the form of the *accounting identity* (or *equation*) that states *assets* ≡ *equities* (*liabilities* plus *owners' equity*). The entity theory recognizes that, while some items on the right side of the identity are often called liabilities, they really are equities with different rights and legal standing in the enterprise. Under the entity theory, an allocation of corporate income to specific equities is possible, but strict adherence to the concept requires that interest on debt be considered a distribution of income rather than an expense.

entrepreneur An undertaker of an *enterprise*; a person who assumes initiative and responsibility for bringing together the various factors of production for the establishment and operation of a business enterprise and takes the risk of its success or failure. An entrepreneur is regarded as hiring both labor and capital for employment in the enterprise rather than being hired by either. The term was borrowed from the French because of connotations of the word "undertaker."

entry 1. The record of a *transaction* in a *journal*.
2. A *posting*.

entry age normal method A *projected benefit-cost method* for allocating the cost of an employee's retirement benefits to particular years and for determining annual funding requirements. The total cost of an employee's projected retirement benefits is ordinarily assigned in level dollar amounts or as a level percentage of compensation to each period from date of entry into the pension plan until expected retirement. A given year's pension cost is generally equal to a *normal cost* which need not equal the retirement benefits accrued during any year.

entry value The estimated price at which an asset which is currently on the books may be purchased. See *exit value*; *replacement cost accounting*.

EOM = end of month.

EOQ = *economic order quantity*.

EOY = end of year.

equal-annual-payment method (of depreciation) See *depreciation methods*.

equalization point = *basing point*.

equalization reserve 1. An absorption account credited at regular intervals by amounts offsetting charges to operations of sufficient proportions to cover expenditures made more or less irregularly during an accounting period, the object being to spread the expense as uniformly as possible over each subperiod's operations or product. At the end of the fiscal year, any balance in the reserve is transferred to the operations or product to which the reserve relates. See *deferred maintenance*.
2. A similar reserve persisting during two or more accounting periods, e.g., a *reserve* for taxes. Reserves of this type have been criticized because of the creation of a provision of an income-tax expense that may never be paid.
3. = *mixed reserve*.

equalizing dividend A dividend paid to correct inequities caused by changes in established regular dividend dates. Example: When a company advances its dividend date or when companies having different dividend dates are consolidated into one company, an equalizing dividend may be paid. See *dividend-equalization reserve*.

equation A relation between two mathematical expressions, specifying that one assumes the same values as the other for some restricted part of the mathematical domain under consideration. See *inequality; identity*.

equipment Fixed-asset units, usually movable, accessory or supplemental to such larger items as buildings and structures; examples: lighting fixtures, lockers, communication devices, air conditioners. Machinery and fixtures are not generally classified as equipment, although they fall under the definition. The term is frequently used in conjunction with some word that limits its application; as, "factory equipment," "delivery equipment," "office equipment," and the like. See *fixed asset*.

Under *Uniform Commercial Code* Section 9-109(2), goods used or bought primarily for use in business (including farming or a profession). To perfect a security interest in equipment, filing is generally required.

equipment-trust certificate An interest-bearing document evidencing part ownership of a trust created for the purpose of purchasing equipment and selling or leasing it to a user. An equipment trust serves as a device for avoiding direct ownership by the user, particularly in the case of railroads and airlines where such ownership would bring the newly acquired asset under existing mortgages and thus make it impossible to have it serve at the same time as security under a conditional-sales or installment-purchase contract.

equity 1. Any right or claim to assets; a *liability* (2). An equity holder may be a creditor, part owner, proprietor, or stockholder.
2. An interest in property or in a business, subject to claims of creditors; *equity ownership*. *Total equity* is an equivalent British term.
3. *Common stock* plus *retained earnings*. See *owners' equity*.

equity capital = *proprietorship; stockholders' equity; net worth*.

equity capital to long-term debt ratio A reciprocal version of the *debt-equity ratio*.

equity capital to total debt ratio A reciprocal version of the *debt-equity ratio*.

equity financing The sale of *capital stock* by a corporation for cash or things of value.

equity method The periodic adjustment of a parent company's investment in a subsidiary, consolidated or unconsolidated, to the book value reflected in the subsidiary's records, and for the *eliminations* common to *consolidated financial statements*.

equity ownership 1. The interest of an owner in property or in a business or other organization, subject, in case of liquidation, to the prior claims of creditors.
2. The interest (*paid-in capital* and *retained earnings*) of a stockholder or of stockholders collectively in a corporation; *proprietorship*. Thus, when income is earned by the subsidiary, a proportional share is debited to the parent's investment account and credited to its revenues. When dividends are received, the investment account is reduced and cash is debited.

equity receiver A person appointed by a court of equity at the request of the owner, or of creditors, to take over the property of an enterprise, reorganize it, and continue its operation until it can be returned to the owner, or wind up its affairs and distribute any assets remaining.

equity security An instrument representing ownership shares (e.g., common, preferred, and other capital stock), or the right to acquire (e.g., *warrants, rights*, and *call options*) or dispose of (e.g., *put options*) ownership shares in an enterprise at fixed or determinable prices. See *marketable securities*.

equity transaction Any transaction having the effect of increasing or decreasing *net worth* or involving transfers between the accounts making up net worth.

equity turnover See *stockholders' equity turnover*.

ERISA = *Employee Retirement Income Security Act*.

error 1. A discrepancy, as between definitions, axioms, and rules of inference employed in a logical argument, or as illustrated in such clerical lapses as a transposition or slide (see *trial balance*).
2. Deviation, inaccuracy, or incompleteness in the measurement or representation of a *fact*. Errors known to be present are sometimes measured and the range of possible errors controlled. The *random* devices of statistics are often employed for this purpose.

Most business decisions are unaffected by small degrees of error, and costs required to increase accuracy may not be warranted. *Value judgments* are required to balance costs of detecting, reducing, or controlling error against benefits that might possibly derive therefrom. Errors arising from carelessness or inadvertence which could have been eliminated by employing usual methods of detection or control are generally held to be not excusable. Accountants are expected to be on the alert for possible sources of errors, to be informed and ready to employ available means for their control or detection, and to assess the possible net benefit to be gained by instituting safeguards.
3. Unintentional mistakes as distinguished from irregularities. They are also further classified into errors in amount (e.g., monetary amounts, inventory counts) and *compliance errors* (deviations from policies or procedures). See *monetary errors*.

escalation price See *contract price*.

escalator clause A clause in a contract which permits adjustments of price or profit, or of allowances for variations in cost under specified conditions.

escapable cost Cost that may be dispensed with upon the contraction of business activity; such cost is conceived as a *net* figure—the savings in cost by curtailing or dropping an activity, less the added cost to other operating units, assuming that any part of the activity must be continued; contrast with *unavoidable cost.*

escape clause 1. A provision allowing one or more of the parties to a contract, under stipulated conditions, to withdraw or to modify promised performance.

2. A clause inserted in tariff agreements under the Trade Agreements Act which allows the U.S. International Trade Commission to recommend that the President withdraw a previously granted concession on the ground that it threatens serious injury to American suppliers.

ESIC = *Enterprise Standard Industrial Classification.*

Establishing Financial Accounting Standards See *Wheat Report (2).*

establishment 1. A plant or group of plants under a single management, engaging in a set of related processes or in the production of a group of related end items. An establishment may be one of several formally recognized entities within a larger administrative organization such as a corporation. An establishment usually has its own receiving and shipping points for rail, truck, or ship transportation, and a separate mailing address. It is ordinarily an *accounting unit.* See *economic unit; business enterprise.*

2. The *establishment.* Loosely, those in power in business, government, or a profession and the system under which such power is exercised, maintained, and extended.

estate 1. Any right, title, or other interest in real or personal property.

2. The property of a person, often a decedent's property in the process of *administration.*

estate accounting The preparation and keeping of accounts for property in the hands of executors, administrators, or trustees acting under the jurisdiction of a probate court or other legal authority.

estate income The revenue or income of an estate as determined under the provisions of a will or deed, or of federal or state laws and regulations.

estate tax A federal *unified transfer tax* has been in effect since January 1, 1977, which subjects cumulative lifetime and death transfers to a single graduated rate schedule. The estate tax is the unified tax applied to transfer at death. See *death taxes.*

estimated cost 1. The expected cost of manufacture or acquisition, often in terms of a unit of product, computed on the basis of information available in advance of actual production or purchase. Broadly, estimated costs include *standard costs;* both relate to future operations, and their amounts may coincide. However, in everyday usage, the terms differ, the former indicating a *projection* of anticipated actual costs and the latter an attainable cost with which actual costs may be controlled and ultimately compared. See *standard cost.*

2. Allocated cost of a unit of product or of one of several departments or product lines. See *cost accounting.*

estimated revenue (state and local governmental accounting) The general-ledger control account which records the total of revenues legally budgeted for a given fund for a given budget period. See *budgetary accounts; budgetary fund.*

estimated salvage value Amount (or price) net of any disposition costs that an entity expects to receive for an asset when it is retired or scrapped. See *salvage (2).*

estimated tax (federal income tax) An estimate of tax liability required of individuals under Section 6015 of the *Internal Revenue Code* on all income earned or received which is not subject to employer withholding. The taxpayer is required to file a declaration of the estimated tax and remit payments on a timely (quarterly) installment basis if (1) expected gross income includes more than $500 of income not subject to withholding or (2) expected gross income from wages subject to withholding exceeds a certain limit (which varies according to filing status).

estimate of cash requirements A forward schedule of cash needed for current operations or capital expenditure at required points or periods of time: a required element in budgeting estimates, often the product of a *cash-flow statement*.

estimating-cost system A method of accounting whereby estimated costs are the basis for credits to work-in-process accounts, thus serving in lieu of actual costs which are accounted for only in total. See *standard cost*.

ethics A system of moral principles and their application to particular problems of conduct; specifically, the *rules (1)* of conduct of a profession sometimes formally expressed and imposed by a profession, or by a professional body, governing the behavior of its members.

Eurobond A bond issued in any country which is denominated in the currency of any other country. In current usage neither country need be in Europe.

Eurocurrency Currency which is deposited in banks outside the country of issue.

European Economic Community (Common Market) An association of Western European countries which has abolished trade restrictions between member countries, adopted a uniform external tariff, and begun to develop as a single economic entity. Member countries are Belgium, Denmark, France, Italy, Ireland, Luxembourg, the Netherlands, the United Kingdom, and West Germany.

evaluation of internal control The process of examination in order to reach a judgment as to how well a system of internal control is functioning. In auditing, the objectives of internal accounting control include providing management reasonable assurance that (1) transactions are executed in accordance with management's general and specific authorization; (2) transactions are recorded as necessary (a) to permit preparation of financial statements in conformity with generally accepted accounting principles or by other criteria applicable to such statements and (b) to maintain accountability for assets; (3) access to assets is permitted only in accordance with management authorization; (4) the recorded accountability for assets is compared with the existing assets at reasonable intervals and appropriate action is taken with respect to any differences. See *Foreign Corrupt Practices Act*.

The purpose of the evaluation of internal accounting control in a regular audit by an external auditor is to ascertain the extent to which internal control can be relied upon for purposes of restricting the extent of substantive *auditing procedures*.

The evaluation of internal control includes both a study of the system of controls and performance of *compliance tests*.

even lot = *round lot*.

event 1. A *process* or part of a process having a particular moment and place of occurrence. A typical event is a *transaction* with an outsider. See *process; condition*.
2. (statistics) A categorical term referring to phenomena observed or recorded by an investigator at a given time and place: a term taken as a *primitive* notion in the theory of *probability*, and interpreted as a class of logically possible observations.

events and conditions A term covering all the phenomena of economic change recognized in the accounting process and constituting the subject matter of *transactions*. *Events* are the usual cause of external transactions, while *conditions* are characteristic of internal transactions.

evidence 1. A collection of *facts*, admittedly or allegedly accurate, relevant, and sufficient, offered in verification of a *proposition*. Its recognition and admissibility are established under rules laid down by courts, learned professions, and other institutions. Evidence differs from belief, which may not be supported by acceptable evidence. An auditor may believe that a given corporate management is competent and able to extricate itself from an important current weakness in financial position, but this belief should have no effect on the accountant's construction and presentation of the evidence of such weakness, as it would ordinarily be disclosed in a balance sheet or operating statement.
2. It is sometimes desirable to distinguish between "data" and "facts" where the latter represent data which have been treated to remove inaccurate materials. "Facts" may then be further distinguished from "information" which is obtained by arranging such facts in different ways intended to be meaningful. Finally, "information" may be distinguished from "evidence," which represents information that has been treated in accordance with rules of admissibility and relevance for points at issue. It is evidence that is sought as a basis for inference or validation in legal proceedings or when inferences are to be made or opinions expressed as part of a completed audit by a professional auditor.

EVSI See *expected value of sample information*.

ex 1. Without, as in *ex-dividend; ex-rights*.
2. (followed by a named location) A term indicating that the price quoted to or paid by a purchaser does not include any transportation or handling costs and that the seller assumes neither cost nor risk beyond the named location (or beyond the moment of time specified in the sales contract) at which the buyer takes delivery.

exact duplicate A copy conforming in every detail with an original.

examination 1. = *audit (1)*.
2. A *limited audit (1)*; when thus employed, the term is accompanied by words or phrases indicating the character of the limitation.
3. A test of competency, suitability, or attainment, as in a CPA examination or a personnel selection test.

examine (auditing) To probe records, or inspect securities or other documents, review procedures, and question persons, all for the purpose of arriving at an opinion of accuracy, propriety, sufficiency, and the like.

ex ante In advance of. A plan of action or decision made on the basis of an assumption about specific facts or data before the latter have occurred.

except-for report See *auditors' report*.

exception 1. A qualification by an auditor in his or her report, indicating a limitation as to the scope of the audit or disagreement with or doubt concerning an item of a financial statement to which he or she certifies. See *auditors' report*.
2. (governmental accounting) A written notification by the Comptroller General to an accountable officer or employee questioning an expenditure; failure to supply a satisfactory explanation may lead to a *disallowance*, following which the officer or employee may be required to recover the amount from the payee, personally reimburse the government, or obtain *relief*.
3. The difference between a *standard cost* and *actual cost*. See *management by exception*.
4. A difference between a balance receivable as recorded and that reported as payable by a customer in reference to a *confirmation* request.

exceptions report A report which focuses on deviations from planned or expected performance. A report which focuses on variance from *standard costs* is an example. The objective is to direct managerial attention to situations where corrective action is needed in the case of an unfavorable difference or where opportunities for improved performance standards may be found in the case of a favorable difference. Sometimes referred to as attention-directing reports.

excess deductions account (EDA) Generally, an accounting record that taxpayers with farm losses are required to keep for federal income-tax purposes (Section 1251). Effective for taxable years beginning after 1969, the purpose is to recapture certain farm losses previously used by taxpayers to offset nonfarm income. The individual taxpayer is affected only if in any year his or her nonfarm adjusted gross income exceeds $50,000, and then only to the extent the farm loss exceeds $25,000 (special rules apply to small business corporations). Each year's farm loss (the excess over $25,000) is set up in an EDA. Farm income in any later year is subtracted from the account. Certain gains otherwise entitled to capital gain treatment will be ordinary income to the extent of the balance in the EDA at the end of the year. Taxpayers who elect to maintain inventories and to capitalize all capital costs need not add to EDA.

excess from recapitalization The amount by which the *book value* (3) of *stockholders' contributions* exceeds the *par* or *stated value* of new securities exchanged therefor. Example: A corporation has outstanding 10,000 $10-par-value common shares of capital stock; its books reflect a *deficit* (2) ("negative" *retained earnings*) of $30,000. Its stockholders surrender their holdings in exchange for 5,000 $10-par-value shares, thereby creating an excess from recapitalization of $20,000 which on a balance sheet may be designated *additional paid-in capital* along with an explanation, or footnote, describing its origin.

excess reserves Reserves held by commercial banks in greater amounts than required by central bank policy. See *reserve*.

exchange 1. The transfer of money, property, or services in return for money, property, or services; or for promises to deliver money, property, or services, or any combination of these items; a *barter*.
2. = *foreign exchange*: the exchange of legal tender or other currencies in ratios authorized by sovereign powers or as transacted in a money market. See *rate of exchange*.
3. A market for a commodity, such as a stock or produce exchange.

exchange check A check given in return for cash or for another check.

exchange controls Governmental actions taken to restrict the convertibility of currency into foreign currency.

exchange depreciation A reduction in the value of one country's money relative to currencies of its trading partners.

exchange exposure See *foreign exchange exposure*.

exchange gain (or loss) 1. The net result in local currency of any completed deal in foreign currency.
2. The net gain or loss resulting from the effect of a change in exchange rates on the carrying amount of assets and liabilities denominated in foreign currencies. Exchange gains or losses result from (a) translation of foreign currency transactions and foreign currency financial statements, and (b) conversion of foreign currency or the settlement of a receivable or payable denominated in foreign currency at a rate different from that at which the item is recorded.

excise tax A tax levied on the manufacture, sale, or purchase of any commodity or service. The basis of tax computation may be *ad valorem* (as in a *value-added tax*) or *in rem* (i.e., on the physical units). See *indirect tax*.

exclusion (insurance) A provision in an insurance contract or bond limiting the scope of the insurance agreement.

ex-dividend A term indicating that the price of shares of capital stock excludes a dividend payable on a certain future date to stockholders of record on a specified preceding date. See *dividend*.

executor A person or one of two or more persons named in a will as the fiduciary who is to take charge of the deceased's estate and administer or dispose of it as directed in the will.

executory contract A contract is wholly executory, partially executory (and partially executed), or wholly executed depending upon the extent to which the substance of the contractual agreement is carried out by the parties involved. In legal literature, executory contracts mean both wholly and partially executory contracts. However, in accounting literature, the term executory contracts normally refers to those contracts that are wholly executory. While a contract remains wholly executory, the present accounting practice does not require a recognition of contractual rights and obligations in financial statements. It is only when a contract is partially or wholly executed that the results of the execution are recorded and reported in financial statements. However, there seems to be a trend toward recognition of contractual rights and obligations in a wholly executory contract as evidenced by the accounting standards on *capital leases*.

exemplary damages See *punitive damages*.

exempt income (federal income taxes) Exemptions from gross income for tax purposes contained in Sections 101-127 of the *Internal Revenue Code*, which include certain death and disability benefits, interest on certain state and municipal obligations, various employee benefits, unemployment benefits, and partial exclusion of qualifying dividends received (a maximum of $100 per year per individual taxpayer). Although not specified in the Internal Revenue Code, social-security benefits are exempt under a ruling from the Treasury Department.

exemption (federal income taxes) A deduction of $1,000 is allowed an individual taxpayer for each exemption claimed by the taxpayer. Personal exemptions are allowed for the taxpayer and the taxpayer's spouse. An additional exemption is allowed if the taxpayer or spouse is blind or over age 65. An exemption is also allowed for each *dependent*. See *personal exemption*.

exempt organizations (federal income taxes) Corporations and trusts which are exempt from the federal income tax. States usually follow suit and such organizations are also exempt from which no income can inure to the benefit of any individual shareholder or member of the organization. The *Internal Revenue Code* does not define the term, but describes more than 20 categories of exempt organizations. Exemption is not automatic. It must be applied for and granted by the *Internal Revenue Service* and organizations can lose exempt status if they do not continue to carry on only qualifying activities.

Corporations which are otherwise tax exempt may be required to pay federal income tax on business income which is unrelated to their exempt purpose. The fact that an organization is tax exempt does not necessarily mean that contributions to it will be tax deductible by the donor. Only a limited subset of exempt organizations so qualify. They are primarily governmental, religious, educational, or charitable in nature.

exhibit A financial or other statement of a formal character prepared for the information of others, as in an auditor's report.

existence (auditing) Refers to two specific related audit *objectives*: (1) that the recorded amounts in a company's financial statements are valid and actually exist, and (2) that all activities and items that did take place and do exist which should be recorded in the financial statements in fact are.

exit value The price or amount at which an asset could be sold or a liability extinguished. It may take the form of *current exit value*, *expected exit value*, or *present value*. See *entry value; replacement cost accounting*.

exordium Preface; introduction.

expectancy = *expected value*.

expected actual capacity 1. The budgeted output level of a production unit to meet budgeted customer demand for a specified interval of time, usually one year.
2. The budgeted profit-maximizing output level of a production unit for the forthcoming period, usually one year.

expected exit value (1) The amount of cash (or its equivalent) into which an asset is expected to be converted in due course of business less direct costs necessary to make that conversion (referred to as "net realizable value") or (2) the amount of cash (or its equivalent) expected to be paid to eliminate a liability in due course of business including direct costs necessary to make those payments.

expected life *Expected value* of length of life or years of service of an asset or asset group at a particular moment of time.

expected value (statistics) The average or mean of a *statistical distribution*; represented in formulas by *E*.

expected value of perfect information (**EVPI**) In *decision* theory, it represents the expected gain if the state of the world were revealed. The relatively easy to compute expected value of perfect information is often used as an upper limit on the *expected value of sample information*.

expected value of sample information (**EVSI**) In *decision* theory, the expected value of sample information is an *a priori* assessment of the expected gain from the information a sample can provide about the true state of the world. The expected value of sample information can be compared with the cost of the sample to decide whether such sampling is justified.

expendable fund A *fund* the assets of which may be applied by administrative action to specific or general purposes.

expended appropriation (governmental accounting) That portion of an *appropriation* equal to the *accrued* expenditures incurred thereunder; the balance of the appropriation may be obligated or unobligated.

expenditure 1. The incurring of a liability, the payment of cash, or the transfer of property for the purpose of acquiring an asset or service or settling a loss. The *accrual basis* of accounting is assumed unless otherwise noted.
2. The amount of cash or property paid or to be paid for a service rendered, or an asset purchased.
3. Any cost the benefits of which may extend beyond the current accounting period.
4. (governmental accounting) The incurring of an actual liability (in distinction to an estimated or contingent liability) pursuant to the authority granted in an appropriation ordinance.
—expend, *v.t.*

expenditure rate An administratively imposed ceiling on the expenditures, usually on an accrual basis, of any organization, organizational subdivision, function, or activity, within any forward period of time.

expenditure tax See *consumption taxes*.

expense *n.* 1. *Expired cost*: any item or class of cost of (or loss from) carrying on an activity; a present or past expenditure defraying a present operating cost or representing an irrecoverable cost or *loss*; capital expenditure written down or off (*writedown, writeoff*): a term often used with some qualifying word or expression denoting function, organization, or time; as, a selling expense, factory expense, or monthly expense.

FASB defines expenses as outflows or other using up of assets or incurrences of liabilities (or a combination of both) during a period from delivering or producing goods, rendering services, or carrying out other activities that constitute an enterprise's ongoing major or central operations.

2. A class term for expenditures *recognized* as operating costs of a current or past period.

3. Hence, any expenditure the benefits from which do not extend beyond the present.

4. Outflows or other exhaustion of assets or incurrences of liabilities (or a combination of both) during a period from delivering or producing goods, rendering services, or carrying out other activities that constitute an enterprise's earning process.

v. To designate a past or current expenditure as a present operating cost or loss; to *write down* or *write off*.

expense account 1. Any *account* (*1*) maintained for a particular expense.

2. A general term for the total *cost of goods sold*, expired services, or irrecoverable losses.

3. A general term for *accounts* (*1*) periodically cleared through *profit and loss* (*1*).

4. A statement of an individual's outlays, usually covering a limited time and purpose.

expense budget The planned cost of the volume at which it is expected that an activity will be undertaken. See *current budget*.

expense center Any location within an organization at which the coincidence of organization and function has been recognized; an *activity*. An expense center may be a machine, a department, or a service shop with which operating costs are identified, its supervisor

deriving his or her authority from and being accountable to a higher level of management. Fixing discretionary responsibilities on supervisors, establishing expenditure limitations, measuring the quantity and quality of work output, and comparing incurred unit costs with predetermined standards and with costs of similar activities elsewhere are features of expense-center accounting.

expense control Any method designed to keep future costs within a predetermined rate or amount. Included are such devices as holding supervisors responsible for restricted functional-cost areas, confining expenditures to certain classes, limiting the amount that may be incurred within a relatively short period of time, and projecting a standard unit cost to which actual cost is expected to conform. See *control*.

expense distribution The identification of an expense with the purpose—for example, a process or product—for which it was incurred. An expense readily identifiable with a particular purpose is a *direct expense*; a joint or common cost that contributes to two or more purposes and is allocable to any one purpose only by some method of averaging is an *indirect expense* or *overhead*. Where it has been decided that a *joint* or *common cost* is to be distributed according to some measure of benefit received, the methods of distribution most often employed are direct-labor cost, direct-labor hours, machine-hours, and space occupied (square feet or cubic feet). See *overhead; direct cost*.

experience rating (insurance) The establishment of a normal rate for a specific risk based on a comparison of the cost of such risk with the average cost of all risks within the class; the adjusted rate may be higher or lower.

experiment 1. A controlled or partially controlled operation, undertaken for the purpose of determining the nature, frequency, or other characteristics of events occurring under stat-

ed conditions. An experimental observation may contribute to or test a generalization.
2. Loosely, anything tried.

expired cost An *expenditure* from which no further benefit is anticipated; an expense; a cost *absorbed* over the period during which benefits were enjoyed or a loss incurred.

expired utility 1. That portion of the anticipated *usefulness* or service yield of a fixed asset no longer to be availed of by or available to its owner, whatever the cause; = *depreciation*.
2. *Accumulated depreciation*.

exponential smoothing A subset of *ARIMA* models used for forecasting in which data are weighted to conform to an exponential function that assigns the heaviest weights to the most recent observations.

Export-Import (Exim) Bank An agency of the U.S. government whose purpose is to aid in financing exports and imports for U.S. and foreign enterprises.

export trade corporation (ETC) A controlled foreign corporation which has at least 90% of its gross income for the immediately preceding three years from sources outside of the United States, and at least 75% of its gross income for the same period from exports to countries other than the United States. The *Internal Revenue Service* allows an export trade corporation's U.S. stockholders to elect to reduce the amount of taxable income below that which would be recognized were the ETC simply a controlled foreign corporation.

ex post Abbreviation of *ex post facto*; after the fact. A plan of action, concept, or decision developed on the basis of facts or data that have already occurred.

exposure (insurance) The extent of a *risk*, measured in terms of payroll, receipts, area, nature of surrounding properties, or other factors.

exposure draft A proposed Statement of Financial Accounting Standards or Concepts issued for public comment by the *Financial Accounting Standards* Board prior to taking final action.

express trust A trust created by specific provision in a deed or other written instrument. See *trust*.

ex-rights A term used in connection with the price of a share of capital stock indicating that a right to subscribe to new shares, formerly attaching to the stock, no longer attaches, the rights having expired or having been retained by the seller. See *right*.

extended coverage An addition or endorsement to a fire-insurance policy that includes such risks as those arising from windstorms, hail, earthquakes, riots, and other possible causes of property damage.

extension of time for filing (federal income taxes) Automatic extensions of the due date for filing income-tax returns are available to individuals (two months) and corporations (three months) if application is made and the estimated tax paid. The maximum extension period cannot exceed six months (except for taxpayers who are abroad), and the reasons for the extension request for the additional four months must be explained and the application approved by the *Internal Revenue Service*. Interest is charged on any balance unpaid from the original due date until date of payment. If the tax remitted by the original due date is not at least 90% of the total tax liability, a penalty is assessed.

extent of tests The number of items or proportion of all possible items to which auditing procedures are applied. This may refer to a group of like items as in a single test—for example, confirming 50% of customer balances outstanding—or it may refer to different items in a common grouping subjected to various tests, for example, visiting five of twenty branch locations for the purpose of observing inventories and testing transactions.

external audit An audit by a person not an employee; an independent audit. See *audit (4)*.

external auditor = *public accountant* or firm of public accountants. Also *certified public accountant*; contrast with *internal auditor*.

external document Documents within an accounting system that have been in the hands of someone outside the organization, e.g., a party to the transactions being documented. In some cases, external documents originate outside the organization and end up in the organization's possession. Examples are: vendors' invoices, canceled notes payable, and insurance policies. In other cases, such as canceled checks, the documents originate within the organization, but go to an outsider who ultimately returns them.

Because they contain some indication of outsider agreement, external documents are generally considered to be more persuasive as audit evidence than *internal documents*.

externalities Consequences attending a transaction which affect others besides the transacting parties, especially when such consequences are not mediated by prices or accompanied by terms of payment as opportunities for negotiation that permit potentially affected *third parties* to influence the transaction. Examples: 1. *Negative externality*: Fabrication of steel in satisfaction of a contract results in smoke and other pollutants that affect the health and property values of persons residing in the vicinity of the mill. 2. *Positive externality*: Execution of this contract results in a pool of skilled labor available for employment by others who are thereby spared the cost of training. Note, however, that subsequent employers might pay a higher price for this labor and subsequent purchases may benefit from the lower price of property in the vicinity of the mill. The externality is then said to have been internalized by means of the resulting market transactions.

external transaction A *transaction* with an *outsider*; known also as a "business" transaction; contrast with *internal transaction*. Sales and purchases of goods and services, collections and deposits of cash, and payments of liabilities constitute the bulk of the external transactions of a business enterprise.

extinguishment of debt, early The reacquisition of any form of debt security or instrument before its scheduled maturity (except through conversion by the holder), regardless of whether the debt is viewed as terminated or held as "treasury bonds." All open-market or mandatory reacquisitions of debt securities to meet sinking-fund requirements are early extinguishments.

extractive industries Industries involved in the activities of (a) prospecting and exploring for wasting (nonregenerative) natural resources, (b) acquiring them, (c) further exploring them, (d) developing them, and (e) producing (extracting) them from the earth.

extra dividend A dividend paid in excess of a previously maintained annual rate, without assurance that the additional payment is to continue; also called "special dividend."

extraordinary depreciation Depreciation that is caused by unusual wear and tear, unexpected disintegration, obsolescence, or inadequacy beyond that attributable to ordinary loss of physical or service life. A provision for depreciation will normally cover both ordinary and extraordinary depreciation. See *depreciation*. Extraordinary depreciation is not usually regarded as a type of *accelerated depreciation*.

extraordinary expense An expense so unusual in type or amount as to be accorded special treatment in the accounts or separate disclosure in financial statements. See *loss; income deduction*.

extraordinary items Events and transactions that are unusual in nature and occur infrequently. The effects of material extraordinary items are segregated in the income statement from income from continuing operations.

extraordinary repairs Repairs making good deterioration attributable to hard use, neglect, or other cause of deferment of normal maintenance or repair; an overhaul correcting both major and minor defects, and often requiring replacements of parts. See *deferred maintenance*.

extrapolation (statistics) An extension or projection to new values lying outside the data, as: an estimate of a country's population two years hence; the probable position of wholesale prices next week.
—extrapolate, *v.t.* or *i*. See *interpolation*.

F = *folio reference*.

face amount (or value) The nominal amount of a bond, note, mortgage, or other security as stated in the instrument itself, exclusive of interest or dividend accumulations. This may or may not coincide with the price at which the instrument was first sold, its present market value, or its redemption price. The nominal amount of each share represented by a stock certificate is usually referred to as *par* or *stated value*.

face-amount certificate A form of contract between certain investment companies and investors whereby the latter agree to make required installment payments to the company until the total called for by the contract has been paid. During the payment period, the certificate has a cash surrender value; at the ''maturity'' date, the surrender value·is the *face amount*, which, because of accruing interest in excess of the loading cost applicable to the certificate, often exceeds the amount paid in by the investor.

facility 1. A coordinated group of *fixed assets*—land, buildings, machinery, and equipment—constituting a *plant*; sometimes called a ''complete'' facility.

2. Any item of physical equipment that contributes to production: a building, machine, or shop; a *factor of production* in the form of any item of plant.

fact 1. A statement embodying *evidence* or findings based on explicitly or partially formulated *rules* of observation not wholly derivable from a structure of logical relations to other propositions. Hence, a fact is at best only probable and not certain; what appears to be fact depends upon the context, state of knowledge, and point of view of the observer.
2. Loosely, any proposition held to be true. This usage fails to distinguish between a simple event or observable characteristic and an inference or systematic statement (such as a *principle, theory*, or other generalization) about a mass of related observations or observable facts. See *evidence* (2).

factor 1. One who buys trade receivables with or without recourse, his or her profit coming from a commission, such as a fraction of 1%, and from interest on advances against receivables. Factoring predominates in the textile industry and is found to a lesser degree elsewhere. Factors were formerly selling agents for merchandise of various kinds, differing from brokers in that they handled the merchandise themselves.

2. (economics) One or more of the contributors to producing goods or services. See *factor of production*.

3. Hence, any component; e.g., any influence that contributes to, modifies, or otherwise affects an endproduct.

4. (mathematics) Any of the numbers or symbols that, when multiplied together, form a product.

factorial The product of a specified number and all the positive whole *integers* preceding it. The factorial symbol is the exclamation point; thus $4! = 4 \times 3 \times 2 \times 1$, or 24; $n! = n(n - 1)(n - 2) \times \ldots \times 2 \times 1$. Factorials quickly become large numbers (e.g., $10! = 3,628,800$), and logarithm tables have been prepared to facilitate their use. See *permutation*. Both 0! and 1! are treated as ''1'' in factorial formulas. See *combination*.

factoring of receivables Process by which *trade accounts (or notes) receivable* are sold, usually without recourse. See *assignment; factor (1)*.

factor of production Any of the various agents (natural resources, labor, processes, capital, the entrepreneur) contributing to the production or supply of a good or service; the combined cost of these factors equals the supply price. See *cost (4)*.

factory cost = *manufacturing cost*.

factory expense 1. An item of manufacturing cost other than raw material and direct labor.

2. Hence, *manufacturing expense; indirect expense; overhead*.

factory ledger A subsidiary ledger containing such operating costs of a manufacturing establishment as materials, labor, and factory overhead. The total of its accounts may be the cost of *goods in process*; or included in the ledger may be inventory accounts for raw materials, supplies, and finished goods, as well as *work in process*.

factory overhead Manufacturing costs which are not directly traceable to units of product. See *overhead*. Also called manufacturing overhead, indirect manufacturing expense or cost, factory burden, *burden*, or *oncost*.

FAF = *Financial Accounting Foundation*.

Fair Labor Standards Act An act originally passed into law in the United States in 1938 to set minimum wages, basic hours of work, and other conditions for workers engaged in interstate commerce. It has been periodically amended to broaden the coverage and to increase the minimum wage.

fair market value 1. Value determined by bona fide bargaining between well-informed buyers and sellers, usually over a period of time. See *market value; fair value*.

2. An estimate of such value, in the absence of sales or quotations.

fairness 1. Adequacy and propriety.

2. The ability of *financial statements* to convey unambiguous, adequate information, particularly when accompanied by the *representation* (in a short-form *auditors' report*) of a public accountant, to ''present fairly'' the detail required by *convention* for depicting *financial position* and *operating results*. This representation—as distinguished from the financial statements themselves—is commonly understood to mean that, without clearly stated *exceptions* or *qualifications*, no less than the following conditions have been complied with by the accountant:

As to the *examination*: (a) his or her independence (observed in the conduct of the examination) is affirmed by the character of his or her report; (b) no limitation, natural or imposed by the client, has reduced the scope of the examination below minimal levels; (c) records and other supporting evidence required have been available to and utilized by him or her; (d) he or she has tested receivables by correspondence, and has substantiated by observation opening and closing inventories that have been valued not in excess of current market; or he or she has satisfied himself or herself with respect to these items by other, not less rigorous, means; (e) he or she has accepted responsibility for the report, if any, of another accountant (e.g., on a branch or subsidiary), which has been combined or consolidated in the financial statements, or he or she has submitted the other's report collaterally; (f) contingencies and other uncertainties that might affect present or future interpretations of the financial statements have been *appraised* (2) by him or her and reported as necessary; (g) his or her short-form-report language follows the professional standard (on occasion modified to express a qualified, adverse, or disclaimer of opinion), or he or she has prepared no report and has disassociated himself or herself from the financial statements; and (h) he or she has exercised professional care and judgment throughout the examination.

As to the client's internal controls and accounting methods during the period reviewed: (i) internal controls have been found adequate; (j) the client's applied accounting principles, policies, and procedures have been acceptable; (k) accounting policies have been consistent during the current and preceding periods; and (1) the books of account have been brought into agreement with the financial statements.

As to the financial statements, including appended notes: (m) terminology common to financial statements has been employed or notes defining uncommon terms are attached; (n) the arrangement of financial-statement items follows the conventional pattern; (o) the financial statements are comparable in form and item with those of similar organizations; (p) unamortized *acquisition cost* which in his or her judgment may be carried forward to the succeeding period is the best basis for asset valuation; any other basis is

described along with the amount by which it differs from acquisition cost less recorded allowances for accumulated depreciation or for loss from expected realization; (q) depreciation methods for both accounting and tax purposes, and current provisions and accumulations, are revealed; (r) more-than-minor (e.g., 5%) differences between net income and taxable income are explained; (s) an unusual large-scale transaction, an important change in activities, or other major post-balance-sheet event or condition is footnoted; (t) annual rentals and other provisions of general interest in long-term leases, pension plans, compensation agreements, and stock-option and bonus plans are set forth; (u) no known misstatement or misrepresentation is reflected in the financial statements; (v) facts and conditions are included without which the financial statements might be interpreted as misleading; (w) information that may contribute to the reader's better understanding is provided, even though without it the statements cannot technically be regarded as misleading; and (x) financial statements and their attachments are management's, although at times prepared by the accountant for management and added to or modified at his or her instance; hence, any item omitted from them and judged to be of importance appears in his or her report.

As to any departure, deemed to be material in character or amount, from any of the preceding conditions: (y) his or her report identifies the item with the financial statements and (z) provides information designed to aid an outsider's appraisal of its significance.

fair-trade price The resale price of a branded product fixed or "suggested" by the manufacturer for the purpose of eliminating or minimizing price competition between wholesalers and retailers. See *fixed resale price; price maintenance*.

fair value 1. Value determined by bona fide bargaining between well-informed buyers and sellers; the price for which an asset could be bought or sold in an arm's-length transaction between unrelated parties; value in a sale between a willing buyer and a willing seller, other than in a forced or liquidation sale.
2. An estimate of such value, in the absence of sales or quotations (e.g., the approximation of exchange price in *nonmonetary transactions*).
3. Reasonable or equitable value; the legal concept of value on which an investor is entitled to a "fair return." The term is often used by public utilities to indicate the basis of valuation employed in the establishment of service rates.

family partnership A partnership whose members are confined principally or wholly to a single family for federal income-tax purposes, such a partnership is not recognized as to any partner who is not considered to be the real owner of his or her partnership interest. Recognition is not denied, however, merely because the capital of one partner is derived by gift from another family partner, nor because tax saving is a motive, provided that capital is a material income-producing factor in the business.

fanout The breakdown of an account into two or more basic accounts.

farm-price method The valuation of the inventory of a farmer, employing market price less any known or estimated direct cost of marketing or other disposition, and sanctioned by income-tax regulations, Section 1.471-6(d). See *unit-livestock-price method*.

FAS = free alongside ship. A symbol indicating that the export price of a given lot of goods includes the obligation of the seller to deliver it to the ship that is to transport it without additional cost to the buyer. See *FAS price*.

FASB = *Financial Accounting Standards Board*.

FAS price The price, when used without further specification, charged a foreign buyer, including inland transportation, warehousing, trucking, lighterage, insurance, and the like, to a point within reach of the loading tackle of the vessel, the seller retaining risks of ownership to this point.

favorable difference (or variance) A term initially applied to (a) the excess of actual revenue over budgeted revenue, and (b) the excess of standard or budgeted costs over actual cost. Reverse conditions are initially labeled as unfavorable differences. Whether such differences are finally favorable or unfavorable and whether they are controllable or uncontrollable and by whom requires careful analysis of the conditions under which the difference arose. For example, the purchasing department may have a "favorable" price variance by purchasing substandard raw material, and this may result in an "unfavorable" usage variance in the production department.

feasibility study Analysis of a proposed course of action to see whether it is *feasible*. Such studies often involve analyses of alternatives to a proposed course of action as in "what-if planning." See *scenario; futurology*.

feasible Operable; practicable. Meeting all conditions of a problem, as in a solution which satisfies all *constraints* of a *mathematical programming* model. Note: such a solution is not necessarily optimal.

Federal Insurance Contribution Act See *FICA*.

Federal Reserve Bank One of 12 central banks, established under federal law, owned by and having broad supervisory authority over member commercial banks.

Federal Trade Commission A quasi-judicial administrative agency of the federal government charged with the general responsibility of maintaining the freedom of business enterprise, curbing monopoly and unfair business practices, and keeping competition "both free and fair." Its basic legal authorities are the Federal Trade Commission Act of 1914 (38 Stat. 717), the *Clayton Act*, passed in the same year, the *Robinson-Patman Act* of 1936, and subsequent amendments. The first of these acts enumerates a number of commercial practices deemed unfair, such as misbranding, misleading advertising, false pricing, threats of lawsuits, filching trade secrets, and various other acts intended to affect competitors adversely. A general intent is to enforce the spirit of fair competition by preventive action or by voluntary settlements, without recourse to the courts unless other measures have failed.

fee Any charge for professional or other services; a *commission*. Its amount is commonly determined by law, custom, or by an estimate, unrelated to cost, of the worth of the service to the recipient.

feedback Any system involving periodic supplying of information on operating performance, comparison of such information with a standard of performance, and taking of corrective action based on the comparison.

feeder organization (federal income taxes) An organization operated for the primary purpose of carrying on a trade or business, the profits of which inure to one or more tax-exempt organizations. It is subject to income tax under Sections 502 and 511 of the *Internal Revenue Code*; before 1951, such income in certain instances was held to be exempt from taxation.

FEI = *Financial Executives Institute*.

fellow subsidiary One of two or more subsidiaries of a controlling company.

fiat Any directive by recognized authority. Usually confined to administrative (as distinct from legislative) directives.

FICA = *Federal Insurance Contribution Act*. Also called "social-security taxes." Under Sections 3101-3126 of the *Internal Revenue Code*, it levies a tax against employees and employers to provide retirement benefits, disability benefits, survivorship benefits, and hospital insurance benefits. Self-employed individuals pay a corresponding tax under Sections 1401-1403 at a rate which is approximately 150% of the rate levied against employees. The fastest-growing component of the total tax structure, with receipts increasing more than 700% since 1960, a majority of U.S. taxpayers now pay more in FICA tax than in federal income tax. See *regressive tax*.

fidelity bond Insurance against losses arising from dishonest acts of employees and involving specified money, merchandise, or other property; persons or positions may be covered.

fiduciary Any person responsible for the custody or administration, or both, of property belonging to another; as, a trustee.

fiduciary accounting 1. The preparation and keeping of accounts for property in the hands of a trustee, executor, or administrator, whether under the direct jurisdiction of a court or acting by virtue of a private deed of trust or other instrument of appointment. 2. *Estate accounting*.

fiduciary funds Any fund held by a governmental unit in a fiduciary capacity, ordinarily as agent or trustee. Also called trust and agency funds.

field auditor An auditor whose function is to audit plants or branches located away from the principal office; a traveling auditor.

field warehousing A method whereby manufacturers, jobbers, wholesalers, and others borrow money using goods which remain stored on their premises as *collateral*. Security is provided by public warehouse companies taking accurate inventories, protecting and safeguarding the goods and issuing warehouse receipts.

FIFO 1. First In, First Out. See *inventory valuation*.

2. (computers) A data structure whereby the first element added to the list is always the first element removed from the list. This data structure is sometimes known as a *queue*. Since this structure has a tendency to propagate through the storage medium, a technique known as a wraparound queue has been developed which goes back and reuses discarded memory locations.

figure of merit A measure used to judge degree of accomplishment as, for instance, a *standard cost* or a sales *budget*. Such a measure is usually formed from several elements—such as labor, materials, overhead, etc.—to which criterion measures are applied.

Noncommensurables such as labor hours and material usage measures are usually converted to comparable units by means of these criterion measures and totaled to an overall figure of merit. The latter may then be compared with similarly stated *objectives* as a basis for evaluating actual accomplishments.

file structure 1. The policies and procedures which govern the way documents or data are to be stored or filed.

2. (computers) The organization which governs the way *data records* are stored in a computer. The most common file structure organization techniques are sequential access, direct access, and index sequential. See *sequential file organization; direct access; index sequential file*.

filing status (federal income taxes) The tax tables or rate schedules an individual should reference in calculating his or her income tax

liability. The family unit to be supported by the income of an individual taxpayer is taken into account with four progressive schedules of marginal tax rates for (1) married taxpayers filing *joint returns*, (2) married taxpayers filing separate returns, (3) unmarried taxpayers filing individual returns, and (4) unmarried taxpayers filing as a *head-of-household*. An unmarried *surviving spouse* may use the joint return schedules for two additional years.

final dividend 1. = *year-end dividend*.

2. The last of a series of *liquidating dividends*.

finance *v.t. & i.* To supply with funds through the sale of stocks or bonds, floating loans, extending credit on open account, or transferring or appropriating money from internal sources.

n. The theory and practice of dealings, including speculation, in money and its investment.

financial Pertaining to money and its management, movement, or objectives; as financial transactions, financial policies.

financial accounting The accounting for revenues, expenses, assets, and liabilities that is commonly carried on in the general offices of a business: a term often limited to the accounting concerned with published financial reports in contrast to internal aspects of accounting such as *cost accounting*. See also *management accounting; administrative accounting*.

Financial Accounting Foundation (FAF) Founded in 1972, the Financial Accounting Foundation is the parent body and source of funding for the *Financial Accounting Standards Board*. Its sponsoring organizations are the *American Institute of Certified Public Accountants, American Accounting Association, National Association of Accountants,*

Financial Executives Institute, Financial Analysts Federation, and the Securities Industry Association (formerly the Investment Bankers Association of America).

Financial Accounting Standards Board (FASB) The designated organization in the private sector formed in 1973 to establish standards of financial accounting and reporting. The FASB is independent of all other business and professional organizations. Although the *Securities and Exchange Commission* (SEC) has the statutory authority to establish financial accounting and reporting standards, FASB standards are officially recognized as authoritative by the SEC and the *American Institute of Certified Public Accountants*.

financial accounts = *financial statements*.

Financial Analysts Journal See *accounting journals*.

financial concept of capital A view that capital is a monetary amount of net assets (stated in either units of money or units of purchasing power). According to this concept of capital, financial resources are invested with the expectation that the investment will generate more financial resources than the amount invested. Recovery of the amount of financial resources invested is a return of capital, and financial resources generated in excess of the amount invested constitute a return on capital (i.e., earnings). See *capital maintenance concept*.

financial condition See *financial position*.

Financial Executive See *accounting journals*.

Financial Executives Institute Founded in 1931 as the Controllers Institute of America, the Financial Executives Institute is an organization composed mainly of corporate controllers and chief financial officers. Through its Corporate Reporting Committee, it has been a powerful spokesman for industry before such bodies as the *Securities and*

Exchange Commission and the *Financial Accounting Standards Board*. FEI has more than 75 membership chapters in the United States, and it publishes the monthly journal, *Financial Executive*. FEI's research arm, the Financial Executives Research Foundation, sponsors and publishes research monographs and books.

financial expense A cost incident to the financing of an enterprise, as distinguished from one directly applicable to operations. Examples: interest on indebtedness; *bond discount* amortized.

financial forecasts A *forecast* of financial positions, changes in financial positions, and results of operations for one or more future periods. Examples include forecasted balance sheets, funds-flow and operating statements. For audit purposes a financial forecast is usually restricted to the most probable set of the values that might materialize. See *forecast; prediction; projections*.

financial highlight 1. In annual corporate reports, a section devoted to items of particular interest to stockholders, prospective investors, and the public; examples: *earnings* (2) and principal reasons for increases or decreases in business as compared with one or more prior years; sales totals for old and new products or activities; working-capital changes; additions and retirements of equity securities; acquisitions and disposals of fixed assets and investments; and so on.
2. Hence, any summary of financial transactions.

financial leverage See *leverage*. The degree of financial leverage is usually calculated by dividing earnings before interest and taxes by earnings before interest and taxes less interest.

financial position (or condition) The *assets* and *liabilities* of an organization as displayed on a balance sheet, following customary practices in its preparation. The term is sometimes applied to a *balance sheet*.

financial projection An estimate of future financial position with results of operations and accompanying changes in *financial position*, often confined only to selected elements such as cash flows and income results. Such projections play a large role in *simulation* studies of a *risk analysis* variety. They may also form a part of the studies leading up to a *financial forecast*. See *forecast*.

financial ratio See *ratio*.

financial ratio analysis See *ratio*.

financial reporting Means of communicating financial information that relates to the information provided by the accounting system. *Financial statements* are a central feature of financial reporting. Information communicated may also take other forms, including corporate annual reports, prospectuses, news releases, or forecasts.

financial risk The *risk* of default on the obligations of a security. Used in contradistinction to *interest rate risk* and *purchasing power risk*.

financial statement A *balance sheet, income statement, funds statement*, or any supporting statement or other presentation of financial data derived from *accounting records*.

financial statement audit The *audit* of a set of financial statements as of a specific date and for a designated period of time. Statements usually include: statement of financial position, statement of net earnings and stockholders' equity, and statement of changes in financial position. The period covered is usually one year when outside financial audits are involved. Interim statements may also be issued on a quarterly or monthly basis, usually without involving outside auditors in their preparation. See *audit*.

financing lease See *capital lease*.

finder One who for a fee brings together a buyer and seller; e.g., in the security field, one who brings together a corporation proposing to issue securities and a firm of investment bankers, his or her fee being a flat sum or a percentage of the underwriting profits.

finished goods (or stock) 1. Manufactured product, ready for sale or other disposition; to be distinguished from finished parts which will enter production or assembly, and *merchandise*, a term covering articles of commerce bought for resale.
2. An account in which appear (a) completed products, e.g., transferred from a *work-in-process account*; and (b) transfers of such products to completed product sold (*sales*), the balance representing completed product on hand: an inventory asset commonly valued at cost or less. See *inventory; inventory valuation*.

firm *n*. A partnership; loosely, a term often used to denote any business organization: a proprietorship, partnership, or corporation. *adj*. Binding; as, a *firm contract*.

firm contract Any contract such as one which obligates a seller to deliver and a buyer to accept at a specified time goods described as to quantity, quality, and price; or one that requires an underwriter to deliver cash from the sale of securities within a specified period of time.

firm policy 1. A *policy* formally adopted and effectively enforced.
2. Hence, a *policy* followed by any individual or organization.

firm price See *contract price*.

first cost 1. = *object cost*. Costs to be found in *primary accounts* are first or object costs.
2. = *original cost* (2).

First In, First Out (FIFO) A method of inventory identification and valuation. See *inventory valuation*.

fiscal agent A bank or other corporate *fiduciary* which performs the function of paying interest on debt or principal of debt when due on behalf of a governmental unit or other debtor.

fiscal period 1. = *accounting period*.
2. The partial *fiscal year* resulting from the formation or dissolution of an enterprise or change in fiscal year.

fiscal year 1. An accounting period of 12 successive calendar months, or of 52 successive weeks plus an additional day (two days in leap years) at the period end; or under strict adherence to weekly accounting periods, the fiscal year may from time to time consist of 53 weeks, thus avoiding a terminal date not more than three days preceding or following the end of the calendar year.
2. A 12-month period ending with the last day of any month other than December: a usage defined in Section 441(e) of the federal *Internal Revenue Code*.

fit 1. (statistics) See *curve fitting; trend analysis*.
2. The relation of the period benefited by a *transaction* and the period during which it is incurred and recorded.

Fitzgerald, A. A. (1890-1969) For many years the doyen of professional accountants in Australia, Sir Alexander Fitzgerald was a prominent figure both in accounting circles and in public service. He has been editor of both the principal professional accounting journals in Australia, and in 1954 he became the first holder of an Australian university chair in accounting.

fixed asset 1. A *tangible asset* held for the services it yields in the production of goods and services; any item of *plant*.
2. Hence, any *capital asset* or *noncurrent asset*.
3. *pl.* A *balance-sheet* classification denoting *capital assets* other than *intangibles* and *investments* (6) in affiliated companies or other long-term investments. In British usage the term may include *intangibles* (2).

Included in the usual fixed-asset categories are land (from which the flow of services is seemingly permanent), buildings, building equipment, fixtures, machinery, tools (large and small), furniture, office devices, patterns, drawings, dies, and often containers; generally excluded are goodwill, patents, and other *intangibles*. The characteristic fixed asset has a limited life (land is the one important exception), and, in organizations where expenses are accounted for, its cost, less estimated salvage at the end of its useful life, is distributed over the periods it benefits by means of provisions for depreciation. See *depreciation; depreciation methods*.

fixed-asset schedule A summary, by classes, of fixed assets, such as that sometimes appearing in annual reports to stockholders.

fixed-assets-to-equity-capital ratio A *ratio* which measures the relationship between long-term assets and the capital structure of a firm. Calculated by dividing net fixed assets by stockholders' equity, it is purported to be an indicator of a firm's ability to meet its long-term obligations. See *debt-equity ratio*.

fixed-assets turnover A *ratio* calculated by dividing sales by fixed assets, it is a measure of the efficiency with which a firm manages its fixed assets.

fixed-asset unit An item or group of items recognized in the accounting processes governing the fixed assets of an enterprise. Five types of units are commonly found, not always clearly differentiated in particular instances; these types and their usual specifications are:

1. The *capitalization unit*: the character of new items that may be added to fixed assets, the minimum expenditure that may be recognized, and the tests to be applied to determine the propriety of the amount capitalized.

2. The *accounting unit*: (a) the control accounts to be carried in the general ledger, and (b) the detail accounts to be carried in plant ledgers.

3. The *retirement unit*: the character and minimum amount of what are to be regarded as items removable from the accounts when taken out of service.

4. The *replacement unit*: the character and minimum amount of what are to be regarded as capitalizable items taking the place of items retired—usually the same as a retirement unit.

5. The *depreciation unit*: the basis—item or group of items—to which periodic depreciation rates are to be applied. See *fixed asset*.

To these is sometimes added the *accountability unit*: the unit ascribed to—and made the basis of observation and reporting by—a person charged with *property accountability*; this unit is the same as (1), (2b), (3), or (4).

fixed budget A budget providing firm allowances for individual activities, allowances that do not vary with the volume of production or other overall measure of work done. See *budget; flexible budget*.

fixed capital The investment in *capital assets*.

fixed-charge coverage ratio A *coverage ratio* which measures the ability of a firm to meet its annual fixed charges, such as interest, rent, and sinking-fund payments, with its regular earnings. It can be calculated by dividing the sum of net income before taxes, interest, and rent by the sum of interest, rent, and sinking-fund payments adjusted for taxes, i.e., sinking-fund payments divided by 1 minus the tax rate. See also *funds-flow fixed-charge coverage*.

fixed charges Unavoidable overhead, particularly interest costs, depreciation, amortization of discount on funded debt and of intangibles, and rent of leased property. The term extends to elements of factory overhead remaining more or less constant under varying rates of production; see *fixed cost*.

fixed cost (or expense) Costs for plant capacity or other long-term assets or obligations which have already been incurred and hence cannot be changed. An operating expense, or operating expense as a class, that does not vary with business volume. Examples: interest on bonds; rent; property tax; depreciation (sometimes in part); minimal amounts of selling and general overhead. A cost designated as fixed is often a function of capacity, and thus, although fixed with respect to volume, varies with the size of the plant which can be altered over time. In this sense, it varies with time (the long run) rather than production volume (in the short run). However, other usages also need to be allowed for. One department of a plant may bear a monthly service charge originating in another department; to the former, the charge is looked upon as a fixed cost beyond its immediate control; to the latter, the charge may in large measure derive from variable costs over which it has primary control. Fixed costs are not fixed in the sense that they do not fluctuate or vary; they vary, but from causes independent of volume. Although usually defined with respect to volume, the term *fixed cost* may also be applied when some other factor is the independent variable, and *cost* the dependent variable. See *semivariable cost; semifixed costs*.

fixed exchange rates The ratio of units of exchange between two currencies set at a constant figure which is to be maintained by agreement between the involved countries. See *flexible (floating) exchange rates*.

fixed liability = *long-term liability*.

fixed resale price The minimum price that a manufacturer or fabricator requires distributors and retailers under contract with him or her to charge on sales of goods purchased. ''Fair-trade'' laws, some declared unconstitutional but others still effective in several states, legalize this type of price fixing by manufacturers of their branded products, but the courts have refused to enforce such laws with respect to resellers not under contract. Many manufacturers now provide a "suggested" retail price, the nonobservance of which may be subject to sanctions imposed by the manufacturer or supplier. See *price; price maintenance*.

fixed trust An organization for the joint investment of funds; it is created by a trust indenture between an incorporated manager, a trustee, and the investors whereby a block of specified units of investments is deposited with the trustee against which one or more certificates of interest are sold to the investor at a price equal to his or her proportionate interest in the current market value of the block plus a loading percentage to cover the expenses and profit of the manager.

fixture Anything attached to a building which cannot be removed without damage to the real estate, usually having utility only in that location (an immovable fixture), or which by custom or under the terms of a lease or other instrument can be detached (a movable fixture). A fixture is classified as a *fixed asset*.

flash report A report covering the elements of financial condition on all or a portion of the operations of an accounting period, prepared before all transactions are known or recorded, or before the books have been closed. Its purpose is to supply information needed by management for immediate review and decision.

flat Without the addition of interest: said of the price of a bond in default, a noninterest-bearing loan, or a bond quoted or sold at a price that does not include accrued interest.

flexible budget 1. A *budget* containing alternative provisions based on varying rates of production or other measures of activity.

2. A budget subject to change as operations proceed. See *budget; overhead*.

flexible (floating) exchange rates The ratio of units of currencies between two countries which are not maintained at fixed levels but are, instead, determined by market forces. See *managed exchange rates; fixed exchange rates*.

flexible standard A *standard cost* determined for a particular class of expenditure, expressed as a formula that provides a stated number of dollars for a fixed or minimum allowance for such an expenditure plus a rate per unit of volume for the variable portion of the expenditure.

flexitime A work program which systematically allows different employees to report for work at different times or for different periods of time.

float 1. Paid or committed cash balances, or similarly liquid resources, on which interest may be earned until the claimant instruments are presented for payment. *Collection float* refers to cases in which interest may be lost and *payment float* refers to cases in which interest may be gained as a result of such delays. See *lock box*.

2. Uncollected deposits that have been credited conditionally by a bank to its customers' accounts. Checks may not be drawn against such deposits until the paper constituting the deposits has cleared; three days or less are normally required for domestic paper. Where the bank's experience with a customer or with certain types of paper has been satisfactory, no such restriction may be imposed. Examples: (i) An outstanding (uncashed) money order purchased from a company such as American Express, Inc. (ii) A draft on an outstanding bank balance which continues to earn interest until the check is presented for payment. As distinct from *kiting* a float does not involve any taint of *fraud* or illegality.

In the case of substantial deposits, many banks have adopted the practice in (2) as a protection against possible collection difficulties.

floating asset = *current asset*.

floating capital That portion of the capital of an enterprise not invested in fixed or other capital assets, but in current and working assets; *working capital*.

floating debt Current or short-term obligations; *current liabilities*.

floating (flexible) exchange rates A market pricing system which allows the price of any country's currency to fluctuate with respect to all other currencies.

floating liability = *current liability; floating debt*.

floating lien *Uniform Commercial Code*, Section 9-204. A security agreement whereby the secured party (creditor) agrees that property acquired in the future may be substituted for the original collateral which may be disposed of in the ordinary course of business; a secured interest in existing and future assets. See *lien*.

floating-point number A computer representation of a numerical value in which the decimal portion of the number is always a fraction between the values of 0 and 1. A *characteristic* or power of a given base is associated with the number.

flow chart 1. A *graph* of operational sequences in the handling of materials or documents, or in the accumulation of costs.

2. A schematic diagram which uses boxes or circles to represent an operation to be performed on a computer, and lines and arrows to represent the logical flow between operations.

flow of cost 1. A list of accounts which follow the steps in a firm's manufacturing process.

2. A standardized list in which it is customary for material cost to enter an inventory account such as "materials inventory" or "stores control." From there, the costs of materials flow into a *work-in-process account*. Labor cost and overhead cost, applied or actual, are added to the work-in-process account. The aggregate cost of units completed flows from the work-in-process account into a finished-goods inventory account. The cost of units sold then flows from the finished-goods inventory account to a cost of goods sold account.

flow statement 1. A depiction in dollars (often with added narrative) of operating performance, by displaying summary movement, often cyclic, from inputs to outputs, i.e., from "primary" to "secondary" to "terminal" positions in the *accounts* (7); a generic term.

2. Thus, in a manufacturing operation, a diagrammatic or tabular tracing of purchases of materials and services through work in process, finished goods, costs of sales, customer receivables, and collections: a *turnover* analysis often utilized in determining the amounts and timing of investment or working-capital requirements for assuring continuous production.

3. A common, long-established, but restrictive tabulation of beginning- and end-of-year balance-sheet differences, formerly known as a "statement of funds received and applied," but now designated *statement of changes in financial position*. The "flow" it depicts is restricted to net changes in balance-sheet categories.

4. More informative summaries of financial variations are obtained from *cash-flow* and *funds-flow statements*. These two statements and the *statement of changes in financial position* are related and one may be derived from the other with the aid of supplemental information.

Of the three varieties mentioned in (3) and (4) above, the funds-flow type is most closely allied to the realities of financial-management activities: a form to which the "changes" statement will likely drift, since it includes operating movements that contribute importantly to changes in asset-and-liability positions.

flow-through method A method of accounting for *investment tax credits* and *timing differences* that allows the related tax benefits to "flow through" to net income as reductions of federal income-tax expense in the year in which the investment tax credits are utilized or the timing differences arise. In contrast to the *deferral method*, in which the credit is spread over the life of the asset. Thus an investment tax credit may be treated as an addition to income during the year in which the asset was acquired (flow-through method) or 1/*n*th of the amount may be added to income in each period of the *n*-year life of the asset (deferral method). The *APB* initially preferred the deferral method but subsequently accepted the flow-through method.

FOB (followed by a named location) = free on board. A symbol indicating that the invoice cost to a purchaser includes the cost of delivery, at seller's risk, to an agreed point, beyond which all transportation and delivery costs and risks must be borne by the purchaser. On domestic shipments, the chances of misunderstanding between buyer and seller are not great: FOB Chicago means delivery by the seller to a freight terminal in that city; freight, handling, or trucking charges thereafter must be paid by the buyer, the seller usually providing a bill of lading or other receipt from the shipping agency. Foreign shipments often give rise to misunderstandings because of unfamiliarity of the foreign purchaser with American commercial practices; in such cases, the original contract between buyer and seller should be specific as to trucking charges, port and customs fees, and loading costs, as well as to the arrangement for special packaging, shipping directions, and other matters peculiar to international trade.

FOB price When used without further qualification, the price charged at a designated location—i.e., farm, factory, wellhead, mine mouth, mill, or warehouse—where the goods were produced, extracted, fabricated, or stored. Although generally restricted to the price charged at the point of shipment, the term may be qualified by specific reference to intermediate points—e.g., FOB port, or even destination—thus making it the equivalent of *delivered price*. Under *FOB pricing*, the seller retains title and the risks of ownership until delivery is made at the FOB point, as evidenced by a carrier bill of lading or other receipt releasing him or her of possession; at that point the purchaser takes title and bears the risks of ownership.

FOB pricing The practice of selling for delivery at the seller's plant, buyers paying the freight from plant to destination. See *FOB*.

folio reference A page number or voucher or other number in a book or document of original or final entry, which refers to the disposition or source of an entry or posting; abbreviated, *F*.

footing test An auditing procedure where the details comprising a total are read as a means of verifying the total. See *mechanical accuracy test*.

footnote (appended to a financial statement) A medium for imparting additional information, usually a narrative, indexed to a particular item. Data thus supplied are required wherever the title customarily attaching to a monetary item is inadequate for informed understanding. Situations demanding footnotes, of importance to financial analysts as well as to stockholders and general readers, include the following:

changes in accounting principles
consolidation policies
stock options
contingent liabilities
unfulfilled contracts
future hazards
depreciation policy and adequacy
asset liens
long-term-loan features
pension accumulations
changes in product lines or processes

Footnotes are so couched as to be understandable to the average reader. See *materiality* ; *subsequent event*.

force account A term employed by engineers to denote that a construction project is undertaken by the owner acting as his or her own contractor; thus, a city may extend its water system by force account, meaning that its own engineers design the work and hire and supervise the labor force required for construction and installation.

forced-sale value The price obtainable from an immediate sale, where the seller is under either legal or voluntary compulsion to sell; *liquidation value*.

forecast An estimate of future *financial condition* or *operating results*, often found in management reports to stockholders, varying in character from qualitative to quantitative projections. A trend to the latter has been noted in recent years, ranging from estimates of sales increases or decreases, in terms of percentages, to summaries of operating budgets. Although in many instances unforeseeable events and conditions may vitiate the accuracy of the lookahead, such estimates supply a useful background for subsequent comparisons with the actual and for management's explanations of basic causes. The public accountant's comments and criticisms on drafts by management of proposed statements of this type are often solicited.

The *AICPA* has amended its rules to permit *audits* of "financial forecasts," defined as: an estimate of the "most probable" financial position of an entity, the results of its operations and changes in its financial position for one or more future periods. "Most probable" is distinguished from *financial projections* and other types of *forward accounting* on the basis that "the assumptions of the forecast accord with management's judgment of the conditions that are most likely to prevail and its most likely course of action." An *external auditor (CPA)* would report on whether the assumptions used as a basis for management's forecasts are reasonable. A recommended standard form is as follows:

We have reviewed the accompanying financial forecast of XYZ Company, which includes the following presentations: forecasted balance sheet as of December 31, 19XX, forecasted statements of income, retained earnings and changes in financial position for the year then ending, and the related summary of significant assumptions. Our review was made in accordance with applicable guidelines of the American Institute of Certified Public Accountants for reviews of financial forecasts and, accordingly, included procedures to evaluate the assumptions used by management as a basis for the financial forecast and to evaluate the preparation and presentation of the financial forecast.

A financial forecast is management's estimate of the most probable financial position, results of operations and changes in financial position for one or more future periods, and reflects management's judgment based on present circumstances of the most likely set of conditions and its most likely course of action. Forecasts are based on assumptions about circumstances and events that have not yet taken place and are subject to variations, and there is no assurance that the forecasted results will be attained.

We have no responsibility to update this report for events and circumstances occurring after the date of this report.

Based on our review, we believe the accompanying financial forecast has been prepared using assumptions which are reasonable as a basis for management's forecast, and is presented in conformity with applicable guidelines established by the American Institute of Certified Public Accountants for presentation of a financial forecast.

This is at least a first step, with more likely to follow. For instance, both data and methodology, including the *models* employed, are usually as subject to scrutiny and evaluation as management assumptions and it is likely that these will all come to be regarded as an inseparable whole. Recourse to experts is unavoidable, but this is not a novel element in auditing. Increasing pressure is being exerted on auditors to review management representations in other parts of the annual corporate report and this is likely to extend to forecasts. See *futurology*.

foreign corporation In state corporation laws, a "foreign" corporation means one created under the laws of another state or country. In federal income-tax law, the term refers to a corporation established under the laws of another country. See *corporation; domestic corporation*.

Foreign Corrupt Practices Act A series of amendments made in 1977 to the Securities Act and other statutes which established: (1) significant penalties for *bribes* made to foreign officials, and (2) the requirement that all publicly held companies must maintain adequate accounting records and a system of *internal accounting control*. See *internal control*. Under an SEC requirement management must review and attest to the adequacy of its internal controls subject to external audit for this purpose. See *audit committee*.

foreign currency translation The process of expressing amounts denominated or measured in one currency in terms of another currency by use of the exchange rate between the two currencies. See *current-noncurrent method; current rate method; monetary-nonmonetary method; temporal method; modified temporal method*.

foreign direct investment The ownership by a domestic entity of specific productive or other business capabilities in foreign countries.

foreign exchange 1. The method by which settlement is made for international transactions. See *exchange*.
2. A generic term applied to bills of exchange and to monetary and credit instruments, such as gold, silver, banker's drafts, letters of credit, and traveler's checks, used in payment of foreign debts, and expressed in the foreign currency.

foreign exchange exposure Also currency exposure and exchange exposure. A measure of the *risk* of loss from holding foreign currencies (or assets and liabilities realizable in foreign currencies) due to changes in the *exchange rates* of national currencies. Given a foreign currency translation method, a firm's foreign exchange exposure is the excess of assets translated at the current exchange rate (exposed assets) over liabilities translated at the current exchange rate (exposed liabilities).

foreign exchange gain (loss) Gain or loss in *local currency* from holding net foreign monetary items during a period in which the exchange rate changes. See *exchange gain (1)*.

foreign exchange risk The *risk* of loss due to fluctuations in the foreign exchange rate of national currencies.

foreign tax credit A credit against the U.S. tax liability of a citizen or domestic corporation for certain taxes levied by foreign governments or U.S. possessions and paid or accrued during the taxable year. *Internal Revenue Code* (Sections 33, 901–905). The amount is generally limited in any one taxable year to the portion of the U.S. tax liability which bears the same ratio as the taxpayer's taxable income from sources outside the United States bears to his or her entire taxable income from all sources. A *carryover* provision allows the taxpayer to carry excess *foreign taxes* back to the immediately preceding two taxable years or forward to the succeeding five years.

foreign taxes *Taxes* levied by any level of a foreign government on U.S. corporate or individual taxpayers. Such taxes are generally eligible for deduction by U.S. taxpayers to the extent that they qualify as trade or business expenses, expenses incurred in the production of income, real estate taxes, or income taxes. *Internal Revenue Code* (Sections 162, 212, 164(a)). Furthermore a taxpayer has the option of claiming foreign income taxes as a credit against U.S. income tax. See *foreign tax credit*. Special rules prevent deductibility of foreign taxes where a portion of the taxpayer's earned income has been excluded from taxation (Sections 265, 911(a)).

foreign tax incentives Tax advantages offered by foreign countries to attract multinational and other enterprises. Such incentives often take the form of reduction, elimination or deferment of *income* or *indirect taxes*.

foreign-trade financing Any of the methods available for the settlement of transactions between persons in different countries. Most of the difficulties of settlement arise out of the use of unlike currencies, necessitating a balancing against transactions flowing in the opposite direction. Many international sales are on an open-credit or consignment basis at the time of shipment; or the shipper may demand settlement when the goods are delivered to the port of exit: an arrangement facilitated through a *letter of credit* or other device instituted by the domestic or foreign bank serving the exporter or importer. See *bank acceptance; letter of credit*.

forgery Any false writing with intent to defraud.

form 1. A document arranged for the entry of *data* or other *information*.
2. (computers) A document containing printed information as well as a location for entering user supplied information.

formal Referring to or derived from the pattern, structure, or rules of organization, rather than from the content of discourse, experience, or social processes.

FORTRAN (*FOR*mula *TRAN*slation) A computer language used primarily for solving scientific-type problems. It efficiently performs limited input and output of numeric data, as well as calculations upon numeric data. It is not as effective as *COBOL* for input and output of large volumes of data.

forward accounting The areas of interest in the preparation of *standard costs*, budgeted costs and revenues, *estimates of cash requirements, breakeven charts*, and *projected financial statements*—and the various studies required for their estimation; also the *internal controls* regulating and safeguarding future operations. Although often based on *historical costs*, forward costs are expected to reflect realistic situations to be encountered and thus may modify existing patterns of operation and costs. The techniques of forward accounting differ from those accompanying historical accounting in that only transaction groups are dealt with, no bookkeeping records are kept, and the major items reflect what are essentially management judgments, projections, and directives. See *forecast*.

forward exchange contract An agreement to exchange currencies of different countries at a specified rate (the *forward rate*) at a specified future date. The purpose of a forward contract may be to hedge either a foreign currency commitment or a foreign-currency exposed net asset or net liability position or to speculate in anticipation of a gain. See *forward rate*.

forward exchange rate = *forward rate*.

forward financial statement An estimate of condition (*balance sheet*), operating results (*income statement*), and funds flow. An endproduct in the preparation of a *budget* for an ensuing period (e.g., a year). See *flow statement*.

Forward financial statements, as of an ensuing 12-month period, may be presented at annual meetings of stockholders, published at quarterly intervals, included in applications for approvals of prospective issues of securities, and in prospectuses; they provide *standards of comparison* for critical *appraisals* of subsequent *variances* (2) in *events and conditions*. See *forecast*.

forward rate The ratio of exchange of units between two currencies or the prices of two commodities quoted for transaction at a future date.

founders' shares A portion of a corporation's capital stock with special privileges or stipulations, issued to its founders or promoters for services rendered. Founders' shares (also called "managers' shares" and "deferred shares") are issued commonly in the United Kingdom, rarely in the United States. Their combined voting power is usually equal to the voting power of the common stock, and they generally have a special claim on earnings, either before or after the payment of dividends to other stockholders. Their participation in the assets of the corporation in the event of dissolution is usually limited to the remaining assets after other stockholders have received the amounts to which they are entitled according to the provisions of the respective issues.

fractile (statistics) = *quantile*.

frame (statistics) A system of records or other assembled collections of data from which samplings are to be taken. Ideally, the identification of the frame should define the scope of the survey as well as other primary categories of the material to be covered; the date, source, and definitions underlying the frame are of central importance. In actual survey design and execution, frames that are initially indicated frequently require amplification and adjustment, e.g., in *multistage sampling*.

franchise 1. A privilege, granted by governmental authority, sanctioning a *monopoly* or permitting the use of public property, usually subject to regulation.
2. The privilege, often exclusive, conferred on a dealer by a manufacturer, to sell the manufacturer's products within a specified territory.
3. A certificate of incorporation.
4. (insurance) The percentage or portion of a *risk* establishing the top limit of loss to be borne by the insured; if the loss is greater, the entire amount is borne by the insurer. Franchise insurance contrasts with "deductible" insurance, where a specified portion of the loss must be borne by the insured, regardless of the amount of loss. See *coinsurance clause*.

fraud The practice of deception or artifice with the intention of cheating or injuring another. Ordinarily fraud involves willful misrepresentation, the deliberate concealment of a material fact for the purpose of inducing another person to do or to refrain from doing something to his or her detriment, or the failure to disclose a material fact; thus a person may be fraudulently misled into giving up a claim to property, waiving legal rights, or entering into a disadvantageous contract. See *negligence; scienter*.

fraud in the execution In the law of negotiable instruments, certain defenses (known as real defenses) will prevent the transferee from becoming a *holder in due course*. Other (personal defenses) are good against a transferee, but not a holder in due course. Fraud here relates to the nature of the document signed or its essential terms and the defense is good against all takers including holders in due course. See *fraud*.

fraud in the inducement (See *fraud in the execution*.) When a person is induced by fraud into signing of the instrument; the defense is not good against a holder in due course.

free currency Money that may be exchanged for the money of another country without restriction. See *blocked currency*.

freedom from bias One of four criteria or requirements for accounting information, advanced in 1966 by a committee of the American Accounting Association, which aims to exclude from financial statements information that is beneficial to one or more groups of users but detrimental to others. The other three criteria were *relevance*, quantifiability (or *quantification*), and verifiability. See *verifiable*.

free on board = *FOB*.

free price The price of a commodity unit sold or purchased under conditions in which each participant is relatively free to effect necessary economic adjustments, including price changes, in response to individual assessment of demand-and-supply relations, while attempting to obtain maximum profits. Such price may be a free competitive price or a free (noncollusive) oligopoly price, depending upon the structure of the industry in which the commodity is being bought or sold. See *price*.

free surplus 1. That portion of *retained earnings* available for common-stock dividends—i.e., after deducting any amounts legally restricted by reason of such items as preferred-stock *dividends in arrears*, the repurchase price of *treasury stock*, or loan agreements calling for a minimum cash balance or a minimum asset-liability ratio.

2. That portion of *retained earnings* not in excess of cash assets over and above *working-capital* or other immediate requirements.

free trade zone 1. Any area of the world in which trade barriers between countries are abolished; e.g., the European free trade zone is comprised of those countries which are members of the *European Economic Community*.

2. A designated area in which goods may be transshipped without payment of the tariffs that would otherwise be applicable.

freight 1. A charge by a carrier for the transportation of goods.
2. Physical cargo.

freight absorption The practice of a seller of not charging the customer with freight out.

freight-in Freight paid on incoming shipments, treated as an element of cost of goods or materials received, or refunded by the seller or deducted on the invoice, according to custom or the terms of sale.

freight-out Freight paid or allowed by the seller on outgoing shipments to customers. In the accounts it may appear as a selling expense or, if included in the selling price, as a deduction from sales.

frequency Relative or absolute number of occurrences of a class of events.

frequency chart A *bar chart* of a *frequency distribution*.

frequency curve A smooth curve formed by *extrapolation* and *interpolation* of values in a *frequency chart*, and intended to portray an ideal or underlying *statistical distribution*.

frequency distribution A statistical series consisting of a number of quantities arranged in the order of their class and number, or frequency of occurrence within each class. See *statistical distribution*.

frequency polygon A geometric picture of a *frequency distribution* formed by connecting the midpoints of the rectangles in a *frequency chart*.

fresh start (federal income taxes) See *carry-over basis (d)*.

fringe benefit A pension provision, retirement allowance, insurance coverage, or other cost representing a present or future return to an employee, which is neither deducted on a payroll nor paid for by the employee. It may be *distributed* with other labor costs or maintained as a separate item on an operating statement.

front-end loading Practice of some *mutual funds* and *investment companies* or *trusts* of deducting the entire amount of administrative, selling, trustee, and/or brokerage fees from the initial deposit or first-year installment on a long-term plan. See *loading (1), (2)*.

full absorption costing The inclusion of all fixed and variable *production costs* (2) in *work-in-process* and *output* costs; contrasts with *direct costing*.

full costing 1. The allocation of all costs to products for purposes of pricing or determining the profitability of product or service lines. As distinguished from "full absorption costing" it includes other costs, such as allocations of selling, general and administrative costs, as well as production costs.
2. In the oil and gas industry, it is the capitalization and subsequent amortization of exploration costs whether successful or not. See *successful efforts method*.

full-cost method An accounting method used in certain extractive industries, primarily in the oil and gas industry, under which all costs incurred in prospecting for mineral reserves and in acquiring, exploring, and developing mineral properties within a relatively large cost center (most often, a country) are (1) capitalized as the historical cost of whatever reserves the enterprise holds within that cost center and (2) charged to expense (amortized) as the reserves are produced. See *successful efforts method*.

full-cost pricing Price set by average cost, generally defined as standard costs of production plus fully allocated overhead, plus a fixed markup.

full-faith-and-credit debt (municipal accounting) Debt of a municipality or municipal enterprise the repayment of which is a direct obligation of the municipality; = *general-obligation bond*. See *revenue bond*.

full liability A liability not shared with others.

full-paid capital stock A share or shares of capital stock on which the whole amount of the par or stated value or the subscription price has been paid. Such stock is nonassessable unless, by law, double or other special liability attaches to it.

fully diluted earnings per share An indicator of operating performance for companies with *complex capital structures* that reflects the maximum reduction in earnings per common share from the assumed conversion or exercise of *dilutive* common stock equivalents and dilutive senior securities. It is computed by dividing earnings by the weighted average number of common shares outstanding during the period plus shares from the assumed conversion or exercise of all common stock equivalents and dilutive senior securities. It must be reported in the income statement before *extraordinary items* and for *net income*; also labeled earnings per common share—assuming full dilution. See *earnings per share; primary earnings per share; if-converted method*.

function 1. Relative utility or usefulness.
2. The general end or purpose sought to be accomplished by an organizational unit. Examples: administration; selling; research.
3. A group of related *activities* serving a common end. See *activity accounting*.

4. (governmental accounting) An *activity* or group of activities charged to an *agency* (2) by legislative or administrative authority. A single classification, for both budgetary and operating purposes, of an agency's income-and-expenditure *transactions* makes possible (a) a controlled diffusion of *expenditure* (and, hence, of *operational*) *authority*, and of responsibilities assumed under such authority, (b) frequent comparisons of budgetary *allocations* with performance, (c) a basis for reporting by activity heads, (d) critical reviews, by supervisory authority and by both *internal* and *external auditors*, of agency accomplishments, especially when compared with *standards of performance*, and (e) the pinpointing by higher authority in applying corrective measures.

5. (mathematics) A statement of the form of the relation to be assumed by two or more *variables* over a defined range of values; generally indicated symbolically by the letters f, F, ϕ, followed by parentheses in which the variables are placed; as, $f(x,y)$; $F(x,y,z)$; $\phi(x,y,z)$. Standard forms for expressing functional relations between two variables are: $f(x,y) = 0$ and $y = F(x)$. The former is referred to as the implicit and the latter as the explicit form. No distinction is drawn, in the first case, between x and y as *dependent* or *independent variables*; the value of either *variable* may be chosen within the range for which the function is defined, and values of the other variable are then determined by equating the result to zero. In the second case, y is explicitly stated in terms of x as the independent variable. Thus, the expression $f(x, y) = ax + by = 0$ defines implicitly a straight-line (or linear) relation between x and y, while $y = F(x) = a' + b'x$ states an explicit relation in which y is the *dependent variable* linearly related to the *independent variable* x through the *constants* a' and b'. Functional relations are not restricted to (a)

the linear forms used for illustration, or (b) only two variables. It is required, however, that the value of y be uniquely defined by whatever values are assigned to x and it is this uniqueness which distinguishes functions from other, more general, types of mathematical relations. Thus, $y = x^2$ is a function but $y^2 = x$ is not, since for each value of x in the latter there are two values of y (viz., positive and negative values) which satisfy the relation. The notion of function includes any number of variables, finite or infinite. Functional *symbolization* is compact and simple and of wide generality; as such, it has proved of great importance in extending the fields of mathematical and related inquiries, such as physics, statistics, and economics. See *production function; statistical distribution; least-squares method; variable*.

functional *adj*. Adapted to and capable of performance, as in a functional part.
n. A *function* or service performed by one *organizational unit* for another.

functional accounting Accounting by *functions* and *activities*; = *activity accounting*.

functional classification A classification of expenditures on the basis of the principal purposes for which they are made. Examples are public safety, public health, public welfare, etc. See also *activity; character; classification; object classification*.

functional cost Any cost identified with a *cost objective*.

functional currency In foreign currency translation, an entity's functional currency is the currency of the primary economic environment in which the entity operates and generates net cash flows. It may be the currency of the country in which the entity operates, as frequently is the case, or it may be the parent's currency in case the foreign operations are a direct and integral component or extension of a parent company's operations.

Any *exchange gains or losses* from the *translation* of foreign financial statements in functional currency into the reporting currency of the *consolidated statements* are not included in the net income of the consolidated entity but are accumulated in a "translation adjustment" account in the shareholders' equity section of the balance sheet.

functional spread (governmental accounting) The *secondary classification* of transactions reflecting their ultimate end uses or the purposes they serve. See *transaction*.

functional statement A statement of costs subdivided by *function* (2) or subfunctions.

fund *n*. 1. An asset or group of assets within any organization, separated physically or in the accounts or both from other assets and limited to specific uses. Examples: a *petty-cash* or *working fund*; a *replacement-and-renewal fund*; an *accident fund*; a *contingent fund*; a *pension fund*.
2. Cash, securities, or other assets placed in the hands of a trustee, principal or income or both being expended in accordance with the terms of a formal agreement. Examples: a *trust fund* created by a will; an *endowment fund*; a *sinking fund*.
3. (governmental accounting) A fiscal and accounting entity with a self-balancing set of accounts for recording cash and other financial resources, together with all related liabilities and residual equities of balances, and changes therein, which are segregated for the purpose of specific activities or objectives usually in accordance with statutes or other types of special regulations, restrictions, or limitations. See *fund accounting*.
4. *pl*. Current assets less current liabilities (on an *accrual basis*): *working capital*; a term used in *flow statements*.
5. *pl*. = *cash*.
v.t. 1. To convert currently maturing liabilities into a long-term loan.

2. To provide for the ultimate payment of a liability by the systematic accumulation of cash or other assets in a separate account or trust.

fund account Any account reflecting transactions of a *fund* (3).

fund accounting 1. A system of accounting for *funds* (1).
2. The systems of accounting for *funds* (3) in not-for-profit institutions and governmental units. The following types of funds are recommended for use by state and local governmental units by the *National Council on Governmental Accounting: general fund, special revenue funds, capital projects funds, debt service funds, special assessment funds, enterprise funds, internal service funds, trust and agency funds*. Additionally, two account groups are recommended: *general fixed-assets account group, general long-term debt account group*.

fundamental analysis An approach in security analysis which assumes that a security has an "intrinsic value" that can be determined through a rigorous evaluation of relevant variables. Expected earnings is usually the most important variable in this analysis, but many other variables, such as dividends, capital structure, management quality, and so on, may also be studied. An analyst estimates the "intrinsic value" of a security on the basis of those fundamental variables and compares this value with the current market price of the security to arrive at an investment decision.

fund asset An asset belonging to a particular *fund* (3) or a group of funds.

fund balance (state and local governmental accounting) The excess of the *assets* of a fund over its *liabilities* and *reserves* except in the case of funds subject to budgetary accounting where, prior to the end of a fiscal period, it represents the excess of the fund's assets and estimated revenues for the period over its liabilities, reserves, and available appropriations.

fund balance sheet A balance sheet divided into self-balancing sections, each of which shows the assets and liabilities of a single fund or group of related funds. This form of balance sheet is more or less standard for various types of governmental bodies and for educational, religious, charitable, social, and other institutions.

funded debt Debt evidenced by outstanding bonds or long-term notes. Floating and funded debt constitute total liabilities to outsiders.

funded deficit A deficit eliminated through the sale of bonds issued for that purpose.

funded reserve A reserve offset by segregated cash, securities, or other assets, available only for a stated purpose.

fund group A group of *funds* (3) of similar character which are brought together for administrative and reporting purposes. Examples: current funds; loan funds; endowment funds; plant funds; agency funds.

funding agency An organization or individual, such as a specific corporate or individual trustee or an insurance company, which assumes responsibility for the accumulation of assets to be used for paying benefits under a *pension plan*; an organization, such as a life insurance company, that provides facilities for the purchase of such benefits. The portion of pension cost that has been paid to a funding agency is said to have been funded.

funding bonds Bonds issued to retire current or long-term indebtedness or to finance current expenditures.

funding decision 1. Any decision to finance a capital investment or a program.
2. An allocation of funds to *decision packages* in a *zero-base budgeting* system. In such a system, this decision usually is based upon an established cutoff level on the ranking made by each budgeting unit. See *decision package*.

fund liability A *liability* of a *fund* which is to be met out of its existing resources.

fund obligation A *liability* or *encumbrance* of a particular *fund*.

fund pool The grouping of *funds* for common investment; consolidated investments.

funds-flow adequacy ratio A *ratio* which indicates the extent to which the funds generated by a firm's operations will cover its investments in assets and its dividend policy, usually calculated by dividing funds from operations by the sum of long-term asset acquisitions, inventory additions, and dividends. The numerator and the denominator may be taken from periods such as five years, rather than from just one year. A ratio value below 1.0 indicates that a firm does not generate enough funds internally to meet its investment and dividends needs.

funds-flow fixed-charge coverage A *coverage ratio* which measures the ability of a firm to meet its annual fixed charges, such as interest, rent, and sinking-fund payments, through the funds it generates from its regular operations. It can be calculated by dividing the sum of funds from operations, interest, and rent by the sum of interest, rent, and sinking-fund payments adjusted for taxes, i.e., sinking-fund payments divided by 1 minus the tax rate. See also *fixed-charge coverage ratio*.

funds-flow statement 1. A statement of *funds* (4) received and expended; a *statement of changes in financial position* or *statement of sources and applications of funds* in which elements of *net income* and *working capital* contributing to an understanding of the whole of financial operations during the reporting period replace totals of these items. Since in the typical business enterprise *fixed capital* and *working capital* are interrelated, interdependent, intertransferable, under common control, and financed from the same sources, this expansion supplies summary fund-management information concerning both *noncurrent assets* and *liabilities* and *operating income* and *expenses* and their joint effects on the components of *current assets* and liabilities.

2. (national income accounting) Statement intended to show all financial (money) transactions in an economy including flows between principal sectors, governments, households, nonfinancial businesses, financial businesses, rest of the world, etc.

funds flow to long-term debt ratio See *cash flow to total debt ratio*.

funds flow to total debt ratio See *cash flow to total debt ratio*.

funds from operations The net amount of *funds* (resources) generated from a firm's profit-oriented activities during a specific period; a major subtotal on a *statement of changes in financial position* computed by adjusting net income for all nonfund items and nonrecurring events in the income statement. Because of ambiguity in the term "funds," "cash provided from operations" or "working capital provided from operations" is preferable. See *statement of changes in financial position*.

funds from operations to current debt ratio A *ratio* which measures a firm's ability to meet its short-run obligations calculated by dividing funds from operations by current liabilities.

funds provided by operations Important subtotal in the *statement of changes in financial*

position in which all items included in the *income from continuing operations* section of the *income statement* have been adjusted (in detailed or summary form) to a funds (usually *working-capital* or *cash*) basis. See *fund (4), (5); funds-flow statement; statement of changes in financial position*.

funds statement 1. = funds flow.
2. = *funds-flow statement*. See *statement of changes in financial position; flow statement*.

fund surplus See *fund balance*.

fungible Of the same class or quality; interchangeable, referring originally to such raw materials as grain in a public elevator. Fungible materials or other assets are those that lose their separate identity in the process of being mixed or stored with items of like kind, notwithstanding the existence of claims or rights which are regarded as attaching to the originally separate assets. Title may pass under some conditions as in the case of stored grains.

furniture and fixtures Office, store, showroom, and hotel equipment, and the like.

future accounting = *forward accounting*.

futures price See *contract price*.

future value The amount to which a present investment, or series of future investments, will grow at some specified future time if the amount(s) invested earns a specified interest rate with compounding each period. See *compound amount of 1* and *compound amount of 1 per period*.

futurology A discipline concerned with methods for predicting the future, often in the form of *scenarios* that emphasize ways in which different *strategies* may be used by management to alter these futures. See *forecast; prediction*.

GAAP = *generally accepted accounting principles*.

GAAS = *generally accepted auditing standards*.

gain contingency A contingency that might result in a gain. Gain contingencies are usually not reflected in the accounts but may be disclosed in notes to financial statements.

gain or loss 1. The net result of a concluded transaction or group of transactions or the transactions of an operating period, following the application of usual accounting rules or rules appearing in income-tax regulations. A *gain*, or *credit*, increases the capital or wealth of the transactor; a *loss*, or *debit*, decreases it.
2. = *profit and loss*.

gains 1. Increases in *assets* or decreases in *liabilities* during a period from peripheral, incidental, or occasional transactions of an enterprise and from other events and circumstances affecting it; they include all increases in net assets or owners' equity other than those from revenues and capital contributions to the enterprise by owners.
2. Any *pecuniary benefit*, profit, or advantage, as opposed to a *loss; revenue* or *income*; as in the phrase *gain or loss*.

3. The excess of revenues over related costs: applicable to a transaction, a group of transactions, or the transactions of an operating period.

game Any collection of rules which govern the conduct of participants in a contest. Example: the body of common law and statutes such as the Sherman Act which guide or govern the conduct of business in the United States. For mathematical analysis, as in the *theory of games*, such rules must be unambiguous and cover all possible contingencies, including (1) the number of players, (2) the choices and the information available to the players at each move, as well as (3) the payoffs to be made (i.e., the scorings) for all possible plays.

game theory See *theory of games*.

game tree A *tree* in which player choices and their consequences are represented as nodes and links, respectively, and in which the payoffs in the form of rewards and penalties for each of the players are represented at the terminal nodes. When chance elements are present (played by yet another player called "nature") the payoffs may assume the form of entire *probability distributions*. Such a tree may be used, at least in principle, to represent any game, and the *chains* leading from origin to termini are called "plays" of the game. The problem of game theory is to choose, or otherwise characterize, a best *strategy* in the form of a rule for effecting choices at each node where a decision is to be made. Such rules may include random choices, in which event the strategy is said to be "mixed." When no random elements are involved in the rules for choices, the strategy is said to be "pure."

gaming 1. Toying with or cleverly manipulating the rules of a *game* for advantage or amusement.

2. The study, usually by laboratory methods, of how choices are actually made. Originally stimulated by inability to arrive at universally acceptable concepts of a solution (i.e., what constitutes a definition of best strategies) in the *theory of games*, most gaming studies are now directed to how choices are actually made, usually under laboratory conditions.

The examples for study are usually drawn from *business games* or else from examples in the theory of games. The Prisoner's Dilemma portrayed in the matrix below provides an example of the latter as follows: P_1 and P_2 are two prisoners. Separately but simultaneously interrogated they are each offered an inducement to confess first. If neither confesses, they will both receive one-year sentences. If one confesses and the other doesn't, the confessing prisoner can turn "state's evidence," and will be freed while the other will receive a life sentence. When both confess, however, they will both receive life sentences.

P_2 P_1	Don't Confess	Confess
Don't Confess	(1 year, 1 year)	(life, freedom)
Confess	(freedom, life)	(life, life)

As is evident, the solution, i.e., the choice of a best strategy, will depend on the assumptions each prisoner makes about the other's conduct as well as the available information (e.g., via prior agreement) at the time a decision must be made. This example thus helps to illustrate the need for expanded concepts of rationality as discussed under *theory of games*, as well as exhibiting the new bases of research it has provided for other disciplines such as sociology, economics, organization theory, and information system design. It also provides an example of a two-person game which is not "zero-sum." See *theory of games*.

Gantt chart A chart, due to Frederick Gantt, which displays both planned and actual performance, as in the following.

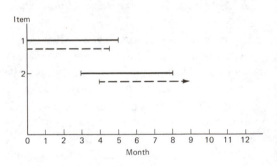

The upper solid line shows that item 1 was scheduled to begin in month 0 with completion scheduled for month 5. The upper broken line shows completion occurred ahead of schedule in month 4 1/2 for this item. The next solid line shows that item 2 was scheduled to begin in month 3 for completion in month 8. The broken line below it, however, shows that its production actually began in month 4 and completion has not yet been achieved in month 9.

GATT = *General Agreement on Tariffs and Trade.*

gearing A British term for *financial leverage*.

general accountant An accountant who deals with any type of accounting problem within an organization.

General Agreement on Tariffs and Trade (GATT) A treaty among most of the economically advanced noncommunist nations guaranteeing bilateral negotiations among participants to reduce tariffs, to lessen trade restrictions, and to extend all lowering of trade barriers between any two nations to all participants. Created as an international organization in 1948, GATT also serves as an arbitrator when violations of international trade agreements are alleged.

general audit = *audit* (*1*).

general average (marine insurance) A loss arising from a sacrifice purposely made for the preservation from common danger of a ship, its cargo, or the persons on board; the loss, incurred for the benefit of all, is made good by a contribution from all; distinguished from *particular average*.

general balance sheet The balance sheet of a governmental body or an educational, religious, charitable, social, or other institution, prepared in the usual commercial form rather than by self-balancing funds.

general cash Cash available for ordinary operating and asset-replacement purposes. See *cash*.

general contingency reserve A *reserve for contingencies* unrelated to any possible future expense or loss; contrasts with *special contingency reserve*.

general expense (or burden) = *administrative expense*.

general fixed assets Fixed assets of a governmental unit not accounted for by a *proprietary fund* or a *fiduciary fund*.

general fixed-assets account group A self-balancing group of accounts set up to account for the *general fixed assets* of a governmental unit.

general fund (governmental and institutional accounting) The assets and liabilities available for general purposes, as distinct from funds established for specific purposes. See *fund*.

generalized audit program An *audit program* which consists of preprinted commonly performed audit procedures, designed to be tailored (added to, deleted from, and changed) to meet the requirements of specific engagements.

general journal The journal in which are recorded transactions not provided for in specialized journals. See *journal*.

general ledger A ledger containing accounts in which all the are classified either in detail or in summary form. See *double-entry bookkeeping*.

general long-term debt Long-term debt legally payable from general revenues and backed by the *full faith and credit* of a governmental unit.

general long-term debt account group A self-balancing group of accounts set up to account for the *general long-term debt* of a governmental unit.

generally accepted Given authoritative recognition: said of *accounting principles* or *audit standards*, and the pronouncements concerning them, particularly, in recent years, those of the *Financial Accounting Standards Board* or the auditing section of the *American Institute of Certified Public Accountants*.

generally accepted accounting principles (GAAP) The conventions, rules, and procedures that define accepted accounting practices at a particular time and provide a standard by which auditors form their professional opinions about financial presentations. GAAP includes not only broad guidelines of general application, but also detailed practices and procedures.

generally accepted auditing standards (GAAS) The standards governing the conduct of external audits by public accountants, as approved and adopted by the membership of the *American Institute of Certified Public Accountants*. There are ten standards divided into three groups, as follows:

GENERAL STANDARDS

1. The examination is to be performed by a person or persons having adequate technical training and proficiency as an auditor.

2. In all matters relating to the examination an independence in mental attitude is to be maintained by the auditor or auditors.

3. Due professional care is to be exercised in the performance of the examination and the preparation of the report.

STANDARDS OF FIELD WORK

1. The work is to be adequately planned and assistants, if any, are to be properly supervised.

2. There is to be a proper study and evaluation of the existing internal control as a basis for reliance thereon and for the determination of the resultant extent of the tests to which auditing procedures are to be restricted.

3. Sufficient competent evidential matter is to be obtained through inspection, observation, inquiries, and confirmations to afford a reasonable basis for an opinion regarding the financial statements under examination.

STANDARDS OF REPORTING

1. The report shall state whether the financial statements are presented in accordance with generally accepted accounting principles.

2. The report shall state whether such principles have been consistently observed in the current period in relation to the preceding period.

3. Information disclosed in the financial statements is to be regarded as reasonably adequate unless otherwise stated in the report.

4. The report shall either contain an expression of opinion regarding the financial statements, taken as a whole, or an assertion to the effect that an opinion cannot be expressed.

When an overall opinion cannot be expressed, the reasons therefore should be stated. In all cases where an auditor's name is associated with financial statements, the report should contain a clear-cut indication of the character of the auditor's examination, if any, and the degree of responsibility he or she is taking.

In support of these broad standards, there is an extensive body of interpretive literature. See *Statements of Auditing Standards; Auditing Standards Board*.

general-obligation bonds 1. Bonds for the payment of which the full faith and credit of the issuer are pledged. See *full-faith-and-credit debt*.

2. (municipal accounting) Bonds payable from *ad valorem* taxes upon all the property assessable by the issuing municipality and from other general revenues.

general operating expense A term often applied to selling and administrative expense and occasionally to production and other costs, such as depreciation, property taxes, rents, royalties, maintenance, repairs, service-contract charges, and other items usually classified elsewhere but which appear separately on an income statement.

general overhead = *administrative expense* and *selling expense*.

general partner(-ship) A partner who alone or with others is liable for the debts of the partnership.

general price level The general level of prices in an economy supposedly represented in an index number such as the CPI (= consumer price index) maintained by the U.S. Department of Labor. As the general level of prices rises (inflation) or falls (deflation), as represented in this index number, the purchasing power of the money unit is supposedly represented by the *reciprocal* of this index number. Conventional financial statements are stated in units of money (nominal dollars) and ignore differences in the value (purchasing power) of the monetary units of economic periods used to measure the items included in those statements. *General price level accounting* (= constant dollar accounting) requires the conventional financial statements to be restated in terms of units of general purchasing power (constant dollars) and to recognize gains and losses from holding monetary items during periods of changing general price levels. See *general price level accounting*.

general price level accounting A method of restating financial statements in units of general purchasing power. See *general price level*. Such restatement changes the unit in which amounts are stated to reflect alterations in the purchasing power of money as measured by some specified *index number*. It does not otherwise change any accounting principle used. For example, depreciation computed by an accelerated method and stated in units of money continues to be accelerated depreciation when restated in units of constant purchasing power. Similarly, the historical cost basis of accounting is retained if amounts stated in units of money are restated in units of constant purchasing power.

Restatement from units of money to units of purchasing power requires, first, the selection of an index of the general level of prices and, second, a decision about whether amounts will be expressed in terms of the general purchasing power of the dollar at the most recent balance-sheet date—''current general purchasing power''—or in terms of the general purchasing power of the dollar as of some date in the past—''base year general purchasing power.'' See *unit of measure (1)*. Starting in 1979, *FASB* is requiring certain large companies to provide supplemental schedules reporting both on a general price level accounting and on a *current cost* basis during a 2-year trial period. The current costs are represented as *replacement costs* and general price level accounting is on a current general purchasing power basis.

general-purpose financial statement Financial report or statement presented to serve all users; this is an objective of financial statements presented in accordance with *generally accepted accounting principles*; contrast with *special-purpose financial statement*.

general records The general ledger and the journals, registers, files, and papers normally supporting general-ledger items.

general revenue sharing An arrangement under which the federal government gives part of its revenues to state and local governments on the basis of predetermined formulas. Unlike *grants in aid*, it is not dependent on agreements to undertake specific activities, and unlike *special revenue sharing*, it is not restricted to specific types of expenditures.

generic expense Expense relating to a class of product or service rather than a particular product or service falling within that class; example: promotional outlays designed to increase the adoption of rotary engines in automobiles. See *institutional advertising*.

geometric mean The number which, when substituted for each of the *factors* of a product, will give the same product as the factors; the mth root of a product of m factors; the number whose *logarithm* is equal to the arithmetic mean of the logarithms of m quantities. Thus, $2 \times 2 \times 4 \times 16 = 256$; hence, the geometric mean of the four factors is $\sqrt[4]{256}$, or 4. Like the arithmetic mean, the geometric mean may be computed in simple or weighted form. The unweighted geometric mean g of a group of m numbers, $N_1, N_2, \ldots, N_m$, is, by definition,

$$g = \sqrt[m]{N_1 \times N_2 \times \cdots \times N_m}$$
$$= (N_1 \times N_2 \times \cdots \times N_m)^{1/m}.$$

In logarithmic terms, this becomes

$$\log g = \frac{\log N_1 + \log N_2 + \cdots + \log N_m}{m},$$

and the *antilogarithm* is, of course, the original expression.

To compute the weighted geometric mean, the weights w are introduced as exponents in the product, and the root to be extracted is equal to the sum of the weights, denoted by $\Sigma w = w_1 + \ldots + w_m$:

$$g = \sqrt[\Sigma w]{(N_1)^{w_1}(N_2)^{w_2} \cdots (N_m)^{w_m}}$$

or

$$\log g = \frac{w_1 \log N_1 + \cdots + w_m \log N_m}{\Sigma w}.$$

If any group of positive numbers is averaged by using the *harmonic, geometric,* and *arithmetic means*, the following relation will be found:

$$h \leq g \leq a.$$

That is, the geometric mean, g, is never greater than the arithmetic mean, a, or less than the harmonic mean, h; it occupies a position intermediate to the harmonic and arithmetic means. This property is sometimes denoted by saying that the arithmetic mean has an upward *bias* relative to the geometric mean, while the harmonic mean has a downward bias. In other words, relative to the geometric mean, the arithmetic mean overstates and the harmonic mean understates the value of the average.

Which particular mean, arithmetic, geometric, or harmonic (or other type of *average,* such as the *median* or *mode*), should be used depends upon the character of the problem. The arithmetic mean may be used when the arithmetic values or absolute changes in magnitudes are of interest, such

as, for example, value of inventory position over a period of years. The harmonic mean is useful when reciprocals are of interest; an average price per unit when commodities are priced at so many units per dollar would be a case in point. The geometric mean is of interest when an average of ratios or rates of change is required.

The geometric mean is often used in compound-interest calculations. For example, it may be desired to find the rate of interest implicit in the investment of a certain sum of money in return for a promise to receive a greater sum at a later date. This is a problem in determining the rate of increase of a sum of money (see *compound; compound amount of 1*). What occurs, under compounding, is the multiplication of an initial sum p_0 by a given rate $(1 + r)$ over n periods to result in a sum p_n. In other words,

$$p_n = p_0(1 + r)^n$$

or

$$r = \sqrt[n]{\frac{p_n}{p_0}} - 1.$$

Thus, if a U.S. Savings Bond yields $1,000 ten years hence for a present investment of $750, as it once did,

$$r = \sqrt[10]{\frac{1,000}{750}} - 1$$

and

$$\log(1 + r) = \frac{\log 1,000 - \log 750}{10}$$

$$= \frac{3.000000 - 2.875061}{10}$$

$$= .012494.$$

Finding the antilogarithm shows that the rate of increase of the $750, i.e., the rate of return, over this period of time is $r = 2.92\%$, not 3 1/3%, the answer secured by use of the arithmetic mean.

In many cases, the arithmetic mean, even though not strictly applicable, serves as an approximation. The geometric mean is more difficult to compute and often not so readily understood. Moreover, if any of the numbers to be averaged is zero, the geometric mean will be zero, since all of the numbers entering into the geometric mean are multiplied together. It is not advisable to use the geometric mean when any of the factors entering into its calculation are negative.

geometric progression A numerical series the values of which increase at a constant *rate*. A formula for the value of the sum S of such a series may be derived as follows: Let

$$S = a + ax + ax^2 + \cdots + ax^{n-1}$$
$$= a(1 + x + x^2 + \cdots + x^{n-1}).$$

Then, multiplying through by x,

$$Sx = a(x + x^2 + x^3 + \cdots + x^{n-1} + x^n).$$

Subtracting the first equation from the second,

$$Sx - S = a(x^n - 1),$$

or

$$S = a\left[\frac{x^n - 1}{x - 1}\right].$$

If $x = 1 + r$ and $a = 1$, the formula gives the *compound amount of 1 per period* for n years:

$$= \frac{(1 + r)^n - 1}{r}.$$

gift (federal taxation) The conveyance of property from one individual to another with less than adequate consideration. A gift is neither a deductible expense to the giver nor taxable income to the recipient, and is to be distinguished from a *contribution* (*1*). Generally the *basis* of property received as a gift is the same as the donor's. But if the value at the time of the gift was lower than the basis, *and* the gift property is sold by the donee at a loss, the donee's basis for computing loss is the value at the time of the gift. As to gifts received on or after September 2, 1958 (or gift property held on that date) and December 31, 1976, the basis is increased by any gift tax attributable to the appreciation in neither instance may this adjustment increase the basis above value at time of gift. Since 1976 gifts have been subject to the graduated *unified transfer tax* rate schedule, which applies to cumulative lifetime (gift) and death (estate) taxes.

gift tax See *unified transfer tax*.

giveup A splitting of a stockbroker's commission with participating brokers: a one-time practice following a large trade; now generally forbidden by the stock exchanges.

GNP = *gross national product*.

GNP deflator A price index to adjust *gross national product* (GNP) measured in current dollars to constant dollars.

goal congruence An attribute of a management control system which encourages consistency between the goals perceived by individuals (employees, managers, etc.) and the goals of the organization.

goal difficulty The extent of effort required to achieve a goal or to be successful in completing a task.

goal discrepancy The difference between an individual's *aspiration level* and the individual's previous performance on a given task.

goal output indicator 1. An *index number* or other measure of attainment for some component program in a *program planning budgeting system*.
2. Any index of attainment.

goal programming A *mathematical programming* problem in which the optimization is directed toward minimizing deviations from a prescribed set of goals. Relative weights may be assigned to deviations from different goals or the weights may be preemptively ordered, in which case even very small deviations from some goals outweigh very large deviations from other goals. Constraints may also be used to rank or order goals, and optimizations may be directed toward minimizing the maximum deviation as well as minimizing the weighted sum of all deviations. Still other optimizations include quadratic and higher-order *functions*.

going concern Any enterprise which is expected to continue operating indefinitely in the future; hence, its collective assets, liabilities, revenues, operating costs, personnel, policies, and prospects: a basic axiom of accounting. See *axiom*.

going-concern value 1. Owners' equity in a business enterprise as disclosed by accounting records and reports; = *book value (3); net worth; stockholders' equity*. It differs from the market value or worth of a business entity as in a prospective disposal or business combination, such worth often being the result of a complex of imponderable, subjectively determined values emerging from considerations of future earning power, product demand, competitive strength, present and prospective governmental regulatory restraints, bargaining concessions, and so on.
2. Hence, worth of any asset or asset group, as determined from similar considerations.

going public Any of a collection of actions related to offering a corporation's shares to the general investing public rather than having them held by relatively few *stockholders*. See *public corporation; closely held corporation*.

good Any item of merchandise, raw materials, or finished goods; a single element of wealth; a commodity.
pl. Loosely, inventoriable items or assets of any kind, including cash, fixed assets, supplies, and items in process of production; as in the expression *goods and services*. See *economic good; service, n.*

goods and services The endproducts of *expenditures*; the initial *distribution (2)* of incurred costs. See *good; service*.

goods in process 1. Partly finished product; *work in process*; raw material and parts on which labor has been expended in the course of converting to or assembling the output of a factory. Under practical operating conditions, the classification may also include raw material and parts removed from stock and waiting the first processing operation.
2. An account or group of accounts in which appear (a) charges for materials, labor, and overhead expended in a manufacturing operation, and (b) credits for product completed or otherwise disposed of, the balance of the account representing partly finished product on hand; an inventory asset valued at cost or less. See *inventory valuation*.

goodwill 1. The current value of expected future income in excess of a normal return on the investment in net tangible assets; not a recorded or reported amount unless paid for.
2. The excess of the price paid for a business as a whole over its *book value*, or over the computed or agreed value of all tangible net assets purchased. Normally, purchased goodwill is the only type appearing on books of account and in financial statements.
3. On a consolidated balance sheet, the premium, or amount paid by the parent or holding company for the shares of its consolidated subsidiaries in excess of their book values at the dates of acquisition, reduced by the discount, if any, at which shares of other subsidiaries were acquired; *consolidation goodwill*.

goodwill method Either of two approaches of accounting for the admission of a new partner into a *partnership* in which an *intangible value*, usually *goodwill*, is recognized. In one approach, the unrecorded intangible value or goodwill of the previous partnership is recognized and the old partners' capital accounts are increased. The new partner, then, is credited with capital equal to the tangible assets contributed. In the second, more typical case, the new partner contributes intangible value or goodwill along with tangible assets and is credited with capital in excess of the amount of tangible assets contributed. Contrast with *bonus method* in which the new partner either gives a "bonus" to the old partners or receives a "bonus" from them, and no intangible value is recognized in the accounts.

Government Accountants Journal See *accounting journals*.

governmental accounting The principles, customs, and procedures associated with accounting for municipal, state, and national governmental units. Characteristics of such accounting have in the past included the entry on bookkeeping records and financial statements of budgetary accounts and other legal or administratively imposed limitations on costs, and the recording of obligations, both of which are now regarded as optional features. In recent years, ordinary accrual accounting has been gradually replacing the older forms.

governmental funds A generic classification adopted by the *National Council on Governmental Accounting* to refer to all *funds* other than *proprietary funds* and *fiduciary funds*. The *general fund, special revenue funds, capital projects funds, debt service funds*, and *special assessment funds* are the types of funds referred to as "governmental funds."

graduated life table The tabular counterpart of a *survivor-life* or *mortality curve*.

grant = *grant in aid*.

grant in aid A donation or contribution usually by a superior governmental unit. Such grants may be for specific purposes, for a category (categorical grants) or a whole block of related uses (block grants).

graph Any series of points linked by relations believed to exist between them. For instance, the relations in the illustration under *network* represent a series of states connected by links with assigned times for the tasks that move the project elements from one state to another. That illustration is in the form of a "directed graph" (also called a "digraph") because movement is unidirectional in the direction indicated by the arrows. (If two-way movement is permitted on any link, the graph is "undirected.")

It is also an example of a "connected graph," as are the *trees* and *chains* shown in it. An example of a graph which is not connected is the following:

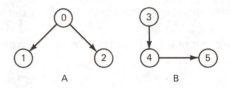

It is not possible to trace a path from any of the nodes of A to any node of B without leaving the graph. The graph in A (a *tree*) and the graph in B (a *chain*) are all connected, however, within each graph. Graphs may also be finite or infinite. The former has only a finite number of elements, the latter an infinite number. The graph of a continuous function provides one example of an infinite graph which is connected, but other relations besides continuous functions can also be represented as graphs.

gray market The buying and selling of scarce commodities by employing business methods generally disapproved; thus, after World War II, certain war contractors, given high priorities from governmental authority during the war, continued as regular customers to purchase the output of steel from steel mills under government-imposed price ceilings in order to resell it at high prices. See *black market*.

gross *adj*. Undiminished by related deductions, except corrections; applied to sales, revenues, income, expense, and the like.

gross bonded debt (municipal accounting) The amount of debt owing before deducting "self-supporting" debt and sinking funds. See *net bonded debt*.

gross book value The dollar amount at which an asset appears on the books, before deducting any applicable accumulated depreciation or other valuation account.

gross cost of merchandise sold (retail accounting) *Invoice cost* (2) of merchandise disposed of by sale, less any return or allowance, plus duty, insurance, and transportation.

gross earnings = *gross income*.

gross income 1. Revenues before deducting any expenses: an expression employed in the accounting for individuals, financial institutions, and the like.

2. = *gross revenue*.

3. Incidental revenue of a manufacturing or trading enterprise. See *income*.

4. (federal income taxes) Section 61 of the *Internal Revenue Code* defines gross income as "all income from whatever source derived ... except as otherwise provided in this subtitle." Certain major categories of income are excluded from gross income, such as life insurance proceeds, gifts and inheritances, interest on state and local obligations, unemployment compensation, and social-security benefits. Thus for tax purposes "gross income" really means "gross taxable income" or income from all sources minus specifically excluded types of income.

gross loss The excess of the cost of goods sold over the amount of sales; "negative" gross profit.

gross margin The excess of sales over cost of products sold. See *gross profit*.

gross (merchandise) margin (retail accounting) *Net sales* less *merchandise costs*.

gross-margin method See *gross-profit method*.

gross-margin ratio A *ratio* which shows the relative *profit margin* available to cover discretionary expenses such as advertising and research and development. This ratio varies greatly from one industry to another so that only comparisons with average *industry ratios* are generally pertinent.

gross national product (national income accounting) The market value of production within the nation during any given calendar year, "production" meaning domestic sales of goods and services to natural persons, and to government, plus the excess of exports over imports. See *net national product*.

gross operating spread (retail accounting) *Gross (merchandise) margin*, less *merchandise procurement cost*.

gross-price method (of recording purchase, sales discounts) A commonly used method for recording sales, but also sometimes used for purchases in which the sale or purchase is recorded at its price or invoice cost and *cash discounts* are recorded, as they are taken, in a *contra account* to "sales" or "purchases." The gross-price method is less commonly used for purchases since it provides no information on the amount of *discount lost*. Most accountants prefer the *net-price method* (of recording purchase discounts).

gross profit Net sales, less cost of goods sold but before considering selling and general expenses, incidental income, and *income deductions*. In a manufacturing concern, gross profit is the excess of net sales over direct costs and factory overhead, and is therefore to be distinguished from *marginal income*, which is the excess of net sales over *direct costs* only.

gross-profit analysis 1. A quantitative expression of proximate causes of change from one year to another in the elements of the gross profits of a business enterprise, the earlier year being the *standard of comparison*; use is made of percentage relationships between the elements, or of unit costs and profits.

2. A similar determination of causes derived from a study of budgeted or standard sales and cost of sales with actual results.

Example of methods of gross-profit analysis (sense 1): Following is a two-year comparison of the sales, cost of sales, and gross profits of the *AB* Company:

Particulars	First Year	Second Year	Increase or (Decrease)
Sales	$650,000	$700,000	$50,000
Cost of sales	430,000	496,000	66,000
Gross profit	$220,000	$204,000	($16,000)
Percent of Sales			
Sales	100.000%	100.000%	— %
Cost of sales	66.154	70.857	4.703
Gross profit	33.846%	29.143%	(4.703)%

If the same conditions obtaining in the earlier year had existed in the current year,

The increase in sales would have yielded a gross profit of 33.846% of $50,000, or	$16,923
But the increase in purchasing costs reduced the gross profit by 4.703% of $700,000, or	32,921
Thus causing a net decline in gross profit of	$16,000

gross-profit method (of inventory) A method of estimating an inventory by subtracting, from the sum of the cost of the beginning inventory and the cost of purchases (or finished goods produced) during the period immediately preceding, an amount equal to the product of the average *gross-profit percentage*, known or estimated, and the net sales for the same period; in a highly refined form, known as the *retail method*. Because of its dependence on estimates, it must be corrected from time to time by a physical inventory. It is used principally in the preparation of monthly income statements within a fiscal year.

gross profit on sales = *gross profit*.

gross-profit percentage See *gross-margin ratio*.

gross-profit ratio *Gross profit* divided by *net sales*. See *gross profit; gross-margin ratio; gross-profit analysis*.

gross revenue *sing.* or *pl.* = *gross sales*.

gross sales Total sales, before deducting returns and allowances but after deducting corrections and trade discounts, sales taxes, excise taxes based on sales, and sometimes cash discounts. See *sale; net sales*.

group accounts (British) = *consolidated financial statements*.

group depreciation See *composite-life method* under *depreciation methods*.

group financial statement A combined financial statement of a number of companies having the same ownership and also having, as a rule, similar structures or types of operation. The usual reason given for a group (rather than consolidated) statement is that the operations of the subsidiaries are of a different order than those of the controlling company, and that more and better information would be the consequence if consolidated statements were avoided; or that the activities of certain subsidiaries involve peculiarities that warrant a separate showing. The possibilities of group statements in annual reports to stockholders have as a rule been greatly underestimated. If, for example, an investment company owns controlling interests in a group of manufacturing companies and in a group of hotels, financial statements of the controlling company, unconsolidated, together with combined financial statements for each of the two groups, would be almost essential in a report of the controlling company to its stockholders. Group statements should be as few as possible; the greater the number, the more difficult the interpretation will be. See *consolidated balance sheet; consolidation policy; conglomerate*.

grouping financial statement A summary worksheet having as its purpose the bringing together of recorded underlying data. Statements of individual subsidiaries or groups of subsidiaries may be published in a condensed form with explanations of intercompany eliminations. Groupings may be made by classes of items ordinarily appearing in detail in other statements, especially where the eliminations applicable to such groupings are minor or wanting entirely. Intragroup profit is always eliminated. It is often desirable to display some detail of the interests of outside stockholders. See *consolidating financial statement; consolidation policy*.

growth curve A time series *graph* in which succeeding *ordinate* values depend on their predecessors.

guarantee *n*. 1. One to whom a guaranty is given.
2. The obligation involved in a guaranty.
v. = *guaranty*.

guaranteed bond A bond guaranteed by a *person* other than the issuer, the guaranty being in the form of an endorsement on each bond, a contract with the issuing corporation, or a contract with the latter's creditors—the last-named device being often employed where the issuing company holds title for (and has leased its property to) a controlling corporation.

guaranteed dividend A periodic dividend on the capital stock of one company, the payment of which has been guaranteed by another.

guarantor One who promises to make good if another fails to pay or otherwise perform an assigned or contractual task.

guaranty *n*. 1. A promise to make good on the failure or deficiency in performance of a good or service.
2. A promise by one person to make good on the failure of another either in payment of a debt or in the performance of a contract or duty. See *warranty; surety*.
v. To execute such a promise.

guidelines Guideposts. Allowable or suggested modes of conduct such as price and wage increases set by government to help lessen inflation.

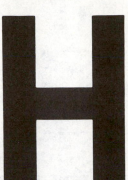

handshaking (computers) Also called *logging in*. A process in which a user interacts with a computer when initially connecting to it. The computer requests identification information which the user provides in order to obtain access to the computer.

haphazard selection A method of taking a *judgment sample* where the sampler attempts to obtain a *representative sample* by going through a population selecting items without regard to their size, source, or other distinguishing characteristic; i.e., without any intentional *bias*.

hardware (computers) The physical computer equipment, such as circuits, wires, and switches. The contrast is with *software* in the form of *computer programs*.

harmonic mean The reciprocal of the arithmetic mean of the reciprocals of a group of numbers; denoted by the symbol h. See *arithmetic mean; geometric mean*. If numbers to be averaged are represented by $N_1, N_2, \ldots, N_m$, and the harmonic mean by h, then,

$$\frac{1}{h} = \frac{\dfrac{1}{N_1} + \dfrac{1}{N_2} + \cdots + \dfrac{1}{N_m}}{m}$$

or

$$h = \frac{m}{\dfrac{1}{N_1} + \dfrac{1}{N_2} + \cdots + \dfrac{1}{N_m}}.$$

The above formula encompasses the simple or unweighted harmonic mean. The formula for the weighted harmonic mean is

$$\frac{1}{h} = \frac{w_1\left[\dfrac{1}{N_1}\right] + w_2\left[\dfrac{1}{N_2}\right] + \cdots + w_m\left[\dfrac{1}{N_m}\right]}{w_1 + w_2 + \cdots + w_m}.$$

As in the case of the *geometric means* and *arithmetic means*, the most common weights (w) are the frequency of occurrence of each value to be weighted.

The harmonic mean is useful for arriving at average unit prices for commodities to be priced in terms of standard units, such as commodity units per dollar. For example, if over a period of time a certain commodity has been observed to sell at 4, 5, and 20 units per dollar, and it is desired to compute the average price per unit, the arithmetic mean $(4 + 5 + 20)/3 = 9\frac{2}{3}$, which suggests that, on the average, the commodity has sold at a rate of $9\frac{2}{3}$ units per dollar, or an average price per unit of approximately 10.34 cents. The harmonic mean, however, shows that, on the average, the commodity has sold at a rate of 6 units per dollar, since

$$\frac{1}{h} = \frac{\frac{1}{4} + \frac{1}{5} + \frac{1}{20}}{3} = \frac{1}{6},$$

and $h = 6$. Thus, use of the harmonic mean results in an average price of approximately 16 2/3 cents (= 6 units per dollar). The result secured by use of the harmonic mean is closer to the ordinary commercial meaning of "quoted unit price." Both the arithmetic and harmonic means used above, however, were "unweighted" (i.e., they were equally weighted). As such, they contain certain assumptions about market behavior. Use of an unweighted arithmetic mean assumes that equal amounts of money were spent at each price, while use of an unweighted harmonic mean assumes that an equal number of units of the commodity were sold at each price. These assumptions may, of course, be modified by introducing weights based on the total number of units sold at each price.

harmonic progression A numerical series the *reciprocals* of which form an *arithmetic progression*.

hashing (computers) A technique used to locate a record within a file. It proceeds via a mathematical *function* which uses the key field of the record as its input and computes an approximate *address* for the location of the record in the file.

Hatfield, Henry Rand (1866-1945) Longtime professor of accounting at the University of California, Berkeley, and author of major textbooks and articles. Served as president in 1919 of the predecessor body of the American Accounting Association (*q.v.*), and was coauthor of *A Statement of Accounting Principles*. Hatfield was a leading accounting theorist and was known for penetrating analyses of other theorists and of accounting practice.

head-end business Property transportation in the form of mail, express, baggage, milk, etc., carried directly behind the locomotive of a passenger train.

head of household (federal income taxes) A single taxpayer who pays more than 50% of the costs of a home he or she maintains for a relative who qualifies as a *dependent* or for an unmarried child whether or not a dependent. The home must be the taxpayer's own home, unless the dependent is the taxpayer's parent, in which case the taxpayer may maintain the parent's home. A married taxpayer who files a separate return may qualify if the taxpayer's spouse does not live in the household but a dependent child or stepchild does for the entire taxable year. The rate schedule then permits the taxpayer to compute the tax at rates approximately halfway between those used by single taxpayers and those for married taxpayers.

hedge Any purchase or sale transaction having as its purpose the elimination of profit or loss arising from price fluctuations; specifically, a purchase or sale entered into for the purpose of balancing, respectively, a sale or purchase already made or under contract, in order to offset the effect of price fluctuation. Hedges are made in the marketing of numerous commodities, and in a variety of ways, but all are attempts to transfer *risk* of price fluctuations from one person or group to others. A firm-price contract for future delivery of a good or service represents a type of hedge under which the purchaser transfers risks of gain or loss from price fluctuations to the seller; a cost-plus-fixed-fee contract, on the other hand, is a hedge in which the seller transfers such risks to the purchaser.

In a restricted sense, the term refers to simultaneous purchase-and-sale transactions having the purpose of offsetting one risk by another more or less equal and opposite. To illustrate this process, assume that it requires three weeks from the purchase of wheat to the sale of flour, that spot prices of wheat are $2 per bushel, that it takes 2.3 bushels of wheat and $1 of other costs to mill 100 pounds of flour, and that flour is selling currently for $6 per hundredweight. With this relation between price and cost, a miller may be willing to engage in purchasing wheat and milling flour; but, in the three weeks intervening between the purchase of the wheat and the sale of the flour, fluctuations may occur in the price of the latter. The miller may hedge against the risk of price fluctuations if a futures market exists in flour or if a firm-price contract for flour delivery three weeks hence can be negotiated. If neither of these conditions exist, it may still be possible for the miller to hedge through the medium of a constituent commodity, such as wheat, the price of which fluctuates in a known manner with the price of flour. Assume that flour prices fall $3 for every $1 decline in the price of wheat, and vice versa. The miller may then hedge fully by selling short three bushels of wheat for every hundredweight of flour he or she expects to mill. If, when the flour is ready for sale, its price has decreased $1, the price of wheat will also have fallen by 33 1/3 cents per bushel. The $1 reduction in flour price will be exactly offset by the $1 gain arising from the short sale of wheat. By selling the flour and simultaneously covering the short sale of wheat, the miller makes 40 cents per unit of flour, assuming that he or she was able to keep other milling costs at $1. He or she loses 60 cents on the barrel of flour but gains $1 on the short sale of three bushels of wheat. The difference of 40 cent is equal to the gain expected to be made on

milling operations when he or she purchased wheat at $2 per bushel for conversion into flour to be sold at $6 per 100 pounds.

A direct price relationship, such as that existing between wheat and flour, is not necessary to hedging. Other items with prices bearing known relations to flour prices offer the same opportunity for hedging; hedging by means of short sales also requires access to organized futures markets. Should foreign currency rates, for example, fluctuate directly with flour prices, they would provide the same protection to the miller. It is only essential that there be correlation between the prices of the items. It is immaterial whether the prices move in the same direction; if wheat prices were to move in a direction opposite to flour prices, the miller could hedge by buying additional wheat long rather than selling it short, for if flour prices should fall and wheat prices rise in response to opposite movements in price, the loss in flour would be offset by the gain in wheat; if flour prices rose, the fall in wheat prices would then eliminate the windfall gain in flour.

Hedging generally is restricted to the elimination of price risks. Hedging against risks such as delayed delivery or physical damage is know as *insurance*. Hedging by locating assets at many different points, or buying them in many different amounts or qualities, is known as *diversification*.

hedge clause A protective statement attached to circulars, advertisements, and letters by brokers, dealers, investment advisers, and others who supply data on securities to customers or clients; its typical postscript form is: "The information furnished herein has been obtained from sources believed to be reliable but its accuracy is not guaranteed." The U.S. *Securities and Exchange Commission* has held that such a statement should not be represented to investors as relieving the broker, dealer, or adviser from liability.

hedge fund A *limited partnership* established by a group of investors and operated by *general partners* for the purpose of speculating through margin buying and short selling, the purpose being to increase the possibility of *capital gains*.

heteroscedasticity Any lack of *homoscedasticity*.

heuristic A plausible method of solution or reasoning—usually employed on complex problems where optimization *algorithms* or completely rigorous methods of reasoning are not available or would require forbidding amounts of time or cost to achieve a ''best'' or ''completely valid'' solution.

hidden reserve Any understatement of *net worth* resulting from such accounting practices as classifying additions to fixed and other assets as expense; overstating depreciation provisions; overaccruing liabilities. On published *financial statements*, disclosure is required for substantial hidden reserves along with reasons, and the amount of their departures from normal procedures.

hierarchical structure 1. An organization design (or element thereof) in which each position is subordinated to another and with a topmost position to which all others are subordinated.
2. (computers) A structure in which some *data records* are considered owners and some are considered members and all except one, called the entry point, have exactly one owner.

highlights 1. Any brief summary of financial or operating data.
2. In annual corporate reports to stockholders: a condensed statement of significant matters derived from and supported by appended financial statements and related data; e.g., total sales for the reported period compared with those of preceding periods, depreciation provisions and the bases therefor, a mounting tax expense, changes in net earnings per share, current ratios, total assets, growth elements. The public accountant who reports on the financial statements is generally regarded as responsible for the *fairness* of highlights relating to past *events and conditions*. See *statement analysis*.

high-low method A process for estimating the fixed and variable components of a *semivariable cost* in which one selects one of the highest and one of the lowest pairs of total cost and activity. The variable component is then estimated by dividing the difference between high total cost and low total cost by the difference between high activity and low activity. The fixed component can be estimated as the difference between high total cost and the product of variable component and high activity. The process can also be used for estimating the variable cost per unit of a variable cost. In this case the fixed component will be zero.

HIP accounting = *human information processing accounting*.

histogram 1. A bar chart.
2. A portrayal of a frequency distribution in which altitudes of rectangles are proportional to frequencies.

historical cost Initially, the amount of cash (or its equivalent) paid to acquire an asset; subsequent to acquisition, the historical amount may be adjusted for amortization. See *cost (1); original cost*.

historical proceeds Initially, the amount of cash (or its equivalent) received when an obligation was incurred by borrowing, as by issuance of bonds; subsequent to incurrence, the historical amounts may be adjusted for amortization. See *bond discount; bond premium*.

historical summary Supplemental data displaying financial statements in condensed form usually for a five- or ten-year period: frequently a feature of annual reports to stockholders. Attached notes call attention to major changes over the years, such as methods of financing, new products, acquisitions of other businesses, increased costs, and the like.

holder in due course A person (holder) taking *commercial paper* under conditions that he or she is given immunity from certain defenses (see *personal defenses*); taking a negotiable instrument under conditions giving him or her more favored treatment than an assignee of a contract.

hold-harmless agreement A *contract* under the terms of which the liability of one person for damages is assumed by another.

holding company A *controlling company* having subsidiaries and confining its activities primarily to their management.

holding gains or losses Gains or losses resulting from holding assets and liabilities while their values change. Holding gains or losses may be realized or unrealized, depending on whether or not an exchange transaction has occurred. Under conventional (historical cost) accounting the *realization principle* requires disposition by actual sale in an *arm's-length* transaction as a basis for recognizing any gain or loss. Exceptions to the realization principle are allowed to recognize changes in market conditions or changes resulting from the passage of time (obsolescence) that significantly affect recorded asset values. These exceptions generally involve reductions in asset values that are expensed in the period of recognition with accompanying notes and explanations in the financial statements. No separate account for holding gains and losses appears on the *balance sheet*. Under *current cost* and *general price level accounting*, holding gains and losses are not exceptions. They occur generally as a result of any changes in pertinent markets or technologies (current cost accounting) or

changes in the index numbers used, such as the *CPI*, to reflect changes in the *general price level*. Hence one or more balance-sheet accounts labeled "holding gains and losses" are generally provided in current cost or general price level accounting.

holding period (federal income taxes) The period during which an asset is owned: a period of importance in the determination of whether sales of securities are *wash transactions* and whether profits from the sale of *capital assets* (2) are to be taxed as long-term or short-term *capital gains*. Generally, in a tax-free transaction, such as a gift or a tax-free reorganization, where the transferee of assets has a substituted basis, the holding period of the transferor is added to the holding period of the transferee.

Hollerith code A coding scheme for computer cards. The code consists of twelve fields on the card. These are the zone fields, 12, 11, and 0, along with nine other fields, numbered 1 through 9.

home office cost (expense) Administrative and other costs and expenses incurred to maintain a headquarters or home office of an enterprise that has operations in different locations. See *branch accounting*.

homogeneous costs Similar or interdependent costs such as those assigned to a *cost pool* and ultimately spread to functions, organizational units, and products on a direction-of-effort, benefit-conferred, or other basis. See *generic expense*.

homoscedasticity Scedasticity refers to scatter and is usually measured by the *variance* of a set of observations. In regression the distribution of the dependent variable is said to be homoscedastic if its variance is the same for all values of the dependent variable(s). Homoscedasticity is a requisite for tests of significance and other parts of ordinary *least-squares regression analysis* and economic series often require transformation to achieve this. The contrast is with *heteroscedasticity*.

horizontal analysis Any *time series analysis* where accounting statements of a given firm are analyzed over several periods of time. For example, see *trend percentage analysis*. Contrasted with *cross-section analysis*, where a firm's accounting statements are compared to those of other firms at the same point (or period) in time.

horizontal audit A method of observing accounting procedures by a public accountant designed to *test* the practical operation of internal controls. Example: tracing a purchase transaction from requisition to order, delivery, inspection, inventory, sales, and collection: included in the auditor's area of inquiry would be the method of procurement; the meaning and sufficiency of inspection and approval; adequacy of documentation; safeguards against inaccuracies, including entry in the bookkeeping records; speed of recording and disposing of discovered errors; smoothness of interdepartmental relationships; and so on.

horizontal combination A business combination of companies with similar functions in production or sale of comparable products.

host country A country other than the home country in which a multinational enterprise operates.

hotchpot A combining of (to put in hotchpot) property of two or more persons in order to effect an equal distribution between them.

human capital The capitalized value of present and future productive services possessed by individuals. See *human resource accounting*.

human information processing accounting *Behavioral accounting* usually focused on cognitive aspects of decision making.

human resource accounting Also called human resource management. Any program for dealing systematically with the human resources of a business firm or other entity such as a government agency or not-for-profit organization. At one stage the effort in human resource accounting was directed toward capitalizing items such as employee training, health programs, etc., on the supposition that this increased their asset value for the employing organization. Practical difficulties in identifying the portion of such expenditures to be capitalized and related issues of depreciating the resulting capitalizations have tended to discourage such attempts at capital asset accounting. At a deeper level one also encounters issues like the assignment of ownership claims to these assets and how such claims might be accommodated in the financial statements. As a result, much of the effort in human resource accounting now bypasses these issues in favor of more careful and systematic attention to the management of human resources as an important aspect of the advantages that may thereby accrue for future as well as present enterprise activity. See *human capital*.

human resource management = *human resource accounting*.

hybrid computer A computer or a group of computers which possess both *digital computer* and *analog computer* properties. The hybrid system is used for control systems problems which make it necessary, or desirable, to be able to perform digital calculations and receive or output data in analog form.

hybrid reserve A reserve serving two or more purposes; usually applied to *appropriations* of *retained earnings* against which costs or losses have been erroneously charged; see *appropriated retained income*.

hypergeometric distribution An extension of the *binomial distribution* to allow nonindependent drawings as in sampling from a finite population without replacement between successive drawings into the sample. Example: drawing a sample of k balls without replacement from an urn with m black and n white gives

$$\frac{C_r^m \, C_{k-r}^n}{C_k^{m+n}}$$

as the *probability* of drawing r black and $k - r$ white balls in the *sample*. See *permutation (4)*. The probability distribution for the hypergeometric is

$$\sum_{r=0}^{k} \frac{C_r^m \, C_{k-r}^n}{C_k^{m+n}} = 1$$

with *mean* $\mu = mk/(m + n)$ and *variance*

$$\sigma^2 = \frac{mnk(m + n - k)}{(m + n)^2(m + n - 1)} \; .$$

hyperinflation Inflation at an extraordinarily high level (100% or more) accompanied, usually, by a variety of other malaises such as high unemployment, unwillingness to save, and a disruption of the usual methods of conducting business because of an unwillingness to hold cash. In general, a situation in which money has completely lost its function as a "store of value." See *money*.

hypothecated asset = *pledged asset*.

hypothecation The pledging of property to secure the payment of a debt: a term sometimes used where a note, acceptance, warehouse receipt, or bill of lading remains in the hands of the debtor, the ledger account or other record being stamped with a reminder that the proceeds therefrom are to be applied to the account of a designated creditor.

hypothesis 1. (logic) A proposition having the status of a *sufficient condition* for a set of other propositions, anteceding the "if" clause in a conditional proposition. In examining a system of internal control, an auditor relies on a hypothesis of adequacy in terms of certain criteria or rules of adequacy. He or she then proceeds to *test* the hypothesis by collecting and sifting *evidence* in accordance with such rules. On this basis, the hypothesis is accepted or rejected. Either eventuality results in the statement of a second hypothesis that provides a *sufficient condition* for a set of propositions concerning the general scope and method to be followed in the remainder of the audit engagement. Other hypotheses will need to be stated, of course, in order to determine in detail what ought to be done in succeeding steps. See *sufficient condition; necessary condition*.

2. (science) A proposition provisionally accepted for the purpose of determining logical consistency between the proposition and an established set or a *primitive* set of propositions; loosely, any conjecture as to the nature or probable causes of events or conditions; a "working hypothesis" is a conjecture which, although not completely verified, is regarded as sufficiently probable to serve as a basis for investigation or other action.

3. (statistics) A proposition involving relations between sets of events, which is to be rejected or tentatively accepted on the basis of sample *evidence* in accordance with stipulated *rules* of *statistical inference*.

hypothesis test See *test; hypothesis*.

IAAA = *Inter-American Accounting Association*.

ICA = *International Congress of Accountants*.

ICAC = *International Committee for Accounting Cooperation*.

IDA = International Development Association. See *World Bank*.

IDC = *intangible drilling costs*.

ideal capacity 1. The output level of a production unit assuming 100%-of-the-time operation. See *theoretical capacity* as a synonym.
2. For an existing plant, the output level which minimizes average total cost per unit of output.
3. In the long run, a scale of plant which will meet customer demand at minimum cost or maximum profit.

ideal standard cost Any projection of a future cost, often differing from and contrasting with *attainable cost* and serving as a hoped-for ultimate goal, standard of comparison, or basis for measuring *efficiency*.

identity 1. A relation between two mathematical functions or logical expressions, specifying that they always assume the same values in a defined domain of all possible values. To distinguish an identity from an equation (the latter specifying a relation that need not hold for any and all values of the variables it contains), and to indicate the greater force of an identity, an additional horizontal stroke is, by mathematical *convention*, added to the equality symbol ($=$) to obtain $\equiv$. The so-called balance-sheet "equation" is actually an identity, since, by the *rules* of double entry, the relation *assets = equities = liabilities + owners' equity* (or *net worth*) must necessarily obtain. When this expression fails to hold, it implies that a mistake is present in the accounting process; but the converse proposition is not necessarily true. Accounting correctness is a *sufficient condition* for satisfying the relation expressed by the balance-sheet identity; it is not a *necessary condition*. In short, if the accounting process is carried out correctly, the balance-sheet identity will be satisfied; but satisfaction of the balance-sheet identity does not imply that the results of following the accounting process are without error. See *necessary condition; sufficient condition; trial balance; equation.*
2. Sufficient continuity to warrant attribution of the same predicates throughout a specified period of time; this may be a legal fiction, as

250

in the case of a machine that retains its identity for purposes of determining legal ownership although all of its parts may have been replaced.

idle capacity 1. The difference between the available capacity of a production unit and its actual utilization level.
2. The difference between the measure of capacity adopted for overhead costing purposes and its actual utilization level.
3. Any unutilized productive potential.

idle-capacity cost The *variance* attributable to failure to utilize facilities at projected rates.

idle time Lost time of workers or machines arising from lack of business or of material, a breakdown of equipment, faulty supervision, or other cause whether or not avoidable. In the distribution of labor and production-center costs, it may be accounted for in a separate operating-expense account and regarded as an item of overhead.

IFA =*International Federation of Accountants*.

if-converted method A method of computing *primary earnings per share* or *fully diluted earnings per share* by adjusting income to reflect assumed conversion of potentially *dilutive* securities at the start rather than the end of the reporting period. Thus, if the security is convertible preferred stock, dividends applicable to these shares are not deducted from earnings to arrive at earnings available for common; if the security is convertible debt, its interest deduction less applicable income taxes is added back to earnings in order to determine if assumed conversion is dilutive. Date of issuance is used if this occurred subsequent to the start of the reporting period. See *earnings per share; primary earnings per share; fully diluted earnings per share*.

illiquid A state of not being *liquid* and hence not being able to meet obligations due for payment.

illusory promise Law of *contracts*. A promise, so conditional that it is not binding on the promisor and thus not sufficient as *consideration* for another promise.

imaginary number A *number* of which $\sqrt{-1}$ is a factor. See *complex number*.

impact statement An analysis which summarizes and documents the estimated effects of a proposed project with special reference to possible *externalities*. Example: An impact statement for a proposed real-estate development might include estimates of the effects of increased traffic congestion that might occur as a result of the proposed development along with proposed remedies and their consequences. A supporting environmental impact statement might include effects on rivers or streams resulting from grading of the property and building of roads. A social impact statement could include projected effects on crime rates, school population, or, more generally, alterations in the types and classes of persons likely to reside in the neighborhood. See also *corporate social report*.

impairment (of capital) 1. The amount by which *stated capital* has been reduced by losses or by dividends or other distributions.
2. The amount by which liabilities exceed assets.

impairment of value Permanent reduction in the economic utility of an asset as a result of which recovery of its cost or *book value* is improbable; generally written down to estimated recoverable cost with immediate recognition of the loss.

implication The relation of a set of *propositions* such that the truth or falsity of one depends upon the truth or falsity of the others.

implicit cost 1. = *opportunity cost*.
2. For bonds, notes, leases, or capital investments, the interest rate which will equate the *present* (or *discounted*) *value* of the cash receipts and cash payments over the relevant life. See *internal rate of return*.

implicit interest method of depreciation See *annuity method* under *depreciation methods*.

implied contract A contract inferred from the actions of the parties, there being no express agreement between them.

implied trust A *trust* where the intent of the parties to create a trust is inferred from the transaction between them.

import quotas Restrictions, usually in physical units, set by a country on the maximum amounts of goods that can be brought into a country from specified sources.

impound 1. To seize and hold in protective custody by means of some legal process, such as a court order.
2. (governmental accounting) To curtail authority to incur *obligations* by withholding portions or all of a congressional *appropriation*; such action by the *Office of Management and Budget* having the effect of modifying the character of an agency's operations. The impoundment authority of the executive, however, has now been limited by the 1974 Budget Control and Impoundment Act, under which (a) any such action by the executive must be referred to Congress which by joint resolution can negate the impoundment and (b) the General Accounting Office is required to monitor all actions that might constitute an impoundment by the executive. Negation by Congress must occur, however, within a specified short period of time or the impoundment stands.

imprest cash = *imprest fund (1)*.

imprest fund 1. A fixed *cash fund* or *petty-cash (fund)* in the form of currency, a bank checking account, or both, maintained for expenditures that must be made in cash, and from time to time restored to its original amount by a transfer from general cash of a sum equal to the aggregate of disbursements: a form of *working fund*.
2. A fund established for a single payroll,

dividend, or other periodic class of payments.

imprest system The system under which *imprest cash* is disbursed and from time to time restored to its original amount through reimbursements equal to sums expended. Implicit in the concept is review by a higher authority of the propriety of the expended amounts before reimbursement.

improvement 1. = *betterment*.
2. The clearing, draining, grading, or other addition to the worth of a tract of land; any cost of developing real estate, whether paid for directly or through special-assessment taxes. See *land improvements*.

impute To assign causality between *variables* which combine to produce a common effect. Imputations are often made by *convention*, even when no specific causal connection can be established between the effect and the variables which have contributed to the end result. An example frequently encountered is the assignment of portions of fixed or common costs to individual items of production. Another example may be found in the distribution of aliquot portions of material and labor costs between items jointly produced. See *joint cost*. Averaging of total costs over a variety of factors is not a satisfactory method of imputation when it is desired to isolate causes of variation in the total cost of joint products. Recourse to *marginal analysis* may be required. See *marginal cost; marginal productivity*.

imputed cost 1. = *alternative cost*; a term often used to indicate the presence of arbitrary or subjective elements of product cost having more than minor significance.
2. A fraction of joint or common costs, including overhead, attributed to any item of goods or services acquired in a *lot* or jointly produced; also, the worth of a *factor of production* joined with and inseparable from one or more other factors in its effects. See *impute; joint cost*.

imputed interest 1. An estimated or *imputed cost* of money or other form of investment often stated as a rate of return relative to some asset or investment base; the best price (= *rate*) at which a loan or an investment of capital may be negotiated. (''Best'' refers to the lowest rate for a borrower and the highest rate for a lender.)

2. An *assignment* (or allocation) of the cost of tying up funds or other resources in a particular class of assets. The reference may be to current assets as when, for instance, a cost of extending credit to customers is estimated. It may also refer to plant, to fixed assets in general, or to a particular capital asset. See *interest on investment* for plant or equipment under construction where, under FASB Statement 34, the portion capitalized is limited to the amount of interest accruing during the reporting period. In some regulated utilities the imputation extends to stockholder net worth and even some types of current liabilities. When the amount to be capitalized exceeds total interest, an additional offsetting credit entry is required. In some cases the credit is to current income. In other cases, it is to a *valuation reserve* which serves as an *equalization reserve* used to absorb part of the higher depreciation in future years caused by the earlier additions to the capitalized value of the asset.

inadequacy The expense or loss of cost caused by insufficiency of capacity or use, necessitating early replacement or abandonment. See *depreciation*. Inadequacy is a factor, with wear and tear and obsolescence, in the determination of depreciation rates.

inadmitted asset (insurance accounting) Any asset having or assumed to have little or no value in liquidation. In reporting the financial position of an insurance company, such assets are segregated and deducted as a group, usually on the face of the report.

incentive stock option (ISO) Created by the Economic Recovery Tax Act of 1981, a *stock option* that meets the conditions specified for the incentive stock option provides a more favorable tax break to employees receiving the option than its predecessor *qualified stock option* did. The employee will have no ordinary income on either at the time of grant or exercise of the option, and will have a capital gain upon the sale of the stock received equal to the selling price less the amount paid for the stock, providing the sale takes place more than 1 year after the date of exercise and 2 years after the date of grant. The exercise of the option does not create a *tax preference* item unlike the qualified stock option. The employer must, however, generally forgo compensation deduction.

in-charge accountant (public accounting) The *manager* or *senior* who assigns and supervises the work of a field staff.

incidence The incurring or sustaining of an expense or loss over which the person affected has little or no control, and for which he or she may be reimbursed by others; example: an *excise tax* paid by a manufacturer on the production of a commodity and added to the selling price paid by the buyer of the commodity.

incidental authority An agent's authority which arises as a reasonable implication to carry out authority expressly given; the acts which are incidentally necessary to carry out express authority given an agent. See *authority*.

incidental beneficiary One who benefits from the performance of a *contract* merely incidental to the benefits for the promisees; one not intended to be a contract beneficiary. The incidental beneficiary has no rights in the contract and cannot recover for a breach. See *externalities*.

income 1. Money or money equivalent *earned* or *accrued* during an accounting period, increasing the total of previously existing net assets, and arising from sales and rentals of any type of goods or services, commissions, interest, gifts, recoveries from damage, and windfalls from any outside source: a generic term. See *revenue; gross income; net income; income realization; profit*.

2. Sales of goods or services; in this sense, the term is less used than formerly, *revenue* now being preferred.

3. An addition; a receipt: often in contrast with *outgo*; as, the income and outgo of stores.

4. Now in restricted senses: (a) the revenues of natural persons, such as salaries, interests, or rents (= *earnings* (*3*)); (b) the remainder of revenue after deducting costs of sales and operating and other expenses (= *net income*); (c) revenues derived from investments and from incidental sources.

5. (economics) The flow of economic goods and services during a period of time: a term frequently contrasted with "wealth"—i.e., a stock of economic goods at a point of time; sometimes synonymous with (a) "net income"—the residual revenue after contractual payments or accruals for land, labor, management, borrowed capital, and risk have been made or allowed for; (b) "money income"—money or money's worth received during a period for services or for the use of property; (c) "real income"—the purchasing power of money income; (d) "psychic" or "subjective" income—the satisfaction of individual human wants. The Hicksian concept of income, defined by J. R. Hicks, states income as the maximum amount one can consume and still expect to be as well off at the end of a period as at the beginning.

In most accounting usage, "income" customarily refers to any factor, other than additional investment, that increases the owner's recorded equity in an enterprise: a concept in harmony with the definition appearing in *Eis-*

ner v. *Macomber*, 252 U.S. 189: "... the gain derived from capital, from labor, or from both combined, provided it be understood to include profit gained through a sale or conversion of capital assets."

income account 1. Any account maintained for a particular item of revenue or income.

2. A general term meaning the current year's revenue and expense, as in the expression, "a charge to income account"; *profit and loss* (*2*).

3. *pl.* Revenue and expense accounts, collectively.

income and expense = *revenue* and *expense*.

income averaging (federal income taxes) An elective relief provision of the *Internal Revenue Code* (Sections 1301—1305) for the individual taxpayer whose taxable income varies widely from year to year. In essence, the excess of current taxable income over 120% of the average taxable income of the past four years is taxed as though this excess had been received in five equal amounts. This tax computation may not be combined with the *maximum tax* computation. See *averageable income; average base-period income*.

income bond An obligation on which interest is paid only if earned; it is like other types of bonds with respect to underlying security, maturity, and other features. Interest may be cumulative or noncumulative; if cumulative, the cumulation may cease after a term of years (often 3). The determination of whether interest has been earned is frequently made dependent on a professional accountant's interpretation of the provisions of the *indenture*, together with what he or she deems to be "good accounting practice." Some income bonds resemble preferred stock so closely that denial of interest thereon as an allowable deduction for tax purposes has been affirmed by the courts.

income deduction One of a class of items making up the final section of the income statement of a business organization, representing expenses (including losses) commonly excluded from operating costs; like other expenses, they are costs necessarily incurred in the conduct of the particular business and are thus customarily regarded as necessary charges before arriving at net income, but as being more in the nature of costs imposed from without rather than costs subject to the controls exercised through everyday operating procedures. They are made up of interest; amortized discount and expense on bonds; income taxes (property taxes being as a rule nominal in character and absorbed as an ordinary operating expense); losses from sales of plants and branches and from other major property disposals; carrying charges on inactive property; prior-year adjustments, as for additional income taxes; charges to contingency reserves; bonuses and other periodic profit distributions to officers and employees; writeoffs of intangibles; adjustments arising from major changes in accounting methods, as in the basis of inventory valuation; flood, fire, and other extraordinary losses; losses on foreign exchange; and the like. For other than interest and income taxes, the usual tests for items in this classification are that they be material in amount and nonrecurrent. Although certain of these expenses are occasionally treated as "surplus charges," it is now considered better practice to include them, with full explanations, in the income statement. See *net income; appropriation of net income; income statement; operating-performance income statement; prior period adjustment.*

income earned 1. *Realized* income.
2. Income realized from services rendered.

income from continuing operations As defined in *APB* Opinion 30, all enterprise revenues, expenses, gains, losses, and changes in accounting estimates less applicable income taxes for the accounting period except for: income (loss) from operations net of applicable income taxes; gain (loss) net of applicable income taxes on the disposal of a discontinued segment; extraordinary gains (losses) net of applicable income taxes; and the cumulative effect of a change in accounting principle (as required by APB Opinion 20 and reaffirmed in APB Opinion 30).

income from discontinued operations As defined in *APB* Opinion 30, income (loss) less applicable income taxes from the *operations* of a segment of the business that has been discontinued during the period or that is in the process of being discontinued. This is reported on a separate line of the *income statement* (separated also from the gain (loss) from disposal of the segment) between *income from continuing operations* and *extraordinary items.*

income in respect of a decedent (federal income taxes) Income earned by a decedent prior to his or her death which was not included in the decedent's gross income for income tax purposes. Under Section 691 of the *Internal Revenue Code*, such income is included in the gross income of the estate or of the beneficiary at the time that the income is received. The income recognized by the estate or transferee is reduced by the amount of federal and state death taxes attributable to the item and also retains the same character (ordinary income, capital gain) when received as it would have had to the decedent.

income per share = *earnings per share.* See *fully diluted earnings per share; primary earnings per share.*

income realization The *recognition* of income, the usual test being the passage of title to or delivery of goods, or the performance of services. See *realize.*

income sheet = *income statement.*

income splitting (federal income taxes) Assigning or allocating income to two or more tax returns to reduce the effects of higher marginal rates of tax which would be incurred if only a single return were filed. Before *joint returns* were permitted, married taxpayers sought to duplicate the tax advantage of *community-property* states by contractually agreeing to split their combined earnings. *Lucas* v. *Earl*, 281 U.S. III (1930), rendered such contracts ineffective, because the income was deemed taxable to the taxpayer who earned it in a common-law state, whereas in a community-property state, state law stipulates that earnings are community property.

Income splitting, or assignment of income, is also used to divert income such as interest, dividends, and rents, from a taxpayer in higher tax brackets to one subject to lower marginal rates. For this approach to be successful, the income-producing property must be transferred to the intended taxpayer. Such a transfer is subject to *gift tax* rules.

incomes policy Government action to limit wage increases for certain classes of workers and price increases for specific types of goods and services.

income statement A summary of the *revenues* and *expenses*, including gains and losses from *extraordinary items* and *discontinued operations*, of an *accounting unit*, or group of such units and resulting in a *net income* figure for a specified period of time.

income tax A tax on annual earnings and profits of any natural person, corporation, or other defined unit. Expressed as a percentage, the rate of tax often varies with the character and amount of the income on which it is based. It may take the form of a *normal tax, surtax*, excess-profits tax, or a combination of any such taxes.

income-tax allocation A financial accounting procedure that does not change the actual income-tax liability for the period but allocates the tax expense to specific events (*intraperiod tax allocation*) or to different accounting periods (*interperiod tax allocation*) to allow for timing differences between generally accepted accounting principles and income-tax allocations.

incompatible functions Any activities within an organization which, if the responsibility of a single individual, would allow that person to commit an unintentional error or an intentional irregularity with a high risk that it could go undiscovered. (See *segregation of duties; error; irregularity*.)

incomplete transaction A *transaction* that in the normal course of events will lead to another; as, a credit sale followed at a later date by a settlement in cash, or a contract in process against which a part of the cost has been incurred and a portion of the prospective profit has been recognized as earned.

incontestable clause A provision in a life insurance policy providing that, after a specified period, the insurer cannot raise certain defenses (or contest the policy) which would be normal defenses in an ordinary contract action, such as misrepresentation or fraud of the insured.

increment An increase over some base value expressed as a difference between the new value and the base. Thus if y_t and y_{t-1} represent new and base values at times t and $t - 1$, respectively, then $y_t - y_{t-1} = \Delta y_t$ is the increment where Δ (= Greek delta) is the usual symbol for the difference in y at t. A positive difference, i.e., $y_t > y_{t-1}$, is called an increment and a negative difference resulting from $y_{t-1} > y_t$ is called a decrement. See *unearned increment*.

incremental analysis Also called *marginal analysis*. A method of analyzing managerial decision problems which emphasizes incremental rather than total costs and benefits associated with an action (or set of alternative actions). Decision makers are thereby freed from considering parts of the decision problem which do not differentiate one alternative from another. Undifferentiating factors (e.g., sunk costs) are generally not helpful in selecting a course of action. They require some time and cost to evaluate and may be misleading for the decisions to be considered.

incremental approach An approach to decision making based only on increments. See *increment, incremental cost, incremental revenue, incremental benefit.*

incremental benefit The change in benefit that accompanies addition or subtraction of a unit of the level of an activity.

incremental budgeting A budget process in which justification is generally required only for *increments* (or decrements) to previous budgeting levels. See *zero-base budgeting; program planning budgeting system.*

incremental cost The change in aggregate cost that accompanies the addition or subtraction of a unit of output, or a change in factors affecting cost, such as style, size, or area of distribution; *marginal cost*. The incremental cost of an independent variable constituting a part of the cost of production or marketing reflects the effect on the choice of an alternative. See *incremental analysis.*

incremental net benefit The difference between the *incremental benefit* and the *incremental cost* it occasions.

incremental revenue The change in revenue that accompanies the addition or subtraction of a unit of sales.

incur To sustain, become liable for: said of a cost, expense, loss, or debt. See *recognize.* —incurrence, *n.*

incurred cost A cost arising from cash paid out or obligation to pay for an acquired asset or service, a loss that has been sustained and must be paid for.

in-cycle work Work performed by an operator while a machine is performing its *cycle* of operations; contrasts with *out-cycle work.*

indebtedness A debt *owing*; any *liability*; an aggregate of liabilities.

indenture An agreement between two or more persons involving reciprocal rights and duties; as, a lease, or a contract between bondholders and the issuer.

independence 1. (logic) The relation between two propositions such that the truth of one does not bear on the truth or falsity of the other.
2. (statistics) The property of two or more chance or *random events*, the *probability* of whose joint occurrence is equal to the product of their individual probabilities of occurrence.
3. The property of a relation between an accountant and a client (or superior) such that the accountant's findings and reports will be influenced only by the *evidence* discovered and assembled in accord with the rules and principles of his or her professional discipline.

independent accountant = *public accountant.* A term used by the U.S. *Securities and Exchange Commission* and others with reference to a public accountant having no financial stake or other interest in the person on whose statements a professional opinion is to be expressed and which, if present, might cause a loss of objectivity or impartiality or otherwise interfere with the free exercise of his or her professional judgment. The SEC has said that "an accountant will not be considered [by the SEC] independent with respect to any person, or any affiliate thereof, in whom he has any financial interest, direct or indirect, or with whom he is, or was during the period of report, connected as a promoter, underwriter, voting trustee, director, officer, or employee" [Rule 2.01(b) of Regulation S-X, as amended]. A similar definition of independence may be found in the AICPA Code of Professional Ethics, Article 1.01.

independent audit = *audit*.

independent contractor One who contracts to perform a service, or work for another using his or her own independent judgment and not subject to the supervision or control of the other person, except to produce the desired result. From the point of view of the internal revenue service if too much supervision or control is exercised, the contractor may be deemed an employee for purposes of withholding and unemployment taxes.

independent variable A variable the value of which, within its defined range, may be assigned without reference to values assumed by other structural elements (variables or constants) in an equation or other mathematical expression. See *variable; dependent variable; function*.

indeterminate appropriation An appropriation which is not limited either to any definite period of time or to any definite amount, or to both time and amount. Distinctions between an indeterminate appropriation and a *continuing appropriation* are as follows: A continuing appropriation is indefinite only as to time where an indeterminate appropriation may be indefinite as to both time and amount. Indeterminate appropriations which are indefinite only as to time may also be distinguished from continuing appropriations in that such indeterminate appropriations may eventually lapse. For example, an appropriation to construct a building may continue in effect until the building is constructed. Once the building is completed, the unexpended balance of the appropriation lapses. A continuing appropriation, on the other hand, may continue forever; it can only be abolished by action of the legislative body.

index 1. (computers) An integer pointer to the location of data stored in the memory of a computer.
2. A table of contents with accompanying page or location references as in the index to an *accounting manual*.
3. (economics) An *index number*.
v.t. To arrange or apply an index in any of the above senses. See *indexing*.

indexation Any arrangement for adjusting the value of a contract to compensate for price changes. Examples: escalator clauses in labor or construction contracts which adjust for specified changes in the *Consumer Price Index* or other costs that are beyond the control of the contractor. Variable rate mortgages will contain clauses allowing for new rates of interest with changing market conditions. Certain countries have official rules to adjust bank loans or other obligations by indexing them for changing price levels.

indexing (and cross-referencing) An organization procedure used by auditors in preparing working papers. Each working paper schedule is given a unique *index* symbol (alphabetic and/or numeric). Wherever numbers of two or more schedules are matched and compared, the index numbers of the related schedules are entered to indicate this cross-reference.

index number An index number shows a change in a variable relative to its base value taken as 100. Thus, if a price of a commodity is currently $6 a unit while its price in a base year (a base price) is $5 a unit, its price index is 120 (100 × $6/$5). If a sales volume of a product in 19X2 is 100,000 units while its sales volume in 19X1, taken as the base year, is 80,000 units, then its quantity index is 125 (100 × 100,000/80,000).

An index number may be "simple," expressing a change in one variable, but more frequently "composite," expressing changes in more than one variable. In the latter case, a group of simple index numbers is aggregated into a single number by taking a weighted average of simple index numbers. For example, if Commodity A's price index is 120 and Commodity B's price index 110, a composite index of the two commodities is 115 if the two price indices (or indexes) are weighted equally. The composite index is, however, 118 if A's index is weighted four times as much as B's ($120 \times 4/5 + 110 \times 1/5$).

Weights that are most commonly used in computing price or quantity indices in business and economics are the value of the commodities. Suppose that A's price went up from $5 to $6 while B's price went up from $10 to $11, and that consumers purchase annually 40 units of A and 5 units of B. Then, A's price index (120) and B's price index (110) are weighted at the ratio of $5 \times 20 = $200 to $10 \times 5 = $50 or 4 to 1. Hence, as computed before, the composite index becomes 118 (120 x 200/250 + 110 $\times$ 50/250). The same result may be obtained by taking the ratio of what the consumers paid in total in the current year ($6 $\times$ 40 + $11 $\times$ 5 = $295) to what they paid in total in the base year ($5 $\times$ 40 + $10 $\times$ 5 = $250), namely 118 (100 x $295/$250).

A problem arises when consumers shift their consumption pattern in response to the price changes. In the above example, suppose the consumers bought 40 units of A and 5 units of B in the base year, but they bought 20 units of A and 10 units of B in the current year, responding to a steeper price increase in A relative to B. The current year's total bill is $6 $\times$ 20 + $11 $\times$ 10 = $230, while the same basket of goods (20 units of A and 10 units of B) could have been bought for $5 $\times$ 20 + $10 $\times$ 10 = $200 in the base year. Hence, if the current year quantities are used, the composite price index becomes 115 (100 $\times$ $230/$200), while if the base year quantities (40 units and 5 units) are used, the index is 118 as computed before.

A composite index is called a "Laspeyres index" if weights used are those in the base year (also called "base year weights") and is called a "Paasche index" if weights used are those in the current year (also called "current year weights"). The price index of 118 computed first is Laspeyres and the price index of 115 computed second is Paasche. Most economic and business indices are Laspeyres. A notable exception is the *GNP deflator*, which is neither Laspeyres nor Paasche.

Being a weighted average, a composite index expresses changes in variables only "on average." It is, however, a useful tool for expressing approximately the changes in the variables, especially when the rates of change among the variables are not widely different.

index number trend series See *trend percentage analysis*.

index of correlation The *coefficient* of correlation for a nonlinear equation, such as $Y = a + bX + cX^2$; usually written ρ (rho) or I; see *coefficient (2)*.

index sequential file (computers) A file organization by which data may be accessed either sequentially or directly using the value of the key filed. This organization is effective for files which require both direct access (as in updating) as well as sequential access (for report generation). It is slower than a simple sequential file for sequential access, however, and it is also slower than a direct access file for direct access. See *file structure (2)*.

indirect business taxes *Sales* and *excise taxes* paid by businesses on the goods and services they purchase.

indirect cost A *cost* not attributed to the *production* of a specified good or service but to an activity associated with production generally: e.g., a variety of factory costs such as supervision, building depreciation, maintenance, heat and light, general and administrative, and selling expense. See *overhead*. The contrast is with *direct cost*.

indirect-cost pool See *overhead pool*.

indirect expense = *indirect cost; manufacturing cost; overhead*.

indirect labor Labor not applicable directly to a product; the cost of such labor. Examples are found in the compensation of janitors, guards, maintenance crews, superintendents, cost accountants. See *indirect cost; direct labor*.

indirect liability 1. An obligation not yet *incurred* but for which responsibility may have to be assumed in the future; as, the possible liability from the premature settlement of a long-term contract.

2. A debt of another, as the result of which an obligation to pay may develop; a *contingent liability*.

indirect material Material not entering directly into a product; the cost of such material. Examples are found in supplies *consumed* in cleaning, oiling, and maintenance generally; replacement of small parts. See *indirect cost; direct material*.

indirect tax A tax which is not borne by the entity on which it is levied, the latter serving merely as a collector from other entities to whom the tax is shifted. Example: a retail sales tax. Such a tax may be shifted forward to consumers by a corresponding increase in sales price or backward to suppliers by a reduction in the price of materials or services purchased. The degree of forward and backward shifts will generally depend on the relative *elasticities* of demand, *q.v.*, and supply, in the affected goods or services. The resulting changes in price may not reflect the whole burden of the tax and they may not be capable of completely separate identification in the prices charged or paid by the entities on which the tax is initially levied. See *direct tax*.

individual 1. A natural person; a human being.
2. (statistics) A unit or element of a *population* or *universe*, or *sample*; an *event*; as, a natural person, a corporation, the toss of a coin, a voucher. The aggregate of individuals making up a *population* or *universe* is conceived as possessing a trait or *characteristic* common to each individual and capable of being measured and expressed in the form of a *number*.

individual level premium method A method for projecting the total cost of an employee's projected retirement benefits by allocating the cost of the retirement benefits in level dollar amounts or as a level percentage of compensation to periods subsequent to entry in the pension plan. With this method, there is no separate measure of past service cost or prior service cost; they are included as part of *normal cost*. See *entry age normal method*.

Individual Retirement Account (IRA) A tax-sheltered retirement plan created by *ERISA* which enables persons not otherwise covered to establish their own individual plan (Sections 219-220). The taxpayer is generally allowed to deduct from gross income annual contributions up to the lesser of 15% of his or her compensation or $1,500. The amounts contributed to an IRA and the income earned thereon are not subject to the income tax until withdrawn by the taxpayer, at which time they are taxed as ordinary income. Special rules govern the investment vehicle to be used, the timing of withdrawals, contributions in excess of deductible limits, and tax-free *rollovers* of funds to and from qualified plans and IRAs.

indorsement without recourse *Uniform Commercial Code*, Section 3-414(1). In the law of negotiable instruments, a *qualified indorsement*, or one that limits the effect of a blank or special indorsement, limiting the liability of the indorser to answer for the default of the person primarily liable. By the use of terms such as "without recourse" the indorser disclaims secondary liability if the instrument is not paid by the party primarily liable.

industrial-accident reserve A reserve set aside by an employer, usually on the basis of a percentage of the industrial payroll, to which payments to injured employees for personal injuries may be charged; it may or may not be accompanied by the setting aside or earmarking of a corresponding amount of assets.

industrial aid bond See *industrial development bond*.

industrial development bond Bonds issued by governmental units, usually not subject to federal income tax, the proceeds of which are used to construct plant facilities for private industrial concerns. Lease payments made by the industrial concern to the governmental unit are used to service the bonds. Such bonds may be in the form of *general obligation bonds* (or *combination bonds* or *revenue bonds*).

Industry Audit Guides A series of small volumes which have been issued since the 1940s by special committees of the *American Institute of Certified Public Accountants (q.v.)*. Each book deals with the auditing procedures and, to a limited extent, the accounting practices relating to the preparation and audit of financial statements of companies in a particular industry. In 1979, the *Financial Accounting Standards Board (q.v.)* decided in principle to assume responsibility for pronouncing upon the distinctive accounting practices of special industries.

industry guide See *audit guide*.

industry ratios Mean or median financial ratios of industries. These ratios serve as bases of comparison for analyses of individual firms. Robert Morris Associates and Dun & Bradstreet are the major publishers of industry ratios.

industry segment A component of an enterprise primarily intended to provide a good or service or a group of related goods or services to unaffiliated customers. Segmentation may also be by geographic areas. It becomes a reportable segment if it satisfies one of the qualifying criteria presented in FASB Statement 14. Also known as "line of business." See *line of business reporting; segmental reporting*.

inequality A relation between two mathematical expressions stating that one is not less than the other. The relation "greater than" is conventionally denoted by the symbol $>$, the open side indicating the greater part. Thus $y > x$ or $4 > 3$ states that the expression on the left is larger than the one on the right; the expression $y < x$ denotes the converse relation. The expression $y > x$ (or $y \geqq x$) denotes that y is greater than or not less than x. The expression $y \geqq x$ means y is greater than or equal to x and is less restrictive than the statement $y > x$, which requires y to be greater than x. Sometimes the two are distinguished by referring to the latter as a "strict inequality." Inequalities represent a more general form of mathematical relation than equations, just as ordinal measures (*ordinal number*) are a more general class than cardinal measures (*cardinal number*). See *measurement*. The relation of inequality may be used to define the notion of equation. Thus, the relations $a \geqq b$ and $b \leqq a$ can be simultaneously true if and only if $a = b$; but the concept of equation or equality cannot be used to define the notion of inequality. Accounting experience confirms the greater generality of inequality and related concepts such as ordinal measures. In cost accounting, for example, it is frequently possible to determine whether the cost of producing a certain item or performing a certain service is increasing or decreasing without being able to determine the precise amount of increase or decrease. Measurements which give expression to such findings are ordinal rather than cardinal in nature. They imply relations of "greater" or "less" without necessarily implying relations of equality. Similar concepts apply to other fields, such as *index number* construction. It may be possible to ascertain whether prices are increasing or decreasing without being able to tell the exact amount of change. If a price index shows a certain value—say, 160—at two different points of time, this does not in itself imply that prices were the same in the two periods; except in unusual circumstances, no meaning can be applied to the notion of equality in interpreting such index numbers. Ordinal indexes are frequently used (or misused), however, in just this fashion. See *index number; measurement*.

inference A judgment or logical conclusion drawn from given assumptions, facts, or other data. A public accountant gives careful consideration to the possible inferences that may be drawn by others from reports he or she has examined or is preparing.

inflation 1. An increase in the general price level of goods and services.
2. Any writeup of asset values.

inflation accounting = *general price level accounting*.

Inflation Accounting Committee, Report of the = *Sandilands Report*.

inflation gain, loss on net monetary items Term used by the *FASB* in its Exposure Draft, "Financial Reporting and Changing Prices" (December 28, 1978), to be used in supplementary financial information to report to a firm's gain in general *purchasing power* during a period of *inflation* from holding net monetary liabilities (more monetary liabilities than assets) or the firm's loss in general purchasing power from holding net monetary assets (more monetary assets than liabilities). The FASB, concerned with the persistence of inflation, did not suggest a term to describe the effects of deflation on a firm's general purchasing power; these are the reverse of the inflation effects: a gain from holding net monetary assets and a loss from holding net monetary liabilities. See *monetary gain, loss; monetary items*.

inflation gains or losses See *holding gains or losses*.

informal record A record that is not a part of the regular bookkeeping system but from which essential or useful information may be derived. Example: a *commitment* listing by a purchasing officer from which may be derived the total of purchase orders issued during a given period, or purchase orders outstanding on a given date.

information See *evidence*.

information economics The study of information in addition to market prices which may affect economic behavior. An important aspect of this research involves the study of information supplied by agents, accountants, and others, for its possible value in dealing with *risk* and *uncertainty*.

information induction A *behavioral accounting* hypothesis which asserts behavioral modification for senders of reports who will try to anticipate reactions of potential recipients and modify their own behavior to influence the behavior of recipients in desired directions. The hypothesis does not refer to doctoring of reports and it distinguishes the part of behavior modification with which it is concerned from that which can occur when a sender acquires information that would cause behavior modification by the sender's part even if the report were not forwarded to any other recipient.

information retrieval The process of retrieving data from a file or storage medium, as in a computer.

information returns (federal income taxes) Information required under the *Internal Reve-*

nue Code and regulations to be furnished by persons who pay income to others. The principal types relate to payments of $600 or more for services rendered if such payments are not shown on Form W-2; dividends and interest in excess of $10; and payments to noncorporate recipients of business rents and royalties of $600 or more. Information returns must also be filed by partnerships, estates, and trusts, including details of revenues and expenses, and distributable shares of net income, if any. Tax-exempt corporations are also required to file annual information returns.

information statistic A statistical version of the information measure which, as developed by Shannon and Wiener, was entirely probabilistic in character. See *information theory*. Also called the Kullback-Leibler statistic, from an extension effected by S. Kullback who was able to show how a very large variety of different statistical methods and approaches could be brought together and unified under this one *statistic*. Subsequently extended by H. Akaike to include both Bayesian and non-Bayesian (classical) statistics. See *Bayes' rule*. Employing the latter rule to choose between two hypotheses H_1 and H_2 on the basis of a sample of observations represented by x, we have

$$P(H_1|x) = \frac{P(x|H_1)P(H_1)}{P(x|H_1)P(H_1) + P(x|H_2)P(H_2)}$$

$$P(H_2|x) = \frac{P(x|H_2)P(H_2)}{P(x|H_1)P(H_1) + P(x|H_2)P(H_2)},$$

where $P(H_i)$ represents *probability*, or, more generally, a *density* associated with H_i, $i = 1, 2$, and $P(x|H_i)$ represents the corresponding *conditional probability* or *density*. In ratio form this gives

$$\frac{P(H_1|x)}{P(H_2|x)} = \frac{P(x|H_1)P(H_1)}{P(x|H_2)P(H_2)}.$$

Taking *logarithms* and transposing terms,

$$\log \frac{P(x|H_1)}{P(x|H_2)} = \log \frac{P(H_1|x)}{P(H_2|x)} - \log \frac{P(H_1)}{P(H_2)}.$$

These expressions are referred to as "log odds ratios." See *information theory*. The expression on the right, referred to as "the weight of evidence," compares the value of the "log odds ratios" with and without the evidence contained in x and shows that the difference is equal to the expression on the left. In fact, setting $p(x) = P(x|H_1)$ and $q(x) = P(x|H_2)$, we can write $p(x) \log p(x)/q(x)$ and define

$$I = \sum_x p(x) \log \frac{p(x)}{q(x)}$$

as the *expected value* of this difference. I, the information statistic is also called the "mean discrimination information" statistic, because it is an *expected value* which summarizes the information in favor of the distribution p relative to q. A further optimization in choosing p on the basis of sample evidence yields the "minimum discrimination information" (= MDI) statistic, in which the resulting minimum $I = I^*$ gives the minimally discriminating power of the evidence in favor of the p distribution relative to the q distribution.

information system 1. Any system for treating *information* or *data*, as in a *file structure*. 2. *Software* associated with retrieval and update of information on a computer.

information theory A branch of communication engineering dealing with the encoding and decoding of signals used to transmit messages, usually in binary (0-1) form. The heart of this theory lies in the number

$$I = \sum_{i=1}^{N} p_i \log \frac{p_i}{q_i},$$

where p_i and q_i represent probabilities (or proportions) of signals sent and received and log (= logarithm to the base 2) is used to reflect the binary (0-1) nature of the signals transmitted. Log p_i/q_i is also called the "log odds ratio" in that p_i/q_i represents the odds in favor of p_i relative to q_i, so that I can be interpreted as the *expected value* of the information received relative to the information sent in terms of their related probabilities (or proportions) for any set of $i = 1, \ldots, N$ messages. Thus I may be used as a measure of message efficiency for a communication channel, a coding device, a decoding device, and so on.

Originally developed by Claude Shannon and Norbert Wiener, the use of information theory has spread beyond communication engineering to a wide variety of fields, such as psychology, economics, and statistics. See *information statistic*. It has also found use in accounting and finance. See *decomposition analysis*.

inheritance tax The term usually applied to a tax assessed by most U.S. states based upon the fair market value of cash or other property received through inheritance. This tax is levied against the recipient, as contrasted to the federal estate tax, which is levied against the estate. The rates of tax, assets exempted (if any), and any automatic exclusions vary from state to state, and usually also vary by the nature of the relationship between the heir and the deceased. Thus in most states a spouse or a child of the deceased is not taxed as heavily as a more distant relative.

in kind See *kind*.

in lieu *adj*. Alternative: as in the expression "in-lieu depreciation" (= *policy* depreciation; see under *depreciation methods*) and "in-lieu taxes" (payments to a governmental unit taking the place of taxes).

input cost Direct and formally allocated indirect variable (and sometimes fixed) costs of activities, functions, and resources devoted to the production of a good or service but excluding administrative, selling, financial, and other expenses relating to general business conduct.

input/output device (computers) Hardware devices used for entering data into a computer and for retrieving and displaying stored data. Typical I/O devices include card readers, card punches, paper tape readers, paper tape punches, line printers, and *CRT* terminals.

input-output statement 1. Any statement (often in *matrix* form) showing movements of quantities from one or more positions or functions to other positions or functions. Examples: Leontief's structural representation of the American economy. Also called an interindustry statement because the values in the cells of the matrix portray flows between industries.
2. A *cost-flow* statement or a *funds-flow statement* may also be put in this form and the same is true for projected flows of traffic or goods moving from origins to destinations.

inquiry An auditing procedure where the form of evidence is a representation by an employee or officer of the audit entity, in response to a specific question by the auditor. Generally, the results of inquiries do not in themselves constitute persuasive *audit evidence* and are usually required to be supported by corroborating evidence.

in rem See *excise tax*.

in short In an adjacent and subordinate column, usually at the left: said of supporting details for which a total appears in any accounting or statistical schedule or table.

insider (Securities and Exchange Act of 1934) A corporate director, officer, or owner of more than 10% of a registered security who acquires knowledge of business through his or her official position. Insiders are prohibited from using such information for their personal gain, and any "insider" profits belong to the corporation.

insolvency 1. Inability or failure to pay debts as they become due. This may occur because the firm is in an *illiquid* state. The term is also used to describe situations in which total liabilities exceed total assets with a negative net worth resulting. More precise usage describes the latter as "bankruptcy" because a firm may be insolvent even in the absence of this situation.

2. The condition of an individual or organization where liabilities exceed the fair and realizable value of the assets available for their settlement (Federal Bankruptcy Law). Note, however, that a firm need not be insolvent in sense 1 even when bankrupt.

inspection (auditing) The act of examining a piece of physical audit *evidence*. See also *statistical quality control*.

Inspector General 1. A federal office created under the Inspector General Act of 1978 which combines investigative and audit functions and which generally reports to the Secretary or Undersecretary of selected federal agencies. This act was prompted by a variety of frauds and other abuses so that, at least for the present, major emphasis has been placed on the "propriety" issues which form one aspect of comprehensive audit. See *audit; Comptroller General*. Only a dozen federal agencies are specified in this law, although other agencies, such as the Department of Defense, have had similar functions for long periods of time preceding the passage of this Act.

2. An officer, especially in the military, who, in common with most auditors, is charged with independent review and appraisal of various management activities. Unlike the Inspectors General of sense 1, who are required to make periodic reports to Congress, these officers in the military rarely make their reports public, and their function is usually regarded as subordinate to members of the general staff or other ranking officers.

installment 1. Any part payment on a debt.

2. One of an agreed series of partial payments on a debt, each of which is specified as to amount and date due, interest often being included.

installment method of accounting A method of recording revenue from an installment sale whereby the gross profit from the sale is *recognized* in any fiscal year in proportion to the portion of the total selling price collected in cash during that year. Example: A piano that cost a dealer $1,600 is sold for $2,400: one-quarter down, the balance to be paid thereafter in equal installments of $30 each. The gross profit is $800 or 33 1/3%, and if $780, including the down payment, is collected during the fiscal year in which the sale is made, the gross profit to be included in that year's revenues will be $800 × 780/2,400, or $260. The same result is, of course, obtained by applying the *gross-profit percentage* to the year's collections (33 1/3% of $780 = $260).

The installment basis contrasts with the *accrual* and *cost-recovery* bases. The accrual basis *recognizes* the full amount of gross profit at the time the sale is recorded. Many retail dealers having installment sales keep their records on the *accrual basis*, especially where the period of payment extends over a period of a year or two. If the *cost-recovery* basis is followed, cash received from the buyer is credited against the cost of the sale until the cost is completely offset; thereafter, any cash received is credited to revenue. This basis may be favored where the likelihood of full payment by the buyer is regarded, for any reason, as uncertain, or where repossession is expected.

Dealers in real or personal property commonly lump together a year's installment sales and costs of sales in order to obtain an overall average gross-profit percentage for that year; then in subsequent years, the same average percentage is applied to the collections on the earlier year's sales to obtain the revenue to be accounted for from such collections.

Where the property in the seller's hands is subject to a mortgage or other lien that is passed on to the buyer, the selling price (and the cost of the sale) does not include the amount of the mortgage or lien. But where the buyer gives back a mortgage or other obligation to the seller, the amount thereof is properly a part of the selling price, subject to realization, as in the case of a contract or note.

A bad debt from an installment sale may be incurred where the cost of the sale exceeds the sum of (a) the collections made to date less the portion thereof accounted for as realized gross profit, and (b) the value of the property, if repossessed, at the time of the repossession, such value having been adjusted downward for the estimated cost of putting the property into resalable condition.

installment sale A sale of real or personal property paid for in a series of equal amounts over a period of weeks or months. The selling price may include a *loading* cost, and a down payment at the time of sale is commonly required. Title may be conveyed with the transfer of the property, subject to a chattel mortgage given to the seller, or subject to lien for the balance of the purchase price; or title may be conveyed to a third person during the payment period. Title may also be passed to the buyer after a certain number of payments have been made, or only following the final payment. See *sale; installment method of accounting*.

Institute of Chartered Accountants in England and Wales Formed in 1880 from the membership of several accountancy bodies founded from 1870 onwards, the Institute of Chartered Accountants in England and Wales is the largest and most influential accountancy body in the British Isles. It examines prospective members, holds an annual Summer School, provides guidance for the information of its members, and publishes a wide range of literature, including two journals, *Accountancy* and *Accounting and Business Research*.

Institute of Chartered Accountants in Scotland Founded in 1854 under the name of the Society of Accountants in Edinburgh, the Institute of Chartered Accountants of Scotland adopted its present name in 1951, when similar societies in Glasgow and Aberdeen amalgamated with the Edinburgh Society. The Institute examines prospective members, publishes committee reports, holds an annual Summer School, issues guidance for the information of members, and, among other things, publishes a journal entitled *The Accountant's Magazine*.

Institute of Internal Auditors An international organization dedicated to the interests of practitioners of internal auditing. Founded in 1941, it issues or sponsors a wide range of publications, including research bulletins and a journal entitled *The Internal Auditor*. The Institute, which has more than 100 affiliated chapters in the United States and other countries, administers the program under which the title *certified internal auditor* is conferred.

institutional advertising Any promotional cost aimed at producing a favorable corporate image or increasing the use of a class of product rather than a particular brand. See *service cost; generic expense*.

institutional buyer Any organization periodically having substantial sums for investment, the principal types being: life insurance companies; educational, charitable, and religious institutions; foundations; commercial and savings banks and organizations; trust companies that have in their possession the funds of individuals and estates; and investment trusts. Life insurance companies are the private sector's largest investors in real-estate mortgages, buy-and-lease financing, corporation bonds, and governmental issues.

institutional investor An organization such as an insurance company, pension fund, or a mutual fund that invests large sums in particular securities.

instrument Any document in writing conferring a right or constituting a contract; examples: stock certificates, bonds, coupons, notes, checks, deeds.

insurable interest A person's interest in or legal relationship with the property of another, such that its damage or destruction would cause him or her pecuniary loss.

insurable value Current replacement cost new, with materials of like kind and quality, less a reasonable deduction for depreciation.

insurance The method whereby those subject to similar hazards contribute to a common fund, out of which any loss sustained by a contributor is paid. The business of assuming the management of such funds is carried on by (a) "stock" companies, i.e., profit corporations; (b) mutual (not-for-profit) companies, whose stockholders insure each other; (c) unincorporated reciprocal organizations, whose members appoint an "attorney-in-fact" as manager to collect premiums in advance, pay losses and expenses, and refund to members any balance remaining at the end of each fiscal year; (d) Lloyd's, an association of underwriters, each underwriter becoming personally liable for the amount of insurance for which he or she subscribes; (e) self-insurers, whose risks are sufficiently numerous and diversified to permit them economically to assume the risks themselves; and (f) governmental organizations established for the purpose of assuming risks, usually when private sector insurance

companies are unable or unwilling to provide the insurance.

insurance fund A fund created for the payment of losses. Sometimes the term is restricted to a person carrying his or her own risks in which case the additions thereto may be based on the premiums which would otherwise be payable to insurance companies, or, more correctly, on a loss factor independently determined for the type of risk involved.

insurance premium The cost to a person of a contract to reimburse him or her for a property or business loss caused by various types of events over which the insured has little or no control; the period covered may range from a year or less to five years. Premium costs are amortized on a straight-line or benefits-received basis over the period of protection. A premium rate is often expressed as "cents percent"—the cost in cents for each $100 of insurance coverage.

insurance register A record of essential facts concerning insurance carried, often including the amounts of premiums expiring in successive accounting periods.

insurance reserve A reserve created on the books of a self-insurer by an appropriation of net income or retained earnings for the purpose of covering fire or other risks. The reserve is appropriated surplus, the preferred practice being to regard losses as operating costs when they occur.

insure To contract with another to assume the financial loss or obligation contingent upon a risk.

intangible (asset) 1. Any "two-dimensional" or "incorporeal" asset; any asset other than cash or real estate; in this sense used by some tax authorities.

2. A *capital asset* having no physical existence, its value being limited by the rights and anticipative benefits that possession

confers upon the owner. See *goodwill; patent; trademark.*

Intangible assets appearing in published financial statements may include goodwill acquired in a purchase of a business, representing the excess of cost of an investment in the partial or total *equity* of another organization over its reported book value at the time of *acquisition.* Patents, copyrights, trademarks, formulas, license franchises, and research-and-development costs are other designations of intangibles of common occurrence, standard practice calling for a disclosure of amortization for those having limited lives.

intangible drilling costs (IDC) (federal income taxes) A term applied to certain expenditures associated with oil, gas, and geothermal resource explorations. Such costs have no salvage value and include the cost of wages, fuel, ground clearing, surveying, and construction of derricks and pipelines incident to the drilling of oil, gas, and geothermal wells. For purposes of federal income taxation, intangible drilling costs may be capitalized or may be expensed currently if so elected. The deduction of IDC expenses may be considered a tax-preference item subject to the *minimum tax* and may be subject to recapture (see *recapture of depreciation*) if the property is disposed of at a gain. Currently expensed IDC are subject to the loss limitation provisions of Section 465.

intangible value The value of an enterprise in its entirety, as a *going concern*, in excess of the value of its net *tangible assets.* Intangible value, arising from a monopoly, secret processes, patents, trademarks, customer goodwill, managerial skill, growth of population, or numerous other possible causes, is often reckoned as the present worth of total earning power in excess of normal return on the value of net tangible assets. See *goodwill; going-concern value.*

integer Any *digit* or any group of digits expressing a *number*; examples: 1; − 24; 63; 762. However, a number containing a fraction, such as 54.25 or 62/7, although a *rational number*, is not an integer.

integer program A *mathematical programming* problem for which only *integer* solutions are acceptable. It may be used to represent a wide variety of nonlinear problems as well as problems in mathematical logic. "Mixed integer programs" extend to cases in which only some of the variables must be integers.

integrated circuit (computers) A *hardware* component consisting of many circuits on a single chip. It replaces discrete components such as transistors, diodes, capacitors, and resistors used in earlier computers. Integrated circuits can be produced at less cost and result in much smaller computers which can operate much faster and use much less power. Decreases in cost of producing integrated circuits represent the primary reason for current decreases in hardware costs.

integration 1. The merger or combination of two separate units as in a *business combination* or *merger.*
2. A concept of taxation which would combine the individual and corporate income-tax structures to avoid or reduce *double taxation.* In its purest form, integration would require income of a corporation to be recognized by shareholders on their individual returns in the year such income is recognized by the corporation, regardless of whether it is distributed. Current variations (in European countries) grant an individual taxpayer credit for the income taxes paid by the corporation on income distributed to individual shareholders. Recipients in turn are required to "gross up" the amount of dividend income received by the amount of tax paid by the corporation.

Another alternative is to allow a deduction to the corporation for dividends paid to individual shareholders.

Inter-American Accounting Association Founded in 1949 as the Inter-American Accounting Conference, it holds congresses every two to three years in different countries of the Americas. Proceedings have been published for most of its conferences, and at each conference the assembled delegations agree on technical recommendations. A full-time Secretariat has been established in Mexico City.

interchangeable part (statistical quality control) Mating or matching components in an assembly which ensure satisfactory functioning even when each component is selected at *random*. Advantages of using interchangeable parts are that it facilitates mass production by eliminating selective assembly, simplifies operations, reduces costs, and helps solve problems of replacement.

intercompany accounts General-ledger records that summarize a specific type of transaction between related or *affiliated companies*. *Intercompany accounts* are usually reciprocal records in the general ledgers of affiliated companies; examples are sales to affiliate and purchases from affiliate, and receivables from affiliate and payables to affiliate. Intercompany accounts are eliminated during the preparation of *consolidated financial statements*. See *intercompany elimination*.

intercompany elimination The subtraction of intercompany investments, receivables, payables, sales, purchases, and other items necessarily omitted in the preparation of *consolidated and group balance sheets* and *income statements*. The principal types of eliminations are: investments in stocks and bonds; advances and current accounts; profit or loss in receivables, inventories, fixed and other assets, valuation accounts, and liabilities; purchases and sales; service, interest, and other income and expense; dividends. It is usually held that eliminations of intercompany gains and losses should be complete, notwithstanding the existence of minority stockholders' interests in subsidiaries; thus, if a parent company owns 60% of the outstanding capital stock of a subsidiary, 100% of the intercompany profit is eliminated from the inventory owned either (a) by the parent or (b) by the subsidiary; in (a), 40% of the inventory profit could be eliminated against the book value of the *minority interest*, or 100% could be absorbed by the majority interest; in (b), 100% would be absorbed by the majority interest.

Where eliminations are numerous and complicated, an *eliminations ledger* may be maintained.

Elimination of intercompany investments in capital stock against the equities shown by the records of the issuing company may give rise to differences that should be distinctively labeled on the balance sheet. The difference between the investment cost and the book equity is in practice variously disposed of. An excess of investment cost has at times been merged in an undisclosed amount with recorded goodwill, added to tangible fixed-asset accounts, shown separately, or subtracted from the combined capital-stock and surplus accounts. An excess of book equity at the date of acquiring control has been merged in an undisclosed amount with "capital surplus," or paid-in surplus, subtracted from tangible fixed-asset accounts, or shown separately. In some instances, both "goodwill from consolidation" and "capital surplus from consolidation" have appeared on the same consolidated balance sheet; in other instances, they have been merged.

Where an excess as to any one subsidiary is substantial (perhaps 20% or more of the investment in that subsidiary), and cannot readily be explained, the subsidiary may not be consolidated; instead, the facts peculiar to that subsidiary can best be displayed in separate financial statements. The excess of investment or book value may be ascribable to an earning power disproportionate to the investment appearing on the subsidiary's books; to the provision of too much or too little depreciation of fixed or intangible assets; or, in general, to asset valuations differing from those on which the controlling company's acquisition has been based. If the cause has been inaccurate bookkeeping procedure, the remedy lies in determining the amount of the excess and correcting it. If the cause has been the earning power of the subsidiary, there can be no objection to adding the subsidiary to the consolidated picture. But if the cause cannot be determined, or if no basis exists for correcting the books of account, the inclusion of the subsidiary with the consolidated group might lead to substantial inaccuracy in interpretation.

If the net excess is one of investment cost, it should not be confused on the consolidated balance sheet with goodwill or another intangible item which bears the label of something acquired in a direct purchase with other assets; it should be designated "excess from consolidation with subsidiaries" or "consolidation excess." This treatment avoids a merging with items usually associated with individual companies. The necessity for such a showing on a consolidated balance sheet has been eliminated in many instances by the amortization of investment cost down to the underlying value reflected in the subsidiary's records.

An excess of book equity at the date of acquisition over investment cost becomes "consolidation surplus." On the consolidated balance sheet, the consolidation excesses should be separated from the consolidation surpluses, in view of the possibility that the former may become a loss and that the latter may ultimately be surplus of the controlling company available for distribution to its stockholders.

Retained earnings on the consolidated balance sheet arising from subsidiary companies is confined to undistributed profits earned since the date of acquisition, without regard to the period prior to that date during which an interest less than controlling may have been owned. Retained earnings applicable to shares acquired after the controlling-interest date is computed only from the date of acquiring such shares.

Shares of the controlling company's capital stock owned by a subsidiary before the date of acquisition may be treated as the equivalent of treasury stock purchased on that date. Any subsequent acquisition or sale by a subsidiary may be treated in the consolidated statements as though it had been the act of the controlling company.

Elimination in consolidation of intercompany investments in obligations against the accumulated obligations shown by the books of the issuing company gives rise to the adjustment of the consolidation excess or surplus or of current loss and gain as the circumstances may require. Any premium or discount at the date of acquisition arising from the difference between the investment cost and the accumulated obligation on the books of the issuer (i.e., face amount less any unamortized discount, plus any accumulated premium to be paid on retirement) is combined with the consolidation excess arising from the subsidiary affected; any differences from acquisitions thereafter may be regarded as current gains or losses.

See *consolidation policy; eliminations ledger*.

intercompany profit Book profit representing the excess of charges by one related company to another for services rendered or goods sold over and above their cost to the related group conceived as a unit. Under standard procedures in the preparation of consolidated statements, intercompany profits are eliminated in their entirety regardless of minority holdings, in order that only profits on sales and services to the public may be shown as having been realized.

intercompany transactions Economic exchanges of goods or services between related or *affiliated companies*.

interdepartmental profit The excess over costs of goods or services charged by one division to another within the same *economic unit*; under standard procedures, they are eliminated in the final accounting, since no profit is realized except through sales to outsiders.

interest 1. The service charge for the use of money or capital, paid at agreed intervals by the user, commonly expressed as an annual percentage of outstanding principal.
2. The return on capital investment.
3. A portion of the *equity* in a business enterprise, expressed as a fraction or in terms of dollars invested.

interest, imputed See *imputed interest*.

interest charged to construction See *interest on investment*.

interest coverage ratio Earnings before interest and taxes for a given reporting period divided by the period's interest payments; a measure of a firm's ability to satisfy its annual borrowing cost from current operations. Also called *times-interest-earned ratio*.

interest formulas A. *Compounding of interest*: Various interest formulas are developed on the basis of interest compounding. Interest is said to be "compounded" if at the end of each period the interest accrued (but not paid or received) during the period is added to the principal in computing the interest in the next period. This is in contrast to "simple" interest where interest is always computed only on the principal regardless of whether there is accrued interest.

B. *Future value of 1*: At an annual interest rate of 10% ($i = .1$), $1,000 now earns interest of $100 at the end of the first year. If the interest is not paid at that time, it is added to the $1,000 principal so that the interest in the second year is based on $1,100, yielding $110 interest at 10%. Thus, at the end of the second year, the $1,000 principal grows to $1,210. The third-year interest is then 10% of $1,210 or $121, and the sum of the principal and interest grows to $1,331 at the end of the third year. Under simple interest, the sum of the principal and interest is $1,300 at the end of the third year since interest is $100 a year.

Thus, generally speaking, $1 deposited now at the interest rate i (stated in fractions such as $i = .1$) grows to $1 + i$ dollars at the end of the first year. In the second year, i is applied to the new balance amounting to $1 + i$, yielding the interest of $(1 + i)i$ dollars. Together with the old balance, the deposit grows to $(1 + i) + (1+i)i = (1+i)^2$ dollars at the end of the second year. Generally, $1 grows to $(1 + i)^n$ dollars in n years if the interest rate is i per year and compounded annually. This is called the *future value (FV)* of 1 or *compounded amount of 1*, which is

$$\text{FV of 1 in } n \text{ periods} = (1 + i)^n. \qquad (1)$$

While the future value has been tabulated in many finance tables, it can easily be computed with a calculator by a repeated multiplication of $1 + i$.

C. *Present value of 1*: The reciprocal of future value of 1 in n periods is called the *present value (PV)* of 1 n periods hence. For example, since the future value of 1 three years from now at 10% interest rate compounded annually is 1.331 ($= 1.1 \times 1.1 \times 1.1$), the present value of 1 is $1/1.331 = .75131....$ Hence, $1,000 to be received 3 years from now is worth $751.31 ($= $1,000 \times .75131$) presently. Thus, $751.31 deposited now at 10% interest will grow to $1,000 in three years, namely to $826.45 (= $751.31 × 1.1) at the end of the first year, to $909.09 (= $826.45 × 1.1) at the end of the second year, and to $1,000 (= $909.09 × 1.1) at the end of the third year.

Therefore, generally, the present value (PV) of 1 to be received n periods hence is:

PV of 1 n periods hence = $1/(1 + i)^n$.   (2)

This may also be computed easily by a calculator with repeated division of 1 using $1 + i$ as the divisor.

D. *Present value of perpetuity*: In financial calculations, it often becomes necessary to compute the present (or future) value of not a single payment, as above, but a series of payments that are to occur at the end of each period for n periods. The present value of a series of payments may be computed by taking the present value of each payment using (2) and adding the results together. The same is true with future values. However, if the payment in each period is the same for all n periods, there is a simpler approach to computing the present value.

To understand the formula, it is convenient to consider the present value of 1 per period in "perpetuity." A perpetuity is a series of periodic payments that continue forever, with its first payment occurring one period from now. If the interest rate is 10% a year, a right to receive $1 in perpetuity is worth $10. This is because $10 deposited at a bank which pays 10% interest can pay $1 at the end of a period and still restore the original principal of $10 to be ready for the next period, and the process can be repeated indefinitely. Thus:

PV of 1 per period in perpetuity = $1/i$.   (3)

E. *Present value of annuity*: An annuity is a series of periodic payments that continue for a given length of time. The present value of 1 per period for n periods with the first payment starting one period from now is given by:

PV of 1 per period for n periods
= $1/i - 1/i(1 + i)^n$.   (4)

Note that the first term $(1/i)$ is the present value of a perpetuity and the second term $(1/i(1 + i)^n)$ is the present value of a perpetuity discounted further for n periods. This makes sense because an annuity is the difference between two perpetuities, one whose payment starts one period from now and another whose payment starts $n + 1$ periods from now. The former is an ordinary perpetuity (whose present value is $1/i$) and the latter is a perpetuity deferred for n periods (whose present value is $1/i$ discounted for n periods, namely $1/i$ multiplied by PV of 1 given in (2) above). Thus, to compute the present value of an annuity by a calculator, first compute the present value of a perpetuity by $1/i$ and reduce it by a fraction $1/(1 + i)^n$ which, as stated before, can be easily derived by repeated division of 1 by 1 + i. For example, the present value of 1 per period for 3 periods at an interest rate of 10% per period is equal to 10 (= $1/.1$) reduced by a fraction $1/(1.1 × 1.1 × 1.1) = .75131$ or 75.131%, which comes to 2.4869. This result may be verified by computing the present value of each of the three payments (the first payment of 1 having the present value of .90909; the second, .82645; and the third, .75131) and adding them together.

F. *Capital recovery factor*: The reciprocal formula (4) for present value of annuity is called the "capital recovery factor," namely:

Capital Recovery Factor
= $i/[1 - 1/(1 + i)^n]$.   (5)

It gives the constant amount of annual payments needed to retire a loan of 1 (or recover the original investment of 1) in n periods at interest rate i.

G. *Future value of annuity*: The value of an annuity may be determined not in terms of its value at its inception (present value) but at its termination (future value). The future value of 1 per period for n periods is given as:

FV of 1 per period for n periods

$$= (1 + i)^n/i - 1/i. \qquad (6)$$

This formula can also be readily understood if viewed as the difference in values of two perpetuities, one which was initiated n periods ago and another which was just initiated and whose first payment is to start one period from now. The former perpetuity was worth $1/i$ when it was installed n periods ago, hence its worth now is $1/i$ times $(1 + i)^n$ using the future value formula in (1). The latter perpetuity is worth $1/i$. Hence, the difference is the future value of the annuity, or the value of the annuity at its termination. A computation of the future value of an annuity by a calculator is likewise a simple matter, calling for an adjustment of $1/i$ by the future value of 1 which can be computed by repeated multiplication of $1 + i$. For example, to compute the future value of 1 per period for 3 periods at 10% interest, the present value of a perpetuity $(1/.1 = 10)$ is adjusted by multiplying it by the future value of 1 three periods hence, which is $1.1 \times 1.1 \times 1.1 = 1.331$, yielding 13.31. This minus the present value of a perpetuity $(1/.1 = 10)$ gives 3.31 as the future value of the \$1 annuity. The result may be verified by adding the future value of each of the three payments. That is, the first payment, which occurred two years ago, is worth $1.1 \times 1.1 = 1.21$; the second payment, which occurred a year ago, is worth 1.1; and the third payment, which occurred just now, is worth 1; the three summing to 3.31, as computed above.

H. *Sinking-fund factor*: The reciprocal of the formula (6) for the future value of annuity is called the "sinking-fund factor," namely:

Sinking-Fund Factor $= i/[(1 + i)^n - 1]. \quad (7)$

It gives the constant amount of annual payments necessary to accumulate to \$1 at the end of n periods. (See *sinking fund*.)

I. *Annuity in advance*: In the above annuity, each payment occurs at the end of the period, hence it is called an "annuity in arrears." If each payment is to occur at the beginning of the period, it is called an "annuity in advance," whose first payment starts now with the last payment at the beginning of the last period. The present value of an annuity in advance is, therefore, equal to 1 plus the present value of an annuity in arrears with one less period. Thus,

PV of 1 per period (at beginning) for n periods

$$= 1 + 1/i - 1/i(1 + i)^{n-1}. \qquad (8)$$

Similarly, the future value of an annuity in advance is equal to the future value of an annuity in arrears with $n + 1$ periods but without the last payment of 1. Thus,

FV of 1 per period (at beginning) for n periods

$$= (1 + i)^{n+1} - 1/i - 1. \qquad (9)$$

J. *Use of finance calculators*: Sometimes, it is necessary to determine the i that yields a given PV or FV and a given n or to calculate the n that yields a given PV or FV and a given i. To derive such a solution, a trial-and-error method may be used, guessing a solution and trying the result to see whether the result overshoots or undershoots the target. The solution is then adjusted accordingly. However, a calculator with finance keys (marked $[n]$, $[i\%]$, [PMT], [PV], and [FV], where the interest rate is given in percentage and not in fraction) can do the iterative computation automatically. Keying in the values of any three (or four) of n, i, PMT (periodic payment), PV, or FV and pressing the key for the unknown yields a solution that satisfies:

$$PV = FV/(1 + i)^n$$
$$+ PMT[1/i - 1/i(1 + i)^n], \qquad (10)$$

where the value of an unspecified variable is

set equal to zero before the iteration takes place.

K. *Internal (DCF) rate of return*: Quite often, a need arises, as in connection with capital budgeting and evaluation of cash flows from a project, to compute the interest rate at which the present value of a series of even or uneven payments becomes equal to zero. Such an interest rate (called the *internal rate of return* or the *discounted cash-flow (DCF) rate of return*) can be computed using a computer or a calculator with a special facility to handle the iterative process. In its absence, a trial-and-error method may be applied using an ordinary calculator.

Suppose a project requires an investment of $10 now but is expected to yield $6 at the end of the first year and $7 at the end of the second year. To obtain the interest rate at which the present value of the cash flows from the project is zero, an initial guess for the rate is obtained by summing all cash flows ($-10 + 6 + 7 = 3$), dividing it by the number of years ($3/2 = 1.5$), and further dividing the result by the initial investment ($1.5/10 = .15$ or 15%). Using this rate, $10 grows to $11.5 at the end of the first year, out of which $6 is recovered, leaving $5.5 outstanding. This grows to $6.325 at the end of the second year at which $7 is recovered, or an overrecovery of $.675. Hence, a higher interest rate is indicated. Revising the rate to, say, 20% and recomputing the future value shows an underrecovery of $.20. The amounts of over- and underrecovery suggest that a breakeven point may lie at (20% $-$ 15%) $\times$ $.20/($.20 + $.675) = 1.15\% below the last number tried, that is, 20% $-$ 1.15% $= 18.85\%$. At this rate, $10 grows to $11.885 which, after a recovery of $6, leaves $5.885; which then grows to $6.994 or an amount approximately equal to the $7 recovery. Hence, 18.85% is the required solution.

This approach makes use of the fact that if the present value of a series of cash flows becomes zero at some interest rate, its future value must also be zero at that rate, and vice versa.

L. *Multiple internal (DCF) rates of return*: In *capital budgeting*, the present value of cash flows associated with a project may become zero at more than one interest rate. Each such rate is an *internal (or DCF) rate of return*. The number of distinct internal rates of return cannot exceed the number of sign changes in cash flows of the project. Multiplicity of IRRs occurs when the project serves as a net source of funds as well as a net uses of funds for at least part of its life.

For example, if an investment of $100 now yields $250 at the end of year 1 but requires an additional investment of $156 at the end of year 2 to liquidate the investment in a way that meets an environmental requirement, the entire cash-flow series from the project is $-100, 250, -156$. This series has two IRRs, 20% and 30%. To verify, at 20% the original cash flow of $-$100 grows to $-$120 in one year. Together with a recovery of $250, the balance becomes $+$130, which grows to $+$156 in one year. This is exactly equal to the amount that must be paid at the end of year 2. Hence, 20% is an IRR. Similarly, at 30%, $-$100 grows to $-$130, and after a recovery of $250, the balance becomes $+$120. This grows to $+$156 in one year, which again is equal to the amount that must be paid at the end of year 2. Hence, 30% is also an IRR.

The multiple IRR ambiguity can be neatly resolved if the interest rate i that is applicable during the financing period is specified. In the above example, year 1 is an investment period and year 2 is a financing period, since the outstanding cash balance from the project is negative (investment) during year 1 and positive (financing) in year 2. Suppose that i is 10%. Then, $-$156 at the end of year 2 is equivalent to $-$156/1.1 $=$ $-$142 at the end of year 1. Hence, out of the recovery of $250, if $142 is reserved, the payment in year 2 can be taken care of. This leaves $108 as the proceeds from investing $100 for 1 year, that is, the IRR r is 8%. Similarly, if i is 15%, $-$156/1.15 = -136; hence $136 must be reserved out of the $250 recovery in year 1, leaving $114. Hence, r is 14%.

This means that if the company values the borrowing (financing) opportunity in year 2 to be worth 15%, the investment return in year 1 is 14%, while if the borrowing opportunity presented by the project is worth only 10%, the investment return is only 8%.

Theoretically, no matter what the cash-flow series may be, and no matter how many IRRs the series may have, r is determined uniquely for any given i, and, conversely, i is determined uniquely for any given r. Thus, the use of a financing rate i is the best way of resolving the multiple IRR ambiguity.

In order to solve for r for any given cash-flow series and a given i, a trial-and-error method will be necessary, in general, starting with an initial guess of r and adjusting it according to the balance at the project termination that the r generates. Under this approach, the outstanding cash balance is carried to the next period at rate r if the balance is negative (investment) or at rate i if the balance is positive (financing). If the cash balance at the project termination computed in this way is positive, r should be increased, while if it is negative, r should be decreased.

M. *Effective interest rate*: Interest rate is normally stated at an annual rate, unless it is specifically said to be a semiannual, quarterly, monthly or daily rate. Compounding period is also normally a year, except when it is specifically stated to be semiannual, quarterly, monthly, daily, or continuous (see below) compounding.

When the compounding period differs from a year while the interest rate is stated on an annual basis, there is a discrepancy between a "nominal" interest rate and an "effective" interest rate. A 10% a year compounded semiannually means that the interest rate is nominally 10% a year but effectively 10.25% a year because it is in effect a 5% interest per six months compounded twice a year, or $1.05 \times 1.05 = 1.1025$, which means 10.25% interest.

The effective interest rate r for a nominal annual interest rate i compounded m times a year is given by:

$$r = (1 + i/m)^m - 1. \qquad (11)$$

As m increases, r increases. For example, for $i = 10\%$, $r = 10.25\%$ for semiannual compounding ($m = 2$) as derived above; $r = 10.38\%$ for quarterly compounding ($m = 4$); $r = 10.47\%$ for monthly compounding ($m = 12$); $r = 10.516\%$ for daily compounding ($m = 365$); beyond this r rarely grows much as m becomes larger. In fact, as m approaches to infinity, r converges to r^*, which is given by:

$$r^* = e^i - 1. \qquad (12)$$

Here, e is a constant given by 2.71828 .... For example, if $i = .1$, then $r^* = e^{.1} - 1 = 1.10517 - 1 = .10517$ or 10.517%. This r^* is called the effective interest rate under "continuous" compounding when the nominal interest is 10% a year.

The computation of e^i and r^* can be carried out in many scientific calculators. However, even without them, they can be approximated reasonably well by the following formula if i is not too large:

$$e^i = (2 + i)/(2 - i) \qquad (13)$$

and

$$r^* = e^i - 1 = i/(1 - i/2). \qquad (14)$$

Namely, the effective interest rate is the nominal interest i on a borrowing of 1 from which a half-year interest is taken out at the time of borrowing $(1 - i/2)$. For $i = 10\%$, the above formula yields $r^* = 10.526\%$ while the true $r^* = 10.517\%$. For $i = 20\%$, the above formula yields $r^* = 22.222\%$ while the true $r^* = 22.14\%$.

N. *Continuous cash flows*: In capital budgeting, cash flows from a project are often assumed to occur only at the end of each year. While this may be acceptable as an approximation, in some situations more precise computations may become necessary since cash flows do occur monthly, weekly, or daily. In such cases, interest formulas under continuous compounding offer a useful means of computing the present or future values of cash flows.

Interest formulas under continuous compounding are very similar to those discussed above under periodic (or discrete) compounding, with the only difference being that e^{in} is substituted for $(1 + i)^n$. Thus:

$$\text{FV of 1 in } n \text{ periods} = e^{in}, \qquad (15)$$

$$\text{PV of 1 } n \text{ periods hence} = 1/e^{in}, \qquad (16)$$

PV of 1 per period (throughout) for n periods
$$= 1/i - 1/[ie^{in}], \qquad (17)$$

FV of 1 per period (throughout) for n periods
$$= e^{in}/i - 1/i. \qquad (18)$$

Note that the i in formulas (15)-(18) is a nominal interest rate under continuous compounding and its effective rate is higher as given in (12).

The formulas (17) and (18) are for cases where cash flows occur evenly throughout each period at the rate of 1 per period. There is no need to distinguish "annuities in arrears" and "annuities in advance" in the case of continuous annuities. Thus, for example, the present value of 1 per period for 3 periods when cash flows are distributed evenly throughout the year under an interest rate of 10% compounded continuously is, from (17), $1/.1 - 1/.1 \times 1.34986 \ (= e^{.1 \times 3}) = 2.5918$.

To make the result comparable to a discrete cash-flow case computed in Section E above, the use of a rate under continuous compounding that effectively yields 10% a year is necessary so that the same effective rate is used in both cases. Solving (12) for i when $r^* = .1$ gives $i = .09531$ (or $i = .09524$ if the approximation formula (13) is used, solving $1 + r^* = 1.1 = (2 + i)/(2 - i)$). Using $i = .09531$ in (17) gives the present value $= 1/.09531 - 1/(.09531 \times 1.331) = 2.6092$ as compared with the 2.4869 obtained in Section E, an increase of approximately 5% when cash flows are assumed to occur evenly throughout the year instead of at the end of the year.

Such a difference can swing a capital budget decision in some cases; hence continuous compounding formulas can be recommended in many business situations.

interest on construction See *interest on investment; capitalization of interest.*

interest on investment 1. The return earned on an investment.

2. The return that should be earned on an investment as an *opportunity cost.*

3. The annual contractual charge for funds borrowed to help finance an investment.

FASB Statement 34 issued in October 1979 now requires capitalizing charges in category (3) and assigning them to assets constructed by an enterprise either for its own use or for lease or sale to others. Such charges are restricted to borrowed funds. *Imputed interest on equity* (in *net worth*) account is not included (as is the practice in some utilities) and the amounts capitalized cannot exceed the interest liability accrued during the period adjusted for amortization of *discount* or *premium*. Such capitalization is not permitted for inventories or other such working-capital items but is restricted to assets, such as capital facilities construction, that require a period of time to get them ready for their intended use. Capitalization ceases when the asset is ready for use, at which time further interest expense is treated as a period cost or charge. Amounts to be capitalized are not restricted to funds specifically borrowed for the assets in question. A weighted average of the rates on other borrowing is also applied—except for clearly unrelated borrowing, such as borrowing by a subsidiary for construction of a facility on its own account. The objective is to capitalize interest cost which could have been avoided not only from additional borrowing but also as a result of inability to liquidate existing obligations.

Cost Accounting Standard 414 of the *Cost Accounting Standards Board* also allows imputed interest on facilities (but not on working-capital items) used to support work on individual defense contracts. The investment base is the historical net book cost of the contractor's facilities and the rate used is determined periodically by the Secretary of the Treasury pursuant to Public Law 92-41. It is applied to the full net cost of the facility without reference to the financial structure of the enterprise. CAS 417 extends this to the cost of capital assets constructed, fabricated, or developed for the contractor's own use.

interest rate The price paid per unit of money borrowed per year, or other unit of time, usually expressed as a percentage.

interest rate risk The *risk* of change in the market value of a security, usually bonds, due to changes in interest rates. See *bond valuation*. Distinguished from *purchasing power risk* and *financial risk*.

interference (statistical quality control) See *tolerance*.

interfund accounts (governmental accounting) Accounts for interfund transactions. See *interfund transfer*.

interfund transfer The transfer of money or other asset or of a liability from one *fund* to another.

intergovernmental revenue Revenue obtained from other governments, such as *grants*, shared revenues, and *entitlements*.

interim *adj*. Occurring between major, fixed, or prominent dates: said of a trustee's report during a period of administration, of financial statements covering less than a full fiscal year, or of any statement for less than the customary reporting period.

interim audit 1. That portion of an *audit* (*1*) conducted while the *accounting period* to be covered by the completed audit is still in progress.
2. An audit of an *interim* period or partial fiscal year.

interim closing Any *closing* of the books other than at the end of a fiscal year, not involving the elimination of income and expense accounts.

interim dividend Any one or more dividends declared during a fiscal year, often quarterly and before earnings are known, as contrasted with a *year-end dividend* declared after the year's net income has been determined.

interim financial information Financial information issued for periods of less than a year. See *interim report*.

interim financial statements *Financial statements* issued for periods of less than one year. See *interim financial information; interim report*.

interim period See *interim*.

interim report A report at any date other than the end of a fiscal year; example: a brief report of a corporation in which profits for the quarter or year to date are announced. The report usually contains a warning that a number of contingencies attach to the figures it contains. Many quarterly reports of corporations disclose only sales, net income, and a few other items, varying in character.

interim statement A statement prepared as at any date, or for a period within a fiscal year or other regular reporting period.

internal accounting See *management accounting*.

internal accounting control Those elements of *internal controls* designed to give management reasonable assurance that assets are safeguarded from unauthorized use or disposition and that financial records are sufficient for the preparation of reliable *financial statements*. (See *internal control; evaluation of internal control*.)

internal audit(-ing) *Audit* within an organization by its own staff. For accounting or accountability types of audits some degree of *independence* and *professional* preparation is required to ensure *objectivity* in the *audit reviews* and *appraisals*. These requirements may be minimal when only routine clerical operations are involved, as in the activity of preauditing *vouchers* that may form part of a system of *internal check*. The requirements of professional preparation and independence may also be extremely high and involve a variety of disciplines when full-scale comprehensive audits are to be undertaken. See *audit (4B)*. To reenforce its independence the activity of internal audit may report directly to a committee such as the *audit committee* of the board of directors in order to help committee members discharge their responsibilities for appraising management and ensuring that all requirements for public and private accountability are met. In most organizations, the internal audit function will occupy a status in between comprehensive audit and clerical status with a major respon-

sibility for relatively independent appraisals involving reviews of the effectiveness of records, controls, and operations within the employing organization where the internal audit function serves as a protective and constructive service to management. This includes activities such as (a) verification and appraisal of the reliability of *accounting records* and *statistical* data; (b) ascertainment that assets of all kinds, both those on hand and those disposed of, are safeguarded and have been accurately and fully accounted for, and that normal accounting processes provide information that discloses losses and wasteful practices; (c) *compliance auditing*, which involves a determination that management-prescribed plans, policies, and procedures are being complied with by operating units. This may extend to the reporting of observations with recommendations for improvement in the various sectors of the business, in which case extended scope or comprehensive audits may become a part of the internal auditing function.

In the majority of business organizations, the internal audit activity is first concerned with the verification of completed financial transactions and records. Using post-transaction verification procedures as base, the internal auditor proceeds to examine and appraise related management policies and plans and records and procedures in terms of their adequacy and effectiveness. An important part of the internal auditor's activities is the review and appraisal of accounting personnel performance under established policies and procedures. *External auditors*, especially CPAs concerned with certification of financial statements, will generally limit the scope of their own reviews when they can rely on adequately functioning internal audit activities. An important aspect of their review then involves an appraisal of the performance of the internal audit function in the development, maintenance, and appraisal of adequate *internal checks* as a part of the process for preventing or early discovery of *fraud* and other improprieties. In the case of broad scope or comprehensive audit, the internal audit function extends beyond the system of *internal check* and includes review and appraisal of the system of *internal control* as well as other aspects of an organization's activities. An evolution in this direction is resulting from events such as enactment of the *Foreign Corrupt Practices Act* together with the SEC requirement that management must now make a statement as to the adequacy of its internal control system in a form that will permit review and appraisal as part of the external audit process.

internal auditor One responsible for the conduct of *internal audit*.

Internal Auditor, The See *accounting journals*.

internal check The design of transaction flows that provide effective organization and operation and protection against fraud or other unauthorized transactions. A principal feature is the allocation of organizational responsibility in such a manner that no single individual or group has exclusive control over any one transaction or group of transactions, each transaction being cross-checked or cross-controlled through the normal functioning of another individual or group. Effective internal check is so devised that a transaction can be consummated only through prescribed operating procedures, of which the mechanism of internal check is invariably an integral part. The term should not be confused with the post-transaction, staff function of *internal auditing* or with overall *internal control*, of which internal check is but an element.

The separation of responsibility for custody and accounting is an essential of internal check which may be best understood by citing several examples taken from practice:

Example 1. The purchasing function in the *W* Company is confined to the responsibility for placing orders and determining prices. Vendors' invoices first go to the voucher-accounting unit to be compared for agreement with the purchase order and with the receiving report from the receiving unit, the latter having neither purchasing nor accounting supervision. Upon finding all in order, the voucher unit prepares a disbursement check. The treasury division, after finding supporting documents in order, indicates final approval by placing a signature on the disbursement check.

Example 2. The receipt, custody, and deposit of the incoming cash of *W* Company are functions of the cashier, whose unit is a part of the treasurer's office and who reports the amount and nature of each item, such as the details of collections from customers, to the accounting unit, where records of total cash in banks and of detailed accounts receivable are maintained.

Example 3. Although the depositing of *W* Company's receipts and the making of disbursements are the responsibility of the cashier, maintenance of the record of cash balance is part of the accounting function. The reconciliation of bank statements, which acts as an internal check on both the cashier and the accounting functions, is assigned to a unit which has no authority or responsibility for either handling or accounting for cash.

These examples illustrate the widely observed principle of internal check: the separation of the responsibility of accounting from that of custody.

Internal check is a deterrent to fraud; a fully developed scheme of internal check makes it difficult for a defaulter to abstract funds or other assets for which he or she is responsible and at the same time cover up manipulations by entering corresponding amounts in the accounting records. As long as accounting and custody are separated, fraud can be completely concealed only through collusion between employees responsible for each of these functions.

Carefully designed internal checks also yield advantages because of the relative efficiency of a specialized operation. An employee preparing disbursement checks continuously tends to become highly efficient in that single operation. If he or she is replaced, a new employee may be readily trained because of the limited part of the work which is comprised in the specialized job.

There is sometimes a tendency to treat certain elements of internal check as axiomatic, and to claim that they must be invariably followed without regard to the conditions surrounding a particular situation. The full development of this notion easily results in overelaboration of records and in a too costly operation. Standards of internal check, particularly the separation of custody and accounting, should be considered as guides to be followed within practicable limits.

Various considerations may dictate a deviation from standards, and the resultant exposure to possible fraud should be recognized and compensated for in other ways, as by more frequent or more comprehensive verification through *internal audit*.

Internal check is so much a part of the organization and the procedures of most businesses that the elements of it may be overlooked. These must always be recognized and given consideration in establishing new procedures and in the appraisal of procedures in use.

internal control The general methodology by which management is carried on within an organization; also, any of the numerous devices for directing an operation or operations generally.

Internal control, a management function, is a basic factor operating in one form or another in the administration of every organization, business or otherwise. Although sometimes identified with the administrative organism itself, it is better characterized as the nervous system that activates overall operating policies and keeps them within practicable performance ranges. A particular system of internal control, notwithstanding its superficial resemblance to common patterns of organization and management, is usually unique in detail, having developed around individuals with varying authorities and capacities of supervision and with varying abilities to delegate or assume authority. In a corporation, internal control commences with the institution and enforcement of top policies established by the board of directors and continues down through the organizational structure, taking form in the development and operation of management policies, administrative regulations, manuals, directives, and decisions; internal auditing; internal check; reporting; employee training and participation. A suggestions plan, for example, is of importance to the scheme of control existing in many organizations. In general, well-designed and carefully operated internal control is said to exist where an organization runs smoothly, economically, and in conformity with top-policy objectives.

An important element in maintaining internal controls is provided in the work of the *internal auditor*. Although the presence of such an auditor may and often does act as a deterrent to departures from required practices, the aim is to neither deter nor enforce, but to investigate and comment. This gives the internal auditor a quasi-independent, professional status and tends to develop and maintain his or her capacity as an unbiased observer and reporter on whom management and the board of directors, including its audit committee, can depend for information concerning the functioning of internal control. Originally the duties of the internal auditor were confined to examinations of the correctness of accounts; in recent years, the field has extended to the examination of all internal controls, often not involving the accounts, and this evolution is likely to be accelerated with passage of the *Foreign Corrupt Practices Act* and subsequent *SEC* regulations; see *internal audit* and the concept of comprehensive audit that extends audit even to appraising the *efficiency* and *effectiveness* of management at different levels. See *audit*.

Policies, administrative directives, and business behavior given life and maintained by internal controls are of three sorts: (1) the formal types, expressed in resolutions of the board of directors, regulations such as an office or accounting manual, or written instructions covering limited activities; (2) the informal type, within the framework of the formal type and given effect by oral directions, such as procedural instructions by a supervisor; and (3) the implicit type—operating habits and standards, unwritten and unspoken, yet nonetheless common to an industry, community, form of organization, or business generally, or accepted human conduct presumably understood and observed by all as a matter of course. The operating quality of any organization is influenced as much by implicit policies and standards as by the explicit types. See *policy; corporate action; administration; administrative action; decision*.

Internal control does not end with the testing of conformance to policies and operating standards but extends to practical operations involving individuals or group decisions or actions that, intentionally or otherwise, are within the discretion of the individual and are covered neither by rule nor convention—as, a determination based on individual judgment to deny credit to a customer. The general characteristics usually attaching to an operating *decision* are its dependence on individual discretion and its freedom from appraisal, at the time it is made, as to its rightness or wrongness. After being put into effect, decisions may be tested on a postaction basis in the normal course of operation of the internal controls.

In December 1977, Congress enacted the Foreign Corrupt Practices Act of 1977, Title I, PL 95-213. Section (102)(2) requires

> Every issuer of a class of securities registered [under the Securities and Exchange Act of 1934] to devise and maintain a system of internal accounting controls sufficient to provide reasonable [sic] assurances that
> (i) transactions are executed in accordance with management's general or specific authorization;
> (ii) transactions are recorded as necessary (a) to permit preparation of financial statements in conformity with generally accepted accounting principles or any other criteria applicable to such statements, and (b) to maintain accountability for assets;
> (iii) access to assets is permitted only in accordance with management's general or specific authorization; and
> (iv) the recorded accountability for assets is compared with the existing assets at reasonable intervals and appropriate action is taken with respect to any differences.

The last of these internal accounting control provisions is codified in Section 13(b)(2)(B) of the Securities and Exchange Act of 1934, 15 U.S.C. 78m(b)(2)(B). These requirements are also reflected in *SAS* Section 320, which seeks to provide guidance for auditor examination of systems of internal control as required under generally accepted auditing standards. Revisions in one or both documents may be expected. For the present, however, distinctions are being attempted between administrative controls and internal accounting controls which are akin to those previously made between *internal check* and *internal control*. There is also an effort to require management representation of the adequacy of internal controls with auditor verification and attestation in a manner analogous to the forms used in auditing financial statements. Evolution toward the ideas and practices of comprehensive audit, however, may set these distinctions aside in favor of auditor evaluation of *effectiveness* and *efficiency* of management control systems. See discussion under *audit*.

internal documents Documents within an accounting system which are prepared and retained within the organization without ever going to an outside party such as a customer or a vendor. Examples of internal documents include duplicate sales invoices, employees' time reports, and inventory receiving reports. Internal documents are generally not considered as persuasive as *external documents* for auditing *evidence*.

internal rate of return (IRR) The rate of interest (return) which equates the initial investment in a project, program, etc., with the present value of future cash flows which are expected to be generated by that project, program, etc.; the maximum capital costs which can be incurred by a firm, profit center, project, etc., without suffering a decrease in profitability. This measure is an alternative to the *net present value* (discounted cash-flow) criterion, which assumes some target rate of return. Although IRR has some popular appeal, it has been criticized for several deficiencies. Among these are the following: (1) the method assumes (often falsely) that the reinvestment rate of return is constant when evaluating projects of unequal length; (2) multiple yields (rates of return) can be computed for a single project; and (3) rankings of projects are inconsistent with a *net present value* criterion under certain cases of capital rationing and mutually exclusive alternative

projects (investments). See *discounted cash-flow method*; *present value; implicit cost (2)*. See also *interest formulas* for a method of computing internal rate of return.

internal reporting The supplying of operating data and other information by one person or unit to another within an organization; as, monthly financial statements prepared by a controller; feasibility reports on proposals for fixed-asset replacements; unit-cost determinations supplied by a cost accountant; purchase orders, expense reports, receiving and shipping notices, collection details, daily cash statements, and other data on recurrent organizational activities that others have an interest in controlling or being guided by.

Internal Revenue Code A codification of federal tax law, first adopted in 1939, to unify some 17 revenue acts which had provided the legal basis of taxation from 1913 to 1939. Revenue acts thereafter were required only to add, amend, or delete specific provisions. The 1939 Code as revised was reorganized into the present Internal Revenue Code of 1954, which has subsequently been amended almost yearly, including major revisions.

Internal Revenue Service An agency of the U.S. Treasury Department responsible for administering the *Internal Revenue Code*.

internal service fund (governmental accounting) A *fund* established to finance and account for services and commodities furnished by a designated department or agency to other departments and agencies. Amounts expended are restored either from operating earnings or by transfers from other funds, so that the original fund capital is kept intact. Also called *working-capital fund* or *intragovernmental service fund*.

internal storage (computers) The hardware used for storing data and programs during a program's execution as in a computer's magnetic memory. It contrasts with external storage which consists of such hardware devices as tape drives and disk drives.

internal transaction A bookkeeping entry reflecting the periodic adjustment of a *prepaid expense*, an *accrual* of a revenue earned or of an expense incurred, the recording of a liability, a *provision* for depreciation, an *allocation* of costs, the correction of an error, and the like; known also as an "accounting" transaction; contrasts with *external transaction* or transaction with an outsider. See *transaction; adjusting journal entry; closing entry*.

internal verification Procedures performed by independent persons within an entity to determine the correctness of the processing and recording of transactions. Part of *internal control*.

international accounting (also **multinational accounting**) Accounting for organizations which conduct activities across national boundaries or maintain operations in countries other than their home country. Thus, international accounting necessarily involves recognition of those accounting practices common to all countries, those practices which differ from country to country, and practices of affiliated organizations in different countries.

International Accounting Standards Committee (IASC) Formed in 1973, the Committee is a collaborative undertaking involving representatives from the principal accounting bodies in the United States, United Kingdom/Ireland, West Germany, the Netherlands, France, Canada, Mexico, Japan, and Australia, for the purpose of proposing accounting standards which merit universal acceptance. Its Secretariat is in London, and its potential influence has been extended owing to the decisions of the principal accounting bodies in more than 40 other countries to become associate members of the IASC. The IASC issues discussion papers, exposure

drafts, and formal Statements which are not legally binding on companies in any country but which have nonetheless carried gradually increasing weight in a growing number of countries.

International Bank for Reconstruction and Development See *World Bank*.

International Committee for Accounting Cooperation (ICAC) A committee composed of representatives from the *American Institute of Certified Public Accountants*, the Mexican Institute of Certified Public Accountants, the *United States Agency for International Development*, the Inter-American Development Bank, and the International Finance Corporation. The committee has as its major objectives the development of accurate accounting information and the improvement of the competency of the accounting profession in developing countries.

International Congress of Accountants (ICA) An assembly of accounting representatives from around the world which meets every five years to discuss international accounting issues. The general objective of these congresses is to advance and harmonize international accounting and auditing practices.

International Coordination Committee for the Accounting Profession (ICCAP) An organization whose membership consists of national accounting bodies of various countries including the *AICPA*; its purpose is to consider, suggest, and possibly adopt uniform solutions for problems involving consolidated financial statements and other matters of common international professional interest.

international corporation See *multinational corporation*.

International Federation of Accountants A confederation of accountancy bodies on a worldwide scale, the International Federation of Accountants was formed in 1977 during the Eleventh International Congress of Accountants, held in Munich. It replaced the *International Coordination Committee for the Accounting Profession*, a loosely knit association drawn from the leading accountancy bodies in 11 countries, which had been set up following the Tenth International Congress of Accountants, held in Sydney in 1972. The purpose of IFA is to develop and enhance ''a coordinated worldwide accounting profession with harmonized standards.'' Although it is associated with the *International Accounting Standards Committee*, the latter retains its autonomy.

International Monetary Fund (IMF) One of two international financial institutions (the other is the *World Bank*) established in 1946. Its objectives are to facilitate international trade and payments, help to stabilize foreign exchange rates, and provide financial aid to member countries.

interperiod tax allocation = *comprehensive income-tax allocation*. A *financial accounting* treatment required when a *material* discrepancy between pretax *accounting income* and *taxable income* results from a timing difference in *generally accepted accounting principles* and income-tax regulations. The annual tax provision is based on pretax accounting income and the tax liability is based on the tax code. The difference between the provision and the liability is a *deferred charge* or *credit*. The deferral or *allocation* results from a timing difference that will reverse in subsequent periods.

Interperiod tax allocation is necessary when both generally accepted accounting principles and the tax code recognize an event or transaction but in different periods. For example, the use of straight-line depreciation for financial reporting and an accelerated method for tax reporting makes pretax ac-

counting income and taxable income unequal in individual years. Because the same total amount is expensed for accounting and tax purposes over the asset's life, the tax deferral in the early years is offset or reversed by higher tax payments in later years. Interperiod tax allocation is not to be used when the discrepancies are permanent. See *partial allocation of taxes; deferred income tax*.

interpolation (statistics) The estimation of intermediate values within a collection of available data; as, an estimate of production for a period the records for which have been lost, based on production data before and after such a period. Compare with *extrapolation*.

interpretation An explanation, often involving the supplying of information concerning the purpose, context, or implications of a statement or action. ''Reasonable'' interpretations are those consistent with the factual information regarded as the most adequate. Because interpretation often involves surmise, individuals differ in the reasonableness of their interpretations because of differences in the character and extent of past experiences with which the instant cases may be compared and because of differences in *bias*.

interpreter (computers) A program which translates, compiles, and executes a single statement in a program before translating and executing the next statement in the program. It is compared to a *compiler*, which translates the entire program first and then executes the program.

interrecord gap (computers) The unrecorded portion of a magnetic tape between two physical records. This unrecorded portion physically separates two records recorded on the tape. It is this interrecord gap that causes tapes to require more storage medium when records are blocked since each *block* is followed by a gap. On a typical tape the interrecord gap is approximately one-half inch.

interval measure See *defensive interval*.

inter-vivos trust A trust created between living persons, as contrasted with a *testamentary trust*. See *trust*.

intestate One who dies without making a will.

intragovernmental service fund See *internal service fund*.

intraperiod tax allocation Distribution of the annual tax provision to the major sections of the financial statements presenting the events responsible for a particular tax effect in terms of the tax consequences of *income from continuing operations*, *discontinued operations*, *extraordinary items*, cumulative effects of an accounting change, and prior-period adjustments.

intrinsic value Amount that an investor considers, on the basis of an evaluation of available facts, to be the "true" or "real" worth of an item, usually an *equity security*. The value that will become the market value when other investors reach the same conclusions. The various approaches to determining intrinsic value in the *finance* literature are based on expectations and discounted cash flows. See *expected value; fundamental analysis; discounted cash-flow method*.

Introduction to Corporate Accounting Standards, An A 156-page monograph published in 1940 by the *American Accounting Association* and written by Professors W. A. Paton and A. C. Littleton. It is known colloquially as "the Paton and Littleton monograph." It has been quoted and cited widely and is accepted as being the foremost explication of the theory generally underlying American accounting practice. It has been translated into Japanese.

inventory *n*. 1. Raw materials and supplies, goods finished and in process of manufacture, and merchandise on hand, in transit and owned, in storage, or consigned to others at the end of an *accounting period*: (a) their aggregate value, usually at cost or some portion of cost; (b) the process of counting, listing, and pricing them; (c) the listing in which they are itemized, showing description, quantities, unit prices, extensions, and totals; (d) a physical inventory.
2. In general, any class or group of materials or supplies, not yet expensed or capitalized; as, maintenance supplies or construction materials.
3. (sometimes *pl*.) The title of a balance-sheet item representing the sum total of finished goods, materials, supplies, and merchandise on hand. Its valuation is cost; cost or market, whichever is lower; or other stated basis. See *inventory valuation; balance sheet*.
4. In the accounts of executors, administrators, trustees, and receivers: (a) the property, tangible and intangible, of an estate or trust, as it existed on a certain date; (b) its estimated or realizable value; (c) the process of taking an inventory of the property of an estate or trust; (d) the list required by law to accompany the accounts or statements filed with the courts.
5. The detailed list of property that often accompanies a bill of sale or a lease of furnished premises.

inventory certificate A representation pertaining to inventories of stock on hand obtained by an auditor from the management of an enterprise under examination. It usually sets forth the method used in determining quantities, the basis on which the items were priced, and other matters relating to ownership, condition, and the like. See *representation*.

inventory control The control of merchandise, materials, goods in process, finished goods, and supplies on hand by accounting and physical methods. An accounting control is effected by means of a stock or stores ledger, mechanical storage records, or a ledger account in which the quantities or amounts (or both) of goods received during an accounting period are added to corresponding balances at the beginning of the period and amounts of goods sold or otherwise disposed of are deducted at a calculated cost based on individual identification or any of various methods of averaging. Physical controls consist of various plans of buying, storing, handling, issuing, supervising, and stocktaking. Stockledger control is made more effective by physical control in the nature of a continuous check of the goods on hand. See *continuous inventory; perpetual inventory*.

inventory equation Beginning (or opening) *inventory* + net additions during the period − withdrawals = ending (or closing) inventory. Usually the additions are net purchases and withdrawals are *cost of sales* (or cost of goods sold). This equation states the essence of the perpetual inventory method. To obtain the periodic inventory method, the ending inventory must be determined (usually by count, weight or measure) and then deducted to determine cost of sales (withdrawals). See *continuous inventory*. When the *retail method* is used, the equation is applied first at retail values to determine the retail value of the ending inventory, which is then converted to cost.

inventory holding gain, loss 1. Under historical cost basis accounting, it is a term frequently used to mean the difference in inventory value resulting from the use of the *LIFO* inventory method versus some other method. See *inventory profit*.
2. Under replacement cost basis accounting, it is the difference between the replacement cost of the inventory and its historical cost. If the replacement cost is the higher value, there is a gain. With respect to items on hand, the difference is referred to as an unrealized holding gain (loss). With respect to cost of goods sold, the difference is referred to as a realized holding gain (loss).

inventory layer Any portion of a total inventory of homogeneous goods which is valued differently from other portions of that inventory. See *LIFO inventory layer; inventory valuation*.

inventory loss See *inventory profit; cost or market, whichever is lower*.

inventory pricing See *inventory valuation*.

inventory profit (or loss) 1. Profit (loss) obtained by holding as distinct from selling inventory. Its amount may be estimated from savings due to not having to replace inventory on a current (replacement cost) basis. It may also be estimated as resulting from variation in the purchasing power of current dollars relative to the dollars in which inventory on hand is stated.
2. Differences between inventory treated on a *LIFO* compared to a *FIFO* basis may also be interpreted as inventory profit (or loss) and the same is true for other alternative ways of recording the consumption and replacement of inventory holding gain (or loss).

inventory reserve 1. A valuation account covering the reduction of inventory cost to market or other less-than-cost basis due to the use of a *LIFO* method of inventory valuation or to price declines, *obsolescence*, shortages, and other causes. The amount of the reserve is customarily supported by details from inventory sheets or records relating to specific items. When any such item is sold, the reserve may be relieved of the amount pertaining to it; or, what is more common, the reserve is carried forward intact until the end of the next year and increased or decreased by inventory requirements at that time, the other half of the adjustment being debited or credited to *cost of goods sold* or its equivalent. If the size of the reserve warrants, its amount at the beginning and end of the reporting period may be a necessary disclosure on the income statement.

2. A *contingency* reserve created for the purpose of absorbing future inventory declines, i.e., declines below market at the latest balance-sheet date. Such a reserve is similar in nature to other contingency reserves: a provision therefor is not an expense, but rather an appropriation of retained earnings, and any charge thereto representing the realization of an inventory decline as described belongs in the income statement for the period in which the decline occurred.

inventory turnover A *ratio* which measures the number of times a firm's average inventory is sold during a year. Considered a rough indicator of a firm's inventory management efficiency, this ratio is best calculated by dividing cost of goods sold by inventory, but, in practice, the ratio of sales to inventory appears to be the most widely used version. This ratio varies greatly from one industry to another, and so comparisons with *industry ratios* are generally pertinent.

inventory valuation 1. The determination of the cost or the portion of cost assignable to on-hand raw materials, goods in process, finished stock, merchandise held for resale, and supplies.

2. The determination of the market price of securities in the case of a dealer in securities or an investment fund or of the pricing of other goods or commodities on hand, where cost or a fraction of cost is not employed as the valuation basis.

Cost. Like other assets, inventories of goods are normally priced at their original cost, or such part of original cost as may be equal to "market" value (see below) or other amount that may "reasonably" be carried forward to the following year. "At the lower of cost or market" is a standard balance-sheet term attaching to an inventory side-head. The *fungible* character of many inventory items, variations in cost-accounting methods, and the individual judgments that enter into determinations of what costs ought to be carried forward create many different valuation patterns.

Materials and Merchandise. The cost of purchased materials, parts, and merchandise is invoice cost, plus transportation, duty, and other direct purchase costs, less discounts and allowances, the former including *trade discounts* and now usually *cash discounts*. Most accountants prefer to see prices net of all discounts, but the idea persists that cash discounts of 2% or less are in the nature of interest and should, therefore, be regarded as belonging to the same category as interest received. Since discounts received are credits, any resemblance to interest must arise from the notion of "prepayment"—that is, payment before the "net" date. Terms of "2% 10 days, net 30" mean that if the interest concept is adhered to, the 2% discount relates to the period lying between the 10th and 30th days, which is 1/18 of a year—an implied "interest" rate of 36% a year. The current rate of interest is too small a portion of this amount to separate.

The cost price to be applied to the units of materials remaining at the end of a fiscal year may not be their individual costs, even though the units may be identified beyond a doubt with particular purchase transactions. The fungible or interchangeable nature of most purchased items gives rise to six commonly employed alternatives as listed on page 288; the use of any or all of them is recognized by many accountants as valid in inventory valuations.

LIFO. The recent widespread use of the Last In, First Out (LIFO) method has arisen from the claim that it more nearly reflects the operating point of view, whether or not selling prices have been affected, since operating people are inclined to think in terms of margins between current market prices—wholesale and retail, or raw material and in-

Basis	Explanation
Actual	Cost relates to specific items.
First In, First Out (FIFO)	Oldest acquisitions are disposed of first: an assumption usually in agreement with fact.
Last In, First Out (LIFO) and base-stock	Recent acquisition costs are most nearly related to the prices at which sales are made; saves taxes on a rising market.
Average	Easily determined; many people think in terms of averages; more consistency between inventory and cost-of-sales bases; often regarded as the most practicable method of imputing costs in a mixed inventory, since in most cases the method results in but minor variation from *actual*.
Standard	More often applied to work in process and finished stock; resembles average cost, except that unusual costs are excluded.
Retail	Also resembles average cost, but results in less than average cost because of markdowns; easily computed; provides for normal margins on future sales.

termediate or finished product. The effect during a period of rising prices is to keep the cost of the inventory at a "safer" lower level than current *replacement cost*, thus reducing margins and making it possible to decrease selling prices, when the market swings in the other direction, without having to provide for inventory losses. If inventory quantities tend to be constant and inventory costs are kept at the lowest point in a long-range price cycle, the "LIFO" method of costing inventories becomes the *base-stock method*. See also *dollar-value LIFO*, where the LIFO method is applied to a group of heterogeneous inventory items.

Market. By "market," as the term is employed in inventory-valuation processes, is meant that portion of inventory cost that can justifiably be carried forward to future periods as the result of giving weight to prices and other conditions likely to accompany disposal, particularly in the local market. It may be equal in amount to a price quotation on an active market at the balance-sheet date, the offering price of a competitor in an inactive market, a "junk" price on a "dead" market, or some other cost fraction that experience and good judgment by management have indicated as a realistic base for application against currently available estimates of possible realization.

As a rule, there should be no reduction of cost to a market figure for that portion of the inventory that will remain in the business as a minimum quantity to be kept on hand, or where the selling price has not yet reacted to a reduction in raw-material cost. Raw material that has been purchased in connection with the manufacture of a product for which a firm price exists and on which a normal profit is expected should never be marked down despite a lower market.

Market price in the case of work in process and finished stock is usually conceived to be the lower of (a) the cost of replacement or (b) the anticipated selling price less the cost to complete, selling expense, and the customary gross margin.

A market quotation should reflect the price on the balance-sheet date of a similar item, which would have to be paid in the area in which the purchase would ordinarily be made for the same quantity usually acquired at one time. Market prices are ordinarily applied to individual items rather than groups or classes, and once a market price has been adopted in an inventory valuation as a basis for the amount of cost to be carried forward, it remains as cost for future reckoning.

Reductions of costs to amounts equal to market are sometimes collected together in an *inventory reserve*. To justify the reserve as a *valuation account* rather than as a subdivision of retained earnings, (a) details of reductions to market by individual items or groups should be available, and (b) in the succeeding period, the reserve is best adjusted as these items are disposed of.

Manufactured Products and Goods in Process. Costing manufactured products and goods in process follows the principles observed in costing sales: the identifying and spreading of *production costs*. These may consist of direct or standard costs of material and labor (*prime cost*) plus an allowance for production overhead determined, e.g., by the application of a percentage to the labor-cost element (see *overhead*). *Variances* arising from differences between the costs thus absorbed and actual cost may be redistributed pro rata to the absorbed cost (*full absorption costing*); more often, they are merged with costs of sales on published income statements, thus eliminating their reallocation. Although the adoption of any one of these somewhat disparate methods may limit the comparability of the balance sheet of enterprises similarly engaged, the effect on income comparisons may be minor because of the limitation to differences between opening and closing inventories.

Markdowns. Markdowns of cost because of age or surplus or slow-moving items may be regarded as equivalent to market reductions, since the common purpose is to carry forward only those costs that may fairly be applied against future realizations. These markdowns are often accomplished by adopting a percentage scale whereby the cost of an item is progressively decreased, as it is continued in stock, until scrap value is reached. In the retail method of determining inventory cost, the same purpose is served by reducing the expected selling price by an average markon percentage.

In all these situations, cost reductions made in accordance with the principles indicated should be justified by past experience or present facts, and should be fairly applied to all inventory items. If the methods adopted differ from those in use at the end of the previous fiscal period, unless the effect is unimportant, the change calls for a balance-sheet footnote, giving some indication of the approximate effect in dollars. An inventory on the LIFO basis is preferably accompanied by a balance-sheet disclosure of the cost that would have been reflected had a FIFO basis been followed.

An allowance for possible future inventory losses, over and above the writedown to current market, is best regarded as a reservation of retained earnings. See *inventory reserve (2)*.

inventory variation The difference between inventories at the beginning and end of a period covered by an income statement, where *perpetual inventories* are not maintained. An increase has the effect of decreasing cost of sales, and vice versa. See *income statement*.

inverted file (computers) A file organization technique in which an individual key value is used for locating all records containing that value.

invested capital 1. The amount of capital contributed to a business by its owners; = *capital (2)*.
2. The amount so contributed, plus retained earnings (or less accumulated losses) and appropriated surplus. See *capital (4); net assets; net worth*.
3. Sum of *net worth* and *long-term liabilities*. See *capital (5)*.

investigate (auditing) To search for and relate underlying causes.

investigation An examination of books and records preliminary to financing or for any other specified purpose, sometimes differing in scope from the ordinary *audit (1)*.

investment 1. An expenditure to acquire

property—real or personal, tangible or intangible—yielding income or services.

2. The property so acquired.

3. = *savings*.

4. A security owned.

5. = *net worth*. "Economic" investment is sometimes described as including long-term debt.

6. *pl*. A balance-sheet title, generally classified into *permanent investment* and *temporary investment*, according to the expected holding periods, and often by phrases indicating the existence of *control* (*3*).

investment adviser (or counsel) One who on a professional or service basis gives advice to another on investment problems. Investment advisers are required by the Investment Advisers Act of 1940 to register with and report to the U.S. *Securities and Exchange Commission*.

investment banker An organization that buys bond or stock issues in their entirety from the issuing corporation, or participates with others in such a purchase; if it distributes the issues to dealers, it is referred to as a "wholesaler"; it is a "retailer" if it sells them directly to investors. Sometimes it does both.

investment center A responsibility unit whose performance is measured in terms of resources committed (capital invested) relative to monetary costs and returns. The two principal means of evaluating profits earned in relation to resources (assets) employed are: (1) the return on investment ratio, and (2) residual income = the difference between monetary receipts and costs. Using these, or similar, measures of performance, management attempts to find a common basis for comparison of major subunits (e.g., divisions in a decentralized organization), while motivating responsible supervisory personnel to consider the cost of financing and the *opportunity costs* of *capital assets* to generate revenues or to control *operating costs*.

investment company (or trust) An organization serving to bring together the savings of individuals for joint investment.

investment in default A security owned on which there exists a default in the payment of principal or interest.

investment in general fixed assets (governmental accounting) An account which represents a governmental unit's equity in the *general fixed-assets account group*. The account is subdivided according to the source of funds which financed the asset acquisition, such as *general fund* revenues or special assessments.

investment tax credit Reduction in the *income-tax* liability granted by the federal government on purchases of qualifying machinery equipment, and other property. The item is a credit that is deducted from the amount of *income tax* payable, not a deduction from *taxable income*; it is calculated as a stated percentage of the cost of qualifying assets purchased during the period. The rates, rules, and qualifying property have changed several times since the investment credit was first granted in the Revenue Act of 1962. *GAAP* continues to view the credit as a cost reduction rather than a tax reduction but permits it to be accounted for by either (1) the deferral method that was preferred in APB Opinion 2, and under which a contra-asset account, *deferred investment tax credit* is established and amortized to reduce income-tax expenses (and increase income) over the life of the purchased asset or (2) the *flow-through method* that was accepted in APB Opinion 4 and that requires all of the reduction in income-tax expense (and increase in income) to be recognized in the year in which the credit arises.

investment turnover See *capital turnover*.

invoice A document showing the character, quantity, price, terms, nature of delivery, and other particulars of goods sold or of services rendered.

invoice cost 1. Cost incurred by a buyer and reflected on an invoice which, unless otherwise specified, is net after deducting both trade and cash discounts.
2. (retail accounting) Billed cost less trade discount, but not less cash discount.

invoice register A book of original entry, often columnar in form, for the consecutive record and summarization of invoices received from creditors; sometimes, another name for a *voucher register*.

involuntary bankruptcy A debtor adjudged a bankrupt not on his or her own petition but on the petition of creditors. If he or she has committed an act of bankruptcy, any individual except a wage earner or farmer may be adjudged an involuntary bankrupt.

involuntary conversion The substitution of one item of property for another as the result of a casualty, condemnation, or other cause over which the owner has no control. In general, under the *Internal Revenue Code* (Section 1033), a loss from such a transaction is recognized, but a gain is recognized only to the extent that the proceeds are not reinvested in similar property within two or three years after the conversion.

IOU An informal document evidencing a cash debt. Under usual standards of *internal control*, an advance by a cashier to an employee is forbidden; in the few instances in which it is permitted, approval in writing by a higher official is customarily required.

IRA See *Individual Retirement Account*.

IRC = *Internal Revenue Code*.

IRR = *internal rate of return*. See also *interest formulas*.

irrational number A number whose terminus has an infinite extension without *repetends*; examples:

$$\pi = 3.1415926536\ldots;$$
$$e = 2.7182818285\ldots;$$
$$\sqrt{2} = 1.41421356237\ldots.$$

See *rational number*.

irregularity Any error in a bookkeeping record. It may be one of principle, a clerical inaccuracy, or a deliberate falsification.

irrevocable trust A trust that cannot be set aside by its creator. See *trust*.

IRS = *Internal Revenue Service*.

ISO (International Standards Organization) An organization of computer manufacturers and users responsible for defining international standards. ISO works closely with organizations such as *ANSI*.

issue 1. To release as in withdrawals of an inventory.
2. To float a *bond* or to release stock as in *issued capital stock*. Any such issue, or proposed issue, of a security in interstate commerce is subject to registration with the *SEC* under the Securities Act of 1933 with the exception of small corporations (size less than 35 stockholders) or in the case of *private placement*.

issued capital (stock) That part of a corporation's authorized capital stock represented by certificates legally issued for cash or other consideration, whether or not such certificates are in the hands of the public or have been reacquired by the issuer. The term thus includes treasury stock, or stock otherwise reacquired, as well as outstanding stock.

itemized deduction (federal income taxes) A deduction allowed an individual taxpayer which is subtracted from adjusted gross income in the computation of taxable income. Specific itemized deductions are those allowed by Sections 161-216 of the *Internal Revenue Code* but which are not defined in Section 62 as being deductible in arriving at *adjusted gross income*. The principal itemized deductions are for interest, taxes, contributions, and medical expenses. Standard amounts of itemized deductions are built into the tax tables, so only the excess of total itemized deductions over the *zero bracket amount* is deductible from adjusted gross income to arrive at tax table income.

JCL = *job control language*.

job control language (JCL) (computers) A programming language for specifying job control statements. The statements are used to request allocation of computer resources as well as to direct the execution of system programs such as *compilers, loaders*, and *utilities*.

job costing = *job-order costing*.

job lot 1. A contract for 1,000 or 2,000 bushels of grain, as compared with the "regular" contract unit of 5,000 bushels: a term employed on grain exchanges; compare with *odd lot*.
2. A miscellaneous collection of goods acquired or salable at a lump-sum price.

job-lot costing A cost accounting method which accumulates the costs of a separately identifiable production run of a homogeneous product as, for example, a run of 200 pairs of one size and style of shoe. Production might be to fill a customer order or might be for stock in anticipation of customer demand. The total cost of the lot includes the costs directly traceable to it and, usually, a share of the nontraceable or indirect production costs. See *job-order costing*.

job order An order authorizing and directing the production of a specified number of units of product, the construction or repair of specified equipment, or the rendition of specified services; known also as a production, construction, repair, or service order, it may serve as the basis for the accounts or subaccounts in which costs are recorded, grouped, and accumulated.

job-order costing A cost accounting method which accumulates the costs of doing a separately identifiable job. Often used by printers, repair shops, and shipbuilding and construction industries. The specifications for the product are frequently set by the customer and production does not occur without a customer order. The total cost of the job includes those raw material, labor, and other costs which are directly traceable to that job and, usually, a share of the nontraceable or indirect production costs. See *job-lot costing* for similarity; *process costing* for contrast.

joint account 1. A record of transactions in which two or more persons or business units have a financial interest.
2. A bank account which may be drawn upon by two or more persons, their rights being similar to those of *joint tenants*.

joint adventure = *joint venture*.

joint-and-several liability A liability for the settlement of which one or all of a group of named persons may be held accountable.

joint cost The *common cost* of two or more simultaneously produced or otherwise closely related operations, commodities, or services. The production of one item, as in a single plant or process, may be possible only if others are produced at the same time; these joint products are called "complementary" if an increase in the output of one of the joint products has favorable effects on the cost of the other. In some cases, the production of one joint product impedes the production of another. Such joint products are called "substitutes"; they constitute that class of products in which the production of both tends to raise the cost of producing each. Costs that are not joint are said to be "independent." Dividing and averaging joint costs that are not independent is always arbitrary, because the level of costs of one product depends in a variety of ways on the level of production of the joint commodity, so that averages tend to lose meaning, except where direct, additional, and independent costs for each commodity are involved. In fact, jointness, to the extent it exists, implies that any decision affecting one commodity cannot be made without affecting the cost of those related to it. See *impute*.

joint-facilities income A term used in public utility accounting to designate revenues derived from facilities operated jointly to produce two or more types of services; as, rental from a power company pole carrying both power and telephone lines.

joint liability A liability for the settlement of which others have equal responsibility. Persons jointly liable must be proceeded against together.

joint ownership The ownership of *real* or *personal property* by two or more persons as either *joint tenants* or *tenants in common*. See *joint tenant; tenant in common*.

joint probability See *probability*.

joint product (or services) A related product or service; a product whose production impedes or facilitates the production of another product. See *joint cost*.

joint returns (federal income taxes) Since 1948, a husband and wife have been entitled to file a single income-tax return jointly even though one of the spouses has neither income nor deductions. The effect of the lower rate schedule for a joint return is to treat the family's income as though it had been earned by both husband and wife equally. This provision permitted the common-law states to achieve parity with the states which have *community property* laws that treat a married couple's income as earned one-half by each. See *income splitting; deductions from gross income; itemized deduction*.

joint-stock association (or company) 1. A group of individuals, acting jointly to establish and operate a business enterprise under an artificial name, and having an invested capital divided into transferable shares, an elected board of directors, and other corporate characteristics, but in most states operating without formal governmental authority; a *common-law corporation*. Its shareholders have unlimited liability for corporate debts and obligations, and it is taxed generally as a corporation. Because of the comparative ease with which a corporation can be created under state laws, joint-stock associations are now rare.

2. (British usage) = *corporation*.

joint tenant Any one of two or more persons who together own *real* or *personal property*, whereby upon the death of any one of them his or her interest passes to the others without becoming a part of the estate. Where, for example, a certificate of capital stock is jointly owned by husband and wife, the owner's name is likely to appear on the certificate thus: "James Smith and Alice Smith as joint tenants with right of survivorship and not as tenants in common." See *tenant in common*.

joint venture A commercial undertaking by two or more persons, differing from a partnership in that it relates to the disposition of a single lot of goods or the completion of a single project. Its duration is limited to the period in which the goods are sold or the project is carried on.

journal 1. Any book of *original entry*; see *double-entry bookkeeping*.
2. The book of original entry in which are recorded transactions not provided for in specialized journals; a *general journal*. See *journal entry*.
3. A journal entry, as in the expression, "to prepare a journal for a given transaction."

journal entry An item in or prepared for a book of original entry, interpreting a business transaction in bookkeeping terms and showing the accounts to be debited and credited, together with an explanatory description of the transaction. Frequently transactions are analyzed in journal-entry form in order to demonstrate their effect on the accounts.
See *adjusting journal entry; compound journal entry; entry; posting; journal; cash journal; book of original entry; double-entry bookkeeping*.

journalize To interpret a transaction in terms of required debits and credits and to give it expression as a *journal entry*.
—journalization, *n*.

Journal of Accountancy See *accounting journals*.

Journal of Accounting and Economics See *accounting journals*.

Journal of Accounting Auditing and Finance See *accounting journals*.

Journal of Accounting Research See *accounting journals*.

Journal UEC See *accounting journals*.

journal voucher A voucher supporting a non-cash transaction. A file of journal vouchers may take the place of a general journal, or journal vouchers may be summarized periodically in the general journal or in a journal-voucher summary.

judgment 1. An amount due to be paid or collected as the result of a court order. In the case of governmental units, judgments include condemnation awards in payment for private property taken for public use.
2. The assertion, implied or explicit, of a proposition concerning the meaning, significance, or structure of a set of concepts, evidence, or actions. By *convention*, the accountant's *judgment* expressed on the basis of his or her audit findings is referred to as an *opinion* appearing as one section of the short-form report accompanied by audited financial statements. See *opinion; fact; valuation; value judgment*.

judgment bonds Bonds issued by a governmental unit to pay judgments against it.

judgment sample A *sample* whose size and the items composing it have been determined by someone who is familiar with the *universe* undergoing the test and capable of exercising informed and unbiased discretion in making the selection. Such samples are sometimes necessary when data are needed quickly or when interest is confined to only a part of the universe. They can be very efficient but they differ from a probability sample in that they provide no basis for objective estimation of *sampling error*.

judgments payable Amounts due to be paid by a governmental unit as the result of court decisions, including condemnation awards in payment for private property taken for public use.

junior accountant An employee of a public accountant who engages in field work and whose activities are closely supervised by a *senior* accountant. Usually an accountant in the first few years of practice.

junior security A bond or mortgage secured by a property on which there is one or more senior or prior issues, and subject to the prior claims of such issues in case of foreclosure or liquidation.

justification (governmental accounting) A narrative analysis of the need for funds.

KD Knocked down; applied to sales or shipments of machines and the like that are to be assembled by the recipient.

Keogh Plans (federal income taxes) Tax-sheltered retirement plans named for Congressman Keogh. Originally enacted in the Self-Employed Individuals Tax Retirement Act of 1962 and amended by the *ERISA* in 1974. Under *IRC* Sections 401-405 they provide proprietors, partners, and other self-employed persons with tax-sheltered retirement income by allowing current deductions from gross income for contributions to such plans and tax-free buildup of income until distributions occur. Rules and limitations include the following: Partners and proprietors cannot benefit themselves unless they provide nondiscriminatory benefits for all 3-year employees. The amount of deductible contributions in any one year cannot exceed the lesser of 15% of earned income or $7,500. The funds contributed to the plan must be placed in a trust, custodial account, or annuity. Distributions cannot begin until the self-employed person reaches age 59 1/2 or is permanently disabled. Distributions are taxed upon receipt by the beneficiary as ordinary income.

key business ratios A series of *industry ratios* published since the early 1930s by Dun & Bradstreet. Median and quartile data of fourteen ratios are presented annually for a wide variety of industries.

kind An *asset* or assets other than cash and receivables; the use of the word is confined to the expression *in kind*.

kiting 1. The act of drawing and cashing an unrecorded check on one bank, followed shortly by a covering deposit in the form of an unrecorded check on another bank that will in turn be covered by a check drawn on a third bank; the process may go on indefinitely among several banks. The time taken for checks to clear through the banking system is thus taken advantage of in order to cover an unauthorized ''borrowing'' or theft of money.

2. Hence, the inclusion in a bank deposit of any item for which no concurrent credit appears on the books of account, the purpose being to cover a concurrent or previous cash theft or shortage.

3. Also, the withdrawal (check or cash) from uncollected bank deposits. Thus, two persons residing in different cities may exchange checks with each other, deposit them in local

banks, draw against the balances thus created, and make covering deposits on or before the collection date of the deposited checks. This can occur only where banks do not prohibit the customer's use of uncollected deposits.

Kohler, Eric L. (1892-1976) A noted accounting author, lexicographer, and practitioner (both government and private practice), with an abiding interest in the development of accounting principles, Kohler was twice president of the *American Accounting Association* and was editor of *The Accounting Review* from 1928 to 1942. He was controller of the Tennessee Valley Authority, Controller of the Marshall Plan, an accounting practitioner both with his own firm and with Arthur Andersen & Co., an accounting professor, and the author of many books and articles. In 1945, he was awarded the Gold Medal of the *American Institute of Accountants*.

kurtosis (statistics) The degree of peakedness or concentration about the central value exhibited by a statistical distribution.

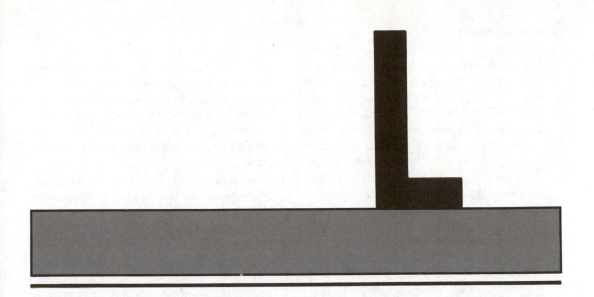

labor-cost ratio *Standard cost* of direct labor divided by *actual cost*.

labor laws Laws governing the conditions of work and the rights of workers. In the United States, the primary labor laws are the National Labor Relations (Wagner) Act of 1935 and the Labor-Management Relations (Taft-Hartley) Act of 1948.

labor quantity variance The difference between the standard and actual direct labor hours of a given type of labor times (usually) the standard wage rate. The labor quantity variance account in the *general ledger* will typically include the quantity variance for all types of direct labor. Also called labor efficiency variance. See *efficiency variance*.

labor rate variance The difference between actual and standard direct labor wage rates for a given type of labor input times (usually) the actual hours worked. The labor rate variance account in the general ledger will typically include the variances for all types of direct labor. See also *price variance*.

labor-saving innovation Any alteration in technique which results in a given amount of product being produced with less real labor expenditures.

laddered portfolios Bond *portfolios*, or portfolios with term investments which are spread relatively evenly in all classes from short-term to long-term maturities. See *barbell portfolios*.

lag The time interval between successive, often related, events such as the receipt and deposit of cash.

lagging indicators Economic *time series* whose turning points generally follow turning points in the overall level of economic activity. See *leading indicators*.

laity The body of persons outside a *profession*; in accounting, those unskilled in the art, particularly those for whom auditors' reports are intended.

land The investment in real estate, usually including *land improvements* completed before the purchase of the real estate but not including buildings or other *limited-life assets*.

landed price The quoted or invoiced price of a commodity, including costs of loading, shipping, and unloading at destination.

land improvements Paving and sidewalks; sewer, water, and gas lines; clearing; grading; fencing; spur-railway tracks; and other items customarily paid for by the owner of a tract of land and installed by him or her or by local government. The term may also include buildings, but generally "building" or "land and building(s)" is the standard of description where a human-made structure has been added to the land. A separate account is maintained where the improvements are being depreciated. The usual practice, however, is to regard improvements as being as durable as the land itself and not subject to depreciation; replacements of paving and other improvement items are then expensed, although if the replacement cost has been greater than the first cost, the excess may be capitalized. See *fixed asset; capitalize.*

language sheet (governmental accounting) A term employed in federal government agencies to designate the administrative draft of the narrative of an appropriation bill accompanying the submission of an agency's budget to the Congress.

lapping The theft, as by a defaulting cashier, of cash received from a customer, made good and credited to the customer's account at a later date by the theft of cash received from another customer, the process continuing indefinitely until the *fraud* is discovered, or until restitution is made or a fictitious covering entry, as to an expense account, can be made.

lapse 1. To expire or be forfeited: said of an insurance policy and the rights and benefits under it upon expiration of the policy or upon cancellation for nonpayment of premium.
2. (governmental accounting) To become unavailable for future spending: said of the unexpended balance of an ordinary *appropriation* at the end of the *fiscal year* or years to which it applies. See *continuing appropriation.*

lapse factor A budget reduction resulting from expected vacant positions in an organizational unit. Particularly in governmental budgeting, lapse factors are estimated to plan for unfilled positions which result from the normal turnover and replacement cycle which occurs throughout the budget period. Salaries and benefits for such vacancies which would be included in a fully funded budget are omitted in the review process. See *decision package.*

lapsing schedule A worksheet on which are entered the costs of individual fixed assets or, more commonly, the total annual additions to a class of fixed assets, together with the details of the distribution of their costs over the accounting periods succeeding their purchase. The purpose of the schedule is to supply the details of an annual or other periodic (a) provision for depreciation, (b) writeoff of costs fully depreciated or of amortized and unamortized costs of items disposed of, and (c) verification of the balance of accumulated depreciation at any time and its identification with individual fixed assets. See *depreciation.*

Last In, First Out (LIFO) See *inventory valuation.*

latency time (computers) The amount of time required for a desired data item to appear below the magnetic head on a disk drive after the head has been positioned above the correct track. On the average this is equal to the time required for 1/2 a revolution of the disk. It is distinguished from the *seek time*, the time required to position the head over the track containing the desired data.

lay days The agreed number of days that a chartered ship may remain in port for loading and unloading without penalty. See *charter party.*

LDC = *less developed country.*

LDCC = *less developed country corporation.*

leading indicators Economic *time series* whose turning points generally precede turning points in the overall level of economic activity. See *lagging indicators.*

lead time The time required after placing an order or adopting a plan of operation or production before materials and facilities can be acquired and made ready and actual production initiated.

learning curve A *curve* describing improvements in the relations between the amount of work (e.g., labor hours) required to make a unit of product and the cumulative production quantity. This improvement is assumed to be due to increases in worker or management skill and knowledge as the production process is repeated. In many applications it has been found that the 80% learning curve is frequently applicable. This means that the average time per unit required to produce $2x$ units is 80% of the average time required to produce x units. Thus, if it takes 10 hours to produce the first unit, it will take 8 hours per unit to produce the first two units, the second unit thus requiring 6 hours. Such curves have received their most extensive use in the production of new products by high-technology companies such as aircraft manufacture or the manufacture of electronic computers.

lease An agreement conveying the right to use property, plant, or equipment (land or depreciable assets), usually for specified purposes and a stated period of time. See *bargain purchase option; bargain renewal option; capital lease; leaseback; leasehold; leveraged lease; term lease*.

leaseback A long-term lease of real estate or equipment which has been sold to an independent or quasi-independent prospective lessor in exchange for cash, any excess of which over *net book value* being customarily credited to and often equal to subsequent rental payments. Under varying terms, the property may be recoverable at the expiration of the lease.

leasehold An interest in land under the terms of a *lease*, normally classified as a (tangible) *fixed asset*.

leasehold improvement Improvement or *betterment* that increases the usefulness of leased property. Costs of such changes are usually amortized over the service life of the improvement or the remaining life of the lease, whichever is shorter.

least-squares method (statistics) The mathematical process for determining the relationship between two or more variables, so that, when expressed as a *curve*, the sum of the distances (deviations) of the available data (observations) from the curve is zero. This condition is met when the curve is so constructed that the sum of the squares of the deviations is less than that obtainable from any other curve of the same type. For most accounting and business purposes, the curve usually employed is a straight line, and the method is applied principally in studies of trends in revenues, costs, production, and other related data, covering past or projected periods and real or assumed operating conditions. The method rests on a statistical *model* in which it is assumed that the data to be treated are subject to two sets of forces: (a) an underlying relation, the general form of which is assumed to be determinable, and (b) *random variations*; it is used to find the best values of the constants in the assumed relation, but the result secured depends to a large extent on assumptions regarding the underlying form of the relation. Even in the case of a straight line, it should be noted that the minimization of the sums of the squares of vertical deviations will not, in general, yield the same values for the constants as the minimization of the sums of the squares of horizontal deviations, since each minimization implies a different direction of application of the random forces.

For a straight-line relation of the form $Y = a + bX$, the choice of values for two constants, a and b, is necessary. These *constants* are obtained by solving the two so-called normal equations

$$\Sigma Y = Na + b\Sigma X$$

and

$$\Sigma XY = a\Sigma X + b\Sigma X^2,$$

where ΣY is the sum of the observed Y values, ΣX the sum of the observed X values, ΣX^2 the sum of the squares of these X values, and ΣXY the sum of the cross-product—i.e., each value of X is multiplied by the value of Y occurring with that same value of X and the results of all such multiplications are then added. N is the number of observations. Solution of these two equations is the equivalent of the least-squares method for determining the values of the constants a and b. Statistical packages for determining these constants and even more general least-squares relations are available on most computers and even on many hand calculators.

ledger A book of *accounts* (*1*); any *book of final entry*. See *general ledger; subsidiary ledger; private ledger; double-entry bookkeeping*.

ledger asset (insurance accounting) A term used in reports to denote any asset appearing on a *ledger*, whether or not stated at its realizable value; both ledger assets and nonledger assets appear on the balance sheet.

ledger clerk One employed in the *posting* and *balancing* of a *ledger*.

ledger control The control of a subsidiary record or ledger by the use of a *control account*. Ledger control is limited to a proof that all items were recorded in the subsidiary record or that they were accurately made, as required, to the *debit* and *credit* sides of that *record*. It does not furnish proof that every item was recorded in its proper account in the subsidiary record.

ledger journal A multicolumnar record that functions as both *journal* and *ledger*. As usually devised, the record contains *debit* or

credit columns or both for the minimum number of accounts, thus providing an all-inclusive record; practicable, however, only when a small number of accounts are required and transactions are relatively few and simple. See *cash journal*.

ledger transfer The now obsolete method of transferring items or balances from one ledger account to another without the medium of a journal; a blind entry.

legacy A gift of personal property by will. A general legacy is one to be paid from the general assets of the *testator*; a "specific" legacy is one involving an indicated sum of money or personal property; a "residuary" legacy is the gift of the balance of a testator's estate after payment of debts, costs and other legacies.

legal capital That part of the paid-in capital of a corporation which by law, agreement, or resolution of directors becomes the *par* or stated value of the *capital stock*; the portion of *net assets* restricted as to withdrawal under corporation law; *stated capital*.

legal debt margin (municipal accounting) The excess of authorized debt over outstanding debt applicable to such limitation. See *debt limit*.

legal entity An individual, partnership, trust, corporation, association, or other form of organization empowered by law or custom to own property or transact business. See *business enterprise; economic unit*.

legal liability 1. A responsibility for some obligation, enforceable at law, e.g., as distinguished from a moral responsibility.
2. (of a public accountant) The *contract* of employment between an accountant and client creates a relationship out of which an obligation arises to perform services with the honesty and due care consonant with his or her profession of special skills and knowledge of the auditing process. The scope of duties may

be either broadened or limited by the terms of the employment contract. It has been asserted that an auditor is liable to third persons whom he or she intends to inform through the medium of his or her report—or, according to another view, who he or she might reasonably anticipate would rely upon the report—provided he or she knows that the report is false or has certified to the truth of the report when he or she had no knowledge of its truth or falsity or when it has been prepared with such gross negligence as to amount to constructive fraud. The accountant's liability to client or to third persons has been modified and in many respects clarified by such statutes as the Securities Act of 1933 and the Securities and Exchange Act of 1934.

Claims against an accountant or firm of accountants by persons who allegedly and to their detriment have relied on financial statements bearing the accountant's certificate have involved extreme carelessness or at best doubtful issues from which general conclusions cannot be drawn.

See *accountant's responsibility*; also *ethics; opinion*.

legal reserve 1. That part of a bank's cash assets that must be kept as a protection for depositors.
2. Any reserve required by law. Examples: the reserves of a life insurance company; the portion of profits that must be set aside under foreign corporation laws.

legal value See *legal capital*.

legend 1. A voucher number or other source reference often supplemented by a descriptive word or phrase that accompanies a journal *entry* or ledger *posting*.
2. A brief summary description accompanying a table or a chart.

less developed country (LDC) (also called developing countries, developing nations, Third World countries) 1. Any country which

has not developed a modern economy with a supporting industrial base.
2. All countries other than those of Western Europe, Australia, Canada, Japan, New Zealand, South Africa, the Soviet Block, China, and the United States. Such countries are given *tariff* advantages by the U.S. government.

less developed country corporation (LDCC) A foreign corporation engaged in the conduct of a business which derives at least 80% of its gross income from sources within *less developed countries*, and which has at least 80% of its assets located in such countries. To encourage investment in less developed countries, dividends and interest received from LDCCs are excluded from a controlled foreign corporation's taxable income if reinvested in these countries.

lessee An entity which has the right to use property owned or otherwise controlled by another entity. Such use is usually limited both as to its nature and time by the terms specified in a *lease*.

lessor An entity which contracts for another entity to use property it owns or controls in accordance with a lease.

less-than-carload lot A term referring to goods the shipment of which requires less space than that available in a single freight car, or to the freight rate applicable to such a shipment.

letter for underwriters Also known as ''comfort letters,'' these are a communication from the *independent auditor* to the underwriter at the time of a registration of securities under the Securities Act of 1933. Before proceeding with the registration these letters give the underwriters some assurance about an auditor's role. They generally refer to such subjects as the independence of the accountants, compliance of statements with the applicable provisions of the Act, and changes in financial statement items subsequent to the statements included in the registration documents.

letter of credit 1. An authorization by a bank to an exporter to draw on it for funds, within a stated amount and time, in payment for specified goods to be shipped abroad. The authorization proceeds from an order of a correspondent bank abroad in which an importer has deposited or will ultimately deposit an equivalent amount in local currency. When the goods have been delivered by the exporter or his or her agent to the inland carrier (*FOB*) or to the port of exit (*FAS*) in accordance with the terms of the letter of credit, the documents evidencing the type and quantity of goods delivered and the fact of their delivery are presented to the bank, which thereupon makes payment to the exporter. See *foreign-trade financing; bank acceptance*.

2. An instrument purchased from a domestic bank by one going abroad, calling for a total amount not in excess of that appearing on its face. The traveler is then entitled to receive from designated correspondent banks the local-currency equivalent of his or her letter of credit either in a lump sum or in whatever smaller amounts the traveler may choose, these amounts being endorsed on the instrument. The bank paying the remaining amount retains the instrument and returns it to the bank of issue; or the traveler is refunded any undrawn amount upon his or her return.

letter of recommendation A letter from an auditor to a client which communicates the auditor's observations and suggestions regarding possible improvements in *accounting practices, internal controls, operating procedures*, and like matters. Considered an important byproduct of the regular audit examination. Also termed *management letter* or *long-form report*.

letter of representation (auditing) A formal letter required on every audit under *generally accepted auditing standards*, from client management to the auditor, in which client management acknowledges that the financial statements are their responsibility and important matters stated to the auditor during the course of the engagement are, in fact, true to the best knowledge and belief of management.

letter rulings (federal income taxes) See *rulings*.

level of effort A measure of the resources required to perform a task or function. Such measures are used in the development of *decision packages* in *zero-base budgeting* systems where, as part of the package, managers identify the costs of operating at different effort levels. For example, the manager articulates the most fundamental and important elements of an activity or function, identified as the "minimum level of effort." Such a minimum typically would not be sufficient to achieve all of the potential in an activity, but it would represent a necessary resource commitment if such an activity is to be pursued. Minimum levels are often substantially below the status quo.

leverage The tendency of net income to vary disproportionately with sales (*operating leverage*), or of *residual net income* to vary disproportionately with net income (*capital leverage* or *financial leverage*). Operating leverage increases as the ratio of fixed costs to total costs increases, since variations in sales then produce much larger variations in net income. Capital leverage, referring to the distribution of income among the equities, is large when most of the capital is in the form of fixed commitments, such as bonded debt and preferred stock, and only a small proportion is in the form of common stock, which receives all income after costs and fixed commitments, such as bond interest, are met; under such conditions, small fluctuations in net income tend to produce large variations in earnings per share of common stock. See also *financial leverage*.

leveraged lease 1. A lease of property that is financed by a long-term creditor other than the lessee or the lessor. The long-term creditor usually does not have recourse to the general credit of the lessor in the event of default.

2. A lease classified and accounted for as a single net investment by the lessor that (a) involves three parties: a lessee, a long-term creditor, and a lessor; (b) involves financing that is nonrecourse to the general credit of the lessor; and (c) requires an initial net investment by the lessor that declines during the initial years of the lease and rises during the later years.

levy *n.* 1. An assessment of taxes.

2. A demand on the members of an organization for a contribution of additional working capital or to make good a loss. See *assessment (5)*. *v.t. & i.* To assess for purposes of taxation.

liability 1. An amount owing by one *person* (a debtor) to another (a creditor), payable in money, or in *goods* or *services*: the consequence of an *asset* or *service* received or a loss *incurred* or *accrued*; particularly, any debt (a) *due* or *past due* (*current liability*), (b) due at a specified time in the future (e.g., *funded debt*, *accrued liability*), or (c) due only on failure to perform a future act (*deferred income*, *contingent liability*).

2. *pl.* The title of the credit half of a *balance sheet*, often including *net worth* as well as obligations to outsiders; when thus used, the inference is that the organization reflected in the balance sheet has a status independent of both its creditors and its owners—to whom it must account in the amounts shown.

3. Liabilities are probable future sacrifices of economic benefits stemming from present legal, equitable, or constructive obligations of a particular enterprise to transfer assets or provide services to other entities in the future as a result of past transactions or events affecting the enterprise.

liability certificate A term applied to a representation or a portion thereof, obtained by an *auditor* from the management of an enterprise under examination, and containing expressions of opinion or fact relating to recorded, unrecorded, and contingent liabilities. See *representation*.

liability dividend A *dividend* paid through the issue of evidences of indebtedness. Example: a dividend paid in bonds or scrip. See *scrip dividend*.

liability for endorsement A contingent or secondary liability usually arising from the endorsement of an obligation owing by another, and continuing until it is ascertained that the original debtor has paid or has failed to meet the obligation; in the latter event, the obligation becomes a direct one of the endorser. See *note receivable discounted; contingent liability*.

liability reserve = *accrued liability*; so called because of the often uncertain amount of *accruals* for such items as income taxes: a term no longer sanctioned by good usage.

liability to an outsider 1. A *liability* other than to an owner, except that a nominal amount owing to an owner or stockholder for services, supplies, or any other usual day-to-day transaction is commonly accounted for and reported as an ordinary liability.

2. In the case of an *affiliated group*, a *liability* remaining as a *consolidated-balance-sheet* item after *intercompany eliminations* have been made.

licensed public accountant One who has registered under state law to practice as a public accountant. Approximately one-half of the states have licensing requirements, and in all but one or two the licensee must be a certified public accountant.

lien The right of one person to satisfy a claim against another by holding the other's property as security or by seizing and converting the property under procedures provided by law.

life annuity An annuity the payment of which ceases on the death of the beneficiary.

life-cycle costs = *complete cycle costs*.

life income funds (institutional accounting) Funds, established to account for assets given to an organization such as a college or university, subject to an agreement to pay the income earned by the assets over a specified period of time to the donor.

life table A table showing additions, retirements, and other mortality and survivor characteristics of a group of assets.

life tenant One entitled to the use or income of property during his or her life.

LIFO 1. = *Last In, First Out*. See *inventory valuation; cost absorption (2c)*.
2. (computers) A scheduling technique in which the last data item stored in a data file is the first to be returned from that file. It is sometimes referred to as a stack.

LIFO inventory layer A pool or group of homogeneous items of *inventory* priced at the same value per unit for *LIFO* purposes. Under the last in, first out cost-flow assumption, ending inventory quantities of homogeneous items are valued at the oldest possible purchase prices. Each quantity using a different price constitutes a layer. Thus, a firm may begin business or adopt the LIFO method when it has 10,000 units on hand at a cost of $1.00. At year end it may have 12,000 units on hand. The first 10,000 units will be valued at $1.00; the remaining 2,000 units (or the layer above the 10,000 units of base stock) will be valued at some purchase price incurred during the year. That price may be based upon any acceptable inventory cost-flow method such as LIFO, FIFO, or average. Under dollar-value LIFO, a price

index approach is used to establish synthetic quantities for nonhomogeneous goods. Reductions in quantity remove the most recent layers first. See *inventory valuation*.

limited audit 1. An audit limited to definite transactions or accounts, excluding all others.
2. An audit (*1*) of all accounts for a short period.
3. An audit in which, usually by agreement, certain customary features have been omitted.

limited company A business corporation; a British term, the abbreviation "Ltd." appended to the corporate name signifying registration under the Companies Act, thus establishing the limited liability of stockholders, as in the case of stockholders of most U.S. corporations.

limited liability A liability restricted by law or contract. Examples: the liability of a special partner in a firm; the liability of a stockholder in a corporation.

limited-life asset Any *capital asset*, as a building, machine, or patent, the usefulness of which to its owner is restricted by its physical life or by the period during which it contributes to operations. See *capital asset; fixed asset*.

limited partnership A partnership in which one or more partners, but not all, have a limited liability to partnership creditors.

limited review *n. Review*; *analytic review*.

linear Having the mathematical properties of a straight line or a plane surface. For example, the algebraic expression $Y = a + bX$ plots as a straight line in a *Cartesian coordinate system*, the constants a and b relating each *abscissa* to its corresponding *ordinate*, so that all pairs of *coordinates* lie on the same straight line. See *coordinate system*.

The constant a is called the "intercept." It locates the ordinate $Y = a$ at the abscissa X

$= 0$. The constant b is called the "slope." It shows the rate of change of the ordinate values per unit change in the abscissa.

linear programming A type of *mathematical programming* for planning an operation; involved is the construction of a *model* of a real situation containing the following elements: (a) *variables* representing the available choices, and (b) mathematical expressions (i) relating the variables to the controlling conditions, (ii) reflecting the criteria to be used in measuring the benefits derivable from each of the possible choices, and (iii) establishing the objective. This provides the setting in which known methods of solution and available computer codes may be used to ensure the selection of the best of a large number of alternatives.

For example, a plan may be sought for the most profitable loading of the available time of 12 hours for machine A and 10 hours for machine B in the processing of two products. These products must be sold together, the condition being that the quantity of the first, which yields a profit of $1 per unit, must be equal to or less than the quantity of the second, which yields a profit of 50 cents per unit. The first product requires 3 hours' time on machine A and 5 hours' time on machine B. The second product requires 2 hours' time on machine A only. To establish the model, these relations are expressed in the form of the following limiting conditions ("constraints"):

$$3x_1 + 2x_2 \leqslant 12,$$
$$5x_1 \qquad \leqslant 10,$$
$$x_1 - x_2 \leqslant 0.$$

The first two constraints refer to the machines and the last to the quantity relations ($x_1 \leqslant x_2$) between the two products. The numbers (*constants*) on the left-hand side of each *inequality* are known as "technological" or "structural" *coefficients*; x_1 and x_2,

the quantities of the two products, respectively, are the *variables*, on which "nonnegativity" conditions $x_1 \geqslant 0, x_2 \geqslant 0$ apply.

Once the objective is prescribed, the methods of linear programming can be used to discover the best of the possible plans. Thus, if the objective is to maximize profit, the solution of $x_1 = x_2 = 2$ is indicated. This program, which returns $3, is said to be an "optimum." Other equally good programs can be determined, such as $x_1 = 0$ and $x_2 = 6$. When this occurs, the model is said to yield "alternate" optima. Lacking such alternatives, the optimum is "unique."

Linear programming can also be availed of for such secondary objectives as disclosing less profitable programs that are less sensitive to possible errors in the basic data. Linear programming methods may also be applied to such diverse problems as determining a product mix that will maximize sales volume or minimize purchase costs; utilizing storage, shipment, or distribution facilities more fully; cutting down on the set-up time in a machine shop; or otherwise making the most economical use of available manpower and physical facilities.

linear trend A trend portrayed in a graph by a straight line. See *trend analysis*.

line item A specific revenue or expenditure separately detailed in a budget. See *line item budget*.

line item budget 1. A budget, usually for a government body, in which budgeted items are grouped only by administrative units and *object costs*. They also tend toward *incremental budgeting* because the comparison provided is only with budgets and expenditure for preceding periods. Output measures and grouping by programs are generally absent. See *program planning budgeting system; zero-base budgeting*.

2. A detailed expense or expenditure budget, generally classified by *object* within each

organizational unit, and, often classified within each object as to authorized number of employees at each salary level within each job classification, etc.

line of business reporting A requirement adopted by the *Securities and Exchange Commission* in 1969 that required registrants to disclose revenue and income before income taxes and extraordinary items for each line of business (as defined by management) accounting for at least 10% of a firm's total revenue and total income before income taxes and extraordinary items. This requirement has since been amended to require *industry segment* information rather than line of business data.

In 1974, the Federal Trade Commission developed a line of business reporting program to accumulate data about corporations engaged in business in the United States. See *segmental reporting*.

line of credit = *credit line*.

line printer (computers) A *hardware* device which outputs data from a computer onto paper. The normal output length of the line of data on a line printer is 132 characters. Modern line printers also provide limited capability for printing graphic data.

lines of business reporting See *line of business reporting*.

link To tie together, as in a *flow chart*. To relate a series of items or transactions as when following an *audit trail* or when calculating a *chain index*.

link list (computers) A technique whereby various collections of data are interconnected through the use of pointers or links. A particular item is located in a link list by beginning at the first data item in the list and following the links from one data item to the next until the specific item is located. The data need not be stored sequentially.

liquid Being in a state where cash or assets readily convertible into cash are available in sufficient amount to meet obligations due for payment.

liquid asset Cash in banks and on hand, and other cash assets not set aside for specific purposes other than the payment of a current liability, or a readily marketable investment. The term is somewhat less restrictive than *cash asset* and more restrictive than *quick asset*.

liquid asset ratios See *liquidity ratios*.

liquidating dividend 1. A pro rata distribution to stockholders or owners by an organization in liquidation, consisting of cash or other assets becoming available from the winding up of its business.
2. A pro rata distribution to the stockholders of a company having wasting assets (as mines, oil wells, timber), representing a return of paid-in capital.
3. A pro rata distribution of assets to stockholders which has the effect of reducing paid-in capital or appreciation surplus; a return of capital.

liquidation 1. Payment of debt.
2. Conversion into cash; examples: the liquidation of accounts receivable, investments, or inventory.
3. The sale of assets and the settlement of debts in the winding up of a business, estate, or other *economic unit*.

liquidation value 1. The price that can be obtained from the sale of assets in liquidation proceedings; forced-sale value.
2. The agreed amount per share to be paid to preferred shareholders upon the voluntary or involuntary liquidation of a corporation.

liquidity *Cash* or *near-cash assets* relative to an entity's need for these items to pay maturing obligations. See *liquid asset*; *solvency ratios*.

liquidity ratios Any *ratios* designed to show a firm's ability to meet its short-term obligations. For examples, see the *acid-test ratio* and the *current ratio*.

listed Admitted to trading privileges: said of a security with reference to an established stock exchange.

list price A printed price, as one appearing in a catalog, subject to trade and cash discounts; hence, any quoted price in excess of that obtaining in an actual sale.

Littleton, A. C. (1886-1974) A prolific author and scholar, A. C. Littleton was a major contributor to the American literature on accounting theory and history. His *Accounting Evolution to 1900*, published in 1933, has become a classic, as has *An Introduction to Corporate Accounting Standards*, which he wrote in 1940 with *William A. Paton*. He was President of the American Accounting Association in 1943 and was Editor of *The Accounting Review* from 1943 to 1946. He was a longtime Professor of Accounting at the University of Illinois at Urbana-Champaign.

loader (computers) A program which takes executable instructions from a disk file and stores them in main memory prior to execution.

load-factor pricing Differential price making at different periods of time for the purpose of maximizing the utilization of production facilities: a principle applied in an effort to overcome seasonal or time-of-day depression in demand, or to attract lower-income groups.

loading 1. The amount often added to an installment contract to cover *selling and administrative expenses, interest, risk*, and sometimes other factors.

2. In an *investment trust* or *mutual fund*, the amount added to the prorated market price of underlying securities, representing administrative and selling costs, trustee's fees, and brokerage.

3. Arbitrary additions used in preparing *statistics* or *indexes* in order to adjust the subject matter to a basis suitable for comparison or presentation.

4. The addition of *overhead* to *prime cost*.

loan Arrangement between an owner (the lender) and another (the borrower) conveying the right to use property for a period of time, usually specified in a formal agreement under which the borrower promises to return the property and usually to pay for using it. Generally in *cash* and the payment for its use is *interest (1)* or *rent*.

loan authority (government accounting) Congressional authority to incur loans relating to designated programs, where repayments are to be made in subsequent *appropriation (1)* periods.

loan capital Long- and short-term liabilities owing to bondholders, owners of debenture notes or bonds, banks, and others; evidenced by instruments having a due date, they are usually interest-bearing. Excluded are payables arising from repetitive transactions in goods and services, accruals of interest and current *operating costs, deferred taxes* and *income, valuation reserves, appropriated retained income* (*earned surplus*), and credits normally classified under *stockholders' equity* (*net worth*).

loan fund (institutional accounting) A fund from which loans are to be made. The term has particular significance in colleges and universities. When both principal and interest of a fund are available for loans, the entire amount is placed in the loan-funds group; when only the income of the fund may be loaned, the principal is included in endowment funds, only the income constituting the loan fund.

loan value (life insurance) The maximum amount that may be borrowed from the insurer on a life insurance contract.

local currency *Currency* of a particular country being referred to; the reporting currency of a domestic or foreign operation being referred to.

local-improvement fund = *special assessment fund*.

lock box An address such as a post office box to which a corporation's customers are directed to remit payment. Lock boxes are usually located in association with an account in a nearby bank which is authorized to open the incoming envelopes and deposit checks to the corporation's account in order to reduce *collection float*. A standard problem in *operations research* is the so-called "lock box location problem," which seeks to minimize the cost of bank and lock box services along with lost interest-earning opportunities. The "corporate payments problem," on the other hand, seeks to extend the *payment float* by selecting the location of banks against which checks are to be drawn in order to increase interest earnings.

log *n.* 1. = *logarithm*.
2. A record or diary as of a ship's voyage.
—*v.t.* to log or enter.

logarithm The power, known also as the *index* or "exponent," to which one number, called the "base," is raised in order to make it equal to another number. Thus, the logarithm of 100 to the base 10 is 2, since $10^2 = 100$, and the logarithm of 1,000 to the base 10 is 3, since $10^3 = 1,000$. The *antilogarithm* is the number obtained when the base is raised to the power specified by a given logarithm; it is frequently called the original number and is signified by N. Thus, the antilogarithm of 2, using the base 10, is 100, and the antilogarithm of 3 is 1,000.

Any positive number may serve as the base but logarithm tables are usually constructed with 10 or $e = 2.718+$ as the base. The former are referred to as common logarithms (also called Briggs logarithms), and the latter as natural logarithms. Each may be related to the other by

$$\log_{10} N = \log_{10} e \ \log_e N \ ,$$

where $\log_{10} N$ and $\log_e N$ refer to logarithms to the bases 10 and e, respectively, and $\log_{10} e = 0.434+$.

The usual rules for exponents apply so that

$$\begin{aligned}
\log N_1 N_2 &= \log N_1 + \log N_2 \\
\log N_1 /N_2 &= \log N_1 - \log N_2 \\
\log N^r &= r \ \log N \\
\log \sqrt[r]{N} &= (1/r) \ \log N.
\end{aligned}$$

This greatly facilitates computation by reference to prepared tables of logarithms. Such tables are expressed in *mantissa* values leaving the user to supply the *characteristic*. Even this simple operation is no longer necessary since computers and even hand calculators are programmed to supply any wanted logarithm value directly.

logging in See *handshaking*.

logical description (computers) A description of the data base as the user sees it. Contrasts with the physical description, which refers to how the data are actually stored in a computer.

logical file (computers) A data set or group of similar records treated as a single entity from the perspective of a user.

logical record A collection of data items as viewed by a user, usually with reference to the problem being solved. It contrasts with "physical records" which conform to the actual storage of this group of data items.

long *n.* A buyer or owner (as distinct from a seller) of stocks or commodities, often on *margin*.
adj. Owning more of a stock or commodity than is owed under contracts to deliver.

long account (brokerage accounting) The account on a broker's books in which the securities or commodities carried for a customer are recorded.

long-form report = *auditors' report* (*2*).

long-lived asset *Asset* that is expected to provide benefits for several years or *operating cycles*; a noncurrent asset usually classified as *property, plant*, and *equipment*, but may also include *investments* and other *intangibles*. See *balance sheet*.

long-range planning See *strategic planning*.

long run (economics) The length of time necessary for a firm to vary all of the factors of production, including those which give rise to its *fixed cost*.

long-term Except as noted below, extending beyond one term.

long-term contract Any contract for goods or services the completion of which extends into one or more succeeding fiscal years. The term is often applied to agreements covering the production of heavy equipment, such as electric generators, construction projects, and ships. The propriety of the accrual of revenue by the producer, as sections of the work are completed, has long been recognized in accounting. See *revenue recognition*. The relative size of the amount yet to be paid may require disclosure in the balance sheet or in a balance-sheet footnote.

long-term debt (on balance sheet) Debt due after one year. The term applies generally to all forms of corporate obligations, secured and unsecured: mortgage bonds; sinking-fund bonds; income bonds; bank loans; debentures (whether or not convertible); loans from insurance companies; and so on. The principal features of each such obligation are disclosed in the *sidehead* or in an appended note; these will include nature of underlying security, if any; rate of interest; redemption rates; convertible privileges. Its position on the *balance sheet* is between *current liabilities* and *stockholders' equity* (net worth); any

portion maturing during the following 12 months usually appears as a *current liability*.

long-term debt group of accounts See *general long-term debt account group*.

long-term debt to equity ratio See *debt-equity ratio*.

long-term holding period (federal income taxes) The period for which a capital asset must be held (currently more than one year) to qualify for treatment as long-term capital gain or loss. See *holding period; capital gain net income; capital loss; capital gain*.

long-term lease An obligation for rental payment on real (and sometimes personal) property over an extended period of years. Present usage of the term applies not only to ordinary or *executory leases* but also to *sell-and-leaseback agreements* and to contracts resembling leases but which are in effect *installment* purchases. Because of the importance and often involved character of this modern type of financing, financial statements containing these items are supplemented by detailed notes, the content of which is outlined in APB 31. See *leaseback; term lease*.

long-term liability An obligation which will not become due within a relatively short period, usually a year. Examples: *mortgages*; mortgage bonds; *debentures*; secured-note issues; *funded debt* generally.

long-term senior securities to total capitalization ratio See *debt-equity ratio*.

loose standards Performance expectations which are set below the normal efficiency level for a given task or set of tasks. Often associated with *budgetary slack*, such standards may lead to underutilization of the productive *capacity*. See *standard cost*.

loss 1. Any item of expense, as in the term *profit and loss*.
2. Any sudden, unexpected, involuntary expense or irrecoverable cost, often referred to

as a form of *nonrecurring charge*, an expenditure from which no present or future benefit may be expected. Examples: the undepreciated cost of a building destroyed by fire and not covered by insurance; damages paid in an accident suit; an amount of money stolen. See *prior-period adjustment; income deduction*.
3. Decreases in assets or increases in liabilities during a period from peripheral, incidental, or occasional transactions of an enterprise and from other events and circumstances affecting it; they include all increases in *net assets* or *owners' equity* other than those from expenses and distributions by the enterprise to owners.
4. = *net loss*.

loss and gain = *profit and loss*.

loss function In *decision* theory, a *function* which records the loss from selecting an action that is not the best one for the state that materializes. The loss is measured relative to the best alternative course of action so that it represents a variant of *opportunity cost* with a cost (= loss) of zero when the best action is chosen.

loss ratio (insurance) The ratio of the losses paid or accrued by an insurer to premiums earned, usually for a period of a year.

lost discount See *discount lost*.

lost units Output units lost either through the *shrinkage* of raw material inputs during the production process or through spoilage of output parts or products. See *shrinkage; spoilage*.

lost usefulness The gradual dissipation, from any cause, of service potential, or worth in exchange; *depreciation*.

lot Any group of goods or services making up a single transaction; if the group consists of a known number of similar items, the price or cost of each is obtained by simple division; if the items are dissimilar and the total price is independent of the prices, if any, of individu-

al items, the cost of each item is usually indeterminable, except by any of several possible methods of imputation. See *imputed cost; job lot*.

lot-acceptance sampling (statistical quality control) = *acceptance sampling*.

lot size See *order quantity*.

lot tolerance percent defective (statistical quality control) A degree of quality, generally in terms of number or percentage of defective items in a *lot* or *batch* of goods, which is generally regarded as just satisfactory or tolerable, the implication being that any quality of lower degree is unsatisfactory; often referred to as "LTPD." A level of quality below which the lot is not acceptable.

lower of cost or market See *cost or market, whichever is lower*.

LTPD = *lot tolerance percent defective*.

lump-sum appropriation (or allotment) An *appropriation* (or *allotment*) for a stated purpose, or for a named department or departmental subdivision, authorizing an aggregate of expenditures, but not specifying beyond general purposes the amounts that may be applied to individual *objects* or *activities* thereunder.

lump-sum purchase The acquisition of a group of assets for an indicated figure, without breakdown by individual assets or classes of assets: a type of transaction often accompanying the purchase of a going concern. For example, the amount paid may have been determined by determining the present worth of future earning ability, by bargaining between individuals whose sense of "values" has little to do with formal records or with reports of earnings, or by other considerations not reflected in the accounts. An appraisal of the acquired assets by engineers may then establish the basis (*replacement cost* or *book value*) for recording the assets, with due allowance for depreciation, any excess of the purchase price over such depreciated basis being regarded as *goodwill*. Where the depreciated basis exceeds the purchase price, the items of which the basis is composed are usually reduced pro rata; or the accrued depreciation, as estimated, is increased. In numerous cases, the book values reflected on the records of the seller are continued on the books of the buyer, particularly where the purchase price has been based on the seller's financial statements, the balancing amount, if any, being designated as an *intangible*. This is the procedure prescribed by regulatory bodies for recording lump-sum purchases of a utility enterprise; the valuation basis thus established is referred to as *original cost*, and the purchase excess as *acquisition adjustment*.

machine-hour rate A rate of cost per hour of work performed by a machine, applied to goods in process. Cost consists of direct and indirect expense—labor, depreciation, power, maintenance, supplies, and often an allocated portion of factory overhead—and may be estimated (a standard rate) or actual. Machine hours, the divisor of cost employed to determine the hourly rate, may likewise be estimated or actual. If the rate is estimated, the difference between estimated and actual, attributable to variations in both costs and hours, and periodically determined, is often spread over the preceding period's production by a supplementary rate or carried into the following (monthly) period for inclusion in that period's estimates. A single, accurate rate is subject to the criticism that its determination delays the postings to cost sheets or other production records for too protracted an interval after the close of the period. See *cost; standard cost; job-order costing; overhead*.

machine language (computers) A *binary coding* system which can be executed directly by the *central processing unit*. Machine language is usually different for each individual type of computer.

machine tool 1. Any device, usually stationary, composed of a number of moving parts, at least partially automatic in action, used for shaping, turning, planing, or assembling.
2. A replaceable part such as a cutting or shaping attachment of such a device.

macro accounting = *national income accounting*.

macroeconomics The study of the determinants of the *aggregate* level of *economic activity* such as *national income* and employment.

magnetic tape (computers) An external storage medium for storage of *binary* bits of data on either plastic or metal tape. Each data item is represented by either seven or nine *bits* of data arranged in a column across the tape and referred to as 7-track or 9-track tape. Only 6 or 8 bits, respectively, are used to store the data and the additional bit is known as the *parity bit*. This bit is either turned on or off so that the entire code is always equal to an even number or odd number in order to permit checking for errors during the read process. This is what is referred to as even parity or odd parity. Each physical read or write onto magnetic tape transfers an entire *block* of data, which may consist of a number of *logical records*.

maintenance 1. The keeping of property in operable condition; also, the expense involved. Maintenance costs include outlays for (a) labor and supplies; (b) the replacement of any part that constitutes less than a *retirement unit*; and (c) major overhauls the items of which may involve elements of the first two classes. Items falling under (a) and (b) are always regarded as operating costs, chargeable to current expense directly or through the medium of a *maintenance reserve* (see *equalization reserve*). Costs under (c) are similarly treated unless they include the replacement of a retirement unit the outlay for which is normally capitalized. See *deferred maintenance*.
2. = any *operating cost*.

maintenance reserve An *equalization reserve* for maintenance costs. See *deferred maintenance*.

majority-owned subsidiary A subsidiary more than 50% of whose outstanding voting capital stock is owned by its parent or by another of the parent's majority-owned subsidiaries.

make-or-buy decision A decision whether a firm should manufacture (make) a certain part, component, or product or whether it should purchase it in the desired quantities from another firm. The decision may be made on the basis of whether the *incremental cost* to make is lower than the purchase price, including applicable discounts, unless the product competes for facilities with other products. The latter situation requires analyses which take into consideration lost profits or investment in new facilities as well as the make-or-buy costs of the product being considered.

makeready time The time spent on the preparation of machines and other facilities before starting production; the cost of labor and other factors applied to such preparation.

See *lead time; setup time*. The term is used principally in the printing trade.

malfeasance The wrongful doing of an act that the doer has no right to do or is contractually obligated not to do. See *misfeasance; nonfeasance*.

malpractice insurance Liability insurance which insures a professional person (doctor, lawyer, accountant) against liability for actions arising out of his or her professional acts.

managed costs An indirect cost whose level is determined by management on a frequent, usually annual, basis. The level of managed costs does not change in response to other activities, such as manufacturing volume, but is subject to review and adjustment by management. The same cost could be a managed cost in one firm and not in another firm. Examples of managed costs include research and development cost, executive training program costs, and advertising. Managed costs are also referred to as programmed costs and discretionary costs. See *discretionary costs*.

managed (band) exchange rates A band involving upper and lower limits for the ratio of units of currencies between two nations which they agree to maintain as limits for allowable fluctuations in their exchange rates. See *fixed exchange rates*.

management 1. Executive authority: the combined fields of *policy* and *administration*: a term often employed as a correlative of *decision making*.
2. As applied to individuals:
    (a) the head of an organization, or
    (b) collectively, the head and his or her immediate staff and any or all persons possessing delegated supervisory authority;
    (c) hence, broadly, the persons within an organization who originate *transactions*.
    It is often said that management ''delegates'' (or assigns or grants) authority to

subsidiary levels of activity, but cannot delegate *responsibility*. The latter can only be "assumed" (i.e., when the delegation has been accepted and agreed to) by the activity (suborganizational, subfunctional) head who operates within the defined limits of the delegation and is *accountable* to (i.e., reports to or has a *feedback* relationship with) the delegator.

Management Accounting See *accounting journals*.

management accounting Accounting designed for or adapted to the needs of information and control at the various administrative levels of an organization. The term has no precise coverage but is used generally to refer to the extensions of internal reporting for the design and submission of which a corporation *controller* is responsible. Repetitive reports on performance involving both product quantities and dollars, special reports covering operational areas undergoing change or proposed for reorganization, and reports of investigations of malfunctioning or suspected inefficiencies are illustrative of the manifold activities in which the present-day controller, frequently with the assistance of a public accountant, is expected to engage. Emphasis is often given to prompt, authoritative, and complete reports that can lead to and even induce management decision making. An illustration of management accounting is *activity accounting*. See *managerial accounting*.

management audit See *audit; internal audit; performance audit*.

management by exception A phrase used in connection with the presumed action required where reports on performance differ from original projections (*actual costs* versus *standard costs* or *budgeting* prescriptions). Characteristically these reports bring out "favorable" and "unfavorable" variances, the latter being the basis for "management

by exception"; see, however, *favorable difference*.

management by objectives (MBO) The joint formulation by a manager and his or her superior of comprehensive goals and plans for achieving the overall objective of the unit for a forthcoming period. The manager's performance is then measured in relation to the agreed-upon goals and plans.

management control See *management control system*.

management control system An organized, integrated process and structure through which management attempts to achieve enterprise goals *effectively* and *efficiently*. It should encompass an organization in its entirety, provide well-defined units of measurement and evaluation, and emphasize continuous comparisons of actual with planned or budgeted performance. Recent literature and pronouncements concerned with division of responsibilities between managers and auditors and the *Foreign Corrupt Practices Act* sometimes distinguish a management control system from an *internal (accounting) control* system by its concern with major methods of organization design, selection of executive personnel and delineation of their duties, and the procedures under which the policies for the direction of an enterprise are to be developed. See *control; internal control; internal check*.

management fraud Intentional misrepresentations by management which affect the financial statements. These may result from the misrepresentation or omission of the effects of events or transactions; manipulation, falsification, or alteration of records or documents; omission of significant information from records or documents; recording of transactions without substance; intentional misapplication of accounting principles; or misappropriation of assets.

management fund (federal accounting) Funds which merge two or more appropriations or portions thereof, in order to carry out a common purpose or project.

management information system (MIS) An information system designed to aid managers in decision-making processes.

management investment company An investment company the management of which is permitted a large discretion in buying and selling securities. There are two principal types: closed-end and open-end companies. The former, also known as *leverage* companies, often have several types of bonds and stocks outstanding, some of which may be listed on exchanges and the prices of which bear no necessary relationship to book values; the latter usually have only a single type of outstanding stock, in which only licensed dealers are permitted to trade and the value of which is based on the market value of securities in their portfolio.

management letter See *letter of recommendation*.

management override The ability or actual act by management to nullify the effectiveness of specific internal accounting controls. Less reliance can be placed on internal accounting control by the external auditor in performing an examination in these circumstances. Where management override can exist, the potential for *management fraud* is increased.

management performance See *operating performance*.

management representations See *representation*.

management review (or audit) An *appraisal* (2) by a public accountant or other professional person of management *performance*: a testing of adherence to governing policy; profit capability; adequacy of operating controls and of operating procedures; relations with employees, customers, the trade, and the public generally; adaptability to and conformity with the current concept of the *public interest*. See *audit* (*4B*).

management science = *operations research*.
1. The field of management problems and their solutions, particularly those of a complex nature, which can benefit from mathematical or statistical modeling or an understanding of which is susceptible to testing, verification, and generalization.
2. The study of new and improved management techniques having general application.

The complexity and subtlety of problems investigated by management often lead to mathematical or statistical *models*; the employment of such models has sometimes supplied a ready means of distinguishing management-science research from other types of investigation in the same area. Thus, the design of an accounting system might take the form of a series of flow charts, manuals, and accompanying codes and account descriptions when executed by an accountant. An *operations-research* specialist might reformulate the design in terms of a mathematical model to study possible variations in accounting structures and their attendant risks and benefits.

management services A division of a public accounting firm, or a unit of a controller's office in a private corporation, which supplies consulting services often of a *management-science* variety.

managements' illegal acts Intentional acts of commission or omission by one or more members of management of an enterprise which violate federal, state, local, or foreign law. Some of the more common serious illegal acts by management include: illegal political contributions, bribes, filing false and misleading reports with governmental agencies, and withholding information from auditors.

manager 1. (public accounting) In the office of a public accountant, a supervisor of audit engagements to whom the field staff reports and to whom varying degrees of authority may be given in the processes of initiating, supervising, closing, and reporting of such engagements.
2. An executive or an *administrator*.

managerial accounting That portion of accounting which attempts to supply management with quantitative information as a basis for decisions. In the view of some it is primarily a planning aid for analyzing different alternatives as a basis for making recommended choices. Its scope, however, varies from firm to firm and may include the design and monitoring of ongoing information and control systems as well as investigation of the potential costs and benefits of alternative future courses of action. Quantitative methods, modeling, statistical analyses, behavioral sciences, and operations research or management science techniques may be employed. See *management accounting*.

mantissa The decimal portion of the common *logarithm*; distinguished from its *characteristic*. Thus, the logarithm of 55, which is 1.740363, displays the mantissa to the right of the decimal and the characteristic (=1) to its left. The logarithm of 550 = 2.740363 has the same mantissa. Thus, logarithm tables conserve space by presenting only mantissa values and allowing users to supply the *characteristic* from the context used. See *characteristic*.

manual of accounting = *accounting manual*.

manual rate (insurance) An established standard premium rate, usually expressed in dollars per thousand dollars of risk.

manufacturing cost 1. Any item of expense occurring in a processing operation.
2. The collective fixed and variable costs of a manufacturing or processing operation; *fac-*

tory cost. Its conventional elements as recognized in accounting are *raw materials* and parts, *direct labor*, and *manufacturing overhead*. See *inventory valuation* (manufactured products).

manufacturing expense The cost of manufacturing other than the cost of raw materials consumed and direct labor; *factory expense; indirect expense*; (factory) *overhead*.

manufacturing overhead = *factory overhead*.

manufacturing statement A statement showing particulars of the cost of goods manufactured. See *cost of goods manufactured statement*.

margin 1. = *gross profit*.
2. The excess of the market price of collateral over the loan it secures, usually required as part of the *short sale* of any security. Thus a rise in the price of such a security may cause the brokers to place additional margin calls to investors involved in such transactions. *Margin requirements* are established by the Federal Reserve System with the objective of reducing speculation and market volatility.
3. The remaining equity of a broker's customer when a security or commodity so purchased is sold.
4. = *marginal income*.

marginal analysis A method of analyzing production costs or revenues by continuous *increments* in order to determine their causes of variation. See *marginal productivity; marginal cost; marginal revenue; incremental analysis*.

marginal balance The excess of revenue over variable cost; see *marginal income*.

marginal cost 1. The increase or decrease in total cost which occurs with a small variation in output.
2. Hence, *incremental cost, differential cost*, or the increase in *direct cost*, excluding any element of *fixed cost*. Ascertaining marginal

cost is of importance in determining whether to vary a rate of production. Fixed or *sunk costs* of facilities will continue whether or not the facilities are put to use; it may therefore be profitable to solicit new business at lower prices even if fixed costs are not completely covered, the test being whether revenues from new business are sufficient to cover the added (marginal) costs of production. At less than *optimum output*, an increase in the rate of production will usually result in a marginal unit cost lower than *average total unit cost*; production in excess of the optimum point will result in a marginal unit cost greater than average total unit cost; at optimum output, the two costs coincide, where optimum refers to the lowest average total unit cost. Thus, marginal unit cost is the lowest amount at which a sale may be made without adding to a producer's loss or subtracting from profits.

marginal costing The assignment of *marginal* or *variable costs* to an activity, department, or product, as contrasted with *absorption costing* and *direct costing*. See *direct costing*.

marginal income The excess of sales over related *direct costs*: the *contribution* (5) of revenues to other costs and profit; also called *contribution margin*.

marginal income ratio The percentage of the sales dollar available to cover fixed costs and profits after deducting the percentage required for variable costs: the complement of the *variable-cost ratio*.

marginal physical product See *marginal productivity*.

marginal productivity An increment in total dollar value (or physical quantity) which results from a one-unit increase in the amount of a *factor of production* employed in any program or process. Completely successful measurement of the marginal productivity of any factor of production can be attained only when it is possible to isolate its variations from other causes of yield variation. In particular, all other factors of production must be approximately constant at known levels before yield variations can be *imputed*, with complete validity, to the factor in question. Such ideal conditions are seldom met with, and it may be necessary to resort to rather complex means for obtaining *approximations* to the desired measures. See *productivity; variance*.

marginal productivity theory The implication of profit maximization that each factor of production should be utilized by a firm until the *marginal revenue product* resulting from increasing each factor equals its price.

marginal revenue The change in total revenue of the firm brought about by the sale of an additional unit.

marginal revenue product The increment in revenue attributable to the employment of an additional unit of a variable *factor of production*.

marginal tax rate Tax on additional dollar of taxable income. Contrast to average tax rate (income tax expense divided by income before deducting income taxes) and statutory tax rate (the rate specified in the income tax law for each type of income or *capital gain*).

marginal unit cost See *marginal cost*.

marginal utility The added *utility* supplied by one additional unit of a good or service. See *utility (1)*.

margin call A demand by a broker to put up additional money or securities when the price of securities purchased on *margin* has fallen since the purchase or the last *margin call*. Also applies to demand by the broker at the time of initial purchase of securities on *margin*.

margin of safety The excess of sales over the breakeven sales volume, expressed as dollars or in other quantity units or as a ratio. See *breakeven chart*.

margin requirements See *margin* (2).

marital deduction (federal income taxes) Both the gift tax and the estate tax contain a marital deduction provision (see code Sections 2523 and 2056, respectively) providing for the reduction of the tax base for the value of property transferred to the spouse of the donor or decedent.

The gift tax marital deduction enables the donor to subtract the value of gifts made to his or her spouse from the amount of otherwise taxable gifts in determining the total taxable base. This deduction is limited by a formula that allows the entire amount of the first $100,000 of gifts to be deducted, none of the second $100,000 of gifts to be deducted, and 50% of the value of gifts in excess of $200,000 to be deducted. The estate tax marital deduction allows for the deduction from the gross estate of an amount equal to the value of property which passes from the decedent to the surviving spouse. This deduction is limited to the greater of $250,000 or 50% of the value of the adjusted gross estate after taking account of any deductions taken for gifts to such spouse in excess of 50% of the value of such gifts.

markdown 1. In retail stores, the reduction of an originally established selling price or *markon*.

2. In banks and investment houses, a revaluation of securities based upon a decline in their market quotations.

3. = *writedown*.

markdown cancellation The portion of original *markon* restored after a *markdown* has been made.

market 1. A geographical area or other arrangement where products and their competitive substitutes can be readily bought and sold by buyers and sellers; hence, any established medium for supplier-consumer communication, such as advertisements in newspapers, catalogs, or door-to-door salesmen.

2. Recent invoice or quoted price at the close of an accounting period, less customary adjustments, including cash discount; the price at which a seller willing to sell and a buyer willing to buy will trade, assuming that both have a reasonable knowledge of the facts, that similar quantities, qualities, and delivery periods are involved, and that the market has been canvassed by both buyers and sellers. In the absence of present or prospective buyers, a market price is conceived (as in the phrase, "the lower of cost or market") to be the lowest price quoted by a prospective seller.

3. The lower of cost or market should not be greater than (a) *replacement* or *reproduction cost* or less than (b) estimated net selling price less estimated costs of carrying, selling, and delivering, and, in the case of unfinished product, less the estimated cost of bringing the product to a completed state, provided that (a) is not applied so as to reduce residual cost to a point below that at which it is anticipated a normal profit can be earned, this being the meaning generally ascribed to the term when used in the inventory valuation method known as *cost or market, whichever is lower*. See *price; inventory valuation*.

4. The price (usually representative) at which bona fide sales have been consummated for products of like type, quality, and quantity in a particular market at any moment of time. See *normal price*.

marketable securities 1. *Equity securities* or debt securities that are actively traded or which can otherwise be bought or sold. A marketable security is one for which sales prices or bid and asked prices are currently available in a national securities exchange (i.e., those registered with the *Securities and Exchange Commission*) or in the *over-the-counter* market. In the over-the-counter market, an equity security is considered marketable when a quotation is publicly reported by the *National Association of Securities*

Dealers' and Quotation Analysts' Automatic. Quotations System or by the National Quotations Bureau, Inc. (provided, in the latter case, that quotations are available from at least three dealers). Equity securities traded in foreign markets are considered marketable when such markets are of a breadth and scope comparable to those referred to above. Restricted stock is not considered marketable.

2. A *balance-sheet* title for negotiable equity securities, excluding investments accounted for by the equity method. Marketable securities may be classified as *current* or *non-current assets* and are generally stated at the lower of the portfolio's cost or market value.

market index of stock prices An aggregate measure of the level of prices of stocks of a given class or those listed on a given exchange. For example, Dow Jones price indexes for industrial, transportation, and utility stocks, Standard & Poor's price index of 500 industrial stocks, and the New York Stock Exchange stock price index.

marketing cost The cost of locating customers, persuading them to buy, delivering the goods, and collecting sales proceeds; *selling expense (cost)*.

market risk 1. In *portfolio analysis*, sensitivity of changes in the price of an individual stock to changes in the *market index of stock prices*. For example, if a change of 10% in the market index is accompanied, on average, by a change of 12% in the price of a particular stock, the market risk of the stock is $12/10 = 1.2$.

2. Ratio of *covariance* of market returns and returns on a given stock to *variance* of market returns. See *systematic risk*. See also *cost of capital; capital asset pricing model*. Usually market risk is estimated as the slope coefficient in a simple *regression* of monthly or weekly returns for the stock on the corresponding returns for the stock market.

3. For fixed-income securities, the risk of change in value of securities due to change in the interest rates.

market structure The organization characteristics of a market in terms of the size, location, and behavior of buyers and sellers. Aspects of such structural characteristics include ease of entry, homogeneity of product, and diffusion of information on buyer and seller actions.

market value = *net realizable value*. See *market*.

markon 1. The amount added to cost, in setting selling prices, to cover operating expenses and profit.

2. Also, the ratio of the added amount to cost (cost markon) or to selling price (selling markon); thus, a cost markon of one-half could yield a selling markon of one-third. See *retail method*.

Markov process A *stochastic* process in which the conditional *probability* for transiting to a future state from the present state depends only on the latter and is unaffected by additional information about the preceding history of the process. See *probability*. The probabilities of moving from one state to another in the next period are known as "transition probabilities" and the *matrix* portraying the transition probabilities from each possible state to every other possible state is known as the transition matrix. If the present state is known, successive multiplication of the known state and the transition probability matrix yields the probability of particular future states. Thus

$$y(t + 1) = My(t) = M^2y(t - 1)$$
$$= \ldots = M^t y(1),$$

where $y(t)$ is the state *vector* with elements $y_i(t)$, $i = 1, \ldots, n$ at stage t; M is the Markov transition matrix with elements $0 \leq p_{ij} \leq 1$, and $M^t = MM \ldots M$ (t times). Each p_{ij} $(i,j = 1, \ldots, n)$ in M represents the conditional probability of transiting from state i to state j in the next period. Thus via the above expression knowledge of M together with knowledge of the state vector in any preceding period, including $t = 1$, suffices to generate all of the future expected states. The values $y_i(t + 1)$ in $y(t + 1)$ are *expected values* obtained by applying M to $y(t)$ as indicated in the above expression on the left to produce

$$y_i(t + 1) = \sum_{j=1}^{n} p_{ij} y_j(t).$$

That is, each $y_i(t + 1), i = 1, \ldots, n$, is the *expected value* of the preceding $y_j(t), j = 1, \ldots, n$, since

$$\sum_{j=1}^{n} p_{ij} = 1,$$

as required for an *expected value*.

markup 1. The amount added to an established selling price for the purpose of determining a new and higher selling price; the percentage of markup is based on the previously established selling price.
2. The total amount by which established selling prices are increased during a given period in setting new selling prices.
3. = *markon*.
4. In banks and brokerage houses, a revaluation of securities based upon a rise in their market quotations.

markup cancellation The elimination of a markup or such portion thereof as pertains to unsold merchandise. See *markup*.

markup percentage *Markon (1)* divided by selling price. Also, expressed as a percentage of cost calculated by dividing *markon* by *cost*.

marshal 1. (applied to assets) To establish the order and classes of assets with respect to their application to the liquidation of liabilities.
2. (applied to liabilities) To establish the classes and priority of liabilities to be liquidated; to arrange priorities so that creditors are equitably treated.

marshalling of assets (partnership law) An equitable principle governing distribution of partnership and individual partner's assets in case of *insolvency*. Firm *creditors* have priority in firm *assets* and individual partner's creditors have priority in the separate assets of partners. The fund belonging to each class of creditors is not available to the other until the priority claims have been satisfied.

martingale A sequence, usually in a *time series*, in which the *expected value* at $t + 1$ equals the preceding value from the already realized observations of a set of *variates* at 0, 1, 2, \ldots, t. Example: a *random walk* in which a particle moves one step forward with probability p and one step backward with probability $1 - q$.

martingale process A statistical time series of a variable in which the expected value of the variable changes randomly from period to period. Therefore, the best estimate of the *expected value* in the next time period is the actually realized value in the most recent time period. This process can be formulated as follows:

$$\hat{X}_t = X_{t-1} + e_t,$$

where $\hat{X}$ = expected value; X = actual realized value; t = specific time period; e = random disturbance term. If a systematic trend is affecting the variable, such as the long-run growth in the economy, a trend or "drift" factor is included in the martingale formulation to form a *submartingale* process. Changes in a variable generated by a martingale process will be statistically independent over time. Historical series of a variable would be irrelevant for predicting future values of the variable. In accounting, the martingale process has served as an important basic hypothesis in empirical research on the statistical properties of earnings.

Massachusetts trust = *business trust*.

master budget A budget which consolidates all budgets into an overall plan, and control document, typically encompassing one year. In business the master budget also 'includes *pro forma financial statements*—including an income statement (operational budget), balance sheet, statement of changes in financial position, and a cash-flow budget—as well as operating and sales budgets. It may also include all or parts of the *capital budget* that are to be accommodated during the budget period so that it can thereby serve as a basis for coordinating all activities.

master control account A control account maintained in the general ledger supported by a subsidiary ledger or other record containing control accounts each relating to a limited number of accounts receivable or other *detail accounts*.

matching 1. The principle of identifying related revenues and expense with the same accounting period. The principle is in most cases observed as a matter of course, since the outgo for the great bulk of operating costs coincides with the inflow of revenue. In recognizing accruals and deferrals, the principle of matching is often invoked. Less common transactions involving income and expense often cannot be "matched." See *income realization; cost absorption; income deduction*.
2. The determination or recognition of items that are to compose an *income statement*.
3. (auditing) A procedure involving a comparison of the contents of two or more documents.

matching grant A *grant* which is conditional on a receiving governmental unit agreeing to commit some of its own resources to the purposes for which the grant is to be given.

material *adj*. 1. Of importance; see *materiality* (*1*).
2. *n*. = *raw material*.
3. *n.pl*. raw materials and finished parts.

material control The supplying of commodities in the amounts required in manufacturing at the lowest cost per unit consistent with required quality and with the least investment in inventory.

material in process = *goods in process*.

materiality 1. The relative importance, when measured against a *standard of comparison*, of any item included in or omitted from *books of account* or *financial statements*, or of any procedure or change in procedure that conceivably might affect such statements. Certain items become material through law, administrative regulation, directors' resolution, or other fiat. Other items are regarded as material because of convention, custom, or current social emphasis, and may differ in importance even among similar organizations. *Value judgments*, the usual and often the only means of determining relative importance, are based on such factors as the relative size and general characteristics of the item and the assumed responsibilities of management to stockholders, employees, and the public. Moreover, the factors of importance today may be of greater or less importance tomorrow. Financial statements, as representations of corporate management, can be prepared intelligently only where value judgments on questions of materiality have been well developed. Unimportant items are merged with other items of the same general class or may perhaps be omitted altogether (e.g., minor *accruals* or *prepayments*); important items may require any of varying degrees of disclosure: a separate listing, a footnote, or parenthetical mention. Some accountants have endeavored to establish standards of materiality by rules of thumb, as, by requiring that any item or item class the money amount of which is 5% or more of total assets or 10% or more of net income appear as an integral detail of a financial statement. Such a rule, however, leaves unsolved the problem of smaller items whose disclosure may be essential, regardless of their size, as where certain items, now of minor importance, may develop into major items with the passage of time or upon the happening of events now contingent or even unknown.

2. The characteristic attaching to a statement, fact, or item whereby its disclosure or the method of giving it expression would be likely to influence the judgment of a reasonable person. See *significant*.

3. (auditing) The relative importance of any audit coverage, such as the testing of accounts receivable by correspondence where circumstances seem to warrant its omission or some departure therefrom, such as the fact that at the time of the audit the accounts have been collected in full; or the relative importance of any impropriety or series of improprieties encountered in the accounts or financial statements, such as a missing document, a wrong classification, an unauthorized transaction, a restriction on information furnished by management, a weak link in internal controls, or a violation of an accounting principle. Here an opinion of materiality, like that attaching to items in financial statements, can be reached only by a value judgment on the part of the auditor provided accepted minimum requirements have been met. The factors of size and recurrability are the more common determinants. Some improprieties, even though minor, may be of such importance as to warrant the auditor's refusal to approve the financial statements; others, of less importance, may justify a qualification in a report and a disclosure of their quantitative effect; others call for discussion with management, looking to the elimination of the impropriety, at least for the future; still others, not being significant amounts, may be ignored altogether.

material price variance A *price variance* in the cost of materials. The difference between the standard and actual price for a specified quantity (usually the actual quantity purchased) of a given type of raw material. Mathematically, it is: (standard price minus actual price) times (quantity purchased). The material price variance account in the general ledger will typically include the difference between actual and standard price for all types of raw materials purchased.

material quantity variance = *material usage variance*.

materials and services A term employed in business generally as an inclusive designation of the immediate objects of expenditure; what is received in, or the cost portions of, *external transactions*. See *object classification; goods and services*.

material usage variance The difference between the standard and actual quantity of a raw material used to produce a given output; usually priced at standard cost. Mathematically it is: (standard quantity minus actual quantity) times (standard price). The material usage variance account in the general ledger will typically include the variance for all types of raw material used. Also called *material quantity variance* and *efficiency variance* (in materials).

mathematical programming A mathematical *model* in which one or more functions is to be optimized (i.e., made maximal or minimal under constraints formulated as other functions. Thus, if $f(x)$ is a goal function and $g_i(x) \geq 0, i = 1, \ldots, m$, then the latter form a set of m constraints to be satisfied in the choice of x, and "optimize $f(x)$ subject to $g_i(x) \geq 0, i = 1, \ldots, m$" is a mathematical programming problem. When $f(x)$ and all of the $g_i(x)$ are linear, then the important special class known as *linear programming* problems emerges.

matrix A rectangular array of numbers or other symbols.

matrix organization An organization structure in which executives are made responsble to multiple chains of commands. Contrasts with scalar structures involving a single dominant chain of command (1 worker, 1 boss) by providing each executive with two or more supervisors. Matrix organizations are usually restricted to middle-management levels with the single chain of command principle being applicable on either side of this level. Example: a multinational enterprise specializing in high-technology products requires both regional and technological expertise on a completely up-to-date basis for success in its sales and services. A matrix organization approach is therefore used in which every plant manager is directly responsible both to a regional vice-president and the corporate vice-president for engineering.

matured liability An obligation due or past due. The term is applied chiefly to the principal amount of a bond or note issue.

maturing liability An obligation that will shortly fall due.

maturity The date on which an obligation becomes due.

maturity basis The basis for calculating bond values and rates of return, on the supposition that the bonds will be held until maturity. See *bond valuation*.

maturity value The amount of cash or other consideration to be paid at the termination of a given period of time (the maturity date) as specified by a contract or obligation; usually the face value of a note or par value of a bond or similar debt obligation.

maximize profit To develop volume to the point where the *incremental cost* of one additional unit equals the *incremental revenue* that can be obtained for it, or where a variation in mix produces a revenue increment which is matched by the resulting increment to total cost.

maximum tax (federal income taxes) The max-

imum tax rate applicable to various types of income. 50% is applicable to the income received by an individual for personal service (primarily salaries, wages, and self-employment income). Other income not earned for personal services—interest, rents, and dividends, etc.—continues to be taxed at marginal rates up to 70%. *Income averaging* may not be elected if a taxpayer utilizes the maximum tax. The 50% maximum rate is applied to the proportion of taxable income received from personal services rather than to total salaries and wages. See *personal service income*.

May, George O. (1875-1961) An English chartered accountant and American CPA, George O. May was the senior partner of Price Waterhouse & Co. from 1911 to 1926 and a forceful leader of the American accounting profession during the second quarter of the century. He developed a collaboration with the New York Stock Exchange with a view toward reaching agreement on broad accounting principles and certain minimum standards of disclosure and was influential in *AICPA* approaches to these same topics. He was an active member of the *American Institute of Accountants* in the 1930s and 1940s, and, in 1938, at the encouragement of the *Securities and Exchange Commission*, he led the Institute's *Committee on Accounting Procedure* in the development and promulgation of its influential series of *Accounting Research Bulletins*. He spoke and wrote widely. His most influential book was *Financial Accounting—A Distillation of Experience*.

MBO = *management by objectives*.

MDI = minimum discrimination information statistic. See *information statistic*.

mean A midpoint in an array of numbers. Operationally defined (see *definition*) by summing their values and dividing by their number. A weighted mean sums their individually weighted values and divides by the sum of the weights. See *arithmetic mean; geometric mean*.

mean discrimination information statistic See *information statistic*.

meaning The referent of a term, statement, concept, or symbol: the object, condition, event, relation, or characteristic intended by a person employing a language. An emotional or emotive attitude or feeling of the user may be implicit in the intended notion in addition to an objective reference.

mean per unit estimator An estimator which does not rely on auxiliary information for projecting *sample* results to estimates of *population* values. In auditing, mean per unit estimates (or stratified mean per unit estimates) are in contrast to difference, ratio, or regression estimates which utilize sample and population book values in addition to audited sample values in making projections to the population.

mean-reverting process A *statistical time series* of a *variable* in which the *expected value* of the variable remains constant over time. Departures from the constant value are simply random disturbances, so the variable will tend to go back to the constant value in the next time period. As a result, a negative dependency exists in the time series of mean-reverting variables. Positive changes will, on average, be followed more frequently by negative changes than by positive ones, and vice versa. The mean-reverting process can be formulated as follows:

$$\hat{X}_t = u + e_t,$$

where $\hat{X}$ = expected value; u = constant value; t = specific time period; and e = random disturbance term. If a systematic *trend* is affecting the variable, such as the long-run growth in an economy, the constant value, u, can be adjusted to make it a function of time.

Historical series of a mean-reverting variable would presumably be very useful for predicting future values of the variable. In accounting, the mean-reverting process has served as an important basic hypothesis in empirical research on the statistical properties of earnings.

mean-variance frontier = efficient (investment) frontier. See *efficiency frontier*. In *portfolio analysis*, for a given set of securities, it is a set of portfolios none of which can be improved in the sense of having both a higher *mean* return and a lower *variance* of returns. For any given variance, the highest mean return portfolio that can be created from the given set of securities is on the efficient frontier (= mean-variance frontier). Similarly, for any given mean return, the portfolio with the lowest variance that can be created from the securities is on the efficient frontier.

measurement 1. The assignment of a system of *ordinal numbers* or *cardinal numbers* to the results of a scheme of inquiry or apparatus of observation in accord with logical or mathematical rules. In the case of ordinal measurement, the following two properties (a) and (b) are exhibited with respect to an ordering or ranking relation, expressed by the sign ''$\geq$'' (read ''ranks''). Among three arbitrary measures 0_L, 0_M, and 0_N found in such notions as preference or valuation, the following relations hold:

(a) One and only one of the three possibilities obtains in the case of two measures 0_L and 0_M: either $0_L \geq 0_M$ or $0_M \geq 0_L$, or $0_M = 0_L$.

(b) If $0_L \geq 0_M$ and $0_M \geq 0_N$, then $0_L \geq 0_N$.

In the case of cardinal measurement, which presupposes the existence of a zero or origin measure as well as a unit measure, the following properties hold in addition to those which apply to ordinal measurement:

(c) $0_L + 0_M = 0_M + 0_L$ (commutative rule of addition).

(d) $k(0_L + 0_M) = k0_L + k0_M$, where k is some real number (distributive rule of multiplication).

(e) $(0_L + 0_M) + 0_N = 0_L + (0_M + 0_N) = 0_L + 0_M + 0_N$ (associative rule of addition).

(f) If $0_L \geqslant 0_M$, then there exist some 0_N such that $0_L = 0_M + 0_N$.

2. In mathematics, any *function* $f(x,y)$ can be used as a measure of the distance between points x and y if it has the following properties:

(a) Nonnegativity: The distance between any two points x and y is always a nonnegative *real number* so that: $f(x,y) \geqslant 0$ with $f(x,y) = 0$ if and only if $x = y$.

(b) Symmetry: The distance from x to y is equal to the distance from y to x; $f(x,y) = f(y,x)$.

(c) Triangle Inequality: The distance from a point x to a point z cannot exceed the distance from x to any other point y plus the distance from y to z; $f(x,z) \leqslant f(x,y) + f(y,z)$.

This last condition is sometimes interpreted via the statement that "a straight line represents the shortest distance between two points." The function to be selected as a suitable measure of distance will depend on the purposes to be served. In addition, some of the three properties may be relaxed when the purpose demands this. For instance, the symmetry property may be omitted or altered to $f(x,y) = (-1)f(y,x)$ when a "signed measure of distance" is wanted.

measurement concept (of accounting) The identification of *economic activity (1)* with time periods whereby for each period the activity can be numerically characterized (or evaluated) and reported; see *continuity; accounting period*.

mechanical accuracy test An auditing procedure designed to determine that the more clerical-type procedures in an entity's ac-

counting system have been performed correctly. These include computations of accounts using prescribed formulas, summarization of details into totals, and transferring of amounts from source documents to records and between records.

median The central item in a collection of numbers arrayed according to size with a like number of items on each side of it. The 50th *percentile* or *quantile*; often represented by the symbol *Md*.

The median is also called an average of position, because of the like number of items on either side of it, notwithstanding the numerical values taken on by the group. It is therefore more stable and less likely to be influenced by extreme values than is the *arithmetic mean*. Thus, the median remains unaffected at 50 when the three values 49, 50, and 54 are changed to 49, 50, and 57; the arithmetic mean, however, changes from 51 to 52. The *mode* (the number appearing with the greatest frequency) is even more stable than the median.

Introduction of extreme values which tend to produce *skewness* in a *frequency distribution* thus has the greatest effect on the arithmetic mean and the least effect on the mode, with the median lying between the mean and the mode. This relation between the mean, median, and mode occurs because the mode is not influenced by extreme values; the median depends only on the position of the extreme values, while the arithmetic mean is directly influenced by extremes. Thus, the introduction of extremes on the high side will tend to move the median above the mode, and the mean above the median; introduction of extremely low values will tend to reverse this relation, with the mean tending to move below the median while the median tends to move below the mode.

It has been empirically established (i.e., by observation) that in a moderately skewed, but continuous, distribution, the median falls about two-thirds of the distance from the mode toward the mean. Mathematically, where $\overline{X}$ is the arithmetic mean, Md the median, and Mo the mode,

$$\overline{X} - Md = \frac{1}{3}(\overline{X} - Mo).$$

This relation can be substituted in the formula given under *skewness*,

$$Sk = \frac{\overline{X} - Mo}{\sigma},$$

to produce the more easily computed value

$$Sk = \frac{3(\overline{X} - Md)}{\sigma},$$

where the denominator, σ, is the *standard deviation*, and Sk the skewness.

In a symmetric distribution, the mean, median, and mode all coincide, and the value of the Sk relation is zero. As skewness occurs, the mean moves increasingly farther away from the median, the direction of skew being determined by whether the mean exceeds or is less than the median.

The value of the median may or may not coincide with the value of any number in the array, depending on whether the number of items is even or odd. If the number of items in the array is odd, the central item is chosen as the median; if the number of items is even, the average of the two central items is chosen as the median. Thus, if an additional value, say, 60, were added to the numbers 49, 50, and 54 given above, the array would have become 49, 50, 54, and 60, and the median (50 + 54)/2 = 52. Whereas 50 can be recognized as one of the items existing in the series, 52 cannot be so recognized. (Note: the same value would obtain for the median if 100 had been added instead of 60; the arithmetic mean, on the other hand, would have been markedly affected.)

mediation Use of impartial arbiters in disputes, usually economic disputes, charged with facilitating negotiations and making recommendations which the disputants can accept or reject.

medical expenses (federal income taxes) Medical expenses incurred for an individual taxpayer, or for a dependent, constitute one of the itemized deductions subtracted from *adjusted gross income* (*IRC*, Section 213). Included are normal expenses for medical care, including the diagnosis, cure, mitigation, treatment, or prevention of disease. Transportation costs may be included, but the cost of lodging and meals may not be included unless they are part of a hospital bill. Premiums for hospital or medical insurance are included, but not premiums for disability insurance. Any medical expense reimbursed by an insurance company or otherwise is not deductible. There are two minimums below which medical expenses are considered to be ordinary personal expenses and therefore not deductible. Thus, the cost of medicines and drugs may be included only in the amount by which they exceed 1% of adjusted gross income. Furthermore, medical expenses in total are deductible only in the amount by which they exceed 3% of adjusted gross income. As an encouragement for individuals to carry medical insurance, Congress has provided that one-half of such premiums (including Medicare) up to $150 per year will be deductible without reference to the 3% floor; the remaining premiums are part of total medical expense subject to the 3% limitation.

memory (computers) Physical hardware which has the property of being able to store information for later retrieval. Major types are as follows: (1) Core or internal memory. Also called fast memory. The magnetic memory directly connected to the central processing unit. This memory offers the most rapid access to information. It is used to store a program and its data during execution. (2) Disk—Information is stored magnetically on flat surfaces or disks which rotate on a cylinder. The head which reads the information moves so that it can align itself with various tracks or cylindrical circles on the disk. The head moves across the tracks while the disk itself turns around in order to make all the information on a particular track available to the reading head. (3) Drum—A cylinder device in which the information is stored on the outside of the cylinder. A disk head is located for each individual track around the cylinder. The cylinder turns around in order to make the information available so that no disk head movement is necessary. (4) Tape—Also called slow memory. Information is recorded magnetically on plastic or metal tape which is stored on a reel. The tape itself is moved past the read/write heads on the tape drive in order to locate the information.

merchandise Purchased articles of commerce held for sale; the inventory of a merchant.

merchandise account A ledger account used for recording purchases and sales, inward and outward freight, returned sales and purchases, and often many kinds of expenses, the balance of which, after making adjustments for goods on hand at the beginning and end of an accounting period, represents gross profit for the period; such an account was formerly in common use, particularly in small retail stores. It has now been displaced by separate accounts for the principal elements.

merchandise cost (retail accounting) Invoice cost less *discount earned*.

merchandise inventory See *inventory*.

merchandise procurement cost *Cost* accompanying a purchase; particularly (*retail accounting*) buying, receiving, transferring, warehouse, and marketing costs pertaining to merchandise acquired for resale. Merchandise procurement cost is deducted from *gross* (*merchandise*) *margin* to obtain *gross operating spread*.

merchandise turnover = *inventory turnover*.

merchant One who buys and sells articles of commerce without change in their form.

merge To join together as in a *merger*. A process by which two individual accounts or files are combined together to form a single account or file.

merger 1. The fusion of two or more enterprises through the direct acquisition by one of the net assets of the other or others. A merger differs from a *consolidation* in that in the former no new concern is created, whereas in a consolidation a new corporation or entity acquires the net assets of all of the combining units.
2. Loosely, any *business combination*.

Metcalf Report A 1,760-page report entitled "The Accounting Establishment" which was prepared by the professional staff of the Subcommittee on Reports, Accounting and Management of the U.S. Senate Committee on Government Operations, and published in December 1976. As the chairman of the subcommittee was Senator Lee Metcalf, the report came to be known by his name. The Report severely questioned the structure and independence of the accounting profession and, among other things, recommended that the federal government establish accounting and auditing standards, rather than leave these to the profession. The subcommittee held hearings in 1977 and published a 2,176-page volume of proceedings entitled "Accounting and Auditing Practices and Procedures." Neither the subcommittee (which has since been reorganized) nor the full committee has thus far proposed legislation based on the Report.

metric 1. A unit of measure in the *metric system*.

2. A measure of distance. See *measurement* (2).

metric system A system of *measurement* based on a unit of length called the meter and a unit of mass called the kilogram. It usually also comprehends the liter as the unit measure of volume, the Celsius (or centigrade) scale for temperature, and a decimal system of monetary units. Some standard conversion formulas are as follows: 1 mile = 1.609 kilometers; 1 ounce = 28.4 grams; 1 quart = .946 liter, and $F = 32 + 1.8C$, where F is temperature in degrees Fahrenheit and C is temperature in degrees Celsius.

MFOA = *Municipal Finance Officers Association*.

micro accounting Accounting for individual, business, nonprofit, or governmental organizations, or for any department or other subdivision thereof. See *macro accounting*.

microeconomics The study of the allocation of economic resources at the level of individual decision-making units such as firms and consumers or their aggregates into specific markets or industries. See *macroeconomics*.

microprocessor (computers) An entire central processing unit contained on a single chip or unit. See *integrated circuit*. The arithmetic or logical functions are all combined into this single unit, which is the central component of the microprocessing computer.

milestone 1. A calendar date set aside in a project schedule for review of accomplishments and possible rescheduling.
2. More narrowly, a node on a *critical path* or *PERT* diagram. See *network*.
v.t. "milestoning."

millnet price See *administered price*.

minicomputer A small computer system which normally has a word size of between 8 and 16 *bits*. Main memory usually consists of from 16 to 32K (K = 1,024) units of storage.

Price range of minicomputers today is around 1,000 to 10,000 dollars. They are usually self-contained in a single unit.

minimum discrimination information statistic See *information statistic*.

minimum level of effort See *level of effort*.

minimum tax (federal income taxes) 1. Prior to taxable years beginning January 1, 1979, a 15% additional tax levied on "items of tax preference," as defined by Section 57 of the *Internal Revenue Code*. For individuals, *tax preferences* included certain itemized deductions which exceeded 60% of *adjusted gross income*, the *net capital gain deduction*, the excess of *accelerated* over *straight-line depreciation* on *real* (Section 1250) *property* and on *personal* (1245) *property* on which the taxpayer is a *lessor*, the bargain element of *stock options*, and certain *amortization* of *intangibles*. The minimum tax base was the sum of the tax preference items reduced by the greater of $10,000 or one-half the taxpayer's regular tax liability. For corporations, tax preference items included those of individuals except that the adjusted itemized deductions were excluded and the net capital gain deduction is replaced by that portion of net capital gain which was excluded from the top corporate tax rate through election of the alternative tax. The minimum tax base was the sum of items of tax preference less the greater of $10,000 or the corporate tax liability computed under the regular corporate rates.
2. For years beginning on or after January 1, 1979, there are two "minimum taxes" to which an individual taxpayer may be subject (the corporate minimum tax remains unchanged). The additional 15% levy is still applied to items of tax preference, excluding "adjusted itemized deductions" and the net capital gain deduction. An alternative minimum tax, as defined in Section 55 of the

Internal Revenue Code, is imposed on a new alternative minimum tax base and will substitute for the individual's regular federal income-tax liability (including the "add-on" minimum tax) if it exceeds such regular tax. The alternative minimum tax base is the individual's taxable income plus the net capital gain deduction and adjusted itemized deductions in excess of 60% of adjusted gross income and reduced by a $20,000 exemption. A three-tier tax rate is then applied to this base to determine the minimum tax.

minority interest The portion of the net worth of a subsidiary relating to shares not owned by the controlling company or other members of the consolidated group.

The amount of outside-ownership equities, consisting of pro rata amounts of *capital stock, capital surplus*, and *retained earnings* as they are reflected on the records of *subsidiaries*, and adjusted by the *elimination* of *intercompany gains or losses*, are desirable details on the face of the *consolidated balance sheet*. A full elimination of intercompany profits and losses (see *intercompany elimination*) necessitates an adjustment of the equities of the outside stockholders of the subsidiary that has taken the profit or loss. This is justifiable, since the purpose of a consolidated balance sheet is to display both assets and equities in the amounts at which they would be stated if the several legal entities composing the consolidated group were reduced to one. Outside stockholders are entitled to know what portion of their book equity is represented by a "controlled" profit—that is a profit that has not yet been realized through a sale to the public.

Minority stockholders' equities, including their shares of the surplus account, are preferably regarded as *liabilities* on the consolidated *balance sheet* rather than as a portion of *net worth*. Although not legal obligations, these equities possess some of the attributes of obligations in that their interests do not parallel those of the controlling equities. This is recognized in the frequent absorption by the controlling company of the entire operating loss or deficit of a subsidiary not fully owned, or in the assumption by the controlling company of all the writedown of an unrealized profit.

The absorption of a loss or deficit is a policy the adoption of which is a matter that warrants the approval of the boards of directors of both the controlling company and its subsidiary. This policy, often followed where the intercompany transactions of a subsidiary have not been maintained at arm's length, should be recorded on the books of the controlling company and the subsidiary by entries covering the entire amount of the subsidiary's loss or deficit, or, better, the amount of the differences attributable to failure to preserve an arm's-length relationship.

Where there are two or more subsidiaries, the balance-sheet summary of outside-ownership equities may be supported by a supplementary schedule if their importance warrants it. See *consolidation policy*.

miscellaneous asset An asset, usually of minor significance, that cannot be classified under any of the other headings or subheadings of the balance sheet.

miscellaneous expense Incidental expense, not classifiable as manufacturing, selling, administrative, or general expense, and appearing on an income statement below operating income or as a subdivision of *income deductions*.

miscellaneous revenue Minor and incidental revenues. Examples: sales of waste paper; occasional rent of unused facilities; interest on bank balances.

misfeasance Doing wrongfully a legal act or an act the doer has a right to do. See *malfeasance; nonfeasance*.

misleading With respect to a financial statement, containing an obscure, *distorted*, or untrue statement; omitting a material fact; or combining or arranging materials in a manner that conceals or diverts attention from matters that would result in different inferences on financial and operating results. See *material*. A financial statement may be judged misleading without regard to the intent of the one who prepared it. The experience, skill, imagination, and independence of a public accountant, together with his or her reliance on accepted standards of auditing practice and statement presentation, are professional safeguards for the prevention of misleading characteristics in financial statements on which he or she reports.

missed discount See *discount lost*.

mixed account 1. An account which includes elements of both a *real account* and a *nominal account*. Examples: a *merchandise account*; an account containing unadjusted prepaid expenses.
2. (brokerage accounting) A customer's account containing both *long* and *short* security or commodity positions.

mixed cost Cost that has both fixed and variable elements. See *semifixed costs; semivariable cost*.

mixed-integer program See *integer program*.

mixed inventory An *inventory* of a class of *goods* the items of which are not or cannot be identified with a particular lot.

mixed reserve An account with a credit balance representing a combination of a *liability*, a *valuation account*, and *appropriated retained income*, or any two of them. Examples: a reserve for plant rehabilitation; an insurance reserve.

mixed surplus A *net-worth* account containing not only *retained earnings*, but also elements of *paid-in capital* or *appreciation credits*, or both. See *surplus*.

mix variance Any difference between expected and actual costs or revenues resulting from changes in proportions. With respect to costs, it can result from using various labor or raw-material inputs in nonstandard proportions. It can also result from a nonstandard percentage composition of various joint products produced. With respect to revenues and gross profits, it may result from the sale of various products in nonbudgeted proportions.

mnemonic system An indexing of accounts or groups of accounts by means of letters or combinations of letters that suggest their name or nature.

mode The item of most frequent occurrence in a group of numbers; often represented by the symbol *Mo*; the class of greatest frequency, or the classes of greatest relative frequency, when there is more than one in a *frequency distribution*. See *median; arithmetic mean; average*.

model *n*. Any system of relations used to represent another system of relations. Examples: A set of algebraic relations used to represent the graphs portrayed in a chart such as a *breakeven chart*. A set of blueprints used to guide the construction of a house or a piece of machinery. A chart or system of accounts with accompanying portrayals of flows that can be used to represent the transactions conducted by an enterprise. Note that in all cases the relation is symmetric since, for instance, the algebraic relations may be modeled by the corresponding geometric figures or the blueprints may be drawn to conform to an already constructed house. For many purposes, one may single out one set of relations to evaluate the other. This is then said to be an evaluation of the model. Such an evaluation may be descriptive as when, for instance, the blueprints are checked against the house that was actually built or when the accounts are examined to see whether they portray the transactions that occurred. The evaluation may also be normative as when the house resulting from the blueprints is evaluated for its structure or esthetic qualities or when the accounting system is evaluated for its efficacy in use. The former are sometimes said to be descriptive models and the latter are referred to as normative models.

v. To erect a system of relations which is to be used as a model.

modem (computers) A contraction of "modulator-demodulator." An electronic device or transducer which allows a computer terminal to transmit its electronic signal via an audio signal over a telephone line. There is a modulator at the terminal end and a demodulator at the computer end and, normally, there is also a return circuit which has a modulator at the computer end and a demodulator at the terminal end.

modified accrual basis The basis of accounting recommended for *governmental funds* (*q.v.*), under which *revenues* are recognized in the period in which they become available; *expenditures* are recognized at the time a *liability* is incurred; and unmatured interest on general *long-term debt* and on *special assessment debt* is recognized when due.

modified cash basis A term sometimes used in place of *modified accrual basis*, but more often to describe a hybrid system in which revenues are recognized when received in cash and expenditures are recognized on the *accrual basis*.

modified temporal method See *temporal method*. A method of *foreign currency translation* that translates cash, receivables and payables, and assets and liabilities carried at present or future prices at the current exchange rate and assets and liabilities carried at past prices at applicable historical rates. Unlike the temporal method, it measures these elements in conformity with *generally*

accepted accounting principles in the United States.

monetary errors Accounting errors which result in misstatement in an account balance or omission of a required disclosure in the financial statements.

monetary gain, loss Gain, loss in general *purchasing power* from holding net monetary liabilities (more monetary liabilities than assets) or net monetary assets (more monetary assets than liabilities) during a period when the purchasing power of the dollar changes. During a period of *inflation*, a firm has a gain in general purchasing power from holding net monetary liabilities and a loss in general purchasing power from holding net monetary assets. During a period of deflation, a firm has a general purchasing power gain from holding net monetary assets and a loss from holding net monetary liabilities. See *inflation gain, loss on net monetary items; monetary items*.

monetary items Cash, claims to cash, obligations to pay cash, and other *balance-sheet* items that are fixed in dollar amounts regardless of changes in prices. If *financial statements* are prepared using *general price level accounting*, gains or losses of general purchasing power from holding monetary items are recognized (charged or credited to income) at the time a pertinent price index changes. Holders of monetary items suffer a loss of general purchasing power during a period of inflation because as the general level of prices rises a given amount of money buys progressively fewer goods and services. Conversely, those who owe amounts payable in a fixed number of dollars gain in purchasing power during a period of inflation. See *general price level accounting; inflation gain, loss on net monetary items; nonmonetary items*.

monetary-nonmonetary method A method of foreign currency translation whereby monetary assets and liabilities are translated into their domestic currency equivalents at the exchange rate in effect at the balance-sheet date, nonmonetary assets and liabilities are translated at the exchange rates in effect when these assets and liabilities were acquired, income statement items (except depreciation and amortization) are translated at some average of current period exchange rates, and depreciation and amortization expenses are translated at the exchange rate in effect when the related balance-sheet items were acquired.

money 1. *Currency* and *specie*, collectively.

2. = *cash*; used in referring to any payment other than *in kind*.

3. See *money supply*.

money capital maintenance concept of income See *financial concept of capital; capital maintenance concept*.

money equivalent The objective value of property or services acquired as the result of a business transaction or a portion of such a transaction not involving the receipt of money or a promise to pay; the stated money amount attaching to a business transaction or a portion of such a transaction involving a barter; it may be equal to the face amount or market value of what is received, or, in certain instances, to the *book value* of the thing given in exchange. See *barter; price*.

money market Market for funds due in less than one year; includes federal funds, Treasury bills, bankers' acceptances, commercial paper, certificates of deposit, discount agency paper, and repurchase agreements. See *capital market*.

money rate of interest = *nominal interest rate*.

money supply In the United States, the different measures and components are defined at levels of aggregation as follows:

1. M-1A—Includes (1) demand deposits at all commercial banks other than those due

domestic banks, the U.S. government, foreign banks, and official institutions less cash items in the process of collection and Federal Reserve float (checks in the process of collection through the Federal Reserve System); and (2) currency outside the Treasury, Federal Reserve Banks, and the vaults of commercial banks.

2. M-1B—Includes M-1A (detailed above) plus negotiable order of withdrawal (NOW) and automatic transfer service (ATS) accounts at banks and thrift institutions, credit union share draft accounts, and demand deposits at mutual savings banks.

3. M-2—Includes M-1B (detailed above) plus savings and "small" (less than $100,000) denomination time deposits at all depository institutions, overnight repurchase agreements of commercial banks, overnight *Eurodollars* held by U.S. residents other than banks at Caribbean branches of member (Federal Reserve Member) banks, and money market mutual fund shares.

4. M-3—Includes M-2 (detailed above) plus "large" (greater than or equal to $100,000) denomination time deposits at all depository institutions and term repurchase agreements at commercial banks and savings-and-loan associations.

5. L—Includes M-3 (detailed above) plus other liquid assets such as term Eurodollars held by U.S. residents other than banks, bankers' acceptances, commercial paper, Treasury bills, and other liquid Treasury securities and U.S. savings bonds.

money's worth = *money equivalent*.

money wages Compensation for services in terms of money received, as contrasted with *real wages*, or the purchasing power of the money over the necessities of life and other things desired by the recipient of the money; also known as *nominal wages*.

monopolistic competition Partial *monopoly* in an ostensibly competitive field.

monopoly 1. Any market situation in which pure competition does not exist.

2. In contrast to *oligopoly*, it involves a market where there is only one supplier or a closely allied group of suppliers and no substitute product is available or acceptable. Examples: a public utility, a government contractor supplying a unique or allegedly unique product.

monopsony A market consisting of a single buyer or group of buyers acting in concert. Thus in contrast with *monopoly* , the imperfections in monopsony occur as a result of buying rather than selling imperfections in a market.

Montgomery, Robert H. (1872-1953) One of the founding partners of the public accounting firm now known as Coopers & Lybrand. He was president of the American Association of Public Accountants from 1912 to 1914 and of the *American Institute of Accountants* from 1935 to 1937. In 1936, he was the chief architect of the merger of the American Society of Certified Public Accountants into the *American Institute of Accountants*. He was the founding author of *Auditing Theory and Practice* in 1912 (now in its ninth edition under the title, *Montgomery's Auditing*). In 1949, he received the Gold Medal of the American Institute of Accountants.

mortality Termination of life or usability. The tendency of an asset to expire or depreciate through use or the passage of time.

mortality curve A *curve* showing the actual or estimated life spans of a large number of persons or things. It differs from the *survivor-life curve* only in method of presentation. While the mortality curve shows the number of persons dying or number of items of property retired over a period of years, the survivor-life curve shows the number of items remaining over a period of years. Both curves are usually computed on a cumulative basis, generally appearing as a less-than (survivor-life) or more-than (mortality) *ogive*.

mortgage A *lien* on land, buildings, machinery, equipment, and other property, fixed or movable, given by a borrower to the lender as security for the loan; sometimes called a *deed of trust* or a "defeasible conveyance." When a mortgage constitutes the security against which bonds are issued, the lien is conveyed by what is ordinarily known as a *deed of trust*. A mortgage bond or note may be designated as "senior," "underlying," "first," "prior," "overlying," "second," "third," and so forth, depending upon the priority of the lien. The first three designations do not always imply a first lien, for such mortgages may be anteceded by a prior purchase obligation. A mortgage may be "closed," which means that its amount may not be altered during its life; or open, which means that the amount borrowed has not reached the sum authorized by the *indenture*. It may also be "variable," to allow for variations in the interest rate that is to be paid or it may be "fixed" when such variations are not permitted. A mortgage may be a "blanket" or "general" mortgage, covering all the fixed and movable property of an enterprise; a "chattel" mortgage, covering specific movable property only; or a "development" mortgage, where funds are raised for the construction or development of property which becomes or remains the underlying security. It may be a "consolidated" or "unified" mortgage, meaning that it takes the place of several previously existing mortgages. Mortgage obligations may become due and payable on a specified date, in definite installments, or by amortization. They are placed on the *balance sheet* among the *long-term liabilities*, except that any amount due within the next succeeding year, as well as any accrued interest, is often classified among *current liabilities*. See *bond; mortgage, consolidated*.

mortgage, consolidated A mortgage that replaces several existing mortgages of one or more creditors into a single mortgage. See *mortgage*.

mortgage, first, second, etc. Qualifications "first," "second," etc. indicate the priority of claims of a *mortgage* in the mortgaged property. Usually, mortgages are ranked in the chronological order in which they are made unless the consent of earlier mortgages is obtained to do otherwise. See *mortgage*.

mortgage bond One of an issue of *bonds* secured by a mortgage against specific properties of the issuer.

mortgagee One to whom a *mortgage* is given as security for funds loaned by him or her.

mortgagor One who gives a *mortgage* as security for funds borrowed.

most favored nation clause The guarantee of one nation to a second that the latter's imports will have tariffs levied which are no greater than those levied against imports from any other nation.

motivational cost A cost which is intended to have motivational consequences for the recipient of a report. This may include withholding a report or it may include adjusting cost data to encourage or to avoid discouraging recipients. Accuracy is not required and these types of cost need not tie into other accounting records.

moving average 1. One of a succession of simple *averages* of groups made up of a fixed number of terms within a series, each group, except the first, being equal to the next preceding group less the first term of that group plus the next following term. For its use in statistical analysis, see *ARIMA*.

Example: The output in tons of a certain plant during the working days of one week was 590, 625, 580, 640, 630, and 450; the following week's output was 550, 601, 592, 584, 630, and 507. The simple average of the first week's production, Monday through Saturday, was 586. The average from Tuesday through the following Monday was 579, a figure obtained from the simple average of the six items involved or from adjusting the previous average by the increased or decreased production of the second Monday as compared with the Monday of the previous week. The latter method is often employed; thus $586 - (590 - 550)/6 = 579$, the moving average for Monday. On Tuesday the moving average declines to 575 [$= 579 - (625 - 601)/6$].

2. The term has sometimes been applied to averaged income-tax statements and to *trend analyses*. See *moving average process*.

moving average method An *inventory* costing method under which the *average cost* of the units on hand is recomputed immediately after each purchase of additional units. Subsequent removal of units from stock are valued at this new average price until it is changed by the next purchase. See *moving average*.

moving average process A time series in which each observation is described as a weighted additive *function* of the past disturbances or shocks to the series. See *ARIMA*.

moving budget $= continuous\ budget$.

moving expense (federal income taxes) When an employee or self-employed person moves to a new job location, both the direct and indirect expenses of the move are deductions for *adjusted gross income*. The direct expenses include the actual travel to the new job site, including meals and lodging, for the taxpayer and family and the cost of moving household and personal goods. Indirect expenses are subject to dollar limitations: the deduction for househunting and temporary living expenses is limited to $1,500; and combined with the costs of acquiring and disposing of a residence, the overall limitation is $3,000. The move must be to a new job site which is at least 35 miles farther from the taxpayer's old residence than was the previous job location.

moving projection 1. The forward view revealed by a *continuous budget*; the phrase suggests a budgeting procedure frequently modified (e.g., monthly), always looking ahead the same number of weeks, months, or other periods, without regard to fiscal years. 2. A *financial projection* developed in an adaptive manner such as by the use of *moving averages*.

multicollinearity A term denoting a *regression analysis* in which two or more of the *independent variables* are linearly dependent on each other. Estimates of the regression coefficients may then be *biased* and they may also exhibit instability that can make any use of the results difficult or dangerous.

multilevel affiliation An arrangement resulting from a series of acquisitions in which a chain of majority controlled companies is established (more than 50% of the acquired firm's voting stock). An ownership configuration in which some subsidiaries have more than one parent company. For example, two-level affiliation exists if company *A* owns a majority of company *B*'s voting stock and *B* owns a majority of company *C*'s voting stock.

multinational accounting 1. = *international accounting*. 2. Accounting for a *multinational enterprise*.

multinational corporation A corporate organization headquartered in one country and possessing substantive production, buying, and/or distribution facilities in other countries. Often distinguished from an *international corporation*, which operates in many different countries but retains close identification with one particular country, sometimes called the headquarter country.

multinational enterprise (also multinational corporation, transnational corporation) An organization, or group of affiliated organizations, which conducts a significant portion of its business activities on a continuing basis in several different nations. Sometimes distinguished from an international enterprise, which is identified with headquarters centralized in a single nation.

multinomial distribution An extension of the *binomial distribution* to permit *probability* calculations for more than two mutually exclusive *events*. Thus, the characteristic term for the multinomial distribution,

$$\frac{n!}{n_1! \, n_2! \, \ldots \, n_r!} \, p_1^{n_1} p_2^{n_2} \ldots p_r^{n_r},$$

gives the probability of observing n_1 items of one kind, n_2 items of another kind, and, finally, n_r items of still another kind in a sample of $n = n_1 + n_2 + \ldots + n_r$ independently drawn observations with probabilities $p_1, p_2, \ldots, p_r$ of occurrence. See *factorial; binomial distribution; permutation*.

multiphase sampling (statistics) A *sample* design or set of sampling procedures wherein certain items of information are collected for all the units of a sample and other items of information on only some of these units, the latter so selected as to constitute a subsample of the units of the original sample; in this case, the sampling would be of two-phase character. This species of design is often adopted on grounds of convenience or economy. Information collected at a second or subsampling phase may be collected at a later time, and in this case information obtained on all the units of the first-phase sample may be utilized, where advantageous, in the selection of the second-phase sample. This type of design may be amplified to permit the addition of further phases.

multiple internal rates of return See *interest formulas*.

multiple-product pricing A method of determining the prices of a seller of two or more products. Producers and distributors of multiple products are the general rule; rare is the single-product firm. The problem of establishing a price for each of several products is a complex one involving the computation of direct cost and the allocation of overhead or fixed-cost burden. In price-competitive industries, multiple-product pricing is employed to ascertain the range of prices for each product within which the firm may profitably react to meet competitors' prices or initiate a price reduction. In nonprice-competitive industries, the method will often require recourse to a formal *model* to suggest the most profitable product mix and price ranges.

multiple regression A *regression* involving more than one independent variable. The general form is

$$Y = a + b_1X_1 + b_2X_2 + \ldots + b_nX_n + e,$$

where e represents an error term and $X_1, X_2, \ldots, X_n$ are the independent variables. X_1 and X_2 may represent different variables or X_1 may bear some functional relationship to X_2. For example, X_2 may be X_1^2 and X_n may be X_1^n, etc. Note that examination for *multicollinearity* or *homoscedasticity* may be required.

multiple sampling See *multiphase sampling; multistage sampling*.

multiple-step income statement A form of the *income from continuing operations* section of the *income statement* in which different classes of revenue, expense, gain, and/or loss items are separated to show intermediate balances and subtotals. It may also be used to emphasize different views of the entity and its relationship to owners and other *equity* holders; for example, enterprise income (income before deducting interest charges and income taxes), income to investors (enterprise income less income taxes), and income to stockholders (income to investors less in-

terest charges) as a more precise description of what accountants report as *net income*. See *entity theory; income statement*.

multiplexer (computers) An electronic *hardware* device which allows a number of different input signals or channels to be transmitted simultaneously over a single channel. The two most common techniques used are frequency and time multiplexing. Frequency multiplexing assigns each input channel to a different frequency within the spectrum of an output signal. Time multiplexing assigns each input channel a portion of time. Multiplexing allows the signals of a number of slower-speed devices to be transmitted simultaneously on a higher-speed channel. A unit is required at the other end which breaks the resulting single signal down into the individual signals.

multiprocessing (computers) A *hardware* configuration which includes more than one *central processing unit* connected to common storage. Each processing unit can simultaneously execute a single program by using the shared resources (including memory and external storage devices) but only one program may be executed on each individual processor at the same time.

multiprogramming A computer configuration which permits more than one program to be executed at the same time on a single computer while *time sharing* the computer's resources.

multistage sampling (statistics) A set of sampling procedures wherein the material to be sampled is regarded as being made up of a number of first-stage units, each composed of second-stage units, and so on, the units at the several stages being selected at preassigned and frequently differing sampling rates. See *sample; random sampling; unit of sampling*.

multivariate analysis The study of relations between two or more variates. The contrast is with univariate analysis which studies the behavior of only a single *variate*. The study of relations between exactly two variates is referred to as bivariate analysis.

municipal bond A *bond* issued by a state or local governmental unit.

municipal corporation The form provided by law under which a county, city, town, village, school district, or other territorial division of a state transacts its business.

Municipal Finance Officers Association An organization of persons interested in state and local governmental finance, accounting, and financial reporting in the United States and Canada. The organization furnishes the secretariat for the *National Council on Governmental Accounting* and publishes statements considered to be authoritative in the state and local governmental accounting field, as well as a quarterly journal *Governmental Finance*.

mutual corporation A form of corporation permitted under state laws, limited mostly to savings banks and insurance companies.

mutual fund A corporation that provides an investment service for its stockholders. Organized under state laws and subject to SEC as well as state regulation wherever its shares are sold, its operations are carried on through an affiliated management company whose officers are usually officers of the fund. Known also as an open-end company, its shares are continuously marketed by the management company. Redemptions may be made at any time.

narrative form 1. = *report form*.

2. (auditing) A form of *systems descriptions* in which procedures are described verbally.

NASDAQ = *National Association of Security Dealers and Quotation Analysts*.

National Association of Accountants (NAA) Founded in 1919 as the National Association of Cost Accountants, it is devoted to the interests of cost and management accountants. It has chapters in many U.S. cities and in a number of other countries. The NAA publishes *Management Accounting* (formerly known as *N.A.C.A. Bulletin* and *N.A.A. Bulletin*) (*q.v.*).

National Association of Securities Dealers and Quotation Analysts An association of securities firms founded in 1939 under provisions of a federal act to self-regulate the over-the-counter securities market. The Association establishes rules of fair practice in the industry and disciplines its members.

National Council on Governmental Accounting A 21-member organization of state and local governmental finance officers, practicing certified public accountants, educators, Canadian finance officers, U.S. federal financial executives, a city chief executive, and a member-at-large. The NCGA,

as it is called, develops, promulgates, and interprets principles of accounting, financial reporting, and related financial management activities for governments in the United States and Canada.

national income The estimate, usually at an annual rate, of a nation's economic productive performance measured by sales and purchases of goods and services; it consists of *personal income* (2) and corporate *net income* before income taxes. Increased by indirect business taxes, business pensions and contributions to pension funds, and the excess of the net income of governmental business enterprises over governmental subsidies paid to business, national income is converted into *net national product* = *gross national product* minus depreciation or consumption of capital during the period. See *national income accounting*.

national income accounting The collection and reporting of financial data, usually on an annual basis, relating to the economic performance of a region or a country. Under current practices, summarized in five sections: *gross national product*—its sources and applications; personal income and outlays; government receipts and expenditures; transactions with foreign countries (imports and exports); and savings and investment. Detailed recommendations for the construction of the summary statement have been published by the United Nations.

natural business year A *fiscal year* ending with the annual low point of business activity or at the conclusion of a season.

natural grouping = *object classification*.

natural interest rate The theoretical rate of interest at which the supply of loanable funds provided by savings is equal to the demand for such funds.

natural number Any of the positive *integers* 1, 2, . . . , *N*, excluding zero. In the Peano postulates, the natural numbers are taken as primitive or undefined (see *axiom*) and the *integers*, *rational numbers*, and *real numbers* are constructed from them.

natural person An individual human being. See *person*.

NCGA = *National Council on Governmental Accounting*.

near-cash asset Asset that can be converted to cash in a very short time, usually no more than a few days or a month. A near-cash asset also is a *quick asset* except that the latter group also includes *cash*. See *liquid asset*.

near monies Liquid assets easily convertible into cash without significant risk of loss of value.

necessary condition A property of a proposition so related to another that the latter cannot be true unless the first is also true. Compare with *sufficient condition*.

negative asset A *liability* (*1*); also, a credit *valuation account*.

negative assurance A form of assurance whereby an auditor, rather than giving a positive opinion, makes a statement of the nature: "However, nothing came to our attention which would indicate that these amounts (statements) are not fairly presented (stat-

ed)." Negative assurance is permissible under *generally accepted auditing standards* only under the following circumstances: in *letters for underwriters* and in *special reports* relative to (1) the results of applying agreed-upon procedures to one or more specified elements, accounts, or items of financial statements and (2) compliance with aspects of contractual agreements or regulatory requirements related to audited financial statements.

negative confirmation See *confirmation*.

negative goodwill See *surplus from consolidation*.

negative income tax A proposal under which the government would contribute funds to persons falling below a specified minimum income level, with the amount increasing at still lower income levels. Thus this "income tax" would be graduated in negative directions just as the present income tax is graduated in positive directions; hence the name. Advanced by the economist Milton Friedman, who proposed to use it as an alternative to all present welfare programs of the government, but the two parts of this proposal are also separable. Currently, the earned income credit under Section 43 of the *Internal Revenue Code* is similar to a negative income tax in some respects. It provides a 10% refundable credit, up to a maximum of $500 on the first $5,000 of earned income. The credit is reduced to zero when either earned income or adjusted gross income reaches $10,000.

negligence Failure to exercise due care.

"Ordinary" negligence arises from errors of judgment attributable, for example, to a lack of seasoned experience, or from oversights and mistakes that might be committed by anyone, but never from willful deceit.

"Gross" negligence adds the element of recklessness and an extreme disregard of common standards—for example, of auditing and reporting.

negotiable Transferable by endorsement and delivery or by delivery in the ordinary course of business, a *holder in due course* being free of the equitable defenses available to prior parties.

net *adj*. Diminished by all relevant and commonly associated deductions. Example: net sales (sales less returns and allowances, discounts, sometimes provisions for bad debts); net income (revenue less expenses recognized during the period covered by the revenue); net assets or *net worth* (assets less liabilities to outsiders); net *current assets* (current assets less current liabilities—i.e., *working capital*); net *fixed assets* (fixed assets at cost less accumulated depreciation); net salvage (selling price or value as scrap less costs of selling and removal); net price (a price from which all discounts have been deducted).

v.t. To subtract a related amount; as, to net current liabilities against current assets.

net assets The excess of the *book value* of the assets of an *accounting unit* over its liabilities to outsiders; = *net worth*.

net avails The net proceeds of a discounted note.

netback price See *administered price*.

net bonded debt (municipal accounting) *Gross bonded debt* less debt self-supporting as to principal and interest requirements, and less the amount of sinking funds available for the payment of other than self-supporting debt.

net book value The difference between the gross amount of an asset or asset group as shown in the books of account and any reserve or other applicable offset, such as *accumulated depreciations*. See *book value*.

net capital gain (federal income taxes) The excess of net long-term capital gain for the taxable year over net short-term capital loss for that same taxable year (Section 1222 of the *Internal Revenue Code*). Net capital gain exists if netting of the long-term capital gains and losses results in a net gain (net long-term capital gain) and if such net long-term gain exceeds any net loss resulting from short-term capital gains and losses (net short-term capital loss). (If no net short-term capital loss exists, as in the case of a net short-term capital gain, then net capital gain is equal to net long-term capital gain.) See *capital gain net income; capital loss*.

net capital gain deduction (federal income taxes) The percentage of net capital gain which is subtracted from gross income as a deduction to arrive at adjusted gross income. The deduction is restricted to individual taxpayers and the percentage of net capital gain which can be deducted is 60% for net capital gains recognized after October 31, 1978.

net current assets = *working capital*.

net cycle time Time for *in-cycle work* plus *out-cycle work*.

net earnings See *earnings*.

net income Revenues less operating costs. The balance remaining to stockholders of a business enterprise after deducting from the gross revenues for a given period all operating expenses and income deductions during the same period.

Under various *APB* and *FASB* pronouncements it is now required to distinguish further between *income from continuing operations* and gains and losses from *extraordinary items* and *discontinued operations*, including their separate income-tax effects. This may be regarded as a compromise settlement of long-standing disagreements on whether the *all-inclusive income statement* or whether the *operating performance income statement* approach should be controlling. Items deemed "unusual" for the current year may turn out not to be so unusual in succeeding years and this may lead to still further evolution in the way these items are reported. The present compromise, however, at least preserves the *clean surplus doctrine* that is associated with the all-inclusive income statement.

net income ratio See *profit margin*.

net income to sales ratio See *profit margin*.

net income to stockholders' equity ratio See *return on equity*.

net income to total assets ratio See *return on investment*.

net loss The reverse of *net income* or profit, determined in a similar manner: the excess of the sum of expenses and losses over revenues and income.

net loss from operations = *operating loss*.

net national product (national income accounting) *National income* plus indirect taxes paid by business, pensions and contributions to pension funds by business, and the excess of net income from governmental enterprises over governmental subsidies. *Gross national product* is net national product plus business and institutional depreciation.

net of tax method An *interperiod tax allocation* wherein the tax effects of timing differences are recognized by adjusting *asset* and *liability* amounts and the related *revenues* and *expenses*. The tax effects are applied to reduce specific assets or liabilities (and related revenues or expenses instead of income-tax expense) on the basis that tax deductibility or tax incurrences are factors in their valuation.

net operating loss 1. = *operating loss*.
2. (federal income taxes) A net operating loss (NOL) occurs when the allowable deductions from a trade or business activity exceed the taxpayer's gross income with certain specific adjustments (*IRC*, Section 172), which include: (1) No net operating loss deduction is allowed. (2) Capital losses can only be deducted to the extent of capital gains. No long-term capital gain deduction is allowed. (3) No deduction for personal exemptions or their equivalent may be taken. (4) Nonbusi-

ness deductions are allowed only to the extent of nonbusiness income. (5) A corporation entitled to a dividends-received deduction (Sections 241-247) may compute such deduction without regard to the taxable income limitations (Section 246).

The amount of an NOL is first carried back to offset the prior 3 years' taxable income with any remaining unabsorbed loss carried forward to offset the succeeding 7 years' taxable income on a chronological basis. The taxpayer may, however, elect to forgo the entire carryback period and apply a net operating loss solely to the 7 successive tax years.

net operating profit = *operating income*.

net present value The difference between the *present value* of the future net cash receipts of an investment project when *discounted* at the firm's *cost of capital* and the initial cash investment in the project. See *interest formulas*.

net-price method (of recording purchase, sales discounts) Approach preferable for recording purchases and sometimes for sales in which the purchase (sale) is recorded at its *invoice price* less all available *cash discounts* under the implicit assumption that all (or nearly all) available discounts will be taken. In contrast to the *gross-price method*, *discount lost* as a result of a failure to pay within the discount period is identified as a separate expense or loss which may be treated as an *adjunct account* to purchases (or sales) for external reporting but which should be reported separately in internal reports so that management and the board of directors will know the amount of discount lost and whether it results from inefficiency, inadequate internal control, and/or lack of *liquidity*.

net proceeds *Proceeds* from the sale or other disposition of property or the marketing of an issue of securities, less costs directly connected therewith.

net profit 1. *Profit* remaining from revenue after deducting related costs. Although it usually designates the final figure on an income statement (= *net income*), some tendency has been noted to confine its application to (a) the excess of *revenues* over *operating costs*: an amount identical with "net income before income deductions"; or (b) the excess of revenues over both operating costs and income deductions, excluding from the latter "distributions" such as income taxes, bonuses to officers, and other items based or otherwise dependent on the existence of such excess. Ordinarily, however, net profit is synonymous with net income, and, unless clearly indicated to be otherwise, the computation of a bonus, for example, designated as a percentage of "net profit," is based on the net-profit amount after deducting the bonus and even an income tax in the computation of which the bonus figures as an allowable expense.

2. *pl.* The profits over a specified period of a corporation or other business after deducting *operating costs* and *income deductions*; = *net income*.

net profit on sales The balance remaining after deducting from *gross profit* on sales selling and other expense varying directly with sales; also known as net *trading profit*.

net purchases The cost of purchases plus freight-in, less returns and allowances and usually cash discounts taken.

net quick assets *Quick assets* less *current liabilities*.

net realizable value See *expected exit value*.

net sales Gross sales less returns and allowances, freight-out, and often cash discounts allowed. In recent years the trend has been to report as net sales the net amount finally received from the customer.

net tangible assets to long-term debt ratio A reciprocal version of the *debt-equity ratio*

which excludes assets presumed to have doubtful values for the coverage of long-term obligations.

network 1. A *model*, usually in the form of a *graph*, consisting of a set of "nodes" with connecting "links." See example below. Other examples may be found under *graph*.

2. For accounting purposes it is sometimes further specialized so that a path may always be traced from any node to every other node and back to the starting node without ever leaving the graph or retraversing any link. Such a path is called a "cycle." Thus, if the nodes are interpreted as accounts, then a path traced in this manner represents an accounting cycle.

Other interpretations and uses are also possible. The example below is from *critical path (= PERT)* analyses such as might be used to schedule construction projects, audit engagements, and many other types of activities. This network fits the modification in (2).

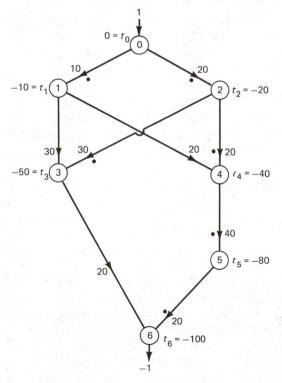

Here the nodes represent states attained after the tasks represented by the connecting links are completed in the times indicated alongside the arrowheads. Ten hours is required for the task going from node 0, the starting node, to the node at state 1. Twenty hours is required for the task going from node 0 to node 2, etc.

To identify the *critical path* (which determines the minimum time for completing the project at node 6) one assigns a time of $t_0 = 0$ to node 0 and cumulatively subtracts the time on the link traversed to the next node. This yields values of $t_1 = -10$ and $t_2 = -20$, as shown. At node 4 a choice of traversed links which could enter into the critical path is apparent. The choice is resolved in favor of the one yielding the smallest (= most negative) cumulative total. This gives $t_4 = -40$ to node 4 and, in a similar manner, assigns a value of $t_3 = -50$ to node 3. The links actively involved in determining these values are indicated by the heavy dots alongside their arrowheads; thus, the link from node 5 to node 6 receives a dot since it wins out on this smallest (= most negative) cumulative value test in comparison to the cumulative value achieved by going from node 3 to node 6.

The time $t_6 = -100$ is the minimum (elapsed) time to complete the project. The lines on the right which have a heavy dot alongside their arrowhead form the "critical path," so named because increases in the times on any of the links in this path will increase the time needed to complete the project. This does not hold, for example, for the link going from node 3 to node 6 or, as a matter of fact, for the links on the possible paths leading into node 3, where slack in the amount of $30 = 100 - (50 + 20)$ units of time is present.

The figure which emerges from all the links with heavy dots at their arrowheads is called a *tree*. As is evident, it has a trunk and branches but unlike the network it does not admit of any cycles. Whereas the network, sense (2), admits of alternate paths between nodes, this is not true for a tree. The path going from one node to another in a tree is always unique.

The "critical path" forms a *chain* along which a continuous flow is possible from starting node 0 to terminal node 6 without going into any dead end, as would be possible in the tree. Thus, if a unit impulse were introduced as shown for the arrow going into node 0, it could continue along the chain until it flowed out as indicated by the −1 assigned to the arrow emerging from node 6.

In this example flow is permitted only in the direction of the arrows. This is therefore an example of a "directed graph" (also abbreviated to "digraph"). When two-way flow is permitted the graph is not directed, and the arrows may be omitted or else the flows may be accorded algebraic signs to show whether flow is in the same or opposite direction to the arrow.

In this example states have been in the form of nodes and the relations between them as links. The opposite convention can also be followed. In any case, these types of graphic devices can be used to model a great variety of phenomena. The flow charts used in audit work represent one class of applications, usually in the form of trees or mixtures of trees, networks (sense 2) and often include chains for critical paths in the determination of time for audit engagements. More generally, the "conservation-of-flow" conditions that enter into electrical, hydraulic, and other types of networks can be given an interpretation in terms of *double-entry accounting* so that the latter can be regarded as an ingredient for all network models. Recent development of ultra-high-speed computer codes specifically designed for network models makes them a likely prospect for extensive use in accounting and financial planning and analytical auditing. The geometric depiction of networks is also easily understood and capable of ready use by persons from a great variety of backgrounds. The fact that all such networks can also be given analytical or algebraic form thus suggests a modeling strategy in which decision makers participate in network depictions of the problem to be modeled while an *operations research* analyst effects further analytical transformations into the corresponding mathematical or computer *models*.

network analysis An analysis based on *network* ideas or related concepts. See *network; graph.*

networking Depicting as a *graph*, activities or jobs in order of precedence all of which must be finished to complete a given project. See *network.*

net working capital = *working capital.*

network model A *model* represented geometrically in *network* form or as an algebraic equivalent. See *network; model.*

net worth (= *owners' equity*) The aggregate appearing on the accounting records of the equities representing *proprietary interests*; the excess of the *going-concern* value of assets over liabilities to outsiders; of a corporation, the total of *paid-in capital, retained earnings,* and *appropriated retained income*; of a sole proprietorship, the proprietor's account; of a partnership, the sum of the partners' accounts. A British equivalent sometimes employed is *total equity = stockholders' equity.*

net-worth method (federal income taxes) An income determination method employed by the *Internal Revenue Service* to estimate the taxable income of taxpayers who do not have adequate accounting records. The method essentially determines the change in the net worth of the taxpayer for the same period to arrive at an estimate of total income. The burden of proof is then on the taxpayer to show that the resulting total income includes exempt income or that additional allowable deductions exist.

net worth to fixed assets ratio A reciprocal version of the *fixed assets to equity capital ratio.*

net worth to long-term debt ratio A reciprocal version of the *debt-equity ratio.*

net-worth turnover Net sales divided by stockholders' equity. See *ratio; stockholders' equity turnover.*

New York Stock Exchange The largest market for corporate securities in the United States. The value of securities listed on the New York Stock Exchange constitutes 87% of all securities listed on the New York Stock Exchange, the American Stock Exchange, and the over-the-counter market.

Next In, First Out (NIFO) A method for determining cost of goods sold under which the units sold during the period are valued at their *replacement cost*, i.e., the prevailing purchase price at the end of the period or the current costs of producing those units in a manufacturing firm. See *replacement cost accounting.*

NIFO = *Next In, First Out.*

NLC (governmental accounting) = *National League of Cities.*

nominal In name only, usually with a connotation that form rather than substance is involved.

nominal account 1. Any of the *accounts (1)* the balances of which are transferred to retained earnings at the close of each fiscal year: so called because such accounts reflect *complete transactions* or *expired costs*; a revenue or expense account: contrasts with *real account.*

2. Any account representing a subclassification of a *real account*; e.g., revenue and expense accounts subsidiary to a retained-earnings account; an account containing disbursements only, subsidiary to a cash account. See *split-account system; cash-flow statement*.

nominal capital The amount of capital represented by the *par* or *stated value* of a corporation's issued stock. See *capital stock*.

nominal damages A sum awarded a plaintiff as damages where the law recognized his or her legal rights have been violated, but where no substantial loss or injury has occurred.

nominal element The portion of an *asset* or *liability account* reflecting *expired* cost or *realized income*, transferable to *profit and loss*.

nominal interest rate The interest rate stated in a security as opposed to the actual yield based on the transaction price and other characteristics of the security. See *effective rate; internal rate of return*.

nominal rate (of interest) = *coupon rate*. The interest rate formally quoted as part of a bond contract or loan agreement and related to the stated amount, due at maturity, from a bond or loan agreement. See *effective rate*.

nominal wage 1. = *money wage*.
2. A token wage.

nominal yield The rate of interest specified in a security. Period interest payment as determined by multiplying the nominal yield by the face or par value. For a *bond*, nominal yield is the same as the *coupon rate*.

nomograph A graphic representation, in a *coordinate system*, of an equation of *variables* so ranged, scaled, and positioned that, given the values of *independent variables*, a *dependent variable's* value can be determined with a straightedge. In its simpler forms, a nomograph is essentially an additive *graph*. Use of nomographs has been greatly diminished by the widespread use of scientific calculators.

nonadmitted asset (insurance accounting) = *inadmitted asset*.

nonassessable capital stock Fully paid capital stock not subject to double or other liability of stockholders: the type of stock ordinarily issued by American corporations.

noncontributory pension plan A pension plan under which employees do not make contributions.

noncontrollable cost 1. Cost that does not fluctuate with volume.
2. Any cost allocated to but not incurred by an operating unit, often identified with supplied goods and services. See *controllable cost*.

noncumulative dividend A *dividend* on *preferred stock*, which, if passed, does not have to be made up at a later date; in some states, the courts have held that such a dividend is in effect cumulative, if earned (e.g., *Day* v. *Cast Iron Pipe Co.*, 96 N.J. Eq. 736).

noncurrent asset See *asset*.

nonexpendable (trust) fund (governmental and institutional accounting) A fund the principal of which must be kept intact; examples: a loan fund, only the income from which is available for loans; an endowment fund; a fund which is subject to an annuity agreement.

nonfeasance Failure to perform a required duty; compare *misfeasance; malfeasance*.

nonledger assets Assets or increments therein that by custom, as in financial enterprises, are not carried on the books of account; as, accruing revenues not yet due; asset appreciation; existing property written off; the amount by which property has been written down below unexpired cost.

nonmonetary items *Balance-sheet* items other than *monetary items* (*q.v.*). Holders of nonmonetary items can gain or lose general purchasing power as a result of holding those items, if the specific prices of those items change more or less than the general price level. If nonmonetary items are measured at their historical cost, gains or losses of general purchasing power from holding those nonmonetary items are not recognized at the time the general price level changes; rather, they are reflected implicitly in the determination of general purchasing power net income when the nonmonetary items are charged or credited to income, for example, via cost of sales, depreciation, or amortization, or when nonmonetary assets are sold or nonmonetary liabilities are discharged.

nonmonetary transactions Exchanges and *nonreciprocal transfers* that involve few or no *monetary items*.

nonnegotiable An instrument lacking one or more of the requirements of a *negotiable instrument*. A nonnegotiable instrument can be transferred by assignment and thus is not the same as a nontransferable instrument.

nonoperating *adj*. Resulting from an incidental activity: said of revenue or expense. See *operating*.

nonoperating company 1. A corporation whose properties, if any, are idle, and whose activities result in wholly incidental (or no) profits or losses.
2. A corporation, its properties leased to and operated by others, which merely distributes its net revenues to its shareholders.

nonoperating expense = *income deductions*.

nonoperating revenue The revenue of an enterprise derived from sources other than its regular activities; = *other revenue*.

nonparametric statistic Also called "distribution-free" statistic. Any *statistic* which does not depend on knowledge of a parent (*population*) distribution for interpretation of its properties. Examples: The *median* represents the 50% point and the first *quartile* represents the 25% point of "any" distribution. Hence knowledge of the parent population distribution is not required when using these sample properties. These values are also called "order statistics" because they usually admit of ordering with the first quartile being smaller than the second quartile and the latter being less than the third quartile, etc.

nonprice competition Competition between rival sellers who charge identical or comparable prices, often mutually agreed to, and who appeal to consumers by claiming superiority in such merits as quality and service.

nonproductive labor A term formerly used for *indirect labor*.

nonprofit corporation An incorporated charity, or any corporation operated under a policy by which no stockholder or trustee shares in the profits or losses, if any, of the enterprise.

nonpublic enterprise An *enterprise* is nonpublic if it meets either or both of the following conditions: (a) its debt or equity securities are not traded in a public market, on a foreign or domestic stock exchange, or in the over-the-counter market (including securities quoted only locally or regionally); (b) it is not required to file financial statements with the *Securities and Exchange Commission*. An enterprise ceases to be nonpublic if its financial statements are issued in preparation for the sale of any class of securities in a public market.

nonreciprocal transfer A transfer of assets or services either (1) from an enterprise to its owners or to another entity or (2) from owners or another entity to the enterprise. Usually thought of as "unidirectional" with an accompanying extinction of the asset or service as in an entity's reacquisition of its outstanding stock.

nonrecurring charge Any expense or involuntary *loss* (2) regarded by management to be of a type not likely to be encountered again; on an income statement it may be classified, if material, as an *income deduction*.

nonrevenue receipts (governmental accounting) Collections, other than revenue, during a given period; applied to receipts from loans and recoverable expenditures.

nonsampling error Any difference between a *population* value and its *sample* estimate which is not due to reliance on sampling procedures. Sources of nonsampling error include errors in the *frame*, errors in the selection or measurement of sample observations, and bias in responses or nonresponses of subjects.

nonstandard material Raw material or a subassembly of a standard above or below that appearing in a standard engineering specification.

nonstandard method See *standard method*.

nonstock corporation A corporation having no issued shares; examples: a mutual savings bank; a savings-and-loan association; a religious or charitable association; a credit union.

no-par-value capital stock Capital stock having no specified par or nominal value, but to which there may attach, under articles of incorporation or by virtue of determinations by stockholders or directors, a specified amount as *legal value* or *stated value*. No-par-value preferred stock usually has a definite liquidation value which must be deducted from total paid-in capital to determine the book value of no-par-value common stock.

norm An authoritative *standard*; a *rule*.

normal capacity 1. Sometimes called average capacity.

2. The average output level required to meet customer demand over several periods of time. See *normal volume*.

normal cost 1. Average or expected cost.

2. *Prime cost* plus *overhead* allocated to products or services produced at a rate established for a predetermined "normal" level of activity and its associated overhead. *Overabsorption* and *underabsorption* of overhead results when actual activity exceeds or falls short of "normal."

3. Under the *actuarial cost method*, the annual cost assigned to each year after the inception of a pension plan or to a particular valuation date. Since the amount represented may be neither "normal" nor a "cost," some prefer to use the term *annual actuarial value*.

normal curve (statistics) A *curve*, also referred to as a "normal function," normal curve of error, or Gaussian curve, used in statistical analysis to describe the behavior of magnitudes subject only to chance or random forces and defined in so-called standardized form, by

$$ y = \frac{e^{-1/2\left[\frac{x}{\sigma}\right]^2}}{\sigma\sqrt{2\pi}}, $$

where e (2.718+) is the base of the natural *logarithm* system, $x = X - \mu$—that is, the deviation of any value X from the arithmetic mean μ— and σ is the *standard deviation*. The curve is symmetric about the mean μ and has a bell-like shape, with y reaching its maximum value at μ and falling off toward zero rapidly on either side. The curve is, however, of unlimited range, so that y never actually reaches zero. There are only two points of inflection, or bend points, where the slope, or shape, of the curve changes sharply; these points give the curve its bell-like shape, and are located at $\pm \sigma$. The quartiles are located at 0.67 units from $\mu = 0$, which forms the basis of the usual probable-error formula $\mu \pm 0.67\,\sigma$, the range of error in which 50% of the cases may be found, if the normal curve applies.

The curve has many uses, the most important of which comes from calculating exact probabilities for the occurrence of events which are subject only to chance causes. Whether the normal curve can be used depends on such factors as the number of occurrences examined, size of sample, etc. Other curves may have to be used, but it is a remarkable property of the normal curve that many other curves themselves tend to become normal under general conditions. Even where *universe* variables are not distributed in the form of a normal curve, the arithmetic means of samples become distributed approximately in the form of a normal curve as sample sizes are increased. See *central limit theorem*. Hence, the standard *normal table* can be used to derive *probability* estimates for such sample values, or to design samples for desired levels of *precision* and *reliability*. See *normal table*.

normal distribution = *normal curve*.

normal hours *Standard machine time* and *standard labor time* for a specified operation.

normal lost units 1. The loss of output units through shrinkage or spoilage which cannot be eliminated cost effectively. The cost of such losses is, therefore, a necessary part of the cost of producing units of good product.
2. The unavoidable loss of output units via shrinkage or spoilage given the existing specification of raw-material inputs, product outputs, and production method. See *shrinkage; spoilage*.

normal overhead Also called normal *burden* (*q.v.*). 1. The budgeted total overhead costs at the budgeted output level for a production unit.
2. The budgeted overhead cost per unit of output at the normal volume of output. See *normal volume*.
3. The budgeted overhead cost per unit of output based upon any preselected notion of capacity or output level.

normal price The value of a commodity resulting from the interaction of economic forces over an extended period of time, as distinguished from those prevailing at a moment of time (i.e., *market price*).

normal return Income on investment at a standard interest rate. The choice of interest rate in computing normal return is usually arbitrary. Often an average rate of return composed of the *geometric mean* of different rates, or an average return from "like investments" is used but both of these averages may include compensation for *risk* as well as return for productivity of capital. The rate of interest on government bonds is sometimes used as a measure free from elements of risk. Standard rates may also be used as a company policy for determining the feasibility of new undertakings.

normal shrinkage 1. Shrinkage which cannot be eliminated cost effectively.
2. Shrinkage which is unavoidable in the circumstances. See *shrinkage*.

normal spoilage 1. Loss of usable parts or salable products which cannot be eliminated cost effectively. The cost of such losses is, therefore, a necessary part of the cost of producing units of good product.
2. Unavoidable loss of usable parts or salable products given the existing specification of raw material inputs, product outputs, and production method.

normal standard cost A standard cost based on the average cost of a number of past periods and on expected future changes in prices, efficiency, or volume. See *standard cost*.

normal table (statistics) A tabular presentation of selected values calculated from the *normal curve*. An example follows.

The normal table is calculated in terms of standard units $x/\sigma = (X - \mu)/\sigma$ (where X represents an individual variable, μ the

NORMAL TABLE OF AREAS UNDER THE NORMAL CURVE

x/σ	P
0	.50
1	.16
1.64	.05
1.96	.025
2.33	.01
4.09	.001

universe mean, and σ the universe *standard deviation*) and shows the proportion of cases which will fall beyond certain limits. Also, taking advantage of the symmetry of the curve, only one-half of the values are reproduced; the other half, or the probability (proportion of cases) falling beyond these limits on either side of the mean, may be found by multiplying the decimal appearing in the body of the table by 2. Thus, values of X in an amount exceeding 1σ more than the universe mean ($X - \mu = 1\sigma$, or $X = \mu + 1\sigma$), will occur only 16+% of the times in the positive direction—read opposite the value 1 in the first column; similarly, such a deviation will occur only 16+% of the times in a negative direction as a result of *random* factors alone. Deviations of this magnitude in either direction will thus occur only 33 times in 100, or .33. Alternatively, about two-thirds of the time, the deviations in either direction will not exceed 1σ.

Under *coefficient of variation*—see *coefficient (2h)*—a problem in determining sample size is illustrated in which it is desired to secure the specified *precision* with a reliability of .95. That is, only .05 proportion of the times is the designer willing to fail in securing the desired precision. Since both positive and negative deviations are equally of interest, the two .025 tails of the distribution are relevant—i.e., only .025 proportion of the times is the designer willing to fail in the positive direction and .025 proportion of the

times in a negative direction. This value, .025, is located in the body of the table, and opposite it is read the value 1.96. Thus, $\pm$ deviations from μ as high as (or higher than) 1.96σ will occur in only 5% of the cases (see *replication*). If deviations in only a single direction were of interest, the appropriate value, 1.64, would be read opposite the probability $P = .05$.

The abbreviated table contains most of the values which are of interest in applied work. The left-hand column contains selected possible deviations of X from μ in standard units x/σ; the right-hand column, or body of the table, states the probability of occurrence (in decimal proportions) of deviations this large or larger. Only one-half the distribution is included in the table; the maximum probability is thus .5—the probability of getting a deviation of zero or greater. To obtain the probability of deviations in both directions, the fraction appearing in the body of the table should be multiplied by 2. It should be noted that a deviation as high as 3σ will almost never occur; for this as well as other reasons, such as convenience, tradition, and caution, this level is used extensively in applied work such as *statistical quality control*.

normal tax (federal income taxes) Prior to 1979, the tax rate structure for corporations was comprised of a normal tax and a surtax. This has now been replaced by a single five-step rate structure reaching 46% for taxable income over $100,000.

normal value The theoretical price that economic forces tend to establish and toward which many market prices are supposed to gravitate.

normal volume The designed capacity or output level of the production unit less an allowance for the average amount of idle time which was expected when the facility was established. See *normal capacity*.

normative Having the property of distinguishing between good and bad or better and worse as in a standard, precept or rule for guiding or evaluating conduct.

normative model See *model; normative theory*.

normative theory Also called "prescriptive theory." A *theory* which prescribes the behavior to be undertaken, or the rules to be followed in pursuit of specified objectives. It differs from "positive theory," which attempts to establish relations between observations; also called "descriptive theory." Mathematics and the natural sciences do not ordinarily use these distinctions. Extensively employed in the social sciences, they may also be used in combination. For instance, in economics, a positive theory of market price behavior may assume the use of profit-maximizing rules derived from normative theories of business managerial behavior. Other uses are also possible. In engineering, for example, a normative theory used to guide the development of a new invention may subsequently be accorded positive status when the resulting invention becomes widely adopted in practice. See *model; hypothesis; theory*.

note A *promissory note*.

note payable 1. A term applied to a *promissory note* with reference to its maker.
2. *pl*. The name of a *ledger account* or *balance-sheet item* showing separately or in one amount the liabilities to banks, trade, and other creditors evidenced by promissory notes.

note receivable 1. A *promissory note* in the possession of the payee or a *holder in due course*.
2. *pl*. The name of a ledger account or *balance-sheet item* showing the amounts owing on promissory notes from customers and other debtors.

note receivable discounted A note receivable not due which has been sold or transferred by endorsement, or otherwise, to a bank or other third party, at face or maturity value, sometimes less a discount representing interest for the unexpired term. The amount of notes receivable discounted is a contingent liability of the endorser and a contingent asset to the one who sells the note with recourse; on a balance sheet, it appears as a reduction of notes receivable, being shown parenthetically or in short, or in a footnote; if there is likelihood of nonpayment by the maker at maturity, it is classed as a current liability.

note register A book in which notes receivable or notes payable are recorded chronologically as received or issued; the details may include date drawn and date due, number, maker, endorser if any, reason for acquiring or giving, amount, and dates and amounts of interest collected or paid.

notes to financial statements See *footnote*.

notice of deficiency (federal income taxes) See *deficiency letter*.

notional Imaginary or unreal: said, for example, of the value of a service not yet rendered, or a liability not yet incurred, but in either case merely in prospect, and hence not to be recorded in the accounts. A long-term lease has been cited as an example of a notional liability.

NSF check Nonsufficient funds check. A check presented for payment but not paid by the drawer's bank because the balance in the drawer's (maker's) account was less than the amount of the check.

nuisance value The premium in excess of fair value that must be paid for a claim, an asset, or an equity in a business or other organization because its existing ownership is damaging to the prospective buyer or to the interest of equity holders, or because of the cost of instituting legal action.

null hypothesis The hypothesis under test. For example, in auditing, the null hypothesis might be that the audited value of the population is equal to the book value. Rejecting the null hypothesis when it is true leads to a *type I error* and accepting it when it is false leads to a *type II error*.

number 1. *n.* One or a series of digits expressing quantity; thus, 0, 1, −4, 486 7/11. See *digit; integer; rational number; irrational number; imaginary number*.

2. Several, as in a number of things.

3. *v.* To assign numbers to things or events as in numbering items of equipment for identification in property records.

OASI (Old Age and Survivors' Insurance) A part of the social-security system of the United States designed to give benefits to young children of deceased workers and pensions to older retired workers. The system is financed through both employer and worker contributions. Benefits are based in part on past earnings of participants.

object The initial designation of an expenditure such as for raw material which, after its initial classification as raw-material inventory, may, with other costs, pass through successive stages to work in process, finished goods, and cost of sales, often, but not necessarily, losing its identity in such transfers. See *cost flow; split-account system*.

object classification 1. The original designation of an acquired good or service pending its spread or absorption.

2. (governmental accounting) The designation of expenditures by types of items purchased or services obtained.

object cost Cost of a good or service in terms of *object*, or what is received in an exchange. Examples: personal service; raw material; equipment. In a subsequent transfer an object cost may lose its identity when merged with other costs; e.g., *raw material* transferred to *work in process*. Costs appearing in *primary accounts* are object costs. See *materials and services; objective statement; cost flow*.

objective *adj.* 1. Having a meaning or application apart from the individual, the peculiarities or the peculiarities of his or her experience; and substantiated or capable of being substantiated by an independent investigator: said of a fact, judgment, or inference; as, objective evidence: often to be interpreted as possessing a doctrinaire, propagandistic, or *ad hominem* tinge. By comparison, one fact may be said to be more objective than another because it is observable by more persons, experimentally repeatable, more promptly recorded after observation, recorded by more competent or more disinterested observers, more precisely determinable, more coherent or interrelated with other generally accepted facts, or observed under less confusing circumstances.

2. *n.* A goal or guide to action with accompanying criteria for evaluating plans or accomplishments. Examples include objectives like ''maximize profit'' or ''maintenance of market share.'' Audit objectives may be associated with particular procedures

designed to ascertain whether all amounts are correctly classified and recorded. They may also extend to more general procedures involving recourse to criteria used to determine whether all items necessary for a fair presentation are disclosed.

3. Pertaining to a classification of transactions or accounts by *object*.

n. A target or goal toward which activity is directed. Complete statement of an objective is accomplished by criteria which facilitate measurement of the degree of accomplishment. See *figure of merit*. For instance, the objective "maximize profit" should be accompanied by criteria in the form of profit measures for each of a specified set of activities so that these in turn may be used to obtain a figure of merit in the form of total profit for comparison with the maximum that forms the stated objective.

objectives of financial reporting Broad designations of audience, purpose, and content to provide direction in the preparation and issuance of financial reports. For example, Statement of Financial Accounting Concepts No. 1 issued by *FASB* describes the objectives of financial reporting by business enterprises as:

> —Financial reporting should provide information that is useful to present and potential investors and creditors and other users in making rational investment, credit, and similar decisions. The information should be comprehensible to those who have a reasonable understanding of business and economic activities and are willing to study the information with reasonable diligence.
>
> —Financial reporting should provide information to help present and potential investors and creditors and other users in assessing the amounts, timing, and uncertainty of prospective cash receipts from dividends or interest and the proceeds from the sale, redemption, or maturity of securities or loans. Since investors' and creditors' cash flows are related to enterprise cash flows, financial reporting should provide information to help investors, creditors, and others

assess the amounts, timing, and uncertainty of prospective net cash inflows to the related enterprise.

> —Financial reporting should provide information about the economic resources of an enterprise, the claims to those resources (obligations of the enterprise to transfer resources to other entities and owners' equity), and the effects of transactions, events, and circumstances that change its resources and claims to those resources.

See *accounting principles; accounting convention; accounting policy (3); Statements of Financial Accounting Concepts*.

objectives of financial statements See *objective* (2). The goals that financial statements, especially published financial statements, should satisfy. These goals are not static, but change over time in response to evolving economic and societal environments. For instance, there seems to be basic agreement at present that the primary purpose of financial statements is to provide information useful for making economic decisions. The first 2 of 12 objectives stated in the Report of the Study Group on the Objectives of Financial Statements (*Trueblood Report*) published by the *AICPA* in 1973 are: (1) to provide information useful for making economic decisions; (2) to serve primarily those users who have limited authority, ability, or resources to obtain information and who rely on financial statements as their principal source of information about an enterprise's economic activities. These objectives reflect the present consensus and the next several objectives stated by the Study Group may by regarded as amplifying or expanding these two. Objective 12, however, is different. As stated by the Study Group this objective is to report on those activities affecting society that can be determined and described (measured) and which are important to the role of the firm in its social environment. Presumably this allows for (or responds to) the kind of experimentation that is already occurring. See, e.g., the discussion in *corporate social report*.

objective statement A statement of expenses in terms of the original objects of expenditure; contrasts with a *functional statement*, in which expenses have been reclassified in accordance with their contribution to the ultimate product or final operating function. Most *income statements* reflect a mixture of the two; in recent years there has been some trend in reports to stockholders to put the income statement on an objective basis.

objective value Value established by competent independent appraisal, or by market quotation for a similar quantity, quality, condition, utility, and place.

objectivity Freedom from bias engendered by the illogic of emotion, prejudice, or hasty surmise.

object program (computers) A sequence of *machine language* instructions used for solving a computer problem. It is the result of the compilation of a source program written in a higher-level *programming language*.

obligated balance (governmental accounting) 1. *Obligations outstanding*: that portion of an appropriation unexpended but committed for expenditure.
2. *Obligations and liabilities outstanding*: that portion of an appropriation undisbursed but "expended" or "committed" for expenditure.

obligation 1. Any kind of indebtedness; a *liability*.
2. (governmental accounting) An *encumbrance* or *commitment*, but sometimes including, as under practices of the Office of Management and Budget, *liabilities*. The "obligations basis" of accounting for the operating expense of a given period is understood to be the *accrual basis* adjusted by *obligations outstanding* at the beginning and end of the period.

obligational authority (government accounting) Legislative permission to incur *obligations (2)*, subject to express limitations of character, money, and other controls. New obligational authority (NOA) = *appropriation (1)*.

obligations incurred (governmental accounting) The whole of the *obligations* entered into during a particular period, expressed as a total of the liabilities expected to arise therefrom. It is equal to the total of recorded expenditures for the period modified by the opening and closing balances of *obligations outstanding*.

obligations outstanding (governmental accounting) The amount of purchase orders or contracts on which goods or services have not yet been received, but sometimes including current and other liabilities. See *obligation (2)*.

observation test An auditing procedure whereby an auditor visually examines activities taking place within the auditee organization — as opposed to the examination of detailed documentation. Observation tests can be performed for *substantive* purposes, as in the observation of physical inventories, or for *compliance* purposes, as in the observation of segregation of incompatible duties among individuals in the EDP department.

observed depreciation 1. *Accrued depreciation* determined not by annual provisions based on expectancy of *service life*, but by physical inspection or appraisal of operating condition, and ordinarily expressed as a percentage of original cost or replacement cost. The numerator of the fraction represented by the percentage is the quantity of services already given off by the referent asset; the denominator, the total quantity, past and future, of the expected service yield of the asset.
2. Estimated deterioration: an engineering or appraisal term bearing no necessary relation

to the accountant's concept of depreciation and sometimes described as the outlay required to restore an asset or asset group to full operating efficiency.

obsolesce To become or cause to become obsolete. See *obsolescence*.

obsolescence The loss in usefulness of an asset occasioned through progress of the arts or by changing laws or social customs. It is distinguished from exhaustion, wear and tear, and deterioration in that these terms refer to a functional loss arising out of a change in physical condition. Obsolescence may be classified as ordinary obsolescence, or loss due to normal progress or development of industry; and extraordinary obsolescence, or loss due to sudden, unforeseen causes, such as an unheralded new invention, unexpected style change, or unanticipated cessation of demand for an article produced. Ordinary obsolescence is customarily included as a factor in determining *depreciation* rates to allow for the gradual lessening of service life through factors other than physical wear and tear. See *depreciation*.

occupancy expense Expense relating to the use of property. Examples: rent, heat, light, depreciation, upkeep, and general care of premises occupied.

Occupational Safety and Health Act (OSHA) Occupational Safety and Health Act of 1970 created a 3-member Occupational Safety and Health Review Commission to handle quasi-judicial functions and gave the Secretary of Labor certain quasi-legislative powers. The Department of Labor has issued detailed rules and regulations setting mandatory occupational safety and health standards applicable to businesses affecting interstate commerce.

odd lot A smaller than customary unit of trade; in stock exchanges, a transaction of less than 100 shares, or, in the case of an inactive stock, less than 10 shares; see *round lot*. —odd-lot, *adj*.

off-balance-sheet financing A term used primarily by specialists in *finance* to describe a use of lease financing that did not meet all of the requirements of a *capital lease* (formerly called a financing lease) so that the present value of the commitment (liability and asset) was not recorded and did not appear on the lessee's balance sheet or the accompanying footnotes. See *operating lease*. This practice was drastically reduced by FASB Statement 13. The term also is used to refer to a form of financial arrangement associated with some *leveraged leases* in which the lender of the funds has no recourse against the *lessor* and agrees to look solely to the *lessee* and the leased asset for repayment of the debt.

office equipment Major items of movable property used in furnishing an office. Examples: office furniture; movable partitions; typewriters; calculating and bookkeeping machines; filing cabinets; duplicating equipment.

Office of Management and Budget (OMB) In the federal government, an administrative unit in the Office of the President, a descendant of the older Bureau of the Budget, responsible for (a) the preparation, and presentation to the Congress, of periodic budgetary documents, and the overall administration of resulting Congressional appropriations, (b) reviewing administrative policies and performance of the government's agencies, and (c) advising the President on budgetary and legislative matters.

officer Any principal executive of a corporation to whom authority has been delegated by the board of directors or the bylaws; often, any member of the top staff of an organization.

offset 1. An amount equaling or counterbalancing another amount on the opposite side of the same or another account or statement. See *absorption account*.

2. An amount having the effect of canceling or reducing a claim of any kind.

offset account An account acting as an *offset (1)*, in whole or in part, to another account; an *absorption account*.

offsetting error An error that eliminates or reduces the effect of another error; thus, a debit of $10.00 posted to an account as a debit of $1.00, and a credit of $65.48 posted to another account in the same ledger as a credit of $56.48: both postings are understated $9.00 and are exactly offsetting, and a trial balance would not reveal either error; but if the credit had been posted as $55.48, the resulting deficiency of $10.00 in credits would have been partially offset by the $9.00 deficiency in debits, causing the trial-balance credit total to be $1.00 larger than the balance debit total. It is always necessary, therefore, to run down and correct a trial-balance difference, no matter how trivial it may appear to be, since an offsetting error may be involved.

ogive (statistics) A cumulative *frequency curve* or *frequency chart*, generally S-shaped. When frequencies are accumulated by addition from lowest to highest values, a "less-than ogive" is obtained; when accumulated values are subtracted from the total *frequency*, a "more-than ogive" is obtained. A *mortality curve* or *retirement curve* is generally presented as a less-than ogive, while a survivor-life curve is generally drawn on a more-than basis. See *mortality curve*.

oil-and-gas payment (petroleum industry) The interest, as of a driller, in the production of crude oil and gas from a particular well or tract of land; it is paid out of production allocable to the *working interest*.

oligopoly A market characterized by a few sellers whose actions influence one another, a homogeneous or slightly differentiated product, and significant barriers to entry by others.

oligopoly and oligopsony prices An oligopoly price is the price that prevails in a market of few sellers and many buyers; hence, a price reflecting the power a few large sellers may exert over the market. An oligopsony price is the price that prevails in a market where buyers are few and sellers numerous; hence, a price reflecting the power a few large buyers may exert over the market.

oligopsony A market characterized by a few interdependent buyers of a homogeneous or slightly differentiated product.

ombudsman An official, usually responsible to the legislative branch of government, whose function is to receive and answer complaints and queries involving administrative practices and to make recommendations for corrective measures under existing and proposed laws and regulations. In the U.S. government, this service is in large measure supplied by the *Comptroller General*. It falls short of what is required of an ombudsman, however, in that the General Accounting Office rarely reports its findings back to the individual complainant, as does, for instance, the Auditor General of Israel.

on account 1. On credit terms: said of a sale or purchase, delivery of which is followed by payment at a later date.
2. In part payment: a term applied to the settlement of a portion of a debt.

on consignment Consigned to another for the purpose of sale, display, or other use.

oncost = *indirect cost*; a British term.

one hundred percent statement See *common-size statement*.

one-transaction method See *cost method*.

on hand In possession, whether or not owned. In a balance-sheet presentation, however, the term connotes "owned," unless explained or qualified by the item title or in a footnote. Thus, *inventory* on hand, without further description, means only items owned and in possession. The term does not include owned items in the custody of others, such as goods in warehouse or on consignment.

open *adj*. In a condition permitting additional entries or postings: said of books of account at the end of a reporting period.

open account 1. Any account not closed out.
2. An unsecured amount owing by a debtor or to a creditor arising through credit sales or purchases, payable in cash, subject to usual trade customs or to specified terms as to discount and payment period; an unsecured loan.

open credit An unsecured receivable or payable not evidenced by a note, subject to settlement in accordance with usual trade or other specified terms.

open-end company (or trust) = *mutual fund*.

open-ended mutual funds A mutual fund that does not have a fixed number of shares, offers new shares to the public and buys back the outstanding shares offered to it by the investors at the market value. Price of the shares is determined by the per share net asset value of the fund's portfolio.

opening balance 1. The balance of an account at the beginning of a specified period, such as a month or a year.
2. *pl*. General-ledger accounts constituting the balance sheet at the end of one year carried into the next.

opening entry 1. An entry or one of several entries by means of which the assets, liabilities, and proprietary interests of a new enterprise are recorded on its books.
2. An entry or one of a series of entries beginning a new system of accounts for an enterprise already established.
3. An entry to reopen the asset and liability accounts at the beginning of an accounting period where they have been closed by journal entry at the end of the preceding period: a practice now largely obsolete.

open market operations Purchase and sale of securities (usually government) by the central bank in order to influence credit conditions.

open market paper rate = *commercial paper rate*.

open mortgage (or bond) A mortgage (or bond) the terms of which provide no limit on the amount that may be borrowed on the pledged security.

open the books 1. To record in a ledger, usually by means of one or more journal entries, the assets, liabilities, and proprietary accounts of an enterprise at its inception or reorganization, or when a new accounting system is installed.
2. To reopen the asset, liability, and proprietary accounts at the beginning of an accounting period, either by means of a journal entry or by carrying down the balances at the close of the immediately preceding period, after the accounts have been ruled off.

open to buy A term used in retailing, particularly department stores, to designate a stated amount of money or merchandise to which a buyer is limited in purchases.

open-to-buy report A statement of existing or expected relations between inventory and sales, used to calculate open-to-buy amounts.

operating *adj*. Pertaining to any usual type of activity in which an organization engages. See *operation; operations; nonoperating*.

operating accounts *Revenue* and *expense* accounts.

operating budget A budget covering recurrent revenue and expense: contrasts with *capital budget*. See *budget*.

operating-characteristic curve (statistical quality control) A curve that portrays graphically the probability of acceptance as a function of submitted quality; generally referred to as an OC curve and most widely known in connection with *acceptance sampling*. Every sampling plan has a unique OC curve which makes clear what protection can be expected from the plan as lots of varying quality are submitted to it for judgment. Valid comparison between various sampling plans as to cost, amount of inspection required, etc., cannot be made unless the plans being compared have approximately "matching" (congruent) OC curves.

Although OC curves originated in the field of acceptance sampling, the concept is of general interest, being applicable to any statistical test based on the use of *random samples*. In fact, the discriminatory power of standard statistical tests cannot be fully understood or utilized efficiently until the associated OC curves have been constructed. Batteries of OC curves for these standard tests appear in statistical texts.

operating company A corporation actively engaged in business with outsiders.

operating cost (or expense) An expense incurred in conducting the ordinary major activities of an enterprise, usually excluding "nonoperating" expense or *income deductions*.

operating cycle The elapsed time between the purchase of inventory items (raw materials or merchandise) and their conversion into cash. The typical succession of transactions involved is (a) the purchase, offset by accounts payable; (b) the liquidation of the payables; (c) the manufacturing operation with its added costs, or the warehousing in the case of merchandise; (d) the sale of the finished product or merchandise; and (e) the liquidation of the amount receivable from the customer. A normal operating cycle—greater than one year, for example, in the business of an installment dealer—is generally regarded as one of the determinants of the character of items classified as *current assets*. It is also of importance in establishing working-capital requirements.

operating expense *Expense* incurred in the ordinary activities of an entity; generally includes *selling expenses*, *administrative expenses*, and general expenses but frequently excludes *cost of sales*, *interest*, and *income-tax* expenses.

operating fund The *fund* for all assets and related liabilities used in the routine activities of a hospital. Also sometimes used in governmental accounting as synonym for *general fund*.

operating income (or profit) The excess of the revenues of a business enterprise over the expenses pertaining thereto, excluding income derived from sources other than its regular activities and before *income deductions*.

operating income to operating assets ratio A version of *return on investment* that focuses on performance in a firm's primary line of business by excluding nonoperating assets. It is normally calculated by dividing net income before interest and taxes by total assets less investments in subsidiaries.

operating lease A lease that is not reported as the acquisition of an asset or the incurrences of an obligation for a lessee. Rental on an operating lease is normally charged to expense by the lessee over the lease term as it becomes payable. See *capital lease*.

For a lessor, a lease that is not recorded as a financing transaction or a sale. The leased property on an operating lease is depreciated by the lessor, and rental income is normally recognized over the lease term as it becomes payable. See *sales-type lease; direct financing lease; leveraged lease (2)*.

operating ledger A ledger containing only *nominal accounts*; i.e., transactions relating to operating revenues and expenses.

operating leverage The tendency of a firm's earnings to change in greater proportion than sales because of fixed costs. The degree of operating leverage can be calculated by dividing contribution margin by earnings before interest and taxes. See *leverage*.

operating loss The reverse of *operating income* and similarly determined. Also called "net loss from operations."

operating margin *Net sales* less *cost of sales*. See *sale (2)*.

operating performance The degree of skill and success attained in any activity.

operating performance income statement An income statement limited to items reflecting revenue and costs of normal operating factors. It differs from the *all-inclusive income statement* mostly in the exclusion from *income deductions* of material amounts of such items as nonrecurring prior-year adjustments, sales of assets not acquired for the purpose of resale, nonrecurrent losses against which insurance would not normally be carried, the elimination of an intangible, and the writeoff of the balance of discount (or premium) and expense following a retirement or refunding of a bond issue before maturity. See *income statement; income deduction; net income*.

operating performance ratio Any *ratio* that has a profits measure in its numerator and sales in its denominator. For example, see *profit margin*.

operating profit See *operating income*.

operating profits to sales ratio See *profit margin*.

operating ratio A *ratio* which measures the proportion of revenue spent on operating expenses, usually calculated by dividing the sum of *cost of goods sold* and *other operating expenses* by *revenue*.

operating report An internal report revealing budgeted costs, standard costs, actual costs, and the like.

operating reserve 1. A reserve created by a charge or charges to operations and deducted on the balance sheet from its related asset; a *valuation account*.
2. = *equalization reserve*.

operating results 1. = *net income* or *net loss*.
2. = *operating income*.

operating revenue 1. Gross sales of goods and services, less returns, allowances, and cash discounts, together with gross amounts received from any other regular income source.
2. Net revenue from sales of services.

operating statement 1. An *income statement*, especially one showing considerable detail.
2. Any statement displaying past financial operations over a stated period; as an *income statement*; a *funds-flow statement*; also a departmental report of income or costs.

operating system (computers) A collection of service routines and utility programs to aid in sequencing and processing *programs* on a computer system. In addition, an operating system performs such tasks as accounting, input/output control, security checks, and aids in execution of programs.

operation 1. An act or a method of acting, usually on a sustained basis in a systematized mode.
2. The performance of any planned work; as, a step or limited series in production or other activity associated with an individual, machine, department, or process.

operational 1. Pertaining to the property of an interpretation placed upon a set of *postulates, theorems*, or individual *propositions*, such that procedures or transactions are specified in correspondence with designated abstract constructs which appear in the propositions. In scientific work, auditing, and certain phases of accounting, such procedures generally refer to the assembly of evidence for the purpose of testing or validating a *hypothesis* or set of hypotheses (see *test*); in administration or business practice, to methods of planning, guiding, adjusting conduct, or internal control. A policy or program stated in such form that procedures cannot be, or are not, specified in a manner that will give effect to the propositions it implies is said to be nonoperational. See *definition (4)*.

2. Pertaining to an *operation*; as, an operational cost.

3. Capable of execution; operable.

operational accountability As distinct from only "dollar accountability," the responsibility of administrators of, e.g., nonprofit organizations to utilize all assets and resources efficiently. The accounting counterpart of operational or comprehensive audits. See *audit (4B)*.

operational audit Also called "management audit" or "performance audit." A special type of comprehensive audit which reviews procedures or past performance with a view to future improvement of operations. It focuses on *efficiency* and *effectiveness*, rather than fairness or propriety. See *audit (4B)*.

operational control The process of conforming specific operations (tasks) to a plan or budget. Its focus is on lower-level supervisors in day-to-day operations. In contrast with *management control*, operational control entails a high degree of structure and predictability in task accomplishment, often permitting the use of mathematical *models* in planning and performance evaluation.

operational gaming Use of *simulations* involving multiple participants, each with partial control over possible outcomes. Long used by the military (e.g., in war games), it received analytic form in the *theory of games*, which awakened interest by others, such as sociologists, who now make extensive use of it to study human behavior under controlled laboratory conditions.

operational research A British term; = *operations research*. See also *management science*.

operations 1. The activities of an enterprise exclusive of financial transactions and those of an extraordinary character; as, *production*, or the rendering of service, distribution, or administration.

2. Hence, the activities generally of an enterprise resulting in charges or credits to revenue or expense.

3. Revenue and expense accounts generally. Example: a charge (or credit) to operations.

operations research See *management science*.

opinion (audit) The written finding of an auditor, following an audit, as to the fairness of the representations of financial position, operating results, and changes in financial position reflected in *financial statements*, and as to the following of *generally accepted accounting principles* in the recording of the underlying transactions and in the preparation of the statements; and the consistency of these principles with those followed in the previous year. These are to be found in the "opinion" or second paragraph of the standard *short-form auditor's report*, the purpose being to inform the reader of the report that what he or she is looking at is subject to the usual interpretations given financial statements. See *judgment*.

A qualified opinion contains the auditor's exception to one or more specified items in the financial statements, and reasons therefore. See *auditors' report*.

Opinions A series of 31 pronouncements issued between 1962 and 1973 by the *Accounting Principles Board*. Normally, these Opinions were endorsed by the *Securities and Exchange Commission* for use by corporations subject to its jurisdiction. See *Statements*.

opportunity cost 1. The value of the alternatives forgone by adopting a particular strategy or employing resources in a specific manner. Prospective change in cost following the adoption of an alternative machine, process, raw material, specification, or operation; see *alternative cost*.

2. As used in economics, the opportunity cost of any designated alternative is the greatest net benefit lost by taking an alternative.

opportunity set 1. The set of *feasible* options available to a decision maker.

2. The set of points which has the *efficiency frontier* as its boundary.

3. In *capital budgeting*, the set of projects to be evaluated for approval or implementation.

optimization *v.t.* Employing procedures or the use of models in an effort to attain an *optimum*.

optimum Best possible. Examples: *mathematical programming* solutions which are directed to maximum profit or minimum cost; the choice of a strategy in the *theory of games* which is best against all possible counter-strategies available to opponents; the choice of a curve of best fit to a set of observations as in the *least-squares method*.

optimum output 1. For an existing plant, the output level which would minimize average total cost per unit.

2. In the long run the output level of the desired scale of plant which would minimize average total cost per unit.

3. For an existing plant, the output level which would maximize profits.

option A legal right to buy or sell something at a specified price, usually within an agreed period of time. See *stock option*.

optional dividend A *dividend* authorized to be paid in more than one form, according to the election of the individual stockholder—e.g., in cash or capital stock.

order cost In economic-lot-size problems, it is the cost to set up or process an addition to inventory which is not affected by the size of the addition. See *economic order quantity*.

order quantity Also called *order size* or *lot size*. The quantity of a storable good to be ordered for inventory. See *economic order quantity*.

order size See *order quantity*.

ordinal number The designation of one of a particular order or series of units in terms of first, second, third, etc. The contrast is with *cardinal numbers*, which express "how many" (e.g., the number of objects in a set) so that the usual rules of addition, multiplication, etc., may be meaningfully employed.

ordinary annuity An annuity payable at the end of each period; contrasts with *annuity due;* = *annuity*. See *interest formulas*.

ordinary depreciation The loss of utility of a fixed asset through normal wear and tear, aging, action of the elements, and the like. See *depreciation*.

ordinary shares = *common stock*; a British term.

ordinate The vertical or *y* axis in a two-dimensional *Cartesian coordinate system*. See *abscissa*.

organic act A law giving authority to a government agency to engage in specified activities, laying down the policies and general method to be followed in its operations, and authorizing subsequent appropriations to support it; distinguished from *appropriation act*.

organization 1. A developed process of administration.

2. Any existing association of people and functions.

organizational slack An existence of resources and authority to use them in excess of what is required for *efficient* and *effective* performance. It may arise from looseness in standards or budgets or it may arise from deficiencies in the design or operation of an *organization* or its *accounting system*.

organizational unit 1. Any administrative subdivision of an *enterprise* or *agency*, especially one charged with carrying on one or more functions or activities; see *activity; activity accounting.*

2. (governmental accounting) The smallest administratively recognized subdivision of an agency.

organization cost (or expense) Any cost incurred in establishing a corporation or other form of organization; as, incorporation, legal and accounting fees, promotional costs incident to the sale of securities, security-qualification expense, and printing of stock certificates. These and similar costs constitute, theoretically, an intangible asset of value which continues throughout the life of the corporation and hence, strictly, do not constitute a deferred charge. However, because the total usually is not large, it has become customary to write off such costs arbitrarily either at once or over the first few years of corporate existence.

Under Section 248 of the *Internal Revenue Code*, organization expenditures of a corporation (such as those for legal and similar services to obtain a charter, fees paid to the state, and expenses of temporary directors) may be amortized over a 60-month period; expenses of issuing stock or of corporate reorganization are regarded as capital expenditures.

original capital The amount of enterprise capital paid in at the time of incorporation or organization.

original cost 1. Outlay for an asset by its owner, not including any adjustments of cost arising from postacquisition alterations, improvements, or depreciation.

2. = *prime cost.*

3. (public utility accounting) Cost of an operating unit or system to the person first devoting it to public use: said of assets coming under the surveillance of governmental utility-control bodies. *Net* original cost re-

sults from the deductions of acquired liabilities.

As used in public utility accounting, the term dates from the early 1930s. In 1933 the public service commissions of 21 states, led by New York, petitioned the Interstate Commerce Commission to prescribe the original-cost basis of plant accounting in the system of accounts for interstate telephone companies over which the ICC then had jurisdiction. Shortly thereafter, the Federal Communications Commission was given jurisdiction over such companies and prescribed the original-cost principle in a system of accounts made effective on January 1, 1936. The system was attacked in the courts by the American Telephone & Telegraph Company but was upheld by the Supreme Court (299 U.S. 232). The original-cost basis is prescribed in other utility-accounting systems, notably the electric (1936) and gas (1939) systems prescribed by the Federal Power Commission and numerous state commissions and the system for steam railroads prescribed by the ICC. Interstate telephone, electric, and gas utilities have been required to state their utility plant in its entirety on an original-cost basis, whereas steam railroads have been required thus to record acquisitions commencing January 1, 1938. See *acquisition adjustment.*

original entry An entry, in proper form for *posting* to a *ledger*, recording a *transaction* in a *book of original entry*. It either includes full information concerning the transaction or refers to supporting vouchers or memorandum books, which contain data, previously recorded, upon which the entry is based.

original issue discount (federal income taxes) The difference between the issue price and the stated value at maturity of bonds or other certificates of indebtedness. Special tax rules (Section 1232, *IRC*) apply if the discount upon the original issuance of the instrument exceeds 1/4 of 1% multiplied by the number of complete years to maturity.

The issuer of a discounted bond treats the original issue discount as an additional cost of borrowing which may be amortized over the life of the bond. See *bond discount*.

origin period (statistics) The point or period of time, e.g., within a time series, selected as the base period.

OSHA = *Occupational Safety and Health Act*.

other assets A balance-sheet term for minor assets not classifiable under other usual headings; its amount is generally a small fraction (e.g., less than 5%) of total assets. Examples: cash advances, cash reserved for nonoperating purposes, cash surrender value of life insurance policies, scrapped equipment held for sale.

other deductions 1. A collection of minor costs in various types of operating statements shown as a single total in order to avoid unimportant detail.
2. = *income deductions*.

other liabilities A balance-sheet figure for minor liabilities not classifiable under other usual headings; its amount is generally a small fraction (e.g., less than 5%) of total liabilities.

other revenue (or income) Revenue from minor sources or from other than the regular activities of a business; nonoperating revenue; examples: interest on customers' notes, installment accounts, and overdue accounts; dividends and interest from minor investments; incidental profit from the disposal of assets other than inventory.

out-cycle work Work performed by an operator while a machine is at rest; contrasts with *in-cycle work*.

outgo 1. = *expenditure*.
2. A subtraction; a disbursement; often contrasted with *income* (2).

outlay 1. The paying out of cash, the incurring of a liability to pay cash, or the issue of a corporate equity or the transfer of property, in exchange for the receipt of goods or services.
2. The purchase price of property or service, measured in terms of the cash or the book value of property given in exchange; *cost*.

outlay cost Cost represented by an expenditure of cash or transfer of property; generally, any recorded cost, contrasting with *imputed cost* and *opportunity cost*.

outlay expiration The reduction of outlay that would normally be recognized by the owner of an asset as the consequence of any related event or condition—e.g., lapse of time, wear and tear, outright destruction, or decline in demand—that diminishes likely future utility or recoverable price as applied to *fixed assets; depreciation*. See *loss; amortization*.

out-of-pocket expense (or cost) 1. An expense incurred by an individual, as on a business trip, paid for in cash, for which reimbursement may be sought; contrasts with *allowance* (3).
2. Any cost, other than a *fixed cost* or *sunk cost* chargeable directly to any product, order, or operation; hence, a cost that may be saved; *direct cost*; a *variable cost*.

output The quantity in volume, cost, sale price, value added, or other measure of goods or services produced in any period. Usually, a rate (= total output per period.)

output cost See *cost of production*.

outsider A person not affiliated or otherwise related. A corporation's outsiders may or may not include stockholders, depending on the context.

outstanding 1. Uncollected or unpaid: said of an account or note receivable or payable, or of a check sent to the payee but not yet cleared against the drawee bank.
2. In the hands of others: said of the units of funded debt of a corporation or of the certificates representing issued shares of capital

stock in the hands of the public; treasury stock is defined in terms of shares issued but not outstanding.

outstanding capital stock Issued capital stock, less treasury stock; capital stock in the hands of the public.

outstanding shares See *outstanding capital stock*.

overabsorption 1. The result produced where the credits in an *absorption account* exceed the total of the account—e.g., a factory-expense account to which it is related; because the corresponding debits may have become intermingled with other expense or inventory accounts, the amount of an overabsorption usually appears on an operating statement. See *variance (2); overapplied overhead*.
2. The amount by which an expected (budgeted or standard) cost is exceeded. This occurs in systems that allocate *overhead* costs at predetermined rates based on an assumed "normal" level of activity. The opposite situation is called *underabsorption*.

overall efficiency See *efficiency (4); variance*.

overall reasonableness test An auditing procedure which has as its purpose assessing the general accuracy, completeness, or correctness of an account balance, rather than verification of its component details. Overall reasonableness tests are generally analytical in nature. See *analytical test*.

over-and-short The name of an account in which appear daily or other periodic and often unavoidable and minor differences between actual cash receipts and payments and the covering documents therefor. At the end of an accounting period it is customarily closed out as miscellaneous expense or income: a procedure usually judged as justifiable in the administration of, for example, *change funds*.

overapplied burden See *overapplied overhead; underapplied burden*.

overapplied burden (or overhead) An excess above actual overhead costs which results from the use of predetermined rates for allocating such costs to products. See *underapplied burden*.

overapplied (overhead) cost See *overabsorption*.

overapplied overhead = *overapplied burden*. See *overhead*. An excess amount of overhead assigned to a product usually resulting from the use of a standard rate of allocation determined by reference to a standard (or normal) volume which was smaller than the volume actually achieved. Also called *overabsorption*. The opposite situation, underabsorption, occurs when the normal volume from which the allocation rate was determined proves to be greater than the volume actually achieved. See *overhead rate*.

overdraft 1. The amount by which a check, draft, or other demand for payment exceeds the amount of the credit against which it is drawn.
2. = *bank overdraft*.

overhead 1. Any cost of doing business other than a *direct cost* of an output of product or service.
2. A generic name for manufacturing costs of materials and services not readily identifiable with the products or services that constitute the main outputs of an operation. Other terms covering the same concept are *burden, indirect cost*, supplementary expense, administrative expenses, and *oncost*. Distinctions sometimes drawn between these terms are not consistently observed.

In speaking of manufacturing overhead, the unit of operation or production needs to be specified, for a cost chargeable directly to a department or work center (e.g., salary of the department supervisor), although a direct cost, constitutes overhead which may be allocated to different product units worked on in the department. Thus there may be product, departmental, and factory overheads. Accountants sometimes speak of "direct departmental overhead," an expression which refers to costs charged directly to the department that are indirect costs of products to which the services performed by the department are applied. The overhead concept often extends beyond the factory and on occasion may be identified with manufacturing, selling, or administrative costs.

Overhead costs were at one time viewed as the result of "nonproductive" factors, particularly when they arose from the presence of personnel not working on the product (supervisors, clerks, accountants, engineers, maintenance workers, and so on). However, much of the progress made in reducing costs of goods and services can be attributed to the use of staff specialists who devise improved methods and organize the information that management uses to direct operations more economically. Similarly, lower product costs often result from the employment of more specialized machinery and less labor, although the proportion of overhead cost may at the same time be increased.

Ratios of overhead to portions of or all direct costs are seldom useful as measures of efficiency between companies or even between plants within a company, because differences exist in the amount and type of machinery relative to labor. Differences in organization and in the classification of costs also affect such comparisons.

Distinctions between overhead costs and direct costs rest upon the methods of measuring unit costs. Direct costs can be identified with units to be costed (i.e., with departments, activities, orders, products) at the time the cost is incurred. This is accomplished by measuring quantities of materials and hours of labor used for each costing unit. Source records are then coded to permit subsequent assembly of the costs for each costing unit. For example, direct-labor tickets may bear both department and job numbers.

Overhead costs cannot, as a practical matter, be traced directly to individual costing units, either because the process of making direct measurements is judged wasteful or because there is no acceptable method of direct measurement available. As an example of a too costly measurement, electric power used by each department in a factory can be measured, but this is not always done because management does not wish to incur the expense of meters and records. Examples of the lack of a method of distribution may be observed in any endeavor to determine how much of the cost incurred for plant protection, accounting, or the president's office applies to each unit of production.

Since overhead costs cannot be charged to individual costing units at the time the costs are incurred, they may be collected as totals and subsequently spread over the various units by allocation. In allocating overhead costs, the accountant proceeds by searching for some index of production that fluctuates with indirect costs and possesses the characteristic of being capable of direct measurement. For example, some indirect costs may vary with the hours of direct labor spent on the various orders. Hence, direct-labor hours can be and often are used as an index for distributing overhead costs to orders. Correlation between an item of overhead cost and the factor used to allocate it does not necessarily hold for short-period fluctuations. For example, building-occupancy cost may be causally related to the total amount of space provided, although changes in the latter occur infrequently. This method is similar in principle to methods widely used in other fields where exactness and accuracy are required, although it often falls somewhat short in the application.

The distinction between direct and overhead costs, most marked in job-order manufacturing, becomes comparatively unimportant in continuous-process manufacturing operations. In accounting for the latter, it is common to include all labor with overhead in costing production.

Accounting for overhead costs has three possible objectives:

1. To provide information useful to management in exercising control over such costs;

2. To determine product costs for inventory-cost purposes by allocating manufacturing-overhead costs to products; and

3. To provide information with respect to variation in overhead costs with changes in volume and other factors for use in profit planning, pricing, and similar problems.

With a carefully designed plan, all three of these objectives can be attained.

Any classification of overhead costs begins with the determination of responsibilities for cost incurrence. For this purpose a responsibility constitutes an organizational unit such as a department having a single head accountable for costs incurred by the activities of the unit. The classification of overhead costs by responsibilities or departments fixes responsibility for control, and at the same time facilitates allocation of the costs to products.

Costs incurred by each responsibility are classified by nature of expenditure or object for which the expenditure was made. This subclassification indicates the costs for which the department head is held responsible. The classification by nature of expenditure is usually uniform throughout an individual company, in order that costs incurred in different departments may be combined whenever desired (for example,

management may wish to know the total cost of supervision for all departments) and to facilitate interpretation of costs on departmental statements. Following is an illustration showing classification of overhead costs in the manner described:

CLASSIFICATION OF OVERHEAD COSTS

Factory Departments	Overhead Expense Accounts
Heavy machine	Supervision
Turret lathe	Clerical
Small machine	Indirect labor
Heat treating	Supplementary
Forge and welding	labor costs
Paint shop	Personnel
General machine	Factory supplies
Power	Maintenance
Repair and	and repairs
maintenance	Insurance
Shipping	Taxes
	Depreciation
	Other factory
	expenses

Reports prepared to assist management in controlling overhead costs provide comparisons between actual costs of the most recent period and costs of a prior period or budgeted costs. When the costs in such reports are limited to those controllable by a single supervisor, it is relatively easy to determine how successful each department head has been in efforts to minimize costs. By study of the details, it is possible to trace variances to individual items of cost.

Accumulation of overhead costs by departments facilitates costing of products by bringing together costs allocable on the same basis. However, for this purpose it may be desirable to subdivide a responsibility or department into cost centers or activities. Where different types of equipment or different operations exist, in a single department, individual cost-center rates may yield more accurate product costs. Multiplication of cost centers increases clerical expense, and hence a practical compromise between accuracy of costs and the amount spent to obtain them must be made.

Departments are divided into two classes: production and service (sometimes called direct and indirect). Service departments are those that provide benefits (e.g., power, maintenance, purchasing, accounting) to other departments but do not work directly on products for sale to customers. Costs of service departments are distributed to producing departments and thus become part of the producing department overhead applied to products.

Another basis used in the classification of overhead costs is variability of costs with volume of production. Separation of fixed and variable components of overhead and determination of rates at which variable elements of each cost should vary with volume assists in controlling overhead costs under conditions of rapidly fluctuating volume. This classification also has a wide field of usefulness for such purposes as profit planning and pricing. In some companies, fixed and variable costs of service departments are distributed to producing departments on different bases.

The classification of overhead costs by variability with volume cuts across classifications by responsibility and nature of expenditure. For this reason, in each overhead account fixed and variable components must be separated. Some accountants incorporate this basis of classification into charts of accounts. Where this is done, there are two accounts for each class of costs containing both fixed and variable components. For example, indirect labor for a given department appears as indirect labor, variable, and as indirect labor, fixed. More commonly the classification is made apart from the accounts.

Predetermined overhead rates are widely used for applying manufacturing overhead to products, because:

1. Overhead rates developed from actual volume make it necessary to delay completion of product costs until the close of the period, because neither the full amount of the overhead cost nor the total quantity of production is known until that time.

2. Wide fluctuations in unit product cost often result from fluctuations in volume of production and as between short periods of time. Irregularly occurring costs have a similar but usually less marked effect on unit cost.

Cost allowances in the standard-volume budget are suitable only for the standard volume of production. When actual volume deviates from the standard, expense components that vary with volume should be controlled with departmental activity. For this purpose, flexible budgeting techniques are often employed to adjust the overhead-cost control budget to the actual volume experienced.

Predetermined rates at which costs should vary with changes in volume is the essential characteristic of *flexible-budget* methods. This proceeds from either of the following approaches:

1. A flexible standard is established for each overhead cost, expressing the cost as a fixed sum plus a rate per unit of volume; the formula sometimes quoted is $y = a + bx$, where y is the amount of overhead sought, a the fixed sum, b the units of volume, and x the rate per unit. From this linear formula the amount of expense allowed at any given volume can be computed and is usually accurate enough for the purpose.

2. Expense budgets are prepared in advance for a series of volumes covering the expected range of activity. For example, budgets may be prepared at intervals of 10% between 50% and 120% of standard capacity.

Expense allowances for any volume within this range are then set by reference to the preestablished budget and may be derived by the formula preceding. This approach allows recognition of a step variation in costs.

Where volume fluctuates considerably from month to month, a flexible budget provides department supervisors with expense goals reflecting the current rate of production and at the same time makes possible the separation of overhead-expense variances into a portion due to over- or underspending and that due to the deviation of actual from standard volume.

A careful study of conditions existing in each situation is needed before bases for allocating costs are chosen. Bases suitable elsewhere are not applicable if equipment, methods of operation, and other conditions differ. For this reason, generalizations with respect to the advantages or disadvantages of specific bases lack significance.

Under some forms of *direct costing*, fixed-overhead costs are treated when incurred as general production expense, and are not allocated to units of production or to inventories; on an income statement they are deducted as a cost-of-sales element or as general expense.

Under other forms of direct costing, fixed-overhead common costs in a multi-product operation are management-allocated to the several lines of product, not necessarily in proportion to labor- or machine-hours or other direct-cost factors, but in proportion to price yields, *price margins*, or relative importance assigned to different product lines. Judgments concerning the relative importance of product lines are necessarily those of top-level management: a principal product, accounting for 60% of direct-labor costs, may be assigned 90% of the common costs,

an assignment that will carry through to residual inventories; a byproduct, none. On the other hand, profitable byproducts supporting a highly competitive major product may be assigned the burden of *absorbing* (3) common costs. As used here, *common costs* are costs of goods and services contributing to two or more product classes, whether or not simultaneously processed; they include *joint costs* serving simultaneously processed or otherwise closely related classes of product. See *direct cost*.

overhead costs = *factory overhead*. See *overhead*.

overhead pool A group of *indirect costs* the total of which by any of various methods is or may be *spread* over intermediate and final-product stages of production. See *overhead*.

overhead rate A *standard* rate at which overhead is allocated; see *overhead*.

overlapping debt (municipal accounting) The proportionate share of the debts of the political subdivisions or special districts lying wholly or partly within the boundaries of a municipality, excluding only the debt of the state government. The municipality's share of the debt other than special-assessment debt is usually determined on the basis of the ratio of the assessed valuation of taxable property lying within the corporate limits of the municipality to the assessed valuation of each overlapping district. Assessed values are used as a basis of allocation because they represent the tax base which will furnish the revenues to be used in paying off the bonds and meeting the interest charges.

To determine the real debt burden carried by taxable real estate within a municipality, it is essential to take into account not only the municipal debt but the overlapping debt as well. Overlapping debt is often greater than direct debt.

In the case of debt payable from special assessments, the total amount of special assessments levied, rather than the assessed values, is used as the basis of allocation because special assessments are based on the relative worth of benefits received rather than on assessed values, and because special assessments will be used to pay the special-assessment bonds and interest. The allocation ratio, computed by dividing the special assessments levied on property located within the corporate limits of the municipality by the total special assessments levied, is applied to the special-assessment debt outstanding.

overriding royalty interest (petroleum industry) The interest, usually of a third party, such as a sublessor of a tract of land, in the production of crude oil and gas from the tract; it is usually a fraction of the original *working interest*.

over-the-counter *adj*. Pertaining to transactions not consummated through an established stock exchange; applied to trans-actions of brokers and dealers in unlisted securities, including government bonds and notes. Over-the-counter markets exist in all large U.S. cities.

over-the-counter sale The sale of an unlisted security.

owe To be under obligation to pay or render something to another in return for something received; to be indebted to another.

owners' equity The interest of stockholders or other owners in the assets of an enterprise (in contrast to claims of creditors and other liabilities) and at any time is the cumulative *net* result of past transactions and other events and circumstances affecting the enterprise. See *net worth*.

ownership 1. The right to and enjoyment of services or benefits with accompanying duties flowing from an asset, usually evidenced by the possession of legal title or by a beneficial interest in the title. See *asset; sale; title; liability; equity ownership; proprietorship*.
2. (auditing) A specific audit *objective* which relates to determining that the assets recorded on a company's financial statements are in fact the legal assets of the company.

Pacioli, Luca (1445(?)-1514(?)) Luca Pacioli (sometimes written as Paciolo), a Franciscan friar, was the author of the first published exposition of double-entry bookkeeping. His treatise appeared as part of a larger work on mathematics, entitled *Summa de Arithmetica, Geometria Proportioni et Proportionalita*, which was published in Venice in 1494. Pacioli was a teacher of mathematics. His work on double-entry bookkeeping was widely imitated and copied throughout Europe, leading to the propagation of the "method of Venice."

paging (computers) A process of transmitting information and data from main to auxiliary storage. Often used when the amount of main storage available is not sufficient for all *programs* during execution in which case various sections of programs are paged in and out as they are required. In a virtual memory system, this paging is performed automatically by the *hardware*.

paid-in capital The total amount of cash, property, and services contributed to a corporation by its stockholders and constituting a major *balance-sheet* item. It may be divided between *capital-stock* and *additional paid-in capital* or *paid-in surplus* accounts; see these terms.

paid-in surplus See *additional paid-in capital*.

paid-up capital The aggregate of par or stated value of capital stock for which full consideration has been received.

paper Bills of exchange and other short-term evidences of indebtedness.

paper profit A profit not realized; anticipatory profit; a profit based on premature, uncertain, or conjectural estimates of operating or trade results. Example: appreciation of unsold marketable securities.

par The nominal or face value of a security.

parameter 1. (statistics) Any measure or set of measures, such as an arithmetic mean or standard deviation, calculated directly from or defined for a universe rather than samples; sometimes referred to as the "true" value a sample is designed to estimate or test.
2. (mathematics) A general *constant* symbolized as $(a, b, c, \ldots)$ which is assigned numerical values $(1, 1/2, -10, \ldots)$ in particular expressions. A constant which is to be varied in any particular expression is said to be "parameterized" as its value is changed from $y = ax$ to $y = \hat{a}x$ in this expression.

parent Any controlling authority.

parent company A *controlling company* having *subsidiaries*. Without a trade or business of its own, a parent company may also be termed a *holding company*.

parent company statements Separate (unconsolidated) financial statements of a *parent company*. Such statements may be more useful to the parent company's creditors and preferred stockholders than if consolidated with its subsidiaries.

Pareto optimality An economically *efficient* allocation of resources, i.e., one in which it is impossible to reallocate resources to make one economic agent better off without making at least one other worse off. See *economic efficiency*.

Pareto optimum Pareto efficiency; see *efficiency (4)*.

parity bit (computers) See *magnetic tape*.

parity price A price level for a particular commodity or service which bears a predetermined relationship to another price or composite average of prices, established on the basis of a historical period, and expressed as an *index number* of 100. As these two sets of prices change, they are reflected in the index number. This measuring device is widely employed in federal farm-price-support programs, and has also been incorporated in industrial wage contracts. Farm prices are supported by the federal government at parity levels through open market purchases and loans (and rates of interest) to producers.

The major significance of the parity-price concept is not in its mechanics, but in the social-control purpose for which it is employed. Underlying its application is an assumption of a need for replacing or supplementing the free-price system by government regulation to achieve a desirable optimum distribution of national income among farmers, laborers, and industry. The parity-price device is one of several means employed by the federal government to alter the distribution of income and influence economic ac-

tivities and falls in the same category as import duties, depletion allowances, social-security benefits, and subsidies.

par of exchange The ratio of one country's unit of currency to that of another country, as defined by the official exchange rates between the two countries.

parole evidence rule The rule which prohibits the alteration of a written contract by use of oral statements made prior to or contemporaneous with execution of the complete written contract unless there is evidence of fraud, accident, or mistake relating to the omission of the oral statement in question.

partial allocation of taxes An *interperiod tax allocation* that restricts the *deferred tax* recognition only to nonrecurring items.

participating capital stock *Preferred stock* which, in addition to having a fixed dividend rate, shares under varying conditions with the common stock in further distributions of profits. See *participating dividend*.

participating dividend A dividend paid to preferred stockholders over and above that paid at a stipulated minimum rate, where preferred stockholders share, to a predetermined extent, in profits that otherwise would be distributable only to common stockholders. In the absence of provisions to the contrary, it is held in some jurisdictions that preferred stockholders are entitled to share pro rata with common stockholders in all dividend distributions after both preferred and common stocks have received dividends at a stipulated rate.

participating preferred stock A preferred stock that entitles its holder to receive, in addition to the regular preferred dividend, a dividend in proportion to the common dividend declared above a specified amount. For example, a participating preferred stock may entitle its holders to receive 8% preferred dividend and share equally any common dividends declared in excess of 10%.

participative budgeting A part of *participative management* that extends to procedures which include the opinions, judgments, and recommendations of subordinates as well as top management in the preparation and revision of budgets and performance standards. A financial planning process conducted in accordance with the principles of *participative management*.

participative management A philosophy of management which seeks to involve subordinates as well as top management in formulating policies and developing the procedures by which their actions are to be guided and evaluated. A motivating idea is that more *effective* performance will result not only by securing such participation in advance of the decisions but also by anticipating problems in securing conformance that might otherwise not come to the fore when courses of action leading to management decisions are being considered. More *efficient* performance may also be secured, it is sometimes believed, especially when carried to the level of ordinary operating employees who hold a reservoir of ideas for improvement and an awareness of problems that arise from their familiarity with actual operations in the plant or in the field. See *Scanlon Plan*.

particular average (marine insurance) An unavoidable loss suffered (and borne) by one of the several interests in a ship and its cargo, arising from damage caused by perils at sea. See *general average*.

partnership A contractual relationship, based upon a written, oral, or implied agreement, between two or more persons who combine their resources and activities in a joint enterprise and share in varying degrees and by specific agreement in the management and in the profits or losses; a co-partnership; a *firm*. A partnership may be general (*general partnership*), in which case the acts of each partner are binding upon the others and each

is liable for all its debts; or it may be limited (*limited partnership*), in which case the liability of certain, but not all, partners is restricted to the amount of their individual contributions to or interest in the firm's capital.

par value The *face amount* of capital stock or other security.

par-value capital stock *Capital stock* each share of which has been assigned a fixed *nominal* or *face value* by the terms of the *corporation's charter*. The par value of each share of capital stock is ordinarily expressed in round amounts, such as $5 or $10 or multiples thereof, but usually not exceeding $100 per share. The corporation laws of a number of states limit minimum and maximum par values.

par-value method See *treasury stock*.

passed dividend A *dividend* not declared on any class of stock at or about a customary dividend date; if relating to *preferred stock*, a *dividend in arrears*.

past due Delayed beyond an agreed time for payment.

past service cost The portion of total pension cost assigned to years prior to the adoption of a pension plan or the first valuation date; the *present value* of pension benefits credited to current or retired employees for service in years prior to inception of a pension plan.

patent A grant by the federal government to an inventor, for a period of 17 years, giving the exclusive right to produce and sell an invention. See *research and development (cost)*.

Paton, William A. (1889 -   ) One of the most influential American accounting theorists of the century, William A. Paton was for many years Professor of Accounting and Economics at the University of Michigan, Ann Arbor. His *Accounting Theory—With Special Reference to the Corporate Enterprise*, published in 1922 and since reprinted twice, has become classic in the field, as has his *An In-*

troduction to Corporate Accounting Standards, which he wrote in 1940 with *A. C. Littleton*. Paton was President of the *American Association of University Instructors in Accounting (AAUIA)*, the predecessor of the American Accounting Association, in 1922, and was founder and first Editor of *The Accounting Review*.

patronage dividend A distribution by a *cooperative* to members and customers; ordinarily it is a rebate on purchases or realizations in profits on sales which have been made on their behalf. Such distributions are deductible by the cooperative on its federal income-tax return, and, in the hands of the member or customer, they are a reduction of the cost of purchases.

payable *adj.* Unpaid, whether or not *due*.
n. A *liability*; a debt owing to another; an *account* or *note payable*.

pay-as-you-go method Phrase used to describe the U.S. system of paying income taxes in the period in which the income is earned by withholding income taxes from employee wages and salaries and by making quarterly payments for estimated income taxes on other nonwage sources of income. Also used to describe an unacceptable method of accounting for an unfunded *pension plan* in which payments to the pension plan beneficiaries are made directly from general corporate funds and not from previous contributions to a *pension fund*.

payback period The time required (usually in years) for estimated future net cash receipts to equal the initial cash outlay for a project. If the estimated receipts are the same amount each year, the payback period is equal to the investment outlay divided by this annual amount. Often used as a constraint to filter *uncertainty* or *risk* arising from reducing a firm's *liquidity* for protracted periods, the payback period may also be used as a criterion of choice in which investments with

shorter payback periods are accorded a preferred status. Used as a risk or uncertainty filter, the payback period is consistent with a use of other criteria of choice such as maximizing discounted returns, *return on investment*, or *implicit rates of return* by selection among alternatives that meet the payback period test.

payback reciprocal One divided by the *payback period*, a reasonable approximation of the *internal rate of return* on a project if net cash inflows after the initial investment are relatively constant and the project's life is reasonably long.

payment The discharge of an obligation by a disbursement of money or by property or services accepted as the equivalent of money; the satisfaction, by or in the name of a debtor, to the creditor, of an amount owing in whole or in part. Where payment is made by check, it is recorded with the issue of the check, although legally such an act constitutes only conditional payment.

payment float See *float*.

payment warrant See *warrant*.

payout ratio Dividend declared on common stock during a year divided by the year's net income usually expressed as a percentage; thus, the percentage of earnings paid out in dividends. See *dividend yield*.

payroll 1. A record showing the wage or salary earned by employees for a certain period, and the various deductions for *withholding* tax, health benefits, and so on.
2. Total wages and salaries accrued or payable for a given period.

payroll cost Payments to employees for labor and services. Payroll costs are usually comprised of two components. One includes cash paid to employees and amounts withheld from employees' paychecks such as federal income taxes, *FICA*, union dues, as well as payments to retirement or other plans which will result in future cash payments to employees. The other component of payroll costs is taxes and tax-like payments an employer incurs as a legal condition of employment. Examples include the employer's share of FICA (social security) and unemployment insurance paid to state and federal governments.

payroll distribution 1. An analysis of the total amount of salaries and wages paid or accrued for a period, showing the component amounts to be charged to the various departments, operations, activities, or products affected.

2. The entry by which the amount of salaries and wages paid or accrued for a period is charged in the required detail to the accounts or records.

payroll records The records relating to the authorization, computation, distribution, and payment of wages and salaries. They include payrolls, time slips, time-clock cards, withholding authorizations, canceled payroll checks or receipts for wages paid, wage and salary authorizations, and individual-earnings records.

payroll taxes Taxes based upon wages and salaries of employees and upon net business income of self-employed individuals. The two federal payroll taxes are (1) social security, which is imposed upon employees and employers equally and also upon self-employed individuals, and (2) the unemployment tax, which is imposed only on employers.

pecuniary benefit That portion of cash or money equivalent remaining from a transaction or group of transactions after deducting applicable costs; see *transaction; profit; cost*.

peer review A process in which activities of a professional are audited by members of the same profession. See *audit*, especially *comprehensive audit*. The activities of profes-

sional organizations as well as individual professionals may be submitted to such processes as when, for example, one public accounting firm engages another public accounting firm to review its auditing practices. The presumption is that the peers engaged for such reviews have levels of ability, reputation, and experience which will qualify them for this undertaking. The reports emanating from such reviews are often given restricted circulation among only a few members of the profession but there seems to be a developing recognition of the desirability of giving wider distribution to these reports.

pegged rates Fixed exchange rates or the ratio of exchange between units of currencies of two countries tied to the value of another currency or *index* agreed to by the countries. See *fixed exchange rates*.

pegging 1. The act of fixing a price by a dealer or other person or group during the initial distribution of a security, or for other purposes; it is accomplished by a series of buying or *wash transactions* and is permitted in certain cases as a stabilizing device under the regulations of the U.S. *Securities and Exchange Commission*. See *stabilization; seasoning*.

2. The fixing of the rate of exchange of one currency with another, usually by a government or an agency authorized by the government.

pension benefits Periodic (usually monthly) payments made to a person under a *pension plan*.

pension cost Annual cost to an employer of providing pension benefits to employees; this consists of the *normal (or current service) cost*, plus some provision for the *prior (or past) service cost*, plus or minus an adjustment for *actuarial* gains or losses as required in the minimum and maximum provisions of *APB* Opinion 8.

pension fund A *fund* for the payment of *annuities* or *pensions*, consisting of actual cash set aside or specific investments in securities, the income from which accrues to the fund. Where title to fund assets rests in a separate organization, such as a trust to which periodic contributions are made under contract with the creator and in accordance with an agreement with employees, the question of whether the creator should report fund assets in its balance sheet has not yet been satisfactorily settled; in general, if the plan is irrevocable, if fund assets cannot be utilized except for pension payments, and if the payment of pensions is not a business obligation but rather an obligation only of the fund, the omission of the fund from the balance sheet of the creator has been regarded as a preferred practice. Where fund assets may legally be utilized for other purposes, and contributions to the fund are voluntary or revocable, they are merely earmarked items and remain as business assets until disbursed. An offsetting *pension reserve*, if any, may be equal to, or greater or less than the fund. See also *pension plan; reserve for contingencies; funding agency*.

pension plan The method adopted by a business or other organization for the payment of *annuities* or *pensions* to retired or disabled employees. If the plan meets the requirements of Sections 401 and 404 of the *Internal Revenue Code*, contributions by the employer organization are deductible in its federal income-tax return, and the employee is taxed only as the pension is received.

pension reserve An obligation recognized in full or in part by an employer as representing a future liability to pay *annuities* or pensions to employees. If created by a charge to expense, such a reserve ordinarily represents a liability. If the plan is a revocable one, the reserve is likely to be regarded simply as a reservation of retained earnings, whether or not it offsets earmarked assets. See *pension fund*.

p/e ratio See *price-earnings ratio*.

percent Any decimal or fraction, times 100. See *ratio*.

percentage depletion (federal income taxes) *Depletion expense* computed as a percentage of *gross income* notwithstanding that the accumulative aggregate of provisions for tax purposes, whether based on income or cost or both, may exceed the cost of the property. Rates currently prevailing, listed in Section 613 of the *Internal Revenue Code*, range from 5% for gravel and certain clays up to 22% for oil, gas, sulfur, and uranium, but the amount thus computed must not exceed 50% of the net income from the property before the depletion deduction. The 22% rate for oil will be gradually reduced to 15% between 1981 and 1984. Percentage depletion is no longer available for the major oil companies.

percentage-of-completion method A method for allocating revenues and costs (with related net income or loss) to projects in proportion to completion. Commonly used on long-term contracts, as in construction projects, the payments are based on pro rata share of progress, usually measured by costs incurred or engineering estimates. See *completed-contract method*.

percentage statement An *operating statement* containing not only monetary amounts but also the *ratio* of each item to any of several bases. In an income statement, the base is ordinarily the total of net revenues; in a manufacturing statement, the cost of goods manufactured or total manufacturing cost; in a balance sheet, total assets. See *common-size statement*.

percentile Any of the values that divide a *frequency distribution* into 100 parts each containing 1% of the total number of items.

perfection standard cost A *standard cost* based on the best possible performance obtainable under the most favorable conditions.

performance A general term applied to part or all of the conduct or activities of an organization over a period of time, often with reference to some *standard* such as past or projected costs, an *efficiency* base, management *responsibility* or *accountability*, or the like.

performance audit An *audit*, instituted internally or by external interests, of organizational activities having as its purpose an *appraisal* of management and accounting *standards, policies*, and general conduct, followed by a report, often informal, of findings. Its scope, carefully defined and delimited, may be overall in character, or one having a restricted application. See discussion of *audit (4B)*.

performance budget (governmental accounting) A budget of outputs, as in a *program planning budgeting system* but often without the accompanying relations to longer-range accomplishments that form an integral part of most PPBS budgets.

performance measurement Quantification of *effectiveness* or *efficiency* in the operations of an enterprise or a segment of it during a period of time. *Income from continuing operations* is an approximation of such a measurement for both effectiveness and efficiency in external *financial reporting*, in a cross comparison between private enterprise *entities*. The emphasis on *realization* rather than on the *earning process* and the inclusion of such items as *holding gains* (or *losses*) may need to be taken into account, however, and allowances should be made for gains or losses from occurrences that are unusual or infrequent and the effects of changes in accounting estimates. See *audit* and especially *comprehensive audit* under *audit*.

perils of the sea (marine insurance) Fortuitous marine perils or risks such as sinking, collision, and unusually heavy weather, excluding those attributable to the ordinary action of wind and weather.

period See *accounting period*.

period cost (or charge or expense) 1. Any expenditure assigned to expense on a time basis rather than on a basis of service yield, although in most instances the two bases coincide; rent, interest, real-estate taxes, and income taxes are examples; contrasts with *product cost*. Straight-line depreciation is often looked upon as a period cost. See *straight-line method; cost absorption; direct costing*.
2. Any cost applicable to the operations of a period without allocation to inventory.

periodic audit 1. An audit covering an intermediate accounting period such as a month.
2. An audit conducted at stated intervals of time.

periodic income Income accounted for proportionately with elapsed periods of time and under varied conditions; as, a part or all of (a) an amount not previously recorded and receivable in the future, as bond interest; (b) an amount already received and recorded, as rent paid in advance; or (c) an amount already recorded (as deferred income) but not yet received, as profit from an installment sale.

periodic inventory A method for determining *inventory* values dependent upon a *physical inventory* taken at the end of each period with the resulting inventory value entered on the books; additions to inventory during the period are charged to a purchases account and not to inventory, as in a *perpetual inventory* system. Inventory book value does not change until the next physical inventory is made.

 Cost of goods sold for a period is calculated by adding the beginning inventory value (the physical inventory value determined at the end of last period) to the period's net purchases or cost of goods manufactured and subtacting the ending inventory value derived from the period-end physical inventory.

periodicity concept (of accounting) The identification of *economic activity* (*1*) with time periods whereby for each period the activity can be measured and reported; see *continuity; accounting period*.

periodic payment accumulating to 1 The amount required, as for a sinking fund, to be deposited periodically at compound interest in order to reach the desired total of 1 at a specified time. See *interest formulas*.

periodic payment with present value of 1 Any of a series of equal periodic payments required to liquidate a present debt of 1 where the unpaid balance draws interest. See *interest formulas*.

peripheral device (computers) An input or output *hardware* device attached to a computer which allows hard-copy output to be generated by the computer or which permits the input of hard-copy data. Peripheral equipment includes such devices as card readers, card punches, line printers, paper tape punches, paper tape readers.

perks See *perquisites*.

permanent asset 1. = *capital asset*.
2. *Land*.

permanent difference A difference between taxable income and pretax *accounting income* arising from a transaction that, under applicable tax laws and regulations, will not be offset in other periods. An example of a permanent difference is amortization of goodwill, which is an expense for accounting purposes but is not deductible for income-tax purposes.

permanent file (auditing) Papers and schedules kept in a separate file for use in succeeding audits. It usually contains copies, extracts, or summaries of such documents as the charter or articles of incorporation; bylaws; trust or partnership agreements; minutes of the board of directors; long-term contracts; progressive schedules of capital stock, surplus, and capital assets; descriptions of and comments on accounting poli-

cies, methods, and internal controls; and other matters of similar import.

permanent investments Investments in securities and other property or rights to property, not held for sale, and hence excluded from the classification of current assets; long-term investments.

permutation Any arrangement or ordering of all or a part of a collection of numbers, symbols, or other units. Example: *a b c d e*, in alphabetical sequence, constitute a permutation, as do also *b a c d e* and *b c e a d*; altogether there are 120 different arrangements of these letters. The varieties of four-letter arrangements of the five letters (e.g., *a b c d, b c d a, a b d e*) are also 120; of three-letter and two-letter combinations, there are 60 and 20, respectively. Or, some of the units may be alike, and indistinguishable from each other; thus, *a b b a b* is one of ten possible permutations of five units consisting of two *a*'s and three *b*'s. The number of permutations under these different conditions may be determined by formulas derived as follows:

1. *No like symbols; each ordered.* Continuing the five-letter illustration, with *a* in any one of five possible positions, *b* can occupy any one of the remaining four, *c* any one of the remaining three, and *d* any one of the remaining two, leaving only one position for *e*. The possible number of arrangements of the five letters is thus $5 \times 4 \times 3 \times 2 \times 1$, or 120, a result that may be referred to as "factorial 5" or "5 factorial" and written as 5!, the exclamation point serving as the *factorial* symbol; or it may be expressed as P_5^5, "the number of permutations of 5 things taken 5 at a time," meaning, in the illustration, the total number of arrangements of the five letters.

2. *No like symbols; not all ordered.* Should it be desired to determine the possible permutations of any four of the five letters mentioned above, with the fifth letter occupying

the remaining position, it will be found that the number is again 120, since $5 \times 4 \times 3 \times 2$ equals that figure. The mathematical expression is P_4^5. Hence, $P_4^5 = P_5^5$. The possible number of permutations involved in placing three letters in any three of the five positions, without regard to the identity of the two letters occupying the remaining position, is represented as $P_3^5 = 5 \times 4 \times 3$, or 60. The ordered sequence of any two of the five letters without regard to the positioning of the remaining three (P_2^5) may be made in 5×4 ways, as may be directly demonstrated by experiment; and, finally, if the number of positions of only one of the letters (P_1^5) is to be reckoned with, only five different permutations are possible. The generalization to be deduced from these considerations is the following formula, where n is the total number of units or items of which the number of permutations (P) of r units is sought:

$$P_r^n = \frac{n!}{(n-r)!}.$$

Thus,

$$P_2^5 = \frac{5!}{(5-2)!}$$

$$= \frac{5 \times 4 \times 3 \times 2 \times 1}{3 \times 2 \times 1} = 20.$$

3. *Some like symbols; each ordered.* The number of permutations discussed in the first formula would have been smaller if two or more of the letters had been the same. Thus, if the letters had been *a a b b c*, the possible permutations would have been

$$\frac{5 \times 4 \times 3 \times 2 \times 1}{(2 \times 1)(2 \times 1)} = 30,$$

or, if the letters had been *a a a b b*, and the number of *a*'s is represented by *j* and the number of *b*'s by *k*, the possible permutations would have been

$$\frac{n!}{j! \, k!} = \frac{5!}{3! \, 2!} = \frac{5 \times 4 \times 3 \times 2 \times 1}{(3 \times 2 \times 1)(2 \times 1)} = 10,$$

and so on, with $0! \equiv 1! \equiv 1$. See *factorial*.

4. *Different symbols, group ordered.* Permutations considered without regard for the sequence or position in which a particular symbol occurs are referred to as *combinations*. Thus, in the selection of any three (r) of the first five letters of the alphabet, *a b c, a c b, c a b*, etc., would be permutations, their number being $r! = 3 \times 2 \times 1$, or 6, but they would constitute only one combination. Hence, the number of permutations, obtained in the usual way, would have to be divided by 6, or $r!$. The formula for combinations is thus expressed as

$$C_r^n = \frac{n!}{r!(n-r)!},$$

and the solution of the illustration would be

$$C_3^5 = \frac{5!}{3! \, 2!} = \frac{120}{12} = 10,$$

a total provable by experiment. A working knowledge of combinations is basic in the study of probability and in the devising of sampling methods. See *probability; sample*.

perpetual bond $= perpetuity$. Same as *annuity bond*.

perpetual budget $= continuous budget$.

perpetual inventory A *book inventory* kept in continuous agreement with stock on hand by means of a detailed record that may also serve as a subsidiary ledger where dollar amounts as well as physical quantities are maintained. Sections of the stockroom are inventoried at short intervals and the quantities or dollar amounts or both are adjusted, where necessary, to the physical count. See *continuous inventory*.

perpetuity A series of periodic payments that last forever. An *annuity* with an infinite life. A perpetuity of \$1 with the first payment starting a year from now has the present value equal to the reciprocal of the applicable interest rate (\$10 if the interest rate is 10%, \$5 if the interest rate is 20%). See *interest formulas*.

perquisites A gratuity or tip. A privilege, gain, or profit incidental to an employment in addition to the regular wage or salary. Any fringe or other benefit made available to an employee because of the employment relationship.

person 1. An *individual (1)*.

2. Any business corporation or other entity given recognition as the possessor of rights, privileges, and responsibilities for which an *accounting unit* has been or can be established. The accounting use corresponds very generally to its legal use.

personal account An amount receivable from or payable to any *person*.

personal defenses In *negotiable instrument* law, limited defenses which are not sufficient to defeat the rights of a *holder in due course* when he or she brings suit on the instrument.

personal exemption A deduction from taxable income based only on demographic characteristics or relations of family support. An individual filing a federal income-tax return is entitled to a "personal exemption" in the form of a $1,000 deduction in computing taxable income. In addition, an exemption is allowed for the taxpayer's spouse if the spouse has no gross income and is not the dependent of another taxpayer (and does not file a return). Additional exemptions are allowed if the taxpayer has attained the age of 65 before the end of the taxable year and/or is blind at the close of the taxable year. These additional exemptions are also allowed for a taxpayer's spouse if the spouse has no gross income and is not the dependent of another taxpayer (and does not file a return). One additional exemption is allowed the taxpayer for each *dependent* claimed on the return, regardless of age or vision.

personal holding company (federal income taxes) A corporation, popularly known as an "incorporated pocketbook," a majority of the outstanding capital stock of which is owned by a small group of natural persons. Current features of the law or regulations provide that (a) stock owned includes stock constructively owned; (b) the number of stockholders collectively owning, directly or indirectly, over 50% of the value of the outstanding shares does not exceed five at any time during the last half of the taxable year; (c) at least 60% of the gross income consists of such items as dividends, interest, royalties, annuities, rents (unless such rents constitute 50% or more of the gross income); (d) regular corporate normal tax and surtax are imposed and a special surtax of 70% on undistributed net income (Section 1541-1 of *Internal Revenue Code*).

personal income 1. The income of an individual, of the type commonly found in an income-tax return.

2. (national income accounting) The income, usually for a year, of the individuals and unincorporated and nonprofit enterprises resident within a country. Under current concepts, it consists principally of wages and salaries from all sources including government; social-security payments by government less employees' contributions to social-security funds; proprietors' income; net rentals, including the imputed rental of owned homes; dividends; interest; and business transfer payments such as uncollectible accounts of private business. See *social accounting*.

personal liability An amount owing by a natural person.

personal property Property or assets of a temporary and movable character, as contrasted with *real estate (or property)*; also known as "personalty."

personal service income (federal income taxes) Income earned as wages, salaries, self-employment income (including professional fees), pensions, and certain other forms of deferred compensation, to which the *maximum tax* rate of 50% may be applied.

Gross personal service income is reduced: (1) by deductions for *adjusted gross income* (AGI) which pertain to employment, (2) by a proportionate share of itemized deductions from AGI and exemptions, and (3) by *tax preferences* other than the net capital gain deduction to arrive at personal service taxable income.

PERT = *Program Evaluation and Review Technique*. A system under which an activity such as construction of a factory is organized and controlled on the basis of the sequential time periods required for each operational step. See *Program Evaluation and Review Technique; network; critical path method.*

PERT cost A networking technique with a superimposed cost accounting system in which managers are assigned to supervise and control costs of individual or groups of activities related by the network.

petty cash (fund) A relatively small amount of cash on hand or on deposit, available for minor disbursements, and usually maintained under the *imprest system.*

phenomenon An appearance; any *event, condition*, thing, or characteristic that is observed or observable; sometimes contrasted with "reality" (i.e., an object independent of possible errors of observation), although the contrast between appearance and reality suggests merely the possibility of correcting observation, since correction must proceed from observation.

Phillips curve A relationship between the percentage of labor force employed and the rate of price inflation. The relationship is such that a decrease in one of these magnitudes produces an increase in the other up to a certain point.

physical asset = *tangible asset.*

physical budget A budget expressed in units of materials, number of employees, or number of labor hours or service units, rather than in dollars.

physical (productive capacity) capital maintenance concept of income Amount that could be withdrawn, consumed, or paid as a dividend during a period of time without reducing an entity's physical productive capacity, its stock of physical (tangible goods) plus its capacity to produce the same quantity of goods and services as at the beginning of the period. Physical productive capacity capital is maintained when the *entity's* net assets remain sufficient to produce the same quantity of goods and services. This concept of income would be applied if, in determining income, expenses were measured on the basis of *replacement cost*, which is the amount needed to maintain the amount of physical capital used up in the *earning process*; thus such income would be the amount that could be withdrawn without reducing the entity's physical (productive capacity) capital. Use of the *LIFO* inventory method tends to yield amounts for *cost of sales* and gross margin (or *gross profit*) that approximate results that would be obtained if the *replacement cost* basis were used. Contrast to financial *capital maintenance concept of income* and *purchasing power capital maintenance concept of income.*

physical concept of capital See *physical (productive capacity) capital maintenance concept of income; capital maintenance concept.*

physical depreciation Loss of usefulness in a fixed asset attributable to purely physical causes; wear and tear. Example: the master plates from which a book is printed may suffer little physical depreciation from wear but a much larger obsolescence from exhaustion of earning power as the book's sales decrease.

physical examination (auditing) the act of performing a *physical observation test.*

physical inventory An inventory determined by observation and evidenced by a listing of the actual count, weight, or measure. Physical inventories are of three types: the *continuous inventory*, supplementing perpetual-inventory records; periodic counts of selected items; and the annual inventory, or overall count and pricing, taken at the end of the fiscal year. The methods followed in each case differ in scope and in the number of protective devices surrounding the operation. The first of these is normally a feature of a perpetual-inventory system, the counting process covering the entire stock being spread over a year or less. The second may be carried on as a part of the *internal audit* program. The third is common even where perpetual records are maintained and may be completed during a period of temporary shutdown at the end of the fiscal year; or it may be instituted before the end of the year and adjusted to the balance at the close of the period through the use of temporary and often informal perpetual records.

physical life Total potential operating life, as of a machine, as contrasted with useful or *economic life*, which may be much less because of the presence of obsolescence or inadequacy, or both. See *service life*.

physical observation test An *observation test* where a specific type of asset is examined. Common examples are cash on hand, securities, inventory, and fixed assets.

physical records 1. Property records, as in a *plant ledger*.
2. (computers) A collection of one or more *logical records* represented as a single unit which is read and written from an I/O (=*input/output*) device in a single operation. Sometimes referred to as a *block*.

physical variance = *efficiency variance*.

pi The ratio of the circumference of a circle to its diameter. An *irrational number* symbolized π, its value is $3.141592653589+$.

piecemeal opinion See *auditors' report*. An expression of opinion by an *external auditor*

as to certain identified items in the financial statements. Such opinions were formerly issued when the auditor disclaimed an opinion or expressed adverse opinion on the financial statements taken as a whole. Because they tend to overshadow or contradict the disclaimer or adverse opinion, they are no longer allowed under current auditing standards.

piece rates A basis for measuring performance according to quantity of production often accompanied by a quota-based performance evaluation scheme.

planned precision The width of the *confidence interval* used in planning a statistical sample. Planned *precision* is usually less than the ultimately desired width (after sampling) and as a safeguard against possible error in predicting the sample *standard deviation* an increase in the planned sample size is required.

planning The process of determining in advance the factors necessary to achieve a set of goals; designing an effective means of achieving some future goals (ends); the process of determining the nature, timing, and rate of resource acquisition and use to reach some desired state of affairs (goal). Such processes may be either long-term (strategic) or short-term (tactical) or a combination of both. These two processes set the stage for the specification of financial plans (i.e., financial means of achieving desired ends) in the budgeting process, and they serve as a reference point for the implementation of management control and performance evaluation. See *management control system; strategic planning; tactics; planning model*.

planning calendar A schedule which relates planning activities to specific completion dates. Each phase of the planning process is specified and time-sequenced to provide coordination in the planning process. See also *planning cycle*.

planning cycle The entire cycle by which plans are developed, reviewed, revised, and adopted, often specified or accompanied by a *planning calendar*.

planning horizon A future time period or date which is to be used for guidance in formulating plans. Long-range planning and short-range planning will generally proceed with different planning horizons and in different degrees of detail. Different horizons are often needed for different *projects* and major decisions such as acquisitions of other companies, the development of new products, or the opening of new markets.

planning model A *model* for delineating or portraying alternative courses of action and their consequences. Sometimes it assumes mathematical form to increase the ranges of alternatives that can be readily considered prior to effecting a choice. Distinguished from a *control model*, which is directed to securing conformance between plans and actions.

planning programming budgeting system See *program planning budgeting system*.

plant 1. Land, buildings, machinery, furniture, and other equipment permanently employed; fixed assets generally.
2. In a restricted sense, buildings only; or land and buildings, as in the term "plant and equipment."

plant asset See *fixed asset*.

plant capacity Maximum potential production within a given plant; expressed in units of product, labor hours, or other measure of full-time employment of the plant's facilities. Deductions made necessary by a single shift, a 5-day week, seasonal or other usual periods of idleness, and other factors yield *practical capacity*.

plant fund (institutional accounting) A fund established for the acquisition of land, buildings, improvements, and equipment.

plant ledger A supporting record of fixed assets owned or controlled, often consisting of one or more subsidiary ledgers and sometimes containing details of accumulated depreciation. See *fixed asset; depreciation*.

The relative importance of the investment in land, buildings, and equipment requires an adequate plan for the orderly maintenance of supporting detail. The justification for such records may be said to be these: (a) at all times the total of the investment in fixed assets is supported by verifiable detail, (b) adjustments can be made readily upon the disposal of additions and retirements, (c) property accountabilities may be more easily assigned and maintained, (d) an insurance basis is provided, (e) an acceptable foundation is assured for reports to tax and regulatory authorities, and (f) more accurate depreciation provisions and accumulations can be supplied.

The scope of plant records is determined by circumstances. The simplest plan is to provide two or more *general-ledger fixed-asset* accounts without attempting currently to maintain details for individual items of property. A somewhat more detailed plan would provide a catalog of individual items of plant without tying in their cost with general-ledger accounts. Such an arrangement would be useful but would not be as accurate or in the long run as satisfactory as the institution of controlling and subsidiary accounts. A fully adequate plan would involve the following:

1. A classification and numbering plan based on the location or characteristics of the items involved;

2. A scheme for maintaining *controlling accounts* governing detailed property records for asset costs and depreciation reserves;

3. A *subsidiary-ledger* card for each significant item or class of plant and equipment; and

4. An established procedure for recording transactions relating to fixed assets, such as original purchases, additions, renewals (replacements), maintenance, retirements, and gains or losses, if any, from retirement.

pledge *n.* 1. = *collateral.*

2. A promise in writing to contribute a stated money amount to a nonprofit organization on or before a given date. Although a pledge may be a legal claim on the donor, enforcement is rarely undertaken, and it is commonly regarded as a *contingent asset* only.

v.t. To transfer personal property to a creditor or trustee for the purpose of partly or fully securing a debt; to *collateralize.*

pledged asset An asset placed in trust or mortgaged to secure an obligation or contract; a collateralized or *hypothecated asset.* It is carried on the balance sheet under its regular heading and, if a current asset, is generally so captioned as to show the extent and purpose of the pledge.

Poisson distribution The *statistical distribution* defined by

$$\sum_{x=0}^{\infty} \frac{m^x e^{-m}}{x!} = 1,$$

where x assumes only integer values within the range exhibited for the summation. Here $e \, (= 2.718+)$ is the base for the natural *logarithms*; m is the mean of x values; and

$$P(X = x) = \frac{m^x e^{-m}}{x!}$$

is the probability that the random variable X will assume a value $x = 0, 1$, etc. Also

$$P(x_1 \leqslant X \leqslant x_2) = \sum_{x=x_1}^{x_2} \frac{m^x e^{-m}}{x!}$$

is the probability that the random variable will be in the interval from x_1 to x_2. Poisson probabilities depend only on the mean so that it forms a one-*parameter* statistical distribution with values of the *mean* and *variance* both equal to m. The Poisson may be roughly characterized as the applicable distribution—as in sampling for defective items or for accounting errors—when there are large opportunities but small probabilities for the occurrence of an event. Also called the "law of small numbers." Tables of its values being widely available, the Poisson is often used to approximate the *binomial distributions* and others when the sample sizes are relatively small.

policy In the field of management, that branch dealing with *decisions* and their planning, formulation, and assessment, establishing the objectives and general methods of administration by which the operations of any organization are conducted; a *rule* or set of rules that guides and governs action; a collection of stated or implied intentions of an organization. "Top" policy in a business enterprise refers to decisions originating as directives from the board of directors, the executive committee of the board, or the president and other principal officers; or it may refer to general principles of conducting business on the basis of which lesser policies, sometimes decisions of subordinate management, and administrative practices are devised and put into channels of control over day-to-day operations. The testing and comparison of an intention or decision with actual performance and the determination of the degree of consistency between the two are functions of both *internal auditors* and *external auditors.* The distinction between policy and *administration* (*1*), or policy and *operation* (*1*), is never entirely clear, although elaborate attempts have been made to draw a rigorous line between them so that the fields of activity of the board of directors, top administrators, and other executives within the organization are cleanly separated and overlap as little as possible. See *administration; corporate action; administrative action; decision.*

policy depreciation See *depreciation methods*.

pool 1. (of accounts) Accounts related to a common service or product, constituting a subfunction which as a group may be *spread* or *allocated* to functions served.

2. A group of related items of inventory or property. See *dollar-value LIFO; composite-life method*, under *depreciation methods*.

pooled income fund (federal income taxes) A *trust* given with an irrevocable remainder interest to a public charity while the donor retains the right to income from the transferred property (*Internal Revenue Code*, Section 642). An income, gift, or estate tax deduction is allowed for the value of the remainder interest contributed to the fund. Various requirements are: (1) the fund must be maintained by the recipient public charity and neither the donor nor the income beneficiary can be a trustee; (2) the income beneficiaries must be paid an annual amount based on the fund's rate of return. No income can be accumulated for any beneficiary; (3) no investments in tax-exempt income securities are allowed; (4) the fund must commingle all property contributed from all contributors when there is more than one donor.

The trust and beneficiaries are taxed under the ordinary rules pertaining to trusts.

pooling of interests A consolidation or merger in which each beneficial interest continues in a new or modified organization with its book value and relative interest in paid-in capital and earned surplus substantially unchanged. See *acquired surplus* (*3*). Since the elements of a purchase and sale are absent, no new costs are established, as is often the case when a *business combination* is brought about by a purchase of the net assets of one company by another. *Accounting Principles Board* Opinion No. 16 specified 12 criteria, all of which must be satisfied as a requisite for pooling. See *purchase method of combination*.

population (statistics) = *universe*.

portfolio A collection of items grouped together for a common purpose of analysis or decision. Example: a collection of different securities or other assets which are to be evaluated in terms of their combined risks and returns. See *portfolio analysis*.

portfolio analysis 1. A detailing of the risks and returns available from different *portfolios* of securities or other assets. An *efficient portfolio* is one in which returns cannot be increased without increased risk or in which risks cannot be decreased without reducing the return.

2. A technique which uses *mathematical programming* models to obtain efficient portfolios, usually with the aid of a computer. A given array of securities such as the stocks on the *New York Stock Exchange* may yield a large number of efficient portfolios as well as many portfolios that are not efficient.

portfolio balancing Equivalent to diversification. The selection of investments for a portfolio which minimizes the *variance* of return for a given expected yield on the assets composing the portfolio.

portfolio risk (portfolio analysis) 1. Contribution of a security to the risk of a portfolio, usually defined as the *covariance* of returns on the security and returns on the portfolio.

2. Sensitivity of changes in price of a security to changes in price of a portfolio. *Market risk* is a special case of portfolio risk in which the portfolio consists of the entire market.

position = *financial position*.

position bookkeeping The procedure involved in keeping a self-balancing section within a double-entry system that indicates the position, long or short, in foreign currency, or in a commodity or security market. It shows, on the one hand, the purchases and sales, usually "futures," in each currency, commodity, or security, and, on the other hand, the obligations to pay to—or the rights to receive from—individual creditors or debtors corresponding amounts of domestic currency.

positive confirmation See *confirmation*.

positive theory See *normative theory*.

post To transfer to a *ledger* the account changes indicated by the record of transactions appearing in journals or other posting mediums. See *enter*.

postaudit An *audit* at some point after the occurrence of a *transaction* or group of transactions. Audits by public accountants are sometimes so called. The term may also be applied to an examination made by an *internal auditor*, in contrast to *preaudit* or *voucher audit*.

post balance-sheet review A set of *auditing* procedures required on all audits which are applied to the period from the date of the audited financial statements to the end of the audit field work. The purpose of these procedures is to determine the occurrence of any significant events subsequent to the financial statement date which have a material impact on their fair presentation.

postclosing balance sheet A balance sheet the details of which are supported by the *open balances* of the *general-ledger* accounts at the end of a fiscal year, after year-end and audit adjustments have been recorded and revenue and expense (nominal) accounts have been closed out.

postclosing trial balance The trial balance of a general ledger at the end of a fiscal period after eliminating the period's revenue and expense or *nominal accounts*. See *balance-sheet account; trial balance*.

postdate To affix a date following the date a document is written or executed: a postdated check cannot be cashed or deposited before the date appearing on its face. See *antedate*.

posterior probability distribution The probabilities associated with various states after the results of an experiment have been analyzed. See *Bayes' rule*.

posting 1. The bookkeeping process of transferring dollar amounts and their accompanying *legends* from a document or book of original entry to a ledger. See *entry*.
2. An item in a ledger; an amount posted.

posting medium 1. A *book of original entry*; a *journal*.
2. A voucher, invoice, or other document, or an intermediate summary from which a posting may be made.

postulate Any of a series of *axioms* or *assumptions* constituting the supposed basis of a system of thought or an organized field of endeavor. The truth of a postulate, like that of other assumptions, is taken for granted as something generally admitted as self-evident, or as being common to other fields, and thus serving as a point of departure in a specialized field. Postulates are chosen for their convenience and fruitfulness in organizing and promoting inquiry or useful action; within the same field, the postulates of one school may differ from those of another, and they may be expected to change as activities within the field are modified, and as the *public interest* in the field alters its views concerning the value of the field to society. Postulates may also have their origins at one or more of the several stages of a process; thus, some may be concerned with moral values, while others may be chosen from among the alternatives present in established customs. See *axiom; principle*.

power of a test The probability of rejecting the *null hypothesis* in favor of the alternative when the null hypothesis is false. Thus, power is one minus the probability of a *type II error*. In general the power of a test is an increasing function of the sample size. Power is also affected by which alternative hypothesis is true. For example, for a given sample size, the power of the null hypothesis that the population mean is 10 vs. the alternative hypothesis that the population mean is 15.

power of attorney An instrument authorizing one person to act as agent for another, either generally or for some specified purpose.

PPBS = *planning programming budgeting system.* See *program planning budgeting system.*

PPS sampling See *probability proportionate to size sampling.*

practical capacity Utilized *plant capacity*: the ratio obtained by dividing anticipated (e.g., budgeted) or actual (after-the-fact) production units by the maximum (theoretical) production units that the plant would be capable of yielding under a 24-hour, 365-day schedule. When applied to *fixed (production or overhead) costs* the ratio yields the portion ascribable to production. Reduced by allowances for nonutilization arising from a single-shift operation and for customary shutdowns or decreased-production periods due to vacations, holidays, inventory taking, cleanup, setup time, and seasonal preparations for new models, the theoretical production is reduced to an attainable level.

practice set A comprehensive problem designed to familiarize students of bookkeeping and accounting with realistic details of transactions, journals, ledgers, adjustments, and financial statements.

preacquisition profits Retained earnings of a corporation prior to the existence of *control* by another corporation. See *consolidation surplus.*

preaudit The examination of (a) creditors' invoices, payrolls, claims, and proposed reimbursements before payment (voucher audit), or (b) sales transactions at or before delivery, as well as (c) verification of an authorization prior to issuing an order to purchase goods or enter into employment contracts within stipulated amounts; also known as *administrative audit.*

Responsibility for preaudit rests on the controller of an enterprise; the frequent testing of the adequacy of preaudit procedures and the effectiveness of their application is a feature of the work of the *internal auditor.* Among activities normally regarded as preaudit functions are: (for costs) the review of contracts before their approval; comparisons of details of invoices or other claims with such contracts, or with purchase orders and other original authorizations; the determination that goods or services of the kind and amount ordered have been received, adequately inspected for quality and quantity, and placed in stock; the verification of price, extensions, additions, returns, and discounts; an inquiry into the authenticity of signatures indicating receipt and approval; (for revenues) review and confirmation of customer's order; independent inspection and delivery; tie-in with shipping documents; delivery receipts from customers; (on cash sales) comparison of sales tickets with cash received.

precious metals accounting A method of accounting for metals like gold or silver which recognizes revenues at the time of extraction or production if there exists a ready market with determinable prices and marketing costs are insignificant. See *production basis of revenue recognition.*

precision 1. Degree of refinement; relative absence of error: the smaller the error, the greater the degree of precision.
2. The closeness with which a measurement agrees with a related set of measurements of the same kind. Thus, the precision of a set of measurements may be said to be inversely related to their *standard error.* See *accuracy; replication; reliability.*
3. (statistics) The magnitude of deviations of any *sample* value or function of sample

values from the population parameter being estimated. See *standard deviation; standard error*.

preclosing trial balance A *trial balance* prepared before giving effect to final *adjusting journal entries* and *closing entries*.

predate = *antedate*.

predecessor auditor The *external auditor* of a company who is displaced by another, *successor auditor*.

predecessor company A business *entity* the net assets and operations of which have been taken over by one or several entities. The successor or successors may be one or more newly formed companies or the party or parties to a *business combination*.

predetermined cost A cost ascertained in advance of the operation for which it is incurred.

predicted cost 1. = *standard cost*.
2. A projection as in a *financial projection* or the result of a time series *regression analysis*.

prediction 1. An estimate of a future operation, event, or condition: often a function of management, depending for its credibility and reliability on the (effective) operation of instituted *controls*. See *forecast; financial forecasts*.
2. A *budget* or any of its component elements; any forward outlook. See *forward accounting*.

predictions = *forecasts* (*q.v.*). Forecasts, however, are also sometimes distinguished from predictions by allowing for the effects of possible courses of management action in the former but not in the latter. See *futurology*.

preemptive right The privilege accorded an existing stockholder under common law to subscribe for a pro rata share of any new capital stock the corporation is about to issue. See *right*. Under the laws of many states, the privilege has been limited and may be eliminated by provision in the articles of incor-

poration or bylaws, or waived by an agreement with stockholders and reflected in each stock certificate.

preferred capital stock The class of stock which has a claim prior to common stockholders upon the earnings of a corporation, and often also upon the assets in the event of liquidation.

preferred creditor A person whose claim against another, particularly an *insolvent* or *bankrupt*, takes precedence over the claims of other creditors. Mechanics' liens, compensation of employees, and state and federal taxes are examples.
pl. The class of creditors ranking highest among claims of creditors generally. See *statement of affairs; marshalling of assets*.

preferred (-stock) dividend A *dividend* to holders of preferred stock, usually at a fixed rate per quarter expressed in a percentage or in dollars per share.

preferred dividends coverage A *coverage ratio* which measures the ability of a firm to pay its preferred dividends, as well as other financial charges, from its regular earnings, usually calculated by dividing net income before taxes and fixed charges by the sum of fixed charges and preferred dividends adjusted for taxes, i.e., preferred dividends divided by 1 minus the tax rate. The "fixed charges" in this ratio normally include interest and rent expense, but sinking-fund payments adjusted for taxes could also be included for a broader version. See also *fixed-charge coverage ratio*.

preferred stock See *capital stock; stockholder*.

preferred-stock bail-out (federal income taxes) A tax-avoidance device under which a corporation would issue preferred stock as a tax-free stock dividend and later redeem the preferred stock for cash which was taxed as a long-term capital gain. Section 306 of the

Internal Revenue Code now provides that such a redemption will be treated as an ordinary dividend and not as a long-term capital gain.

preferred value (statistical quality control) See *basic dimension*.

preliminary audit (auditing) 1. Field work undertaken by an auditor before the close of a period under review, often consisting of a review or testing of *internal controls, records*, and individual *transactions*, the purpose being to expedite the completion of the report after the period has ended. A preliminary audit differs from a periodic audit in that it usually involves no report and is part of a regular annual audit.
2. In an initial engagement, the investigation of the business and its accounting system and operating methods preceding the determination of the *scope* of the audit procedures to be employed.

preliminary balance sheet = *tentative balance sheet*.

preliminary evaluation See *evaluation of internal control*. The preliminary evaluation involves an auditor in the study of a system prior to performing *compliance tests*.

premium 1. The amount by which the price of a security or other asset exceeds its nominal, face, par, quoted, or market value.
2. The amount paid periodically to an insurer or an agent by one insured. See *insurance premium*.
3. The price paid for an option or contract.
4. An amount paid over and above the usual wage, for superior workmanship, loyal service, and so forth.

premium on capital stock The amount in excess of par or stated value received by an issuing corporation for its capital stock; additional *paid-in capital*.

prepaid asset = *prepaid expense*.

prepaid expense 1. An expenditure, often re-current, for future benefits: a type of *deferred charge*. Examples: prepaid operating expenses, prepaid rent, taxes, royalties, commissions; unexpired insurance premiums; stationery and office supplies. Such items are classifiable as current assets and constitute a part of *working capital*; they are charged to future operations on the basis of measurable benefits or on a time or *period-charge* basis. Other types of deferred charges are concluded transactions that are to be applied more or less arbitrarily to the operations of one or more succeeding periods; in contrast, *accrued expense*, a *liability*, is made up of items charged to past operations because of benefits already received.
2. sometimes *pl*. The title of a balance-sheet item representing the portion of outlays for benefits carried into the next accounting period or periods. See *balance sheet*.

prepaid income = *deferred revenue*.

prepaid interest The excess of the face value of a loan over the proceeds of the loan, often classified as a *prepaid expense*. The name is misleading since the amount is to be a future payment. A more logical but seldom followed practice would be to deduct it from the face value of the *liability*.

prepay To pay for a service before its receipt or enjoyment; such prepayment, as for insurance or rent, reflecting long-established commercial practices, contrasts with *accrue* (or the *recognition* of the receipt or enjoyment of other types of services paid for after their receipt or enjoyment). See *deferred charge*.

preproduction costs *Makeready time* and *expense* required to initiate production on particular orders.

present fairly See *fairness*.

present value (or worth) The price a buyer is willing to pay for one or a series of future benefits, the term generally being associated with a formal computation of the estimated worth in the future of such benefits from which a *discount (1)* or compensation for waiting is deducted. See *interest formulas*.

present value of 1 The present sum which, if compounded at a given rate of interest over a given period of time, will yield 1; the discounted value of 1; the reciprocal of the compound amount of 1. See *interest formulas*.

present value of 1 per period The deposit necessary to yield 1 at the end of each of a stated number of succeeding periods, the declining balance remaining on deposit being compounded at an agreed rate of interest per period. See *interest formulas*.

pretax accounting income Income reported for accounting purposes before deduction for income tax.

preventive maintenance *Maintenance* designed to forestall a decline in the current productivity of an asset or process, or to lessen or remove a hazard to life or property. Because it does not add to capacity or usefulness it is *current expense*.

previously taxed income (federal income taxes) In a *Subchapter S corporation*, income of the corporation is taxed to the shareholder in the year earned by the corporation, whether or not distribution of the income is made. Such income, if held by the corporation in subsequent years, is termed "previously taxed income" (PTI). When PTI is later distributed, it is not taxed again to the shareholder but is a reduction of the basis in his or her stock. PTI must be distributed as cash rather than property, and the shareholder's interest in PTI does not transfer with the sale or gift of the stock or to his or her estate. See *undistributed taxable income*.

price 1. The money consideration asked for or offered in exchange for a specified unit of a good or service; in a barter transaction, the ratio at which a unit of any good or service exchanges for a unit of another good or service. Prices are classified in a variety of ways: (a) by their trend over a period of time; see *normal price*; (b) by type of market; see *competitive price; oligopoly and oligopsony prices*; (c) by the freedom of individual business concerns to react to economic forces; see *free price; administered price*; (d) by commercial practices in various industries; see *list price; trade price; cash price; spot price; fixed resale price; FOB price; FAS price; C and F price; CIF price; upset price; contract price; transfer price*; and (e) by their relation to the value of money in exchange for the same goods during different periods of time, independent of the relation to the demand and supply of the commodity; see *current price; real price*.

2. As frequently employed in accounting: (a) the amount received or receivable from a sale; (b) the amount paid or payable for a good or service, in either case less discounts (now often excluding cash discounts); or (c) the amount received in exchange for the issuer's securities (stocks, bonds, and the like).

price ceiling The maximum price of a good or service generally set by government, e.g., to control inflation.

price contract 1. A *contract* between buyer and seller in which a seller agrees to supply a specified item to a buyer at a stated price or under a price formula, with no minimum quantity specified, but usually with a proviso that the buyer will purchase from the seller all required quantities up to a specified maximum quantity.

2. Hence, any contract between buyer and seller, customarily not enforced by the seller should the buyer fail to call for delivery during the contract period. The purpose of such a contract is to protect the buyer by providing

assurance of a source of supply at a price he or she is likely to be willing to pay.

price discrimination The charge by a seller of varying prices under similar conditions of sale. If the effect is to lessen competition or to tend to create a monopoly, federal law may have been violated. When a commodity is sold at a competitive delivered price to customers located nearer competing sellers, it is often necessary for the seller to absorb the excess freight. This freight absorption results in a lower price (*netback* or *millnet*) than that received on sales made to nearby customers on which less or no freight is incurred. If this geographical price discrimination by an individual seller results from an effort to meet competition in good faith, it is not generally held to be illegal. Some latitude is recognized in the exercise of discretion by sellers in charging different prices in consideration of volume sales, terms of payment, and class of customer. Such price differentials can be justified on grounds of lower cost of sales and economic necessity.

price-earnings ratio A *ratio* of the market price of a firm's common stock divided by the *earnings per share* for the past year. It is a popular measure in security analysis and is believed to be an indicator of the market's assessment of the future earnings prospects of the firm.

price efficiency See *efficiency* (*4*); *value variance* (= *price variance*).

price index See *index number*.

price leader An item of merchandise priced abnormally low for the purpose of attracting customers—a device employed by retail stores to increase sales of other products, and by manufacturers and distributors to attract attention to their brands and increase sales of other items. The practice runs some risk of violating federal law. Less diversified competitors are particularly vulnerable to such

competition, their survival being dependent on a normal margin on the price-leader item.

price leadership The practice followed by rival sellers of recognizing and adopting the price established by one or more other members of the industry. Price leadership is usually provided by the largest or dominant firm. A firm may elect to accept the price of a competitor as its own selling price rather than determine its selling price on the basis of other considerations. If the acceptance of a competitor's price is an independently exercised judgment, the risk of violating antitrust acts is probably minimized, since the prerequisites of a conspiracy—a meeting of the minds for the achievement of a uniform price—are lacking. Although adherence to price-leadership practices may be independently decided by individual firms, it may well be dictated by fear of consequences resulting from unilateral price action as well as by anticipated benefits. Industries having only a few large sellers are likely to engage in this practice. As long as the major firms comply, marginal small firms who do not comply are tolerated.

price level 1. A term indicating the average money amount of commodities and services purchased in a given period, usually in the form of a weighted average of the prices of some representative collection of goods and services compared with a similarly weighted average of the prices for the same goods and services in some preceding period;
2. The reciprocal of an *index number* of prices.
3. The general or average price of a firm's sales, as compared with the prices of its trade or industry.

price level accounting The process of measuring and reporting the effects of changes in the general purchasing power of the reporting currency (inflation or deflation) on a business enterprise. Since transactions and events are normally recorded in dollars of varying purchasing power, price level accounting procedures restate and report measures of assets, liabilities, owners' equity, revenue, and expenses in units of equivalent purchasing power. Restatement is based on roll-forward procedures that utilize a general price-level index such as the *consumer price index* or gross national product *implicit price deflator*. See *index number*. Price level accounting is not synonymous with *current value accounting*. See *roll-forward procedure*.

price level gains or losses See *holding gains or losses*.

price maintenance The prescription by a manufacturer or wholesaler of the minimum resale price of a product.

As applied to the sale of securities to the public, prices are maintained by underwriters and dealers during the initial distribution period by purchasing the security when offered by sellers below the fixed price. See *stabilization*.

In the commodity field, price maintenance is a common practice of manufacturers of branded products. Under the Miller-Tydings Fair Trade Act (1937), not only did the manufacturer maintain a fixed sales price level to distributors, but also fixed the price at which distributors and retailers could sell to consumers. This result was achieved by contractual agreement between the manufacturer or distributor and the reseller. Following rejection by the courts of the Miller-Tydings Act and the fair-trade acts of nearly all the states—which had also permitted agreements between the manufacturer or distributor and the reseller prescribing minimum resale prices of a commodity bearing the label, trademark, brand, or name of the manufacturer or distributor—many such agreements have been replaced by the adoption of an almost equally effective producer's "suggested" price.

price margin = *gross margin*.

price system 1. Any comprehensive scheme of determining selling price to the trade, particularly that to which the leaders within an industry subscribe. See *price; competitive price*.

2. (economics) The use of a system of markets for determining the production and distribution of goods and services with resulting incomes to labor and capital.

price variance The variance in cost associated with a difference between the expected (standard) and actual purchase price of a product input. Typically, price variance is related to the acquisition of raw materials or supplies for the production process, and responsibility for it is assigned to the organization's purchasing managers. The price variance (P.V.) is normally measured as: P.V. $= (P_s - P_a)Q_a$, where P_s = the standard price per unit of input (material), P_a = the actual price per unit of input (material), and Q_a = the actual quantity of input (material) "purchased." This formulation assumes that the price variance is measured at the time of acquisition of the materials. If the variance is computed at the time such materials are placed into the production process, Q_a would represent the actual quantity of input (material) "used" in production. See *rate variance*.

pricing policy The body of guiding principles followed over a period of time by the management of a business enterprise in fixing the selling prices of its products or services; contrasts with *ad hoc* price making.

primary account Any account to which *external transactions* are first carried. Some or all of the contents of certain primary accounts, upon clearer identification or determination of activities benefited, are transferred to *secondary accounts*. Examples: an account with a depositary (not transferable); a sales account (ultimately carried to profit and loss); a dividend account (transferred to retained earnings); a *clearing account* (closed out as items are identified); see *terminal account*.

primary classification The initial classification given to an *external transaction*; a component element of a *primary account*; see *secondary classification; basic expenditure*.

primary earnings per share An indicator of operating performance for companies with *complex capital structures* that is computed by dividing a measure of earnings available for common stockholders by the weighted average number of common shares outstanding during the period plus shares from the assumed conversion or exercise of potentially *dilutive common stock* equivalents; presented on the face of an income statement for income before extraordinary items and for net income; also labeled earnings per common share assuming no dilution (e.g., capital structure contains no common stock equivalents) and earnings per common and common-stock equivalent. See *earnings per share; fully diluted earnings per share*.

primary liability (negotiable instruments) The liability of the person on whom rests the absolute requirement to pay a *negotiable instrument*. The maker of a *promissory note* or the drawer of an unaccepted check or draft who assigns it, and the acceptor of an accepted draft, are primarily liable for the obligations upon which their signatures appear. All other parties to such obligations have a *secondary liability*.

prime cost The cost of direct materials and direct labor entering into the manufacture of a product; direct cost, excluding direct (and indirect) overhead.

prime rate The rate of interest charged by commercial banks on loans to preferred customers.

primitive An undefined term or concept used in the construction of *axioms, postulates*, and *definitions*, serving as a starting point in an effort to avoid circular reasoning. Thus, the primitive, undefined terms in the axiom system of arithmetic constructed by Peano are zero, number, and successor. Primitive terms in the axiom system of Newton are force, mass, and acceleration; in Woodger's formulation of the axioms of biology, they are cell, part of, and precedence in time. In accounting, the notion of *transaction* constitutes one such primitive, as do the notions of *claim, property, ownership*, and *continuity*. Primitives in one system may be defined in another. See *axiom*.

principal 1. A sum on which interest accrues; capital, as distinguished from income.
2. The original amount of an estate or fund together with accretions which may, but usually do not, include income; capital sum.
3. A natural or legal person who authorizes another to represent him or her in some business transaction.
4. A partner or other person in a professional accounting firm authorized to deal with clients on major problems and having the responsibility of supervising audit engagements.
5. One primarily liable on an obligation as distinguished from an endorser or surety.

principle A proposition asserted to be controlling in a given system or individual activity and having acceptance among members of a professional group deemed competent in a society; growing out of observation, reason, or experiment, a principle purports to be the best possible guide where a choice of alternatives exists that will lead to the qualities desired in an endproduct. Some principles are *descriptive*; other are *normative* and state what is preferred or prescribed. Among normative principles are definition—the meanings assigned to words—and professional, legal, and moral *norms* or *standards*. Principles are not equally self-evident to all persons. The assertion of a descriptive principle establishes neither the truth nor the wisdom of a normative principle. If a principle is accepted without evidence or proof, it may be called an *axiom, assumption*, or *postulate*.

principle of exceptions A principle which seeks to conserve management time by directing attention only to deviations from planned or expected performance. See *exceptions report*.

prior period adjustment Items of income or expense that relate directly to the operation of a period prior to the date of a published financial statement. Formally corrected financial statements are required to be issued but such adjustments are now usually reflected as adjustments of the opening balance of retained earnings and excluded from the determination of net income for the current period. Current practice (SFAS No. 16) restricts prior period adjustments to (a) corrections of errors in the prior period financial statements or (b) adjustments resulting from realization of income tax benefits of *preacquisition operating loss carryforwards* of purchased *subsidiaries*.

prior probability distribution The assessed probabilities of various states prior to obtaining information from an experiment. The prior probabilities may be specified by the decision maker on a subjective basis or they may sometimes be obtained by objective methods. See *Bayes' rule*.

prior service cost See *past service cost*. *Pension cost* assigned under the *actuarial cost method* in use to years prior to the date of a particular actuarial valuation; prior service cost includes any remaining past service cost plus additional pension costs identified with prior years arising from the pension plan's amendment.

private accountant An accountant whose technical skills and employment are confined to a single organization. See *controller*.

private corporation 1. Any corporation other than one created for the purpose of local government or the administration of a governmental program.
2. A corporation created to promote private interests—business, financial, social, religious—of its members or stockholders. When used in this sense, the term contrasts with *public corporation*. It is synonymous with *closed corporation*. When the shares are held by persons related to each other, it is sometimes called a "family" corporation.

private enterprise The ownership of means of production by private individuals or firms as contrasted to government. A system where production and prices of goods and services are controlled by market forces of supply and demand and individual economic agent decision making.

private ledger A ledger in which confidential accounts are kept; now seldom employed. It is linked with the general ledger through a *control account*.

private offering The sale of an issue of securities by the issuer, rather than through an investment banker. The buyers may be existing stockholders, officers, employees, dealers, creditors, customers, friends of the management, or an insurance company or other institution. The distinction usually drawn between private and public offerings is that the former ordinarily involve but few subscribers who are in a position to be well acquainted with the affairs of the business. Many private offerings are exempt from registration under the Federal Securities Act and state blue-sky laws.

private placement An off-market offering of securities (usually debt) which the issuing corporation generally negotiates with an institutional investor such as an insurance company.

private sector Individual and business activities as contrasted with government activities; see *public sector*.

privileged communication Communication between persons within a confidential relationship (attorney-client; physician-patient) that public policy prohibits disclosure thereof by the person to whom it was made. There is no common-law privileged communication between CPA-client but it has been recognized in some states by statute.

probability 1. Likelihood; belief that a future condition or event will develop or occur.
2. (statistics) A measurement of the likelihood of occurrence of a chance event. The range of probability is between 0 and 1, denoted $0 \leqslant p \leqslant 1$. The "axioms of probability," stated in many different ways, have been subjected to a variety of interpretations. The following formulation is that of the mathematician A. Kolmogoroff.

(1) *The axiom of construction or specification.* There is assumed a *universe* of instances or events, termed "elementary" events, which may be classified into sets. Any class or set is termed a *random* event if it is comprised of elementary events belonging to the universe. The random events are taken to constitute a system having the property that all possible combinations of them in terms of their joint occurrences or nonoccurrence belong to the given system.

(2) *The axiom of classification.* The classification system is taken to be complete in the sense that each elementary event belongs to one or more random events.

(3) *The axiom of measurement.* Given the system of random events, to each random event, which is in effect a class, there is assigned a nonnegative *real number*, written $P(A)$. The event which constitutes the contradiction of A, written not-A, therefore is assigned the probability $P(\text{not-}A)$.

(4) *The axiom of total probability.* Since the universe may always be classified into two mutually exclusive and exhaustive sets, A and not-A, in respect to any random event, it is postulated that the probability of the universe is equal to the number 1, written $P(\text{universe}) = 1$.

Given the above system of axioms and their interpretation, it follows that the probability of an event which is certain to happen is equal to 1, while the probability of an impossible event is 0. When the interpretation placed on the axioms rests on the notion of relative frequency, it follows that if the probability of an event is 0, this does not imply that the event is impossible. In such a case, it may be validly claimed that the probability of occurrence of the event on a single trial is exceedingly small—i.e., that the event will almost never occur on a single trial.

Further refinement is obtained by writing $P(E_i, E_j)$ to represent the "joint probability" for the occurrence of events E_i and E_j together and by writing $P(E_i \mid E_j)$ to represent the "conditional probability" for the occurrence of event E_i when it is known that event E_j has occurred. $P(E_j \mid E_i)$ is interpreted as the conditional probability for the occurrence of E_j when E_i has already occurred. Also

$$P(E_i, E_j) = P(E_i \mid E_j)P(E_j)$$
$$= P(E_j \mid E_i)P(E_i),$$

where $P(E_j)$ and $P(E_i)$ are referred to as the absolute or unconditional probabilities for the occurrence of events E_i and E_j, respectively. E_i and E_j are independent in probability if and only if

$$P(E_i, E_j) = P(E_i)P(E_j).$$

Combining this last formula with the preceding one gives

$$P(E_i)P(E_j) = P(E_i \mid E_j)P(E_j)$$

or

$$P(E_i) = P(E_i \,|\, E_j).$$

In other words, the probability of E_i is not affected by the occurrence of E_j. Similarly, if E_i and E_j are events which occur independently, then

$$P(E_i)P(E_j) = P(E_j \,|\, E_i)P(E_i),$$

so that cancellation of $P(E_i)$ on both sides produces

$$P(E_j) = P(E_j \,|\, E_i).$$

These results taken together mean that E_i is probabilistically independent of E_j if and only if E_j is probabilistically independent of E_i. In other words, the occurrence of E_i does not affect the probability of occurrence of E_j and vice versa. This property does not generalize beyond pairwise independence, but other relations may be examined via *Bayes' rule*.

probability frequency function See *statistical distribution*.

probability proportionate to size (PPS) sampling Technically, PPS refers to the selection of items in which the probability of a particular item being included in the sample is proportionate to its measured "size" on some characteristic. In auditing the selection is usually via a secondary characteristic such as the recorded value of an item (and the primary characteristic is the audited value). The term is also used to refer to the evaluation of PPS selected samples by using a bound based on ranking the monetary errors found in the sample and an *attribute* evaluation of the rate of occurrence. See also *dollar unit sampling; combined attributes and variables sampling*.

probability sample A *random sample* with a computable sampling error. The computed error indicates the degree of representativeness (or lack thereof) to be taken into consideration in interpreting the sample results.

probable event A future event that is likely to occur.

probable life *Age* already attained plus *expected life*.

probable-life curve A *curve*, deduced from a study of *frequency distributions*, of the use of equipment and its accompanying *mortality*.

procedural audit (or review) The critical examination by an *external auditor* of *internal controls* and other procedures employed within an organization, (a) looking to recommendations for their improvement whether by simplification, elaboration, or readaptation, or (b) as a regular feature of a periodic examination. The review may be a general one or may be applied to a segment of the business, often on a rotating basis, as in successive annual examinations; frequently the review involves procedures other than accounting. See *audit; internal control; internal check*.

procedure Any routinization of practices followed in carrying out an authorized function or operation.

proceeds 1. The amount of cash, other assets, and services received from the sale or other disposition of property, from a loan, or from a sale or issue of securities.

2. = *net profits*.

process Any related sequence of acts, steps, or *events*.

process control See *statistical quality control*.

process costing A method of *cost accounting* whereby costs are charged to *processes* or *operations* and averaged over units produced; employed principally where a product is the result of a more or less continuous operation, as in paper mills, refineries, canneries, and chemical plants; distinguished from *job-order costing*, where costs are assigned to specific orders, lots, or units.

process further 1. A decision whether to continue processing a *joint product* after it emerges at the *splitoff point*. The approach is that of comparing the estimated *incremental costs* of additional processing with the estimated *incremental revenues* resulting from such further processing.

2. The act of processing a joint product(s) beyond the splitoff point.

3. Any decision to process a currently produced output into a more finished or different form rather than sell or scrap it in its current form.

processing cost = *manufacturing cost.*

producer(s') capital (economics) *Capital goods* (*fixed assets*) and other *goods* (e.g., *raw materials*) that aid in the production of other goods rather than being used directly to satisfy human wants. See *consumer goods.*

Producers' Price Index (PPI) See *wholesale price index.*

producer's risk (statistical quality control) A calculated *probability* under a given sampling plan that a lot of any given quality will be rejected by the plan. It is generally stated only for lots at the *acceptable quality level* or better; hence the risk (i.e., probability) of rejecting lots of acceptable quality. See *consumer's risk.*

product A good or service resulting from an operation or series of operations. An intermediate product is one on which further operations are to be performed; a final product is any good on which all contributory operations have been completed, or any service that has been fully rendered.

product cost 1. The material, labor, and overhead outlay making up the output of any operation.

2. Material and labor cost of output; in this sense, the term is employed in contrast with *period cost*; see *direct costing; product costing.*

product costing The assignment of costs to units of product. *Process costing* and *job-*

order costing, q.v., represent the two techniques most commonly used for accumulating and assigning costs to units of product. In some cases only *direct costing* is employed. Product costing may be further subdivided since one may assign *actual costs* incurred, estimates of future costs to be incurred, or *standard costs.*

production 1. The making available of *goods* or *services* for the satisfaction of *demands.*

2. The function of making or fabricating, as distinguished from distributing or financing; hence, the addition of value by an *operation* or *process,* reflected in accounting by the recording of the costs of the contributory factors.

3. Output, usually for a specified period.

production basis of revenue recognition See *precious metals accounting.* 1. A method which accords revenue recognition to the production of goods rather than their sale. It can be used if the produced items have stable and determinable market prices, and costs to market them are not material. Examples are precious metals and some agricultural commodities having a ready market.

2. A general classification for revenue recognition methods based on production, e.g., the *percentage-of-completion method.*

production control The planning, routing, scheduling, fabricating, inspecting, and dispatching of the operations of a department producing goods or services, the purpose being to so coordinate workers and machines that established standards of quality, quantity, time, place, and lowest possible cost are fulfilled.

production cost 1. Any cost contributing to *production.*

2. The cost commonly identified with a manufacturing or processing operation; *factory cost.* See *manufacturing cost.*

3. (petroleum accounting) The cost, includ-

ing depletion, of raising crude petroleum to the mouth of a well.

production cost account 1. A ledger account used to accumulate cost for determining the cost of manufactured products. Examples include *direct labor cost, overhead costs, work in process*. Accounts for selling, general, and administrative expense are not production cost accounts.

2. A work-in-process account which accumulates the raw material, direct labor, and overhead input costs of producing products.

production function A listing of the relations between quantities of factors or inputs employed, and quantities of a product, in the maximum amount of output that technology makes possible at each such listing for the resulting output of a salable good.

production method 1. The way in which raw materials are processed into usable parts or salable products.

2. With respect to *depreciation*, the allocation of asset cost on the basis of units produced or hours run. See *depreciation methods*.

production method of revenue recognition See *percentage-of-completion method*.

production statement A summary for a specified period of the elements that comprise production quantities and costs of an enterprise or of a division, plant, department, or product.

productive labor (or wages) Compensation of labor engaged in the physical production of marketable goods or in the physical performance of salable service; = *direct labor*.

productivity The yield obtained from any process or product by employing one or more *factors of production*. Productivity is usually calculated as an *index number*; the ratio of output to input. The usual approach calculates the productivity of different factors separately—the main emphasis being on la-

bor productivity measured as output (usually *value added*) per hour. This approach fails to credit possible sources of variation due to capital investment, improvement in the way labor is managed, or progress in the arts and sciences. Calculating an index of productivity for capital in terms of output per unit of capital investment suffers from these deficiencies and others as well. Interest has begun to shift toward indexes of "total productivity" in which all factors of production are considered simultaneously, but these indexes are difficult to construct in ways which reveal the different sources of variation in total output. Recourse to knowledge of a *production function* would help and could also be used as a measure of "total efficiency" defined as a ratio of actual output to the maximum output made possible by the production function. See *efficiency*. Knowledge of actual production functions is difficult to come by, however, so that separate indexes of productivity for labor and capital continue to be the expedient generally used in practice.

product mix The relative composition of the various products manufactured or sold by a firm. The latter is sometimes referred to as "sales mix." Typically measured in terms of production costs for manufacturing operations and in terms of product prices for sales. Substantial differences may exist in the average production cost and profitability of alternative product mixes and therefore *product line reporting* seeks to portray more homogeneous groups of products (or activities) into subsidiary income statements which provide added insight into this aspect of a company's overall income attachment.

profession A vocation requiring advanced training and (a) generally recognized by universities and colleges as requiring special training of an advanced character leading to a degree distinct from the usual degrees in arts and sciences, (b) requiring principally mental rather than manual or artistic labor and skill for its successful prosecution by reference to common bodies of knowledge, (c) recognizing the obligations of public service and of the public interest, and (d) having a code of ethics generally accepted as binding upon its members.

professional accountant 1. One engaged in accounting.
2. An auditor.
3. A certified public accountant.

profit 1. A general term for the excess of revenue, proceeds, or selling price over related costs; any pecuniary benefit arising from a commercial operation, from the practice of a *profession*, or from one or more individual transactions of any person; usually preceded by a qualifying word or phrase signifying the inclusiveness of the offsetting expense or cost, as ''gross'' or ''net,'' according to and followed by an indication of the source and time covered, as ''from operations for the year.'' Either the singular or the plural of the word may be used where two or more related transactions are considered together. *Net income* is now preferred as a designation of the ending figure of an *income statement*. See *net profit; gains; income*.
2. (economics) A payment or commitment to a person (entrepreneur) undertaking the hazards of enterprise; remuneration or reward for uncertainty-bearing. ''Pure'' profit is a residual and cannot ordinarily be predetermined. By way of contrast, *risk*, being calculable in advance, like rent, and frequently insurable, is a *cost* rather than a profit. Profit can be exactly measured only in retrospect and any preliminary imputation of profit is subjective in character.

profitability index In *capital budgeting*, a measure of relative profitability of a single investment project (i.e., a project that requires a single initial cash outlay followed by cash inflows in the subsequent period). Profitability index is the ratio of the *discounted present value* of cash inflows to the initial investment, which is a benefit-cost ratio as in *benefit-cost analysis*. If *cost of capital* to the firm is used as the discount rate, acceptance of a project with profitability index greater than one will increase the value of the firm.

profit and loss 1. The *ledger account* to which the balances of accounts reflecting revenues, income, profits, expenses, and losses are periodically transferred. Its balance, the net income or net loss for the period, is transferred to *retained earnings* (earned surplus) or other suitable proprietary account.
2. A general term indicating the eventual repository of any gain or loss. Example: a chargeoff to profit and loss.
3. (railroad accounting) = *retained earnings*; also a British usage, particularly when appearing in the adjectival form and followed by *account*.

profit-and-loss statement (or statement of profit and loss) = *income statement*.

profit center A *responsibility center* which accumulates revenues as well as costs.

profitgraph = *breakeven chart*.

profit margin Any *ratio* with measures of profit in the numerator and sales in the denominator. These ratios are important in their own right as measures of a firm's effectiveness in generating earnings for a given sales volume. However, they vary widely from one industry to another, so comparisons with *industry ratios* are generally the pertinent ones. Profit margin ratios are also a basic determinant, along with *turnover ratios*, of *return on investment* and serve an important role in such analyses as the *du Pont chart system*. The most common version of profit margin is simply the ratio of net income to sales. However, some analysts prefer to remove taxes and concentrate on the operating profits to sales relationship. This version of profit margin is calculated either by the ratio of net-income-before-interest-and-taxes plus taxes to sales or the ratio of net-income-after-taxes plus interest-expense-after-taxes to sales. Two other frequently used profit margins are the *contribution margin* and the *gross margin*.

profit planning The process of so conducting operations as to realize a given profit goal: an aspect of an overall budget in which the more important factors affecting profits (e.g., selling prices, volume, prices of cost elements, operating efficiency, etc.) are related to profits, and a plan is prepared which sets forth a desired, presumably attainable, balance between these factors.

profit prior to consolidation *Net income* of any enterprise prior to its acquisition by another through capital-stock control. Such profit does not form part of the consolidated income or *retained earnings* of the group.

profit prior to incorporation A profit made in a business prior to its incorporation. Since a corporation cannot make a profit before it comes into being, such profit is, in effect, represented in the net assets of the business which are transferred to the corporation. See, however, *pooling of interests*.

profit-volume graph See *breakeven chart*.

pro forma *adj.* A term applied to a balance sheet or other statement, or an account (a) which contains in whole or in part assumed figures or other facts, some indication of the character and purpose of the contents of the statement or account and the assumptions on which it is based ordinarily accompanying the use of the phrase; or (b) which contains no figures and is intended to indicate form, range, descriptions, or other characteristics of a proposed presentation.

pro forma balance sheet 1. A *balance sheet* showing hypothetical or tentative amounts, or no amounts, prepared for the purpose of displaying a proposed form or possible future financial condition.
2. A tentative balance sheet.
3. A balance sheet in which effect is given to *transactions* not yet consummated. Example: a balance sheet giving effect to a proposed financing or refinancing whether or not covered by a firm contract. See *financial forecasts*.

pro forma statement 1. A financial statement containing at least in part hypothetical amounts, or no amounts, prepared to exhibit the form in which data of a particular kind are to be presented.
2. A financial statement modified to show the effect of proposed transactions which have not yet been consummated; an "as-if" statement.

program (governmental accounting) 1. Any (or a number) of the major activities of an agency or a group of agencies, expressed as a primary *function*, and covering a fiscal year or larger period.
2. Hence, any major expense within an agency, as contrasted with a *project*; often repetitive from period to period.

program analysis The process of evaluating budget proposals in terms of their consequences for overall organization goals and objectives. See *program planning budgeting system*.

program budget A *PPBS* budget which emphasizes long-range planning and associated accomplishments and resource requirements. See *program planning budgeting system*.

program conversion (computers) The process of rewriting or modifying existing computer *software* in order to move it to a new computer. Careful planning includes parallel execution of the *program* on the old *hardware* and simultaneously on the new hardware as part of the the the test procedures.

Program Evaluation and Review Technique (PERT) A *network*-based technique for planning and controlling projects with several series of steps which must be completed in a specified order. The nodes of the PERT network represent the "event" of completion of an activity and the branches represent the activities required for the event. PERT allows the decision maker to focus attention on *critical paths* which, if shortened, would shorten the completion of the project. See *network*. The technique has also been applied to the control of the cost of completing a project. Such applications are referred to as *PERT cost*.

program flow chart See *flow chart* (2).

programmed costs See *managed costs*.

programming 1. The process of determining the programs (projects, products, etc.) to be undertaken by an organization. Such a process normally follows the specification or reaffirmation of a strategic (overall) plan in which long-range goals and short-range objectives for the enterprise are established. See *strategy; program planning budgeting system*.
2. Loosely, the delineation of a plan.
3. Preparation of instructions for a computer which may be either in *machine language* (*q.v.*) or in a user-oriented language.
4. *Linear programming* or *mathematical programming* models.

programming language A collection of statements which instruct a computer to perform a required task.

program planning budgeting system (PPBS) A budget, usually for a government agency, in which the budget items are grouped under various *programs*. Also called "planning programming budgeting system" but more popularly known as "PPBS." Program outputs are specified along with resulting benefits to the extent possible. The contrast is with *line-item budgets* in which budget items are grouped by administrative categories, and supported with subsidiary schedules in which budgeted amounts are further classified by *object* or *object cost*, without explicit reference to programs or resulting outputs and benefits.

Exhibits I.1 and I.2 provide examples of a line-item (administrative) budget adapted from a budget of the City of Pittsburgh, Pennsylvania. These may be compared with the budget of the City of Sunnyvale, California, which utilizes the following groupings: protection to persons and property, waste collection and disposal, leisure-time activities, water, transportation, maintenance of public property and records, legislative and legal services, and general management and support along with debt service and capital outlays for equipment and capital projects. Supporting detail for library circulation as a part of Sunnyvale's leisure-time activities program is portrayed in Exhibit II. The specification of outputs in the City of Sunnyvale budget, as well as program groupings which are intended to be meaningful to both outside persons and inside administrators and managers, are wholly absent in the City of Pittsburgh budget document. It is sometimes argued that the latter (line-item) type of budget provides controls over expenditures that are required by legislators as well as managers. This can be supplied, if required, by a *cross-walk table*, which is illustrated in Exhibit III by selected groupings of possible budgetary titles from the City of Pittsburgh and the City of Sunnyvale. Further detail by objects of account (= *cost objects*) can be entered in the above overall table or in supporting schedules. In any event the row totals yield the appropriation requests as in a line-item budget while the column totals correspond to projected program expenditures. The latter are supposed to be justified

EXHIBIT I.1

CITY OF PITTSBURGH
COMPARATIVE SUMMARY OF COSTS BY ORGANIZATION UNITS:
GENERAL FUND

	Departmental Estimates for Coming Year	Appropriation for Present Year	Expenditures for Past Year	Increase or Decrease of Estimates over Present Appropriation
Council and city clerk's office				
Mayor's office				
Municipal courts				
Housing clinic				
Service center				
Commission on Human Relations				
City information system office				
Department of City Controller				
Sinking Fund Commission				
Department of City Treasurer				
Department of Law				
Collection of delinquent city and school tax liens				
Civil Service Commission				
Department of City Planning				
Board of Adjustment				
Department of Supplies				
Department of Lands and Buildings				
Department of Public Safety				
Department of Public Works				
Department of Parks and Recreation				
Total				

by *cost-benefit analyses* which enter into the selection of proposed output levels and the costs they entail for the various programs. This also distinguishes it from line-item budgets which tend to focus attention on in-crements and decrements from preceding year appropriations and expenditures and hence emphasize *incremental budgeting*. See the final columns in Exhibits I.1 and I.2. See also *zero-base budgeting*.

EXHIBIT I.2

CITY OF PITTSBURGH
DEPARTMENT OF PARKS AND RECREATION,
GENERAL OFFICE

	Departmental Estimates for Coming Year	*Appropriation for Present Year*	*Expenditures for Past Year*	*Increase or Decrease of Estimates over Present Appropriation*
Salaries and wages, regular employees				
Premium pay				
Miscellaneous services				
Supplies				
Christmas display				
Gas and electric				
Steam				
Purchase of uniforms				
Materials				
Repairs				
Equipment				
Total				

EXHIBIT II

CITY OF SUNNYVALE
RESOURCE ALLOCATION ANALYSIS

Program: Leisure-time activities.
Function: 246.08 Circulation.
Objective: Check out and in all books for continuing use by patrons.

Quality goals:

Keep inventory loss to 1% of stock per year.
Check books out at rate of 1 each 5 seconds.
Check books back in at rate of 1 each 3 seconds.
Reshelve books at rate of 100 per hour.

Fiscal year production plan:

Process 742,441 books.
Handle 15,000 reserve books.
Operate bookmobile to average 50 stops a week.
Issue 6,000 EDP patron files.
Update 54,000 patron files.
Include fines on EDP C-Dek for flow control.

(continued)

EXHIBIT II (continued)

Fiscal Year	Total Cost of Resources	Service-Cost Indices		
		Work Hours	Production Units*	Unit Cost
1969−70 actual	$169,557	30,114	707,845	$.24
1970−71 actual	199,543	35,365	628,786	.32
1971−72 actual	177,022	31,897	685,359	.26
1972−73 estimated	193,558	34,454	720,677	.27
1973−74 proposed	210,857	35,280	742,441	.28
1974−75 projected	216,195	35,450	755,048	.29
1975−76 projected	222,765	35,620	767,049	.29
1976−77 projected	231,051	35,790	780,927	.30
1977−78 projected	240,470	35,960	794,928	.30
1978−79 projected	248,687	36,130	809,052	.31
1979−80 projected	257,989	36,300	823,301	.31
1980−81 projected	267,426	36,470	836,931	.32

*Books circulated.

EXHIBIT III

CROSS-WALK TABLE

Account Titles	Leisure-Time Activities	Protection to Persons and Property	Legislative and Legal Services	General Management and Support	Total
Council and city clerk					
Mayor's office					
Municipal courts					
Department of Parks and Recreation	_____	_____	_____	_____	_____
Total	======	======	======	======	======

program structure A grouping of an organization's activities in terms of the programs in which they participate. A critical part of a *program planning budgeting system*, such structures are intended to provide a better basis for analyzing related activities and costs, and to identify and evaluate the costs and contributions of all activities that contribute to the programs so that trade-offs can be studied and gaps in needed services or activities can be identified. The basic unit for a program structure typically is an organizational subunit within an agency which contributes to one or more programs. See *program planning budgeting system*.

progress billing A trade receivable arising from a contract not yet completed, the corresponding credit on financial statements usually being deducted from work contracts in process.

progression Orderly arrangement in a sequence; examples: a schedule of tax rates varying with income; *arithmetic progression, geometric progression,* and *harmonic pro-*

gression; the first n numbers $1 + 2 + \ldots + n$, which sum to $n(n + 1)/2$; the first n squares, $1^2 + 2^2 + 3^2 + \ldots + n^2$, the total being $n(n + 1)(2n + 1)/6$; the first n cubes, $1^3 + 2^3 + 3^3 + \ldots + n^3$, having the total of $[n(n + 1)/2]^2$.

progressive average One of a series of simple *averages*, each of which is the *arithmetic mean* of a group of items consisting of all the items in the next preceding group, plus a new one. Example:

Series	Items	Progressive Average
A	5, 9, 3, 7, 4	5.60
B	5, 9, 3, 7, 4, 8	6.00
C	5, 9, 3, 7, 4, 8, 5	5.85
D	5, 9, 3, 7, 4, 8, 5, 6	5.87

In this table, a new average can be derived from its predecessor by the formula

$$a_2 = \frac{a_1 n + b}{n + 1},$$

where a_2 is the new average to be determined, a_1 the old average, n the number of items in the series not including the new item, and b the quantity being added to the series. Progressive averages may be used, for example, in statements of earnings, costs, expenses, and the like, that cover the accounting periods since the beginning of the current fiscal year and that show the cumulative averages of a steadily increasing number of periods, usually in comparison with the corresponding amounts of the previous fiscal year or years. See *moving average*.

progressive ledger = *Boston ledger*.

progressive schedule A comparative schedule of financial or operating data to which new data are added as they become available.

progressive tax A tax the rate of which increases with the value of the property or income on which it is levied; contrasts with *regressive tax*.

project *n.* A unit of construction work, or other capital acquisition, such as one undertaken by a governmental unit, the cost of which is accounted for separately from other work and is ordinarily financed by the employment of special funds or by a bond issue. See *program*.

projected benefit-cost methods *Actuarial* procedures for allocating the cost of projected employee retirement benefits to specific years. Rather than recognizing benefit costs as they accrue, these methods usually allocate *pension costs* as a level dollar amount or a level percentage of compensation to the years specified by a particular method. Frequently used versions are the *entry age normal method*, the *individual level premium method*, the *aggregate level cost method*, and the *attained age normal method*.

projected financial statement See *financial projection*.

projections *extrapolations*, *q.v.* Developments or portrayals of possible future states as in the *scenarios* of a *futurology* exercise or *feasibility* or *impact statement study*.

promise to pay An agreement, between buyer and seller or debtor and creditor, that cash will be delivered by the former to the latter on a certain future date or within a certain future period. The agreement may be explicit and hence contained in a *contract* or *promissory note*; or implicit, in accordance with usual trade custom or terms appearing in the seller's advertisement or on his or her invoice.

promissory note An unconditional written promise, signed by the maker, to pay a certain sum in money, on demand or at a fixed and determinable future date, either to the bearer or to the order of a designated person. A promissory note is a *note payable* to the maker and a *note receivable* to a *holder in due course*.

promoter Person who plans the organization and incorporation of a corporation, including selling stock subscriptions and entering into contracts before the corporation is formed.

promotion expense An expense incurred in the formation or furtherance of a new enterprise or activity. See *organization cost; deferred charge*. Thus, advertising expense publicizing a new product, or introducing a product into a new market, constitutes a *deferred charge* amortizable against the revenues of the years to be benefited. Although promotion expenses frequently develop a prospectively continuous benefit, practical considerations and their repetitive character suggest their amortization over a short period and, except where the promotion is out of the ordinary course of business, or where their amounts are sufficient to distort the income of a single year, it is preferable to absorb them against the income of the year in which they have been incurred.

proof of loss (insurance) A formal submission by an insured to an insurer containing sufficient data in support of a claim to enable the latter to determine its liability.

proper In line with common practice; meeting specifications deemed fitting in the circumstances; ethical as well as legal.

property Any asset, including cash, title to which is ordinarily transferable between persons. See *asset*.

property account 1. An account maintained for a *fixed asset*.
2. *pl*. = *fixed assets*.

property accountability The responsibility for observing and reporting on the existence, location, use, and condition of assets, particularly mobile fixed assets, and also small tools and other items which for any of various reasons have not been capitalized. See *fixed asset; internal control*.

property dividend A dividend paid in property other than cash, as distinct from a distribution in cash, scrip, or the company's own bonds or stock; a dividend in *kind*.

property ledger = *plant ledger*.

property plant and equipment A *balance-sheet* classification for long-term *fixed assets* used in business operations. Property, plant, and equipment items are normally grouped and reported at acquisition cost with separate disclosure of accumulated *depreciation* or *depletion* to arrive at a *net* figure. Also referred to as plant assets, operational assets, or fixed assets.

property reserved = *accumulated depreciation*; a British term.

property rights The benefits accruing to the owners of property with specific regard to the property's use and value in exchange.

proportion 1. ratio; as, a/b.
2. A ratio representing the relation to a whole of one of its parts; as, $a/(a + b)$.
3. A ratio, as in sense (2), its source often inferred, applied to an independent quantity; as, $ac/(a + b)$. It is in this sense that the derived adjective, "proportionate," is often used; as, a proportionate part of an annual prepaid insurance premium being charged off monthly—meaning that the quantity thus disposed of during each of 12 months has been one-twelfth of the total premium cost. A further example: proportionate credits of deferred gross profits from installment sales are made to income as the installments are collected. Here either of two ratios may be inferred: g/s or c/s, where g is the anticipated total gross profit, c the installment collected, and s the selling price; the final result is, however, the same, since $(g/s)c$ and $(c/s)g$ both equal cg/s.

proposed dividend The *liability* for a *dividend* recognized in the accounts, but not yet made certain by a formal *declaration;* British usage.

proposition Any declarative statement that may be believed, doubted, or denied, as either true or false: not synonymous with "sentence," since a number of sentences may be required in expressing the statement.

proprietary accounts 1. The accounts, including *nominal accounts*, containing the *owners' equity*.
2. (governmental accounting) The accounts reflecting the *assets* and *liabilities*, and displaying the *results of operations* in terms of revenue, expense, surplus, or deficit. See *budgetary accounts*.

proprietary fund (governmental or institutional accounting) *Enterprise funds* or *internal service funds*.

proprietary interest *Net worth* or a part thereof; the excess of *assets* over *liabilities*; net assets classified as to capital paid in, retained income, and other sources.

proprietor 1. The possessor of a proprietorship.
2. The owner of property such as a stock or bond.

proprietorship 1. = *net assets; net worth; stockholders' equity*.
2. = *sole proprietorship*.
3. Ownership of an unincorporated business by an individual; the business so owned.

proprietorship account The account maintained for the net worth of the business of an individual proprietor.

propriety In conformance with prescribed or accepted values, customs, or procedures: Values may be of an ethical or legal variety and these need not be consistent with each other. They also may not be consistent with customs or perceived procedures. It is a major responsibility of management and of the board of directors to perceive these differences and to determine how they might best be balanced. Some boards have established special committees to deal with issues such as possible conflicts of interest but the ten-

dency is to regard this whole area of corporate activity as something to be monitored actively by the *audit committee*. See *effectiveness; efficiency; propriety* as discussed under *audit (4B)*.

pro rata *adj.* proportional. The term relates to the distribution of an expense, fund, dividend, or other item, the inference being that the distribution is made upon some equitable basis.

prorate *v.* To assign or redistribute a portion of a *cost*, such as a *joint cost*, to a department, operation, activity, or product according to some formula or other agreed-to, often arbitrary, procedure.
n. Proration

prospectus Any written offer to sell a security in which representations, often implied, as to the qualities of the security are made by the seller; specifically, a formal informational document, prepared for prospective investors by the issuer of a security in conformity with regulations under state *blue-sky laws* or the U.S. *Securities and Exchange Commission*. A preliminary prospectus, permitted under SEC rules, is known as a *"red-herring" prospectus*.

Section 2(9) of the Securities Act of 1933 defines *prospectus* as any "…notice, circular, advertisement, letter, or communication, written or by radio, which offers any security for sale…"; the SEC requires the prospectus to contain a fairly extensive disclosure of essential facts pertinent to the security, such as (a) a description of the registrant's business and its development, (b) a description of the principal provisions of the security, (c) certified financial statements, (d) the conditions under which the security is to be sold, and (e) the offering price.

prove 1. To *verify*.
2. Subject to an adequate *test*.

proved developed oil and gas reserves Reserves which are expected to be recovered through existing wells with existing equipment and operating methods.

proved oil and gas reserves The estimated quantities of crude oil, natural gas, and natural gas liquids which geological and engineering data demonstrate with reasonable certainty to be recoverable in future years from known reservoirs under existing economic and operating conditions, i.e., under prices and costs as of the date the estimate is made. Prices include consideration of changes in inventory prices provided only by contractual arrangements, but not in calculations based on future conditions. Depending on their status of development, proved reserves are subdivided into *proved developed oil and gas reserves* and *proved undeveloped oil and gas reserves*.

proved undeveloped oil and gas reserves Reserves that are expected to be recovered from new wells on undrilled acreage or from existing wells where a relatively major expenditure is required.

provision 1. A charge for an estimated expense or loss or for a shrinkage in the cost of an asset offsetting an addition to a *valuation account* such as a reserve for or accumulation of depreciation or the accrual of a liability such as an income tax.
2. (British usage) (a) An amount entered on the books of account covering an estimated or accrued liability. (b) The amount of accumulated depreciation, bad debts, or inventory decline: a *valuation account*.

proxy Written authority to act for another, as in a meeting of stockholders of a corporation.

proxy statement An informational statement accompanying the solicitation of a proxy, particularly one prepared in conformity with Regulation X-14 of the U.S. *Securities and Exchange Commission*. This regulation, relating primarily to solicitations from stockholders on behalf of the management of a corporation the securities of which are listed on a national securities exchange, specifies the minimum content, timing, and other features that attach to such a statement.

prudent investment 1. An investment, as by a trustee, made with the care and judgment reasonably expected of an ordinary businessman.
2. A term employed by the courts and by public utility regulatory boards to denote the minimum outlay for an operating unit or system that a utility management, putting the public interest ahead of interests of stockholders and management, would incur for the same items. Such a theoretical cost, devoid of profits to promoters, "insiders," or affiliates, based on reconstructed need at the time of acquisition, and not infrequently lower than recorded or even original cost, may become a part of the rate base against which a "fair return" to investors is computed. See *original cost (2)*.

public accountant An accountant who offers services professionally to the public. See *certified public accountant; chartered accountant*. The term in the singular may also refer to a firm of public accountants.

public accounting The *profession* of the public accountant; specifically, the offering to the public of independent professional accounting skills consisting principally of the design and installation of financial and cost systems of accounting, audits, investigations, reports (certificates) based on audits, advice on management structure and financial policies, and income-tax service. The services of the public accountant are offered to the public generally, as contrasted with the employment of a private accountant on a full-time basis by a single business enterprise. *Management services* are also increasingly being supplied to clients. The services offered may be general, or restricted to a particular type of accounting service. The public accountant is not required to perform services for all who request them. In every state, practice as a *certified public accountant* is regulated by statute and is confined to those who meet certain qualifying conditions. See *certified public accountant*.

public corporation 1. A corporation that offers its goods or services to the public and the bulk of whose stock is held by persons other than officers or employees.
2. = *municipal corporation*.

public debt The bond indebtedness of the public sector—federal, state, and local governments.

public enterprise fund See *enterprise fund*.

public good Generally a good such that the extent of its consumption by one economic agent does not diminish the amount available for use by other agents as for example, use of parks, individual swimming in a river, use of a highway, etc.

public interest The basic concern of a people as a body in establishing, defending, and from time to time widening its domain by its tolerance or by regulatory and moral prescriptions for private affairs. In the United States, the public interest is conceived by many as a policing operation having as its aim the preservation of the *status quo*; by others as a dynamic force for progress. In either case, it is generally conceded that a *profession* such as that of the *public accountant* must conduct itself in harmony with what appears to be the trend of the public interest and that its moral qualities must be of the highest order if it is to continue freely to lay down the standards to which its practitioners ought to conform. See *public interest accounting*.

public interest accounting The provision of professional accounting services directly in the *public interest*, usually on a no-fee basis,

as distinct from services to special interests for a fee. The absence of a fee permits more attention to the interests served by an engagement and a wider choice in the selection of clients. In actual practice, the selection is usually among clients who would not otherwise be able to obtain such services. In other respects the engagement conforms to high standards of competence and ethics, including the objectivity and independence that are usually associated with professional audits. See *audit*. Engagements include both specific accounting services to the poor and to the not-for-profit sectors and the use of professional accounting skills to provide information and analysis regarding social issues and problems. Examples: 1. A public interest accounting organization was engaged by a volunteer group interested in public health and law to review the applications of certain hospitals for exemption from a provision of the Hill-Burton Act. This act requires a hospital receiving grants to devote a certain percentage of its services to persons who are unable to pay, unless the hospital can convince an overseeing state agency that performance of these services is not "financially feasible." The public interest accounting group's analysis resulted in a new definition of "financial feasibility" that produced positive action by the hospitals and withdrawal of the applications after they were re-reviewed in the light of this new definition. 2. A volunteer organization concerned with ecological effects of a proposed airport expansion asked a public interest accounting organization to review a report prepared by a nationally known public accounting firm on the economic aspects of the proposed expansion. Detailed review of the latter report raised various questions about the nature of its assumptions and the quality of resulting predictions. The ecology interest group (and others) expressed their appreciation for the objectivity and professionalism displayed in the reports of the public interest accounting organization and also commented on the improved quality of subsequent hearings and discussions on the proposed airport expansion.

public offering (Securities Act of 1933) All securities issued to the public in interstate commerce are required to be registered unless some exemption is available, such as an issue not involving interstate commerce. Contrasts with *private offering*. See also *private placement*.

public sector A phrase contrasting with *private sector* to indicate government ownership or field of interest and often extending to the activities of other not-for-profit entities.

public service (or utility) company A corporation supplying to the consuming public services commonly regarded as necessities of life. It operates under a federal, state, or municipal franchise or monopoly and is subject to regulation and control through a commission or other body representing the public. Examples: railroads, electric light, gas, power, telegraph, telephone, and water companies.

punitive damages Also called exemplary damages. Damages in excess of those required to compensate the plaintiff which are awarded to punish defendant for a particularly willful act or to teach defendant a lesson.

purchase An outlay for property or service; the property or service acquired.

purchase allowance Reduction in the purchase invoice price granted because the goods were slightly damaged, delivered late, or fell short of what was stipulated in the order in some other way. The goods are retained by the purchaser but at a lower price than was agreed to originally.

purchase and leaseback See *sale-and-leaseback*.

purchase contract (securities) See *underwriting contract*.

purchase discount Reduction in the purchase invoice price for payment within a specified period. See *cash discount*.

purchase group (or syndicate) = *underwriting syndicate*.

purchase method of combination The accounting technique for a business combination which fails to satisfy all 12 criteria presented in *APB Opinion* No. 16 for a *pooling of interest*. Under this method, the cost of the acquired company is allocated to its net assets based on their fair market values at the date of combination. See *intercompany elimination*. The purchase method establishes a new basis of accountability for the acquired net assets and is generally consistent with accounting principles for the acquisition of any asset or group of assets.

purchase-money obligation A mortgage or other form of debt secured by a *lien* having priority over any lien subsequently created.

purchase order A document authorizing a vendor to deliver described merchandise or materials at a specified price. Upon acceptance by a vendor, a purchase order becomes a contract. Several copies of a purchase order are customarily prepared. In a typical case, the copies are distributed as follows: one (the original) to the vendor; three to the receiving department, of which, following the receipt of the goods, one is returned to the purchasing department and another is sent to the accounting department; one to the accounting department, serving as a basis for a commitment record; two remain in the purchasing department, one serving as the basis of a purchase record, the other being placed in a follow-up file.

purchase records Records relating to the purchase of merchandise, materials, supplies, and similar items. Examples: vouchers and invoices; voucher or purchase register; creditors ledger; purchase contracts, orders, and requisitions; the files of a purchasing department.

purchase tax See *turnover tax*.

purchasing power 1. The ability to buy; hence, (a) the quantity of a particular class of goods or services that may be purchased for a given sum of money, such as one dollar, or (b) the percentage relationship of such a quantity to that so purchasable at some preceding point of time.
2. The reciprocal of the *price level (1)*.

purchasing power capital maintenance concept of income Amount that could be consumed, withdrawn, or paid as a *dividend* during a *period* of time without reducing the general purchasing power of an *entity's* net assets. Purchasing power capital is maintained when the value of the net assets measured in units of general purchasing power remains constant. This concept of income would supposedly be applied if net income determined on a *historical cost* basis were restated for changes in the general price level. Contrast to "financial" *capital maintenance concept* of income and "physical" ("productive capacity") *capital maintenance concept* of income.

purchasing power risk Risk of change in the real value of a security due to changes in the purchasing power of the monetary units. It is distinguished from *interest rate risk* and *financial risk*.

pure profit Net income in excess of returns, including *imputed interest (1)*, on the several *factors of production*, usually arising from entrepreneurial activities and risk bearing.

put A transferable option or offer to deliver a given number of shares of stock at a stated price somewhat below current market at any time during a stated period, usually not exceeding three months. Such an option is purchased by a speculator who looks forward to a price decline during the period to a point below that appearing in the option; should that event occur, he or she will purchase the shares on the market and deliver them to the maker or issuer of the option or offer, thus gaining a profit; should the price remain unchanged or rise, the holder of the option will allow it to expire, with a loss equal to his or her cost. See *call; straddle*.

pyramid analysis A British system of *ratio* analysis of the determinants of *return on investment*. The top, primary level, of the "pyramid" consists of a *return on investment* measure, the secondary level consists of a general *profit margin* and *total assets turnover*, and the lower levels consist of various expense to sales ratios and specific *turnover ratios*. This system is similar to the *du Pont chart system*, but it is usually more elaborate.

pyramiding 1. In finance, the use of multiple layers of *holding companies* to control a relatively large amount in corporate assets through ownership of a small amount of capital invested in the stock of the firm at the top of the pyramid.
2. In the stock market, an increase in the holding of a stock financed out of the *margin* created by a rise in the price of stock already owned.

qualification 1. A statement in an auditor's *report* or certificate directing attention to any important limitation attending the examination or to his or her doubt or disagreement as to any item reported; distinguished from *disclosure*, the latter relating to facts of interest to readers revealed on financial statements, in accompanying footnotes, or, less frequently, in the report or certificate. See *exception (1); footnote; opinion*.
2. An exception or reservation attaching to a statement or a proposal as in a bid or offer which will not be binding unless certain conditions are met.
3. Ability to perform a specified task or function, e.g., as determined by an *examination*.

qualified indorsement See *indorsement without recourse*.

qualified opinion See *opinion; auditors' report*.

qualified report (or certificate) An audit report containing one or more *qualifications* or *exceptions*.

qualified stock option (federal income taxes) A privilege granted an employee of a corporation to purchase at a specified price a limited number of shares of its capital stock, under conditions laid down in the *Internal Revenue Code* (Section 1.422-2). Qualified stock options were completely phased out in 1981. See *incentive stock option*.

quality control 1. Any of the policies and procedures, especially those relating to plant and product design and operating and output inspection, used to determine and maintain a desired level of operations or products. See *statistical quality control*.
2. In an audit by a public accountant, the development and maintenance of high levels of field performance, critical supervision by supervisors (managers and partners), and informative reporting based on conformance to professional standards and independent judgements. See *quality review*.

quality review A term applied to a mutually arranged testing of one accountant's professional practices by another, or by a professional body created for that purpose; included in the test may be reviews of audit programs and reports, working papers, supervisory practices, relations with clients, training programs, and so on. See *peer review*.

quantification Any statement expressed in numbers; particularly, a *proposition* expressed or restated in numerical terms.

quantile (statistics) Any of the values that

divide an array or frequency distribution into stipulated proportions of individual units. See *quartile; decile; percentile*.

quantity discount An allowance given by a seller to a purchaser because of the size of an individual purchase transaction. This practice is not in violation of federal laws dealing with price discrimination provided the allowance granted represents a saving in selling costs.

quantity variance = *usage variance*. The variance in cost associated with the difference between the expected (standard) and actual quantity of a production input (e.g., raw materials or direct labor). The standard quantity should be related to the measure of activity, such as the amount of goods (output) to be produced during the period of analysis. Responsibility for the quantity variance (Q.V.) rests primarily with production managers. The variance typically is measured as Q.V. $= (Q_s - Q_a) \times P_s$, where $Q_s =$ the standard quantity of inputs; $Q_a =$ the actual quantity of inputs; $P_s =$ the standard price per unit of input.

quartile (statistics) The value of any of three points (upper quartile, *median*, and lower quartile) setting off four proportionate divisions of a frequency distribution each containing 25% of the total number of individual observations.

quasi contract An obligation imposed by law for the purpose of preventing an injustice or an unjust enrichment; its imposition is independent of any agreement or any indications of the parties' intent.

quasi endowment fund (institutional accounting) Funds established by a governing board of an institution to account for assets to be retained and invested as if they were endowments.

quasi-public company A corporation operated privately but for purposes in which the public

has some general interest. Examples: charitable and religious corporations.

quasi-random number One of a series of numbers generated by a process which is almost *random*, or sufficiently random for most applications in accounting and auditing. Tables of such numbers are available in sources like *Random Decimal Digits*, published by the U.S. Interstate Commerce Commission. Recourse to such tables, however, has largely been supplanted by use of computers with random number (really only quasi-random) generating capabilities. See *random numbers*.

quasi rent 1. That portion of a producer's gross revenue attributable to some unique operating efficiency or other low-cost factor not available to a competitor. See *rent (3)*.
2. Consideration for the use of another's property other than real estate; = *rent*.

quasi reorganization A recapitalization, a principal feature of which has been the absorption of a deficit; specifically, the procedure whereby a corporation, without the creation of a new corporate entity or the intervention of a court, eliminates an operating deficit or a deficit resulting from the recognition of other losses, or both, and establishes a new *retained earnings* (earned-surplus) account for the accumulation of net income subsequent to the effective date of such action. See *dated earned surplus*.

questionable payments (or sensitive payments) Includes bribes, kickbacks, illegal political contributions. Payments sometimes made by American companies to foreign governments or persons to gain favor are interdicted by the *Foreign Corrupt Practices Act, q.v.*

queue 1. A line of customers, a file, or a list of items waiting for service.
2. (computers) A list of jobs waiting to be serviced. A "queue discipline" such as *FIFO*

or *LIFO* may be imposed to indicate the order in which jobs or items are to be processed.

quick asset A current asset normally convertible into cash within a relatively short period, such as a month. Examples: cash, call loan, marketable security, customer's account, a commodity immediately salable at quoted prices on the open market.

quick ratio See *acid-test ratio*.

quotas 1. A specified amount as, for instance, the number in specified minority groups who must be recruited for given categories of jobs. See *trigger price*.

2. Maximum or minimum allocation of product in a market to buyers and sellers.

quoted price (of a security) On listed stocks, price per share stated in dollars and eighths; on corporate bonds, price per one-thousand-dollar bond stated in dollars equal to one-tenth of its face value; on government bonds, a percentage of a one-thousand-face-value bond with fractions in thirty-seconds; on other types of securities, price per share or per bond, or both bid and asked prices.

R

R and D (R&D) expenditure = *research and development cost.*

random Arising from chance alone, in contrast with haphazard or systematic; as, a random defect in the output of a machine. See *statistical quality control.* When a process is random, it obeys known (or unknown) laws of chance behavior; even when unknown the law is discoverable, at least in principle, by applying methods of *statistical inference* to regularities in the behavior of sample observations; when haphazard, the mixture of chance and other elements is so compounded that it is impossible to take advantage of any laws of behavior. Although containing errors of a statistical variety (e.g., *sampling error*), random error is distinguishable in principle from systematic error. Systematic error, or *bias*, if known and measurable, may be allowed for, thereby improving estimates, predictions, or tests. Where the amount of bias is unknown, mixture with random behavior has the same practical effect as that of haphazardness. See *haphazard selection.* Randomization requires careful planning to make certain that only chance elements are present, or that bias, if present or introduced, is known and measurable.

random number generator (computers) A computer *program* that generates *random numbers.* See *quasi-random number.*

random numbers A set of numbers formed at random—i.e., obtained from a random process, such as throwing dice or tossing coins—and generally arrayed in tabular form to assist in sample selection. Note: It is not the numbers but their arrangement or order in which randomness is reflected. Hence, it is the process used to generate the numbers from which the randomness (if present) will flow. M. G. Kendall and B. B. Smith, *Tracts for Computers No. 24* (Cambridge, 1939), contains an arrangement of 100,000 such numbers, flagged at various places where lack of randomness may be present. Availability of random number generators on electronic computers, however, has largely replaced such tables. Usually capable of generating only *quasi-random numbers*, the use of computers is justified not only by considerations of convenience but also by the ease with which an almost unlimited number of such numbers can be generated.

random sample (statistics) A *sample* in which all the elements have been drawn at *random*, or according to the laws of chance. The *pro-*

cedure by which the sample is constructed characterizes a random sample, rather than its specific content. See *stratified sampling; systematic sampling; multiphase sampling; multistage sampling; replication.*

random sampling (statistics) A procedure for selecting a sample of arbitrary size *n* with preassigned probability from a given *universe;* exemplified by the use of *random numbers.* The universe may be finite or infinite. See *unit of sampling.*

random variable See *variate.*

random variation (statistics) 1. A fluctuation resulting from chance alone. In *statistical quality control*, a random variation is defined as a fluctuation in quality or quantity not attributable to an assignable (nonchance) cause.

2. In time series analysis, as used in economics, the term is sometimes used to denote a variation in data which is (a) explainable, and (b) the result of more or less unique, nonrecurring events. A marked fluctuation in the price level caused by a war may be classified as random to distinguish it from movements or variations caused by *trend, seasonal*, or *cyclical* factors.

random walk A time series in which all successive values of a variable are independent of previous values. Therefore, the past history of the variable cannot be used in any systematically meaningful way to predict future values of the variable. The random walk hypothesis has played an important role in empirical research on stock market behavior and the statistical effects of accounting earnings reports. See *efficient market hypothesis.* The minimum variance forecast for the value of the next observation in such a series is the value of the last observation in the series. See *martingale process.*

range The difference between the largest and smallest items in a group of numerical data. See *dispersion.*

rank correlation A measure of the degree of relationship between variable ranks or orderings. A variety of such measures which are distribution free (*nonparametric statistics*) may be employed. A widely used measure is Kendall's tau, defined by

$$\tau = \frac{2S}{n(n-1)},$$

where

$$S = 2p - \frac{1}{2}n(n-1)$$

and *p* is called the positive score. For a number of observations, *n*, greater than 10, the quantity *S* is distributed approximately in the form of a *normal distribution* with *mean* zero and variance $n(n-1)(2n+5)/18$. The following example involves the analysis of the average annual price of a stock for the presence of a downward trend:

Price	Rank	Positive Score
94	8	0
74	1	6
75	2	5
92	7	0
84	5	1
82	4	1
88	6	0
79	3	0
		13

The highest price, 94, which occurred in year 1, is given rank 8, while 74, which is the average price for the second year, is given rank 1. The other average annual prices are accorded the ranks in between these two values, as shown. To derive the positive score of $p = 13$ we count the number of items below any designated item which have been accorded a higher rank and enter it in the column marked positive score. Thus the score of zero is assigned to the first item because none of the succeeding ranks exceed 8. On the other hand, there are 6 items exceeding rank 1, which occurs in the second row, and 5 items with ranks exceeding 2 after the third item recorded in year 3. Rank 7, which occurs in year 4, is not exceeded thereafter, and hence the value 0 is entered for its contribution to the positive score. Continuing in this manner and totaling the results yields $p = 13$ and $S = 2 \times 13 - (1/2) \times 8 \times 7 = -2$ to obtain the tau coefficient of $\tau = 2(-2)/(8 \times 7) = -.07$. This slight negative value could easily have occurred by chance and hence the evidence does not support the hypothesized downward trend.

rapid amortization (federal income taxes) As an incentive for the acquisition of certain types of buildings and equipment, Congress has from time to time allowed a fact writeoff of the original investment. See *accelerated cost recovery system; accelerated depreciation (d)*.

rate 1. The price of a unit of service over a unit of time; as, a labor rate of $2 per hour.
2. The measure of movement over a unit of time; as, a rate of speed in miles per hour or a monthly rate of production.

rate of exchange The *ratio* between a unit of one currency and the amount of another currency for which that unit can be exchanged at a particular time. The historical exchange rate (the rate that was in effect at the date a specific event or transaction occurred) and the current exchange rate (the rate in effect at the balance sheet date) are used in foreign currency translation. See *exchange (2); foreign exchange; consolidated financial statement*.

rate of return 1. Return on an investment expressed as a percentage or ratio, as in annual return divided by investment. Rates for other periods of time are obtained by adjusting the numerator in this expression to the desired period and amounts. Annual or other return is always calculated after allowance for depreciation or other measures of capital consump-

tion. See *accounting rate of return; return on common equity*.
2. For capital budgeting decisions, it may be calculated as a simple interest average or it may be determined via compound discount formulas to obtain an *internal rate of return*. See *interest formulas*.

rate-of-return pricing A method of determining prices by adding a *markup* on costs which will produce a predetermined return on investment. This method is comparable to target pricing in price-competitive industries. A dominant firm that establishes price in a price-leadership industry may employ this method to determine a price level not only for its own products but also for those of competitors. See *price*.

rate of turnover See *turnover (1); turnover ratios*.

rate variance The *variance* in cost associated with a difference between the expected (standard) and *actual cost* of product inputs, particularly direct labor. The responsibility for *labor rate variances* rests with the production manager. Similar in concept to a *price variance* for raw materials, it is typically measured as: R.V. $= (R_s - R_a) \times Q_a$, where R_s = the standard rate per unit (hour) of labor, R_a = the actual rate per unit (hour) of labor, and Q_a = the actual quantity of labor units (hours) used.

ratification 1. Acceptance, as in the signing or other formal acknowledgment of a proposed *contract* or agreement.
2. The adoption or acceptance of an act which has been performed, but not authorized at the time. The ratification, in effect, accepts the act and the legal consequences. Thus, a principal may accept an agent's previously unauthorized act, or a minor may ratify an act after attaining majority.

rating 1. The financial or credit standing of a person as determined by a mercantile agency.
2. The relative worth of a security as deter-

mined by any of several investment advisory services.

3. A projected *rate* (2) of working.

4. Any ranking or ordering of items or relations.

ratio The relation of one amount, *a*, to another, *b*, expressed as "the ratio of *a* to *b*"; *a:b* ("*a* is to *b*"); or as a simple fraction, integer, decimal fraction, or percentage; thus, the ratio 6:5 may also be written as 6/5 or 1.2 (or "1.2 to 1") or 120%. Financial ratios are those derived from comparisons of balance-sheet items, or of balance-sheet items with income-statement items; operating ratios are those derived from comparisons of items of income and expense. The purpose of ratios is to epitomize and facilitate comparisons with periods, another organization, or an industry average.

In accounting, a numerical relation of component parts of *financial statements* to each other. These numerical relationships are expressed as ratios, decimal fractions, or percentages. Ratio relationships are computed to obtain information about various characteristics and conditions of firms. For example, the ratio of current assets to current liabilities would presumably provide some insights about a firm's ability to meet its short-term debt. In general, ratios are calculated to make financial statement analysis easier and more effective.

Many ratios can conceivably be developed from the various items in financial statements, but they usually fall into the following categories: liquidity ratios; long-term solvency ratios; turnover ratios; and profitability ratios. Liquidity ratios are indicators of a firm's ability to meet its short-term obligations. Some examples of liquidity ratios are the *current ratio* and the *acid-test ratio*. Long-term solvency ratios are measures of a firm's ability to meet its long-term financial obligations. Some examples of long-term solvency ratios are various versions of the *debt-equity ratio* and of the *coverage ratios*, such as the *times-interest-earned ratio*. Turnover ratios measure the efficiency of a firm in the usage of its resources. Some popular examples of turnover ratios are *accounts receivable turnover*, *inventory turnover*, and *total assets turnover*. Profitability ratios are indicators of a firm's effectiveness in achieving profits in relation to sales volume and investments. Some examples of profitability ratios are *profit margin* ratios, especially the net income to sales ratio, and the *return on investment* and *return on equity* ratios. Profitability and turnover ratios are often combined into integrated systems of ratio analysis, such as the *du Pont chart system*, to provide insights on underlying causes of profit levels.

The choice of ratios ought to be determined by the objectives of an analysis, but the overall criterion should be the ability of a particular ratio to predict the economic conditions of the firm being studied. A parsimonious selection should normally be employed because some ratios reflect the same information as other ratios and including them could hamper and confuse the analysis. Ratios can be analyzed for one period of time through a *cross-section analysis* or they can be studied in a *horizontal analysis*. Also, groups of ratios can be combined as in *discriminant analysis*, to provide a general statistical score.

Ratios have always been a basic tool of financial statement analysis, and although they have been subjected to frequent criticism, they have proven to be useful as explanatory and predictive variables in a wide variety of analyses.

ratio estimator A *statistical* estimator in *ratio* form which typically employs auxiliary information for securing *population* estimates from *sample* results. Example: The book value for an item in inventory is y. A sample is drawn with book value Y and audited value X. The ratio X/Y is used to obtain $x = (X/Y)y$ as the estimated audited value for this item of inventory. The ratio estimator is generally biased since, using E for *expected value*,

$$E(X/Y) = (EX)/(EY) - \text{cov}(x/y,y)/(EY),$$

and the right-hand side is not equal to x/y unless $\text{cov}(x/y,y)$—i.e., the *covariance* between y and the x/y ratio—is zero. See *bias (2)*. It is a consistent estimator, however, which means that the bias disappears with increasing sample size and its efficient use of readily obtainable and obviously pertinent auxiliary information has made it attractive for widespread use in accounting and auditing. Finally, a use of regression equations of the form $x = a + by$ offers yet another alternative, which is unbiased and efficient but somewhat more troublesome to calculate to obtain the a and b values by *least-squares methods* from the sample X and Y data.

rational number An *integer* or the quotient of two integers; as, 1; -173; 3/4 (= 0.750); $0.142857+$ (= the *repetend* of 1/7). Every rational number employed as a single number or as a fraction can be expressed in terms of a decimal, called a terminating decimal with a *repetend* (e.g., 5/1 = 5.0). An *irrational number* has no repetend and hence cannot be so expressed.

raw material Goods purchased for use as an ingredient or component part of a finished product. They range from goods in their natural state requiring further treatment or fabrication, to finished parts that may be assembled without further processing. They do not include *supplies* used in the manufacturing process that do not become a part of the product.

reacquired stock *Capital stock*, title to which has reverted to the issuing corporation, fol-

lowing repurchase, donation, or settlement of a debt to the corporation. If the reacquired shares are kept alive, i.e., the certificates are not canceled, they are known as *treasury stock* (or *shares*). If the certificates are reacquired in accordance with a plan of redemption, as in the case of certain types of preferred stock, cancellation is usually deemed to have occurred simultaneously with the act of repurchase, the "treasury" status thus being bypassed, and the shares are said to be retired. See *redemption*.

real account A *ledger account*, the balance of which is carried forward into a succeeding fiscal period; hence, any *balance-sheet* item; distinguished from *nominal account*.

real cost 1. Cost expressed in terms of physical units of measurement; as, tons, bushels, miles, labor hours; or in terms of some measure of prices obtaining on a base or comparison date.
2. Money cost reduced to a common measure of sacrifice attendant on an economic activity.

real defenses In *negotiable instruments* law, a defense inherent in the subject matter and thus good against anyone suing on the instrument including a *holder in due course*. These defenses (such as forgery, incapacity, etc.) are good against all transferees because in essence no *contract* was formed.

real estate (or property) *Land* and *land improvements*, including buildings and appurtenances; also, standing timber and orchard trees.

realizable value *Market value* or *net realizable value*. See *market (2); realization criterion*.

realization 1. A concept which gives accounting recognition to an exchange transaction, such as a sale of goods or services, only when an inflow or outflow of cash or cash equivalents results. See *realize*.

2. The *realization principle* holds that revenue should be recognized with accompanying gains or losses at the point of sale in an *arms'-length transaction* if the earnings process is virtually complete. This is a widely used practice. However, revenue (or loss) can also be recognized on other bases. See *revenue recognition; precious metals accounting*.

realization criterion An accounting practice (principle or convention) which recognizes gains or losses only on evidence of a bona fide sale.

realization principle = *realization criterion*.

realize To convert into cash or a receivable (through sale) or services (through use); to exchange for property which at the time of its receipt may be classified as, or immediately converted into, a *current asset*. See *revenue recognition; depreciation*.

realized depreciation = *recapture of depreciation*.

realized gain, loss Difference between proceeds from sale and cost or book value of the asset sold. "Realized gain (or loss) on marketable equity securities" is the title of the account that would appear on the income statement to report the difference between the net proceeds from the sale and the *cost (1),(3)* of a marketable equity security sold. FASB Statement 12 also requires that a loss be reported as realized (1) if the classification of a marketable equity security is changed between current and noncurrent portfolios and the market value of the security was less than cost at the date of transfer, and (2) if the market value of the security has declined below cost and the decline is considered to be other than temporary, in either of these cases, a new, lower-cost basis is established.

realized revenue (or profit) *Profit*; a profit in the form of cash or some asset which at the time the transaction was consummated could have been converted immediately into cash or another *current asset*.

real number A number in the system of *rational* and *irrational numbers*. Hence, a number which may have either property— i.e., it may be a *rational* or *irrational number* but is never an *imaginary number*.

real price (or value) 1. The price of record during different periods subject to *index-number* adjustment to include a change in money value. See *price*.
2. The value of a product of land in terms of its purchasing power over the necessities and luxuries of living desired by the producer.

real time information system (computers) A system which provides information continuously in a manner that enables the user to control the activity being modeled. The term real time thus refers to the time requirements of the activity being modeled, especially when these requirements are very demanding as in certain chemical and biological processes.

real wages The purchasing power of money wages; the ability of money wages to purchase goods or satisfactions.

reappropriation (government accounting) Legislative action permitting the incurrence of obligations under an expired or about-to-expire *appropriation (1)*.

reasonably possible event A future event whose chance of occurrence is more than remote but less than certain.

reasoning 1. The use of any or all of the processes, or the processes themselves, by which arguments are conducted or conclusions are reached.
2. Inference; mental activity involving the consideration of data for the development of evidence or for the purpose of reaching a conclusion concerning such evidence.
3. Any formal sequence of thought or exposition beginning with *assumptions* (whether or

not capable of proof), *axioms*, or first principles, followed by premises and a conclusion; as in a syllogism.

rebate 1. An allowance; a deduction; a refund of a part of the price paid for a good or service.

2. In banking practice, discount deducted when a loan is paid before maturity.

rebudgeting The process of revision of previously formulated budgets due to unanticipated circumstances which arose during the budgetary period.

recap = recapitulation; also, a resume of mixed data by principal classes.

recapitalization Any major change in the character and amount of the outstanding capital stock or paid-in surplus of a corporation, including the absorption therein of a deficit. See *reorganization; quasi reorganization.*

recapture of depreciation (federal income taxes) Gain on disposition of equipment is taxed as ordinary income to the extent the gain represents recovery of prior depreciation deductions (Section 1245). In general, depreciation of buildings is recaptured as ordinary income only to the extent that prior depreciation deductions have exceeded straight-line depreciation (Section 1250).

receipt 1. The acquisition of cash or any other asset.

2. A written acknowledgment of something acquired; hence, an accounting document recording the physical receipt of goods; a receiving ticket or slip.

3. *pl.* Cash or other assets acquired, from any source.

receivable *adj.* Collectible, whether or not *due*.

n. 1. An account or note *receivable*.

2. *pl.* The title of a *balance-sheet* item representing the sum total of accounts and notes receivable (i.e., amounts due from customers); classified as a current asset. A split in the item is made if amounts owing from persons other than customers—e.g., officers—has been included, unless such amounts are nominal, arise from ordinary sale transactions, and are to be collected within the usual credit period accorded customers. Amounts owing from officers and employees are given a separate classification beneath current assets if they are not currently collectible. Sometimes notes receivable are distinguished from customers' accounts and displayed separately, where they are of an unusual character; in the case of a material amount of installment notes or accounts, the separation is accompanied by some indication of the *range* and *mean* of due dates. Installment accounts not to be collected within a year are sometimes excluded from the current-asset classification; however, trade practice in that type of business permits their retention. If an allowance for bad debts is required, the amount of the allowance (reserve) is deducted and only the net amount appears on the balance sheet.

receivables turnover *Sales (net)* divided by average *receivables* during the sales period.

receive To acquire cash, any other asset, or a service.

receiver 1. A person appointed by a court to take charge of property pending its disposition or the attainment of an imposed objective.

2. One appointed to receive money or goods; a cashier or receiving clerk.

receiver's certificate An evidence of indebtedness issued by a *receiver* from the proceeds of which he or she has secured funds or other assets necessary for the preservation or operation of the property in his or her charge; it constitutes a lien on the property, ranking ahead of other secured liabilities.

recession A downswing in the level of economic activity. A commonly used rule of thumb to identify a recession in the United States is that *GNP* falls for two successive quarters.

reciprocal (of a number) The quotient obtained by dividing any number into 1. Thus, the reciprocal of 12/17 is 17/12, also expressible as a decimal. See *repetend*.

reciprocal population A *population* used to assess possible understatement of another population due to errors or omissions. For example, bills of lading or shipping invoices might be sampled for overstatement to detect omissions from recorded accounts receivable.

reclassify To break down a transaction or transaction group into *secondary classifications*, usually accompanied by transfers to *secondary accounts*.

recognition See *recognize*, below.

recognize 1. To accept, submit, or give reality to.
2. To determine the amount, timing, *classification*, and other conditions precedent to the acceptance and entry of a *transaction*.
3. Hence, to give expression on books of account; said of transactions. See *transaction; accrue; revenue recognition; cost absorption*.
—*recognition, n*.

Recommendations on Accounting Principles A series of 29 pronouncements issued by the Council of the Institute of Chartered Accountants in England and Wales between 1942 and 1969. The Recommendations were intended to be guidance statements only and were not binding on members of the Institute. The series of Recommendations was superseded by the *Statements of Standard Accounting Practice* issued by several accountancy bodies in the United Kingdom and Ireland beginning in 1970.

reconciliation 1. Determination of the items necessary to bring the balances of two or more related accounts or statements into agreement. Example: In the reconciliation of a depositor's bank balance, outstanding checks which have not been presented to the bank for payment, deposits not credited by the bank, collection fees, protest fees, and the like, charged by the bank but not entered on the customer's books, drafts collected, rebates of interest, and so forth, credited by the bank but also not entered on the customer's books, are factors the net amount of which will bring the balances between the depositor and the bank into agreement when added to the smaller or subtracted from the larger of the two balances.
2. A statement of the details of the difference between any two or more accounts. Thus, a reconciliation of an account of home-office books containing transactions with a branch would involve a showing of the balance of that account and of the corresponding account (with the home office) on the branch-office books, and a listing of the details making up the difference.
—reconcile, *v.t.*

reconciliation of surplus A statement of changes in surplus accounts during an accounting period.

reconciliation statement = *reconciliation* (2).

record *n*. 1. A book or document containing or evidencing some or all of the activities of an enterprise or containing or supporting a transaction, entry, or account. Examples: a book of account; subsidiary ledger; invoice; voucher; contract; correspondence; internal report; minute book.
2. *pl.* = *books of account*. The expression "books and records," though redundant, is in common use.
v.t. To give expression to a transaction on (or in) the *books of account*; to *enter*.
3. (computers) A named collection of one or more *data items*.

recordable event = *accounting event*.

record date See *stockholder of record*.

recording medium The cash voucher, journal, journal voucher, or other document, summary, or book employed as the means of giving initial expression to a transaction and serving as a basis for transferring the amount of the transaction to a ledger; a *posting medium*. Examples: a journal entry; a voucher evidencing a payment, from which a ledger posting is made in detail, or, joined with other similar items, in total.

recoup To recover an outlay through sale, use, or charge to profit and loss; to *realize*.
—recoupment, *n.*

recover 1. To convert into cash or other current asset: said of all or part of the cost of a good or service, or operation, upon its sale or upon the recognition of its contribution (as of depreciation) to production; to *realize*. See *recognize; transaction*.
2. To repossess a previously sold item or to receive damages for loss or a theft.

recovery The absorption of cost as the result of sale, use, or depreciation or other process of allocation; realization. See *cost absorption*.

recovery cost (or expenditure) 1. = *residual cost*.
2. (governmental accounting) An expenditure for or on behalf of another governmental unit, fund, or department, or for a private individual, firm, or corporation, ultimately to be recovered in cash or its equivalent.

recovery value 1. Estimated revenue from the resale or scrapping of a fixed asset; *salvage* (*2*).
2. = *residual cost*.

redeemable bond = *callable bond*.

redeemable preferred stock Preferred stock that permits the issuer to redeem it at specified prices and times.

redemption The retirement of stocks or bonds by the issuer by means of repurchase, usually at a preagreed rate.
—redeem, *v.t.*

redemption fund = *sinking fund*.

redemption premium The premium paid on the retirement of a security, in accordance with the terms of the contract between the issuer and the original security purchasers. It is a financial expense in the case of bonds, and is recorded when paid or accrued as is *bond discount*. A premium paid in the retirement of capital stock is accounted for as a charge to paid-in surplus or earned surplus, or both, following the rule applying to the acquisition of *treasury stock*.

redemption value Price, usually stated in the contract, to be paid by the issuer to call *bonds* before maturity, or *preferred stock* for repurchase and *retirement*. See *call price*.

red-herring prospectus An announcement and description of an anticipated issue of securities, given restricted circulation during the "waiting" period of 20 days or other specified period between the filing of a registration statement with the U.S. *Securities and Exchange Commission* and the effective date of the statement. It generally takes the form of the final prospectus, except that the offering price, commissions to dealers, and other data dependent on price are omitted; also emblazoned across each page is an inscription printed in red, stating that the document is not an offer to sell or the solicitation of an offer to buy and that neither kind of offer may be made until the registration statement has become effective. See *prospectus*.

red-ink entry 1. An entry made in red to indicate its subtractive effect upon the aggregate. Example: a credit in a column or book where ordinarily only debits are entered. The use of symbols such as a minus sign or parentheses obviates the use of red ink.

2. Any item in an account having such an effect; as, an encircled posting or one preceded by a minus sign.

3. = *loss*.

rediscount *n*. A *negotiable instrument*, previously acquired by a bank at a discount, sold to a Federal Reserve Bank.

—*rediscount*, *v.t.*

rediscount rate The rate charged member banks by the Federal Reserve System for borrowing funds.

redistributed cost Any *cost* which is reassigned to another *cost account*. For example, factory service department costs are first assigned to the department in which they arose and subsequently allocated to other service and production departments which they have served. See also *allocation of variances; circulation of costs*.

reducing-balance form = *report form*.

reducing-balance method See *depreciation methods*.

reentrant computer code A computer *code* which has the properties that it may be reentered and reexecuted after being permitted to go to another *program*.

reference *v*. To determine the accuracy of the facts and figures in a draft report or letter by comparison with working papers or other data and by recomputing totals, extensions, and other derived amounts.

refund *n*. An amount paid back or a credit allowed on account of an overcollection or a return of an item of sale; a *rebate*.

v.t. 1. To pay back or allow credit for an overcollection.

2. To provide for the payment of a loan by means of cash or credit secured by a new loan.

refunding bond One of an issue of *bonds* having as its purpose the retirement of a bond already outstanding. The new issue may be sold for cash and the proceeds applied to the redemption of the outstanding bonds, or the new bonds may be exchanged for the outstanding bonds.

register A record for the consecutive entry of any class of transactions, with notations of such essential particulars as may be needed for subsequent reference. Its form varies from a one-column sheet to one of many columns on which entries are distributed, summarized, and aggregated as a means of determining periodic adjustments or totals. It may serve as a journal, a subsidiary ledger, or both. See *journal*.

registered bond A *bond* the *principal* of which, and usually the *interest*, are payable only to the person whose name is recorded on the books of the obligor or trustee.

registered warrant (municipal accounting) A *warrant* registered by the paying officer for future settlement because of present lack of funds, and payable in the order of registration. In some cases a warrant is registered when issued and in other cases it is registered when presented to the paying officer by the holder. See *warrant*.

registrar An agent, usually a bank or trust company, officially appointed by a corporation to account for the original and subsequent issues of its capital stock, the cancellation of certificates presented for transfer, and their reissue. This agent maintains the corporation's stock register, by means of which an overissue is prevented. His or her signature validates each outstanding certificate, and a registrar's statement of the number of shares outstanding is accepted by the public accountant as a confirmation of a client's book record. The office of registrar is often combined with that of *transfer agent*.

registration (of securities) The process of qualifying a security for sale to the public, accomplished by filing documents in acceptable form with state blue-sky commissions or with the U.S. *Securities and Exchange Commission*; frequently public hearings are required, especially where deficiencies are found in the information filed, and these may be sufficient cause for the postponement or suspension of the normal effective date of the registration, which, under SEC regulations, is normally 20 days after the filing date. See *stop order*.

registration statement 1. A formal statement by a corporation filed with the U.S. *Securities and Exchange Commission* or other government body, containing financial and other data for the information of buyers in a proposed sale of securities.
2. A similar statement required by a state or local authority.
3. The statement required to be filed with the U.S. Securities and Exchange Commission by a national security exchange.

regression analysis See *least-squares method*.

regression coefficient The *coefficients* expressing the relationship between the independent and dependent variables in a *regression equation*.

regression equation An equation expressing average relationships between two or more variables. This term and equivalent terms, such as lines of regression, derive their names from Francis Galton, who, in a study of relationships between heights of children and parents, believed he detected a tendency for the former to regress toward average heights. For example, regardless of whether the height of fathers was above or below the average, sons, Galton believed, tended to go back or regress toward the mean. See *least-squares method*.

regression estimate An estimator (or sample evaluation technique) in which auxiliary information in regression form is used to obtain an estimate for the variable of interest (the dependent variable) or to project a sample result to the population. See *ratio estimator*. Any estimate from a *regression equation*. See *scatter diagram; least-squares method*.

regressive tax A tax levied at rates which vary inversely with the size or value of the property or the amount of income. Thus, a flat per capita tax, such as a poll tax, is regressive when measured relative to differing total amounts of income or property owned. Contrasts with *progressive tax*.

regulated investment company (federal income taxes) Defined in Section 851 of the *Internal Revenue Code* as companies which are registered under the Investment Company Act of 1940 and which receive at least 90% of their income from dividends, interest, and capital gains. They may not own more than 10% of the outstanding voting securities of any one company, and they may not invest more than 5% of their funds in any one company. They are exempt from income tax if they distribute currently at least 90% of their income other than capital gains.

reinsurance An agreement between two insurers whereby one assumes all or part of the risk of loss on a policy issued by the other: a practice followed, for example, where large single risks are underwritten.

related company = *affiliated company*.

related cost 1. A *cost* incurred in securing a sale or other revenue; any *variable* or *semivariable cost*.
2. A *cost* consequent upon or leading to another cost.
3. = *common cost*.

related party transactions *Transactions* with persons or entities with some special relationship to the subject entity. This may include: *affiliates*: principal owners, management, and members of their immediate families; and investee entities. Generally, related parties are involved when one party has the ability to significantly influence the management or operative policies of the other.

relational data model A *model* which represents the information in a *data base* as a series of simple tables. The language capability involves operations which combine various tables and remove rows and columns from those tables in order to extract the information desired.

release (of a mortgage) A formal document, recorded in the same manner as a *mortgage*, stating that the obligation under the mortgage has been discharged.

relevance A quality of accounting information which makes it useful to a decision maker. Sometimes accorded almost the status of an *axiom* in the form of a standard or norm for guiding accounting developments, the quality of relevance may need to be balanced against other considerations such as accuracy and reliability.

relevant cost *Cost* or components which enter into a choice between alternative courses of action.

relevant range A *range* of values for activity or volume within which an organization (or subunit) is likely to operate within a given time period. This range normally is viewed in the context of *variable budgets* and *cost-volume-profit analysis*. Outside this range the relations assumed, as in a *breakeven analysis* may need to be reexamined. See *breakeven point*.

reliability 1. (auditing) The measure of confidence that may be placed in a set of records or reports or the system of procedures and controls under which they were produced. The test of reliability is whether a reconstruction, following accepted accounting practices, would yield approximately the results actually obtained. The closeness with which the records or reports conform to the results thus theoretically obtainable constitutes the degree of reliability. See *replication*.

2. The confidence generated in a reader of financial statements by their appearance, fullness of information presented, and general capacity to communicate both favorable and unfavorable information.

3. (management) The condition of operating effectiveness in which continuity of function, adherence to present standards, capacity for avoiding failure, and other desirable factors are believed to be present.

4. (statistics) Ability to repeat results in a given experiment. See *precision; accuracy; trend analysis*.
—*reliable, adj.*

reliance on internal control A result of the auditor's *evaluation of internal control*, in which the evaluation becomes the basis for restricting the extent of *substantive tests*.

relief (governmental accounting) The allowance of credit to an *accountable officer* or employee for an amount "disallowed" or a charge made by the *Comptroller General*, in compliance with a specific direction of the Congress or as the result of the exercise of the Comptroller General's statutory authority.

remainderman One entitled to the corpus of an estate upon the expiration of a prior estate, such as life tenancy. See *life tenant*.

remittance slip A printed form accompanying a remittance, indicating what debt it is meant to cover and detailing any adjustments, corrections, or deductions. A check or voucher may also supply this information.

remote data terminal (computers) A terminal located at a facility separate from the location of the main computer. Normally used for input and output between the main computer and the remote site.

remote event A future event whose chance of occurrence is slight.

renegotiation The procedure used to adjust a contract price or contract amount, sometimes after delivery has been made and the profit determined.

renegotiation reserve A current liability estimated to be the amount refundable under contracts subject to *renegotiation*.

renewal 1. The replacement of a part, having more than a nominal value or having a life generally of more than a year; of a machine; or of any unit of plant and equipment: an addition to fixed assets accompanied by the removal therefrom of the item replaced. See *cost absorption*.
2. The cost of replacing a part, having a small value or having a life ordinarily not exceeding a year, of a machine or other unit of plant and equipment: usually classified as a repair and constituting a charge to operations.
3. *pl.* The cumulative costs of the replacements in sense (2) over a period of time, as a year, the ledger account consisting of such costs, often combined with repair costs and commonly entitled Repairs Renewals. See *replacement*.

renewal (or replacement) fund Cash or securities set aside to provide for the replacement or renewal of plant and equipment: a procedure occasionally followed by a public utility, less often by a commercial enterprise.

rent 1. Compensation for the use of land or buildings, or of equipment or other personal property. The amount paid constitutes income to the owner of the property and an expense to the tenant or user of the property.
2. One of a series of *annuity* payments.
3. (economics) Payments or commitments to factors of production, the terms of which, if modified, will not alter the supply. Like *costs*, rents are known, with certainty, in advance. But, unlike costs, they represent a surplus over and above necessary payments to secure a particular volume of product. A tax which affects costs will thus generally affect supply and price. A tax whose *impact* or

incidence is entirely on rents will not affect either supply or price. See *quasi rent*.

rent of an annuity The periodic payment or payments to or from an *annuity fund*.

rent of ordinary annuity See *compound interest*.

rent roll A landlord's or agent's record of rentals periodically receivable from each property or subdivision thereof owned or managed, and showing also vacancies, arrears, recoveries of arrears, and other information concerning deviations from the regular terms of the lease. It may have characteristics of a journal and subsidiary ledger.

reorder point The level of inventory at which an order for replenishment should be placed. In *economic lot size* problems the reorder point is determined by balancing the cost of possibly being out of stock against the cost of carrying excess inventory during the lag between order placement and receipt. This sometimes takes a "two-bin" form in which the emptying of one bin signals the need for an order for replenishment before the second bin is also emptied.

reorganization 1. A major change in the financial structure of a corporation or a group of associated corporations resulting in alterations in the rights and interests of security holders; a *recapitalization, merger*, or *consolidation*.
2. A realignment of or change in management.
3. A major change in business policy or in production or trading methods.

repair 1. The restoration of a capital asset to its full productive capacity, or a contribution thereto, after damage, accident, or prolonged use, without increase in the asset's previously estimated service life or productive capacity. The term often includes *maintenance* primarily "preventive" in character, and capitalizable *extraordinary repairs*.

2. The charge to operations representing the cost of such restoration.

3. *pl*. The cumulative costs of such outlays over a period of time, as a year. See *renewal (3)*.

repayment with penalty A phrase used to indicate that section of certain loan agreements imposing a charge (usually stated as a percentage) against a borrower should he or she pay off an indebtedness (or any installment or other fraction) before its due date. Presumably the charge represents compensation for a break in the lender's investment program, for the waiting period preceding the reinvestment of the funds, and for the risk of a possible decline in interest rates at the prepayment date (a frequent cause for prepayments followed by refinancing elsewhere).

Forestalling possible prepayments, lenders (e.g., insurance companies) have been known to lower interest rates voluntarily and to extend due dates when faced by competition from other lenders.

repeating audit = *periodic audit*.

repeating decimal See *repetend*.

repetend The repeating or circulating series of *digits*, including zeros, appearing in the quotient, when sufficiently extended, of any integer divided by any other integer; thus, $1/3 = .\dot{3}\ldots$; $2/37 = .\dot{0}5\dot{4}\ldots$; $5/21 = .2\dot{3}809\dot{5}\ldots$. The dot ($\cdot$) above the number 3 indicates that 3 is the repetend; the dots above the numbers 0 and 4 as well as 2 and 5 indicate that these decimal fractions may be carried out to further places by repeating the included series of digits; thus $2/37 = .054054054\ldots\infty$. See *rational number*.

replacement 1. The substitution of one fixed asset for another, particularly of a new asset for an old, or of a new part for an old part. On the books of account, the recognition of the cost of the new asset requires the elimination of the cost of the asset it replaces. See *fixed asset; renewal (1)*.

2. = *renewal (2)*; in this sense, the often-encountered phrase "renewals and replacements" is a redundant one.

replacement cost The *current cost* of replacing an existing asset with one of equivalent productive capacity. See *reproduction cost*. The term is also used in a more general sense as the cost at current prices, in a particular locality or market area, of replacing an item of property or a group of assets.

replacement cost accounting A proposed alternative to historical cost based accounting which considers the effects of changing prices for those things purchased and sold within the specific firm by valuing assets, liabilities, and expenses at their *replacement cost*. Differences between replacement costs and historical costs result in *holding gains or losses*. Often called the "specific price level approach" because many replacement cost estimates are obtained by applying special *index numbers* such as construction cost indices and also to distinguish it from the general "price level approach," which attempts to reflect the effects of price level changes in financial statements by means of general indices of prices which reflect changes in monetary purchasing power. See *exit value; entry value*.

replacement-cost method of depreciation 1. The computation of depreciation cost or expense for a period using the *replacement cost* of an asset rather than its *historical cost*. For example, with the straight-line method of depreciation the charge would be determined by: replacement cost minus salvage value divided by estimated useful economic life.

2. It is sometimes argued that the foregoing approach is inadequate to provide for replacement because the replacement cost of the asset increases from one period to the next, thus the computation should be as above plus allowances for any deficiency resulting from applying that method for all previous periods.

replacement method (of depreciation) See *depreciation methods*.

replacement unit An asset or asset part taking the place of a *retirement unit*, and hence capitalized; a *capitalization unit* or part thereof. See *retirement unit*.

replication The repetition of methods by which evidence is gathered. Thus, if under similar conditions of selection and verification, two independent testchecks are made of a group of vouchers, each is a replication of the other, although the particular vouchers examined may not be the same.

In statistics, replication and randomization together constitute the basis of modern experimental and survey design. What these terms mean may be clarified by an example:

Assume that it is desired to test the relative speed of two machines for a certain kind of calculation. An operator might be assigned to each machine by a random choice, as by tossing a coin, each operator being assigned the complete set of calculations to be run. Where one operator is more skilled than the other, as on one type of calculation, the results of the test will necessarily reflect a mixture of operator and machine efficiencies. A more refined test could be instituted by replicating the experiment in a variety of ways, and with varying efficiencies, thus yielding different types and degrees of information. If it is desired to determine merely which machine is faster, a very simple replication design may suffice. If it is desired to determine "how much" faster, or how much faster on certain operations, a more complicated set of replications may be necessary.

Having one operator assigned to each machine, as noted above, may introduce an operator bias. Another method might be to exchange operators and machines after the first calculations. But even this may prove unsatisfactory, since the switch might tend only to confirm the operator bias. Moreover, it might not be sufficient to compare the results of the same operator on each of the two machines, because both operators might show an improvement on the second machine. An enlarged replication might consist of having a series of operators, each of whom is assigned by a random process to one of the machines for a run of computations— the amount and character of the runs also being chosen at random. Similarly, the two operators may be assigned to each machine for short runs, and several complete runs essayed in this manner until the desired information is secured.

Every process of auditing carries with it the notion of replication, the assumption being that the repetition of the same auditing procedures by others having equal skills would produce the same general conclusions. The replication of audit methods may be regarded as a test of the *precision* with which the procedures were carried out. The standard form of audit certificate implies not only a high degree of *precision*, but *accuracy* and *reliability* as well. See *accuracy; validity*.

report 1. A body of *information* organized for presentation or transmission to others. It often includes interpretations, recommendations, and findings with supporting *evidence* in the form of other reports. Example: an annual corporate report with accompanying financial statements and auditor opinion. See also *financial statement; auditors' report*.
2. The type of report issued by an auditor. In the case of an external auditor these are either "short form" or "long form." See *auditors' report*.

reportable segment An *industry segment* that is significant to an enterprise as a whole. The significance of a segment may be assessed by relating its identifiable assets, revenue, or operating profit or loss to those of the combined enterprise. Information presented for reportable segments in the financial statements of public enterprises includes information about revenue, profitability, and identifiable assets. See *segment information*.

report form 1. The style usually followed in presenting an income statement whereby the subject matter is read from top to bottom, beginning with sales and ending with net income, with subtotals at various points between. See *income statement*. The report form of balance sheet is sometimes encountered. See *balance sheet*, and illustrations thereunder.
2. The type of report issued by an auditor. In the case of an external auditor these are either "short form" or "long form." See *auditors' report*.

report generator (computers) = *report program generator*.

reporting The giving, often periodically, of information to others; particularly (a) *internal reporting* as by an *internal auditor*, and (b) *external reporting*: the supplying of financial data by the management of a corporation to stockholders, government agencies, and the public; or the furnishing by a public accountant of an *opinion*, information, or comments at the conclusion of an *audit*. Among commonly recognized essentials of reporting are: brevity; the simplest language permitted by the complexity of the subject matter; intelligibility to the widest possible audience; inclusion of all essential items; and consistency and continuity with the next preceding report of the same type. See *audit; auditors' report; accountability; feedback; internal reporting; report*.

reporting currency The monetary unit in which a particular set of financial statements is expressed.

report program generator (RPG) (computers) A high-level *programming language* for generation of output reports. The language consists of filling out a series of forms containing descriptions of input/output *files* and the type of processing to be performed on the *data* in those files. This information is then entered into the computer. A program is then generated which is then *compiled* and *executed*.

representation 1. (auditing) A written statement of fact or opinion requested of and obtained from the management of an enterprise under audit. The representations customarily obtained by the auditor from management in the course of an audit provide a form of evidence relative to various *objectives (2)*. At the end of an engagement a *letter of representation* is obtained to acknowledge detailed representations and to cover other broader representations as well.
2. The statement in the public accountant's short-form report that a client's financial statements "present fairly" *financial position* and *operating results*. See *auditors' report; fairness*.
3. Any statement of fact or opinion, such as one of those attributed to the management of a corporation and appearing in its published financial statements or in a prospectus. Management's representations as to published financial statements aside from those given to the auditor (see above) are, with respect to others, usually implicit but are generally understood to cover not only the auditor's representation of *fairness* but also the broader aspects implied in the continuation of the *going concern*. When an auditor certifies to financial statements only on condition that they are in agreement with the books of account, management's representation is made to cover the whole field of the auditor's examination.

representative sample A *probability sample*. Any *random sample* selected for observation, whether or not containing a determinable error.

reproduction cost The *current cost* of replacing an existing asset in kind—that is, replacing it with an identical one—usually with an allowance for *depreciation*. See *replacement cost*.

repurchased stock Reacquired capital stock that has been bought from stockholders. See *reacquired stock; treasury stock*.

request for proposal See *RFP*.

requisition A formal written demand or request, usually from one department to another within an organization, for specified articles or services.

research and development (cost) Two activities often grouped together. Research is planned activity aimed at discovering new knowledge often with the hope that such knowledge will be useful in developing new products or services or that it will lead to improved processes or techniques. Development is the translation of research findings or other knowledge into new or improved products, services, or processes.

FASB Statement 2 requires that the *cost* of such activities be charged to *expense* as incurred because the uncertainty of future benefits is too high to justify recording them as an *asset*. The only exception is for firms that conduct research and development activities for others on a contractual basis where the costs incurred are treated like work (or contracts) in process and then the applicable rules and principles are those that apply to accounting for contracts.

(federal income taxes) Under Section 174 of the *Internal Revenue Code*, research and development expenses which are not included in normal operating expenses and are not capital expenditures eligible for ordinary depreciation may be deducted currently or may be capitalized and amortized over a period not to exceed 60 months.

reserve 1. A segregation or earmarking of retained earnings (earned surplus) evidenced by the creation of a subordinate account; *ap-propriated retained income*: a "true" reserve. The earmarking may be temporary or permanent, the purpose being to indicate to stockholders and creditors that a portion of surplus is recognized as unavailable for dividends. Examples: reserve for contingencies; reserve for improvements; *sinking-fund reserve*.

2. The total amount of recognized shrinkage in the cost of any fixed asset or class of fixed assets, credited to a separate account; a *valuation* or *allowance* account. Examples: *reserve for bad debts; reserve for depreciation (accumulated depreciation); reserve for amortization* (of intangibles); see these terms.

3. = *accrued liability*; as, reserve for federal income tax.

4. The understatement of financial condition as employed in the phrase *secret reserve* or *hidden reserve*.

5. In the federal government, an appropriation or a part thereof not *apportioned* but set aside for possible future use or for return to the Treasury.

Uses of the term other than in senses 1 and 5 are declining, the substitution of *allowance* having gained considerable support in recent years.

6. A store of assets such as (1) wasting assets, as in *reserve recognition accounting*, or (2) inventory or generating capacity held to meet peak demands.

reserve account = *retained earnings*; British usage.

reserve adequacy The sufficiency of the amount of an existing *reserve*, or of a reserve being accumulated at a planned rate, to offset a given cost or loss; as, the ability of a *depreciation reserve*, by the time the retirement of a fixed asset takes place, to absorb its *depreciable cost*; or the ability of a *pension reserve* to cover prospective payments to retired employees over a specified period of time. A material inadequacy in a reserve must be disclosed in a financial statement.

reserved surplus = *appropriated retained income*.

reserve for accidents Retained earnings appropriated for possible future accidents. Amounts estimated to be payable for accidents that have already occurred are ordinary liabilities, provision for which is made through profit and loss.

reserve for amortization A *valuation account* set up to reduce the investment in an asset, in recognition of a plan for the extinction of such investment within a specified time, regardless of its physical condition. The term is applied principally to the accelerated writedown of assets having a legal or physical life greater than their economic life, such as patents, copyrights, franchises, and other intangibles, and of tangible assets such as leaseholds, leasehold improvements, mine equipment, and timber roads. See *amortization*.

reserve (allowance) for bad debts A valuation account set up to reduce the recorded amount of notes and accounts receivable to the amount anticipated as collectible; it is credited periodically with amounts offsetting provisions for estimated losses from receivables, and debited with the losses from the accounts against which the reserve was originally created. See *bad debt*.

reserve for contingencies An amount of *retained earnings* earmarked for general undetermined contingencies or for any indefinite possible future losses. Like other appropriations of retained earnings, a reserve for contingencies is a component of stockholders' equity and is shown within the stockholders' equity section of a balance sheet. Such reserves are seldom found in current accounting practice. See *appropriated retained income*.

reserve for depletion The credit offsetting depletion provisions, less retirements; the account in which these items appear. See *depletion*.

reserve (allowance) for depreciation The credit offsetting depreciation provisions, less retirements; the account in which these items appear. See *accumulated depreciation*.

reserve for discounts A valuation account reflecting the estimated shrinkage in receivables that may result from the granting of *cash discounts* to customers in the settlement of their outstanding accounts. A *provision* (*1*) for such a reserve is not a standard requirement, usually because the amount involved is not *material*.

reserve for encumbrances (governmental accounting) A *reserve* set up to record reductions in appropriated amounts occasioned by anticipated expenditures. See *encumbrance*.

reserve for inventory (governmental accounting) A reserve segregating a portion of *fund balance* to indicate that assets equal to the amount of the reserve are invested in inventories and are, therefore, not available for appropriation.

reserve for overhead See *equalization reserve*.

reserve for renewals and replacements See *equalization reserve*.

reserve for repairs See *equalization reserve*.

reserve for retirement of preferred stock Retained earnings (earned surplus) appropriated as a feature of a plan for the gradual reacquisition and cancellation of an outstanding issue of preferred stock.

Often required by the original agreement with preferred stockholders, the reserve may also be created voluntarily by board resolution; in either case, it serves to earmark earned surplus, thus forestalling demands for additional dividends by common stockholders. The total amount of the reserve may include the premium, if any, and the anticipated expense of retirement, the latter consisting primarily of advertising and fees of banks, brokers, or other appointed agents of the issuer; or the expense, if small, as is usual, may not be provided for in advance where the preferred stock was sold at a premium or where the issuer has been gradually acquiring it on the open market and has been able to repurchase it at less than par, the paid-in surplus account or accounts thus created serving as a part of the retirement-reserve requirement. When the retirement has been completed, the account maintained for the preferred stock will have disappeared; the paid-in-surplus accounts will have been absorbed (or diminished) by a portion (or all) of the retirement premium; a charge will have been made to retained earnings (earned surplus) for any portion of the retirement premium not absorbed by the paid-in-surplus accounts arising out of transactions in preferred stock; remaining will be the retirement reserve, intact, the amount of which is the sum total of the successive provisions therefor, and the balances, if any, of the paid-in capital; the former, being a subdivision of retained earnings (earned surplus) as are all appropriated-surplus items, is restored intact to its source.

Interim retirements of preferred stock should have no effect on succeeding provisions for the retirement reserve, since roughly the same total quantity of liquid assets will have to be expended on the repurchasing operation regardless of the time of its occurrence. A retirement reserve, whether pertaining to bonds or stock, serves no really useful purpose and is actually unnecessary in a well-operated corporation unless required by contract with security holders. The board of directors could as easily permit the earned-surplus account to grow, explaining the need for its continued growth in a balance-sheet footnote, and contracts with stockholders have sometimes thus provided. The reserve serves only as an assurance to the security holders that the board will be barred from dissipating as dividends the presumably liquid assets acquired through earnings—the normal source of funds for retirement.

reserve for uncollected taxes (state and local government accounting) A reserve segregating a portion of a fund for taxes receivable, thus effectively placing the fund on the *cash basis* of revenue recognition.

reserve for wear, tear, obsolescence, or inadequacy = *reserve for depreciation*.

reserve fund Cash or securities segregated from working capital for some specific purpose, often accompanied by a corresponding liability or appropriation of surplus.

reserve recognition accounting (RRA) An accounting procedure required by the *SEC* under which oil and gas companies must issue supplemental income statements which include the discounted value of any new proven reserves discovered during the year as well as revision in the values of such reserves reported in previous years. Elements of uncertainty include not only the size of the reserves and projected selling prices but also the timing of discoveries and similar ambiguities concerning where such reserves are "proven." Similar difficulties that would attend the choice of a *discount* rate are replaced by other difficulties that accompany the specification of an arbitrary 10% rate for this purpose by the SEC. All of the above problems are compounded many times when the oil and gas company statements must include foreign reserves which may involve co-ownership with foreign governments as well as other oil companies. It thus appears unlikely that reserve recognition accounting is an improved alternative to present practices although the reporting of such reserves can have value as supplementary information in the reports of oil and gas companies.

reserve requirements The amount of reserves that each bank must keep either in currency or on deposit with the central bank. Often specified as minima that must be achieved in accordance with regulations of the Federal Reserve System. Usually expressed as a percentage of each bank's total deposits.

residual 1. A remainder amount.
2. The debit or credit balance remaining in an account, such as for a *sinking fund*, after giving effect to all disbursements and receipts for which the account was established.
3. (statistics) The difference between an observed and an estimated or forecasted value. In *regression analysis* it is the portion of an observed value not explained by the independent variables. See *scatter diagram*.

residual cost (or value) 1. Cost (of an asset) less any part of cost amortized or treated as an expense or loss; *book value; residuary outlay; recovery cost*; distinguished from *salvage*, which implies that the usefulness or recoverability (other than from the sale of scrap) has been reduced to zero.
2. For leases, the estimated fair value of a leased asset at the end of its lease period.

residual income A means of measuring decentralized divisional performance which stresses the profit responsibility and the financial management efficiency of the division managers and typically computed as the difference between divisional profitability and a charge for capital resources committed to the decentralized unit.

residual net income (or profit) Net income remaining for common stock after satisfying fixed obligations to prior income claimants (operating costs, preferred stockholders). See *leverage*.

residuary legatee One entitled to receive the balance of an estate after specific bequests, taxes, and other liabilities have been satisfied.

residuary outlay *Outlay* less any outlay expiration; *residual cost*.

resolution 1. An action or proposal for action by the board of directors of a corporation ranging from a directive to management (e.g., the declaration of a *dividend*) to expressions of opinion, thanks, censure, and the like.
2. Any expression of a desire or intent.

resource 1. = *asset*.
2. *pl.* An inclusive term often applied to the assets of a bank or other financial institution; as commonly used it may also include unrecorded sources of assumed organizational strength such as management, repeat customers, and so on.

respondeat superior The maxim—let the master answer—holds the principal or employer liable for the acts of the agent or employee committed in the scope of the agency or employment.

responsibility 1. The acceptance of assigned *authority*.
2. The obligation prudently to exercise assigned or imputed *authority* attaching to the role of an individual or group participating in organizational *activities* or *decisions*. See *authority*.

responsibility accounting A method of assigning costs to organization units. The purpose is to secure control at the point where costs are incurred instead of assigning them all to products and processes remote from the point of incurrence. See *responsibility costing*. It thus represents a type of "organization unit" costing in contrast to *product* and *process costing*. It differs from *activity accounting* in that the latter assigns an account and requires identification of an organization unit wherever budgetary authority exists for the expenditures of funds. Activity accounting thus provides criteria for accounting and organization system design which are further extended by requiring distinctions between "programs" and "projects" such as are found in *program planning budgeting systems*.

responsibility center Any *organizational unit* accountable to higher authority for performance of assigned functions, usually including its incurrence of specified costs under *budget limitations and control*. See *cost center*.

responsibility costing A method of accounting in which costs are identified with persons assigned to their control rather than with products or functions. It differs from *activity accounting* in that it does not in itself (a) require an organizational grouping by activities and subactivities or (b) provide a systematic criterion of system design. See *responsibility accounting*.

responsibility drift The gradual shifting of responsibility within an organization, caused by the almost inevitably imperfect fitting of delegations of *authority* with assumptions of *responsibility*. Unforeseen overlapping of authority, changes in personnel, the growth of individual management capabilities and interests, and informal modifications of objectives and of the operating environment are causes.

restatement (of financial reports) The recasting of a previously determined (and published) balance sheet or operating statement, and its republication where there has been a substantial change in *accounting principles* or *policies*. See *financial statement*.

restate-translate approach A *foreign exchange translation* method which takes into account the effects of inflation. This approach requires the restatement of foreign account balances to reflect changes in purchasing power of the foreign currency and then the translation of these adjusted amounts to their domestic currency equivalents.

restricted assets 1. (governmental accounting) Assets (usually of an *enterprise fund*) which may not be used for normal operating purposes because of the requirements of regulatory authorities, provisions in bond indentures, or other legal agreements, but which need not be accounted for in a separate *fund*. 2. (business accounting) Assets, such as *pledged assets* which have restricted uses by virtue of contracted agreements.

restricted cash Cash deposits that can be withdrawn in whole or in part only under special conditions or for specified purposes. A separate bank account is usually required.

restricted fund (institutional accounting) A *fund* established to account for assets with uses limited by the requirements of donors or grantors. Hospitals may have three types of restricted funds: specific purpose funds, endowment funds, and plant replacement and expansion funds. These are distinguished from *board-designated funds*.

restricted random sampling See *systematic sampling; stratified sampling, multiphase sampling; multistage sampling*.

restricted receipts Receipts earmarked for specific purpose.

restricted retained earnings That portion of *retained earnings* not legally available for dividends, as where *preferred-stock dividends* are in arrears, *working capital* or the working-capital ratio falls short of the minimum specified in a loan agreement, and so on; also retained earnings made unavailable for dividends by voluntary action of the board of directors. On a financial statement containing such an item, the nature of the restriction is disclosed in the accompanying sidehead or in a footnote.

restricted stock option (federal income taxes) Since 1950 Congress has provided tax provisions which allow corporations to issue *stock options* to corporate executives, whereby the executives may gain certain tax advantages primarily through the *capital gain* rules. From 1950 to 1964 the restricted stock options rules provided that the option price was required to be at least 85% of the fair market value of the stock on the date that the option was granted; the executive could later exercise the option and hold the stock long enough to qualify for long-term capital gain, and then sell the stock with the preferred tax treatment on the entire gain. The value of the option at the grant date was not recognized as income to the executive. The ''bargain purchase'' at the date of purchase was not recognized as income and eventually the gain on sale was given capital gain treatment. In 1964 restricted stock options were replaced by ''qualified stock options'' with more stringent requirements. The employer was allowed a tax deduction for the amount of that bargain. Qualified stock options were completely phased out in 1981. The Economic Recovery Tax Act of 1981 introduced a new type of stock option called *incentive stock option*.

results from operation *Net income*, sometimes before adding other income and before subtracting *income deductions*.

retail accounting The accounting methods of retail stores, particularly the methods advocated by the National Retail Dry Goods Association.

retail cost A term indicating that the *retail method* has been used in determining cost of sales or inventory.

retail method (of inventory) A method of maintaining a *book inventory* by which the *cost of sales* and *inventories* of department and other retail stores are determined at the close of intermediate accounting periods without a physical stocktaking. Generally, the method involves ascertaining the ratios between costs and selling prices of purchases, including the beginning inventory, and applying this percentage to net sales to obtain cost of sales. *Markons, markdowns*, and revisions of both also enter into the computation. As in the case of any book inventory, a periodic physical verification is an invariable accompaniment. Under the retail method, physical inventories are valued at selling prices and reduced to cost by application of the computed percentage. See *markon*.

retail price maintenance agreement A technique used by a manufacturer of a brand-name product to have the retail price kept at or above some minimum. The most common method is to come under a state Fair Trade Law, which permits an exception to the *Sherman Anti-Trust Act*.

retained earnings (or income) Accumulated *net income*, less distributions to stockholders and transfers to paid-in capital accounts. It may be appropriated, but an *appropriation* (5) remains as a subdivision of retained earnings, ultimately to be returned without diminution. Also known by the older title *earned surplus*.

retained earnings statement A statement portraying the reconciliation of beginning and ending balances in the *retained earnings* account. Required by *generally accepted accounting principles* whenever a *comparative balance sheet* and *income statement* are presented either in a separate statement (probably the most common practice) or in a combined statement of income and retained earnings, or in a statement of owners' equity in the balance sheet.

retirement 1. The removal of a *fixed asset* from service, following its sale or the end of its productive life, accompanied by the necessary adjustment of fixed asset and depreciation-reserve accounts.
2. The asset so removed.
3. The cost of such an asset, particularly (*pl.*)

the cumulative amount of such costs over a period of time, as a year.

4. The cancellation of reacquired shares of capital stock by a corporation. Retirement generally refers to the permanent removal of corporate shares as opposed to holding them as *treasury stock* or the extinguishment of bonds or other evidences of debt. See *treasury stock; outstanding capital stock.* —retire, *v.t.*

retirement accounting (or method) See *depreciation methods.*

retirement allowance A sum paid or payable to an employee retired from active service; an annuity or pension.

retirement curve = *mortality curve.*

retirement fund See *pension fund.*

retirement of debt See *retirement (4).* The liquidation or settlement of a liability; the extinguishment of a debt obligation. May be accomplished by repayment, conversion, contract modification or composition agreement with creditors, or refunding. Also see *extinguishment of debt, early; debt restructuring.*

retirement of stock See *retirement (4).*

retirement plan A plan providing for *retirement allowances.*

retirement unit An asset or asset part the replacement of which is accompanied by the removal of its costs from the *asset account.* It is the credit counterpart of a replacement unit and may be the same or more or less than a *capitalization unit.* If less than a capitalization unit, its minimum dollar amount is often specified, in order that the capitalization of small items may be avoided. See *fixed asset; depreciation.*

retrospective rating (insurance) A method of adjusting the amount of a premium to the actual loss experience during the period of protection, subject to maximum and minimum limits.

return 1. A statement of information required by governmental bodies from individuals and business enterprises. Example: an income-tax return.

2. (with *on*) Earnings on investment, i.e., *income*, also, gross revenues or sales.

3. *pl.* Goods sent back to the seller, the amount being deducted by the seller from gross sales and by the purchaser from gross purchases.

return on assets See *return on investment.*

return on capitalization A version of *return on investment* in which only long-term equities are included in the investment denominator. Its simplest form is net income divided by the long-term capital, i.e., total assets less current liabilities.

return on common equity An accounting rate of return on the book value of the common shareholders in a corporation computed by dividing net income less preferred dividends by average book value of common equity during the period. The computation excludes the dividend claims of preferred shareholders from the numerator and the book value of their equity from the denominator. See *accounting rate of return; return on investment; price-earnings ratio.*

return on equity The basic *ratio* measure of a firm's profitability from the viewpoint of the owners or stockholders. It is usually calculated by the simple ratio of net income to owners' equity. When preferred stock is present, a slightly more complicated version can be used, by dividing net income less preferred dividends by stockholders' equity less preferred stock equity. The return on equity ratio also provides estimates of the internal growth prospects of a firm when combined with the *dividend payout* ratio. The expected growth rate is the average rate of return being earned adjusted for the resources leaving the firm in dividends. This relationship can be calculated by multiplying return on equity by 1 minus the ratio of dividends to net income. Return on equity is often broken down into its component parts, somewhat along the lines of the *du Pont chart system*, by relating profit margin to *stockholders' equity turnover*, i.e., return on equity equals net income per dollar of sales times stockholders' equity turnover, which is sales divided by stockholders' equity.

return on investment (ROI) An overall, ultimate, *ratio* measure of the profits achieved by a firm through its basic operations. It is considered a useful indicator of management's general *effectiveness* and *efficiency*. Return on investment has a number of versions. The simplest is the ratio of net income to total assets. However, some analysts prefer to focus strictly on operations by excluding taxes and financial charges, such as interest expense, from the numerator, namely by dividing net income before interest and taxes by total assets. A slightly different version considers taxes to be an operating expense but not interest expense, i.e., divide the sum of net income after taxes and after-tax interest by total assets, where after-tax interest is interest times 1 minus the tax rate. Also, some analysts prefer to measure the return on only long-run sources of funds, i.e., "capitalization," and, thus, use total assets minus current liabilities as the denominator. Return on investment is usually the apex measure of the *du Pont chart system*, where *profit margin* and *total assets turnover* are related to each other to determine the reasons for a particular rate of return.

return on owners' equity See *return on equity*.

return on total assets See *return on investment*.

revaluation excess (or surplus) The *valuation account* created when the *book value* of capital assets is adjusted to a higher level in accordance with an appraisal of such assets. See *appraisal surplus*.

revenue 1. Sales of products, merchandise, and services, and earnings from interest, dividends, rents, and wages; *transactions* resulting in increases in assets.

FASB defines revenues as inflows or other enhancements of assets of an enterprise or settlements of its liabilities (or a combination of both) during a period from delivering or producing goods, rendering services, or other activities that constitute the enterprise's ongoing central or major operations.

2. (governmental accounting) The gross receipts and receivables of a governmental unit derived from taxes, customs, and other sources, but excluding appropriations and allotments.

3. *pl.* The principal classes of gross operating income of common carriers and other public utility companies; corresponds to *sales*.

revenue anticipation note (municipal accounting) Notes issued in anticipation of the collection of revenues from specified sources to be repaid upon the collection of the revenues.

revenue bond (municipal accounting) One of an issue of bonds by a governmental unit for the purpose of financing the construction, purchase or additions to income-producing enterprises, where repayment of the bonds and periodic payments of interest are made dependent on earnings. Construction or purchases thus financed include bridges and toll highways, airports, housing projects, school dormitories, electric plants, water plants, transportation terminals, markets, street-railway and bus systems, and public garages.

Revenue bonds are issued by three types of governmental organizations: states, local governments such as cities, and agencies established for the sole purpose of operating a revenue-bond-financed enterprise (e.g., a toll-bridge authority). From the standpoint of security, the type of issuing agency is ordinarily of little importance, since neither a state nor a local government can use its general credit to support such bonds. The safety of the investment is dependent on the profitability and good management of an income-producing venture.

One of the reasons for the emergence of revenue bonds has been the exhaustion of the legal *debt limit* of many governmental units. Revenue bonds are not as a rule held to constitute a part of a governmental indebtedness for the purpose of computing such a limit. Even if a governmental unit has an ample margin, it may nevertheless decide to issue revenue bonds instead of *full-faith-and-credit debt* in order to avoid the possibility of having to pay for the bonds and interest from other sources if the earnings of the enterprise should be insufficient. If the operations of an enterprise involve more than one governmental unit, revenue bonds may be the only source of construction funds.

The disadvantages of revenue bonds are twofold. Because they are payable solely from the revenue of the enterprise, they may represent (1) a high risk and thus carry (2) a higher interest rate than full-faith-and-credit bonds.

From the standpoint of the investor, revenue bonds offer a better yield and at the same time retain many of the advantages that full-faith-and-credit bonds possess. For example, the interest on revenue bonds may be exempt from federal income and other taxes. Revenue bonds are usually considered to be legal investments for banks, insurance companies, and trustees. While they do not have the backing of the governmental unit's taxing power, considerable protection is provided for the bondholder. The bond indenture usually provides that the governmental unit must charge sufficiently high rates for the service it renders in order that periodic costs, including depreciation, interest, and principal, may be met. Sometimes depreciation charges are not included among the operating expenses in computing required earnings on the theory

that it is unfair to expect the users of the service to pay for the old plant (in the form of debt-service charges) and also for its eventual replacement (in the form of funds built up from depreciation charges). The indenture usually contains a pledge of the revenues of the enterprise for the payment of debt-service charges, thereby preventing their pledging for any other purpose. Another protection is the usual requirement of an annual audit by public accountants. Another customary remedy is the possibility of a mandamus to force the management to take whatever action is necessary to protect bondholders' interests, or an injunction prohibiting officials from incurring certain expenses or performing any acts contrary to the provisions of the bond indenture or likely to injure the bondholders' investment.

Moreover, the bondholders may also have a mortgage on the property, and are thus in a position to foreclose in the event of default. Foreclosure may, however, do more harm than good, since a public enterprise frequently receives open or hidden subsidies from the governmental unit in whose territory it operates. These subsidies may consist of (a) the payment of higher charges for services than are paid by other customers of the enterprise, (b) free engineering, legal, and accounting services, or (c) the exemption of the enterprise from state and local taxes. Should the bondholders take over the enterprise, these benefits would likely be lost. A better solution, although not a complete one, is for the bondholders to appoint a receiver and work out a plan of reorganization for getting the enterprise back on its feet.

revenue center A *responsibility center* within a firm that has control only over *revenue* generated; contrast with *cost center* and *profit center*.

revenue deduction (municipal accounting) An expense, tax, or uncollectible account receivable of a municipal utility or other self-supporting enterprise.

revenue expenditure An expenditure charged against operations: a term used to contrast with *capital expenditure*;
= *expense*.

revenue ledger (governmental accounting) A subsidiary ledger which supports both the estimated revenues control account and the revenues control account of a fund.

revenue realization See *revenue recognition*.

revenue receipts Revenue collected in cash during a given period.

revenue recognition To *recognize* revenue in the form of an inflow of assets resulting from the profit-oriented activities of a business. The *realization principle* is widely used as a basis of recognition in accounting but alternative bases for revenue recognition may be used as in the *percentage-of-completion method* for long-term construction contracts or in the *precious metals accounting* used for some types of mineral and farm products. See *realization*; *revenue*.

revenue reserves That portion, or any detail thereof, of the *net worth* or *total equity* of an enterprise representing *retained earnings* available for withdrawal by proprietors; a British term, contrasting with *capital reserves*.

revenue rulings (federal income taxes) See *rulings*.

reverse splitup Also called *reverse stock split*. The calling in of shares by an issuer, followed by the issuance of fewer shares in exchange; also known as "splitback" or "splitdown." See *splitup*.

reverse stock split See *reverse splitup*.

reversing entry An entry in which all the debits are identical as to account and amount with all the credits in a previous entry, and all the credits are identical as to account and amount with all the debits in the same previous entry. It is frequently employed at the beginning or end of an accounting period when, in the preceding *closing*, record was made of revenues not yet received, of liabilities for which no bills had been rendered, or of other *transactions* the exact amounts of which were unknown. The use of reversing entries makes possible a record of actual receipts and disbursements in the regular manner as if no adjustments had been recorded in the preceding period. See *adjusting journal entry*; *journal entry*.

review *v*. To examine critically any operation, procedure, condition, event, or series of transactions: a general term the application of which remains obscure unless accompanied by a statement of procedures or objectives.
n. (auditing) An analysis such as an *analytic review* to determine overall reasonableness.

revocable trust A *trust* terminable at the pleasure of or under certain conditions by its creator. See *trust*.

revolving credit agreement See *credit agreement*.

revolving fund 1. A fund from which moneys are continuously expended, replenished, and again expended. Examples: *imprest cash; working fund*; assets available for loans the repayments of which are available for other loans.
2. (governmental and institutional accounting) A fund created by an appropriation or issue of securities for the purpose of providing working capital that is to be replenished through revenues or transfers from users of the fund's facilities.

RFP = *request for proposal*. An announcement of a willingness to consider bids for performance of a specified *project* or a component thereof as in a research *program*.

Richardson Report Formally known as the *Report of the Committee of Inquiry into Inflation Accounting*, this document was published in 1976 by the New Zealand government. Evidently inspired by the *Sandilands Report*, the New Zealand Minister of Finance appointed the committee in December 1975. Its chairman was I. L. R. Richardson, a prominent Wellington barrister. Three of its five members were chartered accountants. The committee accepted with some modifications, the recommendation of the *Sandilands Report* on current cost accounting, but disagreed that the financial statements should not disclose the inflationary effects of carrying monetary assets and liabilities. The Richardson committee recommended a two-stage accounting recognition of gains and losses on monetary items. The Richardson Report has had considerable influence on standard setting in New Zealand and has been frequently cited overseas.

right 1. A claim having a natural, moral, or legal justification.
2. The privilege of a stockholder to subscribe to a proportionate share of any new issue of capital stock by a corporation, usually at a price somewhat less than market, unless, under the articles of incorporation or by agreement, the privilege has been waived; the existence of this privilege makes it possible for a stockholder to preserve his or her relative equity (*preemptive right*) in the business and at the same time maintain an undiminished interest in the retained earnings. It generally takes the form of a transferable subscription warrant issued by the corporation which must be exercised within a specified period of time. A single right is the privilege attaching to each old share of capital stock to buy a designated number of shares (or a fractional share) of the new capital stock. The relation of the market value of a right to the market value of the old stock is sometimes expressed by the formula

$$m_1 = \frac{m - s}{n + 1},$$

where m_1 is the market value of one right, m the market price of an old share, s the subscription price of one new share, and n the number of old shares required to obtain the right or rights to purchase one new share. Thus, if m is 22, s is 20, and n is 4, the market price of a right to purchase 1/4 share may be expected to be 40 cents.

right-of-way A *leasehold* or *easement*, temporary or permanent, permitting the construction and operation of a railway, road, power line, or pipeline over another's land. The cost of right-of-way is a *fixed asset*, and is subject to depreciation only following a decision ultimately to abandon.

ring structures (computers) A data structure which is generated by the use of *link lists*. It has the property that the last element in the list is connected to the first element in the list, thus forming a complete loop (or ring).

risk *n*. 1. Chance of loss: the subject matter, person or thing, of insurance; degree of probability of loss; the amount of insurance underwritten. See *probability*.
2. In sampling, the probability that the *confidence interval* projected from a sample does not contain the true audited population value.
3. (auditing) (a) The subjective likelihood that the financial statements certified to do not in fact present fairly the auditee's financial position and results of operations in accordance with *generally accepted accounting principles*. (b) The characteristic of an auditee entity or audit area which represents a high likelihood that a material misstatement may exist and may not be discovered upon audit.
4. The amount of insurance underwritten.
5. A *statistical* measure representing an average amount of opportunity loss. Commonly used measures such as the *coefficient of variation* or *variance* (*3*) are not satisfactory since the choice of favorable as well as unfavorable events is included in their values.

A modification of the latter value is the semivariance, which is calculated by the formula for the variance after excluding favorable outcomes—i.e., after excluding deviations above the mean or expected value. A better measure is the area in the lower tail of the *probability distribution* since this is the area where the chances of occurrence of extremely unfavorable events are concentrated. In some cases the entire probability distribution is used as a basis for decisions under risk. See *risk analysis (2)*. Insurance practice customarily uses such probability distributions in the form of *mortality curves* to identify different classes of risk as a possible basis for charging different premiums for the amounts at risk in each class. See *risk index*.

v. To undertake a venture with possible losses or unfavorable consequences.

risk-adjusted discount rate In *capital budgeting*, the discount rate used to compute net present value of a project is *cost of capital* unless the project is more (or less) risky than the firm, in which case the discount rate is adjusted upward (downward) according to

riskiness of the project and the risk aversion of the firm. The use of risk-adjusted discount rates is an alternative to using *certainty equivalents* in evaluation of risky projects.

risk-adjusted rate of return 1. In capital budgeting, same as *risk-adjusted discount rate*. A rate of return that is considered normal or minimum desirable from projects of the given level of riskiness.
2. In evaluating performance of securities, the rate of return earned by an investment less the rate of return expected of investments at that level of riskiness.

risk analysis 1. Any analysis of unknown or chance events for purposes of effecting or evaluating decisions in terms of possible penalties and benefits attending those events.
2. More narrowly, a method for generating the different probability distributions with accompanying costs and benefits that may attend different courses of action. Usually confined to large investment proposals, risk analysis generally uses *computer simulations*.

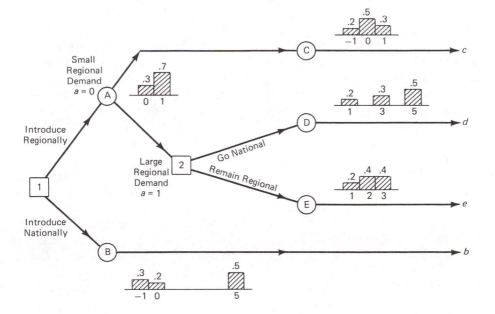

The illustration on page 443 provides an example of risk analysis as it might be used in marketing a new product. The alternatives are represented in the form of a *decision tree*. The nodes at 1 and 2 are where decisions are to be made; the nodes at A, B, C, D, and E are where chance factors come into play. Thus, if the decision is to introduce the product nationally, then the *frequency distribution* at B shows a 50% *probability* of netting 5 (= $5,000,000) to be weighed against a .2 probability of no profit and a .3 probability of losing 1 (= $1,000,000). (See the values −1, 0, and 5 with their associated probabilities for the *frequency distribution* diagrammed at the bottom of the figure.) This is to be compared with other alternatives developed as follows.

The link associated with a decision to introduce the product regionally leads to node A, where chance factors are encountered in the form of a frequency distribution which gives a .3 probability of generating a small regional demand (with a return of $a = 0$) and a .7 probability of yielding a large regional demand (with return $a = 1$). In the former event the product will be marketed only regionally, after which chance factors determine the returns with the frequency distribution shown at C. In the event that a large regional demand is encountered at A, a further decision will then be made at node 2. The potential results of the latter choices are then indicated by the frequency distributions at nodes D and E, respectively.

Each of the following three strategies is being considered: (i) introduce nationally; (ii) introduce regionally and if a large demand materializes then go national; (iii) introduce regionally and if a large regional demand materializes then remain regional. It is assumed that a small regional demand will negate any decision to go national. The frequency distributions at B and C may be used

without modification to portray these portions of a risk analysis. The others involve probabilities that are conditional on the outcomes of preceding stages and these are obtained from repeated simulations that generate the following as a basis for choice:

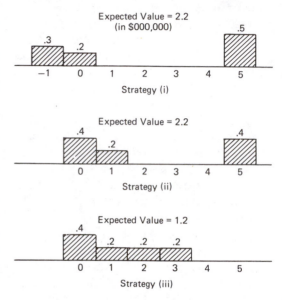

Evidently strategy (i) has the same *expected value* as strategy (ii) but the *probability distributions* differ since (i) admits of a loss which is offset by a larger probability of obtaining a gain of 5 (= $5,000,000). In addition strategy (ii) admits of a larger range of choices (i.e., it is more flexible in its response possibilities) than strategy (i). Finally, strategy (ii) is superior to strategy (iii) in that the .2 probability of a return of, respectively, 2 and 3 is dominated by a .4 probability of 5 (= $5,000,000), while the other parts of these two probability distributions are the same.

Most marketing managers would probably choose strategy (ii), although some might be tempted by the higher probability of a 5 (= $5,000,000) return from strategy (i). Moreover, the possibilities of (unexpected) competitive reactions to a successful new product might also incline a manager to strategy (i). On the other hand, additional chances for exploiting the flexibility of strategy (ii) are present since it will also generate new data which can be used to test old hypotheses and formulate new ones.

These latter considerations indicate that it may be desirable to extend the above decision tree. Such extensions might also include cash flow and financing considerations to unify marketing and finance aspects of these decisions. Notice, for instance, that the events at A and B materialize before those at D or E. Presumably this is taken into account in the net *present values* represented by the "returns" in the above frequency distributions. Additional conditions such as effects on liquidity ratios and other aspects of risk—including a possible loss of better opportunities from marketing still other new products during the periods in which funds are tied up in this one—would require adding new elements to the decision tree or perhaps modeling the relevant processes in other ways.

risk aversion Tendency to avoid uncertainty in favor of certainty. An aspect of behavior exhibited in insurance buying and willingness to accept smaller returns from investments of lower risk.

risk index A measure of the risk of an investment. Several different measures are in use, all of which rely, at least in part, on the extent of dispersion of returns from the investment: (1) variance of returns, (2) range between minimum and maximum returns, (3) mean absolute deviation, (4) covariance of returns with the returns on the portfolio of interest, (5) covariance of returns with the returns on the market portfolio, and (6) the ratio of covariance with the market portfolio to the variance of market returns, also called *market risk* or *systematic risk*. All of these

measures reflect favorable as well as unfavorable outcomes in their magnitude. When this is to be avoided an adjustment may be made by using the semivariance, which is the portion of the variance reflecting only unfavorable outcomes. Another (and better) alternative uses the area under some range of unfavorable values in the tail of the probability distribution of these returns. See *risk (5)*.

risk premium An extra amount paid to compensate a party for bearing more than normal risk. In investments: (1) the rate of change of expected return per unit of risk, and (2) the difference between return on a risky investment and the return on a riskless rate of return. See *risk-adjusted discount rate*.

risk-return frontier In capital budgeting, the set of investment opportunities that cannot be improved upon by other investment opportunities in the sense of higher expected return without higher risk or in the sense of lower risk without lower expected return. In *portfolio analysis*, the set of portfolios that cannot be improved upon by other portfolios in the same senses. See *efficiency frontier; mean-variance frontier*.

Robinson-Patman Act A federal law (49 Stat. 1526), passed in 1936 as an amendment of the *Clayton Act*, its primary purpose being to specify additional competitive practices designated as "unfair." Ingredients, nature of manufacture, and origin of product were required to be disclosed; price differentials were permissible only where differences in cost could be demonstrated.

robustness (statistics) The relative insensitivity of an estimator to variation in the statistical properties (or assumed properties) from which it is derived. See, e.g., the discussion under *median*.

ROE = *return on equity*.

ROI = *return on investment*.

roll-forward procedure The technique for

translating historical cost-based financial information to dollars of general purchasing power as measured by some *index number* (usually the *CPI*) at the end of a reporting period. The objective is to measure all items in common units of general purchasing power at the end of the reporting period. Translation is accomplished by multiplying the book value of a *nonmonetary item* by the ratio of the value of a general price level index at period end to the general price level index value at the time the item being translated was initially recorded. For revenue and expense items assumed to be generated uniformly throughout the period, translation is accomplished by multiplying the recorded amount by the ratio of the period-end price level index to the average index value for the period. See *price level accounting*.

rollover The renewal of a *short-term debt* at the option of the borrower, under informal or formal agreement with the creditor. Such a debt is classified as a current liability, but the possibility of a renewal may call for a balance-sheet footnote.

round lot A trading unit of 100 shares or multiples of 100 shares of an active stock; a stock-exchange term which may also be applied to units and multiples of 10 shares of an inactive stock.

round off To simplify the presentation of a quantity by omitting its terminal digits, with the express purpose of displaying only *significant* figures.

round sum A number remaining after *round off* of digits.

routine *adj.* Regular; customary; ordinary; repetitive; everyday; performed at the point of operations.
n. A relatively unvarying procedure.

routinize To reduce to *routine*; said of methods of operation, particularly those surrounding *transactions* that recur in volume,

the objective being speedy and accurate processing with a minimum of supervision and cost. Many *internal checks* and *controls*, including *internal-audit* programs, are concerned with the constant testing of these methods and with the institution and maintenance of shortcuts and other improvements of routinized procedures.

royalty Compensation for the use of property based on an agreed portion of the income arising from such use; as, the periodic payment to the owner of land for oil, coal, or minerals extracted; to an author for sales of his or her book; to a manufacturer for use of its processing equipment in the production operations of another firm.

royalty interest (petroleum industry) The fractional interest of the owner or lessor of a tract of land in the production of crude oil and gas from the tract; a fraction often encountered is 1/8. See *working interest; overriding royalty interest; oil-and-gas payment*.

RRA = *reserve recognition accounting*.

rule 1. An order, directive, or instruction, usually detailing something to be done or a prescribed operation; contrasted with *principle* or *policy*, a rule covers a narrower field of activity and allows less discretion in its application.

2. A statement, explicit or implied, governing meanings, procedures, interpretations, or inferences belonging to subordinate languages, systems of analysis, or sets of operations and decisions. Since a rule governs the subordinate system, its validity cannot be logically proved or disproved within the same system; the logical demonstration of the validity of a rule is demonstrated by reference to a more *primitive* set of rules. The validity of the "realization rule" for measuring operating income, for example, cannot be tested by reference to whether it conforms to the policies of a particular com-

pany. A challenge to the validity of such a rule requires reference to more primitive rules concerned with more basic objectives of accounting per se. Policies and procedures of particular companies are judged in the light of rules thus derived, rather than the reverse.

3. A procedure which can be completely routinized because its application is definite and unvarying. This usage is intended to contrast with a *policy* in that the latter may require some uses of judgment in its application.

rule off To underscore the last entry in a journal or the last posting in a ledger account for the purpose of indicating a total and preventing any further entry or posting thereabove; a process often followed by bookkeepers at the end of accounting periods when the books are closed, or when an account balances.

rule of reason A general approach of the courts in the area of antitrust agreements including interpretation of the *Sherman Anti-Trust Act*, in which restraint of interstate commerce is unlawful only when the restraint is unreasonable.

rule of seventy-eight (78) A rule sometimes used by finance companies to allocate earning on annual bonus to be paid in equal monthly installments. The name derives from the fact that the sum of 1 through 12 (12 months) is $n(n + 1)/2 = 12 \times 13/2 = 78$. Thus, allocating 12/78 of the total earning to month 1 followed by 11/78 to month 2, etc., accounts for total earnings and return of principal with decreasing amounts allocated to the former and increasing amounts to the latter.

Example: A loan of $1,500 is to be repaid in 12 monthly installments of $151 each, totaling $1,812 (= 151×12). The interest portion, $312 (= $1,812 - $1,500), is allocated as follows: $312 \times 12/78 = $48 to the first month, $312 \times 11/78 = $44 to the

second month, ..., and $312 \times 1/78 = $4 to the twelfth month. Hence, the refund of the principal is: $151 - $48 = $103 in the first month, $151 - $44 = $107 in the second month, ..., and $151 - $4 = $147 in the twelfth month.

rule of seventy-two (72) Rule-of-thumb formula for approximating the number of periods in which a given amount of money invested at $i \times 100\% = r\%$ per period will double; it is: $72/r$ periods. It is not as accurate as the *rule of sixty-nine*.

rule of sixty-nine (69) A formula for *approximating* the number of periods required for a sum of money to double at $r\% = i \times 100\%$, where i is the per period rate of interest to be used. The name derives from the formula, which is $(69/r\%) + .35$ period. For instance, at 10% per annum, $n = 69/10 + .35 = 7.25$ years. A check on this approximation is obtained from $2 = 1(1 + i)^n$ via log $2/\log(1 + i) = n$. The latter formula is exact. See *interest formulas*. For $1 + i = 1.1$, reference to a table of *logarithms* gives $.30103/.04139 = 7.273+$, which differs only by .023 from the previously calculated 7.25 years. The rule of 69 yields fairly good approximations (to within 1/10 of a period) for interest rates up to 100%.

rulings (federal income taxes) *Rules* (2) of the *Internal Revenue Service*. Also called *revenue rulings*, they are intended to provide guidance to taxpayers but do not carry the authoritative weight assigned to *regulations* issued by the Treasury Department. If the subject matter is of general interest, the rulings are published. Since 1976, letter rulings to individuals and other tax-paying entities on private tax matters have also been available to the public after identifying information has been deleted.

running form = *report form*. See also *account form*.

safeguarding of assets Protecting the assets of an entity, by means of *internal controls*, from loss due to *errors* or *irregularities* in processing transactions and handling the related assets.

safe harbor rule A provision in a law or regulation that protects those who have met certain requirements from possible legal actions by not allowing others to challenge the consequences or making it difficult for others to do so by shifting the burden of proof to them. For example, under the Economic Recovery Tax Act of 1981, if a lease meets certain requirements, the *Internal Revenue Service* is not allowed to challenge it even if the substance of the deal is obviously not a lease. This opened a door for a company in a tax-loss position to ''sell'' its *investment tax credits* and the tax benefits from the *accelerated cost recovery system* by means of a *sale-and-leaseback* arrangement with a tax-paying company, making investment tax incentives available to profitable as well as unprofitable companies. Similarly, if a company files its financial forecasts with the *Securities and Exchange Commission*, users of the forecast cannot sue the company for damages caused by acting on the forecasts as long as the forecasts are prepared on a reasonable basis and in good faith.

safety stock A quantity of inventory held to meet unanticipated demand during the time between placement and receipt of an order for inventory. In *economic lot size* problems, the optimal safety stock balances expected stock-out costs against the expected carrying cost of the safety stock.

salary The compensation paid periodically for managerial, administrative, professional, and similar services; contrasts with ''wages''; deducted from salary amounts are withholding tax and benefit provisions, leaving ''take-home'' pay.

salary roll The payroll for salaried employees.

sale 1. A *business transaction* involving the *delivery* (i.e., the giving) of a *commodity*, an item of *merchandise* or *property*, a *right*, or a *service*, in exchange for (the receipt of) *cash*, a *promise to pay*, or *money equivalent*, or for any combination of these items; it is recorded and reported in terms of the amount of such cash, promise to pay, or money equivalent. A sale is sometimes distinguished from an *exchange (1)*, particularly in the phrase ''sale or exchange,'' where the latter is confined to transactions involving no cash or an incidental amount of cash, thus being used in the sense of *barter*; except for such use or where specifically qualified, the term extends to any *transaction* where something is parted with and as compensation therefor something is received. A sale differs from a *gift*, for which there is no consideration; from a *bailment*, which involves no transfer of *title*; and from a *chattel mortgage*, under which a transfer can occur only in case of default on the obligation it secures.

2. *pl.* The aggregate of such recorded and reported amounts during any given accounting period, appearing on books of account as a credit. On an *income* statement, unless otherwise qualified, sales are *net*, i.e., gross less returns, allowances, discounts, and (rarely) provisions for uncollectible accounts.

sale-and-leaseback A transaction involving the sale of property and the seller's simultaneous lease of the property from the purchaser.

sales allowance See *allowance* (2).

sales discount See *discount*.

sales journal The *book of original entry* in which sales are recorded individually or in groups; it may also contain columns classifying sales by departments, products, and the like.

sales load Selling commission and other expense, sometimes added to the net asset value of an open-end investment company's shares, in determining the share price to the investor.

sales mix See *product mix*; *breakeven chart*.

sales records Books and documents that serve as the evidence or record of cash and credit sales, including sales orders, tickets, slips, invoices, journals and summaries, and customers' ledgers.

sales return See *return*.

sales revenue Total *sales*, usually with reference to a given period.

sales to accounts receivable ratio See *accounts receivable turnover*.

sales to current liabilities ratio A *ratio* which purportedly indicates a firm's potential ability to obtain short-term financing. It seems to be used infrequently.

sales to fixed assets ratio See *fixed assets turnover*.

sales to inventories ratio See *inventory turnover*.

sales to other assets ratio A *turnover ratio* that relates sales volume to intangible assets and deferred research and development costs. It seems to be used infrequently.

sales to stockholders' equity ratio See *stockholders' equity turnover*.

sales to total assets ratio See *total assets turnover*.

sales to working capital ratio See *working-capital turnover*.

sales-type lease A lease that gives rise to a manufacturer's or dealer's profit or loss to the lessor—i.e., the fair value of the leased property at the inception of the lease is greater or less than its cost, or carrying amount, if different. Normally, sales-type leases arise when manufacturers or dealers use leasing as a means of marketing their products.

sale value The price at which an asset of any kind can be sold, less whatever cost is yet to be incurred.

salvage 1. Value remaining from a fire, wreck, or other accident or from the retirement or scrapping of an asset.

2. Actual or prospective selling price as secondhand material or as junk or scrap, of fixed assets retired, or of product or merchandise unsalable through usual channels, less any cost, actual or estimated, of disposition; *scrap value*. See *residual cost*.

3. (marine insurance) The award to those

who have voluntarily given aid to the saving of marine property in peril.

salvage value = *salvage (2)*.

sample *n*. 1. (statistics) A portion of a *universe* of data chosen to reflect or assist in determining the accuracy, validity, or other characteristics of the whole. Sampling is an important element in the process of auditing See *testcheck*.
2. A physical specimen used for selling or testing a quantity of goods.
v.t. & i. To select a sample.

sample size The number of items in a *sample (1)*.

sampling 1. Obtaining a group of values to represent a total population from which those values are drawn.
2. Passing out specimens of a product especially a new product, as in an advertising and promotion campaign.

sampling distribution (statistics) The mathematical form of the *distribution* taken by the value of any *statistic* or set of statistics calculated from samples of a given size. For example, the *arithmetic means* of sufficiently large samples drawn at random from any *universe* tend to array themselves in a *normal distribution* with *expected value* equal to the universe mean. See *central limit theorem*.

sampling error The difference between a *population* value and a sample estimate of that value resulting from the fact that only a sample has been observed. See *standard error of estimate*.

sampling inspection (statistical quality control) See *acceptance sampling*.

sampling unit See *unit of sampling*.

Sandilands Report Formally known as the *Report of the Inflation Accounting Committee*, this 364-page document was published in 1975 by the British government. It resulted from an 18-month inquiry commissioned by the government's Department of Trade and Industry and carried out by a special 12-member committee chaired by F. E. P. (later Sir Francis) Sandilands, an insurance company executive. In its report, the committee recommended the use of *current cost accounting* in companies' financial statements, and eschewed the use of general price level accounting (or any kind of general index adjustment). The report has been influential not only in the United Kingdom but elsewhere. See *Richardson Report*.

satisfice *n*. 1. An *aspiration level* with an associated *probability* of achievement sufficient to induce an individual to undertake or continue an activity directed to its achievement. When the risk of nonattainment is too high, an individual must either (a) reduce his or her aspirations to a lower level, or (b) revise the originally estimated probability of achievement—i.e., experience a greater risk of nonachievement—or (c) search for a new alternative. Coined by Herbert A. Simon, the concept has been used in research on budgeting and goal-setting activities by managers as well as in the study of various types of accounting controls.
2. Loosely, a level of attainment which an individual regards as sufficient.
v.t. To satisfice.

satisficing Seeking (1) the first available satisfactory alternative in a decision context rather than exhaustively searching for the best or most optimal alternative as well as (2) rejecting the decision context and searching for a new one when a satisfactory alternative cannot be found.

savings 1. The excess of income over consumption (sometimes stated in the form of purchases of consumers' goods and services) during a given period; often referred to as "current savings."
2. Accumulated holdings of liquid assets and investments, including hoarded money, bank accounts, securities, real estate, machines;

for the national economy as a whole, often referred to as the "stock of savings." Total savings are stated on a gross or net basis, depending upon whether liabilities to third parties have been deducted.

savings-and-loan association A type of *cooperative* having as its purposes the promotion of thrift and home ownership. It exists in the form of state-incorporated building-and-loan associations and federally incorporated savings-and-loan associations.

scale economies Decreases in average unit cost of production as output increases. Hence, the opposite of scale diseconomies. See *efficiency*.

scan (auditing) To look at the entries in an account, accounting record, or group of accounts or records, for the purpose of testing general conformity to pattern, noting apparent irregularities, unusual items, or other circumstances appearing to require further study. The term indicates a general and rapid review as opposed to a detailed examination or substantiation of each item, and often a review requiring the skill of an experienced auditor and having as its purpose the discovery of the qualitative aspects of a procedure, classification, or collection of transactions. See *analyze*.

Scanlon Plan A *participative management* plan in which workers (or their union representatives) and management agree on productivity improvements, the way they are to be measured, and the proportions in which the resulting benefits are to be divided with the workers. Named after Peter Scanlon, an official of the United Steelworkers, the plan has achieved some success in smaller companies or plants but has been less extensively used in large companies or plants, possibly because of the multiplicity of different worker interests and jurisdictions that need to be accommodated.

scarce 1. In short supply.
2. (economics) Not "free"; said of any commodity or service which must be paid for to be acquired.

scarcity (economics) Any good or service which requires economizing. A condition of insufficiency to supply all levels of demand.

scatter diagram (statistics) A diagram consisting of coordinate axes and points designed to show relations between two or more variables; generally restricted to statistical data. Its purpose is to portray, simultaneously, central tendencies, such as *regression* relations, and tendencies toward scatter or dispersion in the observed data.

scenario 1. A scene or series of scenes or segments with accompanying notes and descriptions, including actor entrances and exits, to be used in producing a play or a movie.
2. A portrayal of various possible states, e.g., marketing states, which may emerge under different management *strategies*. See *futurology*.

schedule 1. A supporting, explanatory, or supplementary analysis accompanying a balance sheet, income statement, or other statement prepared from the books of account.
2. An accountant's or auditor's working paper covering his or her examination of an account or group of accounts.
3. Any written enumeration or detailed list in orderly form.
4. *v.t.* To position or sequence in time. Examples: assigning orders for processing; assigning auditors to different engagements or to different parts of an audit.

scheduled cost = *standard cost*.

schema 1. A conceptual portrayal, often in the form of *graphs* or *networks*, to represent entities, states, or operations and their relations to one another as in a *chart of accounts*.
2. (computers) A logical description of all

items stored in a data base along with a logical description of the relationship between them. A subschema is a description of some portion of that data base which is used for an individual application program. The schema and subschema concepts are used extensively in the *CODASYL* data base model.

Schmalenbach, Eugen (1873-1955) One of the preeminent theorists in the field of business economics in Germany during the first half of the century, Eugen Schmalenbach propounded the theory of "Dynamic Accounting." A renowned writer, editor, and teacher, Schmalenbach led a school of thought which has served as a lightning rod for competing theories.

science Knowledge systematized by general principles, and by methods leading to its correction and expansion.

scienter Knowingly; willfully. Such knowledge as establishes responsibility for the consequences of an act. Hence an act for which one can be held fully *accountable*.

scientific management A school of management thought which emphasizes the development of clearly defined, fixed principles of work. This school of thought dates back to the late 19th century and has as its base a strong bias toward production standardization. The foremost exponent of this approach to management, Frederick W. Taylor, stressed the need to eliminate the exercise of personal authority in favor of scientific selection and development of the work force. See *time and motion study*. *Standard costs*, especially engineered standard costs and traditional budgetary control, has scientific management at its roots.

scope (auditing) The characteristics of an *audit*, primarily with reference to the procedures followed in a particular case, or the extent to which the transactions, records, or accounts examined serve as a basis of adequate testing and substantiation. The "scope" covered by the first paragraph of the uniform short-form financial audit report sets forth (a) the nature of the audit (usually an examination of the financial statements of a specified company), (b) the period covered, (c) that "generally accepted" audit standards were followed, and (d) that other tests or procedures were instituted as the auditor deemed necessary. See *opinion; auditors' report*.

scope of examination See *scope*.

scorekeeping The process of data accumulation or recordkeeping which enables interested parties (internal and external) to ascertaining how an organization is performing. It is sometimes viewed as one of a triad of accounting functions which include attention directing and problem solving as well as scorekeeping functions for management and others interested in an organization's functions.

scrap value = *salvage* (2).

screening (statistical quality control) A sorting operation involving complete inspection of all items in some designated segment of production, such as a submitted lot of goods, a day's production, etc., the purpose of the operation being to find and remove from this segment of production all defective items present in it; often referred to as "100% inspection."

scrip 1. A fractional or temporary share of stock or other security, issued in connection with a recapitalization or reorganization, and ultimately convertible into regular certificates.

2. The obligation issued by a corporation in connection with a *scrip dividend*.

3. Paper "money" issued by corporations to pay wages and accepted by company stores.

scrip dividend 1. A dividend paid in promissory notes called *scrip*. The notes may be negotiable, bear interest, mature at different dates, and call for payment in cash, stock, bonds, or property. Scrip dividends are rare. They are occasioned by lack of cash, as when the business of a corporation is highly seasonal. See *liability dividend*.

2. That portion of a stock dividend representing a fractional share, taking the form of a certificate exchangeable for cash or, in combination with other similar certificates, for whole shares.

search A process of locating a single item or group of items from a list of data items. Two types of search are: (1) *Binary* search, which involves dividing the list in two, determining which half the item appears in and discarding the other half. This process is then repeated with the half that is kept and continued until the individual item is located. The technique requires the list of data items to be ordered in some manner based on the value of the key data item. (2) Block search, in which the data are divided into blocks. The first data item in each block is checked until the block containing the item is located. The latter is then searched until the item is located. This technique requires the items to be stored in an order which is based on the value of the key field. Other more sophisticated methods of search are also available.

search theory The part of the discipline of *operations research* which is concerned with determining optimal search strategies under various conditions such as (1) when limited resources or time are available, or (2) when the object for which the search is being conducted can take evasive action, as in antisubmarine warfare.

seasonal variation (statistics) Changes within a year, tending to follow the same pattern from one year to another. An example is the tendency of retail sales to rise before Easter, fall during the summer, and climb to a peak in December. For this reason, comparisons of current figures are often made with those of corresponding periods of preceding years.

seasoning The period of time required for the stabilization or market acceptance of a security, following which only minor fluctuations in its market price are expected to occur. The term "seasoned security" often refers to a listed stock having such a market price, yielding regular quarterly dividends, and backed by net assets and an earning capacity deemed adequate for the protection of the investor.

SEC = *Securities and Exchange Commission*.

secondary account An account built up from *internal transactions* involving transfers from *primary accounts* and other secondary accounts; examples: a finished-product account, a bad-debt account, a retained-earnings account. See *terminal account*.

secondary classification The reclassification or any of a series of reclassifications of a transaction or transaction group following initial entry; thus, the total of a payroll-expense (or -clearing) account eventually distributed to other expense accounts reflecting the nature of work performed or of products on which the labor has been expended.

secondary distribution The sale of a block of securities by an investment dealer as an "off-the-board" offering to other dealers or to the members of the exchange on which the security is listed. The source of the offering is usually an institution, an investment trust, or sometimes an individual whose investment policies compel the sale of the block as a single lot. The plan for the disposal in certain cases must be filed with the U.S. *Securities and Exchange Commission*. The reason for this method of sale is that, if the block were offered on the floor of the exchange, the price of the security might be unduly depressed. Commissions to dealers who resell to their customers are generally higher than those of regular trading transactions. During the process of disposal, the price of the security may be stabilized.

secondary liability The liability of a party to a *negotiable instrument* that is contingent upon the failure of the party primarily liable to liquidate the obligation at maturity. It attaches to the endorsers of a check, to the drawer of an assigned acceptance, and to a guarantor or surety on a note.

second mortgage A *mortgage* on real estate already encumbered with a first mortgage. See *mortgage*.

secret reserve = *hidden reserve*.

Section 306 stock (federal income taxes) In general, capital stock (other than common stock) received on or after June 22, 1954, as a tax-free dividend on common stock or as a redistribution in a tax-free reorganization. The proceeds are taxed as ordinary income when sold; or, if redeemed, at the time of redemption. Under the 1939 *Internal Revenue Code*, gains from the sale or redemption of such dividends were referred to as "preferred-stock bailouts," taxable as long-term *capital gains*, a loophole closed by Section 306 of the 1954 Code.

Section 531 surtax (federal income taxes) = *accumulated earnings tax*.

secular Continuing over a long period of time, as in *secular trend*.

secular price A price resulting from the interaction of economic forces over a term of years. See *normal price*.

secular trend (statistics) The growth or decline reflected in *time series data* based usually on assumptions as to occurrences of events over extended periods of time; applied to population growth, price levels, interest rates, consumption of electric power, and many other collections of useful data. To evaluate management effectiveness, for example, it may be necessary to eliminate from

a time series such secular trends as population growth.

secured account 1. Any account against which *collateral* or other security is held.
2. The state of being safe or protected or the processes involved in bringing about such a state as in the measures used to protect a *data base*.

secured creditor A person whose claim against another is protected by *collateral* or by a *mortgage* or other *lien*; if the protection is ample, the claim is designated as "fully secured," if the protection is not complete the claim is designated as "partially secured."

secured liability An obligation against which specific assets have been pledged or guarantees given.

secured transaction = *Uniform Commercial Code*, Article 9. An obligation where a borrower or buyer provides *collateral* to a lender or seller to ensure that the obligation will be paid.

securities acts 1. The federal legislation which governs the registration, sale, and trading of securities in the United States. The two basic statutes are: (1) the Securities Act of 1933, which deals with the initial distribution of securities, and (2) the Securities and Exchange Act of 1934, which deals with trading in outstanding securities. In addition to establishing filing and disclosure requirements, the Securities and Exchange Act established the Securities and Exchange Commission to carry out the statutes, including enforcement and the issuance of regulations that extend to auditing and accounting standards as well as regulation of the securities markets.
2. More generally any acts or regulations by states or other governmental entities that apply to the sale and purchase of *securities*. See *blue-sky law*.

Securities and Exchange Commission = (SEC) An independent federal regulatory agency created by the U.S. Congress in 1934 to administer the federal *securities acts*. In accordance with these acts, as amended, the Commission (frequently called the SEC) possesses authority to specify the accounting principles (or standards) and auditing practices used in the financial statements filed with the Commission by corporations issuing securities in interstate markets, with minor exceptions, or whose securities are traded on national securities exchanges. Since 1937-1938, the Commission has looked to the organized public accounting profession—successively, the *Committee on Accounting Procedure*, *Accounting Principles Board*, and *Financial Accounting Standards Board*—to furnish it with pronouncements and other forms of guidance on accounting principles (or standards). In the area of auditing, it has relied on the *Committee on Auditing Procedure* and the *Auditing Standards Board* for pronouncements. The Commission has, however, issued *Accounting Series Releases*, and its accounting staff has issued *Staff Accounting Bulletins* to advise interested parties of Commission and staff policies, respectively. The Commission's views are also reflected in its Annual Reports to the Congress, and clues to thinking within the Commission may be gleaned from speeches and articles of Commissioners and members of its staff. See *securities acts*.

security 1. A general term for any kind of transferable certificate of ownership or indebtedness. It is applied primarily to permanent or long-term equities or obligations, such as stocks and bonds, and rarely to notes, acceptances, and other short-term evidences of indebtedness, unless they are of the type traded in on an established exchange.
2. Collateral adequate in amount to protect a debt.

security income and expense Income from dividends and interest, and profit or loss from the acquisition and sale of stocks and bonds held for short-term or long-term investment: an item (or one bearing a similar title) of frequent appearance in income statements.

seek time (computers) The time required to position the read/write heads on a magnetic disk drive directly over the track containing the desired data. See *latency time*.

segment 1. Any division of an organization, authorized by board action or management fiat, custom, or tolerance, to operate, within prescribed or otherwise established limitations, under substantial controls by its own management.
2. Any functional or geographical region or a product line breakdown, as in *segment reporting*.

segmental reporting Also called *line of business reporting*. Annual disclosure of financial information disaggregated to a firm's reportable industry segments, its foreign operations and export sales, and its major customers as prescribed by *FASB* Statement Nos. 14 and 21 and *SEC ASR* No. 236. For each reportable segment, disclosure includes sales to unaffiliated customers and sales or transfers to other segments, its operating profit or loss, the aggregate amount of its identifiable assets, its aggregate depreciation, depletion, and amortization expense, and its capital expenditures.

A reportable industry segment is an industry segment determined to be significant to the business as a whole by passing a revenue test, an operating profit test, or an identifiable asset test. See *industry segment*.

segment information 1. Information included in financial statements about the *reportable segments* of a business enterprise. The disclosures required of public enterprises for each reportable segment include information about revenues, profitability, and identifiable assets; aggregate amounts of depreciation, depletion, and amortization; capital expenditures; equity in the net assets of unconsolidated subsidiaries and certain other equity method investees; and the effects of any change in accounting principles. See *industry segment*.

2. Financial information that, in addition to the information described above in (1), includes information about an enterprise's operations in different geographical areas and its major customers.

segment of a business A component of an entity whose activities represent a separate major line of business or class of customer. Such a component may be represented by a plant, a division, or a subsidiary. Its assets, results of operations, and activities should be clearly distinguishable, physically and operationally, from the other assets, results of operations, and activities of the entity for financial reporting purposes. Segment of a business is not to to be confused with *industry segment* as that term is used in financial reporting for segments of a business enterprise.

segment profit The excess of a *segment's* sales over its product costs and operating expenses.

segment reporting See *segmental reporting*.

segregation of duties The design of an accounting system and a concomitant designation of responsibilities so that no one person performs *incompatible functions*. The four primary types of segregation of duties are: (1) separation of operational responsibility from recordkeeping responsibility; (2) separation of the custody of assets from accounting; (3) separation of the authorization of transactions from the custody or related assets; and (4) separation of duties within the accounting function.

self-balancing Containing equal debits and credits, as in a *general ledger*; but not appli-

cable to a subsidiary ledger unless it contains an account complementary to a general-ledger controlling account.

self-employment income (federal income taxes) Income of self-employed persons up to an amount equivalent to wages currently covered under the social-security tax—subject to social-security tax at a special rate, approximately 50% more than the tax on employees.

self-employment retirement plans (federal income taxes) Also known as *Keogh Plans* or as H.R. 10 plans.

self-insurance The assumption by a person of a risk of loss arising out of the ownership of property or from other cause. See *insurance*.

self-sustaining fund A fund which generates from its operations revenues at least equal to its operating costs computed on a *full accrual* and *full absorption basis*.

sell-and-leaseback agreement A term applied to an arrangement whereby a business enterprise owning and occupying improved real estate sells it to an investor, such as an insurance company, and takes back a long-term lease on the property and often, in addition, an option or agreement to buy, effective at the termination of the lease. This arrangement, which may also apply to personal property (machinery and equipment), has certain tax advantages, serves the purpose of minimizing the investment in *fixed assets*, and simplifies the financial structure of the lessee; in a footnote to the balance sheet of the lessee, disclosure is made of the number and character of such leases, together with the amount and nature of the minimum and conditional rental obligation thereunder, the years effective, and the obligation of the lessee upon the expiration of the lease. See *long-term lease*.

sellers' market A favorable condition for sellers within an industry characterized by an excess of demand; contrasts with *buyers' market*.

selling and administrative expense A composite class of expenses standing on an *income statement* between *cost of sales* and *income deductions*. See *selling expense; administrative expense; general operating expense*.

selling expense (cost) Any expense or class of expense incurred in selling or marketing. Examples: salesmen's salaries, commissions, and traveling expense; advertising; selling-department salaries and expenses; samples; credit and collection costs. Shipping costs are often so classified.

selling syndicate (or group) A group of persons, usually security dealers or brokers, each of whom agrees to assume the responsibility for the distribution of a part of an issue of securities. They are usually selected by the manager of the underwriting syndicate for their established ability in disposing of allied issues; if the issue is subject to the federal *securities acts*, their appointment is not confirmed until the effective date of the registration statement filed with the U.S. *Securities and Exchange Commission*, and then only if they accept the offering price and the number of shares or bonds allotted to them. The term "selling group" often refers to selling arrangements where the participating dealers are given the right to enter into firm commitments up to specified limits, and to "subscribe" for additional shares, the latter subject to the overall allotment by the manager.

semantics The relationship between a set of symbols and their desired meaning. Also the study thereof.

semifixed costs *Fixed costs* which assume different values over different ranges of activity. Examples: A second foreman must be hired or a new building leased because of increased volume. In general the behavior of such costs is not symmetric so that a subse-

quent decrease in the volume of activity is not necessarily accompanied by a reduction in the thus incurred levels of semifixed costs until after some time has elapsed. See *stepped cost; semivariable cost*.

semisenior accountant An accountant employed on the staff of a public accountant, acting under the general direction of a senior accountant, ranking midway between junior and senior classifications and capable of assuming responsibility in well-defined areas without close supervision.

semivariable cost A cost that includes both variable and fixed components. At zero level of activity, a semivariable cost may be equal to some nonzero amount. As activity increases, the semivariable cost grows at a constant rate. At certain points this *rate* of cost increase may change to a new constant value as volume continues to increase and so on. Unlike *semifixed costs*, however, the changes in the total do not vary in "jumps," i.e., discontinuously. Maintenance expense is an example since some level of preventive maintenance cost is usually incurred and additional maintenance cost is incurred in direct proportion to the level of activity with alterations in the rate of increase in such additional maintenance cost increasing at extremely high volumes. The term is also used to mean an item of indirect factory expense that varies, but not necessarily at the same rate, with the quantity of goods manufactured.

senior *adj.* A term applied to a class of securities or to a bond, note, or share of that class to indicate its preference, in case of liquidation, over another class; antonym: "junior." Examples: a first-mortgage bond is a senior security as compared with a second-mortgage bond; preferred stock is senior to common stock.

senior (accountant) 1. An accountant employed on the staff of a *public accountant*, qualified by training and experience to conduct an *audit* under the supervision of a *principal*. His or her duties usually include the formulation of an audit program subject to review by a manager or partner, the carrying out of the approved program either directly or through assistants, the preparing of financial statements and reports reflecting the results of the examination, and the exercise of professional judgment in making decisions on accounting and auditing matters arising during the course of his or her examination. Often the term has no precise application but is used generally to describe the relative ranking of a public accountant in terms of ability, experience, and responsibility.

2. = *accountant in charge*; the word is employed in this sense in textbooks and manuals.

senior security See *junior security*.

sensitivity analysis The process of identifying data variations for which optimal solutions and resulting decisions or estimates change, possibly drastically, with perhaps small changes in the data.

separable cost A cost that may be identified with a particular product or service, as distinguished from one common to joint products. See *common cost; joint cost.*

separate return (federal income taxes) Rather than filing a *joint return* married individuals may file separate returns, each stating their own income and applicable deductions, exemptions, and credits. A married couple filing separate returns must both use the *zero bracket amount* or they must both *itemized deductions*. Because of the lower joint return rates, it is seldom advantageous to file separately unless both spouses have separate income and one has significant medical expenses, or both have capital losses.

sequential file organization (computers) A file organization technique whereby individual data records are stored physically contiguous to each other. The process of locating an individual data record involves searching from the beginning of the file until the desired record is located. Updating a sequential file to add new data items or modify existing data items usually involves recopying the entire file while making corrections as copying takes place.

sequential investment decisions An *investment* effected in a manner that makes each component of the total investment contingent on what has materialized from previous decisions and any other developments that may have occurred.

serial bonds 1. An issue of bonds redeemable in installments.

2. A set of *bond* issues, all issued at the same time but each with a separate maturity and interest rate. Distinguished from *series bonds*.

serial correlation The lagged correlation between two different *time series*. See *autocorrelation*. A serial correlation *coefficient* may be calculated to measure the degree of correlation on different *lead* and *lag* periods to ascertain where greater and less degrees of serial correlation occur between the two series.

series bond Group of bonds issued at different maturities and interest rates but under the same *indenture*. Distinguished from *serial bonds*.

service *adj.* Capable of being used; useful; contributing to the production or operations of its owner; said of a limited-life asset employed, for example, in a manufacturing plant, its application being confined principally to the expression *service life*.

n. The useful work done by a person or machine. The object of every expenditure is the acquisition of either an asset or a service, present or past, the difference between them being that an asset is acquired for its convertibility into another asset or into a future service or a series of future services, while a past or present service is an *expense* the whole benefit from which will have been ended during the *accounting period* in which the *expenditure* is incurred; = *benefit*.

service capacity The greatest number of service units that a machine, operation, or plant can yield within a specified period of time; productive capacity.

service center An organizational unit or staff furnishing maintenance and other specialized service, or office or other supplies to other units within an organization; its costs, often expressed in the form of *standard rates*, may be passed on to users.

service cost 1. The cost of any *service*.
2. The amortizable cost of a limited-life asset; i.e., the asset cost, less estimated recovery, if any, from resale or scrap. Service cost is the amount to be depreciated over the useful life of a fixed asset; *depreciable cost*. See *depreciation base*.
3. The operating cost of a *service department*.

service department 1. A department rendering a distinct class of services to other operations. Examples: a power plant; a paint shop; a factory-accounting department.
2. A department that repairs and reconditions articles or merchandise returned by customers.

service life 1. The period of *usefulness* of an asset or asset group to its owner; hence, the period during which depreciation is accrued; *useful life*. The original estimate of service life when the asset, asset group, or asset class is first acquired is the basis for the initial depreciation rate; subsequent revisions of the estimate, up or down, may be necessary as experience with the asset or asset type grows. Economic service life may be less than physical service life because of such factors as *obsolescence* and *inadequacy*. See *depreciation; depreciation methods*.
2. Hence, the age of an asset upon retirement.

service potential The future *benefits* expected to be received from an item that qualify it for classification as an *asset*.

service unit An item of work done; a single performance or operation, as of a machine. The cost of a machine or other fixed asset may find justification in the reasonableness of the cost of each item, or group of items (such as 100, 1,000, etc.), of useful work, such item cost being determined by dividing depreciable cost by the estimated number of items or groups of items that the asset is expected to yield over its life. The estimated number of service units may also supply a basis for depreciation on a production basis; see formula (1) under *depreciation*.

service-yield basis (of depreciation) The method of computing and recording depreciation whereby cost is spread over useful life in proportion to service units consumed; the *production method* of depreciation. See *depreciation*.

set of accounts The journals, ledgers, forms, classification of accounts, and records and files generally maintained under a system of accounts; *books of account*.

settlement (government accounting) Formal approval by the *General Accounting Office* of one or more *disbursements*, or a group of disbursements, following a *testcheck* of *transactions*, an examination of administrative procedures, controls, and supervision maintained by a *disbursing officer*.

settlement warrant (governmental accounting) See *warrant*.

setup time 1. The time required in changing over a machine or method of production from one product or production plan to another. See *starting-load cost; lead time; make ready time*.
2. The cost of any such changeover.

SFAS = *Statements of Financial Accounting Standards*.

shadow price An imputed value. An *opportunity cost*. The maximum amount an economic agent would be willing to pay for the addition of another unit of a constrained resource. The implicit value of a resource, as in the optimal solution to a *linear programming* problem where it assumes the character of the opportunity cost of altering a particular constraint.

share One of the equal parts into which each class of the *capital stock* of a corporation is divided.

share bonus = *splitup*; a British term.

share capital *Capital* (*3*) represented by shares of capital stock; a British term.

shared revenue Revenue which is levied by one governmental unit but shared on a predetermined basis, usually in proportion to the amount collected, with another unit of government or class of governments. See *general revenue sharing*.

shareholder = *stockholder*.

shareholders' loan equity (a British term) Long- and short-term corporate liabilities to bondholders, owners of debenture notes or bonds, banks, and others; excluded are accounts payable arising from repetitive transactions in goods or services, accruals of interest, incurred current *operating costs*, and voluntary reserves, appropriated *retained earnings*, and other elements normally associated with *net worth*.

share-premium account = *paid-in surplus*; a British term.

Sherman Anti-Trust Act A federal law (26 Stat. 209), passed by the Congress in 1890 and administered by the U.S. Attorney General, its objective being to discourage activities that would lessen competition and often taking the form of legal action against agreements, contracts, and business combinations that restrain interstate trade or create monopolies. In 1914 it was supplemented by the *Clayton Act*, and the Federal Trade Commission Act and it has since been supplemented in other ways.

short *adj.* 1. Unable to account for the disposition of cash or other property.
2. (brokerage accounting) Owing securities or commodities.
3. Subordinated in position; see *in short*.

short account (brokerage accounting) An account representing the speculative interest of a customer in securities or commodities not owned but sold, usually with the hope of a later purchase to cover the sale following a decline in price. See *short sale*.

short covering The purchase of a security or commodity for the purpose of making delivery on a short sale.

shortfall Gain from the sale of an *investment* (*6*) owned for a brief period (e.g., six months).

short-form report See *auditors' report* (*1*).

short rate An insurance rate based on a period less than a year; a rate proportionately higher than the annual rate; used in determining the cancellation value of a premium but disregarded in the computation of unexpired premiums in a going concern.

short run The length of time in economic decision making during which there must exist at least one fixed factor. See *long run*.

short sale The sale of a security or commodity for future delivery and prior to its purchase, with the expectancy that the market price will decline by the time a covering purchase must be made.

short swing profits (Securities Act of 1933) Profits realized by persons (insiders) who take advantage of inside information to realize personal gain. Short swing profits may be recovered by the corporation or by a shareholder through a *derivative suit*.

short tax year (federal income taxes) See *tax year*.

short-term debt Any *current liability*, including the maturing portion of a *long-term liability*. See *term loan*.

short-term debt ratio A *ratio* of debt maturing in the short term (usually defined as three to five years) to total debt. It is considered an indicator of short-run financing needs of a firm.

short-term lease See *term lease*.

should cost Any estimate of the cost of a product based on attainable efficiencies and economical operation.

shrinkage 1. The natural loss of *raw materials, work in process*, or *finished goods* in terms of weight or volume due to the nature of the product or the methods employed for production, transportation, and storage. Once it has occurred, shrinkage usually cannot be restored.
2. Spoilage in the sense that fruits and vegetables may spoil or dehydrate and become unsuitable for sale or further processing.

SIC = *Standard Industrial Classification*.

sidehead A horizontal title of an item in a financial statement.

sight draft A *draft* payable by the drawee upon demand or presentation; distinguished from *time draft* or *acceptance*. An employee or agent may be given the right to draw sight drafts on his or her principal for advances to cover purchases or to cover his or her travel or other expense. Sight drafts are sometimes used by creditors in attempts to collect overdue accounts.

sight test (auditing) To examine accounts without formal analysis; to *scan*.

significant 1. Of sufficient magnitude, as measured by a departure from some norm or standard, to raise doubt that the deviation is the result of chance, *random*, or compensating factors; hence, indicating behavior calling for a better awareness or understanding of the cause, the removal of the cause, or a modification of the *standard* because of its inadequacy.
2. Of sufficient importance to warrant *disclosure* or the treatment accorded larger or more important items; likely to influence *judgments* or *decisions*: said of individual *transactions*, transaction groups, or other *events* or *conditions* peculiar to a given establishment. See *materiality*.

significant amount A number resulting from a *round off* intended to convey to the observer the same impression as would the fully expressed quantity. Thus the total assets of a certain bank were recently reported as $4,935,468,311.89. To the average stockholder or depositor, the significant figure would probably be a rounded-off $4.9 billion, an amount informative to him or her and readily recalled. To the bank's *controller*, however, who must test total assets against total liabilities, the significant quantity would be no less than all 12 digits. In many reports to stockholders, larger corporations now omit cents, substitute zeros for hundreds, often thousands of dollars. For most readers, only the first two or three digits of any item in financial statements have significance.

simple average An unweighted (really equally weighted) arithmetic *mean*; obtained by dividing the sum of differing items in a series or group by the number of such items, regardless of the frequency of any one of them.

simple interest The charge for the loan of money or for a deferment of the collection of an account, computed by applying a rate (of interest) against the amount of the loan or account; contrasts with *compound interest*.

simple journal A *book of original entry* containing but two money columns, one for debits, the other for credits. See *journal*.

simple trust (federal income taxes) A *trust* that must distribute its income currently but does not distribute corpus before its termination. See *complex trust*.

simplex method A commonly used method for solving a *linear programming* problem through a well-defined iterative process.

simulation A method of studying operational problems, whereby a *model* of the *system* or *process* is subjected to a series of manipulations to reflect varying assumptions. Often the simulation is effected via a computer, especially when the behavior of a large and complex system is involved.

simulation program A *computer code* which represents behaviors of certain features of a system to be studied. Simulation is often contrasted with optimization, although the two may be used together in various ways. A number of specialized languages are available which are useful for developing simulation programs. Two such languages are SIMSCRIPT and SIMULA.

single-entry bookkeeping A system of *bookkeeping* in which only records of cash and of personal accounts are maintained; it is always incomplete *double-entry bookkeeping*, varying with circumstances. There is usually no detailed record of gains or losses; a statement of financial condition is prepared from whatever data are available from the records or by inspection or count, and the new profit or loss for a period is derived from a comparison of financial condition at the close of the period with that at the beginning, unless adequate profit-and-loss data can be derived from cashbook distribution totals. Where transactions are infrequent and receivables, payables, and assets other than cash are few, single-entry records, carefully maintained, may be adequate.

single-step income statement A form of *income statement* in which all the elements of expense appear in the same section, thus eliminating such intermediate remainders as gross profit, gross income, and operating profit; contrasts with *multiple-step income statement*.

sinking fund Cash or other assets, and the interest or other income earned thereon, set apart for the retirement of a debt, the redemption of stock, or the protection of an investment in depreciable property; sometimes paralleled by a *sinking-fund reserve*. A sinking fund established for the purpose of extinguishing indebtedness or reacquiring capital stock may also be known as a *redemption fund*. See also *fund*.

sinking-fund bond Any of an issue of bonds where the indenture requires the issuer to set aside periodically a sum which, with interest, will be sufficient to meet the redemption price of the bonds or to equal a specified fraction of the total, the balance unprovided for being left for refunding.

sinking-fund depreciation method See *depreciation methods*.

sinking-fund method (of depreciation) See *depreciation methods*.

sinking-fund reserve An appropriation or earmarking of earned surplus, usually in the form of planned periodic transfers, for the purpose of providing an equity counterpart for assets being accumulated, sometimes in a separate *sinking fund*, for the retirement of an outstanding security. See *appropriated retained income*.

site audit (governmental accounting) An audit conducted on the premises of the organization under examination: a term now obsolescent; contrasts with an older form of examination whereby the organization's vouchers were reviewed in the Washington office of the *Comptroller General*.

skewness (statistics) Lack of symmetry between the two sides of a *curve*. In a symmetric curve, the *arithmetic mean, median*, and *mode* coincide. The mean deviates increasingly from the mode as skewness develops; moreover, it deviates in the direction of the skewness. By comparing the difference between mean and mode, it is possible to define a measure of skewness.

To facilitate comparisons between curves, Pearson's measure in standard units is employed:

$$Sk = \frac{\overline{X} - Mo}{\sigma},$$

where $\overline{X}$ is the arithmetic *mean*, Mo the *mode*, and σ the *standard deviation*. Another more easily calculated measure (Bowley's) is

$$Sk = \frac{q_2 - q_1}{q_2 + q_1},$$

where q_1 is the first *quartile*, and q_2 the second quartile or *median*. See *median*.

slack variable A term used in *linear programming* to denote a variable whose values represent the portion or amount of a constrained resource which is not used in a particular solution to the problem.

small business corporation (federal income taxes) 1. Under Section 1244 of the *Internal Revenue Code*, a corporation which has received for stock, as a contribution to capital, and as paid-in surplus, a total amount of cash and property (adjusted basis) not in excess of $1,000,000. Losses on the sale of small business corporation stock can be treated as an ordinary (as opposed to a capital) loss by an individual under conditions prescribed in Section 1244 of the Internal Revenue Code. 2. Under Subchapter S of the Internal Revenue Code (Sections 1371 *et seq.*) a domestic corporation which: (a) is not a member of an affiliated group; (b) does not have more than 15 shareholders; (c) does not have as shareholders persons other than individuals, estates, and certain trusts; (d) does not have a nonresident alien as a shareholder; and (e) does not have more than one class of stock. Such corporation (also known popularly as a Subchapter S corporation) can elect to be ex-

empt from the corporate income tax and pass its taxable income or loss through to its individual shareholders, who report their respective proportions on their individual returns. See *undistributed taxable income*.

smoothing Any treatment designed to remove irregularities in data, such as unusual peaks or valleys in a curve, that may be the result of nonrecurring operating conditions.

social accounting The systematized treatment of *social indicators* which represent quality-of-life conditions in a country, region, or other geographical unit. Many governments in Western Europe (and Japan) now issue periodic reports, often in narrative form with accompanying data and charts, to portray areas of social concern. (The OECD Working Party on Social Indicators in its 1973 report defines these as "social goal areas" in which there is an identifiable and definable aspiration of fundamental and direct importance to human well-being.) Also, starting in 1973, the U.S. government began to issue *Social Indicators*, a report containing charts, tables, and accompanying explanatory and interpretative text organized around the following eight social concerns: health, public safety, education, employment, income, housing, leisure and recreation, and population.

Although a use of subjective measures of feeling, attitudes, and opinions is also appropriate, nearly all of these reports are concerned almost entirely with objective measures of areas of social concern. See A. Charnes, W. W. Cooper, and G. Kozmetsky, "Measuring, Monitoring and Modeling Quality of Life," *Management Science*, 19, no. 10, for an example of a subjective system at a local government level.

The table on pp. 464-65 from N. Terleckyj, *Improvements in the Quality of Life* (Washington, D.C.: National Planning Association, 1975), is an example of such an ob-

Goal Output Indicators

Activity	Total cost: 1974-83 (billions 1973 dollars)	1. Average life expectancy at birth, years	2. Percent of population with major disabilities	3. Number of violent crimes per 100,000 persons per year	4. Index of mean performance in grade 12 based on standard tests	5. Percent of students 3 or more years behind 1973 average	6. Number of persons completing college, thousands	7. Number of persons not in the mainstream of labor force, millions	8. Median earnings of individuals, thousands 1973 dollars	9. Percent of population below poverty standard	10. Percent of population in near-poverty conditions	11. Percent of population with living standard loss of over 30 percent	12. Family income ratio: 20th to 90th percentile	13. Mean family income, blacks as a percent of whites	14. Hourly earnings of women as percent of earnings of men	15. Percent of persons living in adequate housing	16. Percent of persons living in adequate neighborhoods	17. Percent of population affected by bothersome pollution	18. Percent of persons regularly taking part in outdoor recreation	19. Index of preservation of life and natural forms	20. Number of scientists active in basic science, thousands	21. Number of active artists, thousands	22. Discretionary time, hours per person per year	23. GNP, billions 1973 dollars
Base 1973 / Base 1983	—	71.3 / 72.7	17.5 / 16.8	668 / 668	100 / 105	24 / 19	957 / 1342	11.1 / 8.8	5.9 / 7.8	11.4 / 8.7	4.8 / 3.5	8.6 / 8.7	25 / 25	65 / 70	60 / 60	88 / 92	77 / 87	62 / 46	21 / 54	100 / 110	81 / 139	265 / 323	2111 / 2199	1275 / 2033
1. Change in health-related habits and patterns	$64	5.3	-3.3	-129								.9							25				57	
2. Health services related to specific conditions	66	1.7	-3.1	-69								.4											53	
3. Special health services for vulnerable population groups	91	2.5	-1.0																					
4. Improvement of law enforcement systems	26			-180										2										
5. Employment and other opportunities for the young	51			-240	5	-4		-1.5		-.9	-.4		2	1										
6. Remedial and augmenting educational inputs	73				16	-11	50		.1				1											44
7. Improved educational technology and approaches	183				21	-14	50		.2				2											60
8. General day care for children	126							-1.8	.2	-1.7	-1.3		1		3								117	43
9. Universal access to higher education	273						1050														20	32		29
10. Structural improvements in higher education	70						350		.1												20	11		10

No.	Description																							
11.	Maintenance, updating and improvement of job skills	342						650	3.4	.2	.9	.9		2	4	6						10	16	34
12.	Specialized training for those outside mainstream of labor force	94							5.0	-1.3	.4	.4			3									21
13.	Private savings, insurance, pension plans	200							.9	.6	4.3			1	1									
14.	Old age pensions at 40 percent of current median earnings	30							-1.7	.6	2.6			1	1									
15.	Extended welfare program: tax and transfer to abolish poverty and near-poverty	76							8.7	3.5	1.3			3	3									
16.	Aid to depressed communities	171							1.8	.2	.9	.9		1	2	4	5	5	.2					17
17.	Construction and maintenance of houses	108							.4	.4							8	5	.2						
18.	Design and testing of new neighborhood, city and regional environments	202														2	10	.9	3						
19.	Innovations in cars, roads and other transportation system components	155																.4	4					71	
20.	Pollution control	171																5	.29						
21.	More basic environmental improvements	332																	.17	4					
22.	Recreation facilities in neighborhoods	127	1.1	.4														5	12						
23.	Major parks and facilities	80																5			10				
24.	Preservation of wilderness and scenery	26																		10	50				
25.	Pure science—institutions, education, communication	36																				51			
26.	The arts—institutions, education, subsidies, new forms	28																					300		
27.	Reduction in working time	107												1	2									60	
28.	Time saving innovations	91									.4								4					319	50
	TOTAL LISTED (output not additive)	(3,399)	(8.9)	(6.8)	(448)	(27)	(16)	(1300)	(7.2)	(1.4)	(8.7)	(3.5)	(6.9)	(9)	(12)	(11)	(8)	(13)	(.37)	(28)	(60)	(81)	(315)	(677)	(160)

jective system for the United States. Utilizing *PPBS* concepts it is also an example of how *double-entry principles* may be extended for multidimensional applications in order to obtain more systematic portrayals and summaries.

Using reports and work by others going back as far as the 1960 "Eisenhower Commission Report," Terleckyj and his associates selected for study those that are listed at the top of the table. They then selected the indicators for each such area that are shown by the grouping of the respective column captions.

The numerical values at the top of each column represent the estimated indicator value in 1973 and its projected value for 1983 if present "trends" are continued and no new programs are activated. Possible progress that might be additionally activated is listed by programs in the stub followed by estimates of a 10-year total program cost which would produce the incremental effects shown in the cells of the corresponding row of the table.

We illustrate what is involved by reference to the $64 billion program listed in row 1 for which Terleckyj supplies further details as follows:

Title of Activity	Total Cost 1974–83 (billions of 1973 dollars)
Change in health-related habits	$ 5
Fitness and diet improvements	35
Accident prevention	1
Alcoholism abatement	17
Drug abuse abatement	6
Total	$64

These expenditures would then affect health and safety in the amount obtained by reading from the cells in row one as follows: average life expectancy would increment by 5.3 years, so that by 1983 this expectancy would be 78 years instead of 72.7; percent of population with major disabilities would decrement further by 3.3% from 16.8% to 13.5% in 1983; and number of violent crimes per 100,000 persons per year would decrement by 129 from its projected 1973-1983 standstill level of 668.

Impacts across different areas of social concern are brought out and so are areas of concern where no impact is expected. Thus the program of row 1 is not expected to have significant impact on any of the listed dimensions of education, skills, and earnings or economic equality. Via the projected .9% reduction in the percent of population exposed to a living standard loss of over 30% (in any one year), however, it does affect the area of concern labeled adequacy and continuity of income and finally it also affects art, science, and free time by an estimated additional 57 discretionary hours per person living in 1983.

No increment to GNP is estimated from the program in row 1 but the annual increment for some of the other programs would be substantial by 1983. This may be seen by reference to the last column on the right in this table. Of course, this last column could be further extended to a measure of economic welfare by first replacing GNP by net national product and then reducing this to a per capita basis after adjustment for nonmarket activities and after removing portions of net national product which represent accounts that do not conform to reasonable conceptions of "economic welfare." Another approach would replace the above 10-year result with an annualized version in order to study possible reallocations of such GNP increments in order to effect still further improvements in other areas of social concern.

Any approach along the latter lines would need to take account of dynamic interdependencies and interactions. As a start in that direction it may be observed that the estimates in the columns are not additive, as is indicated by the numerical value in parentheses at the foot of the table. For instance, even if all 28 programs were activated at the levels indicated in the table, the estimated maximum increment to life expectancy would be 8.9 years and not the 10.6 years obtained by totaling the entries in column 1.

social audit An examination of the performance of an *accounting unit* in various areas of social concern. See *social accounting*. Such activities include independent review and appraisal of social and environmental consequences of corporate activities. These reviews may be part of regularly performed *internal audits* or they may involve special arrangements with an outside group retained for the purpose. See *corporate social report*. It is not customary for the resulting reports to be released publicly as is the case for typical business financial audits. Even internal distribution of reports may be restricted. The review thus tends to lose its third-party orientation and to take on the character of an internal consulting arrangement rather than an *audit*.

social concern An area of activity which impinges on areas of immediate importance for human well-being and thus is readily identifiable for purposes of social goal formation. See *social accounting*.

social costs The costs or reductions in value associated with *externalities*.

social indicator Any measure, usually in the form of an *index number*, which is used to represent conditions in an area of *social concern*. Examples are indexes of crime, longevity, and health. See *social accounting*.

social inventory A detailed list of an organization's activities, often without accompanying measures, which affect society or the physical environment in which it operates.

social report A *report* of activities or the state of affairs in one or more areas of *social concern*. Such reports may proceed from a single entity, as in a *corporate social report*, or they may be for an entire society or region, as in *social accounting*.

social-security tax A flat-rate tax levied on the earned income of employees and self-employed persons which is designated for the maintenance of the social-security program. The tax levied on wages of employees is paid equally by the employer and employee. In all cases, there is a maximum amount of wages subject to the tax. The flat rate is composed of three separate taxes, the revenue from which is used in the maintenance of the three separate social-security benefit programs: old age and survivors insurance, disability insurance, and hospital insurance. (Also known as FICA tax because of its authorization by the Federal Insurance Contributions Act.) See *FICA*.

software Computer programs usually supplied by the manufacturer of the computer which make possible the use of the computer by a user. Typical software items on a computer include such things as system programs, assemblers, compilers, and operating systems, as well as programs for scientific calculations and statistical analysis. See *hardware*.

sole proprietorship A business enterprise the net worth of which belongs entirely to one individual.

solvency ratios Any *ratio* that measures the relative amount of debt used by a firm in its capital structure, especially in regard to the ability of the firm to meet its debt obligations.

sorting The process of arranging items into a desired sequence or order.

sound 1. Conforming to tradition; consonant with the views, often of untested objectivity, of the practical person; leading to a profitable end or meeting some other measure of commercial success.

2. Hence, in harmony with accounting or management doctrine of purported general acceptance.

sound value *Replacement* cost less observed *depreciation* and *deferred maintenance; present value* as determined in an *appraisal*: a term used principally in *fixed-asset appraisals*.

source and application of funds A statement summarizing the flow of *funds (4)* (= *working capital*). Within an organization, the purpose being to depict the leading *events and conditions* and principal financial changes during a designated period of time; now known as *changes in financial position*.

source document The documents upon which evidence of an *accounting transaction* are initially recorded. Source documents are often followed by the creation of many additional records and reports which do not, however, qualify as initial recordings. Examples of source documents are purchase orders, payroll time cards, and customer orders.

sources of evidence The persons, actions, records, and documents which provide the information gathered by an auditor as a basis for rendering an opinion. See *evidence*.

span of control The extent of a supervisor's jurisdiction, often represented in organization charts by subordinate lines of authority extending to activities or subunits; a term formerly employed in referring to an asserted limitation on the number of persons that could effectively report to another.

special agent See *agent*.

special-assessment bonds (municipal accounting) *Bonds* of a municipality issued for public improvements, and repaid from assessments levied against benefited properties. If the bonds are issued not only with the understanding that they will be paid from special assessments, but, in addition, with a pledge for the *full faith and credit* of the municipality, they are known as "general-obligation special-assessment bonds."

special-assessment fund (municipal accounting) A fund set up to provide for financing improvements or services out of *bond* issues or proceeds of *assessments* levied against the properties benefited. See *fund*.

special audit An audit having a limited, specified scope: a *limited audit*.

special contingency reserve A *reserve for contingencies* related to one or more specific items of possible future expense or loss. Like other contingent reserves, it is classified as a subdivision of *retained earnings*; but if such a reserve is actually a *liability* already incurred, it is so classified for balance-sheet purposes.

special district (municipal and governmental accounting) An independent unit of local government organized to perform a single governmental function or restricted number of related functions. Special districts usually have the power to incur debt and levy taxes. Examples of special districts are water districts, drainage districts, flood control districts, hospital districts, fire protection districts, transit authorities, port authorities, and electric power authorities. Some of these, like power authorities, are entirely dependent upon enterprise earnings and cannot impose taxes.

special fund (municipal accounting) A *fund* that must be used in accordance with specific legal or administrative restrictions; any fund other than the general fund. See *fund*.

specialist On stock or commodity exchanges, one who represents a single stock, industry, or commodity (known as a "specialty"). He or she operates at a designated "trading post" on the floor of the exchange, executes brokers' orders, and, in general, endeavors to maintain an orderly market for this specialty.

special order = *job order*.

special-purpose financial statement A financial statement having limited use or application. Public accountants as a rule report only on *all-purpose financial statements* around which standard practices of presentation, disclosure, and qualification have grown. Some corporate managements follow the practice of accompanying special-purpose statements with certified all-purpose statements, or the latter may be supplied in lieu of the former. Special-purpose statements are encountered primarily in connection with forms used in the compilation of statistics by trade or governmental bodies.

special reports A special class of *auditor's reports* issued in connection with: (1) financial statements that are prepared in accordance with a comprehensive basis of accounting other than *generally accepted accounting principles*; (2) specified elements, accounts, or items of a financial statement; (3) compliance with aspects of contractual agreements or regulatory requirements related to audited financial statements; (4) financial information presented in prescribed forms or schedules that require a prescribed form of auditor's report.

The work performed by an external auditor leading to a special report is covered by *generally accepted auditing standards* with additional specific reporting requirements relating to each general special report type.

Common types of special reports are: financial statements prepared on a tax basis, cash receipts and disbursements statements, reports relating to royalties, and reports in connection with proposed acquisitions.

special-revenue fund (municipal accounting) A fund used to finance particular activities and created out of receipts of specific taxes or other revenues. Such a fund is usually authorized by statutory or charter provisions to pay for certain activities with some special form of continuing revenues. See *fund*.

special revenue sharing (governmental accounting) An arrangement under which the federal government apportions part of its revenues to state and local governments for purposes of community development. Unlike *general revenue sharing*, use of funds is restricted in the manner of a *block grant* and, in fact, the program replaces the previous block grants program for community development.

specie Metallic or "hard" money, as compared with paper money; sometimes limited to gold or silver coin.

specification cost = *standard cost*.

specific cost Cost readily identifiable with a particular product or service; *direct cost; historical cost; actual cost*; used principally in contrast with *average cost, FIFO, LIFO*, and *retail cost*.

specific-order cost system See *job-order costing*.

specific performance An equitable remedy requiring performance on a contract as agreed, as opposed to allowing collection of damages, on the theory that damages are not an adequate remedy.

specific price change Change in the *market* price or *replacement cost* of a single good or services or a group or interrelated or similar goods and/or services. Contrast to general price level changes that would relate to a broad spectrum—or all—of available goods and services.

specific price index Measure of the relative change in the price(s) of a single good or a group of interrelated or similar goods and/or services at a given time as compared to a base time or period. Contrasted with a general price index, such as the gross national product (*GNP*) price deflator. See *index number*.

specific purpose fund (institutional accounting) A *fund* classification provided for hospitals to record the principal and income of assets which may be used only for purposes specified by a donor. If the assets are restricted to use for plant replacement or expansion, they are accounted for in the plant replacement and expansion fund, not a specific purpose fund. If the donor has specified that the principal must be held inviolate, the principal is accounted for as an endowment fund; if the donor has further specified the purposes for which the endowment income may be used, the income is accounted for by a specific purpose fund, if the use of the income is not donor restricted, the income is accounted for by the hospital's *operating fund*.

speculator One who deals in *risk* and *uncertainty* usually by undertaking the purchase or sale of foreign exchange, a security, a commodity, or a service in anticipation of a shortage or surplus at different times or places, hoping to gain thereby.

spending variance The portion of variable *overhead variance* not attributable to deviation between *standard* and *actual* levels of activity; the overhead counterpart to a *price variance* for materials or a *rate variance* for direct labor.

spinoff (federal income taxes) The transfer by a corporation of a portion of its assets to a newly formed corporation in exchange for the latter's capital stock, which is thereupon distributed as a property dividend to the stockholders of the first corporation. Also, distribution by the parent corporation of the stock of an already existing subsidiary. See *splitoff; splitup* (2) .

split-account system A bookkeeping process whereby accounts are supported by two or more "nominal subaccounts" each containing—and limited to—a single class of transactions, the relationship being similar to that of a *retained-earnings* account and income-and-expense accounts.

split dollar life insurance An agreement between employer and employee whereby the benefits and premiums under an insurance policy are split. Employer pays that part of the annual premium equal to the yearly increase in the cash surrender value with the employee paying the balance. On the death of the employee all proceeds are nontaxable.

split gifts (federal income tax) An election granted by Section 2513 of the *Internal Revenue Code* which allows spouses to treat a gift made by one of the spouses (donor spouse) as if it were made one-half by each of the spouses. Included in the *unified transfer tax*, it was also available under the prior federal gift tax and is intended to help establish equity between donors in community property states and in common-law states. It allows each spouse the opportunity to use the $10,000 per donee annual exclusion provided by Section 2503(b), and the benefit, which reaches $600,000 in 1987, that can be transferred tax free. The election is made for each quarter in which a gift is made and binds the spouses to treat all gifts made in that quarter by either spouse as being made one-half by each.

splitoff 1. (federal income taxes) The transfer to its stockholders by a parent corporation of the capital stock of a subsidiary corporation in exchange for a pro rata surrender of their stockholdings in the parent. Compare with *splitup* (2); *spinoff*.
2. See *splitoff point*.

splitoff point 1. The point in the production process where *joint products* emerge with separate identities from common raw material and other inputs. At this stage decisions with respect to further processing or other disposition of each product must be made. See *process further*.

2. A point in the production process where *joint costs* end and costs traceable to the now separate products begin.

splitup 1. The issue to present stockholders of additional shares of a corporation's capital stock without changing the amount of paid-in capital applicable to outstanding shares. It may be accomplished by calling in outstanding shares and issuing in their stead a larger number of shares each with a lesser par value; or an additional number of no-par shares may be issued pro rata to existing stockholders. Also called a *stock split*. Where outstanding shares are called in and fewer shares issued in their place, the transaction is known as a *reverse splitup* or a *reverse stock split*. A transfer of *paid-in surplus* to *capital-stock account*, accompanying the issue of additional shares, does not alter the character of a splitup, but a transfer out of *retained earnings* (earned surplus) causes the issue to take on the appearance of a *stock dividend*, unless the amount so transferred is small in relation to the fair value per share of the stock outstanding.

2. (federal income taxes) A corporate reorganization whereby two or more new corporations replace a previously existing corporation with the stockholders of the old owning the stock of the new, and the assets of the old being divided among the new; also, a distribution in liquidation by a parent corporation of its stock in two or more already existing subsidiaries. See *spinoff; splitoff*.

spoilage 1. The loss of usable parts or salable products due to defective raw materials, machine performance, or workmanship during the production process. In some cases it is cost efficient to rework the defective part or product.

2. Sometimes used as a general term for all types of losses arising during handling, storage, or processing.

3. The natural loss of raw materials or products such as spoilage of fruits and vegetables.

spooling (computers) The process of temporarily collecting process data for use at some later time. A typical application involves an "output spool" in which an amount of desired output from a disk file is collected and subsequently shipped to a desired printer.

spot cash Cash immediately available as for a purchase.

spot exchange rate The exchange rate for immediate delivery of currencies exchanged.

spot price The price of a commodity available for immediate sale and delivery, the commodity being referred to as a "spot" commodity. See *price*.

spot rate The rate of interest or price being charged currently.

spot sale (or purchase) The sale (or purchase) of a commodity for immediate delivery, often on a cash basis.

spread *v.* 1. To *enter* or *post*, often in detail; as, "to spread on the records"; "to spread over (certain) accounts."

2. Hence, to divide, as in proportion to *benefits* conferred, a *joint cost* or a *common cost* or group of such costs between two or more *cost objectives*.

3. Periodically to allocate a *pool* of such costs to *cost objectives*.

n. 1. The act of journalizing or posting the detail of one or a group of transactions.

2. The excess of selling price over direct cost; *gross profit*; hence, a gross-profit percentage.

3. Underwriters' commission. See *underwriting contract*.

4. The range between the bid and asked prices of a stock or commodity.

5. A combination of *put* and *call*. Also, a transferable option entitling the holder either to buy or sell within a stated period a given number of shares of stock at stated prices.

spread sheet 1. A *worksheet* providing a two-way analysis or recapitulation of costs or other accounting data. If used as a basis for postings, it may be regarded as a journal, necessitating its preservation like any other *book of original entry*.

2. Specifically, a worksheet (see next page) containing an analysis of a group of related accounts or classes of accounts, e.g., horizontal rows representing *debits* and vertical columns *credits*; the amount, if any, appearing at one of their intersections, often obtained by analysis, represents the total of the transactions debited to the account or account class named by the sidehead and at the same time credited to the account or account class named by the column head; when prepared as an exhibit, sometimes referred to as an *articulation statement*. See *cash flow; cost flow*.

stability A tendency to remain in or return to a given state when displaced or disturbed. Stability may also be present in a dynamical system as in, for instance, the tendency to return to a *trend line* or *curve*. The device of "hidden reserves" is closely associated with attempts to produce the appearance of stability, or of greater stability than actually exists, in profits or liquid position, etc.

stabilization A term applied to the pegging or fixing of the price of a security on the market by the issuer or dealer to prevent or retard a decline during the period beginning with the original offering and usually ending with the absorption of the issue by the public. See *pegging; seasoning*.

—stabilize, *v.t.*

stabilized accounting Term used by *Henry W. Sweeney* to describe his approach to *general price level accounting*.

Staff Accounting Bulletins A series of "interpretations and practices" adopted by the Division of Corporation Finance and the Office of the Chief Accountant of the *Securities and Exchange Commission*. The SABs (as they are known) were begun in 1975 and do not purport to represent the official view of the Commission. The SABs are normally more specific and technical than the Commission's *Accounting Series Releases*.

staff auditor 1. A field representative of a public accountant.

2. An *internal auditor*.

standard 1. A mode of conduct of general application arising from *convention* or advocated or imposed by higher authority.

2. A desired objective; a performance goal; a *model*. Established by custom, common consent, scientific, professional, or government bodies, administrative action, or law, usually after extensive observation, experimentation, research, testing, or planning, and often compromised, a standard, whether or not attainable, normally falls short of an ideal and its duration may be limited; its purpose is to serve as a working basis for the institution of procedures that will assure conformity or coordination on the part of a group or groups of persons, within the ranges of technological, institutional, or other limiting conditions under which they operate, and to provide a criterion for a medium of control over future activity when activated by inspection, reporting, publicity, or other device at the level at which enforcement can be best applied. Standards, human-made, grow out of efforts to meet proximate needs and sometimes to justify or freeze attainable practices; often they originate in different fields of interest and may conflict. To keep

M COMPANY
ACCOUNT ANALYSIS, YEAR 19–1
(in dollars, 000.00 omitted)

Account Debit	Credit*	Cash	Invest-ments	Receiv-ables	Inven-tory	Pay-ables	Capital Stock	Sales	Pur-chases	Ex-penses	Totals (Debits)
Cash	(a)		1.0	21.5			20.0			0.3	42.8
Investments	(b)	5.1									5.1
Receivables	(c)							32.4			32.4
Inventory	(d)								5.6		5.6
Payables	(e)	28.8									28.8
Capital stock											—
Sales	(f)			0.8							0.8
Purchases	(g)					28.7					28.7
Expenses	(h)			0.2		6.3					6.5
Totals (credits)		33.9	1.0	22.5	—	35.0	20.0	32.4	5.6	0.3	150.7

* (a), Sale of investments, collections of accounts, sale of capital stock, refund of overcharge; (b), purchase of investments; (c), sales of merchandise; (d), purchases unsold; (e), payment of liabilities; (f), return of sale; (g), purchases of merchandise; (h), bad debt written off, operating expense.

pace with a changing world, old standards may give way to new. See *accounting standard; accounting policy*.

3. Any quality or measure agreed to as between persons, e.g., specified in a *purchase contract*.

4. A cost yardstick. See *standard cost; standard of comparison*.

standard comparison See *standard of comparison*.

standard cost (cost accounting) A forecast or predetermination of what actual costs should be under projected conditions, serving as a basis of cost control and as a measure of productive efficiency (or standard of comparison) when ultimately aligned against actual cost. It furnishes a medium by which current results can be compared and the responsibility for deviations can be placed. A standard-cost system lays stress upon important exceptions and permits concentration upon inefficiencies and other conditions that call for correction; it is usually less expensive to maintain than a *job-order* or *cost-finding system*, for the work of repeatedly calculating the cost of normal production activities is eliminated. To give maximum utility, standard costs must be relatively stable and subject to change only when important increases or decreases occur in the cost of materials or labor or in operating conditions. *Variances* between actual and estimated expense arise in every accounting period; because of inflation, seasonal fluctuations, and other causes, they are usually accumulated to the close of the fiscal year and written off as a general processing expense. A standard-cost system preferably ties in with the financial records.

A standard cost is a form of *estimated cost*; the latter, however, may refer to any prediction of cost, without the discipline in its computation that customarily attaches to standard cost, and in practice it may be subject to revisions as operations progress. Standard costs remain relatively fixed over a period of time except, as already stated, for major changes necessitated by new and severe economic conditions or drastic alterations of production methods. In most systems of estimated costs, the chief emphasis is on *actual costs*, whereas with standard costs a more nearly ideal cost is predetermined as a measuring standard for actual performance. See *basic standard cost; current standard cost; ideal standard cost; normal standard cost; perfection standard cost*.

A standard cost is thus a carefully formulated advance estimate of what a future cost should be under conditions expected to prevail. More specifically, it represents the costs that should be incurred if prescribed procedures are followed. Ideally such procedures should include carefully applied engineering studies of the equipment to be utilized along with its location and maintenance, related work motions and times, types of material to be utilized, etc. While predetermined costs in the form of estimates have long been used by business management, the present-day concept of a standard cost is a product of the *scientific-management* movement. The leaders in this movement have stressed improvements in manufacturing methods, the increased ability of management in exercising *controls*, and the embodiment of approved methods in standards which serve both as goals toward which to work and as measures of performance.

Such standards were a great improvement in the basic data used by management for two reasons; they were based upon systematic observation, measurement, and controlled experiment—all factors which mean a marked increase in *reliability*; and they were recorded and made generally available within the company. These standards are engineering or quantitative standards expressed in methods of operation, units of material, and hours of labor. They are basic standards. See *basic standard cost*.

Since the ultimate objective of improved manufacturing methods is a better product at a lower cost, it was soon seen that basic standards could be translated into cost standards.

In most modern applications, standard costs serve primarily as attainable goals to be striven for in management's attempt to control production. From comparisons with actual costs, variances are computed. These constitute loss or gain occasioned by failure or success in observing the preestablished standards.

Although standard costs may be employed for purposes of cost control without incorporating them into the accounts, experience has shown that their usefulness is strengthened by doing so. Predetermined overhead rates, which were essentially standard costs, were employed for some years before predetermined costs for direct labor and direct material came into use. The bookkeeping techniques generally used are similar to those of the so-called estimating-cost systems. However, instead of adjusting the predetermined costs when the actual costs are found to differ, the standard-cost approach has viewed standard costs as "command" costs through managerial action.

A variety of terms for what are now generally called standard costs are found in the early literature on the subject.

In cost systems where the primary objective is to provide data to be used by management in exercising controls over costs, the following features are evident:

1. The primary classification of accounts is by responsibility for cost incurrence, with a secondary classification by nature of expenditure. This plan of classification tells, first, who is responsible for the cost and, second, for what the money has been spent. (See *activity accounting*.)

2. Costs to be given expression in the accounts are predetermined.

3. Actual costs are compared with the standard costs. By comparison, it is possible to measure the success management has had in achieving planned costs, i.e., controlling costs.

4. Variances—differences between actual and predetermined costs—are analyzed to determine why they arose.

5. Managerial action is taken to prevent unfavorable differences from recurring in the future.

6. Standard rates are reviewed at least once annually.

Reports to management follow the *principle of exceptions* and emphasize variances. The point of view is that management needs to concern itself with costs only when they deviate materially from those established beforehand as valid costs. Supervisors are thereby freed from the necessity for having to examine large masses of figures to keep themselves informed as to current performance. However, see *favorable difference; management by exception*.

Quantitative standards are usually developed by engineers or others qualified by technical knowledge and experience with production processes.

Types and quantities of materials and labor which should be consumed are usually established. However, the fact that overhead cost represents a variety of different items, many of which are either difficult or impractical to measure closely, commonly leads to the expression of *overhead* standards in terms of dollar cost without underlying quantitative standards. In some cases, quantitative standards are set for important components of overhead cost (e.g., indirect labor) while dollar allowances are used for the remainder.

Not all expenses incurred at the production level may be included in production (factory) overhead. Certain items may be regarded as general expenses rather than production costs, and thus be excluded; e.g., (1) administrative (and sometimes selling) costs identified with certain plants having a large degree of independent management; (2) *sunk costs*, such as depreciation expense, over which local production management has little or no control; (3) research-and-development expense and other costs that have been identified with other functional activities (e.g., customer service) at the scene of production or elsewhere and are under external controls. Determining the content and boundaries of overhead flowing into product costs is thus a responsibility and function exercised at a higher level of management.

Standards for nonmanufacturing activities are set in a similar manner when standards are applied to such operations. For example, standard quantities are set for materials used in packing products for shipment, and operation time standards are determined for shipping-department labor. Time standards may also be set for typing, posting entries, and other repetitive clerical operations. Activities of field sales personnel, technical staff employees, and executives are usually so varied that reliable standards are difficult to set. See *work sampling*.

Problems of coordinating standard costs with the accounts arise when the standard costs are used as a basis of reporting.

Cost systems with standard costs incorporated into the accounts follow the general procedure outlined below:

1. Actual costs of cost factors used in manufacturing are charged to variance or clearing accounts.

2. Work-in-process accounts are debited the variance accounts credited with standard cost of production. Variance balances accumulate for the fiscal period.

3. Transfers from work-in-process to finished-goods accounts are made at standard cost, leaving the work-in-process inventory at standard cost.

4. Transfers from finished-goods inventory to cost-of-goods-sold accounts are made at standard cost, leaving the finished-goods inventory at standard cost.

5. Balances in the variance accounts are closed to cost of goods sold or prorated between inventories and cost of goods sold.

Process methods are generally followed where standard costs are in use. Standard costs suffice for costs of individual products or orders. Actual costs are accumulated only as totals by elements and departments. However, where desired, actual costs can be accumulated by job orders and comparisons of actual and standard cost can be determined for each order.

Raw materials are frequently costed at standard prices on receipt of the materials. Hence, the raw-materials inventory is stated at standard cost and the material-price variance is developed and absorbed in the period in which the materials are purchased.

Under a different bookkeeping routine sometimes used, charges to work in process for direct materials and direct labor are made at actual cost. Credits to work-in-process account are entered for the standard cost of production completed and transferred, and for the closing inventory of work in process. The remaining balance in the work-in-process account then represents the variances from standard cost.

For bookkeeping purposes, variances need be determined only at the close of the period. The number and classification can be limited to those considered necessary for purposes of variance disposal. For this reason, variance accounts are usually few in number, although numerous variances may be calculated and reported statistically. For purposes of cost control, variances should be known as soon as possible after the event which caused them to arise. It is also desirable to report them at their source. Therefore, variance reports are generally prepared to inform operating management of variances on a current basis. Examples are reports of labor variances (often reported daily), of scrap and spoilage, and of departmental-overhead-expense variances. Periodic summaries of these reports may later serve as a basis for accounting entries.

The method of determining actual cost through the use of ratios to base is a form of averaging, and the resulting actual costs are average costs. In setting up the inventory accounts, care is taken to avoid grouping together materials or products exhibiting diverse cost fluctuations, for otherwise the ratios made may be distorted.

Variances are unabsorbed cost balances which may be viewed either as *period costs*, to be charged in their entirety against income of the period in which they arise, or as product costs, to be divided at the end of the period between inventories and cost of goods sold. Under the first of these views, inventories are costed at standard cost of the products contained therein. Either method is generally acceptable provided it has been consistently employed from year to year.

Opponents of standard costs for inventories may, however, accept standard costs for measuring efficiency, facilitating bookkeeping, and disclosing variances due to idle plant capacity. Variances arising from other causes are excluded from the general accounts or proportionately divided between inventories and cost of goods sold.

Inventories priced at standard cost are subject to the usual end-of-period adjustments for obsolescence, physical condition, and realizable value (see *inventory valuation*). A reduction in book costs to a lower market figure is often accomplished by adjusting inventories to revised standard costs. Thus, a decrease in material price is reflected in a new standard cost at which the costing inventory is stated. In general, the use of standard costs for pricing inventories offers no special problems, for the comparison with market prices can be applied to standard costs in the same manner in which it is applied to actual costs.

standard costing The process followed in pricing goods sold, and often inventories, at *standard cost, q.v.*

standard-cost system A method of accounting whereby *standard costs* are the basis for credits to work-in-process accounts; standard costs may also be applied to charges of materials, labor, and other costs to work in process, and to physical as well as book inventories; differences between actual costs and standard costs are carried to *variance* accounts. See *standard cost*.

standard deduction (federal income taxes) A deduction which an individual taxpayer may elect in lieu of itemized deductions. See *zero bracket amount*.

standard deviation (statistics) A measure of dispersion; the square root of the average of the squares of the differences between a group of numbers and their arithmetic mean; usually denoted by σ (sigma). Also called "root-mean-square deviation," especially when the deviations are measured from some value other than their *arithmetic mean*.

The ability of an arithmetic mean or other measure of *central tendency* to represent a group of numbers is determined by the amount of dispersion or variation in the numbers. Thus, it is much more meaningful to say that the average variable cost is $50 per unit when this cost is identical for every unit or ranges from $45 to $55 than when the costs range from negligible to very large amounts as from $1 to $1,000.

Although other measures of dispersion, such as *range* and *average deviation*, are available, the preferred measure of dispersion in statistics is the standard deviation, σ, especially when the mean is used as the representative measure. The standard deviation takes into account not only the spread between lowest and highest, but also the intermediate values; it logically relates the amount of dispersion to the arithmetic mean, and leads directly and easily to the statistical relations commonly employed such as the *least-squares method* and related *correlations*.

The mathematical expression of the standard deviation is

$$\sigma = \frac{\sqrt{\Sigma\, f(Y - \overline{Y})^2}}{N},$$

where σ is the standard deviation, which is always positive, Σ is the "sum of," f is the frequency (the number of times each Y occurs), N is Σf or the number of Y's, Y is any value, and $\overline{Y}$ is the arithmetic mean of Y's.

standard error (statistics) The *standard deviation* of a *sampling distribution*.

standard error of estimate (statistics) The standard deviation about a *regression* line, usually denoted as S_y or S_x.

Standard Industrial Classification (SIC) A system for classifying business establishments (generally, individual plants, stores, banks, etc.) by the type of economic activity in which they are engaged. The system uses 1-digit, 2-digit, 3-digit, and 4-digit SIC industry codes, each of which is described in detail. At the 1-digit level, the SIC classifies business activities into 11 divisions: agriculture, forestry, and fishing; mining; construction; manufacturing; transportation, communications, electric, gas, and sanitary services; wholesale trade; retail trade; finance, insurance, and real estate; services; public administration; and nonclassifiable establishments. Each of these divisions is subdivided into 2-digit major groups which, in turn, are further subdivided into 3-digit industry groups. The 3-digit SIC industry groups are still further subdivided by product lines into over 1,000 narrower 4-digit industry groups. Metalworking machinery and equipment (a 3-digit industry group), for example, is divided into metal cutting machine tools, metal forming machine tools, power-driven hand tools, rolling mill machinery and equipment, and so on.

standard labor rate Base pay plus incentives and premiums estimated attainable under efficient working conditions. See *standard cost*.

standard labor time Labor hours of specified quality, determined by an engineering study and required for the production of a given quantity of goods or services or for the performance of a specified operation. See *standard cost*.

standard machine time The time normally required for a machine or group of machines to produce a specified quantity of goods; such data may include setup and teardown as well as operating time. See *standard cost*.

standard material Raw material or a subassembly conforming to predetermined engineering specifications which may cover both quantity and quality. See *standard cost*.

standard method A prescribed set of operations determined by engineering study to be desirable in executing an assignment, work order, or other operation. See *standard cost*.

standard of comparison 1. Any *model* serving as a basis for judgment or evaluation.
2. In the analysis of financial statements, any basis against which income statement and balance-sheet data may be compared. These bases might be budgeted figures or other managerial forecasts, criteria recommended by professional advisers, financial data of previous time periods or of another company in similar circumstances, or the comparison

may be based on *industry ratios* or other *standard ratios*.

3. Hence, deviations from standards, even those painstakingly determined by management for application to special situations, do not in themselves warrant ready conclusions, favorable or unfavorable. The chief function of the continued employment of standards of comparison is to keep management aware of the peculiar and often variant conditions and procedures that reside within its domain of operations. With the passage of time, even increases in departures from standards do not lend themselves to immediate inferences, for the same unprojected events and conditions that have given rise to the variances may have altered the standards themselves. See *favorable difference*.

Both *internal-audit* and *external-audit* procedures call for the use of a variety of standards of comparison as a prelude to *judgments* concerning the accuracy, meaning, and general propriety of financial-statement components; these often lead to reductions or extensions of audit *scope*.

standard of performance A projection of operations and their subsequent appraisal under known or estimated and attainable operating goals, evidenced by a *budget*, programmed output quality or quantity, *standard costs*, personnel limitations, and other imposed conditions. See *function; standard of comparison*.

standard preparation hours A standard value or other measure for *setup time* or *makeready time* determined from an engineering or statistical study.

standard price The price of raw materials estimated to be obtainable by the exercise of prudent procurement practices.

standard profit The net amount that should be earned per unit when a job is executed or a service is performed under a *standard method* employing *standard material* and *standard labor time*.

standard purchase price = *standard price*.

standard ratios Prescribed *ratio* criteria which firms should presumably meet. They are usually *industry ratios*.

standard-run quantity = *economic lot size*.

standard short-form report See *auditors' report (1)*.

standby costs = *fixed cost*.

standby equipment One or more machines or other fixed assets considered necessary to production but remaining idle during periods of offpeak or otherwise limited operations. Where carefully maintained, a standby asset may be subject to a separate depreciation policy—i.e., to a lesser rate of depreciation than that applicable to similar equipment employed full time.

standby underwriting An agreement to purchase the balance of an issue of securities remaining after a portion of the stockholders have exercised their preemptive rights or have absorbed, under an optional arrangement, new securities in exchange for old, as in reorganization or recapitalization following bankruptcy proceedings. See *underwriting contract; underwriting syndicate*.

standing cost (charge, or expense) = *fixed cost*.

standing order 1. An order authorizing broad classes of work that must be performed regularly in the operation of a plant or a division of a plant. Examples: an order for the general repair, upkeep, and maintenance of property and often the standards therefor that are to be maintained; an order for the generation of power, heat, and light.

2. A continuing *work order* directing the production of an item to meet specified inventory requirements, or to fill gaps in a productive period or process.

staple 1. The chief commodity traded in a market.

2. Raw material on hand.

3. A linen, wool, cotton, or artificial fiber; the commonly expressed fiber quality such as length.

stare decisis The legal doctrine that court decisions should stand as precedent for future guidance.

starting-load cost The cost of preparing to operate; cost of designing, tooling, recruiting, and training the labor force before production starts; a term having reference to the opening of a new plant or department, the reopening of a plant or department after a shutdown, or the beginning of work on a new or altered method of production or product. See *lead time; setup time*.

stated capital 1. The amount contributed to a corporation by the purchasers of its capital stock; or, under varying state laws, the portion of the amount contributed by purchasers of no-par-value stock that is credited to the capital-stock account, the balance, if any, being credited to *paid-in surplus*; a distinction, comparable to that accorded *par value* and paid-in surplus. Often the state law or the regulations thereunder require that the articles of incorporation or bylaws disclose the division between the two accounts; in some instances, the decision may be made by the stockholders or board of directors as an issue or a block of no-par-value stock is sold. See *paid-in capital; additional paid-in capital*.

2. *Legal capital*.

stated liabilities *Liabilities* as they appear in the *books of account* or in a *financial statement*. The term is often used when no proof of accuracy exists, as in the case of an unaudited statement prepared from books and records which may be incomplete and may or may not give evidence of errors after an examination has been made; or when the amount of liabilities taken over from partici-

pants in a merger or purchase of net assets is subject to subsequent adjustment.

stated value Stated capital per share; stated value of new stock issued is determined by dividing the stated capital resulting from the new issue by the number of shares issued; this will change if an additional block of shares of the same class is assigned a disproportionate amount of stated capital, the stated value of each old and new share then becoming an average.

statement 1. A formal presentation of account names and amounts, usually in conventional order, or groups of such accounts, prepared for the purpose of displaying financial condition, operating results, and the like.

2. A summary of transactions between a debtor and a creditor for an accounting period, presented by the creditor to the debtor to show the amount due or owing; a statement of account.

3. A *proposition*, sometimes further restricted to statements given under oath.

statement analysis The study of financial statements for making predictions about a firm's economic performance and condition. The principal tools of statement analysis are *ratio* analysis, *cross-section analysis*, or *horizontal analysis*. Such techniques as *comparative analysis*, *common-size statements*, *trend analysis*, and a variety of forecasting techniques from mathematics and statistics can be used. More sophisticated statistical and mathematical models are being employed not only because of the increasing power resulting from progress in these methods but also because of increasing availability of improved electronic computers and computer codes.

statement form = *report form*.

statement heading The title of a *balance sheet* or other *financial statement*; three elements are commonly regarded as a minimum requirement: name of organization, name of statement (or descriptive phrase indicating content, if there is no common name), and date or period. Other title content sometimes found in accounting exhibits includes: (a) name incorporation, an addition common a generation ago when the effect on financial statements of a series of new state business-corporation acts then being adopted was uncertain, but now considered unnecessary; (b) the name of a principal subsidiary or names of principal subsidiaries forming a part of consolidated figures.

statement of account A *report* of *transactions* between debtor and creditor, usually prepared by the creditor, and concluding with the open or unpaid balance, if any. Examples: a monthly bill from a retail store to a customer; a bank statement (here prepared by the debtor).

Statement of Accounting Principles, A A 138-page monograph published in 1938 by the *American Institute of Accountants*. It contains an extensive analysis of contemporary accounting practice and was written by two accounting academics, Thomas H. Sanders and Henry Rand Hatfield, and a law professor, Underhill Moore. It was a controversial publication at a time when the American accounting profession was debating its role in codifying *generally accepted accounting principles*.

statement of affairs 1. Any statement showing the assets, liabilities, and net worth of an enterprise.
2. A tabular projection of the estimated effects of immediate liquidation, a recent balance sheet serving as the starting point. Although prepared principally in cases of actual or pending bankruptcy, it is occasionally employed where a creditor or prospective creditor wishes to observe the results that would follow the enforcement of a claim. Four classes of creditors are commonly

recognized: preferred, fully secured, partially secured, and unsecured, the form of the statement centering about them.

statement of assets and liabilities (or of financial position) 1. = *balance sheet*; these alternative names are occasionally encountered.
2. A statement prepared for an organization that does not maintain double-entry records, or that keeps no records.

statement of changes in financial position A *report* showing the inflows and outflows of funds (resources) with resulting changes in *assets, liabilities*, and *owners' equity* between successive *balance sheets*; a financial report intended to provide a comprehensive disclosure of the financing and investing activities of a company during a particular time period prepared in accordance with *APB* Opinion No. 19. Financial reports containing a balance sheet and income statement should also include a statement of changes in financial position.

For this statement, *funds* are usually defined as all financial resources; however, *funds* may mean cash, plus cash equivalents, or working capital. See *statement of sources and applications of funds*.

statement of changes in working capital See *statement of changes in financial position; statement of sources and applications of funds*.

statement of financial position (or condition) = *balance sheet*.

statement of loss and gain (or profit and loss) = *income statement*.

statement of realization and liquidation A statement showing in summary form the results of winding up the affairs of an enterprise going out of business: the amounts received from the sale of the various classes of assets (realization), the amounts paid toward the settlement of various classes of liabilities (liquidation), and a statement of the operating revenue, expense, and losses for which the liquidator has been responsible.

statement of receipts and disbursements A list of incoming and outgoing cash during any specified period of time; usually classified on an *object* basis; see *cash-flow statement*.

statement of resources and their application = *statement of sources and applications of funds*.

statement of sources and applications of funds A report summarizing the flow of *funds (4)* (= *working capital*) within an organization during a designated period of time, the purpose being to depict, on an accrual basis, the leading events and conditions, and trends and other changes during the period; the source: differences between *comparative balance-sheet* items, supplemented by breakdowns of certain items.

Further breakdowns of balance-sheet and income-statement variances yield a *cash-flow statement*.

Of these three statements, the cash-flow variety, essentially a statement of receipts and disbursements, appears to be best suited as a budgetary vehicle. The sources and applications statement, which follows the form now in use, displays only a partial movement of an organization's available funds during any given period and will doubtless yield in time to the funds-flow form when it is realized that the movement of funds in operations is of equal importance to and is always closely interrelated with the management of the funds that make up working capital.

statement of stockholders' equity (or investment or net worth) A financial statement in annual reports to stockholders which shows the amount of *paid-in capital* and *retained earnings* and the changes therein since the preceding report.

Statements 1. See *Statements of Financial Accounting Standards; Statements of Financial Accounting Concepts*.

2. A series of four advisory pronouncements issued between 1962 and 1970 by the *Accounting Principles Board*. Unlike the Board's *Opinions*, its Statements were not regarded as obligatory. Statement No. 4, issued in 1970, consisted of a codification of *generally accepted accounting principles* then in use by most companies, and it has been, and continues to be, widely quoted.

Statements of Auditing Procedure The term used prior to 1972 to refer to pronouncements now referred to as *statements of auditing standards*.

Statements of Auditing Standards The official pronouncements of the American Institute of Certified Public Accountants relating to external audits by public accountants. These are codifications containing the ten *generally accepted auditing standards* and the various pronouncements and interpretations to be followed in applying them. These statements are published frequently by the *Auditing Standards Board*. See *audit guide*.

Statements of Financial Accounting Concepts Pronouncements issued by the *Financial Accounting Standards Board* that set forth fundamentals on which financial accounting and reporting standards are to be based. They are intended to establish the objectives and concepts to be used in developing standards of financial accounting and reporting. Topics include the objectives of financial reporting, definitions of the elements of financial statements, and measurement of the elements of financial statements.

Statements of Financial Accounting Standards (SFAS) Standards of financial accounting and reporting issued by the *Financial Accounting Standards Board*. These standards are, in effect, rules governing the preparation of financial reports.

Statements of Position A series of opinions on accounting policy issued since 1974 by the *Accounting Standards Executive Committee* of the *American Institute of Certified Public Accountants*. The SOPs (as they are known) are not binding on Institute members but are issued in the public interest and as recommendations to the *Financial Accounting Standards Board*. In 1979, the FASB decided in principle to assume responsibility for developing *Statements of Financial Accounting Standards* on specialized accounting practices that hitherto were the subjects of SOPs, *Industry Audit Guides*, and *Industry Accounting Guides*.

statements of revenues and expenditures 1. A statement identical with an income statement, or with an income statement to which the cost of assets acquired during the same period has been added.
2. (municipal accounting) A statement prepared for a municipal fund or department, except utilities and other self-supporting enterprises, setting forth the revenues earned, the expenditures incurred, and the excess or deficiency of revenues compared with expenditures.

Statements of Standard Accounting Practice A series of official pronouncements issued since 1970 by the councils of several accountancy bodies in the United Kingdom and Ireland. While not binding on companies, the Statements nonetheless possess considerable authority, and the financial press regularly comments on companies that depart from these standards. The bodies whose councils approve the Statements are the *Institute of Chartered Accountants in England and Wales*, the *Institute of Chartered Accountants in Scotland*, the Institute of Chartered Accountants in Ireland, the Institute of Management Accountants, the Association of Certified Accountants, and the Chartered Institute of Public Finance and Accountancy.

The Statements are drafted in the first instance by the *Accounting Standards Committee*.

statistic Any value, such as an arithmetic mean, median, or standard deviation, calculated from a sample rather than a universe. It may, when suitably modified, be used to estimate a universe value or *parameter*. More generally, but loosely, any numerical measure of a physical or economic condition or activity, as a wage, a national-income total, or a summation of assets.

statistical distribution A mathematical function specifying the *probability* of occurrence of any *random* event in a designated system of random events, where the random events are characterized by the relation $P[x_1 \leqslant X \leqslant x_2] = k$. This relation specifies that the *probability* of a chance or *random variable*, X, exhibiting a value greater than or equal to some real number x_1 and less than or equal to x_2 is equal to k, where k is a number such that $0 \leqslant k \leqslant 1$. Such probabilities are obtainable from a statistical distribution defined over all possible values of the random variable.

statistical inference 1. The use of a limited quantity of observed data as a basis for generalizing on the characteristics of a larger, unknown universe or population.
2. The study, methodology, or use of relations between statistics and parameters. See *statistics (1); descriptive statistics*.

statistical quality control The application of statistical science, in conjunction with other disciplines, to the field of *quality control*. The American Society for Quality Control, a professional engineering society, was founded in 1946 "to create, promote, and stimulate interest in the advancement and diffusion of knowledge of the science of quality control and of its application to industrial processes." Like other professional societies, ASQC publishes a journal, *Industrial Quality Control*, and sponsors other publications that serve the objectives of the Society. Among these, the *ASQC Standard A1-1951* defines basic terms and symbols for control charts as formulated by the Society's Standards Committee. A projected standard will define basic terms and symbols for acceptance sampling.

Pioneering work in statistical quality control was undertaken by Dr. W. A. Shewhart of the Bell Telephone Laboratories in the early 1920s as the outgrowth of an investigation to develop a scientific basis for attaining economic control of quality of manufactured product through the establishment of control limits to indicate at every stage in the production process from raw materials to finished product when the quality of product is varying more than is economically desirable. Since that time, and particularly since World War II, the field of statistical quality control has undergone rapid development and extension first in the United States and now in Japan. In the field of accounting, its principles may be applied to budgeting, cost and inventory control, and other fields such as forecasting and financial analyses.

Statistical quality control is divided into two major but closely related parts: (1) process control and (2) *sampling inspection* or *acceptance sampling*.

Process control is primarily concerned with infinite *universes* of repetitive operations, such as continuing manufacture of similar parts; it attempts to analyze production operations both as a means of anticipating and forestalling trouble and as a means of eliminating useless investigations, slowing or shutting down of operations, or resetting of machines caused by variations which may appear significant but are actually only *random* in character.

Acceptance sampling is generally concerned with sampling from finite universes, such as a "lot" of completed or purchased product, for the purpose of reaching a decision, based on the evidence available in the sample, concerning what disposition to make of the lot.

The principal tool of process control is a control chart which serves as a guide for decisions on the process. The principal tool of acceptance sampling is a battery of standard sampling plans providing enough flexibility in lot sizes, sample sizes, and risk control features to make possible the selection of a plan (or plans) to be used on submitted lots for the purpose of reaching a decision regarding disposition of these lots. Choosing a plan is a matter of seeking to strike an economic balance between the risks of making wrong decisions on the lots and the cost of reducing these risks by more inspection. The protection features possessed by a proposed sampling plan are graphically portrayed by its associated *operating-characteristic (OC) curve*; its corresponding inspection cost features are graphically portrayed by its associated average-sample-number curve.

Both process control and acceptance sampling seek to deal with the inherent variability of all phenomena by systematic statistical means. In a group of "identical" parts there is present not only variation resulting from differences in materials and the machines and quality of labor applied in the preparation of the parts, but variation in the quality of inspection and reporting itself.

The use of *tolerances* and *allowances* in manufacturing and design constitutes evidence of widespread recognition of this inherent variability. It remained for statistical quality control to recognize that all variability could be systematically grouped into two classes: (a) those variations resulting from *random* or chance causes which cannot be eliminated and which make detailed investigation of individual variations useless, and (b) those variations which are the result of assignable or nonrandom causes and which are possible and profitable to discover and eliminate. Recognition of these two broad groups of causes made it possible to specify limits of variation of product within which a state of statistical control may be said to exist and beyond which statistical control does not exist. These limits, known as "control limits," (see *control chart*) are constructed so that variations of product within this range should represent only random variations, while variations beyond this range, or other evidence of lack of control (such as trends) imply either lack of control or the fact that the process is moving out of control.

Control limits are not, generally, the same as *tolerance* limits. It has been one of the contributions of statistical quality control to test the feasibility of design specifications against actual production capabilities, forcing, where necessary, alterations in either design or production methods. But tolerance limits and control limits may, under certain circumstances, be combined or coordinated by the use of "modified control limits."

With systematic recognition of the presence of random variation, it has often been possible to substitute sample inspection for 100% inspection, or *screening*. This has resulted not only in reduction of inspection costs but in substantial improvement of inspection results as well. A reduced burden of inspection makes possible the use of a more carefully selected and trained staff and allows this staff to devote more careful attention to the items which are inspected.

Process control and acceptance sampling constitute what have been called the routine "bread-and-butter" areas of statistical quality control. A third area, now recognized to be of fundamental importance in this field, is that of planned investigation in research and development, pilot runs, laboratory work, and direct manufacturing operations. This area of application involves modern concepts and techniques of experimental design and calls for a fairly high degree of statistical maturity on the part of personnel responsible for its initiation and administration in industrial operations.

Not the least of the accomplishments of statistical quality control has been the development of orderly and systematic *feedback* reporting, with concomitant beneficial effects on production and supervisory personnel. From the need for carefully devised records and reports has arisen also the articulation of *standards* which worker, supervisor, and all others concerned with quality of product can respect and accept. Opinion and "judgment" backed by authority and the mysteries of managerial "know-how" are replaced by the careful marshaling and analysis of evidence in a form which is readily comprehended and appraised by all concerned. The result is often not only improvement in quality and quantity of product at reduced cost but improved employee morale as well.

statistical series (statistics) A group of numerical data arranged according to magnitude, time, position, class, or other systematic order; examples: a frequency distribution; a time series.

statistics 1. The discipline that deals with the study of *universes* (*populations*) through the medium of samples and their interrelationships; it is often described as having two branches: *statistical description*, involving the condensation of large masses of material to a few significant features, and *statistical inference*, or the study of the relations between populations and samples. The major problems of statistical inference may be divided into three categories: estimation, the testing of hypotheses, and prediction.
2. A number, such as an arithmetic mean, or

an array of numbers, such as the set from which the arithmetic mean is calculated; usually represented by $\overline{X}$.

3. In accounting practice, "statistics" are sometimes distinguished from accounting data by the fact that the former may not tie in directly with the books of account and thus be subjected to the discipline of double-entry bookkeeping.

statute of frauds Statutes existing in all states requiring certain transactions (for example transactions involving real property) to be in writing to be enforceable.

statute of limitations The limitation set by law on actions that may be taken on matters involving the title of property, contracts, crimes, and torts. Particularly, the period of time set by statutory law within which recovery may be had for a right to which the litigant might otherwise be entitled; for example, Section 6511(a) of the *Internal Revenue Code* provides that a taxpayer may not recover an overpayment of tax unless he or she submits a refund claim within three years from the time the return was due or within two years from the time the tax was paid. Again, Section 6501 of the Code provides generally that no income tax may be assessed more than three years after the return was filed. These limitations do not apply where fraud exists, no return has been filed, or waivers have been signed by the taxpayer and the Treasury Department has extended the period.

statutory audit An *audit* done in order to comply with the specific requirements of some governing body.

stepped cost A cost such as a *semifixed cost* that advances by steps with increased volumes of activity.

stewardship A custodial or management function which carries with it an accountability for the custody and safekeeping of enterprise resources, for their efficient and profitable use, and for protecting them from unfavorable economic impacts including impacts from factors in the economy which are beyond the control of managements such as changes in price levels or technology.

stochastic As applied to a *system* or *process*: developed by chance; functioning on the basis of *probabilities*, usually with an emphasis on chains of conditional probabilities.

stock 1. The legal capital of a corporation divided into shares. See *capital stock*.

2. A stock certificate.

3. = *inventory*.

stock appreciation rights Awards entitling employees to receive cash, stock, or a combination of cash and stock in an amount equivalent to any excess of the market value of a stated number of shares of the employer company's stock over a stated price. The form of payment may be specified when the rights are granted or it may be determined when the rights are exercised; in some plans an employee may choose the form of payment.

stock company A corporation whose capital is divided into shares evidenced by transferable certificates.

stock discount The excess of *par value* over *paid-in capital*; once treated as a *deferred charge*, it is now generally regarded as a debit *valuation account* to be combined with the capital-stock account to which it is related before the appearance of the latter on a balance sheet, or subtracted on the face of the balance sheet from that account. Under the laws of most states, the discount is in effect an unpaid subscription and, in case of insolvency, collection from original subscribers can be enforced. Ultimate absorption of the discount by charging it to earned surplus does not relieve the stockholder of the contingent liability. The liability does not attach to a subsequent purchaser of the stock from the original stockholder unless he had notice or should have known of the existence of the discount.

stock dividend A dividend in the form of shares of any class of the distributing company's own stock. It may be charged to retained earnings, or to any other surplus account legally available for such use. The distribution of a stock dividend charged to retained earnings has the effect of capitalizing past earning. A distribution of shares of another company's capital stock held by the distributing company is not a stock dividend but a property dividend. A stock dividend charged to retained earnings should not be confused with a *splitup*.

stockholder The legal owner of one or more shares of the *capital stock* of a corporation. Stockholders have the rights to attend annual and special meetings or give their voting proxies for such meetings to others, usually a management group. They are expected to authorize or ratify, usually at management's initiative, charter amendments; amendments of bylaws, unless control over bylaws has been passed to the board of directors; a merger or consolidation with another company; sale of a major portion of the corporate assets or business; dissolution of the corporation; assessments on stock; election or removal of directors; approval of acts of directors and management during the fiscal period immediately preceding.

Stockholders, as owners, have the power to establish basic corporate policies, but in the case of publicly owned companies, stockholders only rarely take concerted action except to adopt or approve policies fixed by and originating with management. It is sometimes said that such independent action is exercised infrequently because its possibility imposes restraints on those who would not adequately safeguard stockholders' interests; but the primary cause lies elsewhere: stockholders of public companies have no readily

available means for acting as a unit. Management, on the other hand, has devices in its favor that are supported by law and custom and that tend to perpetuate it: an annual meeting with stockholders that management usually dominates with ease; stock control secured by direct ownership, voting trusts, or proxies; and bylaws that give management technical advantages in meetings and elections. Individual stockholders representing only a minority interest are given the right, by most states, to examine the *books of account* and to procure other information, and the courts have often aided them in preventing undesirable management actions. But for the most part, stockholders who are not numbered among the management play no role in policymaking or in administration; in the average case, stockholders undoubtedly regard their everyday interests as being too far removed from management affairs to justify any active participation on their part. Thus, left to its own devices, management perpetuates itself and the policies it devises.

Individual nonmanagement stockholders, however, occasionally have more influence on corporate affairs than stockholders acting as a unit. A single stockholder or a group of minority stockholders, in possession of factual material and a strong popular or public-service point of view, for example, can be and often has been instrumental in instituting and modifying management policies, sometimes through court action, but more often by publicity.

stockholder of record A stockholder whose name is registered in the corporate transfer books. The term often appears in dividend resolutions, accompanied by a date, the purpose being to provide a point midway between the date of the resolution and the date of payment that will permit a verification of the records and the preparation of dividend checks so that payment can be made at the appointed time. See *dividend*.

stockholders' contributions = *paid-in capital*.

stockholders' equity The recorded *proprietary interests* of stockholders in a corporation, consisting of the *going-concern value* of assets over liabilities to outsiders; the total of *paid-in-capital, retained earnings*, appropriated and unappropriated = *owners' equity*. Where assets have been revalued, the excess from revaluation over *book value* may also be included under this head. See *realized gain, loss; revaluation excess*.

stockholders' equity to total capital ratio A reciprocal version of the *debt-equity ratio*. Its denominator consists of all long-term sources of assets.

stockholders' equity turnover The *ratio* of sales to stockholders' equity. It is used mainly, along with *profit margin*, in analyses of the determinants of *return on equity*.

stock in trade Merchandise held for sale in the regular course of business.

stock on hand The inventory of raw materials, supplies, finished and partly finished product, merchandise, and like items; see *inventory*. A British term.

stock option The right, under stated conditions of time, price, and amount to purchase shares of a corporation's capital stock. Often such rights are given to corporate officers or to underwriters or promoters as compensation for services. The transaction may be one of simple sale and purchase, in which case the recording of the transaction follows ordinary procedures. But where the option is given in part compensation of an officer or employee, the price paid for the stock may be and usually is less than its market price, thus making it possible for the individual exercising the option to have at least a potential profit at the moment of acquisition. Most option agreements provide that the purchaser must retain the stock for a minimum period, thus elim-inating to some extent the possibility of speculation. The amount of compensation is measured by the excess of the market price of the stock over the amount to be paid in by the individual. The time of the accrual on the books of the corporation has on some occasions been the time at which the option becomes the property of the individual—whether thereafter exercised or not. The entry required is a debit to current (compensation) expense for the excess of the market price over the option price and a credit to "Option rights outstanding"—the latter account being a separate balance-sheet item appearing as paid-in capital; should the option not be exercised or exercised only in part, a reversal of the entry is not made, but the credit becomes a part of paid-in surplus because of its character as contributed capital. If exercised, the full credit is made to capital stock. Because the exercise of the option will in most cases be dependent on the existence or emergence of a market price greater than the option price, a more realistic date for the initial entry would be that on which the option is exercised: the date on which the possibility of the stock purchase becomes for the first time anything more than a mere contingency. The date of exercise will usually be the date on which a similarly measured amount becomes taxable income to the individual and deductible expense for the corporation for federal income-tax purposes. In all cases, a full disclosure of the details of the option agreement is required in a balance-sheet footnote. See *restricted stock option; incentive stock option*.

stock-out cost The cost associated with exhaustion of the supply of inventory, including the loss of customer goodwill and lost orders the cost of production shutdowns and premiums that must be paid for special inventory orders, etc.

stock-purchase warrant A privilege (in the

form of a coupon or certificate) sometimes attached to preferred stock or to a debenture or other type of bond, giving an owner the right to purchase an indicated number of shares of stock at a specified price within a specified time. See *warrant; right*.

stock register A corporate record, usually kept by a registrar, containing the details of the issuance of stock certificates and of the disposition of those returned for transfer or cancellation.

stock right See *right*.

stock split See *splitup (1)*.

stock-transfer book A record in the nature of a journal wherein transfers of capital stock are entered, usually for posting to the individual shareholders' accounts in a capital-stock ledger. It is kept by the company or by its transfer agent.

stop order (securities) An order issued by a regulatory body or court suspending the sale of a security until specified remedial action has been taken by the seller. Under federal law and the regulations of the U.S. *Securities and Exchange Commission*, a stop order may be issued by that body suspending the effectiveness of a *registration statement*. Such an order is usually the consequence of the finding, after a hearing, that the registration statement contains an untrue or misleading statement of fact; the order ceases to be operative and the registration becomes effective when the registration statement has been amended to meet the Commission's objections. See *registration* .

stores *Raw materials* and *supplies* (*3*) used in the manufacture and distribution of goods or in the upkeep of plant and equipment. The term is rarely applied to finished goods or materials in process of manufacture.

straddle The purchase of both a *put* and *call* for a single security at the same market price. The purchase of two puts and one call is re-ferred to as a *strip*; and of one put and two calls, a *strap*.

straight-line method The assignment of equal segments of the *service cost* of any item to the benefits to be yielded by the item: a procedure followed in *depreciation* computations and in the *spread* of *prepaid expenses* and *bond discount* or *premiums*. In practice, a *period charge* for depreciation is usually substituted for a more exact measurement of benefits yielded because of (a) its relative simplicity, (b) the presence of only minor differences between the two methods, (c) the impossibility of estimating with any degree of realism the total prospective output of services, as in the case of many types of machinery, or (d) the absence of any readily determinable unit of service, as in the case of buildings. See *depreciation; depreciation methods; period cost; bond discount; cost absorption; deferred charge*.

strap See *straddle*.

strategic planning The process of discovering, evaluating, and selecting among alternatives which will give direction to an enterprise or program. See *corporate strategy*. Usually restricted to major directional considerations as in the following examples: (1) Evaluating whether a proposed acquisition will alter a company's image and thereby divert it from its present line of business. (2) Deciding whether to undertake a large-scale expansion of overseas activities or whether the resources needed for such an endeavor might be better devoted to domestic activities. (3) Analyzing existing and projected competitor activities to assist in deciding whether to move to a *matrix organization* approach.

strategy 1. A *plan* of action.
2. A plan used to govern or guide other plans.
3. A *formula* or *rule* which will unambiguously designate the choice to be effected at every move in any play of a *game*.

The specializations in senses 2 and 3 further distinguish the sense 1 usages as follows: Sense 3 is required for mathematical uses as in the *theory of games* where absolute rigor and unambiguity are required to an extent that may not be desirable for other contexts and uses. Sense 2 distinguishes different layers of *control* and supporting detail as in a *corporate strategy* which governs a marketing strategy, and so on. The sense 1 usage is general, or generic, and covers all of these possibilities and others as well. See also *tactics*.

stratified sampling (statistics) Drawing of *random samples* within strata or relatively homogeneous subgroups of the *population*. Generally, the strata are sampled independently so that sample results in one stratum do not affect sampling procedures in other strata. The data may also be classified into strata on the basis of cost, ease of handling, and other criteria, as well as statistical homogeneity.

strip See *straddle*.

structural analysis The use of *common-size statements* in an analysis.

stub-survivor curve (statistics) A *survivor-life curve* which is not extrapolated to zero survivors, generally because of lack of sufficient information with which to validate the extrapolation.

stumpage 1. Standing timber or the log feet derivable therefrom.
2. The price paid for the privilege of removing timber from land.
3. The portion of the cost of timberland assigned to timber removed.

Subchapter S corporation (federal income taxes) Refers to a corporation which has made an election under Subchapter S of the *Internal Revenue Code* of 1954 (Sections 1371 *et seq.*). In general, the corporation which makes this election is not subject to the corporate income tax for the years in which the election is in effect. The shareholders of the corporation, however, are taxed on the income of the corporation whether distributed as dividends or not. (The undistributed taxable income is treated as dividend income to the shareholders.) Likewise, a corporate net operating loss is deductible by shareholders on a pro rata basis as a trade or business expense.

In order to qualify for the election, a corporation must meet certain requirements. These requirements restrict the number and types of shareholders as well as the type of stock issued by the corporation. Although corporations making the election are sometimes referred to as small business electing corporations, Subchapter S imposes no restrictions on the size of qualifying corporations.

The election of Subchapter S status must be made prior to the 75th day of the taxable year for which the status is to be effective. All shareholders must consent to the election. The election can be revoked in subsequent years by the shareholders of the corporation. See *small business corporations (2); undistributed taxable income*.

subjective 1. Having a meaning or application reflecting the characteristics of an individual, the peculiarities of his or her experience or environment, not independently substantiated: said of an event, fact, judgment, or inference. See *objective*.
2. In a pejorative sense, expressing disparagement of another's view.

subjective value 1. Value assigned to an asset, as by a corporate management, without independent verification.
2. Value not independently determinable because of the impossibility of *replication*, arising from any of numerous causes, such as intractability of materials or lack of adequate records.

subject to A phrase sometimes employed in audit reports to introduce a *qualified opinion*, indicating that the auditor's endorsement of the financial statements is tempered by the existence of a material uncertainty the outcome of which is yet undeterminable, or by the limited scope of the examination.

subject to opinion = *qualified opinion*. See *opinion; subject to*.

sublease An agreement between a lessee and a third party conveying the lessee's right use the leased property.

submartingale A sequence in which the *expected value* at $t + 1$ equals or exceeds the value of the preceding item in the series. This *inequality* condition extends the equation condition which is applicable to a *martingale*. Stock prices and sometimes accounting profits seem to reflect such processes.

subordinated debt A *debt* ranking below those owing to general creditors; such an arrangement may be agreed to in the case of a financially embarrassed debtor where a creditor has faith in the debtor's business future.

subrogation The substitution of one creditor for another, as where an insurer, following the settlement of a loss, acquires part or all of the insured's right of indemnification from third persons.

subroutine (computers) A portion of a main *program* which performs a particular set of tasks usually in more than one part of the program.

subsampling The process of selecting a sample of the items contained in a sample. Also called multistage sampling. See *cluster sampling*.

subschema See *schema*.

subscribed capital stock That part of the capital stock of a corporation against which unpaid subscriptions are outstanding. It is sometimes found in corporate records as a credit account offsetting subscriptions, portions of it being transferred to the capital-stock account (and sometimes paid-in surplus also) as subscriptions become fully paid and stock certificates are issued.

subscription 1. An agreement to buy a security; the contract between a corporation and a purchaser of shares of its capital stock.
2. A written agreement to make a contribution to a fund for a charitable, educational, political, or other purpose.
3. An agreement to pay for a publication or a series of publications to be issued in the future.

subscription right (or warrant) A transferable instrument evidencing the right of a corporate stockholder to buy a proportionate amount of new shares about to be issued by the corporation. See *right; preemptive right; warrant; stock-purchase warrant*.

subsequent event (or condition) An actual or potential major change in financial condition, or in earnings or earning capacity attributable to and normally a matter for future accounting periods. Examples: new litigation; acquisitions and disposals of business and assets; changes in product lines; possible losses from added risks; effects of new government regulations; and so on. *Materiality* is the test of whether such items require disclosure, usually in the form of *footnotes*, in published financial statements.

subsidiary (company) A *corporation* owned or controlled by a *holding* or *parent company*, most often through the ownership of voting stock. See *control (3)*.

subsidiary accounts A group of similar accounts relating to the same activity or object, maintained in a separate record and controlled by an account in the general ledger. Examples: customers' accounts; factory accounts. See *control account; subsidiary ledger*.

subsidiary-company accounting The method followed by a subsidiary company in recording transactions with its parent or controlling company. It is not uncommon among manufacturing and trading enterprises to find wholly owned branches separately incorporated but with assets and liabilities merged with the parent's. Many practical difficulties arise from such situations, including the confusion which results from attempts to prepare financial statements and tax returns of any one of the corporate entities. Not only is it essential to maintain separate records for each subsidiary, but the transactions of each subsidiary should be, as far as possible, on an arm's-length basis; particularly is that basis desirable where there are outside creditors and stockholders. An exception is necessary for a public utility subsidiary against which charges are made by the controlling company or other affiliated company for construction or services, notwithstanding the relative importance of minority interests; under such circumstances, the *public interest*, represented by public utility regulatory boards, generally requires that these less-than-arm's-length acquisitions be valued at their prudent-investment cost or original cost. See *original cost* (2).

A division of the surplus accounts on the subsidiary's books between the period prior to the date of acquisition and the period thereafter, and the indication by directors of the source of declared dividends, are helpful devices in the preparation of *consolidated statements* and in the recordkeeping of the *controlling company*.

subsidiary ledger A supporting *ledger* consisting of a group of accounts the total of which is in agreement with a *control account*. Examples: a customers' ledger; a creditors' ledger; a factory ledger; an expense ledger; a plant ledger; a branch or departmental ledger.

subsidy 1. A grant of financial aid, usually by a governmental body, to some person or institution for particular purposes. See *grant*. 2. = *subvention* (1).

substance over form (federal income taxes) The right of the *Internal Revenue Service* to look through the form of a *transaction* to its substance. Taxpayers may properly structure their affairs in such a way as to minimize their taxes legally. However, if the form of the transaction has no valid business purpose other than to save taxes, the IRS will often be allowed to ignore it. The IRS will, at times, look through a series of transactions (step transactions) and tax the result as though only one transaction had taken place.

substantial authoritative support Statements or expressions of opinion by *authorities* [see *authority (3)*] or by authoritative bodies or an existence of extensively used practices which can be referenced to support particular accounting and reporting practices. Appeal to "substantial authoritative support" by practicing certified public accountant has become less frequent since they can no longer deviate from an opinion of the *Accounting Principles Board* or a statement from the *Financial Accounting Standards Board* on the basis that a client's accounting procedure has substantial authoritative support.

substantial performance A doctrine in equity that permits recovery by a contractor who has substantially performed the contract in good faith in all material particulars.

substantiate To ensure the accuracy of, by the weight of evidence; to *verify*.

substantive test An auditing procedure or test the purpose of which is to obtain evidence about (1) the monetary correctness of transactions or balances that are or should be recorded in the books and records of an audit entity, or (2) the adequacy of disclosures necessary for the fair presentation of the financial statements have been made. Substantive tests may be applied to transactions or financial statement balances; they may be analytical or detailed in nature. Contrast with *compliance test*.

substituted basis The basis of valuation under the *Internal Revenue Code*, Section 1016(b) for (1) property received from a donor, grantor, or transferor—e.g., a partner transferring assets to his partnership—or for (2) replacement property such as property acquired in an *involuntary conversion* a tax-free (like-kind) exchange for shares of stock in a corporate reorganization. The substituted basis in (2) is determined by reference to other property held by the person for whom the basis is to be determined. In (1) it is determined by reference to the basis of the property in the hands of transferor, donor, or grantor. See *carryover basis*.

subvention 1. A grant, as by a foundation to an individual or organization, for some charitable, literary, scientific, or other purpose. 2. = *subsidy* (*1*).

successful efforts method An accounting method used by some enterprises in the oil and gas and other extractive industries in which (except for acquisition costs of properties) a direct relationship is required between costs incurred and specific reserves discovered before costs are identified with assets. Costs of acquisition and exploration activities that are known not to have resulted in the discovery of reserves are charged to expense. Capitalized costs relating to producing properties are amortized as the reserves underlying those properties are produced. See *full cost method*.

successor auditor The *external auditor* of a company who displaces another, *predecessor auditor*.

sufficient condition Property of a *proposition* so related to another that the latter follows logically or is deducible therefrom; hence, the truth of the first proposition is denied if the second is not admitted. Compare with *necessary condition*.

sum 1. An amount, as of money. 2. An aggregate or total.

3. *v.t.* The act of forming such an aggregate or total.

summary prospectus A short form of prospectus permitted under *Securities and Exchange Commission* regulations relating to promotional activity of dealers in SEC-registered securities.

summons A writ issued by a court directing the sheriff to notify the defendant of plaintiff's alleged cause of action and that defendant must answer within a specified period, or judgment by default will result.

sum-of-the-years-digits method (of depreciation) See *depreciation methods*.

sunk cost A past cost which cannot now be revised and hence cannot (or should not) enter into current decisions for increasing or decreasing present profit levels.

sunshine laws Specific legislation passed by states or the federal government providing that meetings of specific agencies must be open to the public.

supplemental actuarial value The amount assigned to years prior to a given date under the *actuarial cost method* in use.

supplemental appropriation (governmental accounting) A Congressional grant of spending power having the effect of adding to an *appropriation* previously approved; made necessary by the anticipated insufficiency of an original appropriation or by the imposition of new powers or responsibilities for which no financial provision had previously been made.

supplementary cost The cost of a product other than *prime cost*.

supply 1. The quantity of an economic good made available for sale by a producer or distributor. 2. The sum total of such quantities made available by all producers or distributors: in economics, a series of prices and the quantity (= rates of supply) of the commodity or service sellers are willing to offer when the price stands at that level or higher represents a "supply curve."

3. *pl.* A classification often used for minor items of inventory, too small or of too little value to classify as raw material; also, items, sometimes not inventoried, but expensed when purchased, and having use primarily in offices, such as stationery, carbon paper, and cleaning compounds; *stores*.

supply price The price that must be paid to obtain over a specified period of time and at a specified place a given quantity (=rate of supply) of a commodity or service. See *supply (2)*.

supporting record A group of cards or ledger sheets that assist in maintaining the accuracy of a *ledger account*.

support price See *administered price*.

surety One who guarantees the performance or faithfulness of another; differs from a guarantor in that he or she is a promissor or debtor under the original agreement and is primarily liable with his or her principal for every default. The guarantor's obligation is a contingent one, and is a separate undertaking.

surplus 1. = *earned surplus*.

2. Stockholders' equity in a corporation in excess of the par or stated value of capital stock: a generic term covering paid-in, earned, and appraisal surplus. Its use in a *balance sheet* requires a qualifying adjective disclosing its nature.

surplus analysis 1. A worksheet or exhibit displaying the sources and disposition of the various forms of *surplus* or of changes therein during a given period.

2. The process of determining the sources and disposition of a corporation's *surplus (2)*.

surplus at date of acquisition = *acquired surplus*.

surplus charge Any expense, loss, or other cost charged to (earned) surplus directly rath-

er than through the medium of the income statement. For the principal classes of such charges, see *net income*.

surplus from consolidation The excess of book value at the date of acquisition over cost at which a parent or holding company has acquired shares of certain subsidiaries, less premiums on the purchase of other shares acquired. On the balance sheet, it appears usually as paid-in surplus; but circumstances may warrant its deduction along with a reserve for depreciation from the amount of fixed assets. See *consolidation policy*.

surplus-fund warrant See *warrant (4)*.

surplus reserve = *restricted retained earnings*.

surrender value The portion of premiums paid or other amount recoverable on an insurance policy or other contract if immediately canceled.

surrogate 1. A person vested with authority to act for another under defined circumstances; as, a corporate vice-president, acting, by virtue of custom, law, regulation, or delegation, as president in the latter's absence or inability to serve.

2. Hence, anything that serves as a full replacement, substitute, or replication of any other thing.

3. Probate judge.

surtax The added tax resulting from a stepped up tax rate applied to income above specified amounts. In federal income taxes the term is generally restricted to the corporate income tax. For taxable years ending after December 31, 1974, and before January 1, 1979, the first $50,000 of corporate income was exempt from surtax. Prior to that the exemption was $25,000. For taxable years beginning on or after January 1, 1979, the term has been abolished and a five-tier tax rate structure has been substituted in its place. See *normal tax*.

surtax exemption (federal income taxes) The portion of corporate taxable income for years before January 1, 1979, which was exempted from the corporate surtax imposed by Section 11 of the *Internal Revenue Code*. See *surtax*.

surviving company An entity which, as the result of a business combination, has acquired the net assets and carries on the operations of one or more predecessor companies. It may be newly organized at the time of the combination or it may be one of the predecessor companies.

surviving spouse (federal income taxes) The surviving member of a married couple. A taxpayer may use the favorable tax rates applicable to joint returns if the spouse died during either of the two taxable years preceding the current taxable year and the taxpayer maintains a household for a dependent child. A joint return may be filed for the year of the spouse's death; the surviving spouse category is therefore significant only in the year following death.

survivor-life curve See *mortality curve*.

suspense account An account in which receipts or disbursements are temporarily carried pending their identification. It does not appear in financial statements.

suspension (of the sale of securities) See *stop order*.

sustain = *incur*.

Sweeney, Henry W. (1898-1967) An accounting and tax practitioner who is regarded as the author of the first definitive work on general price level accounting in the United States. His pioneering book, *Stabilized Accounting*, was published in 1936 and reprinted twice; it was particularly influential in the early years following World War II.

S-X Regulation S-X, the *Securities and Exchange Commission* (*SEC*) regulation that specifies the form and content of financial reports required to be filed with the SEC.

SYD = *sum of the years digits*. See *depreciation methods*.

symbolic logic Any process of *deduction* through the use of symbols representing *classes, systems*, or *propositions*, commencing with and dependent on *postulates, definitions*, and other *assumptions*.

symbolization 1. The assignment of a letter, number, or other mark or character as a title or as a supplement to the title of a ledger account. Each symbol is intended to have the same meaning wherever used and to suggest immediately and accurately the thing to which it relates as well as its place in the classification of accounts. The careful devising of symbols can result in the saving of much time and space in compiling records and in adding to their precision and accuracy. 2. The assignment of a word, typographical mark, sign, name, or linguistic shorthand term to an object that forms the subject matter of an inquiry, as a convenient aid to reference, discussion, or formal manipulation. A symbol is sometimes contrasted with a sign in the sense that a symbol is a conventional sign which has the same meaning or referent for all parties to a discussion. The degree of abstractness in symbolization is determined by training and convenience. Persons untrained in highly abstract symbolization may contrast "symbolic expressions" with expression in ordinary language: e.g., the instruction in common words for calculating a compounded amount as contrasted with the formula $s = (1 + i)^n$. But the instruction in ordinary language is only a less abstract symbolization which quickly loses its initial advantage of familiarity when the calculation is complicated. In accounting, as in other disciplines such as mathematics and logic, progress is facilitated in dealing with increasingly complex phenomena by developing symbolization. The "symbolization of place" denoted by "Dr" and "Cr" in double-entry bookkeeping, for example, has made it possible conveniently and efficiently to deal with a much wider range of problems than was possible under the more limited symbolization of single-entry bookkeeping. By this device more elaborate explanations accompanying many entries under the older and "simpler" system have been dispensed with.

syndicate A term for a joint venture or short-term partnership, applied principally to a security-distribution operation and to other joint undertakings in the financial field. Its existence is often evidenced by an informal exchange of letters among participants, appointment of a manager with specified powers, transacting business and keeping an independent set of books under the manager's direction, and concluding with a wind-up of the business at hand and with a final distribution of the assets.

synergism A relationship, as between two combining companies, such that the resulting value is greater than the sum of its individual parts; e.g., as in 2 plus 2 equals 5, where the 2's represent values of the separate entities and 5 represents their value in combination.

system 1. A collection of related elements, especially when the relations are complex or the elements numerous.
2. A collection of objects or events conforming to a plan; the plan itself.

systematic random selection A means of selecting a *probability sample* in which there is a nonrandom element in the selection process. For example, selecting a customer account at random from the beginning of a file to the fortieth account and every fortieth account thereafter throughout the file is a systematic selection process. Since such a process is not strictly random, it may lead to biased results especially when *serial correlation* is present. See *systematic sampling*.

systematic risk The relative volatility of returns on individual securities associated with the returns on the market as a whole. Since this volatility results from factors that affect all securities, it is a risk that cannot be eliminated through investment diversification. See *market risk*.

systematic sampling (statistics) A *sample* design or set of sampling procedures, frequently employed, wherein sampling units are selected at some fixed and designated interval, e.g., every fifth file card in a file system. A systematic sample qualifies as a *random sample* if the starting element is selected at random and every kth element (k, an integer) of the *frame* is selected thereafter. If a population is of size N, then this population may, where possible, be viewed as decomposable into k samples (k, an integer) of size n; i.e., $N = kn$. In a systematic sample with random start, a number between 2 and k selected at random, the element in the *frame* with this number constituting the starting element in the sample; every kth element thereafter is then included in the sample. A systematic sample design with random start is far easier to execute than a completely *random sample* design—the latter having a probability of selection of the sample of $1/C_n^N$ and the former a probability of $1/k$. See *combination; permutation*. The *sampling errors* underlying a systematic sample are, typically, more difficult to calculate.

system design 1. The deliberate arrangement of the elements and relations forming a *system* such as are involved in *internal control* or *internal check*.
2. The specifications of a *system of accounts*.

system of accounts The classification of accounts, and the books of account, forms, procedures, and controls by which assets, liabilities, revenues, expenses, and the results of transactions generally are recorded and controlled. See *accounting system*.

systems descriptions (auditing) The representation of accounting systems and their attendant controls for the purposes of analysis and evaluation. Generally systems descriptions take one or a combination of three forms: flow charts, narratives, or questionnaires.

systems program See *application program*.

systems strength (auditing) Those elements of an accounting system which constitute controls; i.e., assure the accomplishment of one or more control objectives. See *internal control*; *evaluation of internal control*.

systems weakness (auditing) An absence of controls (see *systems strength*) to the extent that there is a significant risk that the objective of internal control will not be met.

S-Z SEC Regulation S-Z. See *Securities and Exchange Commission*.

table lookup (computers) A technique in which desired data values are looked up in a table. *Logarithms* and interest rates for *present value* calculations are often stored in the form of tables for which table lookups are employed.

t-account A form of account often used for demonstrating the effect of a transaction or series of transactions, or for solving short accounting problems. It takes the general form of the letter T, the space above the horizontal line being used for the name of the account, the space thereunder serving for debits (on the left of the vertical line) and credits (on the right of the vertical line).

tactics A set of *plans* with objectives which are subordinate to other (strategic) objectives and are to be evaluated accordingly. Example: It is planned to lose a particular battle as one part of a strategy for winning a war. The tactical objective is to lose this battle in a manner that will best further the indicated strategy. See *strategy* (2).

takeover The acquisition of a going business by another through outright purchase, exchange of capital stock, or other device; see *business combination*.

tangible asset Any asset having physical existence; any asset other than an *intangible*.

tangible value 1. The worth of tangible assets, such as plant and equipment and current assets: *going-concern value* of assets other than intangible.
2. That part of the value of a business enterprise which can be imputed to its tangible assets.

tare An amount included in the gross weight of an article such as the weight of a truck, barrel, package, crate, or other carrier or container. Net weight is the gross weight less the tare.

target cost = *standard cost*.

target price See *contract price*.

target rate of return pricing Pricing to recover total costs plus a markup on either total costs or invested capital.

tariff 1. A *tax* levied on goods imported or exported. Under the U.S. Constitution, a tax on exports is forbidden.
2. The fares and related rules and regulations applicable to a regulated carrier, as the tariff charged for specified classes of freight shipments.

tax A *levy* backed by the force of laws which unilaterally determine the payors and terms of payment to a governmental unit. Especially any levy imposed for general governmental support as distinct from fees, licenses, tolls, or similar payments for specially identified services or privileges provided by a governmental unit. Levies such as special assessments to pay for improvements which supposedly benefit particular pieces of property occupy an intermediate category which may be identified with one classification or the other on different occasions.

taxable income 1. Income subject to tax by any governmental authority.
2. The amount of income subject to tax under the law.

Tax Adviser, The See *accounting journals*.

tax-anticipation note (or warrant) (municipal accounting) A note issued in prospect of collection of (property) taxes and repaid from them.

tax avoidance Minimization or reduction of taxes by legal means. For instance, by the use of tax shelters, by the timing of transactions, or by careful tax planning in accordance with Judge Learned Hand's assertion that "nobody owes any public duty to pay more than the law demands" (*Commissioner* v. *Newman*, 159 F.2d 848, 2d Cir.1947). The contrast is with *tax evasions* which involve illegal means that go beyond what Judge Hand's statement allows.

tax-benefit rule (federal income taxes) The provision in the *Internal Revenue Code* (Section 111) permitting the omission from gross income of items such as a bad-debt recovery if the related deduction in an earlier year did not have the effect of reducing the income tax paid in that year or any year to which a net operating loss of the year of the related deduction is carried.

tax certificate A certificate issued by a governmental unit as evidence of the conditional transfer of title to tax-delinquent property from the original owner to the holder of the certificate. If the owner does not pay the amount of the tax arrearage and other charges during a specified period of redemption, the holder can foreclose to obtain title. Also called "tax sale certificate" and "tax lien certificate" in some jurisdictions. See also *tax deed*.

Tax Court (federal income taxes) An administrative court comprised of 16 judges whose purpose is the resolution of disputes arising between the *Internal Revenue Service* and taxpayers. The judges normally sit individually and hear tax cases in cities throughout the United States. Access to the court is limited to taxpayers who petition the court within 90 days of the receipt of a statutory notice of deficiency. Although a jury trial is not available in the Tax Court, the taxpayer can petition the court and litigate with the *Internal Revenue Service* without having paid the proposed tax deficiency. Appeal to a U.S. Circuit Court of Appeals is also possible. CPAs who have passed a special examination as well as attorneys may represent a taxpayer in the Tax Court. A small claims division (tax deficiencies under $5,000) will resolve disputes informally without resorting to judicial precedent and without appeal to a Circuit Court of Appeals.

tax deed A written instrument by which title to property sold for taxes is transferred unconditionally to the purchaser. A tax deed is issued upon foreclosure of the *lien* obtained by the purchaser at the tax sale. A grace period is usually allowed during which the owner may redeem property through paying the delinquent taxes and other charges. See also *tax certificate*.

tax election (federal income taxes) In several hundred very specific situations taxpayers are allowed to elect the tax treatment of a transaction or the form or timing of reporting. In some instances an election must be made in advance, e.g., Subchapter S status, while in many cases the election is made by filing the tax return, e.g., method of depreciation. Many elections are binding for future years until a change is permitted by the Commissioner of Internal Revenue, e.g., filing of consolidated returns, whereas others may be changed annually by the taxpayer, e.g., filing of joint or separate returns. A few elections may be changed or rescinded retroactively, even after the return is filed, e.g., filing of a separate return, while many may not be changed after the filing or due date, e.g., filing of a joint return.

taxes receivable (municipal accounting) An account the balance of which represents the portion of current and delinquent taxes levied by a governmental unit remaining uncollected.

tax evasion Avoidance of taxes by illegal means. See *tax avoidance*.

tax-exempt organization (federal income taxes) See *exempt organizations*.

tax-free exchange (federal income taxes) A transfer of assets between taxpayers where one of the taxpayers is not taxed on the exchange. Such an exchange might occur where a taxpayer receives "like-kind" assets in a direct exchange of business assets or in an exchange of assets in certain corporate organizations, mergers, and recapitalizations. (See *Internal Revenue Code*, Sections 1031 and 351 *et seq.*) The gain or loss on a tax-free exchange is not recognized in the year realized, and instead, is utilized to adjust the tax basis of the assets received in the exchange. See *substituted basis* (2).

tax havens Countries which offer permanent tax incentives in order to attract *multinational enterprises*.

tax lien A claim of a governmental unit upon a property pending the payment of taxes levied against it or its owner; a recorded lien.

tax preference (federal income taxes) Selected items of exempt income and deductions, as defined in Section 57 of the *Internal Revenue Code*, which otherwise would cause income to go untaxed, but which are subjected to a special tax treatment under the *minimum tax* or the alternative minimum tax. Included in tax preferences are such items as: the *capital gain* deduction for individuals, excess of accelerated *depreciation* on buildings over *straight-line depreciation*, excess of five-year *rapid amortization* over normal depreciation (e.g., pollution control devices, child-care facilities), excess of *percentage depletion* over the adjusted basis of the property, excess of *intangible drilling costs* over *straight-line amortization*, and certain excess itemized deduction amounts.

tax rate The amount of tax stated in terms of a unit of the tax base; for example, 25 mills per dollar of assessed valuation of taxable property.

tax rate limit The maximum rate at which a governmental unit may levy a tax. The limit may apply to taxes raised for a particular purpose, or to taxes imposed for all purposes; and may apply to a single government, to a class of governments, or to all governmental units operating in a particular area.

tax ratio The *ratio* of income tax expense to net income before taxes. Many analysts will investigate income tax expense further if this ratio deviates significantly from the prevailing income tax rate.

tax shelter (federal income taxes) Any of a number of investments which generate losses, usually due to noncash deductions such as depreciation or depletion, or due to accelerated payments which flow through to individual taxpayers and can be used to offset other income, thereby lowering the individual's taxable income. Common tax shelters include investments in real estate, livestock, and railroad rolling stock.

tax supplement A tax levied by a local unit of government which has the same base as a similar tax levied by a higher level of government, such as a state or province. The local tax supplement is frequently administered by the higher level of government along with its own tax. A locally imposed, state-administered sales tax is an example.

tax table income (federal income taxes) The *adjusted gross income* of a taxpayer reduced by any *itemized deductions* over the *zero bracket amount*, or in some circumstances increased by an unused portion of the zero bracket amount. Taxpayers falling within certain tax table income ranges (generally below $20,000) and having the requisite number of personal exemptions (generally below 9) must use the tax tables to calculate their gross tax. See Internal Revenue Code, Section 3.

tax year The period for which a tax is computed and filed. For federal income taxes a taxpayer must use the calendar year for tax reporting purposes unless a different accounting period has been elected. Other reporting periods which may be elected are any 12-month period ending on the last day of any month, or a 52- to 53- week year ending within a few days of the end of any month. A new corporation, trust, or estate may elect any allowable tax year. A new partnership must elect the same year as that used by the principal partners. Prior permission from the *Internal Revenue Service* is generally required before a tax year may be changed. Such change usually creates a "short tax year" for the months between the close of the old year and the start of the first new period.

Specific rules are provided for the filing of the return for such short period (Section 442, *Internal Revenue Code*).

technical efficiency See *efficiency* (*4*); *efficiency variance*.

technology The state of the art for transforming materials or generating increased value from economic resources.

telecommunications (computers) The transmission of data between one or more computers and remote terminals using communications lines such as are provided by telephone companies or other communications companies.

teleprocessing system The computer hardware and software used in connection with a *telecommunications* system.

temporal method A method of foreign currency translation whereby cash, receivables, payables, and assets carried on foreign financial statements at current value are translated into their domestic currency equivalents at the exchange rate in effect at the balance-sheet date, assets and liabilities carried on foreign statements at historical cost are translated at the exchange rates prevailing when these assets and liabilities were acquired, income-statement items (except depreciation and amortization) are translated at some average of current period exchange rates, and depreciation and amortization expenses are translated at the exchange rate in effect when the related balance-sheet items were acquired. See *current-noncurrent method*.

temporary investment 1. The amount expended for a security or other asset representing the investment of excess cash.
2. *pl.* The title of a *balance-sheet* item classified as a *current asset*. The standard for valuation is cost, or the amount representing current market value, if less, or the value to be received, if liquidation will yield less than cost. Without qualification it may be assumed

to be available for conversion into cash that may be applied to any ordinary working-capital purpose, thus excluding investments held for other purposes, notwithstanding their marketability. The term contrasts with *permanent investments*. See *balance sheet; cash fund*.

tenancy in partnership The form of ownership of partners in property owned by the partnership in states which have adopted the *Uniform Partnership Act*; the legal rights of partners in partnership property.

tenant in common Any one of two or more persons who together own an item of real or personal property, whereby upon the death of one, the share of his or her property is included in the estate, there being no right of survivorship as in joint tenancy. See *joint tenant*. Tenancy in common of a certificate of corporate capital stock is indicated by an ownership inscription such as "James Smith and Alice Smith." See *joint tenant*.

tender To present for acceptance, as in a bid for a contract or a proposal to buy property. See *tender offer*.

tender offer A tender made directly to shareholders to purchase stock, usually restricted by conditions requiring the right to require all or a controlling portion of the company's voting stock at a fixed price per share before a certain date.

tender of performance An unconditional offer to perform a contract in the manner specified and at the time specified. If the contract requires performance of an act, tender of performance will discharge the offeror, whereas if the contract requires payment of money the offeror will not be discharged from performance.

ten-five-three depreciation See *accelerated cost recovery system*.

ten-K (10-K) The principal periodic report filed by most companies registered under the *securities acts*. Filed annually, Form 10-K is divided into two parts: Part I contains information about the registrant and its business; Part II contains financial and related information, including basic financial statements.

ten-Q (10-Q) Form 10-Q is a quarterly report submitted to the *Securities and Exchange Commission* by most companies with registered securities. The primary contents of Form 10-Q are interim *financial statements*.

tentative balance sheet A balance sheet not final as to form or substance, or both, prepared for discussion or other limited purpose

Tentative Set of Broad Accounting Principles for Business Enterprises, A Published in 1962, this was the third in a series of Accounting Research Studies published under the authority of the Director of Accounting Research of the *American Institute of Certified Public Accountants*. Its authors were Robert T. Sprouse and Maurice Moonitz. It was envisaged that this third Study, predicated on *The Basic Postulates of Accounting*, would enable the *Accounting Principles Board* to base its future *Opinions* on a foundation of accounting theory and derived principles.

term bonds Bonds all of which mature on the same date

terminal account A general-ledger or expense-ledger account appearing as an item on a balance sheet or income statement, or as one of a group constituting such an item; a terminal account may be a *primary account* or a *secondary account*; an account in which transactions remain without further reclassification or *allocation*.

terminating decimal = *repetend*. See *rational number*.

term lease An obligation for rental payments on real (and sometimes personal) property over an extended period of years. Three years has been used as a criterion in some cases for classifying leases as short-term or long-term, but the short-term, long-term distinction is no longer significant in accounting for leases.

term loan A form of loan by banks to business enterprises taking the form of five- to ten-year unsecured notes, the proceeds often being used in the purchase of equipment. The agreement with the borrower usually provides for such safeguards as restrictions on additional loans, secured and unsecured, maintenance of a specified working-capital level, management compensation, and dividend limitations. The term may also be applied to similar loans by insurance companies.

terms of trade 1. In general the ratio of the average price of a country's exports to the average price of its imports.
2. The quantity of domestic goods that must be sacrificed to obtain a unit of imported goods.

term structure of interest rates A profile (or graph) of interest rates for current borrowing as a function of term to maturity. For a loan with a given risk, the *yield to maturity* (determined by the market conditions) varies with the term of the loan. The longer-term rates are not necessarily higher or lower than the shorter-term rates, but they tend to vary less than the shorter-term rates.

test 1. A specified procedure or set of procedures, including rules for assembling *evidence*, making interpretations, and determining significance for accepting or rejecting *hypotheses*. A test may be purely logical, as when a criterion of consistency or independence is applied; or it may refer to empirical material (see *fact*) as well. Where the latter type of test is involved, it becomes necessary to recognize that errors are to be expected, but that such errors can be limited to a specified magnitude or relative frequency of occurrence (see *probability*). Generally, in ex-perimental design (see *experiment*), two types of error are traditionally recognized: type I error, rejection of a true hypothesis, and type II error, acceptance of a false hypothesis: by *probability* methods the risk of occurrence of each type of error may be calculated. It has become increasingly common to recognize that indeterminateness, a third outcome, is possible for given levels of risk of these errors. Where indeterminacy results, the implication is that insufficient evidence has been assembled to arrive at a conclusion under the rules of the test so that further evidence should be assembled. See *hypothesis; rule; testcheck*.
2. As applied to the quality of a commodity or of a performance, a *sample* or *sampling*.
v.t., The conduct of a test, as in (1) above.

testamentary Pertaining to a *testator* or his or her estate.

testamentary trust A trust created by will. See *trust*.

testator One who makes a will.

testcheck *v.* To verify selected items in an account or record for the purpose of arriving at an opinion of the correctness of the entire account or record; to *sample*. Provided the selection has been sufficiently *representative*, absence of error or the limitation of error to a given range is regarded as warranting the assumption that the remaining items are of like accuracy or quality. See *sample; test; detailed audit; audit test*.
—testcheck, *n.*

test data approach (auditing) A method of verifying processing steps in an electronic data processing system, whereby data are processed and the computer-produced results are compared to predetermined results.

text (of a report) The narrative supplementing and interpreting a presentation of financial statements, as in a report by an auditor to a client, or by management to stockholders.

theoretical capacity 1. The maximum possible output of a machine or other production unit per time period, assuming no interruptions, delays, or downtime during that period. Also called designed capacity. It is usually achievable only for relatively short periods of time.

2. The theoretical maximum ability of a plant to produce a specified product(s) over a year's time via a specified production method(s) assuming continuous operation of at least one limiting (bottleneck) productive unit 24 hours per day, 365 days per year.

3. The same as definition 2 except that it is determined for less than 24 hours per day and/or less than 365 days per year.

theory 1. A set of *propositions*, including *axioms* and *theorems*, which, together with definitions and formal or informal rules of inference, is oriented toward the explanation of a body of acts or treatment of a class of concrete or abstract operations. In well-defined fields, the support of a theory derives from two considerations: (a) its logical structure with respect to *consistency* and *redundancy* of propositions, as well as its deductive potential, (b) the manner in which propositions dependent on the theory (axioms or theorems) may be placed in correspondence with data incorporated in facts relative to rules of measurement, testing of hypotheses, or more generally accepted "rules of evidence."

Choices between theories rest not only on the seeming fitness of their expression but also on (a) their adequacy in explaining bodies of facts, (b) their tendency to lead to the discovery of new problems and facts, and (c) their persuasiveness in formulating or reformulating related theories and hypotheses. Further discrimination between theories may be made on the basis of *judgments* concerning their *operational* or nonoperational character. For example, some persons have adopted the theory that accounting ought to be "completely" truthful, or "as truthful as possible." Such a theory usually is nonoperational, although it may suggest numerous problem areas for investigation as well as other theories which are highly operational; the conditions of consistency and completeness for such a theory are usually impossible to determine, since its *primitives, axioms,* and *rules of inference* are not often stated in a manner that allows logical examination of the relations between the theory and the theorems presumably deduced therefrom. Without rules of measurement and testing it is impossible to invalidate the theory or delimit its applicability. For the most part, therefore, it is probably better to regard such theories as *heuristic* and more nearly related to *common sense* rather than to logical or scientific analysis.

2. The body of systematic knowledge concerning a field of inquiry or an art.

3. A proposition advanced to guide investigation.

4. (colloquial) A statement rejected as false, misleading, or irrelevant, especially if emanating from a person lacking in practical experience, or from one concerned with only one or a few factors in a situation that cannot be understood or controlled without reckoning with many factors. Those who decry "theory," however, may do so in order to secure a hearing for their own theory which they dub "practical experience" and to avoid the need for the critical examination of *evidence*.

Theory and Measurement of Business Income, The A highly influential book written by two economists, Edgar O. Edwards and Philip W. Bell, and published in 1961 by the University of California Press. Quoted and cited extensively in the accounting literature, the book contains a cogent argument for the use of *current cost accounting* in *financial statements*.

theory of games A mathematical discipline concerned with *strategy* choices among players (= participants) with at least some degree of conflict in their objectives. See *strategy (3)*. As distinct from *gaming, q.v.,* the theory of games is usually concerned with optimal (= best possible) choices from among the strategies that are available.

The following classifications are often employed because of the differing mathematical properties that emerge from them: the number of players (one, two, or *n*-person = more than two players) in the game being analyzed, its reward structure (zero-sum or otherwise), number of moves (finite or infinite), and the state of information (perfect or imperfect) available at each move. The following diagram represents a two-person zero-sum (one player's gain is equal to the other's loss), finite move, imperfect information game:

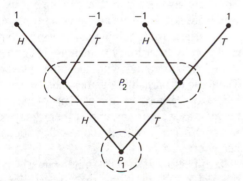

The players are here designated as P_1 and P_2, respectively, and each is positioned relative to nodes that represent a move—i.e., a stage of play where the designated player may effect a choice of an *H* (= heads) or *T* (= tails) branch, as in the game of "matching pennies." The game is scored with P_1 as the player who wins when the coins match. Thus, if P_1 and P_2 both choose *H*, then the play starting with P_1's choice of the branch labeled *H* emanating from his or her node

moves upward along the two left-most branches, where the value "1" indicates the payoff to P_1 for the situation in which the revealed choices show a match.

The payment is from P_2 to P_1 and P_2 is the one who pays the winning amount to P_1, so one's gain is equal to the other's loss. This same zero-sum property would be evident if P_1 chooses *H* and P_2 chooses *T*, in which case the value "−1" represents the resulting payment to P_1 (a negative value corresponding to the amount P_1 loses) from the resulting failure to attain a match.

The fact that there are only three nodes in any such set of choices (called a "play") exhibits its character as a finite-move game.

The broken-line circles and ellipses are "information sets" used to represent the state of information. Thus, since P_1's choice of *H* or *T* is not disclosed, player P_2 does not know whether he or she is on the left-most or right-most node when making choices. Hence this is an "imperfect information" game. If P_1's choice were revealed before P_2 makes his or her decision, then the game would be one of "perfect information." Chess and checkers, for instance, are perfect information games and each node would be portrayed in a different information set.

A collection of branches and nodes arranged as in the above diagram is called a "dendrogram" or *tree*. Any *game* may be represented in this form, and when labeled and interpreted as above, it is called a "game tree." The representation of the game is then in "extensive form."

An alternative representation, called the "normal form," is portrayed in the following *matrix*. The rows and columns of the matrix are arranged so that P_1 chooses a row and P_2 chooses a column with the consequent intersection resulting in a cell showing the payoff from P_2 to P_1. As in the extensive form, a negative value for the payoff is equivalent to

P_1 \ P_2	H	T
H	1	−1
T	−1	1

P_2 receiving that amount from P_1.

A strategy is any rule which unambiguously determines a player's choice at every possible move in any play of a game. The rules "always choose H" and "always choose T" fit this definition. They are called "pure strategies." A "mixed strategy" alternates between H and T in prescribed proportions. The mixed strategy is "randomized" when these choices are effected by a randomizing device—such as the toss of a coin.

The adverse consequences from one opponent's discovering another's strategy are held to a minimum by such randomization since then neither P_1 nor P_2 can know the particular choices in advance. Thus an analysis of best possible strategies is usually restricted to the class of randomized strategies whenever a best mixed strategy is to be used. For the case of pure strategies such randomizations may also be employed, but then it offers no extra protection since the resulting choices are predictable in any case.

The "normal form" of representation displays the payoffs associated only with the pure strategies such as "always choose H" or "always choose T." The mixed strategies are then obtained by mathematical manipulations to ascertain the best *probability* (i.e., randomized) combinations for both players. In the above game the best strategy for either player is mathematically demonstrated to be "Choose H with probability 1/2 and hence also choose T with probability 1/2."

The above game is said to be fair since the expected value is zero for each player under the indicated best strategy choice. It is not the case, however, that all zero-sum games are fair. The zero-sum property refers only to the fact that what one person gains the other loses. A game which does not have this property is said to be "non-zero-sum." Example: two firms competing for market share in a certain product undertake advertising campaigns which increase the total market demand for this product. Hence both may gain in absolute market share even if neither gains in relative share.

More than two players with differing objectives—the situation of an n-person game—gives rise to possibilities for the formation of coalitions in which various persons may cooperate to achieve a greater payoff than the sum of what they could otherwise obtain. This possibility gives rise to side-payment games in which players may bargain for advantageous divisions of this total. This may also occur in "bargaining games" which are not zero-sum and in which a player may refrain from joining an advantageous coalition in order to try to increase his or her share by bargaining with the other player. The topic of bargaining games thus naturally leads to "games of threat" in which all players, as well as any one of them, may be worse off as a result of supposedly rational behavior.

Two-person zero-sum finite games lend themselves to solutions, called "minimax strategies," in which each player can guarantee a minimal return or maximal loss no matter what strategy the opposing player employs. Attempts to provide satisfactory concepts of a solution for other types of games have not been successfully resolved. New and broadened definitions of rationality, however, have been developed which differ from those of classical economics in that the possible behavior of other players is taken into account as part of any proposed theory of strategy choices along with the state of information when choices are to be effected. Also, *gaming* methods for studying actual behavior under varying conditions have now evolved along with new disciplines such as *decision theory* which try to match the value of information against its cost of acquisition as part of a general theory of rational behavior. See *gaming; decision tree; agency; information economics*.

thin incorporation (federal income taxes) A corporation with a capital structure heavily weighted toward the use of loans from shareholders rather than equity investment. Two tax provisions encourage an excessive debt-equity ratio (usually exceeding 3 to 1): (1) deductibility to the corporation of interest paid on debt in contrast to dividends paid on equity and (2) treatment of debt repayment as a tax-free return of capital without regard for the status of earnings and profits which would result in a taxable dividend if paid to an equity holder. If a corporation is considered to be thinly capitalized, a portion of its debt will be reclassified as equity. Factors distinguishing debt and equity are set forth in the *Internal Revenue Code*, Section 385.

third party A person or group including their representatives such as corporations, unions, and government agencies or legislatures which have interests that are affected by transactions to which they are not an immediate party. See *audit; externalities*.

third person 1. A person with whom an *arm's-length* relationship is maintained.
2. A person affected by but not directly involved in a transaction.

three-five-ten depreciation See *accelerated cost recovery system*.

throughput (computers) The total amount of information processed by a computer in a specified time period.

throughput accounting An accounting system

so devised that original *objects* of expenditure in *primary accounts* may be identified in *secondary accounts* and *financial statements*, particularly the *income statement;* see *objective statement; activity accounting; spread sheet*. For this purpose, a *split account system* may be maintained—a procedure that lends itself well to mechanical recording and reporting. See *cash flow; cost flow*.

tickler A file or record of maturing obligations or other items maintained in such a manner as to call attention to each item at the proper time. Examples: in a bank, the note tickler; in an insurance office, the policy-expiration tickler and the premiums-due tickler.

tick marks Checks or other symbols used by auditors to indicate the work done on detailed items subject to their examination. Tick marks are indicated by the individual items presented in the working paper schedules and explained in a legend.

tight standards Standards, as in *standard costs*, or budget levels which are set above the efficient levels of performance normally expected for a given task or set of tasks.

time and motion study A method of determining labor-efficiency standards based on the principles of *scientific management* which usually proceeds as follows: The work required for production is first studied and an attempt is made to render it efficient by means of suitably designed tools and positioning of materials and machines to be used. The work tasks are then subdivided into elementary motions. The latter are then timed either by reference to a standard table of times for these motions or else by a stopwatch with direct observation. Allowance for differences between work and rest periods, machine downtime, and rework and defective materials also enters into the determination of a resulting standard time for performing the task (the process is called ''leveling''). These times then become a basis for *control* and evaluation as in a *standard cost system* or a budget. They also provide a basis for estimating costs and prices in contract bids and related activities. Recent years have seen extensions of these techniques to nonstandardized areas such as selling and administration by means of *work sampling*.

time cost = *period cost*.

time deposit A deposit that cannot be withdrawn for a specified period without incurring a severe penalty.

time draft A draft payable within a specified time after acceptance by the drawee, usually 30 days; an *acceptance*.

time preference theory of interest An explanation of interest as a price people are willing to pay for delaying current consumption in favor of increased consumption in the future, or *vice versa*.

time series A set of quantitative or qualitative measures defined for or related to a number of successive or intermittent time periods. *Trend analyses* are frequently prepared from the numerous time series common to business enterprise.

time series analysis Classification and study of business, economic, or related movements. The term is usually applied to the decomposition of an economic series (such as prices, production, etc., occurring at different times or over succeeding periods of time) into *trends* or *cyclical, seasonal*, and *random* (or other) movements.

time sharing (computers) An operation of a computer such that many different users can perform many different tasks in an apparently simultaneous manner. Actually the computer gives each user an individual slice of time in rapid rotation. It operates so rapidly that it is not apparent that other users are getting a portion of the computer time. See *time slice*.

times-interest-earned ratio The basic, most popular *coverage ratio*. It is an indicator of the margin of safety for interest payments to creditors. It is calculated by dividing the sum of net income before taxes and interest by interest.

time slice 1. (computers) The time interval in which an individual user gets access to the computer on a time-sharing system.
2. A more or less arbitrary interval of time used for analytical purpose as in a *time series analysis*.

time value of money Value derived from the use of money over time to increase its magnitude by investment and reinvestment. It follows that a stipulated sum of money is less ''valuable''—i.e., it has a smaller magnitude—at the end of a period of time than at the beginning when such investment opportunities can be availed of. This also forms the basis of discounting and present value calculations in which end-of-the-period value is measured by the discounted *present value* when the interest rate used reflects the lost opportunities for return in alternate investments. That is, the interest rate then serves as the *opportunity cost* of an investment. See *interest formulas*.

timing difference Difference between the period in which a transaction affects taxable income and the period in which it enters into the determination of pretax accounting income. Timing differences which originate in one period may reverse or ''turn around'' in one or more subsequent periods. Examples of timing differences are (a) recognizing revenues from installment sales at the time of sale for accounting purposes and recognizing revenues as cash installments are received for income-tax purposes and (b) depreciating an asset using the straight-line method for accounting purposes and using an accelerated method for income-tax purposes.

title The right to property; the means by which such right is established.

title insurance A guaranty, by a title insurer or by a political subdivision of a state, that the title to real estate is vested in a named person on a certain date.

tolerance (statistical quality control) 1. The amount and direction (+ or − or both) of deviation from a *basic dimension* named as acceptable in a specification.
2. A permitted difference in dimension between two mating parts. As distinct from *tolerance,* an *allowance* is designed to provide the degree of tightness or looseness required for assembled parts. Thus, parts within tolerance, e.g., a shaft at maximum tolerance and a hole at minimum tolerance, may fail to provide a required allowance despite the fact that each part is within tolerance. Where an internal part is smaller than an external part, allowance is known as "clearance." If an internal part is larger than an external part, allowance is known as *interference*. See *basic dimension*. The American Standard series provides a choice of seven different classes of fits: free, medium, snug, tight, medium force, heavy force, and shrink.

tool 1. Any instrument for manual use that aids a mechanical operation; examples: a saw, a hammer, or other hand tool.
2. A cutting or shaping part in a machine.
3. = *machine tool (1)*.

top down approach An approach to management which emphasize central (i.e., top level) direction and control. In computers it is an approach to system design in which the overall control routine is developed first, after which second level modules which augment the top module are then developed and the process is repeated until the lowest level modules have been developed and tested. The contrast is with *bottom-up approach*.

topical Current (problems, needs, articles, pronouncements); of local or limited application; not related to or assisting in the solving of fundamental problems.

total assets turnover The *turnover ratio* of sales to total assets. It is considered a general measure of asset management efficiency. It is also an important variable in *return on investment* analyses, such as the *du Pont chart system*. This ratio varies greatly from one industry to another, so it should be compared with *industry ratios* when analyzed alone.

total debt to total capital ratio A version of the *debt-equity ratio* in which total assets serves as the denominator.

total equity = *equity (2)*.

tour of offices, plants An audit procedure followed in most audits to gain general background knowledge of the business. This procedure recognizes that in order to evaluate the financial data to be examined, the auditor must understand the physical processes from which they result.

trace (auditing) To ascertain whether an item has been disposed of in accordance with source indications.

traceable cost 1. Any cost whose original transaction character is maintained or can be followed after its transfer or allocation to another account. See *split-account system*.
2. = *direct cost*.

trade acceptance A noninterest-bearing bill of exchange or draft covering the sale of goods, drawn by the seller on, and accepted by, the buyer. Its purpose is to put into negotiable form an open account having a short maturity. To be eligible for discount, it must contain a statement that the acceptor's obligation arises out of the purchase of goods from the drawer, and it may be accompanied by a record of the purchase. Attempts to popularize the use of trade acceptances have not been generally successful in the United States. See *draft*.

trade account payable A liability on open account for the purchase of commodities or services used in the regular course of business.

trade account receivable An amount owing from a customer for goods or services sold in the regular course of business, as distinct from a receivable growing out of other transactions or a receivable differing in form from the ordinary unsecured debtor's account.

trade association A nonprofit organization, local or national in character, serving common interests of enterprises engaged in the same kind of business.

trade credit Terms of credit extended only to members of a particular industry or customer group.

trade deficit The difference between a country's exports and imports when imports exceed exports calculated in an appropriate currency. See *trade surplus*.

trade discount The discount allowed to a class of customers on a list price before consideration of credit terms; as a rule, invoice prices are recorded in the books of account net after the deduction of trade and quantity discounts.

trade investment (British usage) An investment by one business corporation in another often regarded as permanent for the purpose of protecting or enlarging the former's activities; usually represented by a *minority interest* in *capital stock*.

trade liability A current account, note, or acceptance payable for goods purchased and services received in the ordinary course of business; ordinarily, any current liability, excluding wages and taxes unpaid.

trademark A distinctive identification of a manufactured product or of a service taking the form of a name, sign, motto, device, or emblem. Under federal law, a trademark may be registered for 28 years and the registration may be renewed for another 28 years, thus preventing its use by another person.

trade name The name by which a product is known in commercial circles. It may or may not be registered as a *trademark*.

trade note receivable A promissory note from a customer in payment for goods supplied or for services rendered.

trade or business (federal income taxes) See *business* (*1*). Although the term is not defined in either the *Internal Revenue Code* or the Income Tax Regulations, it is a requirement of Section 162 of the Internal Revenue Code that the taxpayer be engaged in a "trade or business" in order for expenses incurred in such activity to be deductible in calculating adjusted gross income. Generally, it must be a relatively full-time activity for the taxpayer. In *Deputy* v. *Dupont* (308 U.S. 488) the Supreme Court ruled that "carrying on a trade or business ... involves holding one's self out to others as engaged in the selling of goods or services." The determination of whether a taxpayer is engaged in a trade or business often involves a factual determination and is a much litigated area.

trade payable 1. An amount owing to a creditor, usually due within a short period, e.g., 30 days.
2. *pl. = payables*.

trade price The price charged to regular distributors who generally buy either continuously or in large lots; usually, the *list price* less *trade discounts*.

trade receivable 1. An amount billed to a customer, usually collectible within a short period, e.g., 30 days.
2. *pl. = receivables* (*2*).

trade surplus The difference between a country's exports and imports when exports exceed imports calculated in an appropriate currency. See *trade deficit*.

trading on the equity The increase in profit return resulting from borrowing capital at a low rate and employing it in a business yielding a higher rate.

trading profit 1. = *gross profit*; the first item usually found in a British *income statement*.

2. Profit arising from speculation, as from purchases and sales through stock and commodity exchanges.

transaction An *event* (*1*) or *condition* (*2*) the *recognition* of which gives rise to an entry in *accounting records*. Expressed in money amounts, a transaction as conceived by the accountant is made up of an equality between *credits* and *debits*, the former representing the source, the latter the immediate identification and disposition.

The moment for recording a transaction is dependent on the nature and occurrence of the *event* or the existence of the *condition*, the customary timing of its recognition, ascertainment of the money amounts involved, a determination of the accounts affected, and an *administrative audit (or review)* of the adequacy of referable supporting data serving as objective evidence of its component elements. For the bulk of transactions, these *decisions,* conforming to general business policy, traditional trade customs, and local conventions, are a vital part of the daily *routine* on which the mechanics of accounting are dependent. See *events and conditions; deal; double-entry bookkeeping*.

transaction cycle A segment of an accounting system containing interrelated types of activities, transactions, and accounts. Major transaction cycles common to many companies are (1) sales, collections, and receivables, (2) payroll and personnel, (3) purchases, disbursements, and payables, (4) inventory and warehousing, and (5) capital acquisition and repayment. Systems are generally described in terms of transaction cycles for the purpose of evaluating *internal controls*.

transactions review Application of review procedures (in contrast to auditing procedures) to a set of *transactions*.

transactions test An auditing procedure which involves the selection and examination of transactions and related documentation as opposed to account balance information (although for certain accounts they may be the same). Such procedures may have either *substantive* or *compliance objectives*.

transcribe 1. To post as from an *invoice* to a *journal*, from a *journal* to a *ledger*, or from a *ledger* to a *trial balance* or *financial statement*; any act of transferring a dollar amount or units of goods or services from one record or account to another.

2. To prepare typed copy from a tape or record.

transfer 1. A passage of property, usually with title, or of service from one *person* to another, in exchange for other property or service; a *sale*.

2. Any passage of property or service between *affiliates*, branches, departments, or locations, usually recorded by the transferee at (depreciated historical) cost to the transferor plus the expense of moving and installation.

3. (government accounting) A conveyance of all or part of an *appropriation* (*1*) from one *agency* or other appropriation unit to another.

transfer agent An agent, usually a bank or trust company, officially appointed by a corporation to make legal transfers of the shares of its outstanding capital stock; the agent may, in addition to keeping the current stock-transfer books, keep the shareholders' ledger, in which case he or she prepares a list of shareholders for the use of the corporation whenever needed for the payment of dividends, the issue of stock warrants, shareholders' meetings, and other corporate purposes. The agent may also distribute the dividends, warrants, and so forth. The office of transfer agent is sometimes combined with that of *registrar*.

transfer and counter warrant See *warrant* (*4*).

transfer ledger A binder for filled ledger sheets or *closed accounts*.

transfer payments (national income accounting) Payments to individuals, usually via government mechanisms, which are not generated from current productive activity. Examples are welfare payments, unemployment compensation, social security, etc.

transfer price The amount charged by one internal organizational unit for providing a product or service to another internal organizational unit; the value placed upon a good or service which is transferred by one responsibility center to another in an organization. Ideally, a transfer price system should be designed to motivate managers to behave in a manner that best serves the overall enterprise and at the same time effectively measures the profit performance for each responsibility center affected. Sometimes transfer prices can be set without interference by centralized management personnel. Problems arise when *externalities* are present. For example, a transfer price which is adequate to cover *marginal cost* plus a contribution to *overhead* in the center may nevertheless cause a loss because an externality effect increases costs to other parts of the enterprise. Conflicts with other parts of *management control* systems also occur. For instance, the purchasing responsibility centers which wish to effect purchases of certain goods or services may be given access to outside vendors as added protection against inefficiencies or gouging from internal units. The latter may have been handicapped in this competition, however, because of their inability to secure management approval for capital expenditures needed to modernize their facilities. In general, therefore, one can expect that transfer price systems will require supplementation and guidance from top management to be successful.

transfer tax (on stocks) The tax levied by a state (principally New York) upon the sale or other transfer of a share of stock.

transition matrix The *matrix* of *transition probabilities* from one set of states to another set of states to which a system might move. The important special case of a *Markov process* provides an example.

transition probability The *conditional probability* of moving from one state to another. In the important case of a *Markov process* the transition probabilities are not time dependent but in other cases, including quasi-Markov processes, time dependent features of these probabilities are taken into account.

translate (foreign exchange) To determine the equivalent, in local currency, of the amount of any item expressed in foreign money by application to the latter of a *rate of exchange*.

translate-restate approach A foreign exchange translation method which takes into account the effects of inflation. This approach requires the translation of foreign account balances to their domestic currency equivalents, and then restatement of these translated amounts to reflect changes in the general purchasing power of the domestic currency.

translation See *foreign currency translation*.

translation gains or losses Gains or losses resulting from *foreign currency translations*.

translator (computers) A *computer program* which converts a series of statements from one language to another. The translator may be used to convert programs from one computer to another. It may also be used to convert a higher-level *programming language* to a lower-level, more basic, computer programming language.

transportation cost The cost of freight, cartage, handling charges, and the like, relating to goods either purchased, in process, or sold.

travel expenses (federal income taxes) Expenses which are deductible for income-tax purposes if incurred by the taxpayer in the active pursuit of a *trade or business* or in an investment capacity. For employees and self-employed individuals, business-related travel expenses are deductible in arriving at *adjusted gross income* (*Internal Revenue Code*, Section 62). For tax purposes "travel expenses" are distinguished from "transportation expenses." A taxpayer who is away from home overnight for business-related reasons may deduct meals, lodging, and incidental expenses as well as the cost of transportation. Travel expenses are also subject to special substantiation requirements and foreign travel expenses are subject to additional restrictions (see IRC, Section 274).

traveling auditor A staff auditor who examines the accounts at branches and other outlying points as an aid to head office control. See *internal audit*.

Treasury bill A noninterest-bearing obligation of the U.S. government, payable to the bearer, maturing in less than a year from the date of issue. Bills are sold at a discount from the face value and the amount of discount constitutes the interest income to the holder of the bill.

treasury bond 1. Bonds authorized but unsold by the corporation.
2. Corporate bonds that have been reacquired from the bondholders and held in the corporate treasury.
3. A coupon security of the U.S. government, usually carrying a maturity of ten years or more from the date of issue. See *Treasury bill; Treasury note*.

Treasury certificate A U.S. government obligation of maturity no more than one year from the date of issue and paying interest on a coupon basis.

Treasury note A coupon obligation of the U.S. government of maturity one to ten years from the date of issue.

treasury stock (or shares) Fully paid capital stock reacquired by the issuing company through gift, purchase, or otherwise, and available for resale or cancellation. Neither gain nor loss is recognized and if held for resale, it is shown as a deduction from stockholders' equity. Treasury stock is not a part of capital stock outstanding; and the term does not apply to unissued capital stock, or to shares forfeited for nonpayment of subscriptions. No dividends may be paid or accrued on treasury stock and no voting rights attach to it.

treasury stock method A method of calculating the diluting effect on earnings per share that would result from the issuance of common stock under option and warrant agreements at prices below the current market prices. The method assumes that any proceeds obtained upon exercise of options and warrants would be used to purchase common stock at current market prices.

treasury warrant An order on the U.S. Treasury to pay a specified amount in the form of an ordinary bank check.

tree A connected graph which has no cycles. See *network; graph*.

trend analysis The averaging of *time series* data, in order that a smooth *curve* showing general growth or decline may be developed for some past period of time. Four methods in common use involve the superimposing of a curve on a graph of the data:
    1. Freehand method. A trend may be fitted (or averaged) by drawing a freehand line on the face of the graph.
    2. Semiaverage method. The data are first divided into two or more equal time subperiods; the simple average for each period is then plotted at the center of each subperiod, and a curve is drawn through the points.
    3. Moving average method. The principle of the *moving average* is applied, using as a basis a *cycle* of years or less.
    4. Least-squares method. The curve is so drawn as to minimize the sum of the squares of the deviations of the data from the curve.

A trend curve is simply an average to which old as well as newly emerging causative factors contribute; it is not a reliable basis for estimating future growth except in those instances where it is known or is assumed that the same factors will influence the future with the same effects as in the past.

trend percentage analysis In statement analysis, a *time series analysis* in which each *financial statement* item in a particular year is divided by the same item in some base year to form an *index number*. The items in the base year are all assigned an index number of 100, and the indices in subsequent years go up and down relative to the base year. Trend patterns, if present, should be more readily apparent in the index numbers than in the original accounting data.

trial balance A list or abstract of the balances or of total debits and total *credits* of the accounts in a *ledger*, the purpose being to determine the equality of posted debits and credits and to establish a basic summary for financial statements. See *double-entry bookkeeping*. The term is also applied to a list of account balances (and their total) abstracted from a customers ledger or other subsidiary ledger for the purpose of testing their totals with the related control account.

Before abstracting a trial balance, as for a general ledger at the end of a month, the bookkeeper makes sure that all the postings have been made in the ledger that are necessary to assure equal debits and credits. If columnar journals or their equivalent are in use, the bookkeeper determines that the column totals crossfoot and have been posted to control accounts in the usual manner, and that all the postings of detail items in the latter part of the month have been completed. Where the accounts contain principally summary postings, as is usually the case in the general ledger of a large enterprise, the postings will be relatively few in number and are easily reviewed for completeness.

Where postings in a ledger are numerous and no rigorous method has been instituted for proving the correctness of individual postings, trial-balance totals may at the outset be unequal, and the bookkeeper is faced with the necessity of locating and correcting the error. A small error, often the composite of offsetting errors, must be paid the same attention as a large one. Not infrequently offsetting errors of the same magnitude may remain undiscovered for a considerable length of time; when one is disclosed, it is necessary to return to the period between balancing trial balances in which the error occurred and search for the matching item. Thus, an error in addition of $100 may have been made when adding the details of each of two accounts, one on the debit side and the other on the credit side; or the errors may be attributable to different causes: for example, one an error in posting, the other an error in bringing down a balance.

Various devices are employed by bookkeepers in locating the more common types of error; these include:

1. A recheck of the trial-balance items with the account balances appearing in the ledger, and a refooting of the trial-balance columns.

2. A difference equal to a single digit may be caused by errors of addition in the ledger; a recheck of the ledger additions and balances since the last correct trial balance may disclose it.

3. Where the difference is divisible by 2, a posting equal to one-half the difference may have been made on the wrong side of the ledger; thus if the trial-balance debits exceed the trial-balance credits by $267.12, it may be that through a clerical error a credit item of $133.56 has been posted in the ledger as a debit. The bookkeeper would therefore scan for that amount on the debit side of the ledger accounts, covering all postings made since the last correct trial balance.

4. The difference may indicate a posting completely omitted; the excess of $267.12 just described may thus turn out to be an omitted credit posting of that amount, and the bookkeeper would search for such an item among the credit entries in books of original entry. At the same time, he would look for items to which no posting references had been attached, since the difference might have been caused by the failure to post two or more items.

5. A difference made up of two integers (excluding zeros), their sum being a multiple of 9, may point to a transposition or slide as now described. Thus, if a debit of $5,396.75 had been posted incorrectly as a debit of $3,596.75, the trial-balance total of credits would be larger than the debit total by $1,800.00; or a credit of $2,459.89 posted incorrectly as $4,259.89 would have precisely the same effect. 18 is twice 9, the difference between the transposed integers is 2, for the reason that the difference between any two digits (e.g., $7 - 3 = 4$) is always the same as one-ninth of the difference between the two digits (when combined as a single number) and their transposition (i.e., $73 - 37 = 36$; $36 \div 9 = 4$). The trial-balance difference divisible by 9 may thus point to its own resolution. Hence, in this case, the bookkeeper would scan books of original entry for debits the thousand digit of which exceeds the hundred digit by 2, or for credits where the hundred digit exceeds the thousand digit by the same number.

6. The preceding paragraph covers an error resulting from a transposition. A slide is the movement of a number right or left one or more decimal points. If the trial-balance difference, particularly one containing several digits, is divisible by 9, a slide may have occurred; to spot the source of the error, the bookkeeper would look (a) for 1/9 of the excess among the ledger postings on the side opposite the excess; if such an item is found,

it may be that ten times the item is the figure that should have been posted; or, if not found, (b) for 10/9 of the excess among the ledger postings on the same side as the excess; if found, it may be that 1/10 of the item found is the figure that should have been posted. Thus, a trial-balance credit excess of $4.68 might mean that a debit amount of $5.20 was improperly posted as $.52, or that a credit amount of $.52 was improperly posted as $5.20.

7. A two-point slide may be indicated if the trial-balance difference is divisible by both 11 and 9; in that event, the bookkeeper would look (a) for 1/99 of the excess among the ledger postings on the side opposite the excess; if such an item is found, it may be that 100 times the item is the figure that should have been posted; or, if not found, (b) for 100/99 of the excess among the ledger postings on the same side as the excess, if found, it may be that 1/100 of the item found is the figure that should have been posted. Thus a trial-balance credit excess of $51.48 (=$52 minus $0.52) might mean that a debit amount of $52.00 was wrongfully posted as $.52 or, on the other hand, that a credit amount of $.52 was wrongfully posted as $52.00.

8. A three-point slide may have occurred if the trial balance is divisible by 999. The procedure to be followed for locating a source of error may be inferred from the two preceding paragraphs.

9. A *spread sheet* or articulation statement may also be used to locate errors.

Trial balances are used in auditing to present details supporting account balances. See *aged trial balance; classified trial balance; working trial balance*.

trial-balance schedules See *trial balance*.

trigger price (international trade) The price of a country's imports below which either *tariffs* or *quotas* will be imposed.

troubled debt restructuring See *debt restructuring*.

true and fair view (British) The phrase "give a true and fair view": the British equivalent of *present fairly* in the *opinion* section of the audit *short-form report*, *q.v.* See *fairness*.

Trueblood, Robert M. (1916-1974) An active practitioner respected as an intellectual leader of the American accounting profession, Robert M. Trueblood was Chairman of the Board and a senior partner in the firm of Touche Ross & Co. He was President of the American Institute of Certified Public Accountants in 1965-1966 and was chairman of the Institute's blue-ribbon Study Group on the Objectives of Financial Statements from 1971 to 1973.

Trueblood Report See *objectives of financial statements*.

true reserve An appropriation of *retained earnings*; a *surplus reserve*.

trust A right, enforceable in courts of equity, to the beneficial enjoyment of property, the legal title to which is in another. The person creating the trust is the creator, settler, grantor, or donor; the holder of the legal title is the trustee; and the holder of the beneficial interest is the *cestui que trust* or beneficiary. A trust may be either express or implied. An express trust is created by specific provisions in a deed, will, or other writing. An implied trust is one where the intent of the parties, although not made explicit, may be inferred from the nature of the transaction; it includes a resulting trust, arising from the nature of the transaction or the relationship of the parties, as where in the purchase of property one person pays the purchase price and another takes the deed, and a constructive trust, where one person in a fiduciary capacity is in a position to gain by fraud or otherwise an advantage for himself at the expense of the person to whom he owes a duty. See *cestui que trust; business trust*.

trust-and-agency fund (municipal accounting) See *fiduciary funds*.

trust deeds An indenture conveying title to a mortgaged property from the mortgagor to the trustee, the latter holding it in trust, as mortgagee, for the owners of the obligations secured by the mortgage. It describes the mortgaged property, the duties, obligations, powers, and rights of the trustee, and the terms of the mortgage; it also contains the transfer of title, and the covenants of the mortgagor to pay principal and interest and to maintain and insure the property, and describes the procedure in case of default.

trust fund 1. A fund held by one person (trustee) for the benefit of another, pursuant to the provisions of a formal trust agreement. The investment of the principal of a trust established under the law is restricted by statutory provisions in the various states.
2. Generally, any asset or group of assets owned by or in possession of one person, but in equity belonging to another; sometimes referred to as a quasi trust fund. When such assets have been mingled with other assets, the balance sheet is so drawn as to call attention to the fact.

turnover 1. The number of times that various assets, such as raw material or other items of inventory, personnel, and the like, are replaced during a stated period, usually a year; the rate of such replacement.
2. See *turnover ratios*.
3. = *sales*; British usage.

turnover ratios Any *ratio* in which sales is the numerator and a balance-sheet item is the denominator. (In the case of inventory turnover ratio, cost of sales may be used in place of sales.) Turnover ratios relating sales to various asset items are intended to be measures of asset management efficiency. However, the purpose of turnover ratios relating sales to various equity items is unclear, so they are seldom used.

turnover tax (also purchase tax) An indirect tax usually assessed on an *ad valorem* basis at one or more stages of the production/ marketing process. E.g., in Canada, the tax is imposed when production is complete; in the United States, a sales tax is imposed when goods are retailed. Imposed at more than one stage, the tax has a cumulative tax-on-tax effect which VAT (value-added tax) is intended to eliminate.

two-bin policy See *reorder point*.

two-class common stock A class of common stock with different rights than the basic ownership common stock which enables its owner to share in earnings potential on sub-stantially the same basis as common stock even though the security may not be exchangeable for common stock.

type A *model*; a class of items, events or individuals with common characteristics. Some theorists have asserted that a typology is the most systematic knowledge possible in much of what is called the social sciences, in contrast to the greater systematization of the physical and biological sciences. See *norm*.

type I error The error of rejecting the *null hypothesis* when it is true.

type II error The error of accepting (i.e., not rejecting) the *null hypothesis* when it is false.

UCC = *Uniform Commercial Code.*

UEC = *Union Européenne des Experts Comptables, Economiques et Financiers.*

ultra-vires Beyond its powers; exceeding legal authority: applied principally to the acts of a corporation in exercising powers or a degree of power that it does not possess under its charter or under the law. Although ultra-vires acts may technically be void, the corporation and parties dealing with it may nonetheless be bound thereby. Thus, a corporation is liable for a tort committed in the course of an ultra-vires transaction, and a party contracting with a corporation, not knowing that the transaction is beyond the corporation's powers, may hold the corporation to this contract if the corporate agent had apparent authority to enter into it.

unadmitted asset (insurance) = *inadmitted asset.*

unallotted appropriation (governmental accounting) The balance of an *appropriation* available for *allotment* for purposes authorized within an appropriation act.

unamortized bond discount The portion of *bond discount* remaining to be *amortized* and added to interest expense for the borrower (or income to the lender) during future periods. Unamortized bond discount is presented on a balance sheet as a deduction from the amount of the liability (asset) to which it relates. Two methods of amortization which may be used are the interest method and the straight-line method. If the interest method of amortization is used, the net liability (asset) represents the present value of future interest and maturity payments discounted at the historical interest rate—that is, at the effective interest rate (yield rate) determined by the price at which the bond was actually issued (purchased); if the straight-line method of amortization is used, the net liability (asset) only approximates that present value. The amount of the periodic amortization is added to interest expense (income) to reflect the effective interest rate at which the bond was issued (purchased). See *bond discount; unamortized bond premium.*

unamortized bond premium The portion of *bond premium* remaining to be amortized and subtracted from interest expense for the borrower (income to the lender) during future periods. Unamortized bond premium is presented on a balance sheet as an addition to the amount of the liability (asset) to which it relates. If the interest method of amortization is used—see *unamortized bond discount*—the net liability (asset) represents the present value of future interest and maturity payments discounted at the historical interest rate—that is, at the effective interest rate (yield rate) determined by the price at which the bond was actually issued (purchased); if the straight-line method of amortization is used, the net liability (asset) only approximates that present value. The amount of the periodic amortization is subtracted from interest expense (income) to reflect the effective interest rate at which the bond was issued (purchased). See *bond premium; unamortized bond discount*.

unapplied cash (municipal accounting) Cash not reserved for a special purpose, available for any use within the *fund* of which it is a part.

unappropriated budget surplus (municipal accounting) The excess of the estimated revenues of a fund for a given period over the appropriations made therefrom.

unappropriated income (institutional accounting) An account set up for budgetary control to which is credited the excess of the estimated income over estimated expenses as shown by the approved budget.

unappropriated retained earnings (earned surplus) That part of retained earnings which has not been transferred to a subordinate account or otherwise earmarked for any specific purpose, thus remaining available for the absorption of dividends.

unasserted claims *Claims* which have yet to be filed or made against an entity by allegedly damaged parties, but which are considered possible or probable because of circumstances or events.

unaudited information Information contained in audited financial statements which has not been audited. This most commonly arises from requirements from the *Securities and Exchange Commission* for specific disclosures for which the audit requirement is waived. See *associated with*.

unaudited statements *Financial statements* issued by a company which the auditor has been engaged to prepare or to assist in preparing. This type of engagement is an accounting service as distinguished from an examination of financial statements in accordance with *generally accepted auditing standards* and the auditor will not have applied *auditing procedures* to the statements which are sufficient to permit him or her to express an *opinion* concerning them.

All such statements with which the external auditor is associated must be clearly marked "unaudited," and they must be accompanied by the auditor's *disclaimer* of opinion in a form such as:

> The accompanying balance sheet of X company as of December 31, 19—, and the related statements of income and retained earnings and changes in financial position for the year then ended were not audited by us and accordingly we do not express an opinion on them.

unavoidable cost Cost that must be continued under a program of business retraction; fixed cost. See *sunk cost*. Contrasts with *escapable cost*.

unbilled cost Recoverable cost identified with uncompleted contracts for goods and services, less advances and progress payments from the contractee: classified separately as a current asset or appearing parenthetically with receivables from customers, no element of profit being included.

uncertain 1. Impossible to calculate exact results or to assign probability measures at any point within a range of possible outcomes. Uncertainty may be said to be present when objective calculations of *risk* are impossible or difficult to make. This usually occurs as a result of either (a) a lack of relevant information or (b) the impossibility of *replication*. Thus, insurers may be unable to calculate premiums required to insure the profits of a speculative venture because (a) they have been unable to acquire or assess relevant information, or (b) the enterprise is too dependent on the personal characteristics of a single individual. See *profit* (2).

2. Improbable.

uncertainty 1. A state of *risk* in which the relevant probabilities are not known and cannot be reliably estimated in advance of a decision.

2. A state in which favorable as well as unfavorable outcomes are to be considered in a decision that must be made in the absence of any knowledge of their probability of occurrence.

unclaimed dividends 1. The amount of dividend checks not cashed by stockholders. Often no record is kept in the accounts of the corporation, and only reconciliation of bank statements or examination of the accounts of the paying agent will show the obligation and the funds available for their payment.

2. Dividends received by stockbrokers or bankers, as stockholders of record for their customers, not claimed by or allocated to the rightful owner.

unclaimed wages Wages earned but not claimed by employees; the liability to employees or former employees for sums left over from amounts originally drawn for payrolls; wage checks not presented for payment.

uncollectible accounts (receivables) 1. Amounts owed to a business, usually expressed as specific accounts or notes receivable, for which ultimate collection is not possible or is highly unlikely.

2. Debtors owing payment to a business, primarily as a result of credit sales, who will not discharge their obligations. See *allowance for doubtful accounts; bad debt*.

unconsolidated subsidiary A *subsidiary* with separate financial statements that are not included in the *consolidated financial statements*. A subsidiary may not qualify for consolidation if control by the parent is temporary, if effective control does not lie with the parent (e.g., a foreign subsidiary with important restrictions imposed by its local government), or if operations of the parent and the subsidiary are not compatible (e.g., a manufacturing company and a bank). Unconsolidated subsidiaries are accounted for by the equity method.

underabsorption The amount by which the debits to an *absorption account* fall short of the total. This occurs in *cost accounting systems* which provide for *allocations* of *overhead* at rates based on an assumed "normal" volume that fails to materialize. See *overabsorption; volume variance*.

underapplied burden A deficiency of overhead costs which results from the use of predetermined rates of allocation. See *overapplied overhead; underabsorption*.

underapplied overhead See *underabsorption*.

underlying company = *subsidiary (company)*; a term usually limited to a subsidiary that owns franchises or other rights that are not transferable but are essential to the operation of the economic unit.

underlying security A *security* (1) issued by a subsidiary company, the return on which is assured by a direct guarantee by the parent company or by a contractual or other relationship.

underwrite To perform the duties of an *underwriter*.

underwriter 1. A person, usually an investment banker, who (a) has agreed, alone or with others, to buy at stated terms an entire issue of securities or a substantial part thereof for resale to the public, (b) has guaranteed the sale of an issue by agreeing to buy from the issuing party any unsold portion at a stated price, (c) has agreed to use his or her "best efforts" to market all or part of an issue, or (d) has offered for sale stock he or she has purchased from a controlling stockholder. The definition appearing in the federal Securities Act of 1933 (Section 2 [11]) is "any person who has purchased from an issuer with a view to, or sells for an issuer in connection with, the distribution of any security, or participates or has a direct or indirect participation in any such undertaking, or participates or has a participation in the direct or indirect underwriting of any such undertaking; but such term shall not include a person whose interest is limited to a commission from an underwriter or dealer not in excess of the usual and customary distributors' or sellers' commission." See *underwriting syndicate*.

2. A person or concern assuming an insurance risk in return for compensation: a profit corporation, or mutual or reciprocal organization; also an agent accepting such business. See *insurance*.

3. The guarantor of the liabilities of any venture.

Underwriters' Laboratories A nonprofit service organization sponsored by the National Board of Fire Underwriters for the examination and testing of devices, systems, and materials as to their relation to life, fire, and casualty hazards, and for crime prevention; if approval is given, a "UL" label is attached to the product.

underwriting contract (securities) An agreement between the issuer of a security and the *underwriter* or underwriters or *underwriting syndicate* that is to market the issue, providing for the outright purchase by the underwriter(s) of the entire issue, or any part of the issue not taken by stockholders in exercising their preemptive rights, or simply for the application of what amounts to the underwriter's "best efforts" to sell the issue to the public. An increase in the last-described type of contract has been brought about as the result of the federal Securities Act and regulations that attach more responsibility to the investment banker and prescribe a 20-day "waiting period" during which marketing conditions may change materially.

underwriting syndicate A group of persons, usually investment bankers, that agrees, pursuant to the terms and conditions of an *underwriting contract*, to assume the risks involved in buying and marketing all or a part of an issue of securities; the group consists of the originating person and participating persons, and from their number a manager is chosen to represent them. The agreement between syndicate members or underwriters is in the form of a contract; its duration generally includes the price-support or stabilization period.

undisclosed principal (law of agency) A principal whose identity is not known to the third party who deals with the agent of the principal. Where the agent acts for a principal without disclosing to the third party that he or she is an agent or the principal's identity.

undistributed profit The profit of a *partnership, trust, syndicate*, or *joint venture* before division among the parties interested; *retained earnings; earned surplus*.

undistributed taxable income (federal income taxes) The portion of income earned by a Subchapter S corporation which has not been distributed to shareholders during the corporation's tax year or within the first 75 days of the subsequent tax year. See *small business corporation* (2). Although not distributed, this income is taxed on a pro rata basis to each taxpayer as a nonqualifying dividend. The amount of income recognized as undistributed taxable income is added to the tax basis of the shareholder's stock for determining gain or loss upon subsequent sale or disposal. Because this undistributed income is taxed currently to the shareholders, it may be subsequently distributed tax-free. See *previously taxed income*.

undiversifiable risk See *market risk*.

undivided profit The undistributed amount of a corporation's net income not yet formally transferred to retained earnings: a term in general use on the financial statements of banks, where undivided profits are often combined with earned surplus under the heading "Surplus and undivided profits."

undue influence Where one party is under the domination of another and is induced by unfair persuasion of the dominant party to follow a course of action which he or she would not have followed of his or her own free will. The party induced may void the agreement entered into.

unearned increment 1. A *windfall*.

2. An increase in the value of property attributable, not to any expenditure thereon of money or effort by the owner, but to circumstances beyond the owner's direct control. See *increment*.

unearned revenue (or income) 1. Revenue (or income) received but not yet earned; = *deferred revenue*.

2. (taxation) Revenue from sources other than personal services.

unencumbered allotment (governmental accounting) Part or the whole of an *allotment* neither expended nor *encumbered*.

unencumbered appropriation (governmental accounting) Part or the whole of an *appropriation* neither *expended* nor *encumbered*.

unencumbered balance (governmental accounting) Part or the whole of an *appropriation* or *allotment* neither *expended* nor *encumbered*.

unexpended appropriation (governmental accounting) Part or the whole of an *appropria-*

tion not yet *expended*, though possibly *encumbered* in whole or in part.

unexpended balance (governmental accounting) That portion of an *appropriation* or *allotment* which has not been expended, though possibly *encumbered* in whole or in part. See *encumbrance*.

unexpired cost Any expenditure benefiting the future; any asset, including *prepaid expense*, normally appearing on a *balance sheet*.

unfair competition The employment of practices by a seller designed to obtain a larger share of the market by false or misleading advertising, adoption and use of a rival's trademark, discriminatory pricing, selling below costs or dumping, preclusive buying of raw materials, establishing exclusive selling contracts with distributors, securing rebates from suppliers, or adopting any other device that unfairly takes advantage of a competing firm. The *Federal Trade Commission* is authorized by law to investigate trade practices and is empowered to issue cease-and-desist orders prohibiting acts in violation of the antitrust acts. Its orders are enforceable in the federal courts. Damaged competitors may bring a civil action under the *Clayton Act* and *Sherman Anti-Trust Act* against unfair competitors for treble damages.

unfavorable difference (or variance) See *favorable difference*.

unfunded supplemental actuarial value = *actuarial liability*.

unified transfer tax In 1976, Congress substituted a single, graduated tax on the privilege of transferring property by gift or at death for the previous gift tax and estate tax. This unified transfer tax applies on a cumulative basis to transfers during lifetime (gifts) and to transfers at death. The Economic Recovery Tax Act of 1981 reduced tax rates and increased the deductions and exclusions.

In order to prevent normal gifts such as

birthday, Christmas, and wedding gifts from being involved in the gift tax, a donor may exclude up to $10,000 of gifts per year to each separate donee. In addition, $600,000 may be transferred tax-free when the 1981 Act becomes fully effective in 1987 (lower in earlier years). Above this amount the graduated rates range up to 50% (in 1985 and after, higher in earlier years) are applied. An unlimited amount of *marital deductions* are available for both lifetime transfers and death transfers between spouses. Married taxpayers may also make *split gifts* to third parties where each spouse reports one-half the gift regardless of which party provides the property to be transferred.

uniform accounting system A system of accounts common to similar organizations, such as those developed or promoted by *associations* and those promulgated by federal and state regulatory bodies such as public utility commissions.

Attempts to establish uniform accounting for an industry or for an industry or for other or all forms of human endeavor have been unsuccessful, at least in the United States, because the principal objective has been the development of elaborate, categorical *classifications of accounts* designed to aid in making comparisons, or to facilitate the construction of macro statistics, whereas the aim in *micro accounting* has been to provide information peculiar to the self-contained self-concerned organization or individual: information not readily adaptable, without substantial adjustment, to a macro buildup.

Uniform Commercial Code (UCC) The most encompassing act formulated by the National Conference of Commissioners on Uniform State Laws—a group concerned with promoting uniformity in state laws. It deals with all phases of commercial transactions, from start to finish, which may ordinarily arise. It has been adopted by all states.

uniformity Adherence to an imposed regulation or established rule or custom.

Uniform Partnership Act (UPA) A body of law proposed by the National Conference of Commissioners on Uniform State Laws intended to cover the basic law of partnerships. The UPA has been adopted in several states.

Uniform Warehouse Receipts Act See *warehouse receipt*.

unilateral contract A contract where the offer on one side is a promise and the doing of an act is the acceptance; a promise for an act. See *bilateral contract*.

Union Européenne des Experts Comptables, Economiques et Financiers Founded in 1951, the Union Européenne des Expert Comptables, Economiques et Financiers (known as the *UEC*) is a federation of more than 25 accountancy bodies from most of the nations of Europe. It issues recommendations and publishes a lexicon of accounting and commercial terms in several languages, an Auditing Handbook, sundry other volumes (including proceedings from its Congresses), and a quarterly, *Journal UEC*.

union shop A place of employment where union membership is a condition of continued employment for eligible workers.

unissued capital stock That part of the authorized capital stock, whether or not subscribed, which has not yet been issued.

unit (of fixed assets) See *fixed-asset unit*.

unit cost The *cost* of a selected unit of a *good* or *service*. Examples: dollar cost per ton, machine hour, labor hour, or department hour. See *cost unit*.

unit credit method See *accrued benefit-cost method*.

unit-livestock-price method The valuation of the inventoried draft, breeding, or dairy animals, or animals raised for sale, of a farmer or livestock raiser whereby the number of each class and age of animal is multiplied by an average unit cost of raising the animal to that age. For federal income-tax purposes, each unit cost employed is expected to fall within a given range.

unit of measure 1. A unit in a scale of *measurement*, such as an inch or a minute; in financial accounting, the unit in which the elements of financial statements are measured—for example, units of money or units of general purchasing power. Historically, financial accounting measurements in the United States and in most other countries were in units of money. In a few countries in which the decline in the purchasing power of the monetary unit has been dramatic, financial accounting measurements in terms of units of purchasing power have been adopted and are in use—for example, Argentina, Brazil, and Chile. See *general price level accounting*.

2. Foreign currency accounting: In U.S. accounting practice any non-U.S. currency in which assets, liabilities, revenues, and expenses are measured.

unit-of-production method (of depreciation) = *production method*. See *depreciation methods*.

unit of sampling A characteristic element in a defined *population* to be subjected to sampling. The sampling unit may be determined by physical conditions, administrative expediency, or cost considerations. From a statistical point of view, the unit of sampling constitutes a classification of the fundamental population under inquiry, where the classification may be broad or may coincide exactly with the units of substantive interest.

In sampling a cabinet file of cards, where the results of specific transactions are recorded, in order to obtain an estimate of the total volume of a set of transactions, a variety of sampling units may be defined. First, the sampling unit may be the individual file card in the cabinet. Second, the sampling unit may be the cards within file partitions. Third, the sampling unit may be, say, three inches of consecutive file cards in the cabinet. In the last two cases, grosser classifications of the filecard population are involved, and the classifications may be considered as *universes* in their own right: viz., the universe of folders or partitions in the cabinet and the universe of three-inch file sections. Finally the sampling unit may be the dollars in an account as in *dollar unit sampling*.

In practice, sample designs may incorporate a hierarchy of sampling units, where the fundamental population of substantive interest is subjected to two or more levels of classification. To each classification level there corresponds a stage of sampling and a population of sampling units. In such a design there will accordingly be primary, secondary, tertiary, etc., units of sampling. In each of the stages, *samples* of the corresponding units of sampling are selected from the defined population of units. An illustration may be given of the sampling of designated economic and demographic characteristics of families in a specified city for a given period. In this case, the city might be classified by enumeration districts according to U.S. Census Bureau criteria; the set of enumeration districts would then constitute the universe of primary sampling units. Second, all primary sampling units might be further classified by individual city blocks or other defined areas; the set of city blocks would comprise the universe of secondary sampling units. All city blocks might then be classified by dwelling units, the tertiary universe. Finally, the set of all dwelling units might be classified by families dwelling in the units. The last or quaternary *universe* coincides with the universe of units on which immediate interest centers.

Given the above four-stage classification scheme, the sample design might specify the following instructions: (a) select a random sample of *m* out of the *M* enumeration districts in the city, (b) select randomly from each of the enumeration districts drawn every *k*th (*k*, an *integer*) block in the enumeration district, (c) select randomly from each of the blocks drawn every *p*th (*p*, an integer) dwelling unit, (d) list the families in all the dwelling units drawn, classified by number of families in the dwelling units. Select randomly every *r*th (*r*, an integer) family from the set of one-family dwellings, select randomly every *s*th (*s*, an integer) family from the set of two-family dwellings, etc. The numbers *m*, *k*, *p*, *r*, *s*, etc., would be determined in the design by reference to certain population *parameters* and specified costs of travel and enumeration. See *random sample; random numbers; probability.*

unit record equipment (computers) Output devices which are used to read and write data from a unit record or IBM punched card. These devices include the card reader, card punch, card sorter, and collater.

univariate analysis See *multivariate analysis.*

universe 1. The whole of the subject matter of whatever is under consideration.
2. (statistics) The entire array or group of data from which samples may be drawn; sometimes referred to as a *population*. A universe may be either (a) existent, such as the total number of persons in the United States at a given moment of time, or (b) hypothetical, such as the values which may be assumed in successive throws of a pair of dice. A *frame* is the medium generally employed for actual sample design and execution since universes and populations do not readily lend themselves to actual implementation but serve rather to clarify what is intended in the selection of a *frame*.

unlimited liability Legal responsibility not restricted by law or contract. Example: the li-

ability of a general partner for the debts of a firm.

unliquidated encumbrance (governmental accounting) An *encumbrance* not paid or approved for payment.

unpaid dividend 1. A dividend declared but not yet paid.
2. An *unclaimed dividend*.
3. A passed dividend on cumulative preferred stock.

unproductive wages A term sometimes employed for *indirect labor*.

unqualified opinion See *auditors' report.*

unrealized appreciation The amount by which a *revaluation excess* is greater than the *book value* of assets at the time of its revaluation and recording, less allocated depreciation provisions thereon.

unrealized holding gain, loss Generally, a *holding gain (or loss)* or *inventory profit* that has not been realized by a *sale* or exchange transaction and thus has not been *recognized* in the *accounts*; for an exception, see *unrealized loss, gain.*

unrealized loss, gain *Income statement* account title to report the change during the period in the amount by which cost exceeds market of the firm's *current* portfolio of marketable *equity securities*. *FASB* Statement 12 requires that marketable equity securities be valued at *cost or market, whichever is lower* and that a *valuation allowance* (a *contra account* to the *asset, marketable securities*) be used to report the amount by which the aggregate cost of the portfolio exceeds its market value. If the amount of the *valuation* allowance for the current portfolio of marketable equity securities increases from the beginning to the end of the period, an unrealized loss is included in *income* although it has not been realized. Further, if the amount of the *valuation allowance* on the current portfolio *equity securities* decreases from the beginning to the end of the period, the change is included in income as an unrealized gain, often in an account called "recovery of unrealized loss on marketable securities."

unrealized revenue Revenue attributable to a completed business transaction but accompanied by the receipt of an asset other than cash or other form of current asset; as, an installment sale (gross revenue) or the prospective profit from such a sale (net revenue). See *realize*. Although expressed on books of account, it does not appear in the *income statement*, unless minor in amount, until the asset has been realized. The term is sometimes confused with *deferred revenue*.

unrecovered cost 1. The portion of original investment not amortized through the process of *depreciation* or *depletion*.
2. Uninsured losses from extraordinary obsolescence, fire, theft, or market fluctuations.

unrelated business income (federal income taxes) That portion of the income of a *tax-exempt organization* which, under Sections 511-514 of the *Internal Revenue Code*, is subject to the corporate income tax because the activity producing the income is unrelated to the exempt purposes of the organization.

unrestricted assets (institutional accounting) Assets which may be utilized at the discretion of the governing board of a governmental or nonprofit entity.

unrestricted funds (institutional accounting) *Funds* which are established to account for assets or resources which may be utilized at the discretion of the governing board. Antonym of restricted funds.

unrestricted random sampling See *random sampling*.

unsecured account A personal account supported by the general credit of the debtor against which no collateral or guaranty is held.

unsecured liability A *liability* for which the creditor holds no security.

unsystematic risk The variability in security returns caused by factors that are unique to a particular firm. This risk can be eliminated through portfolio diversification, so it is considered irrelevant in the determination of market returns on a security. See *capital asset pricing model*; *API (3)*.

UPA = *Uniform Partnership Act*.

upset price The lowest price at which a seller is willing to sell; the initial price asked at an auction before bidding commences; in equity proceedings (bankruptcy), the amount established by a court as the lowest acceptable price for a corporation's assets.

usage variance See *quantity variance*.

use-and-occupancy insurance See *business-interruption insurance*.

useful Having some advantage: sometimes said of an accounting concept, principle, or practice favored over another because of its ease or breadth of application, familiarity, or other cause not always disclosed.

useful life Normal operating life in terms of utility to the owner: said of a fixed asset or a fixed-asset group; the period may be more or less than physical life or any commonly recognized *economic life; service life*. See *depreciation; economic life*.

usefulness 1. The property of being *useful*.
2. That property of an outlay causing it to have continuing value. Originally applied to expenditures for fixed assets, it is often extended to other types of expenditures the value of which is not exhausted within the current accounting period. See *fixed asset; cost recovery; deferred charge; utility*.

user charge (governmental accounting) A charge levied against users of a service or purchasers of a product of an *enterprise fund* or an *internal service fund*.

user cost *Cost* incurred or *loss* sustained on a *fixed asset* as the result of (a) continuing it in service rather than disposing of it through sale or as scrap, or (b) giving it restricted use. See *cost; rent; profit*.

USPC = *U.S. Possessions Country Corporation*.

U.S. Possessions Country Corporation (USPC) A U.S. domestic corporation which has at least 80% of its gross income for the immediately preceding three years from sources within U.S. possessions (excluding the Virgin Islands) and at least 50% of its gross income for the same period from the active conduct of a business. In order to encourage investments in U.S. possessions, the *Internal Revenue Service* allows a special tax credit for U.S. Possessions Country Corporations. See Section 921 of the *Internal Revenue Code*.

usury laws At the state level of government in the United States, maximum allowable interest rates on various types of indebtedness.

utility 1. Capacity for satisfying wants or fulfilling a particular purpose. Because there is often more than one purpose or want in a situation where utility is judged, the same object or act may have both utility and disutility. See *service; benefit; marginal utility; depreciation*.
2. = *public service company*.

utility fund See *fund*.

utilization variance = *volume variance*.

valid 1. Accurate, precise, reliable, authorized, and relevant.

2. True or correct.

3. Enforceable.

validate 1. To test for or to certify or attest to accuracy, *precision, reliability*, and *relevance*.

2. To do what is necessary to make anything effective or legal.

validation (statistics) The determination of whether a test yields desired results with the necessary elements of *accuracy, precision, reliability*, and *relevance*. For example, a test of accounting students may be undertaken to determine their aptitude for the profession. At a subsequent date, the test may be validated by undertaking a survey to determine which of the students subjected to the test had entered upon accounting careers and how their employers had rated them. High positive correlation between the results of the test and the subsequent survey would tend to confirm the validity of the test. But one such test and survey may not be enough. Continued testing and surveying by *replication* with resulting correlation coefficients of approximately the same magnitude may be required to obtain *precision* and *reliability*. Reference

to the career situation toward which the test is oriented confirms the *relevance* of the test; continuation of the tests with approximately the same results confirms their precision and reliability. Correspondence between test and career is a means of determining *accuracy*. A combination of all of these measures is encompassed in the term *validity*.

validity See *valid; validation*. As used in deductive logic, propriety established by a strong inference in which no inconsistency appears.

validity tests (auditing) Auditing procedures or *tests* which are intended to determine that recorded items are *valid*.

valorize By law, regulation, or other governmental action, to give a commodity a value differing from its economic or market value.

valuation 1. = *accounting valuation*.

2. A judgment expressing or implying preference, or relative approval or disapproval, often expressed ''better'' or ''worse'' or ''first'' and ''second'' (see *ordinal number*) but sometimes expressed in money; see *measurement*; when based on a careful weighing of *evidence*, related experience, training, native shrewdness, and other fac-

tors, as is often the case, it may not coincide with a judgment following the formal exercise of logical principles. Valuation methods and bases are numerous and varied. The judgment may be expressed quantitatively and in monetary terms, as in a bid or offer or acceptance, an assessment of real estate, or a balance-sheet or other financial-statement expression. Application may be made to a single asset, a group of assets, or an entire enterprise, as determined by various bases and methods. See *going-concern value; liquidation value; cost; cost basis; cost of reproduction; present value; market value*.

valuation account (or reserve) An *account* which partly or wholly offsets one or more other accounts; for example, accumulated depreciation is a valuation account related to specified depreciable assets and allowance for bad debts is a valuation account related to accounts receivable. If a valuation account is deducted from the related asset or liability it is sometimes referred to as a contra-asset or contra-liability account. See *contra account*.

valuation allowance See *valuation account*.

valuation excess = *unrealized appreciation*.

valuation reserve = *valuation account*

value *n*. 1. Any preferred object or interest there in.
2. Attributed worth, expressed in money and applied to a particular asset, as the value of an automobile; to services rendered, as the value of a man's labor; to a group of assets, as the value of a company's patents; or to an entire business unit, as the value of a plant or business enterprise. Without qualification or more limited definition, including specific, operationally feasible, and generally agreed-to rules for measurement, the term has only subjective significance, and should not be confused with, even though often identified with and measured by, cost. See *accounting valuation; cost basis*.

When market value is less than cost and the cost of an inventory item is reduced to an amount equal to market in accordance with common inventory-valuation procedures, it is often said that the "value" adopted is market. However, since the practice is not to raise cost to market if market is greater than cost, it is apparent that the value basis is still cost: i.e., original cost has been brought down to a fractional-cost basis justified by— rather than valued at—market. See *inventory valuation*. A similar argument applies to the book value of fixed assets—cost less accumulated depreciation, the last-named being the fraction of cost estimated to have been consumed, absorbed as an operating expense; the net figure is the cost balance carried into—and presumably benefiting—succeeding periods.
3. Hence, loosely, the amount at which an item appears in the books or on a financial statement; cost, or a portion of cost judged to be of benefit to one or more future periods.
4. (economics) The quantity of other goods (or money) required to be given in exchange for a particular good; a *rate of exchange*; the monetary measure of exchangeability of a good; an economic phenomenon based on the process of *exchange* in monetary terms in a market. The term is closely related to the concept of price, the monetary measure of exchangeability of one unit. The value of a quantity of a product is found by multiplying quantity by price.
v. 1. To express individual relative preference for an object or mode of conduct.
2. To assign a monetary amount to an asset or a claim.

value added 1. Any of the segments of the selling price of a commodity or service attributable to the present or a prior stage for its origin: thus the price (e.g., $10) paid by the consumer of a given product may be assumed to have its origin in the respective selling prices of (a) the "producer" of a component raw material—e.g., an ore ($2); (b) the "processor" of the raw material, who disposes of the output at a price ($6) that includes processing costs and profit; (c) the "distributor," who wholesales the product ($7); and (d) the "retailer," who in turn retails the product ($10) to the "consumer." Hence, by omitting successive costs of constituent materials and services which have already been accounted for as sales, these four stages may be said to have contributed "added (dollars of) value" of 2, 4, 1, and 3, respectively, for the total (and only the total) final selling price of $10.

2. The contribution to *gross national product* of an *accounting unit* to the economic activity of a nation, perhaps subdivided into domestic and foreign trade components.

value-added statement 1. A report showing the amount and sources of *value added* during some specified period of time. An illustrative example is shown on p. 531.

2. When present, construction of plant and equipment with a company's own (*force account*) labor minus materials and supplies used in such construction will need to be included in order to complete the above as a statement of contribution to *gross national product* during the period. See *value added (1)*. The reference to operations is then omitted from the title of the statement.

3. A value-added statement for tax purposes, an example of which appears below.

(Adopted from the statement on p. 531.) See *value added (1)*. It omits construction as well as increments (decrements) in finished goods and work-in-process inventories.

The $500,000 net in the example below may be left without any further description, as above, or it may be distributed in detail, as before, or an in-between course may be elected by noting that this amount was distributed to employees, stockholders, other providers of capital, and government (corporate income tax = $100,000). The $50,000 reduction in going from the first to the second statement is due to the omission of the finished goods and work-in-process inventory change with a resulting equal reduction in employee wages and to pension contributions (including FICA).

value-added tax (VAT) A percentage tax on the *value added* of a commodity or service as each constituent state of its production and distribution is completed: essentially a sales tax divided among the *economic units* contributing to the production and availability of the commodity or service. As compared with the more common form of *sales* or *turnover tax*, an added-value tax reaches back in time and assessment to earlier completed transactions; and by circumventing the compounding effect of a succession of taxes on gross sales it may have to be imposed at a somewhat higher rate than the ordinary form of sales tax it replaces in order to yield a comparable total.

Sales, net of returns and allowances		$1,000,000
Less: Purchases of materials and supplies (excluding $75,000 increase in raw materials inventories)	$400,000	
Rent	50,000	
Total		450,000
Value added for tax purposes		550,000
Less: Value-added tax		50,000
Net		$ 500,000

COMPANY
STATEMENT OF VALUE ADDED BY OPERATIONS
19–1 to 19–2*

Outputs		
Sales, net of returns and allowances		$1,000,000
Additions to inventory		
Finished goods	$100,000	
Work in process	(50,000)	
		50,000
Value of output		$1,050,000
Inputs		
Purchases of materials (less applicable discounts of $1,000)	$375,000	
Less: Additions to materials inventories	75,000	
		$ 300,000
Other supplies used		100,000
Rents		50,000
Value of input		$ 450,000
Total value added		$ 600,000
Applied as follows:		
To employees		
Wages and pension contributions, including FICA		$ 300,000
To providers of capital		
Interest on loans		50,000
Dividends to shareholders		25,000
To government		
Corporate income tax		100,000
Other taxes		50,000
To provide for maintenance and expansion of assets		
Depreciation		50,000
Retained earnings		25,000
Total value added		$ 600,000

*Only results from operations are included in this statement. Nonoperating items such as dividend or interest income are excluded as well as gains or losses on sales of capital assets. Estimates may therefore be required to eliminate the effects of such nonoperating items in the application (or distributions) of value added shown in the above statement. The total outputs and inputs that enter into the total value added produced, however, supply a control for this purpose.

Many governments which use VAT also rebate all or part of the tax as a *duty drawback* on exported goods in order to avoid competitive disadvantages in foreign markets.

valued policy (insurance) An insurance contract, illegal in many states, under the terms of which the parties have agreed to the value of the property covered and the amount to be paid in case of total loss.

value in use The *present value* of future net cash flows (including the ultimate proceeds of disposal) expected to be derived from the use of an asset in the enterprise. See *value to the business*.

value judgment A choice or approval based on individual or group preference. It is distinguished from a technical judgment of means to achieve a specified result. Value judgments may be impulsive, habitual, or reflective; they may be derived by various patterns of reasoning and combinations of such patterns: e.g., a ranking of purposes according to ultimate worth or urgency, an analogy to approved precedents, a deduction from an established set of general policies or moral principles, a rejection of undesirable extremes, a limitation of resources, consideration for the desires of other people, a prediction of advantageous and disadvantageous consequences, and so on. Such reasoning may be difficult to reduce to precise quantitative determinations, and, since it often involves a conflict of purposes, it may be controversial. Acceptance by others of a value judgment having general application is often dependent on its *commonsense* appeal; in a restricted area, acceptance may rest on the esteem in which the author of the judgment is held, or on his or her position (for example, as a manager). A value judgment is sometimes regarded merely as subjective opinion, sometimes as no more than whimsy: qualities differing in degree rather than in fundamental character.

value to the business An asset measurement based on how much better off an enterprise is as a result of its ownership of the asset. Value to the business is often computed by measuring the adverse effects on net cash inflows assuming an enterprise is deprived of the use of an asset (deprival value). Several assumptions underlie the measure of value to the business: (a) acquisition cost approximates an asset's cash-flow potential at its acquisition date; (b) at subsequent dates, measures based on the current cost of that asset provide a useful approximation of its cash-flow potential; (c) in some circumstances, the cash-flow potential of an asset may be impaired to the extent that the enterprise would not wish to buy the asset at its current cost if it did not already own one; and (d) value to the business cannot exceed the maximum sum that an enterprise would be willing to pay to possess an asset. Therefore, value to the business is *current cost* or a lower appropriate value (i.e., *expected exit value* or *value in use*).

value variance = *price variance*.

variable (mathematics) A symbol of classification intended to represent a range or a subdivision of a range of values defined in terms of a particular *model* or set of structural relations, such as an *equation*.

Variables may be dependent or independent, and are generally defined relative to each other by elements, such as *constants* or *parameters*, appearing in an equation. As usually applied in mathematics, both are represented by abstract symbols, the former by the last few letters of the alphabet ($\ldots$, x,y,z), and the latter by the first few letters of the alphabet ($a,b,c,\ldots$). This device (see *symbolization*) facilitates investigation of general properties of equations by abstracting elements peculiar to a given situation. Thus, in the equation for a straight line, $y = a + bx$, x is the independent and y the dependent variable, and a and b are parameters of intercept and slope, respectively, which become constants when assigned particular numerical values. In terms of the structure specified by this equation, the range of variation may be as great as $-\infty$ to $+\infty$, although interest may attach only to some subdivision of this range, for example, $-10 \leqslant x \leqslant 10$.

By *convention*, independent variables are written on the right and dependent variables on the left side of equations, as above.

Within the defined range of variation, x may be assigned any value, and this value will, through the other elements, such as the constants in an equation, define the value of y, the dependent variable. In the indicated equation of a straight line, the value of y is thus defined uniquely; but this need not be the case: in the equation of a parabola, $y^2 = a + bx$, for example, each value of x, the independent variable, defines two values of y, since $y = \pm\sqrt{a + bx}$; see *function* (5); if only *real numbers* are of interest, values of x which yield *imaginary numbers* are not admissible in the defined range of variation for x; if a and b are positive, values $x < -a/b$ are then not admissible.

The two-variable linear equation, $y = a + bx$, states certain properties of all straight lines. The intercept with the y axis is given by the parameter a, and the rate of increase of y relative to x is given by the parameter b. For example, if $a = 1$ and $b = 2$, a particular straight line $y = 1 + 2x$ is secured in which y increases twice as fast (the slope $b = 2$) as x and the intercept is 1 ($a = 1$) gives the value of y when $x = 0$. The presence of two parameters shows that only two points, or one point and the value of one parameter, a or b, are needed to determine any line because by substituting two points such as $x = 2$, $y = 5$ and $x = 0$, $y = 1$ in $y = a + bx$,

$$5 = a + 2b$$
$$1 = a + 0b.$$

By solving these two equations the values of the constants $a = 1$ and $b = 2$ are obtained, thus yielding the particular straight-line equation, $y = 1 + 2x$.

More than one *independent variable* may appear in an equation. Thus, in the equation of a plane, $y = a + bx + cz$, the variables x and z are both independent, while y is the dependent variable; x and z may be assigned any values within the range $-\infty \leqslant x \leqslant \infty$, $-\infty \leqslant z \leqslant \infty$ without reference to each other; but, once these values are selected, the value of y is completely determined. As in the case of the straight line, this general form of equation provides a symbolic device for the study of relations between variables and parameters for planes; the intercept with the y axis is given by a; the rates of increase, or slopes, of y relative to x and z are given by b and c, respectively; three points determine a plane; and so on.

Use of variables is not restricted to equations. They may be employed, for example, in an *inequality*, such as $y \leqslant a + bx$, or *functions* (5), such as $f(x,y) = 0$.

variable annuity A contract between an insurance or investment company and an investor under the terms of which periodic distributions differ as changes take place in the value of underlying securities.

variable budget = *flexible budget*.

variable cost (or expense) 1. An operating expense, or operating expenses as a class, that vary directly, sometimes proportionately, with sales or production volume, facility, utilization, or other measure of activity; examples: materials consumed, direct labor, power, factory supplies, depreciation (on a production basis), sales commissions, etc. See *fixed cost; semifixed costs; semivariable cost; direct costing.*
2. That portion of factory or processing expense represented by such costs.

variable-cost ratio The ratio between sales revenue and variable costs.

variables sampling A sampling application in which a quantitative characteristic of the sampled items is considered. In auditing, sampling for monetary error in substantive testing is an example of variables sampling. See *dollar unit sampling.*

variance 1. The difference between corresponding items in comparative balance sheets, or in income and other operating statements.

2. The difference for a year or less between the elements (direct material, direct labor, factory overhead) of standard cost and actual cost. See *standard cost*. The term applies to (a) a money difference or (b) any change in the character or purpose of amounts expended. See *standard cost; favorable difference; management by exception*.

3. (statistics) The square of the standard deviation; usually denoted by the symbol σ^2. However, when variance is the *statistic* to be computed, it is the usual practice to employ the divisor $N - 1$—i.e., to define variance as $\sigma^2 = \Sigma (X - \overline{X})^2 / (N - 1)$. This convention has the property of making the sample variance an unbiased estimator of the variance in the universe from which the sample came. It is important to note that, contrary to appearances, the square root of the sample variance as defined above is not an unbiased sample estimator of the *standard deviation* in the universe from which the sample came. Variance, a statistic important in the analysis and design of experiments, is extensively used in *statistical quality control*, although when samples are small it may be replaced by the *range* as another measure of scatter or lack of homogeneity in data.

variate A *random variable*. A *variable* with values assigned at least in part by a *random* process. Hence a variable for which each possible value, or range of values, has an associated *probability* of occurrence.

VAT = *value-added tax, q.v.*

vector An ordered array of numbers such as observations of monthly sales of each of three items in a retail store arranged either in the form of a column or a row such as

$$\begin{bmatrix} x_1 \\ x_2 \\ x_3 \end{bmatrix}$$

or

$$(x_1, \ x_2, \ x_3).$$

The former is referred to as a column vector and latter as a row vector. It is important to maintain the integrity of each position since the same numerical value in one position has a different meaning when assigned to another position. A bill of materials order in which different lines refers to different parts provides an example. The concept of a vector also coincides with the concept of a point when the values in different positions are interpreted as the values of the *coordinates* on different axes (or dimensions) of the space. Each row or column of a *matrix* may also be regarded as *vector*.

venue Relates to the place (county) within which either party may require a case to be tried.

verifiable Susceptible to *verification*.

verification 1. The procedure by which *validity* is ascertained. The thoroughness with which evidence is sought and investigated and strictness is observed in applying *rules* of evidence ordinarily varies in accordance with the importance of the item and the cost involved. Thus, the weight of packaged coffee need not be verified to the second decimal, although that may be necessary in the case of fine watch parts. Circumstantial *evidence* may be regarded as establishing a loss of papers due to rats nesting in a warehouse, but insufficient to verify a theory explaining a net loss shown in an annual report. A foreman's testimony may be sufficient to verify a rumor that a given machine is eccentric in its behavior but not that all machines of the same model are similarly eccentric.

2. (auditing) The process of substantiation involved in proving by customary audit procedures that a statement, account, or item is accurate and properly stated, or is within permissible or reasonable limits.

verify (auditing) To confirm the truth, accuracy, or probability of, by competent examination; to *substantiate*.

vertical analysis The use of *common-size statements* in an analysis.

vertical combination A *business combination* involving companies with supplier-customer relationship. The relationship may be immediate or indirect and remote but the combination is vertical when the union enables a combining company to expand its operation either toward its customer or its sources of supply.

vested benefits Benefits in a *pension plan* that are not *contingent* on an employee's future service.

viability Power or ability to live or survive, or to operate and develop satisfactorily; said of an economy or nation, less frequently of an industry, a business enterprise, a process, a plan, or an agreement.

virement 1. = allocation, see *allocate* (3).
2. Any transfer from one account to another.

vis-à-vis Face-to-face: a term used variously by social scientists as a noun, adjective, verb, adverb, conjunction, or preposition, and signifying an opposing or contrasting position or proposition, opposite to, to oppose, to stand opposite to or in contrast with, oppositely, contrastingly, as compared with, in relation to, or with respect to.

volume cost A term usually signifying a lower cost or a particular cost effected by volume.

volume discount An allowance given by a seller to a purchaser because of the aggregate size of the purchases in a series of transactions over a given period of time; distinguished from *quantity discount*.

volume variance A variance in fixed *overhead (production) cost* which arises when the actual production level (volume) differs from the expected level used in the computation of predetermined fixed overhead rates for prod-

uct costing purposes. Volume variance supposedly measures departures from the cost of *ideal capacity*; however, these departures may also result from unrealistic planning of sales volume, production scheduling, and fixed overhead (production) costs. The volume variance (V.V.) typically is measured as: $V.V. = (Q_b - Q_s) R_s$, where Q_b = the quantity of activity (usually production hours) budgeted in computing the predetermined fixed overhead rate for product costing, Q_s = the standard quantity (hours) allowed for the level of actual production output during the period, and R_s = the standard, predetermined rate for applying fixed overhead cost to production. See *overabsorption*; *underabsorption*.

voluntary reserve An allocation or earmarking of *retained earnings* (earned surplus), as for insurance, retirements, and other items not evidenced by *contracts, commitments* to outsiders, or sustained *losses*.

vote 1. An act or action formalizing a preference or expressing a choice, as in a *resolution* of a board of directors.
2. = *fund* (3); a British term.

voting trust A limited-life trust established for the purpose of concentrating the control of a corporation in the hands of a few persons, known as "voting trustees." The device is often used in *reorganization* proceedings. Stockholders consenting to participate in the plan transfer their shares to the voting trustees and receive in exchange transferable certificates of beneficial interest in the trust; the stock is then registered on the books of the corporation in the names of the trustees.

voting-trust certificate A certificate of beneficial interest issued by or in the name of voting trustees following the deposit with them of stock for the purpose of placing the voting control of a corporation in the hands of a limited number of persons for a stated period of time.

vouch 1. To ascertain the nature, propriety, and amount of items of revenues, expenditures, assets, or liabilities by examination or testing of supporting data; to test by comparison with evidence.

2. To attest the propriety of an expenditure as by approving it for payment.

voucher 1. A document which serves as evidence of the disbursement of cash. Examples: a receipted bill; a canceled check; a petty-cash receipt; the carbon copy of a check.

2. A document serving as evidence of the *authority* to *disburse cash*. Example: an approved invoice from a supplier.

3. A form (used with a *voucher system*) to which bills, receipts, and other evidences of indebtedness are often attached, showing the authority for the payment, the particulars of settlement, and other relevant details; a disbursement voucher.

4. The written evidence of a *business* or *accounting transaction* sometimes contained in a single document without attachments. Example: a journal voucher.

voucher audit 1. The examination and approval by administrative authority of a proposed disbursement; = *preaudit*.

2. (governmental accounting) The postaudit of individual disbursements formerly made by the *Comptroller General* (General Accounting Office).

voucher check A check showing such particulars of a payment as date, amount, discount, other deductions, and invoice number or other reference to goods or services received or to be received; it may combine the features of a check, a formal receipt, and a detachable remittance slip.

voucher index An alphabetical list of payees' names often used in conjunction with a *voucher register*. It may be a card index, on which voucher numbers and amounts recorded are listed; or a file of carbon copies of vouchers, arranged by names of payees. As a record of the business done with each payee, it may also serve as a *creditors' ledger*.

voucher register (or journal or record) A record for the entry and registry of vouchers, usually columnar in form, permitting their summarization, distribution, and posting to ledgers, individually or in the aggregate. It may serve as both a *book of original entry* and a *book of final entry*.

voucher system A system by means of which invoices and other evidences of liability are collected, audited, recorded, and settled. It involves the use of vouchers, voucher checks, a voucher register, etc., and is an important feature of any system of *internal control*.

vouching 1. The preparation under a *voucher system* of invoices or other statements of liability for entry, distribution, and payment. See *vouch*.

2. The process of verification

walk-through test An auditing procedure where transaction documentation is examined from the point of initiation through the processing steps applied by the entity's accounting system to final disposition in the accounts. Generally the purpose of a walk-through test is to allow an auditor to gain familiarity with the accounting system and provide assurance that descriptive information about the system is reasonably accurate. However, under generally accepted auditing standards, a walk-through test alone would not be considered adequate for a *compliance test*.

warehouse receipt The evidence of title given to the owner of goods placed in a public warehouse. Transfer of title is effected by assignment of the receipt. In the event the goods are *fungible*, the warehouseman may make delivery of a commodity of like quality and weight. A *negotiable* warehouse receipt is made "to bearer" and may be transferred without endorsement, often serving in this form as collateral on bank loans. A non-negotiable warehouse receipt is made to a specified person or to his "order," and must thus be endorsed when transferred or surren-

dered. Warehouse receipts are governed by the *Uniform Warehouse Receipts Act*, in effect in most states for many years.

warrant 1. An obligation of a governmental body issued in settlement of debts and payable immediately by the treasurer of the governmental unit; also known as a "warrant-check."
2. A short-term, interest-bearing obligation of a governmental body issued in the settlement of debts and payable from taxes or other revenues to be collected for a designated period; a *tax-anticipation note* (or warrant).
3. A certificate, either separate or attached to a bond, short-term note, or certificate of preferred or common stock, that entitles the owner to purchase, usually within a stated period, shares of stock at a specified price per share. See *right*.
4. In municipal accounting, the term "warrant" is used in three senses, the most common of which is to designate a draft on the treasurer by an accounting officer to pay money to a payee designated in the warrant. In this form it resembles a check except that it does not indicate a bank of payment. The payee presents it to the treasurer and receives

a check, or cashes it at his or her local bank, the bank forwarding it to the municipal treasurer for reimbursement.

A second use of the term in municipal accounting is as a general title to a short-term, interest-bearing obligation. There are two types: tax-anticipation warrants and registered warrants. *Tax-anticipation warrants (or notes)* are issued in anticipation of taxes to be collected and are made payable solely from the collections of the particular tax levy against which they are issued. The warrants are usually issued only against a certain percentage of the tax levy (for example, 75%) but the collections therefrom cannot be used for any purpose until all of the related warrants, and any interest thereon, have been paid.

Registered warrants are documents evidencing unpaid obligations "registered," rather than paid when presented to the municipality's paying officer, because of lack of funds. These obligations do not start to bear interest until registered, and they must be called in and paid in the order of registration. In some cases, the warrants are automatically registered when issued; in others, when the claim is presented by the holder.

Least frequently, the term is used in municipal accounting to designate a written order by an accounting officer to the treasurer to accept money. Such warrants are used for the purpose of making sure that the money is credited by the treasurer to the proper funds and accounts, so that there may be no conflict in applied uses. The deposit warrant indicates the accounts and funds to which the money is to be credited and bears the approval of the accounting officer.

warrants payable Warrants outstanding and unpaid.

warranty A promise by a seller to defend title and possession of real estate or to make good

on a deficiency as to quantity, quality, or performance in a product or service. The character of the deficiency and the period covered are usually attached to the bill of sale or to the product itself.

wash sale (federal income taxes) See *wash transaction* (2).

wash transaction 1. A transaction reversed or offset shortly after its occurrence. Wash sales between two persons, at one time commonly carried on in listed securities, are now prohibited by stock-exchange rules; their purpose was to make an artificial showing in trading activity and price; and thus induce investors to buy at the price thus established. 2. As defined in the *Internal Revenue Code*, a wash sale is a sale of a security at a loss, preceded or followed within 30 days by the purchase of, or agreement to purchase, the same security; only dealers are excepted from the rule that such a loss is not recognized currently, but is added to the tax basis of the replacement security.

waste 1. Resources of labor or material consumed or produced in a given operation and not returning an economic benefit. 2. (economics) Ability to improve output without increasing any input or ability to reduce some input without reducing output. Sometimes referred to as "technical efficiency" (or inefficiency), it is represented by failure to achieve the maximum output that the *production function* made possible from the inputs that were utilized. See *efficiency*.

wasting asset 1. A fixed asset having a limited useful life, and subject to depreciation; hence, any fixed asset other than land the outlay for which, less estimated terminal value, is allocable over the period of usefulness; a *limited-life asset*. See *fixed asset; depreciation*. 2. An asset that diminishes in value by reason of and commensurately with the extraction or removal of a natural product such as ores, oil, and timber, which it contains.

watered capital The excess of capital stock issued, at its par or stated value, over the fair value of the assets contributed in exchange.

wealth Anything having *value* or *utility*. In the possession of persons, wealth is often identified with *capital* or *capital goods*; in *economics* the passage or flow of wealth from one person to another may be designated *revenue* or *income* for purposes of *national income accounting* when it represents a market or other exchange between them, but not when it represents a gift or transfer. See *transfer payments*.

wear and tear That portion of depreciation attributable to ordinary use, disuse, lapse of time, or action of the elements. See *depreciation*.

weighted average An *average* or *mean* in which each item is assigned a relative importance, called a weight. Often the weights assume the form of relative frequency or number of occurrences. Example: purchases of certain raw materials are made during a given month as follows:

Units	Price Each	Total Cost
150	$1.50	$225.00
175	1.40	245.00
50	1.32	66.00
65	1.30	84.50

The simple average of prices paid is $5.52/4, or $1.38, but the weighted average would be the total cost divided by the number of units purchased, $620.50/440, or $1.41. The latter result is also obtained by weighting each price by its relative frequency.

weighted average cost of capital See *cost of capital*.

Western Hemisphere Trade Corporation (WHTC) A U.S. domestic corporation all of whose business is conducted in North, Central, or South America or the West Indies which has at least 95% of its gross income for the immediately preceding three years from sources outside of the U.S., and at least 90% of its gross income for the same period from the active conduct of a business. In order to encourage a favorable balance of trade in the Western Hemisphere, the *Internal Revenue Service* taxes WHTC's at a lower rate than other domestic corporations. See Section 921 of the *Internal Revenue Code*.

Wheat Report 1. A report published in 1969 by the *Securities and Exchange Commission*, which examined the operation of the disclosure provisions of the Securities Acts. Entitled *Disclosure to Investors*, the study was prepared by a team of Commission staff members under the direction of Commissioner Francis M. Wheat.
2. A report published in 1972 by the *American Institute of Certified Public Accountants*, which proposed the establishment of the *Financial Accounting Standards Board*. Entitled *Establishing Financial Accounting Standards*, the report was prepared by a blue-ribbon Study Group chaired by former SEC Commissioner Francis M. Wheat. The principal recommendations of the Study Group were adopted in 1972 by the *AICPA* Council.

wholesale price index A composite index showing changes monthly in the price of commodities and goods sold to manufacturers, distributors, and retailers. Now called *Producers' Price Index*.

WHTC = *Western Hemisphere Trade Corporation*.

will A document prepared by a natural person in contemplation of death and containing instructions for the disposition of his or her property.

windfall An unexpected gain. Often with a further connotation of not being justified by the result of an expenditure of effort or money by the beneficiary.

window dressing The making of, or attempt to make, a favorable showing of financial position or operating results, sometimes with fraudulent intent, as by (a) not accounting for all expenses, (b) anticipating sales, (c) concealing liabilities, (d) burying unfavorable transactions, (e) delaying writeoffs, (f) underproviding for depreciation, (g) not revealing the mortgaging or pledging of assets, (h) devising transactions designed to produce a more favorable financial showing, and the like.

withdrawal 1. Cash or property paid to an owner or stockholder and accounted for (a) as a *dividend* or other distribution of profit (and charged to the proprietor's account or to *retained earnings* (*earned surplus*) or (b) as a reduction of paid-in capital (illustrated by a repurchase of capital stock or a *liquidating dividend*). Unless accompanied by an acquisition of shares of stock, a withdrawal of unrestricted corporate funds by a stockholder is generally presumed to be a distribution of the retained income of the corporation, and only a return of its capital paid in when retained income has been exhausted.
2. Cash obtained from a checking or savings account in a bank with a corresponding reduction in the remaining balance.

withholding The process of deducting from a salary or wage payment an amount, specified by law or regulation, representing the estimated federal or state income tax of the individual that the employer must pay to the taxing authority. The term is also applied to deductions from interest, dividends, and other periodic payments to nonresident aliens (Section 1441 of the *Internal Revenue Code*).

word 1. A unit of language.
2. (computers) A sequence of *bits* or *bytes* which are treated as one unit for storage and access on word-oriented machines.

work center = *cost center*.

working asset Any asset other than a capital asset.

working capital Capital in current use in the operation of a business: the excess of *current assets* over *current liabilities*; net current assets. See *current asset; current liability; balance sheet; statement of sources and applications of funds*. The amount of working capital, supplemented by the ratio of current assets to current liabilities (known as *working capital ratio*), has long served as a credit test and often as a measure of debt-paying ability. One attempting to apply such a test, however, recognizes that other factors, equally and not infrequently more important, remain to be considered before the meaning of working capital in any given situation can be comprehended. The following example, and comments in the paragraph that follows, will illustrate.

Current assets		
Cash	$158,265	
Receivables	287,932	
Inventories, at market which is less than cost	843,679	$1,289,876
Current liabilities		
Accounts payable	$130,481	
Accruals	177,112	307,593
Working capital (net current assets)		$ 982,283
Working-capital ratio		4.1

The working capital of a retail store at the end of its fiscal year consisted of the items shown listed above. The management, in applying to its bank for a 6-month loan of $500,000 at the beginning of the following year, disclosed: (a) that obligations arising out of purchase commitments as a *hedge* against rising prices amounted to $800,000 and would have to be met within the next few months after deliveries had been made; (b) that the rate of merchandise turnover for the coming year would probably not exceed the rate of 3.5 enjoyed during the past year and might be as low as 2.0 because of larger average inventories (an estimated average of $1,400,000 as compared with $840,000) and possibly a 10% decrease in sales attributable to overstocking by customers in recent months. The conclusion of the bank was that, despite a record annual profit of $200,000, a gross margin of 25%, working capital of $982,000, and an ostensibly healthy working-capital ratio of 4:1, the risk was a poor one, and the loan was refused on the ground that the situation pointed to a no-profit year and that, other things being equal, in six months' time available cash would be insufficient by several hundred thousand dollars for repaying the loan. Instead, the bank suggested commitment cancellations and retrenchment measures. This illustration serves to indicate that, without a considerable amount of collateral data, particularly information concerning the immediate future, working-capital information alone may be misleading.

Principal working-capital sources in a business enterprise are (1) net income from sales of products, merchandise or services, and sales of other assets; (2) sales of capital stock and long-term obligations (usually segregated apart from working capital); (3) provisions for depreciation; and (4) additions to other *valuation accounts*.

working-capital fund (municipal accounting) A name sometimes given to the type of *fund* designated as an *internal service fund* by the *National Council on Governmental Accounting*. Formerly also called intragovernmental service fund or *revolving fund*. See *fund*.

working-capital ratio = *current ratio*. The ratio of current assets to current liabilities.

working-capital turnover A *turnover ratio* relating sales to current assets minus current liabilities. It is a measure of a firm's efficiency in working-capital management. Since the denominator can take on negative values, some analysts prefer to use the reciprocal of this ratio. See *ratio*.

working fund Cash advanced for working-capital or expense purposes, and replenished from time to time as needed. It is not on an *imprest-cash* basis wherever, for various reasons, replenishments are not equal in amount to reported expenditures. See *imprest cash*.

working-hours method (of depreciation) See *depreciation methods*.

working interest (petroleum industry) The fractional interest of the lessee of a tract of land in the production of crude oil and gas from the tract; a fraction often encountered is seven-eighths. The remainder is known as the *royalty interest*. See also *oil-and-gas payment; carried interest*.

working papers (auditing) The schedules, analyses, transcripts, memoranda, and so forth, prepared or collected by an auditor while making an examination, and serving as the basis and record of his or her report.

working trial balance (auditing) A *trial balance* to which *adjustments* are appended in supplementary columns; many public accountants make use of the working trial balance as an index to their *working papers*.

work in process (or in progress) The partly finished product of a manufacturing operation, also known as *work in progress* or *goods in process*. It is usually included in the inventory at the cost of direct material and labor, plus a portion of *factory overhead* (or *indirect expense*) or is valued at the *lower of cost or market*. If *direct-costing methods* are in use, overhead may be excluded.

work measurement A *cost control* method which relies upon formal analysis of the operations required to complete a project; a set of techniques which attempts to determine the workload required for a project and the resources required to complete it efficiently. It includes *time and motion studies*, *work sampling*, and other methods to analyze input/output efficiencies of employees.

workmen's compensation A system providing payments to workers injured from a risk arising in the course of employment, payment occurring without consideration of the negligence of either party.

work order The written authority on which the performance and record of substantially all the work in a factory is controlled.

work program 1. A *plan*, including the estimated cost, of work to be done.
2. (municipal accounting) Hence, the division of a *lump-sum appropriation* of a department for *current operating expenses* to activities or departmental units so that each will get its administratively determined share of the whole. See *allotment*.

work sampling An extension of *time and motion study* methods from factory production to sales and other areas which involve non-repetitive actions that are less subject to direct managerial control. The process involves an application of *statistical sampling*, or other types of sampling, to ascertain a representative mix of the activities involved. These are then studied for possible improvements or simplifications including improvements in layout. The results are then timed in a manner analogous to that used in ordinary time and motion studies. The results serve as a guide for *budgeting*, workload planning and *control* and evaluation of operations.

work study Any method of investigation designed to provide better job or machine performance.

work unit A unit of measure, often commonly accepted, for determining *average cost*, time, or efficiency, thus making possible (a) comparisons of one operation with another or with the same operation in a preceding period, and (b) estimates of future operations.

World Bank (International Bank for Reconstruction and Development) One of two international financial institutions (the other is the International Monetary Fund) established in 1946. Its purpose is to promote the international flow of long-term funds for construction and development in developing countries by selling its own bonds or by guaranteeing loans made and encouraging cofinancing from other private and public sources. More risky development loans, at especially low rates of interest, are the business of its affiliate, the International Development Association (IDA).

worth Value expressed in terms of some standard of equivalence or exchange; *value*; as, *cost; replacement cost; market value*.

writ A legal document commanding the sheriff to give notice of pending legal action.

write down To transfer a portion of the balance of an asset account to an expense account or to profit and loss.
—*writedown, n.*

write off To transfer the balance of an account previously regarded as an asset to an expense account or to profit and loss.
—*writeoff, n.*

write up To record an increase in the book value of an asset, not represented by an outlay of cash or other property or an inflow of capital.
—*writeup, n.*

year-end adjustment A modification of a *ledger account* at the close of a *fiscal period* arising from an accrual, prepayment, physical inventory, reclassification, policy change, audit adjustment, or other unrecorded-nonroutine transaction. The term does not ordinarily embrace a correction arising from a clerical error.

year-end dividend A dividend declared after the year's net income has been more or less accurately determined; sometimes employed in contrast with *interim dividend*.

yield *n*. 1. The actual, as distinct from the nominal, rate of return on an investment; the *effective rate*. See *bond valuation*.
2. The dividends paid during a given year divided by the number of outstanding shares of common stock at the end of the year.

v. 1. To give forth; produce: said of interest or other return from an investment or of services or benefits as from a fixed asset.
2. To give way or to concede a point as in an argument or debate.

yield to maturity *Effective rate* of return on a bond calculated from its market price, face value, coupon rate, and the time remaining to maturity. See *bond valuation*. Since most bonds carry half-yearly coupons, it is conventional to state bond yields on a "six-monthly" compounded basis as opposed to "annually" compounded. Thus, a bond yield of 8% means 4% per six months, six-monthly. See *interest formulas*.

zero-base budgeting A budget process which requires managers to justify each requested budgetary expenditure anew every year. It contrasts with *incremental budgeting* in which changes (increments or decrements) from preceding budget or expenditure levels become the focus for justification. In practice, however, the situation is mixed since prior budget levels weigh heavily in zero-base budgeting if only because that is where experience is centered, while budget totals as well as increments may be questioned even under a *line-item* incremental approach. The processes used and the emphases in incremental and zero-base budgets do differ. Major inputs to a zero-base budgeting system involve the development and ranking of *decision packages*. Persons with responsibility for funding decisions are thus supposedly presented with a description of all potentially fundable activities and the consequences of funding these activities at different *levels of effort* as well as the minimum levels needed to continue them at all. Proponents of zero-base-budgeting argue that such a system compels detailed planning and constant reconsideration of the importance of various activities and goals. See *budget; program planning budgeting system*.

zero bracket amount (federal income taxes) A flat amount built into the tax tables and tax rate schedules designed to eliminate a portion of a taxpayer's personal expenditures from taxation. Formerly termed the standard deduction, the zero bracket amount allowed to single persons and heads of household after 1978 is $2,300, and to those filing a joint return, $3,400. A taxpayer whose itemized deductions exceed the zero bracket amount may deduct the excess itemized deductions to determine *taxable income*.

zone system (of pricing) See *basing point*.

INDEX OF ENTRIES

No mark means a minimum definition of the term in one or two lines; often only a reference to another term.
• means a definition, often with alternatives and a brief discussion up to several lines.
•• means the definition is accompanied by a medium-sized discussion of up to a half column or about 30 lines.
••• means a detailed accompanying discussion ranging from half a column to several pages.